CHILDREN   SEA

DAISUKE IGARASHI

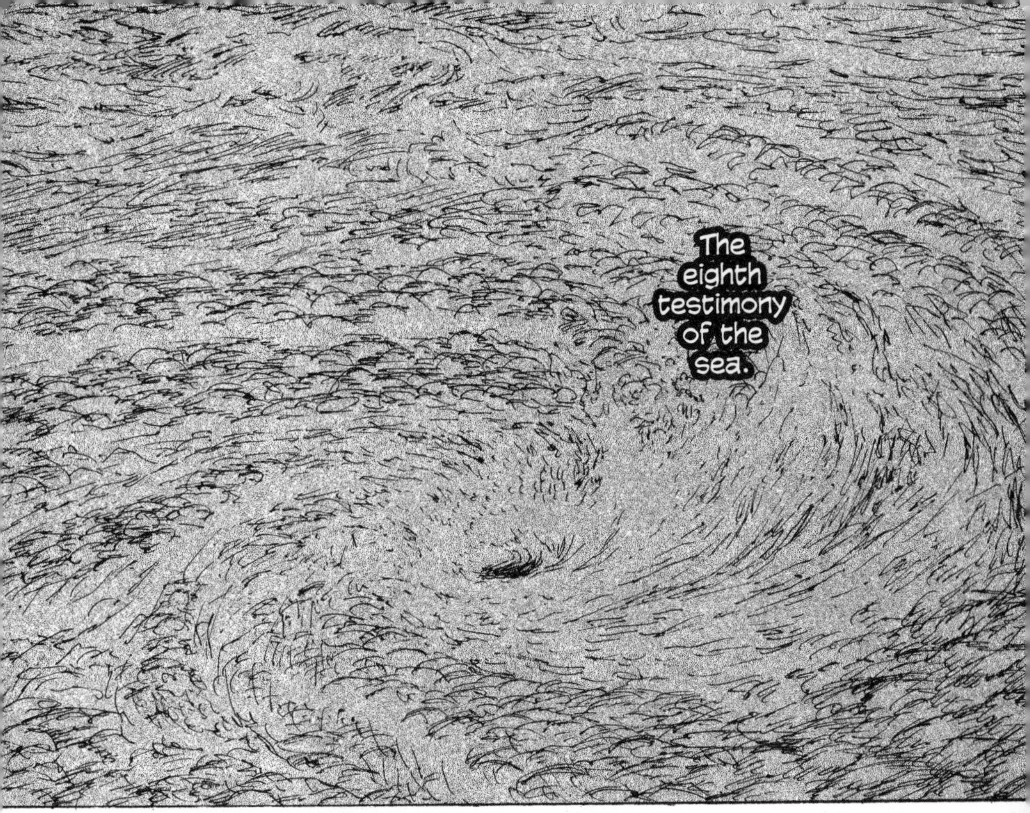
The eighth testimony of the sea.

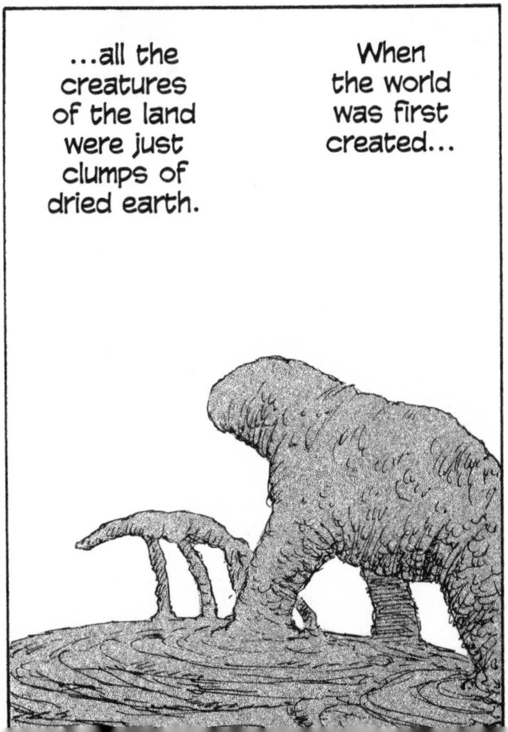
When the world was first created...
...all the creatures of the land were just clumps of dried earth.

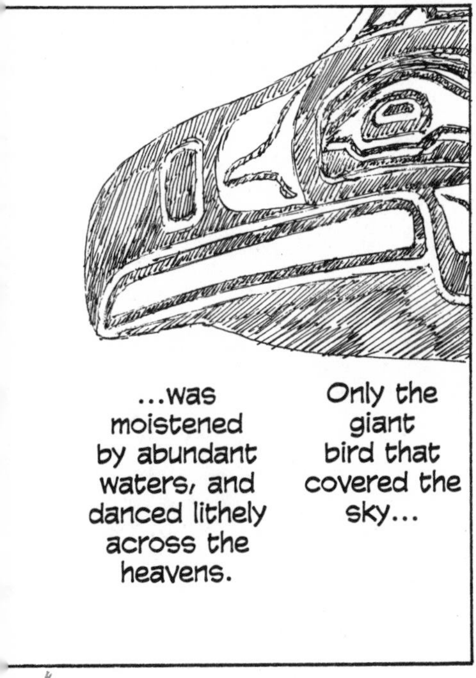
Only the giant bird that covered the sky...
...was moistened by abundant waters, and danced lithely across the heavens.

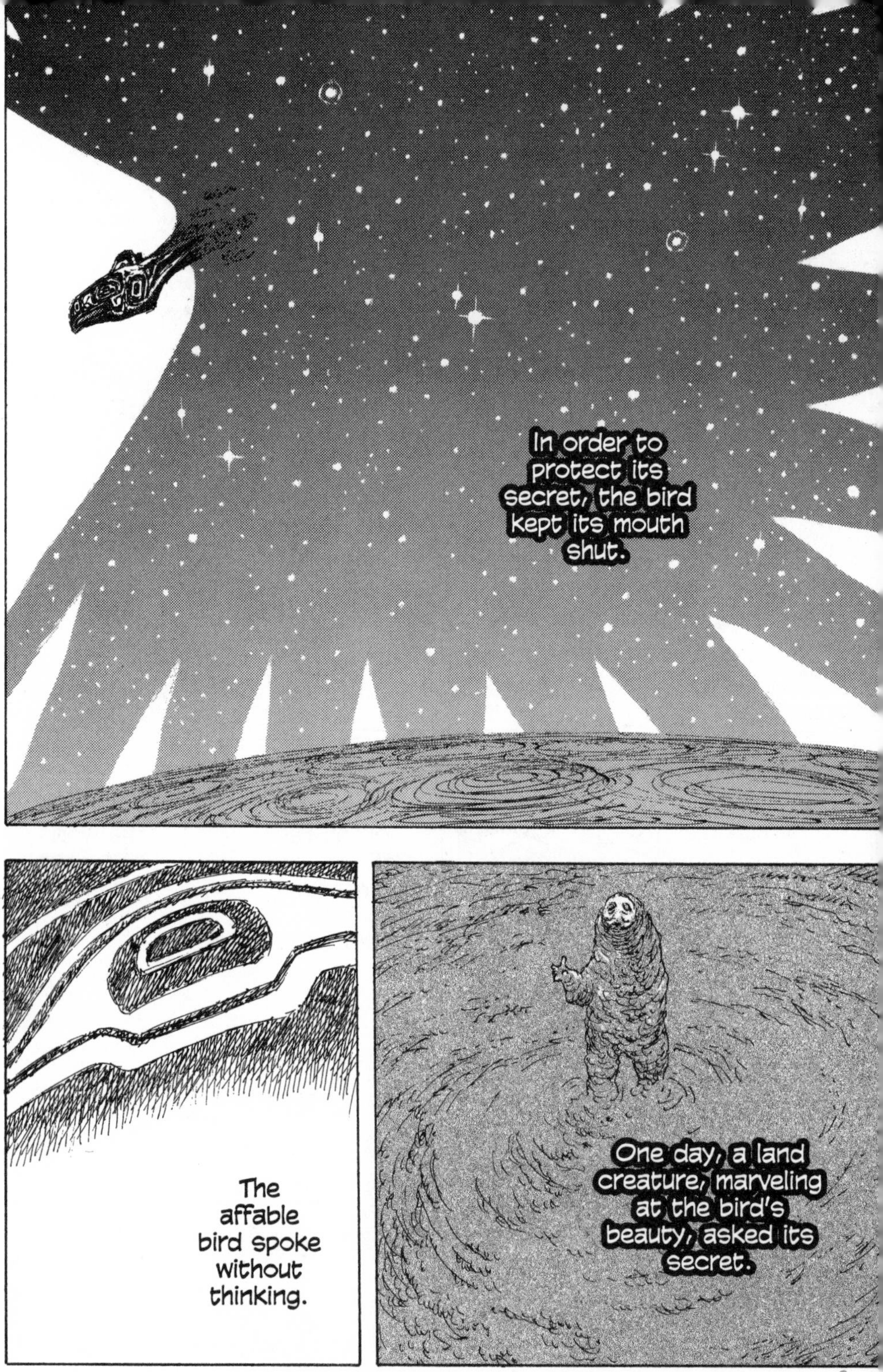
In order to protect its secret, the bird kept its mouth shut.
One day, a land creature, marveling at the bird's beauty, asked its secret.
The affable bird spoke without thinking.

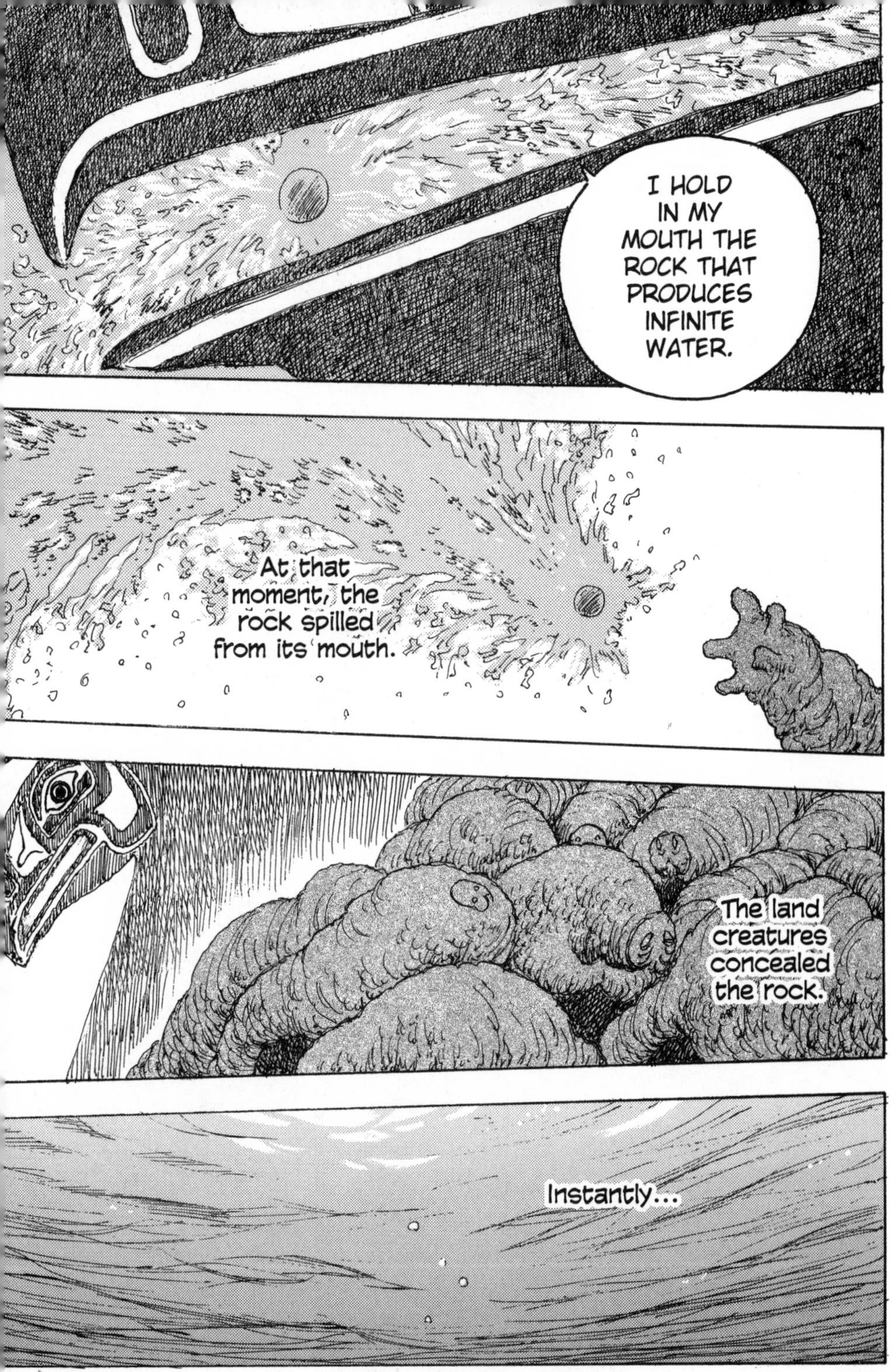
I HOLD IN MY MOUTH THE ROCK THAT PRODUCES INFINITE WATER.
At that moment, the rock spilled from its mouth.
The land creatures concealed the rock.
Instantly...

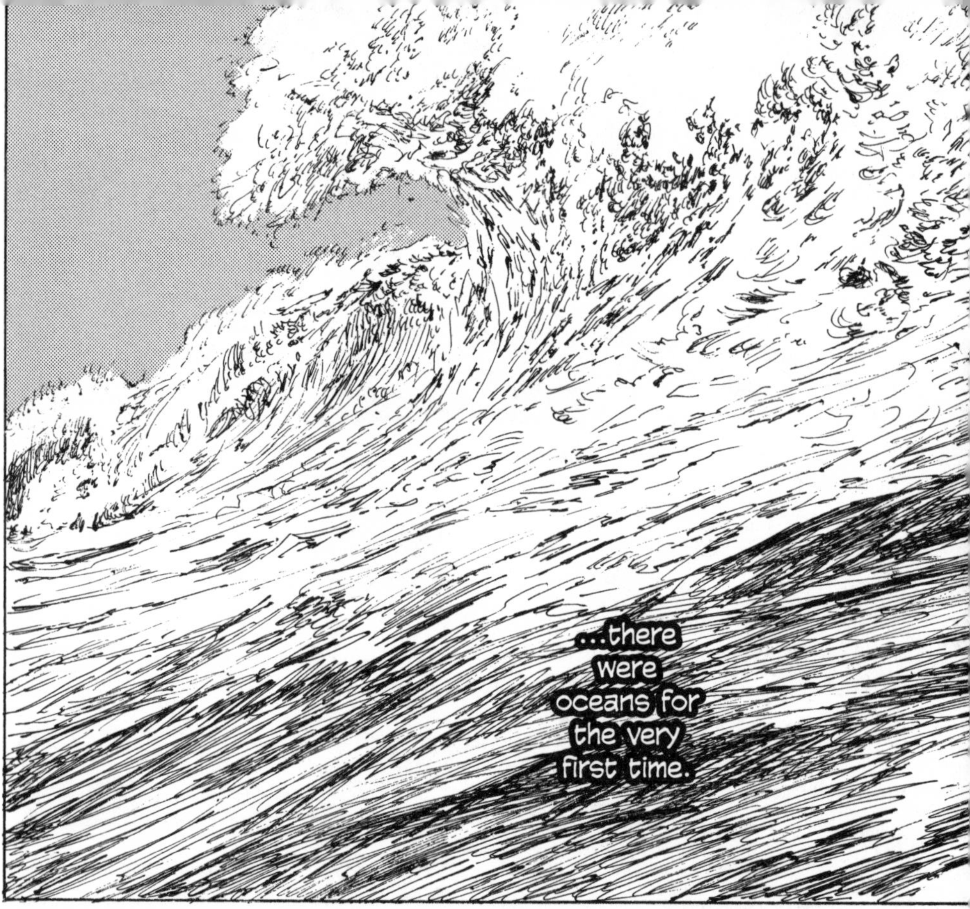
...there were oceans for the very first time.

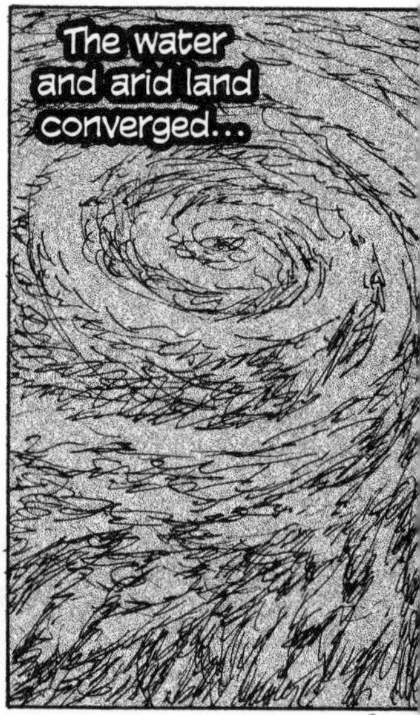
The water and arid land converged...

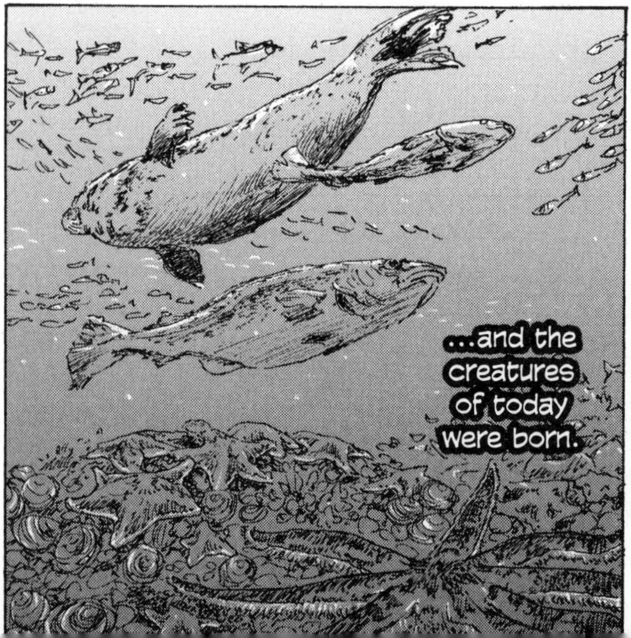
...and the creatures of today were born.

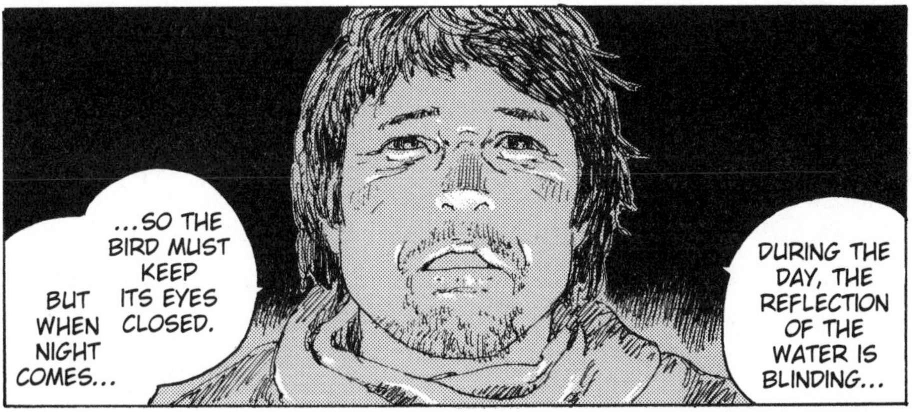
DURING THE DAY, THE REFLECTION OF THE WATER IS BLINDING...
...SO THE BIRD MUST KEEP ITS EYES CLOSED.
BUT WHEN NIGHT COMES...

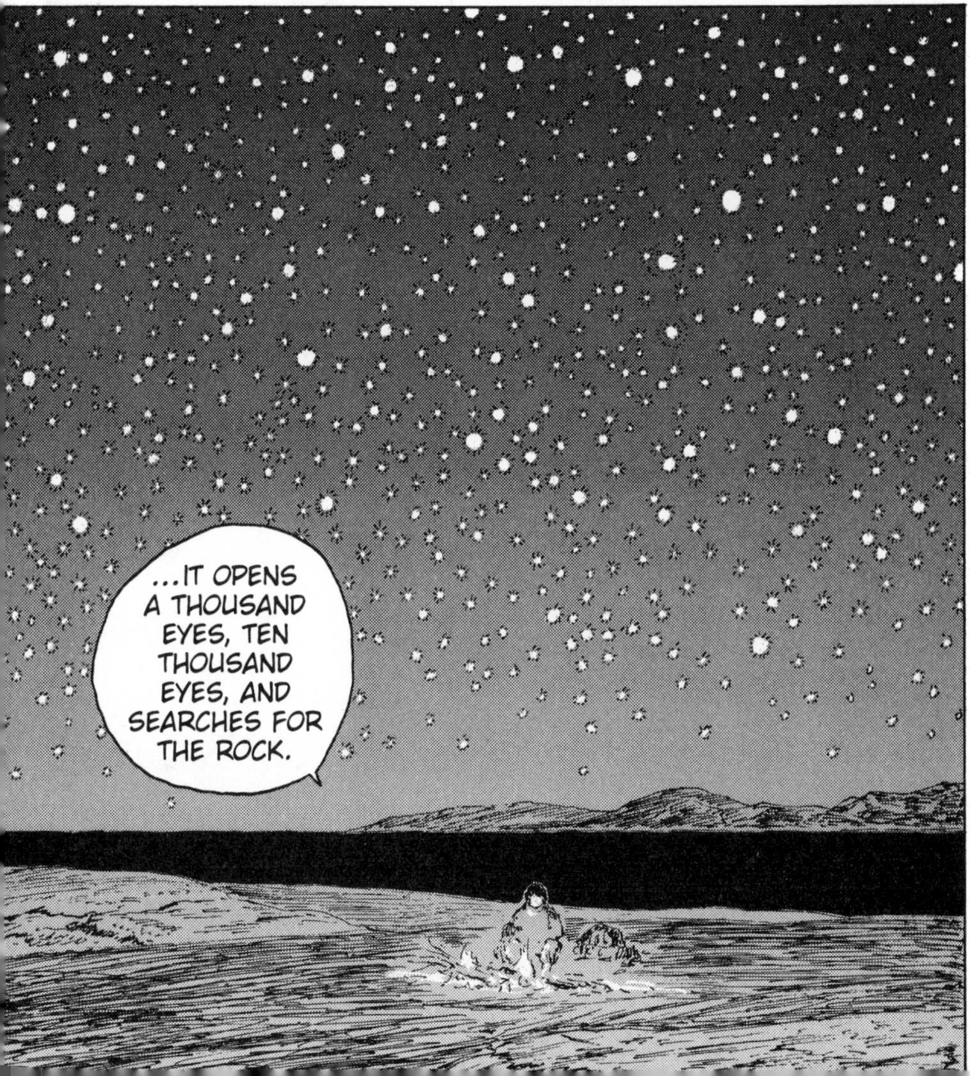
...IT OPENS A THOUSAND EYES, TEN THOUSAND EYES, AND SEARCHES FOR THE ROCK.

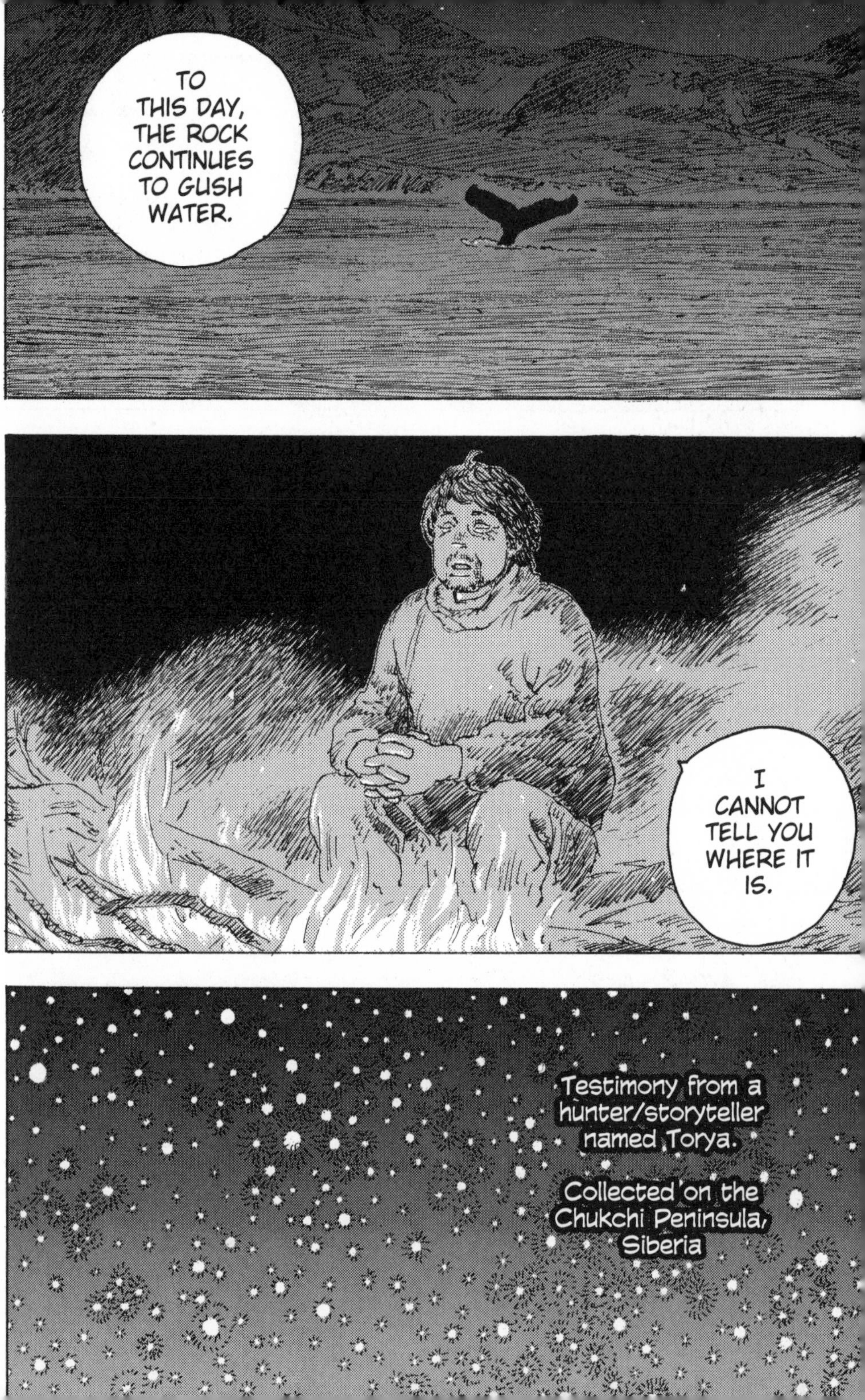
TO THIS DAY, THE ROCK CONTINUES TO GUSH WATER.
I CANNOT TELL YOU WHERE IT IS.
Testimony from a hunter/storyteller named Torya.
Collected on the Chukchi Peninsula, Siberia

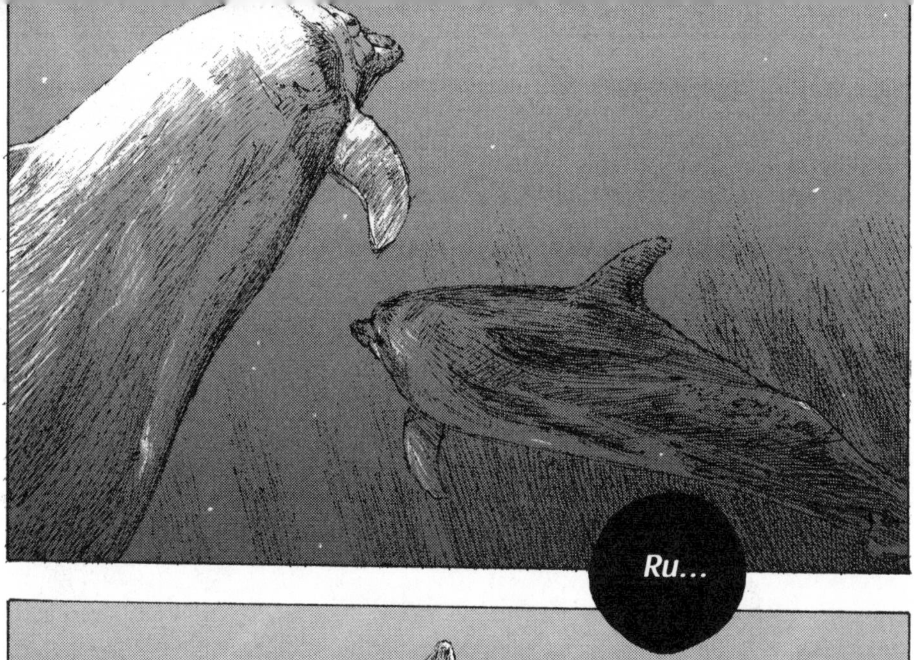
Ru…
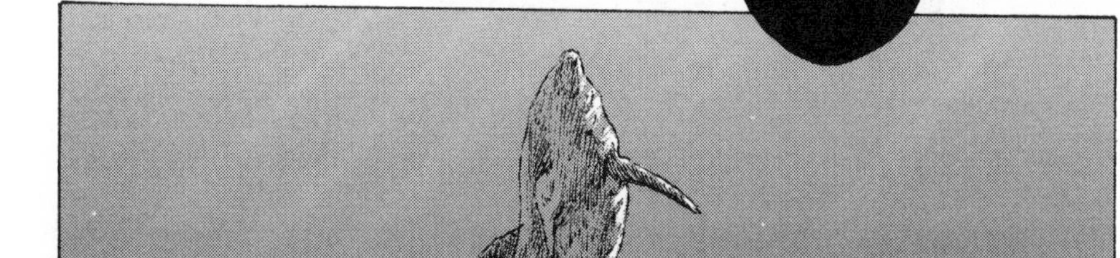
Ru…
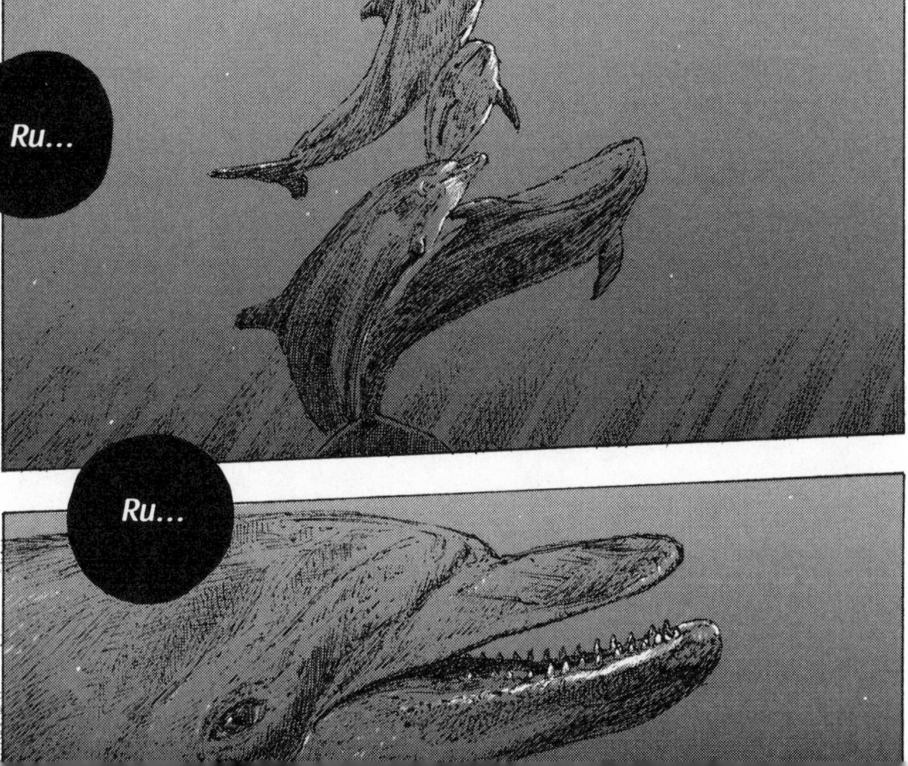
Ru…

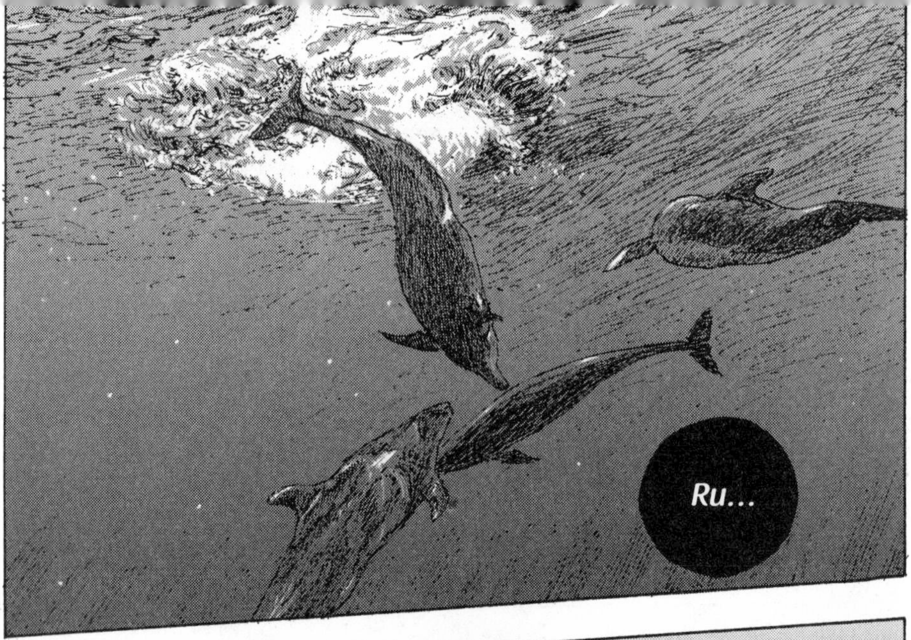
Ru...
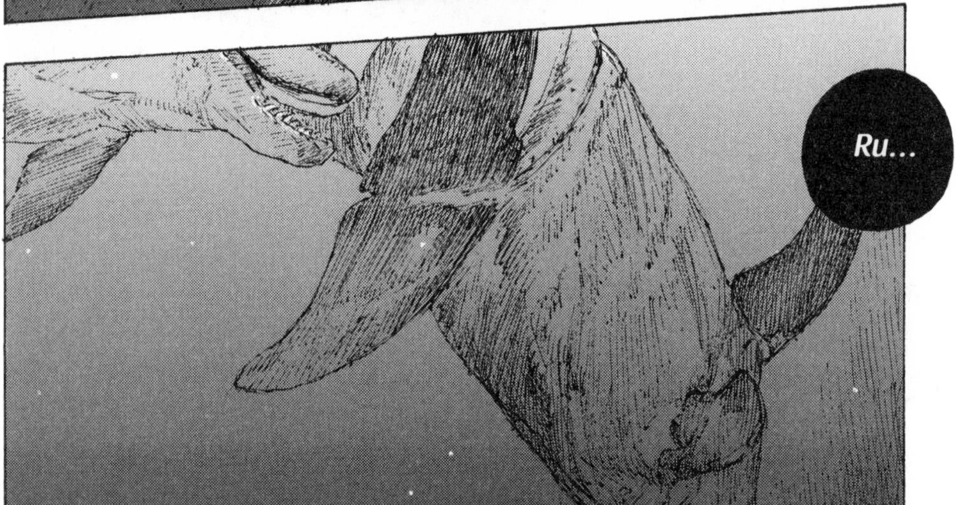
Ru...
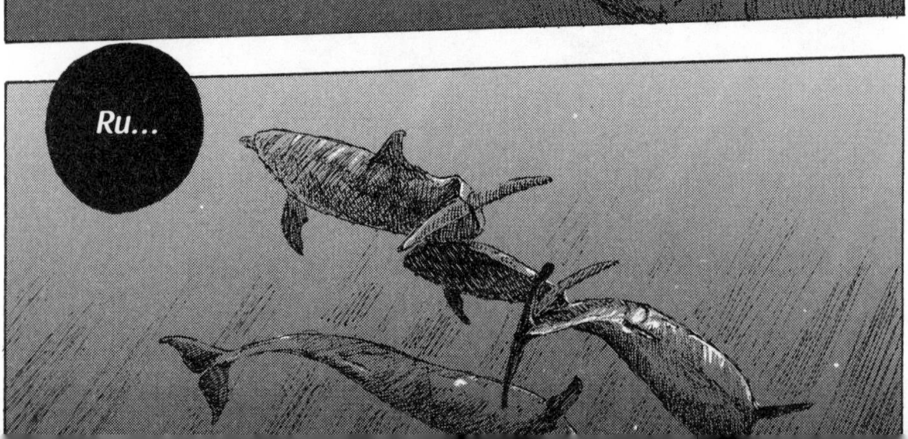
Ru...

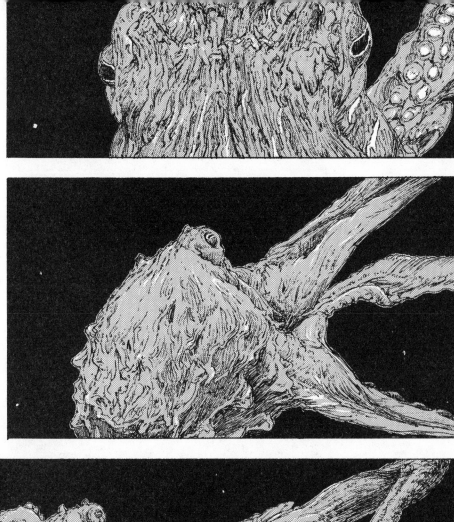
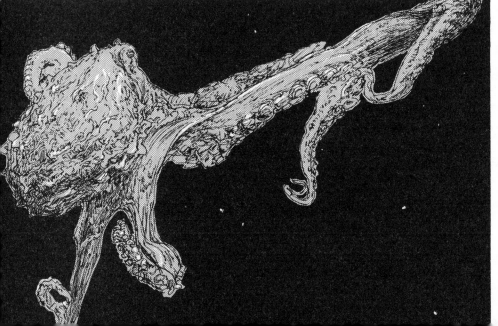

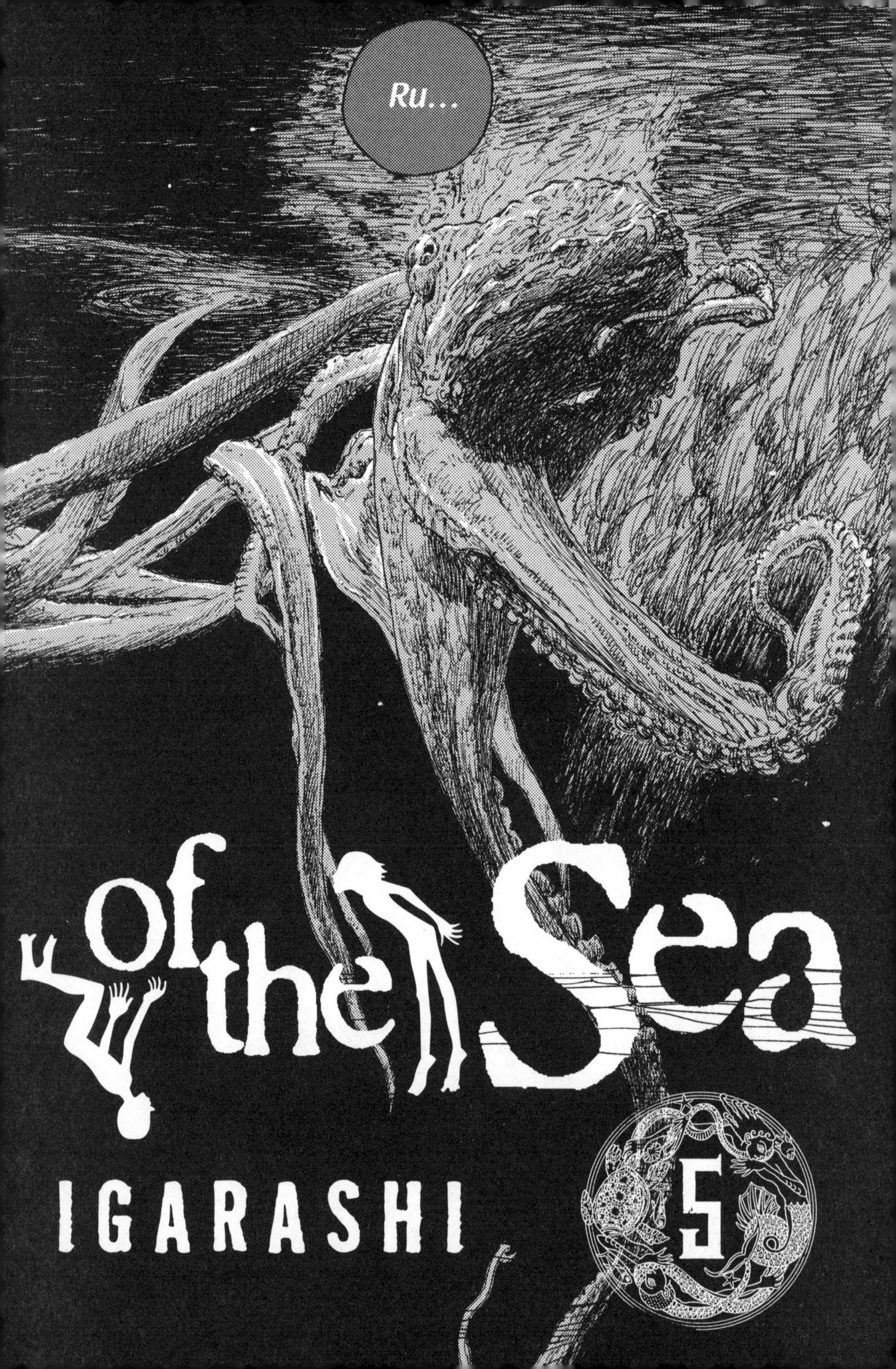
Ru...
of the Sea
IGARASHI
5

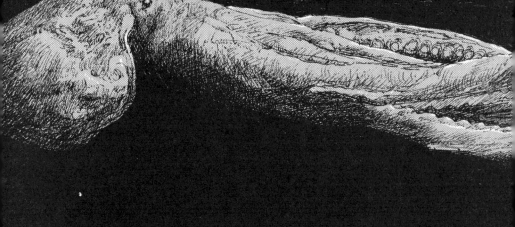

Ru...

Children

DAISUKE

Children of the Sea

THE STORY THUS FAR

During summer vacation Ruka meets Sora and Umi, two boys who were raised by dugongs. After meeting the boys, strange things begin to happen. A mysterious shooting star appears, fish turn into light and disappear...

One night, after entrusting Ruka with a meteorite that fell in Ogasawara, Sora turns into light and disappears. Ruka and Umi set sail with Anglade and are swallowed by a singing whale. Kanako and Dehdeh set sail to search for Ruka and Umi while Jim and Anglade wait for the “real show,” which they believe holds the key to Umi and Sora. Jim and Anglade have been waiting patiently for six years since the incident in the Antarctic, perhaps even longer...

Just what is this “real show”?

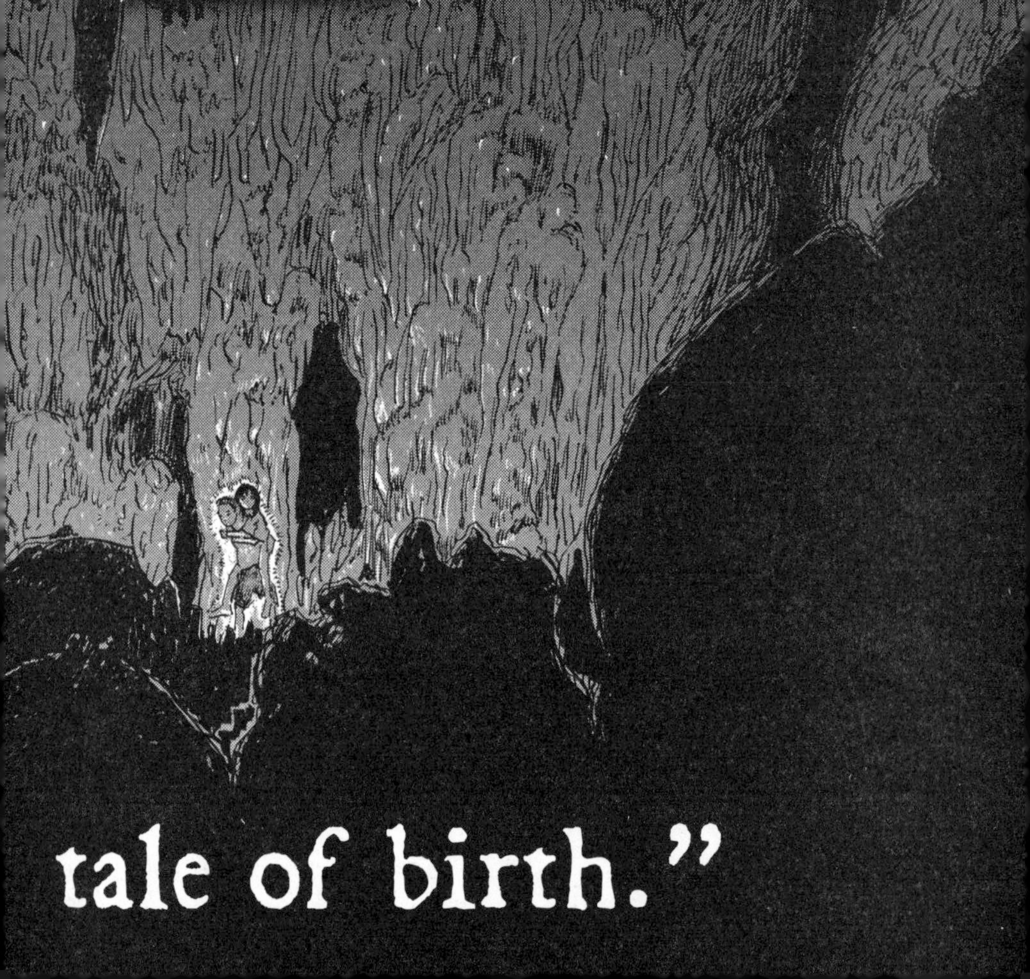
tale of birth.”

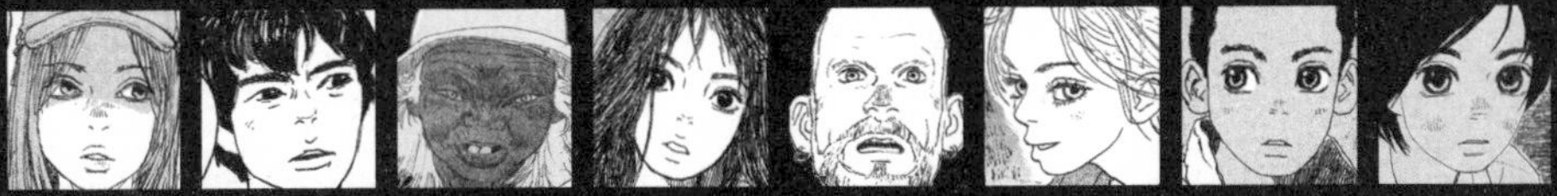

KANAKO AZUMI

Ruka's mother. She was raised as a traditional shell diver.

MASĀKI AZUMI

Ruka's father. He works at the aquarium.

DEHDEH

A jack-of-all-trades. She was the one who brought Jim to Umi and Sora when they were first captured.

ANGLADE

A gifted young marine biologist. He was Jim's partner once but now has different priorities.

JIM CUSACK

A marine biologist. Forty years ago he was responsible for the death of a young boy who looked like Sora. Since then he has been pursuing the mystery of the ocean children.

SORA

Raised as Umi's older brother. He is physically weak and is often in the hospital. He turned into light in front of Ruka and then disappeared.

UMI

A boy found off the Philippine coast over ten years ago. The aquarium has been taking care of him and Sora. He has opened up to Ruka.

RUKA AZUMI

A middle school student who has a hard time articulating her feelings and tends to use her fists and not her words. Her parents are separated and she lives with her mother.

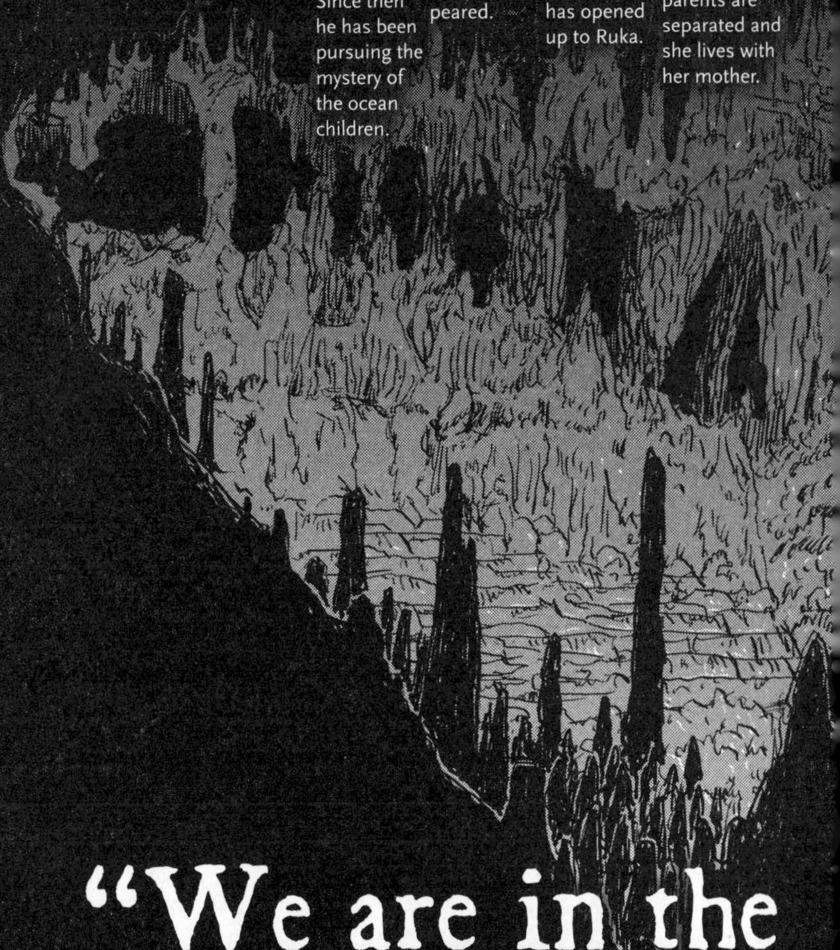

"We are in the

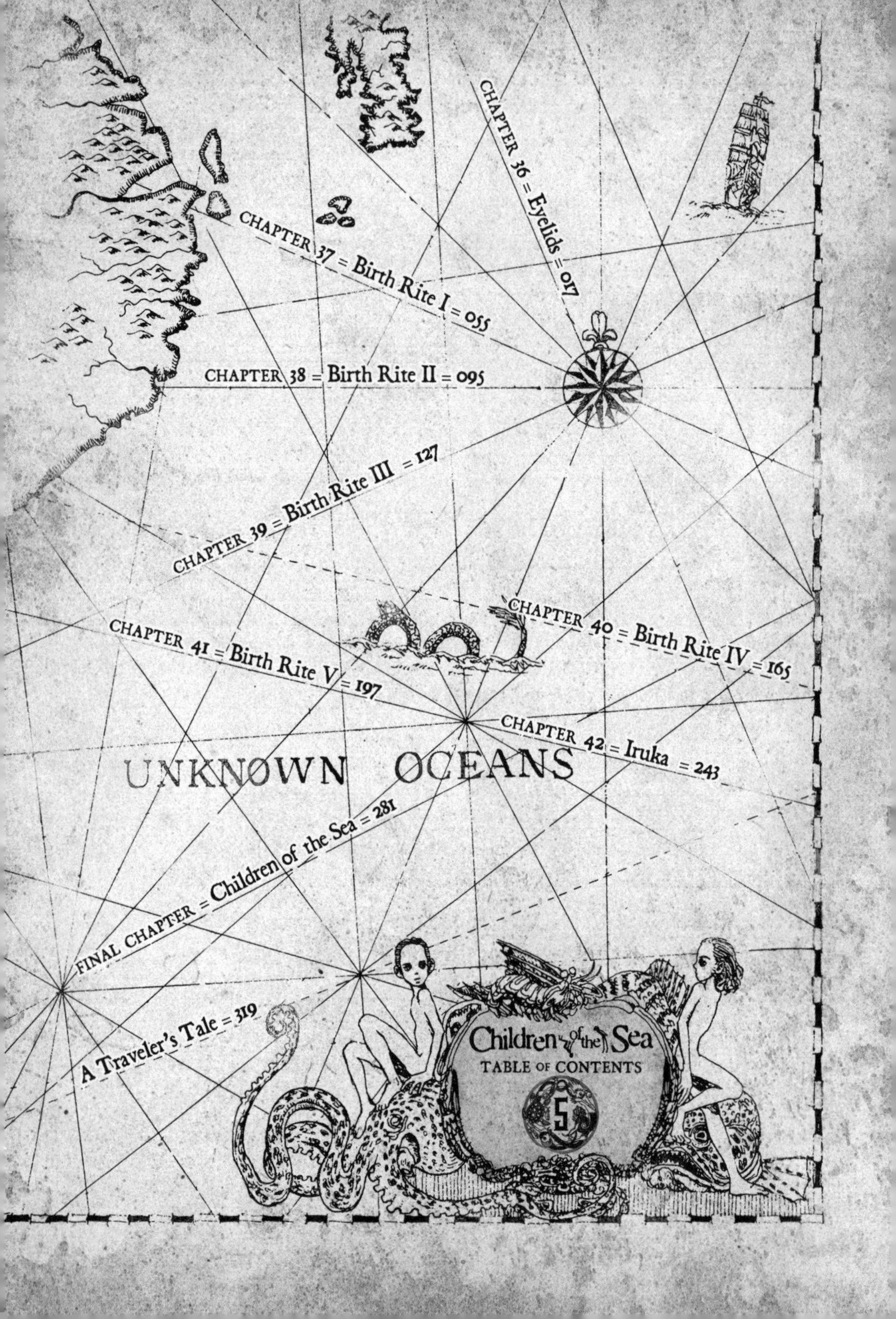
UNKNOWN OCEANS

Children of the Sea

TABLE OF CONTENTS

5

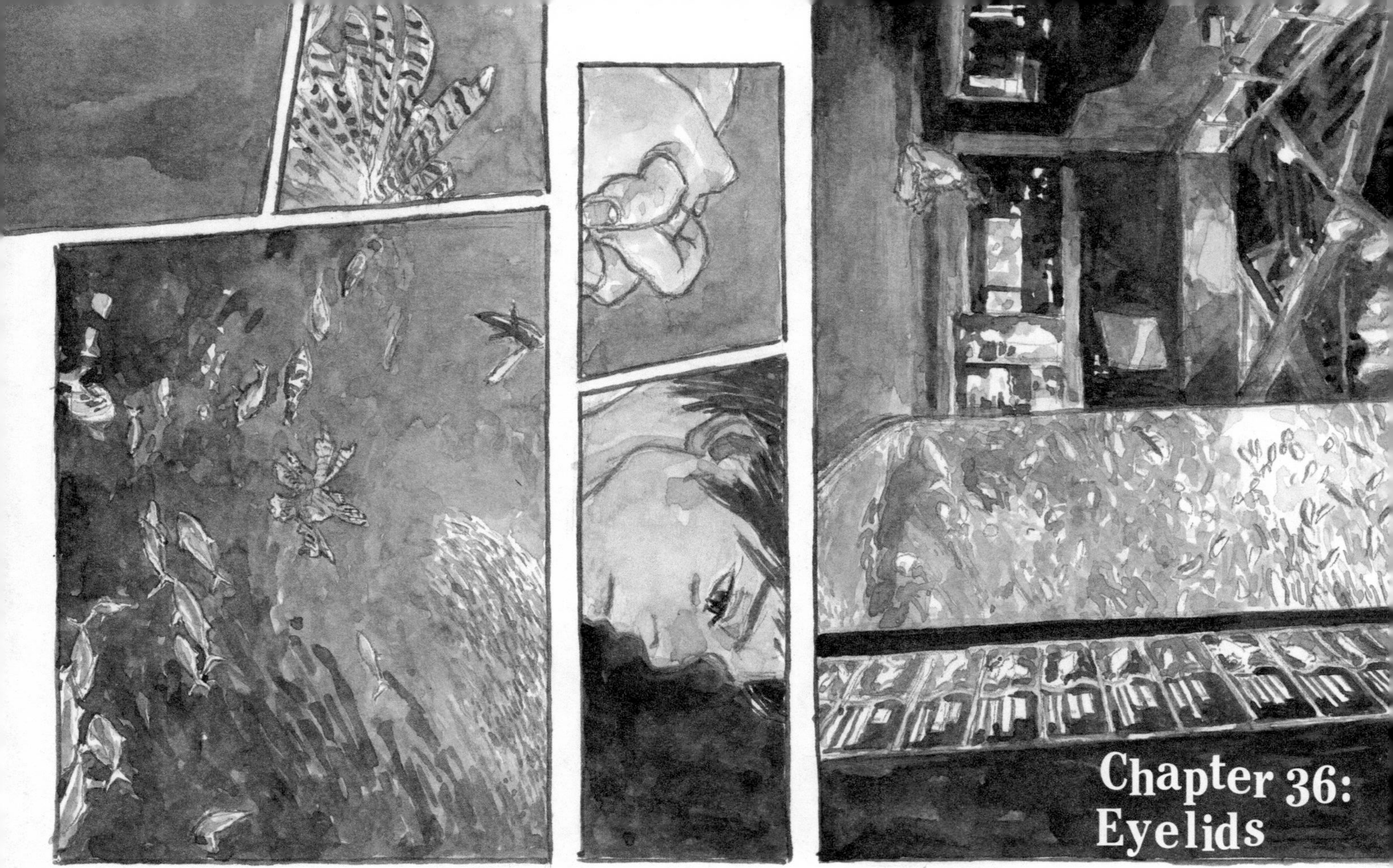
Chapter 36:
Eyelids

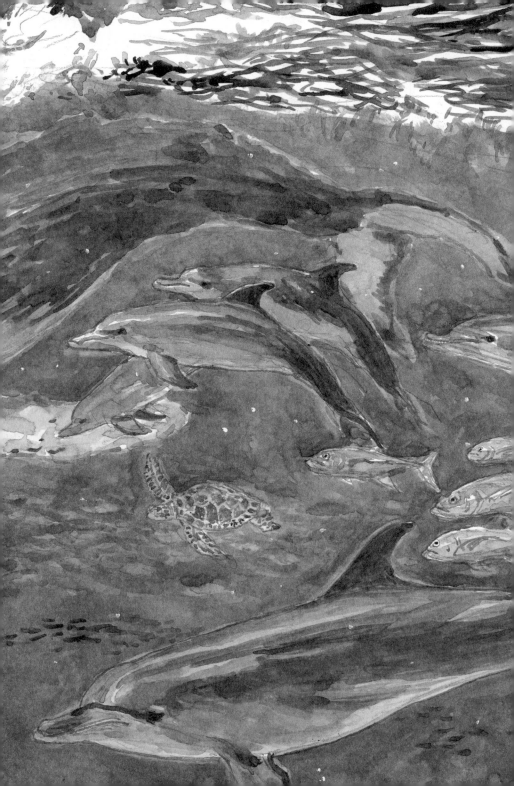

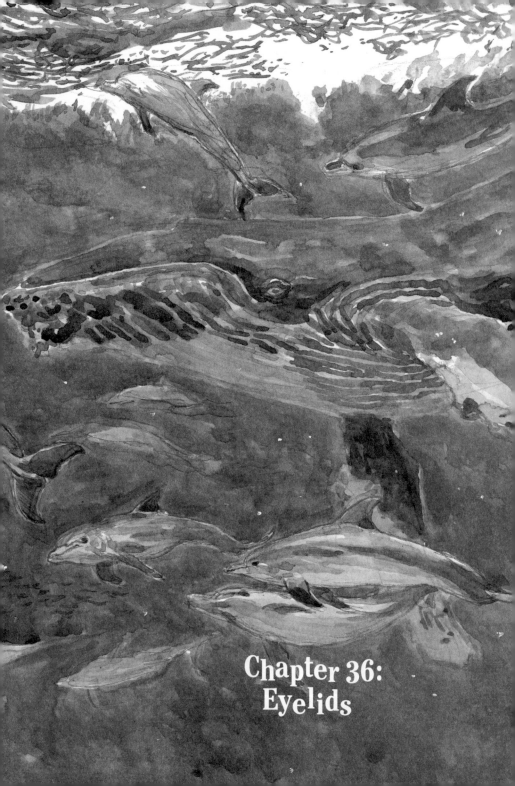

Chapter 36:
Eyelids

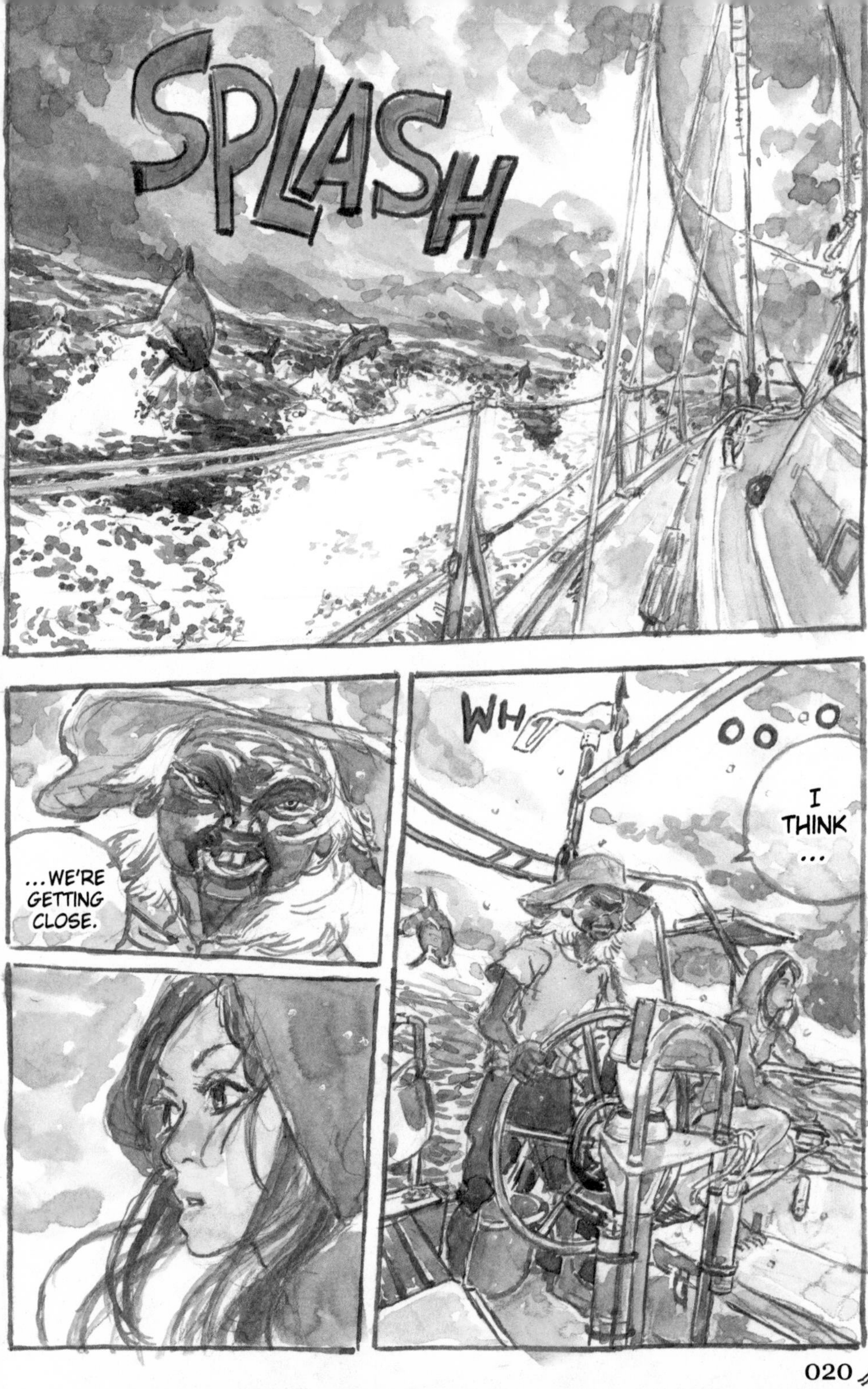
SPLASH
WH
I THINK ...
...WE'RE GETTING CLOSE.

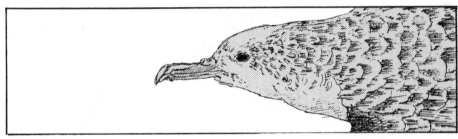

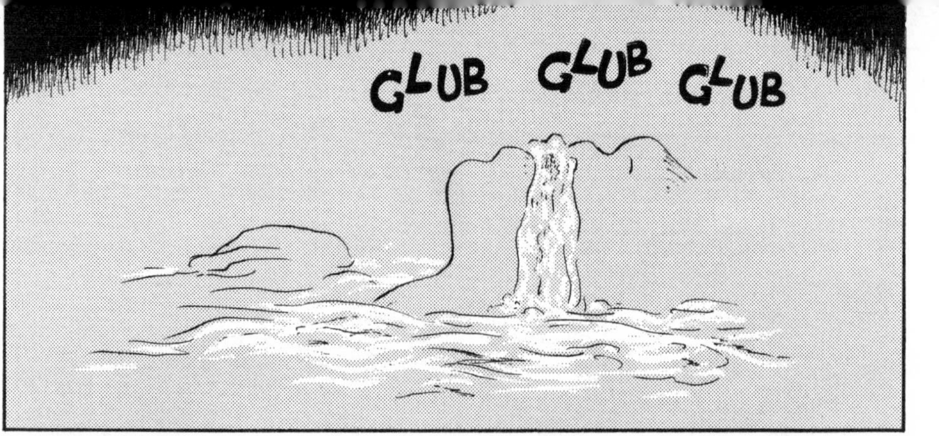
GLUB GLUB GLUB
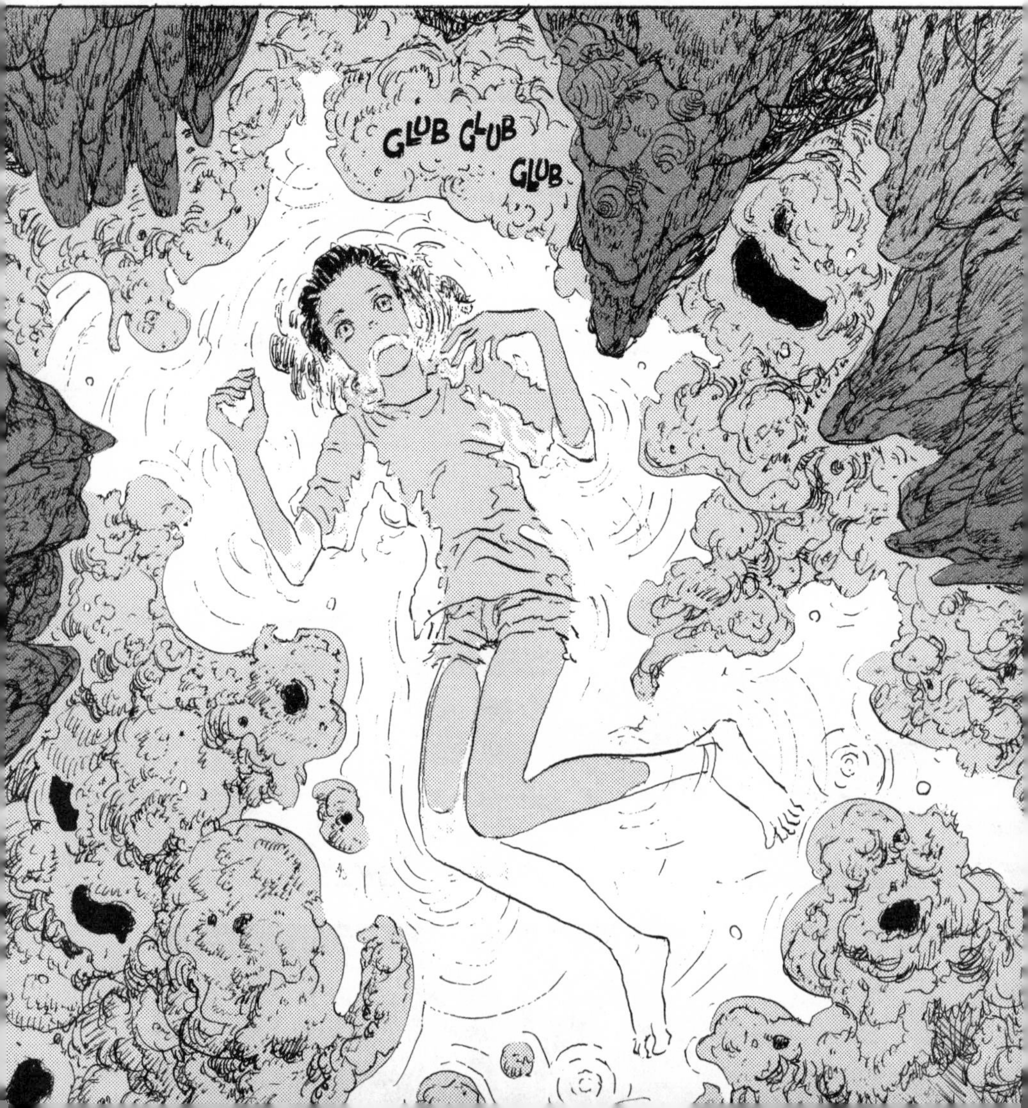
GLUB GLUB
GLUB

plip plip
plip
plip
splat
drip
Ru...

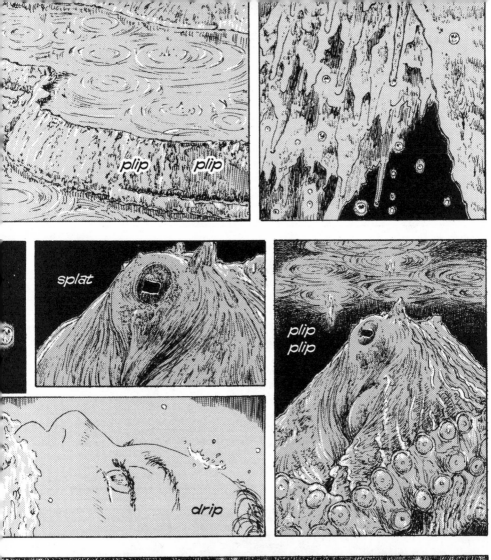

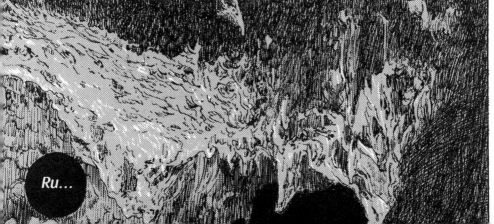

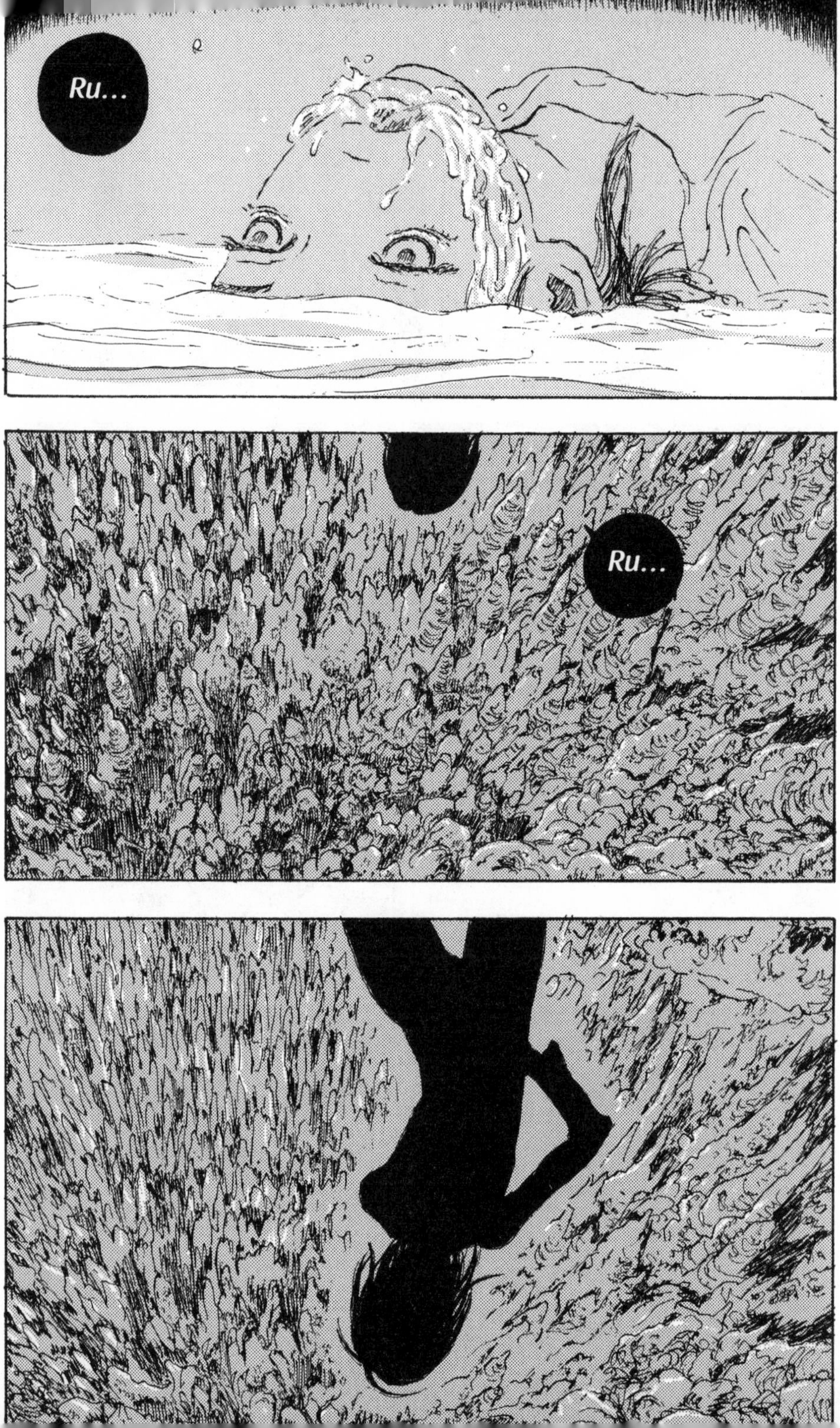
Ru...
Ru...

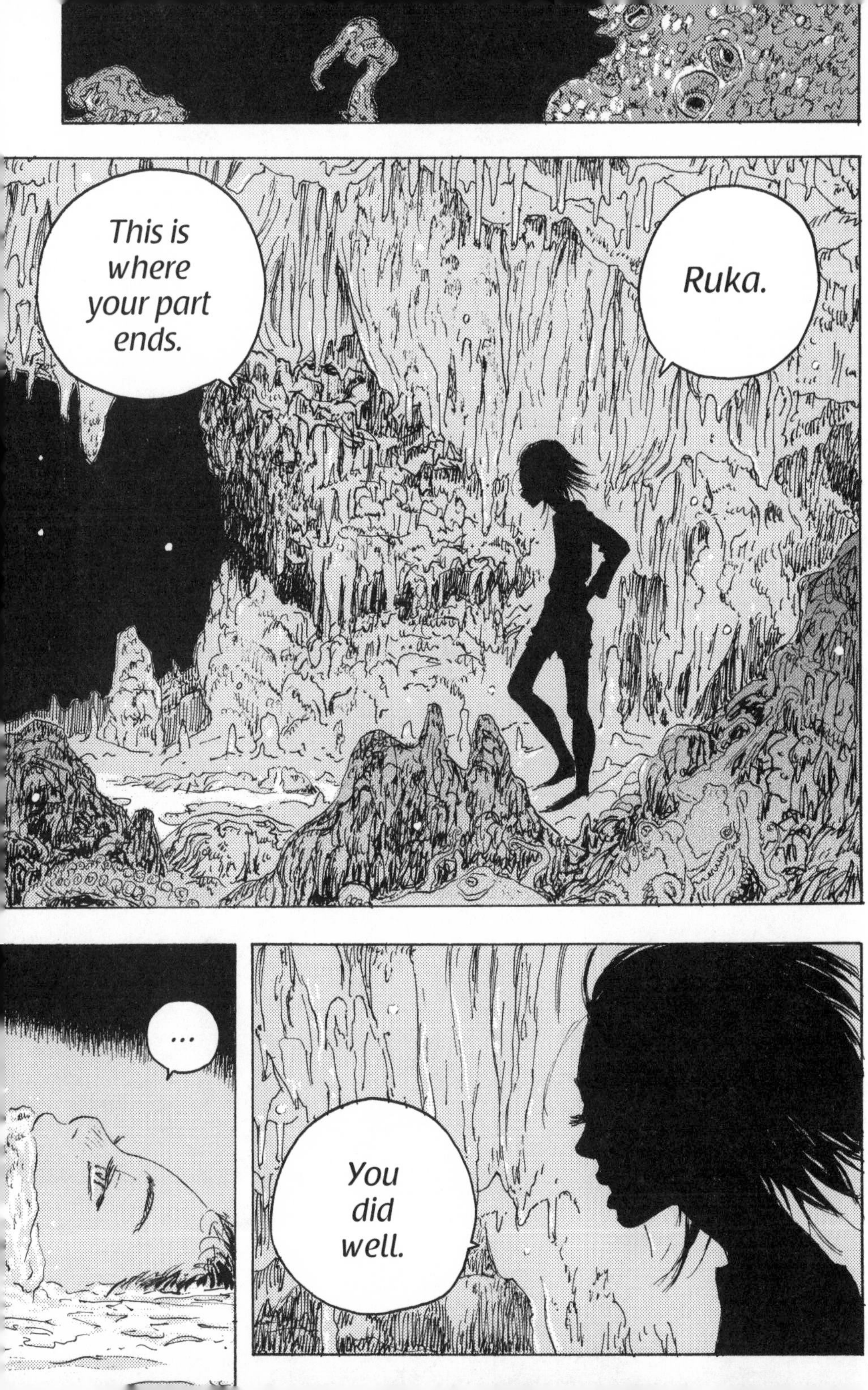
Ruka.
This is where your part ends.
You did well.
...

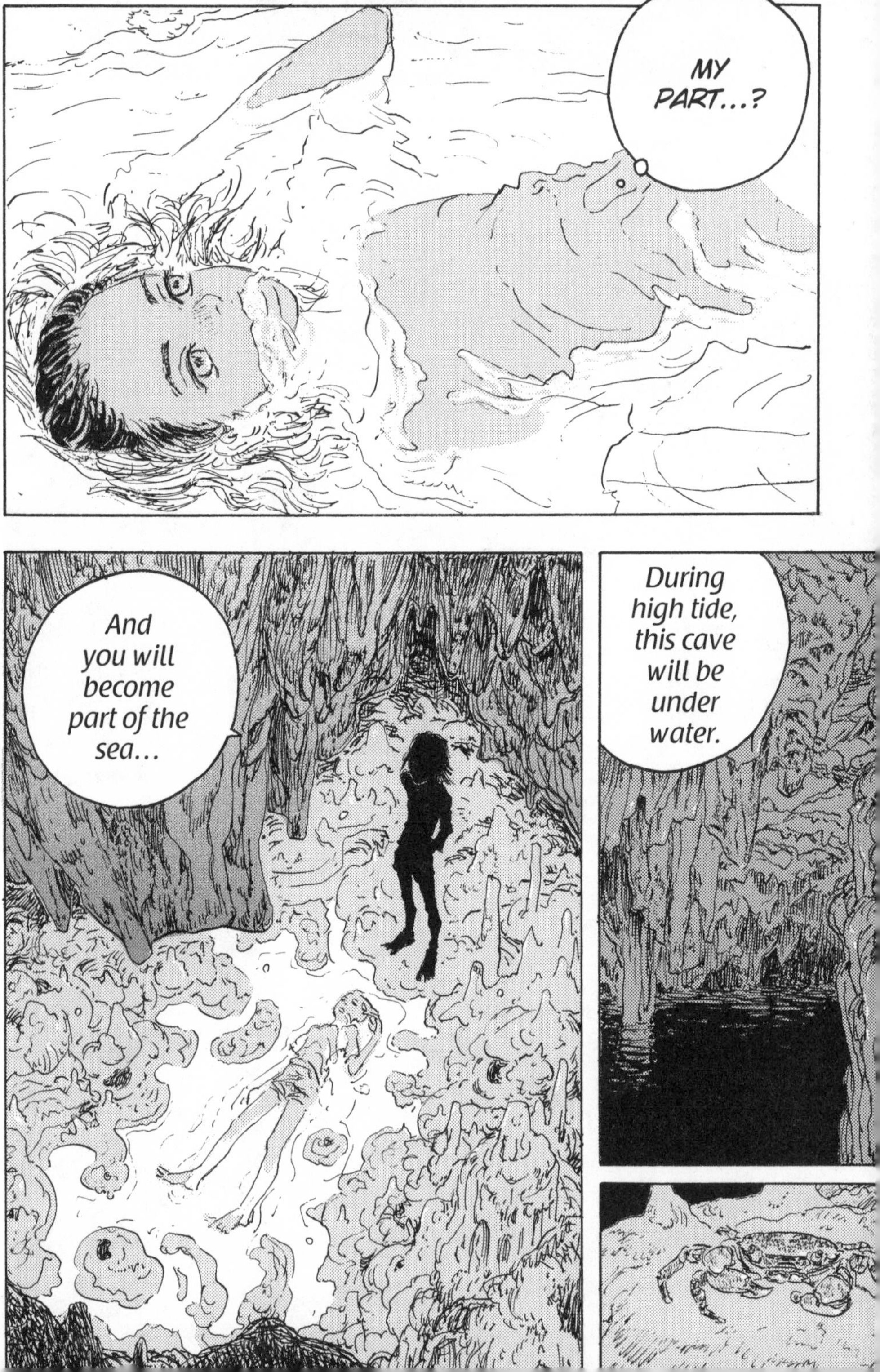
MY PART...?
During high tide, this cave will be under water.
And you will become part of the sea…

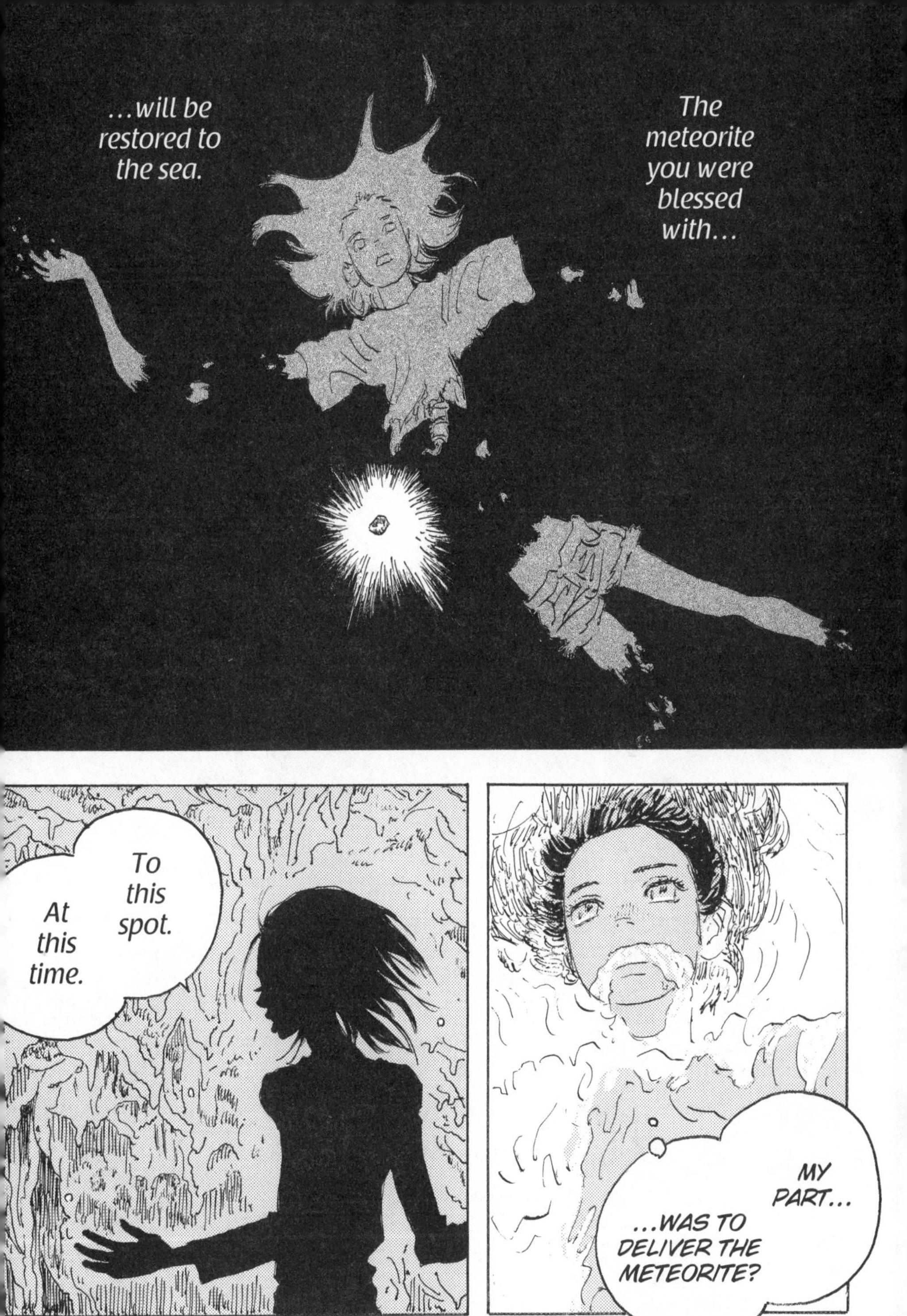
The meteorite you were blessed with…
…will be restored to the sea.
MY PART… …WAS TO DELIVER THE METEORITE?
To this spot. At this time.

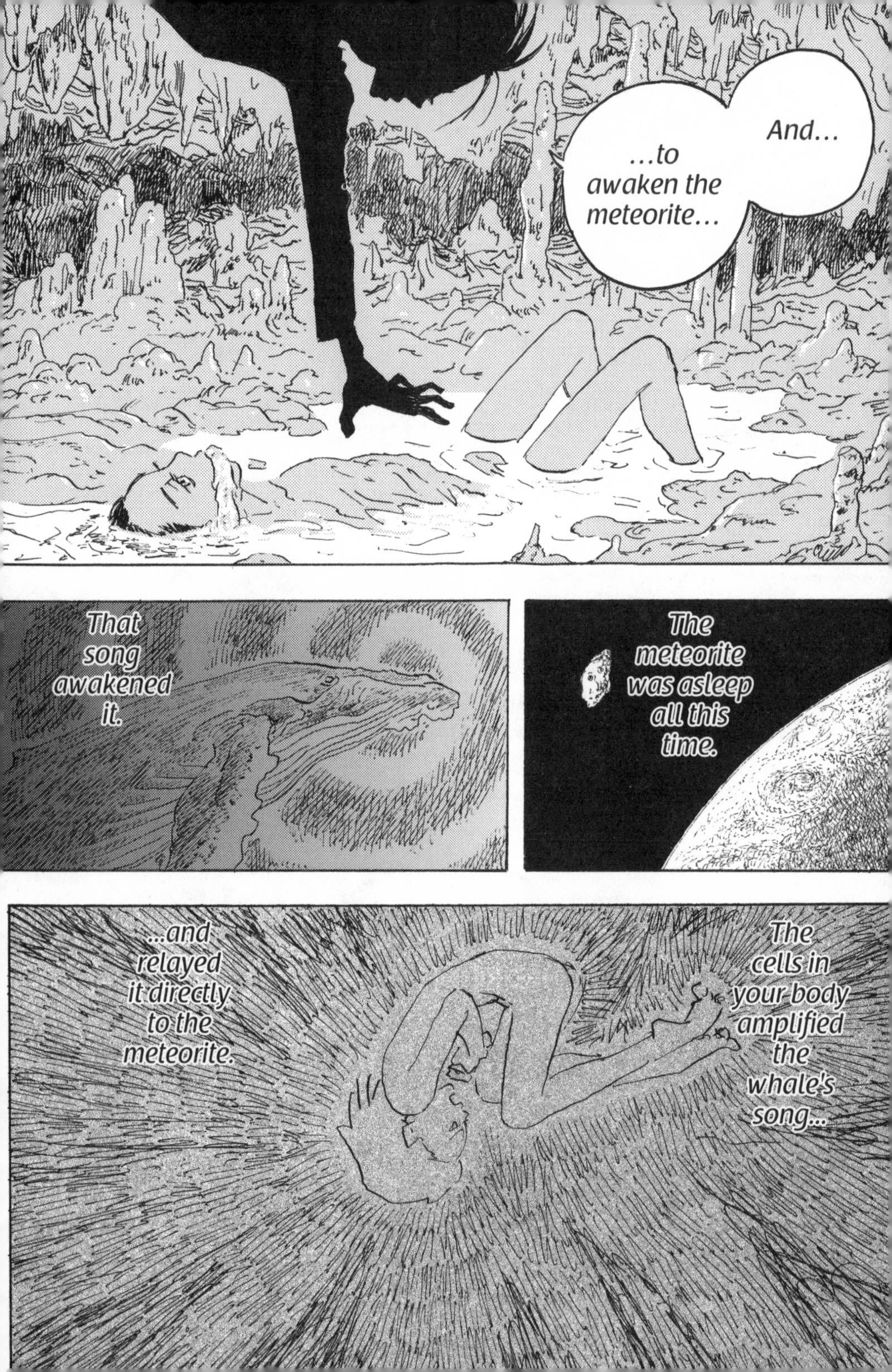
And…
…to awaken the meteorite…
The meteorite was asleep all this time.
That song awakened it.
The cells in your body amplified the whale's song...
...and relayed it directly to the meteorite.

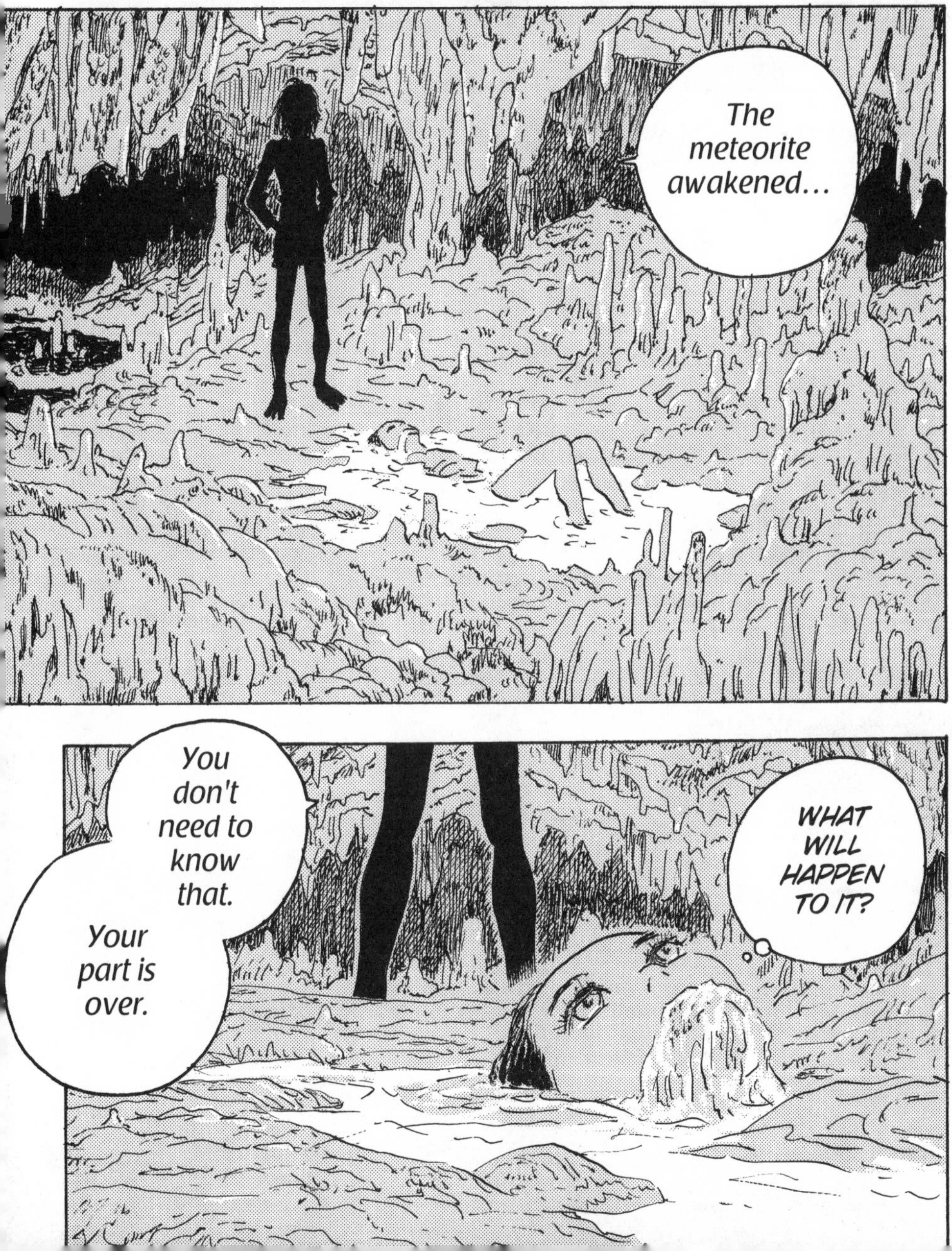
The meteorite awakened…
WHAT WILL HAPPEN TO IT?
You don't need to know that.
Your part is over.

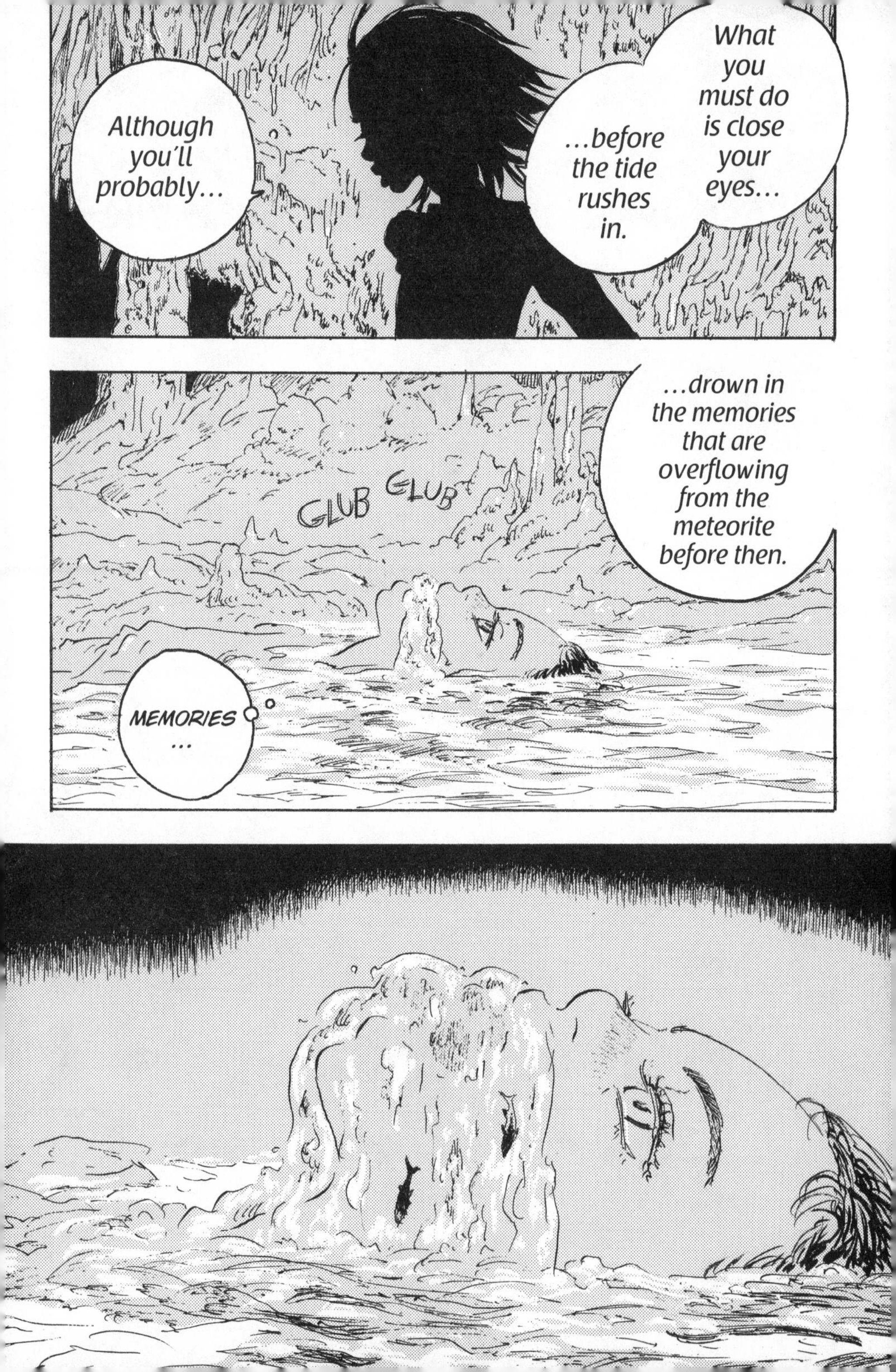
What you must do is close your eyes…
…before the tide rushes in.
Although you'll probably…
…drown in the memories that are overflowing from the meteorite before then.
GLUB GLUB
MEMORIES …

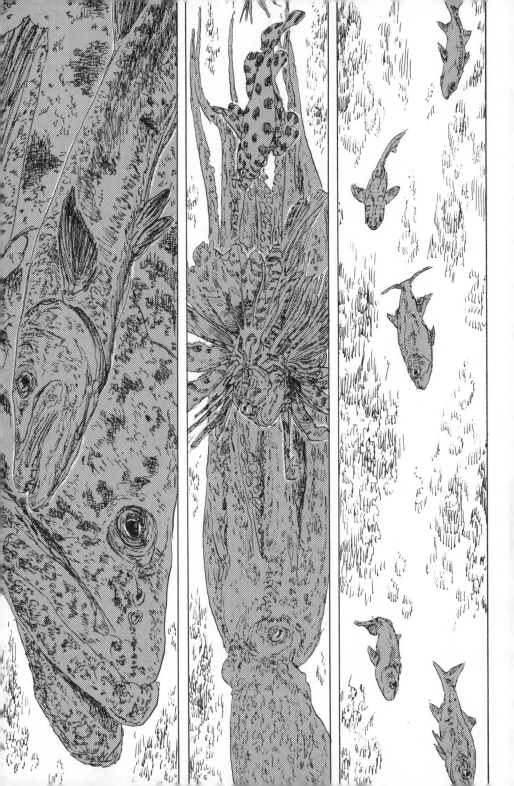

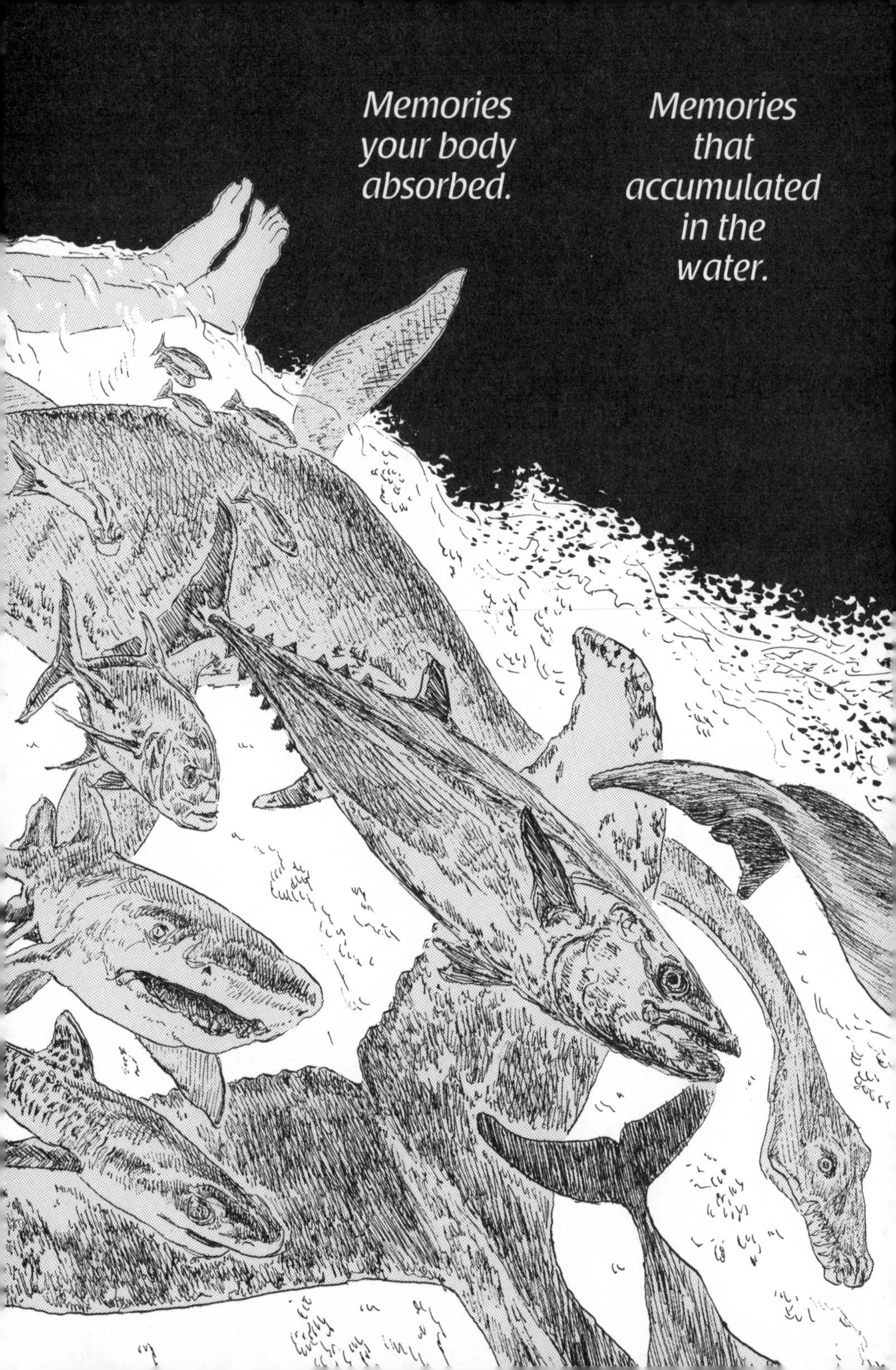
Memories that accumulated in the water.
Memories your body absorbed.

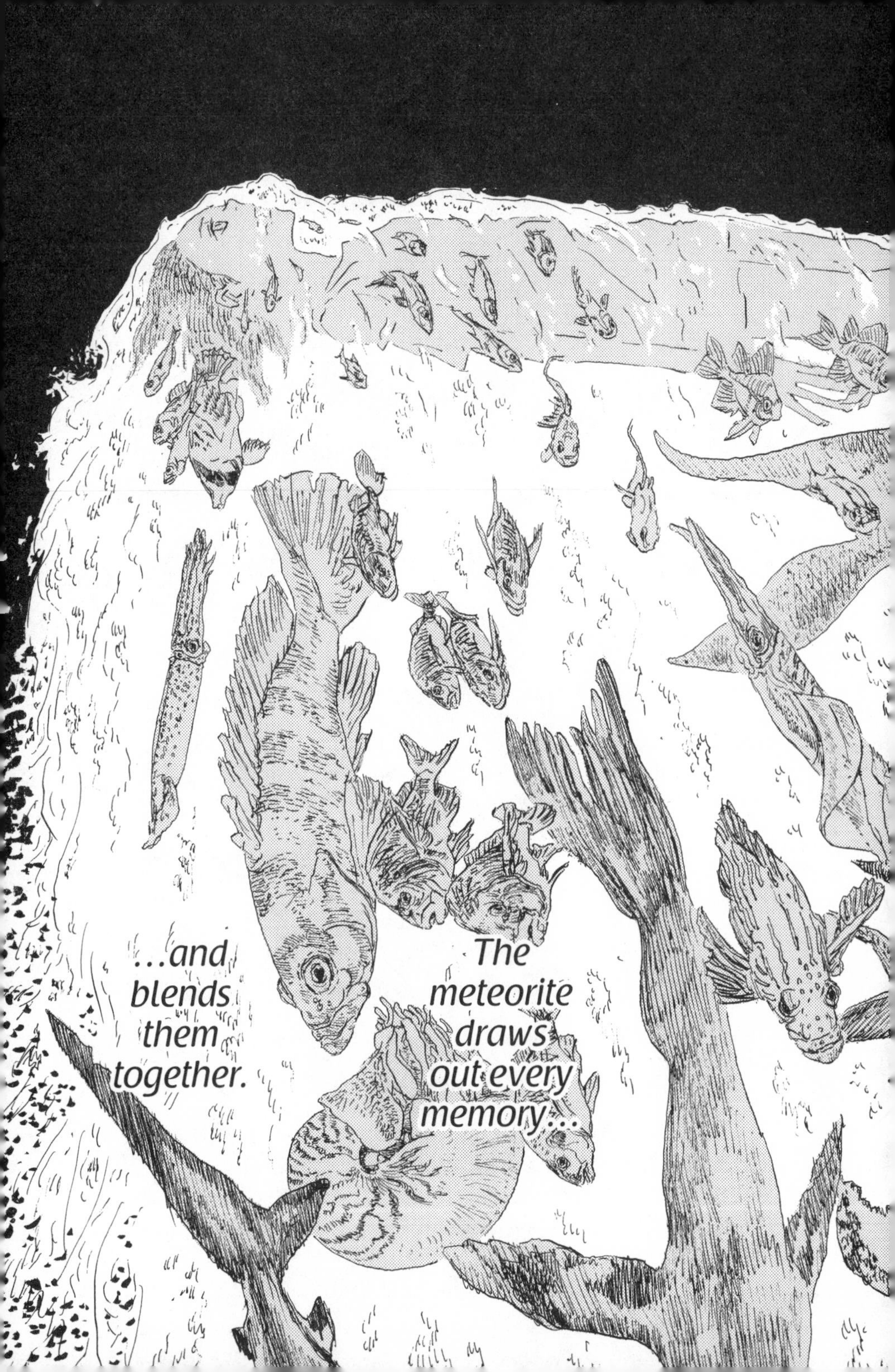
The meteorite draws out every memory...
...and blends them together.

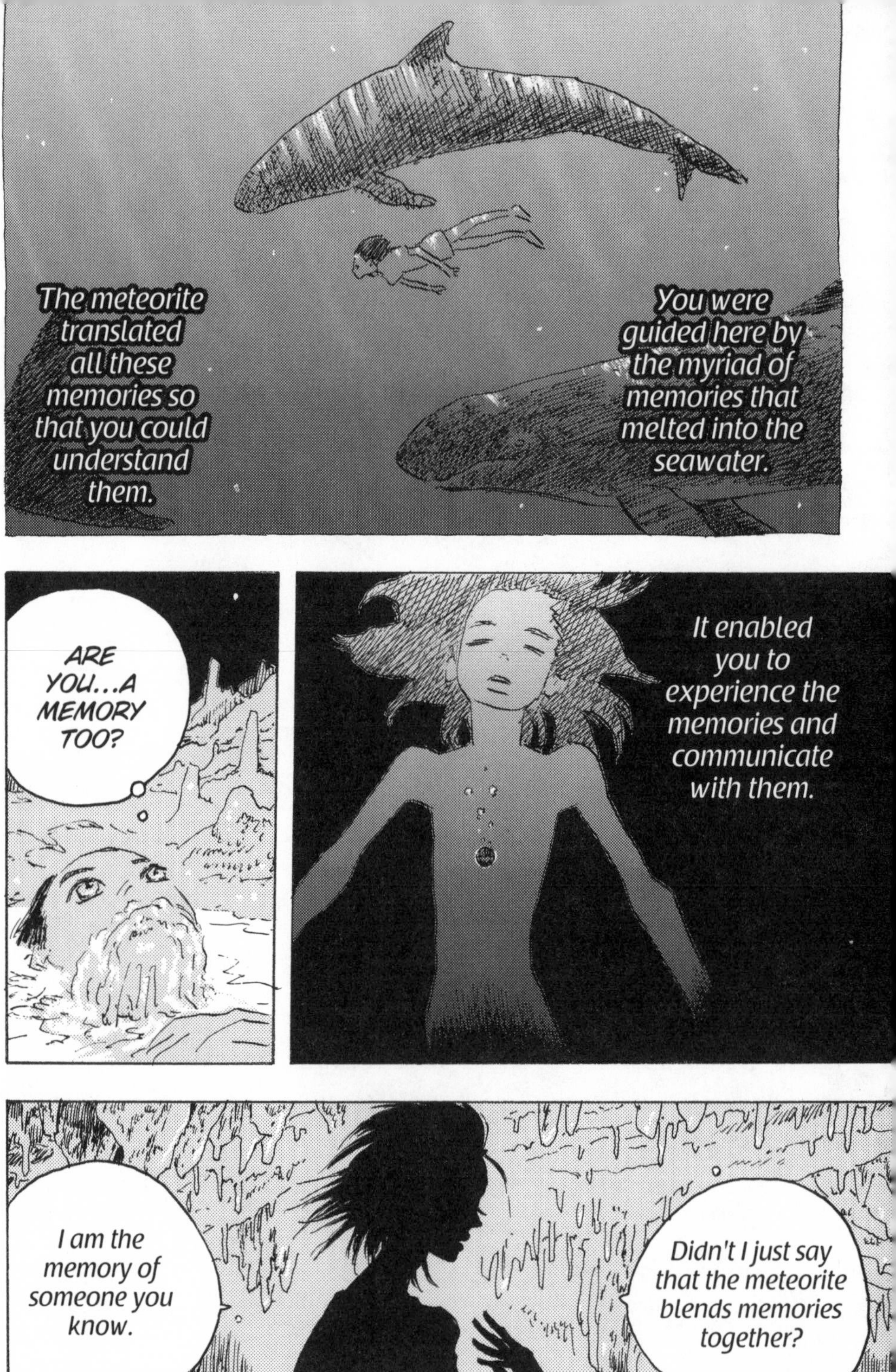
You were guided here by the myriad of memories that melted into the seawater.
The meteorite translated all these memories so that you could understand them.
It enabled you to experience the memories and communicate with them.
ARE YOU...A MEMORY TOO?
Didn't I just say that the meteorite blends memories together?
I am the memory of someone you know.

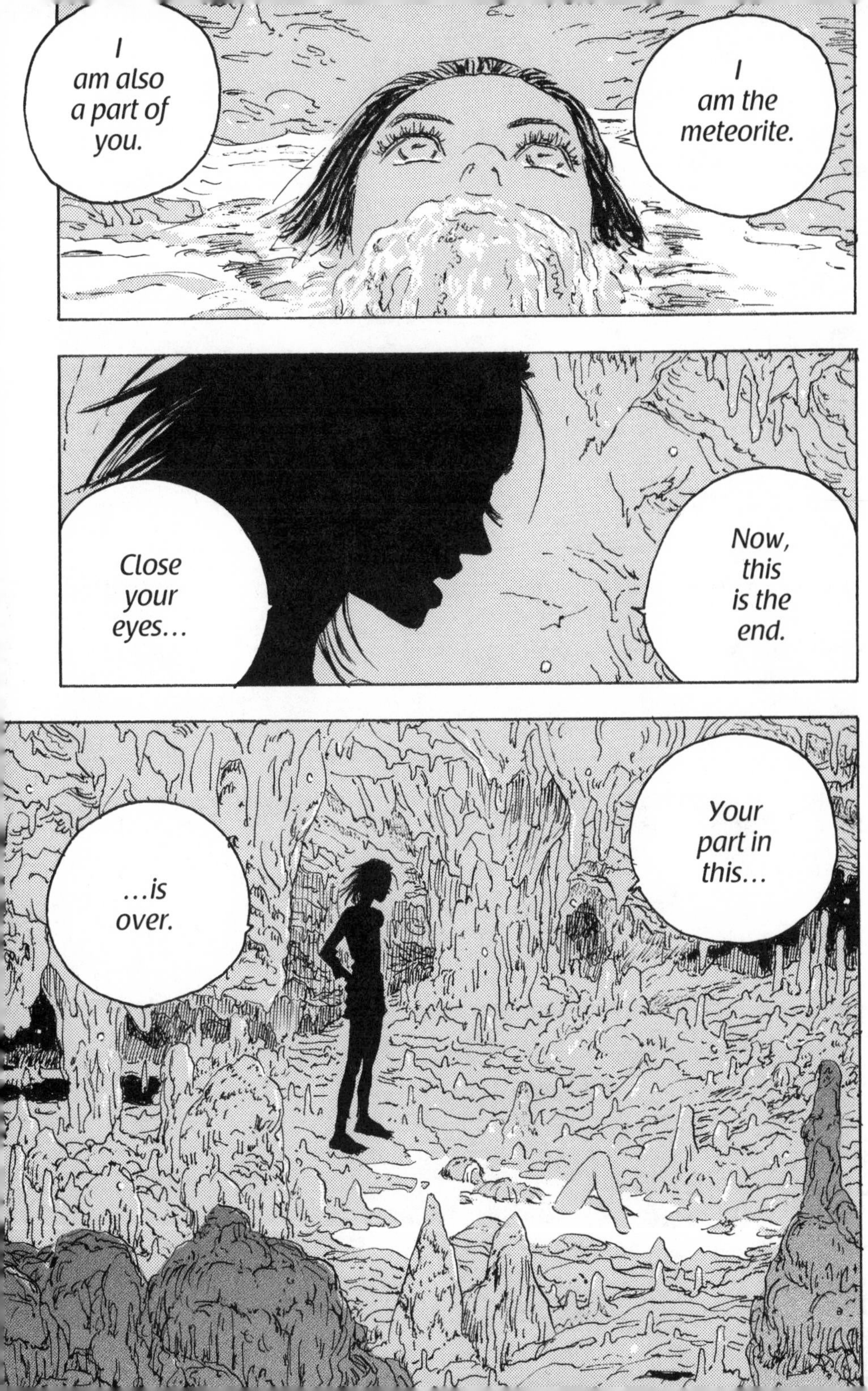
I am the meteorite.
I am also a part of you.
Now, this is the end.
Close your eyes…
Your part in this…
…is over.

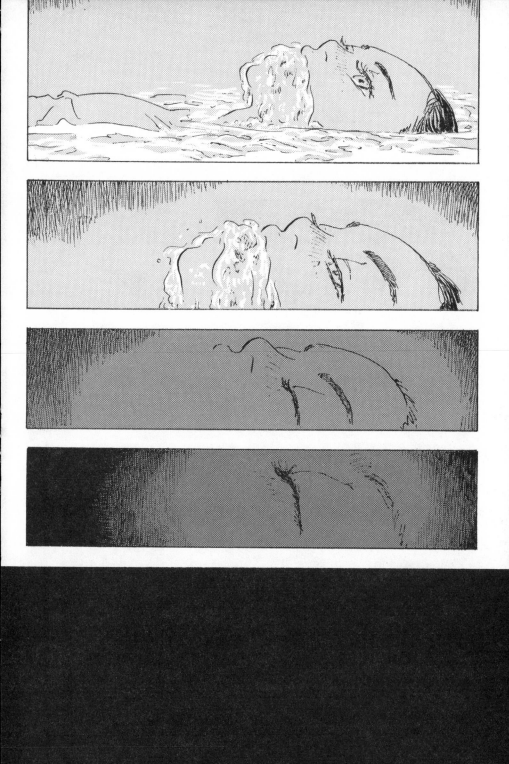

BUT...

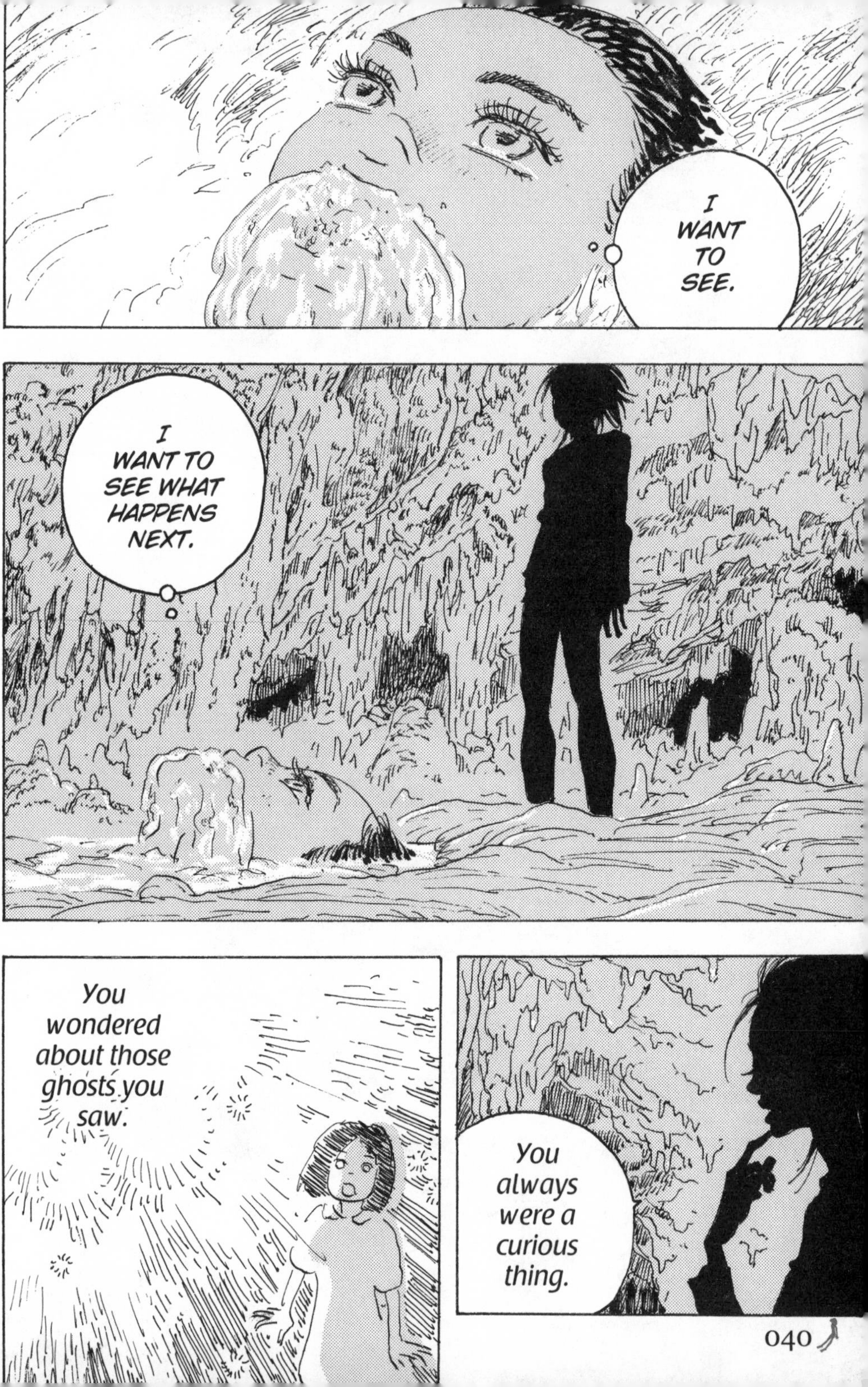
I WANT TO SEE.
I WANT TO SEE WHAT HAPPENS NEXT.
You always were a curious thing.
You wondered about those ghosts you saw.

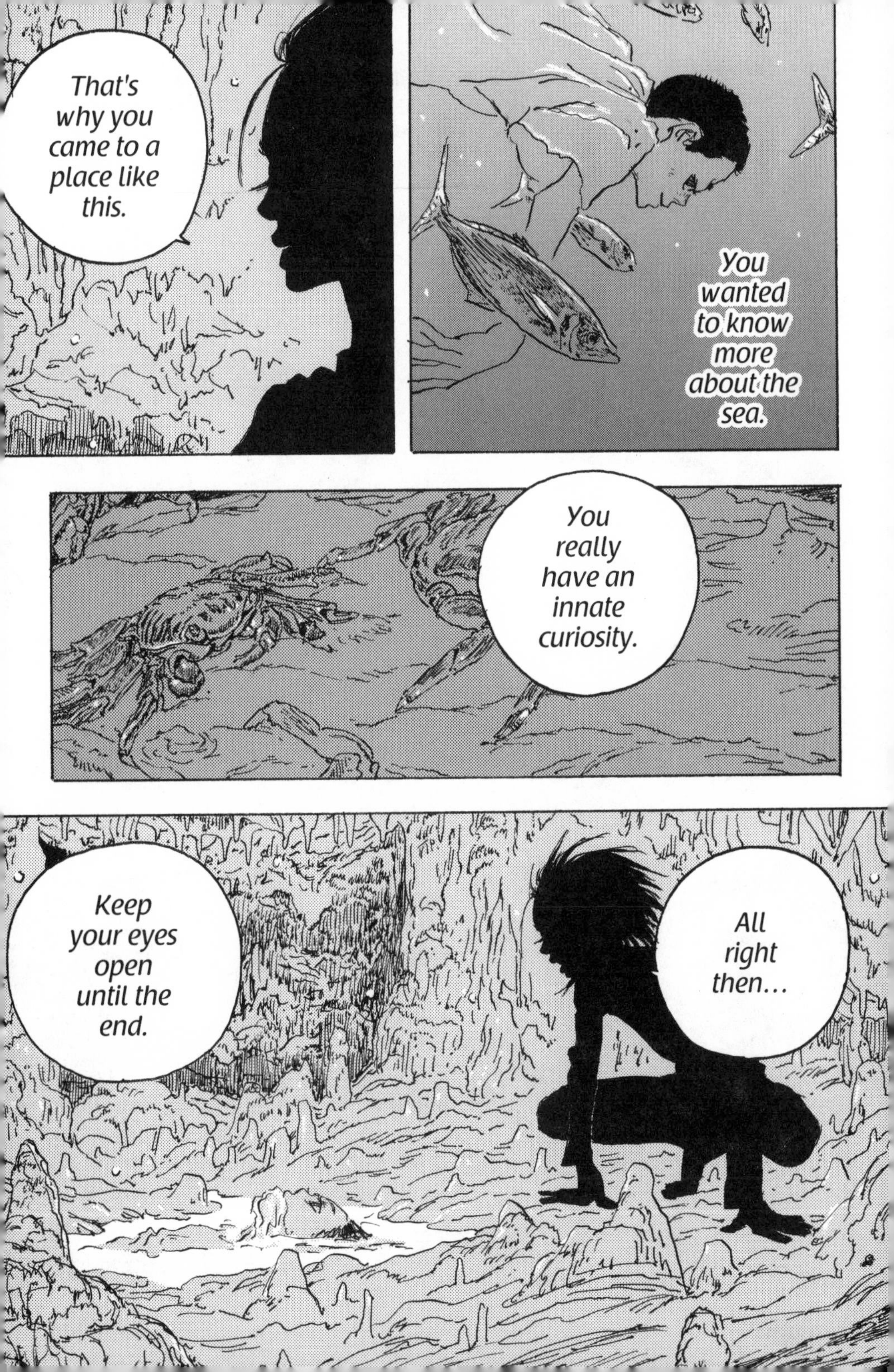
You wanted to know more about the sea.
That's why you came to a place like this.
You really have an innate curiosity.
All right then...
Keep your eyes open until the end.

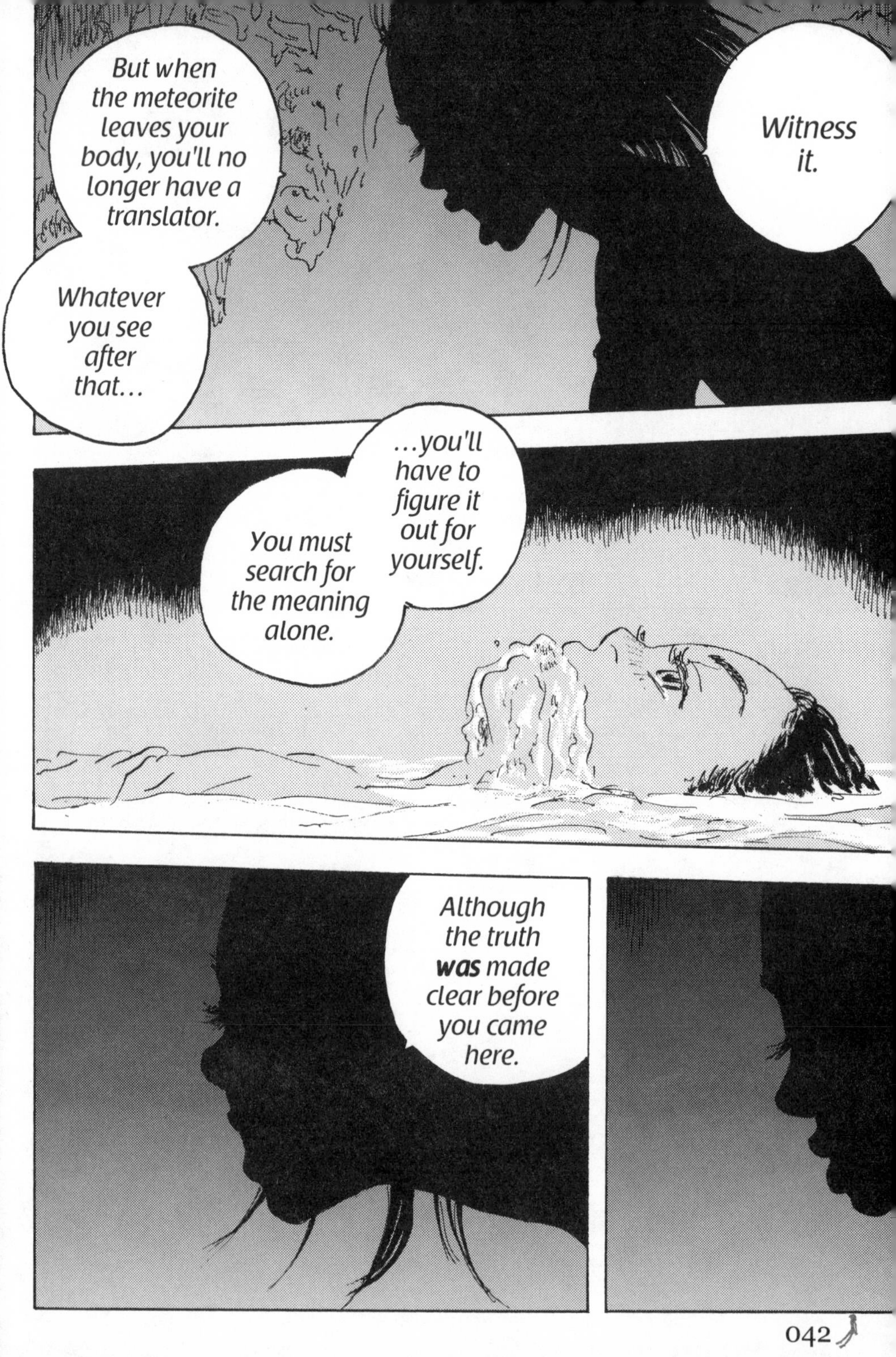
Witness it.
But when the meteorite leaves your body, you'll no longer have a translator.
Whatever you see after that…
…you'll have to figure it out for yourself.
You must search for the meaning alone.
Although the truth **was** made clear before you came here.

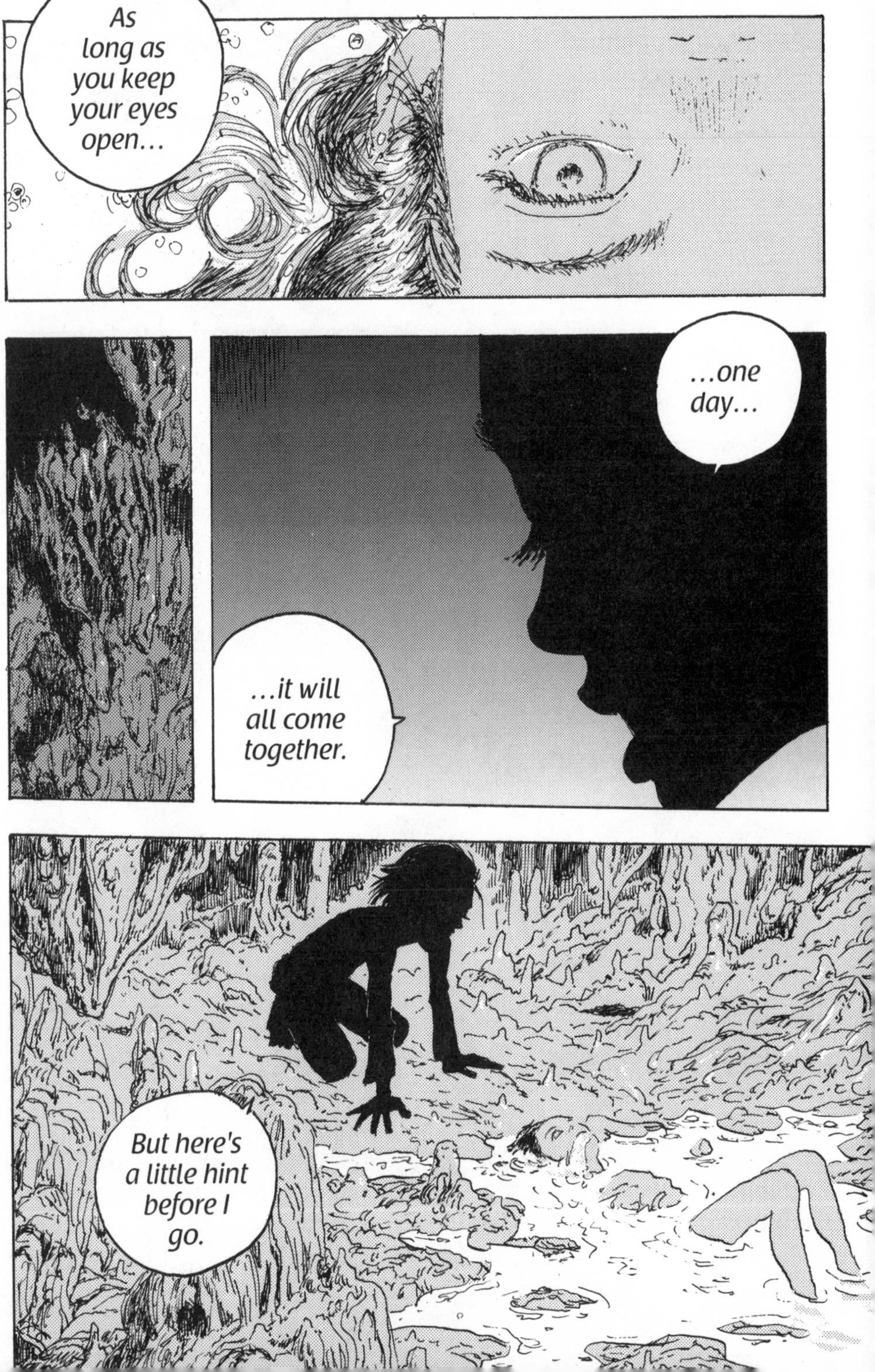
As long as you keep your eyes open...
...one day...
...it will all come together.
But here's a little hint before I go.

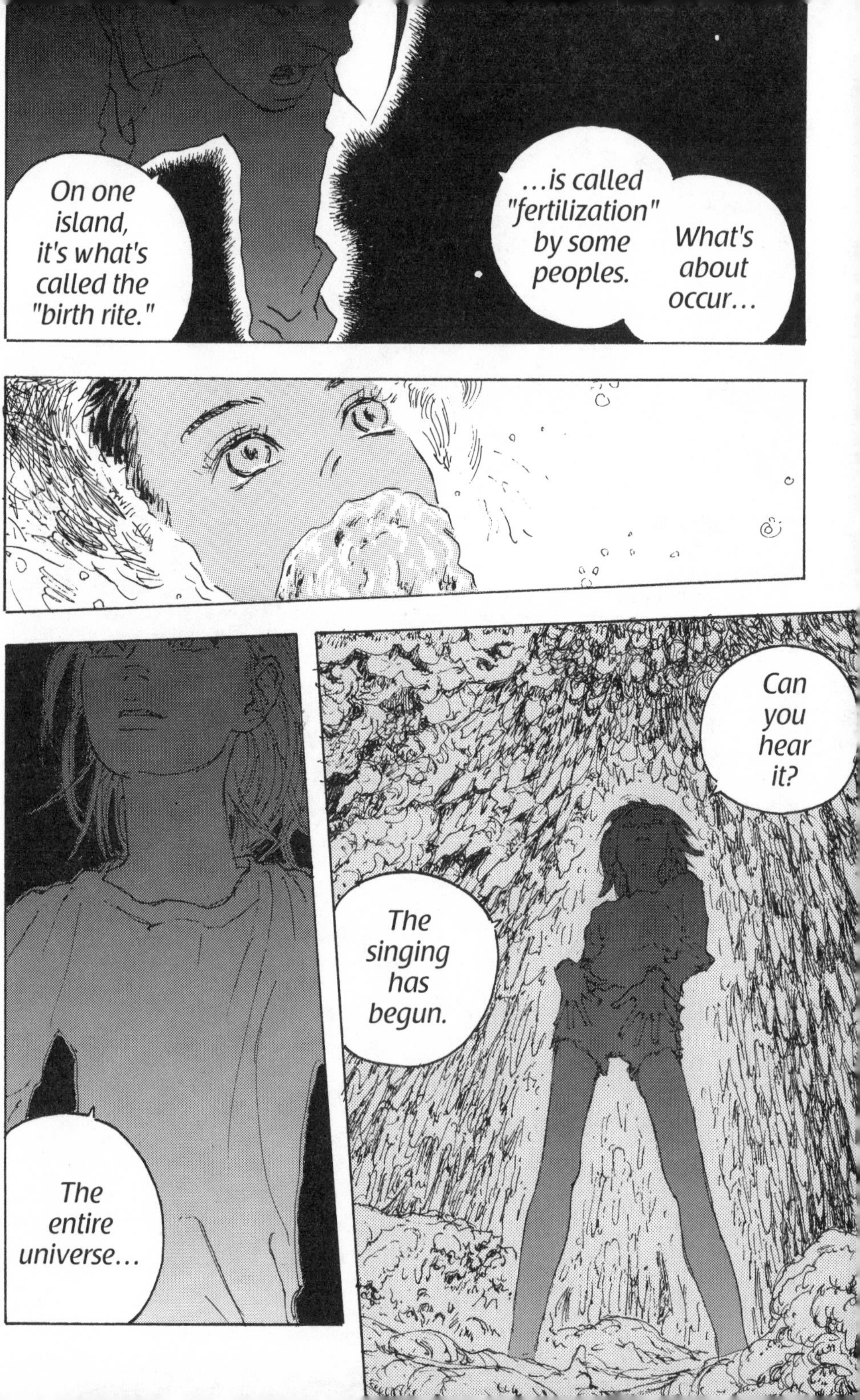
What's about occur…
…is called "fertilization" by some peoples.
On one island, it's what's called the "birth rite."
Can you hear it?
The singing has begun.
The entire universe…

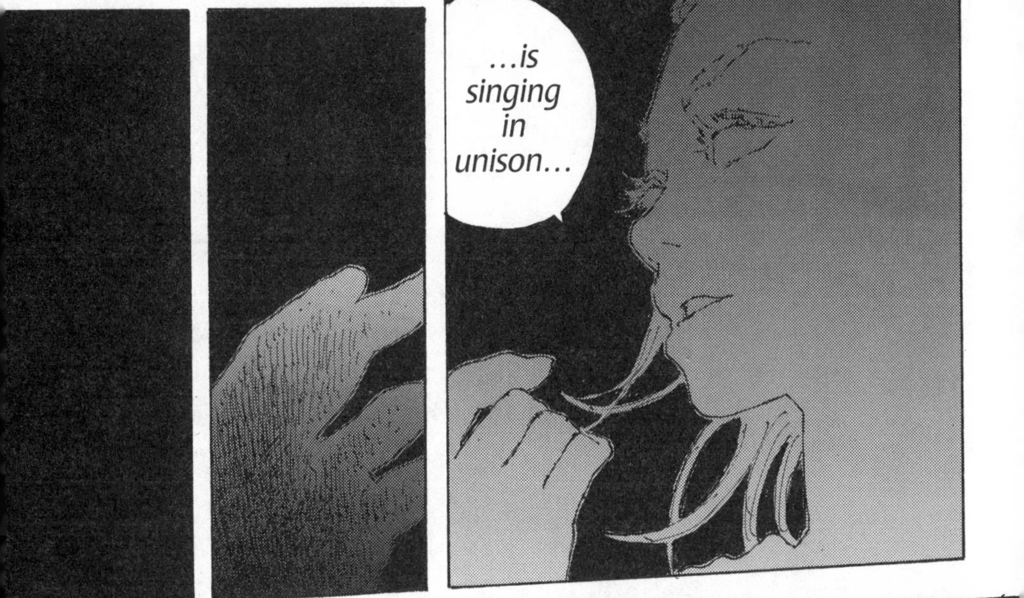
…is singing in unison…
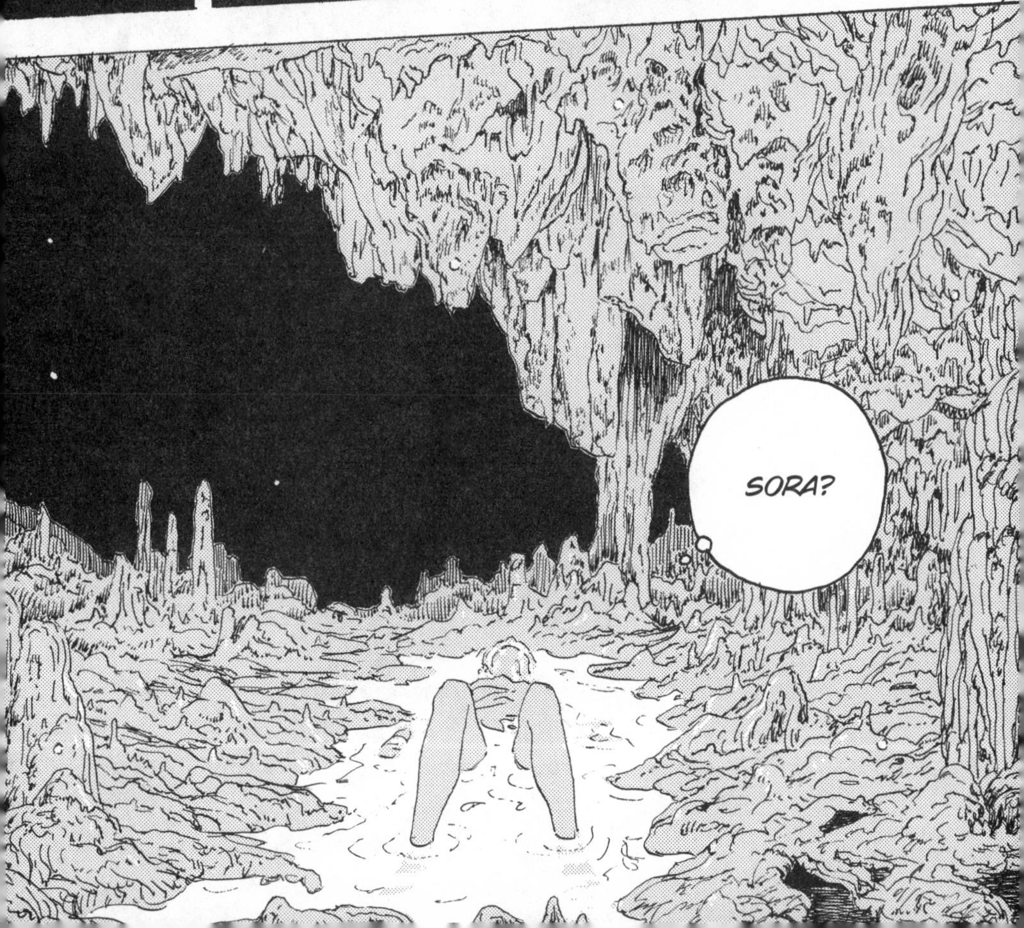
SORA?

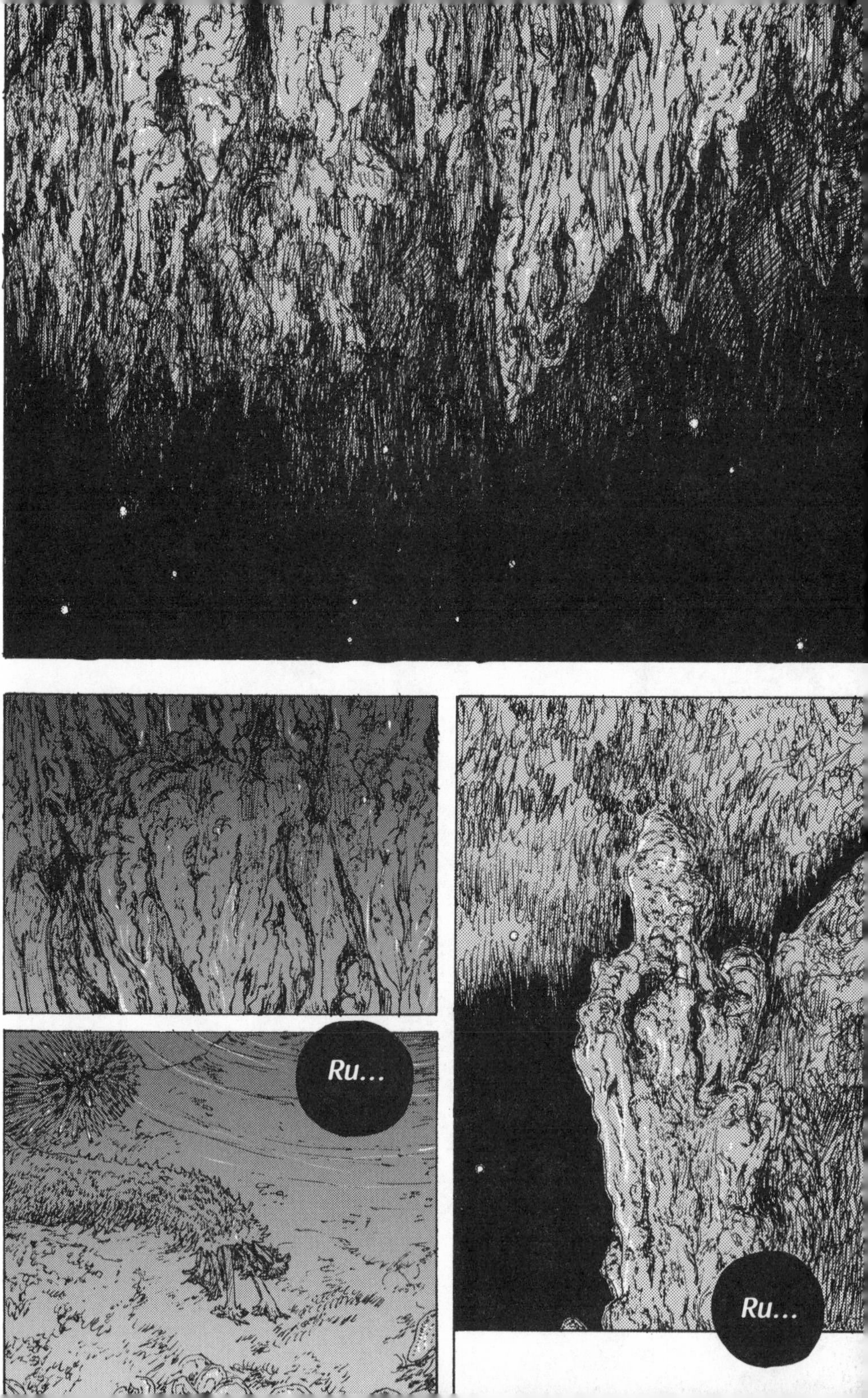
Ru...
Ru...

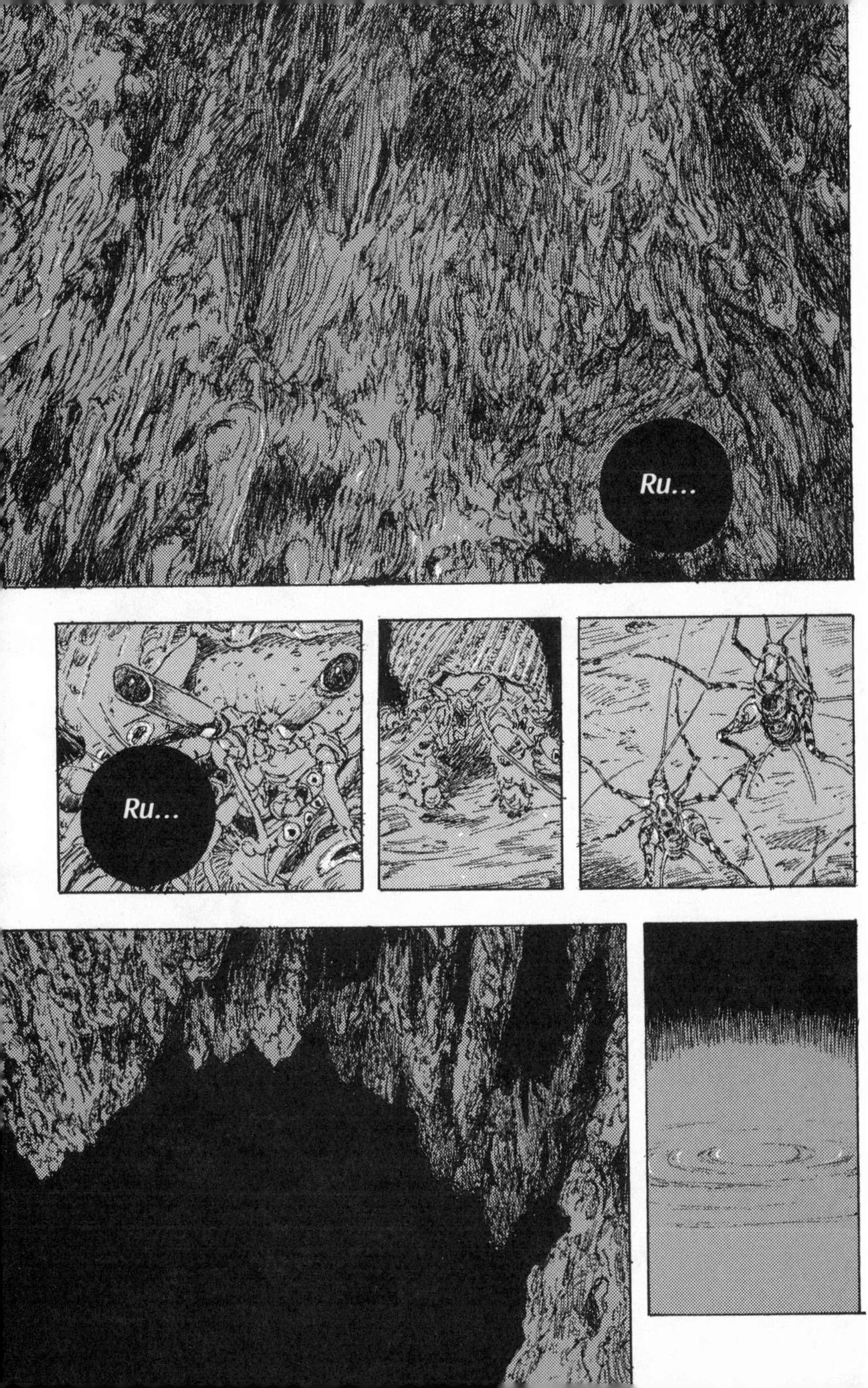
Ru…
Ru…

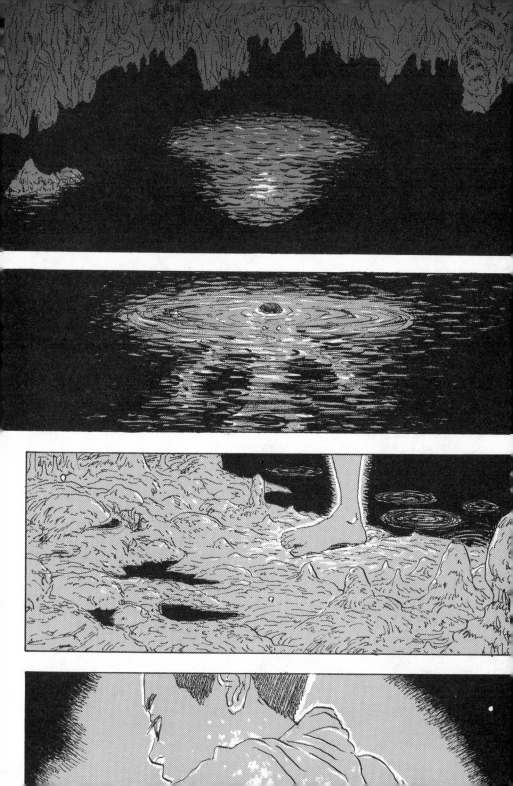

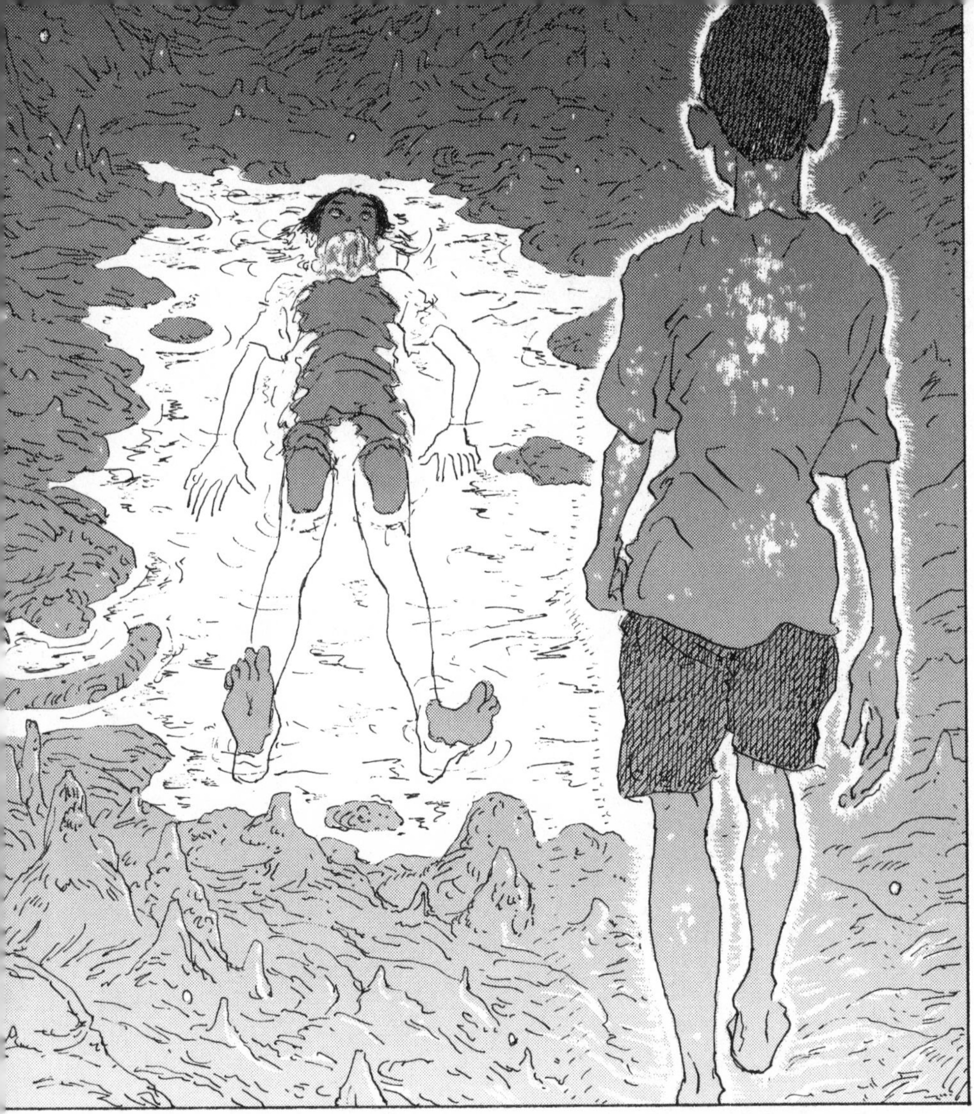
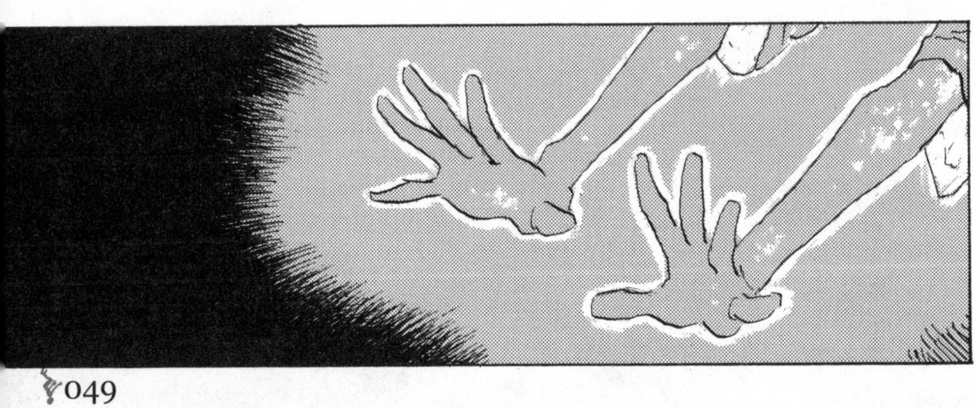

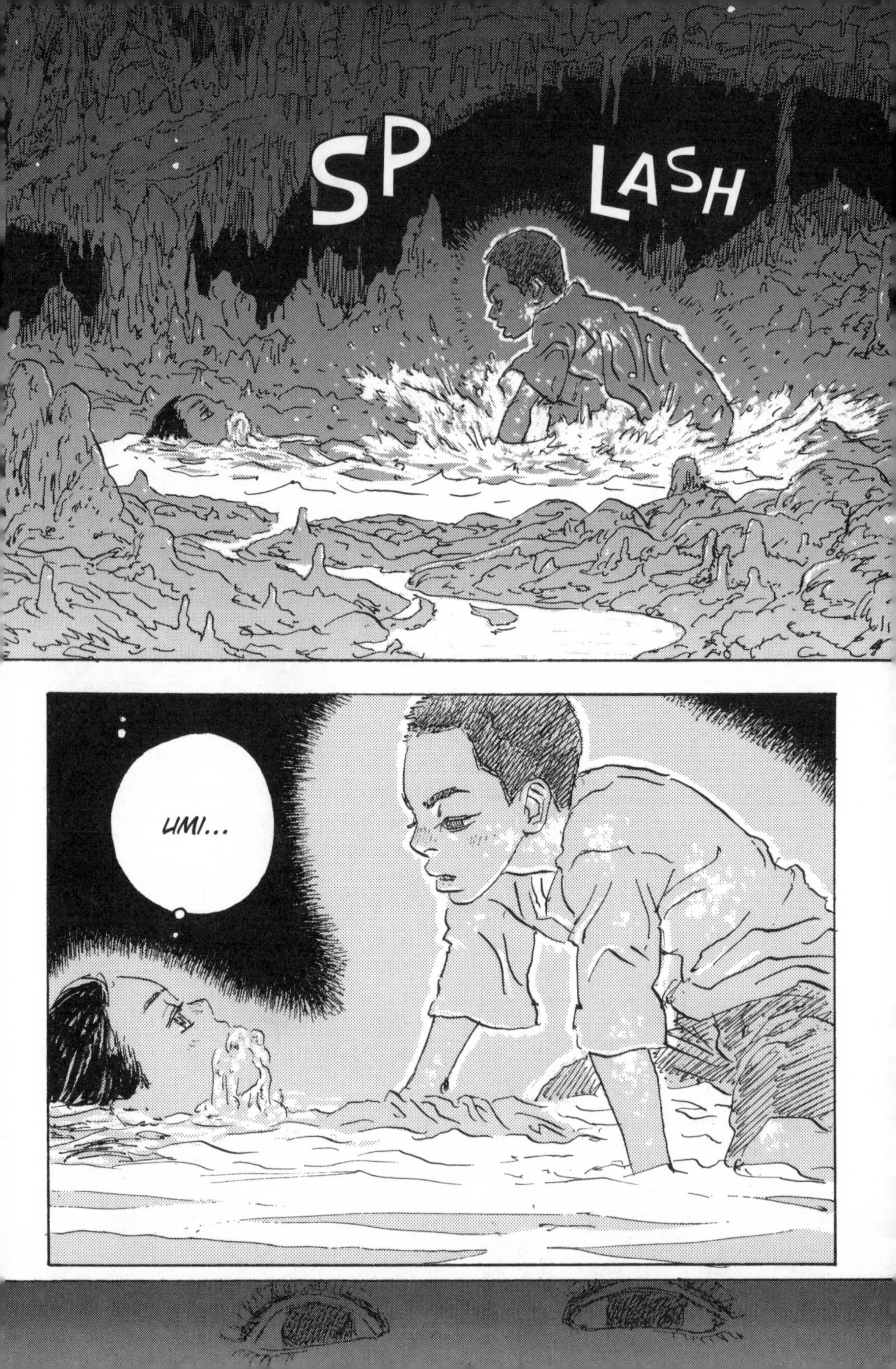
SPLASH
UMI...

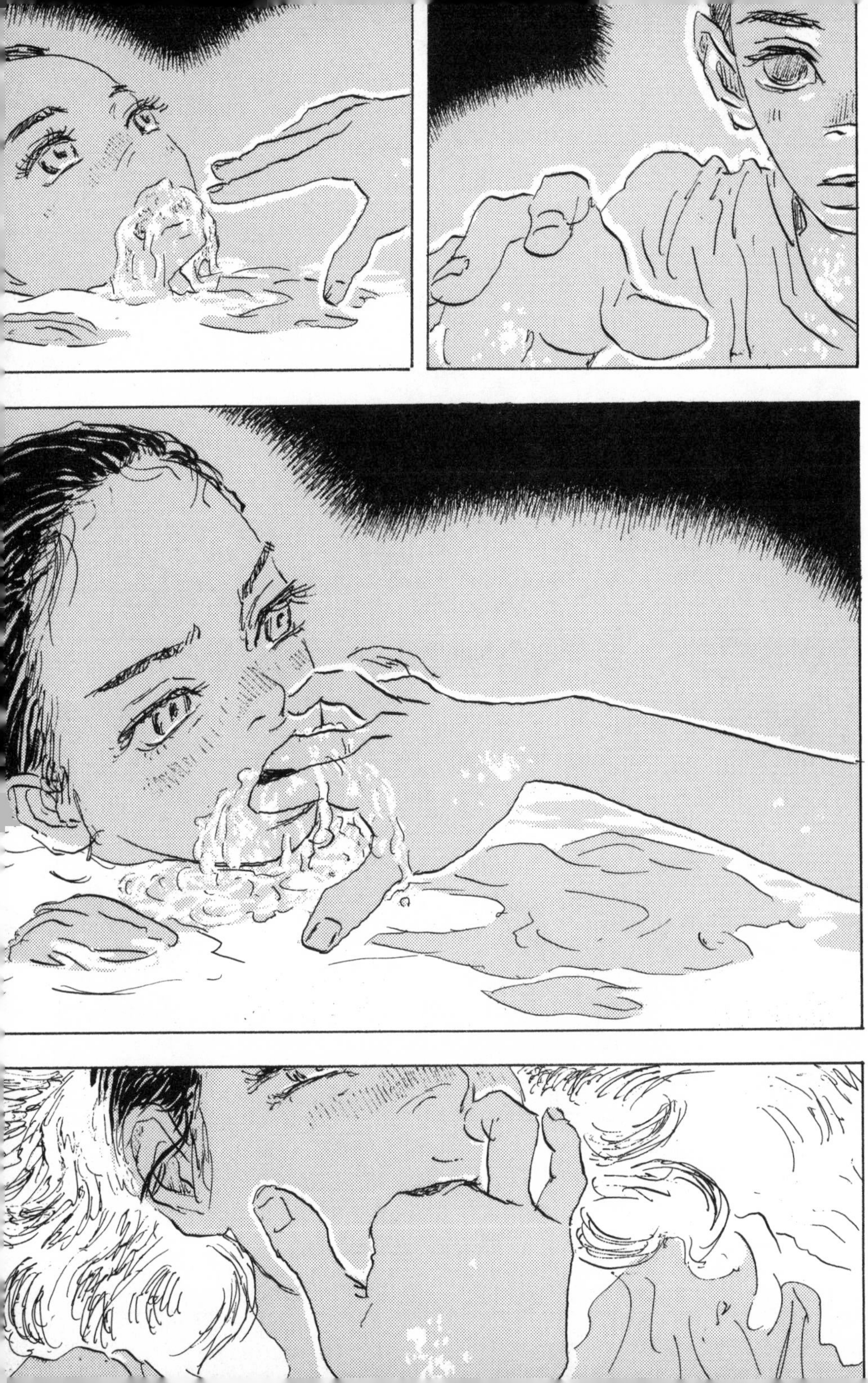

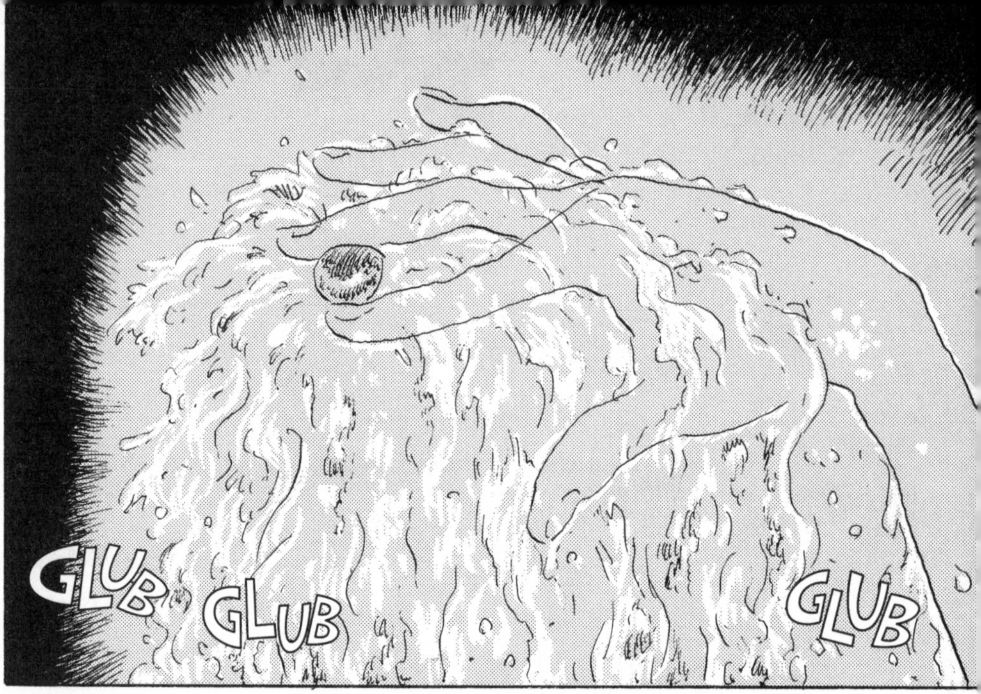
GLUB
GLUB
GLUB

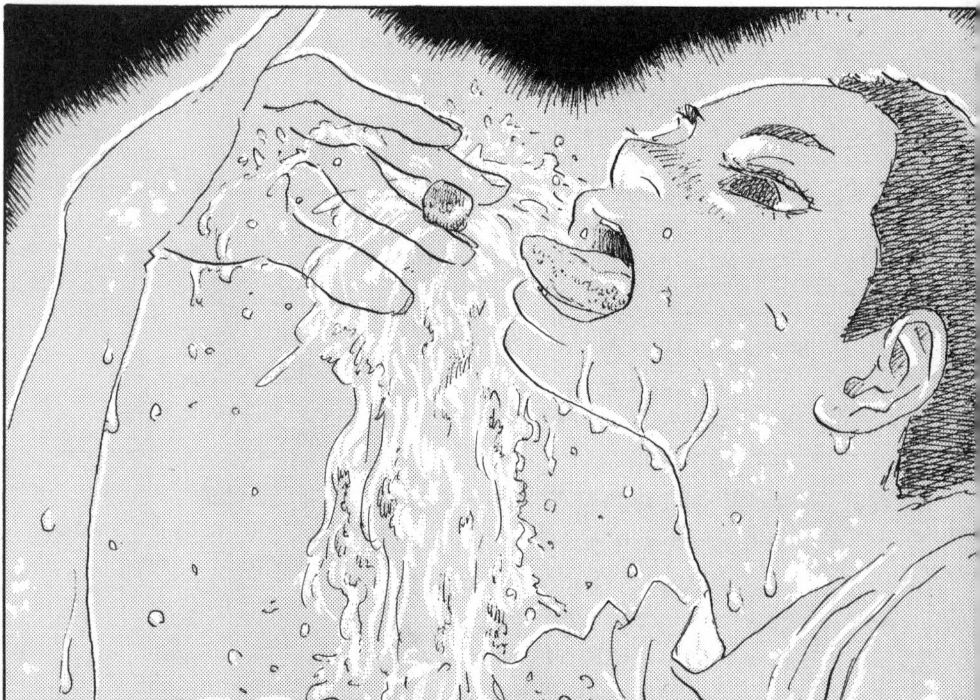

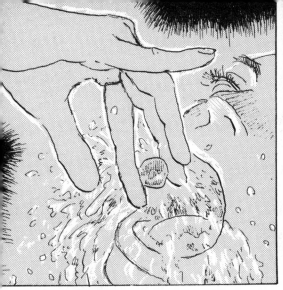
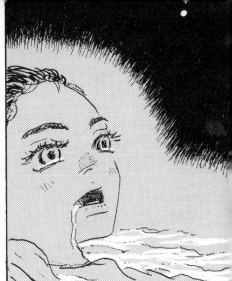

SH HU U

EVERY LEGEND IS THE SAME...

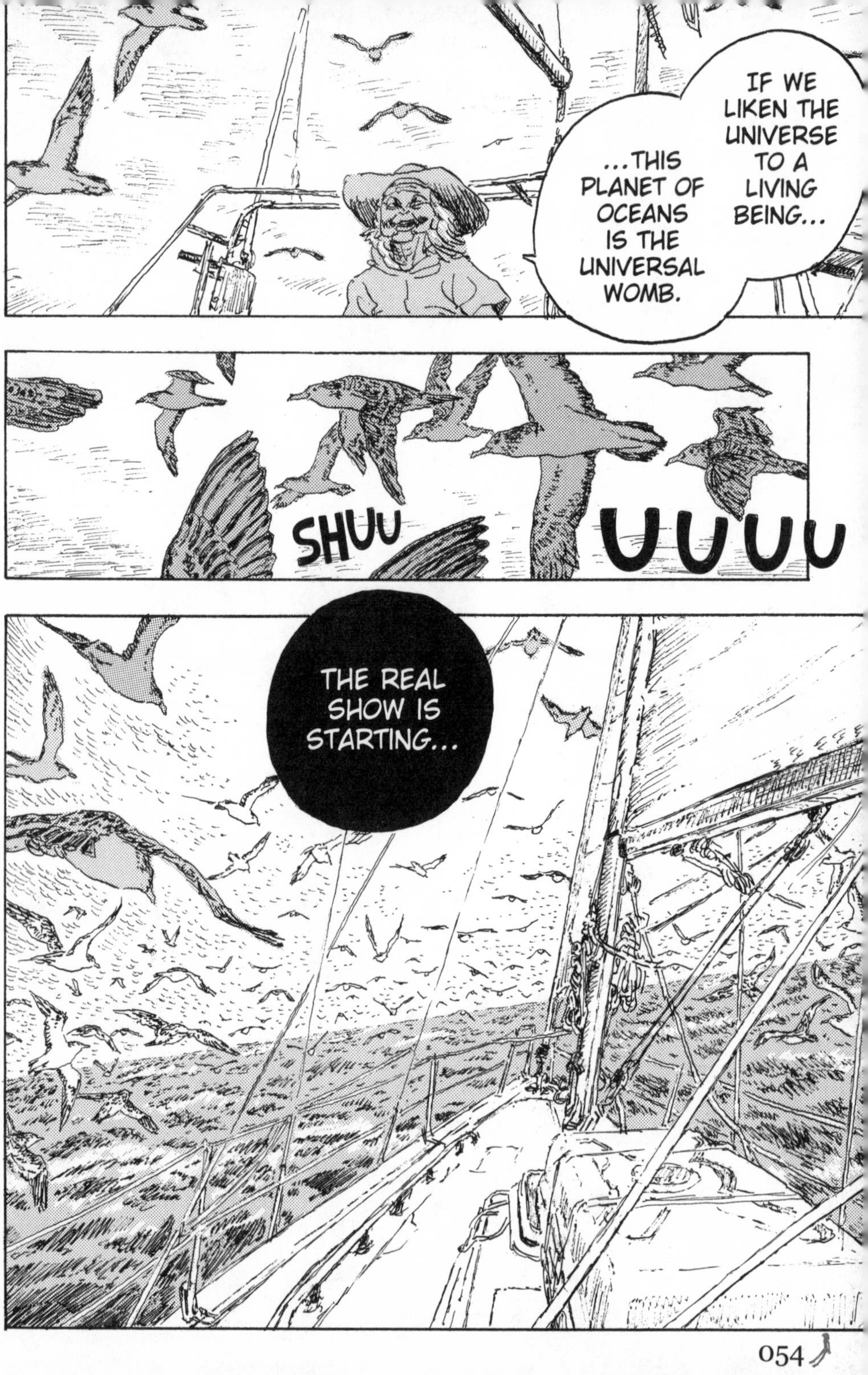
IF WE LIKEN THE UNIVERSE TO A LIVING BEING...
...THIS PLANET OF OCEANS IS THE UNIVERSAL WOMB.
SHUU UUUU
THE REAL SHOW IS STARTING...

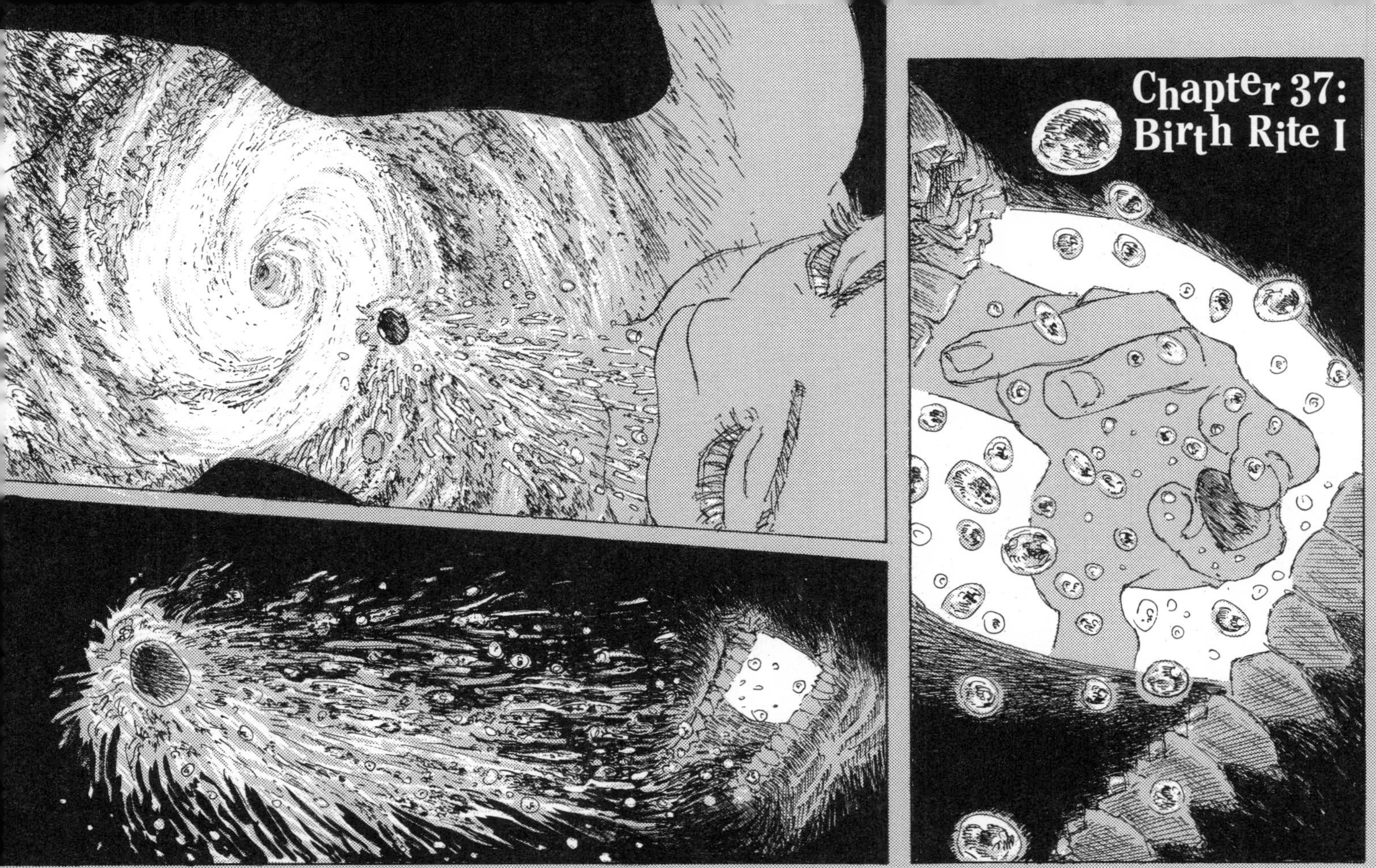
Chapter 37:
Birth Rite I

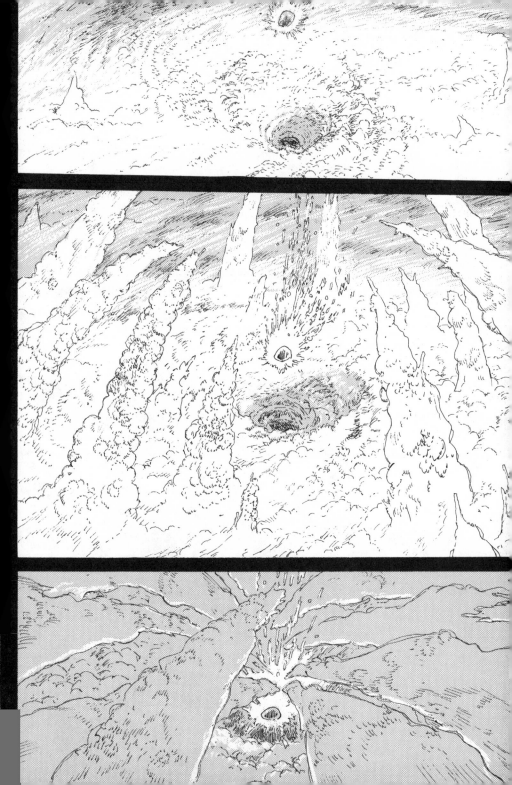

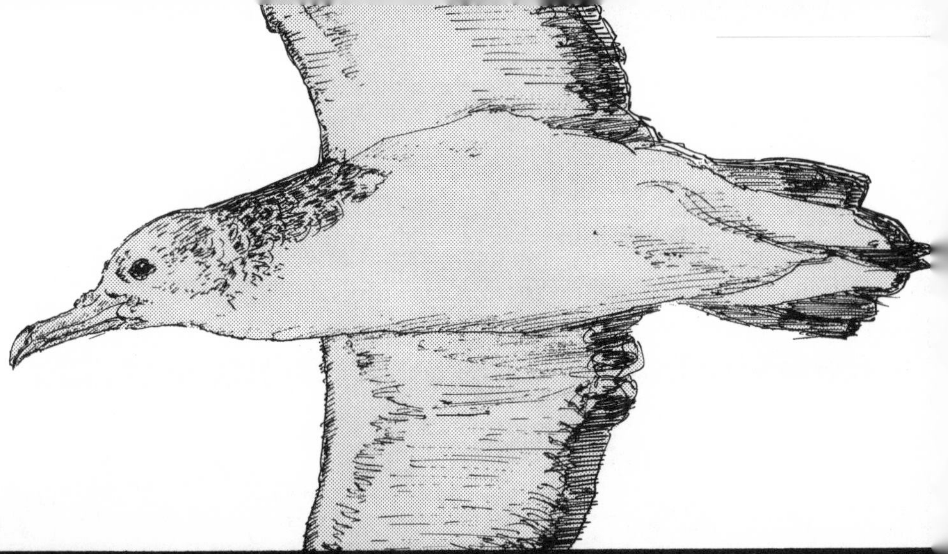

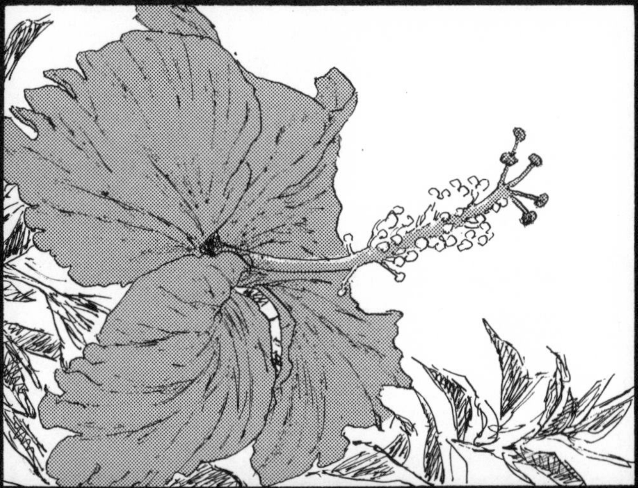

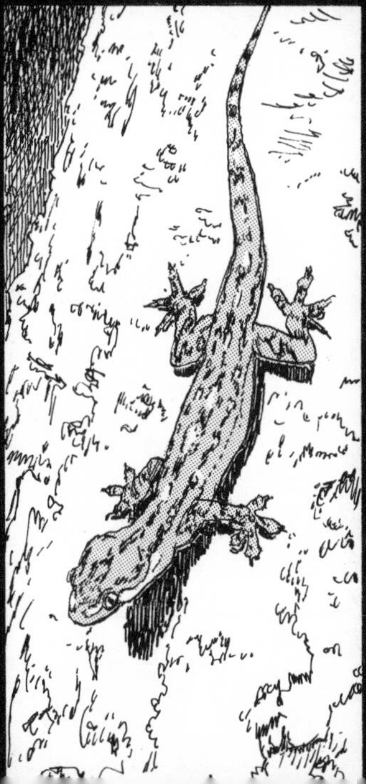

Chapter 37: Birth Rite I

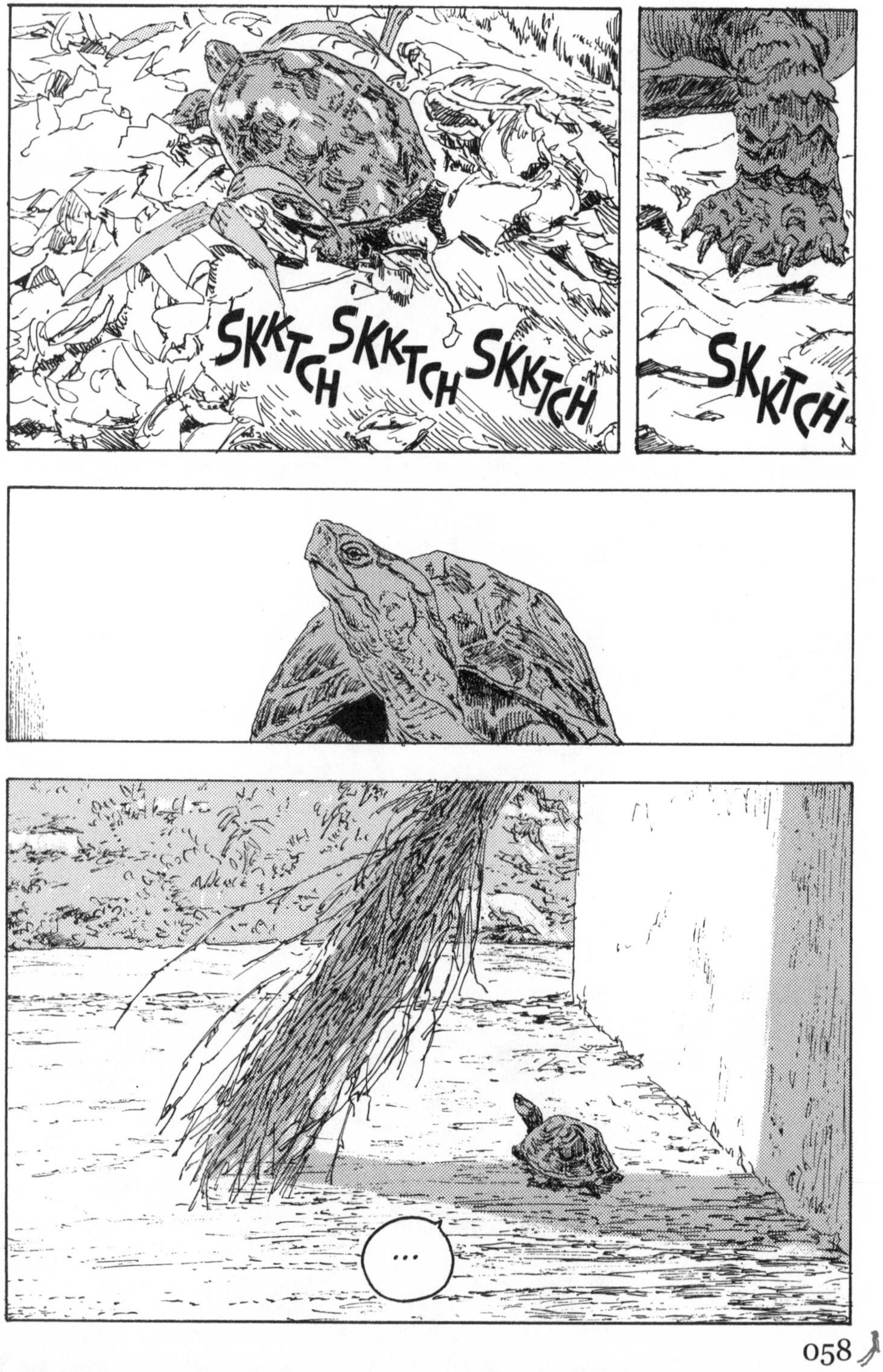
SKKTCH
SKKTCH
SKKTCH
SKKTCH
...

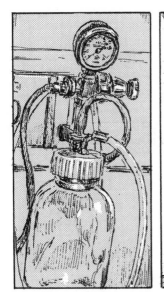

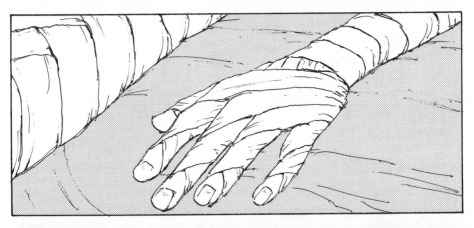
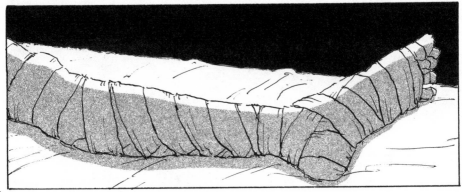

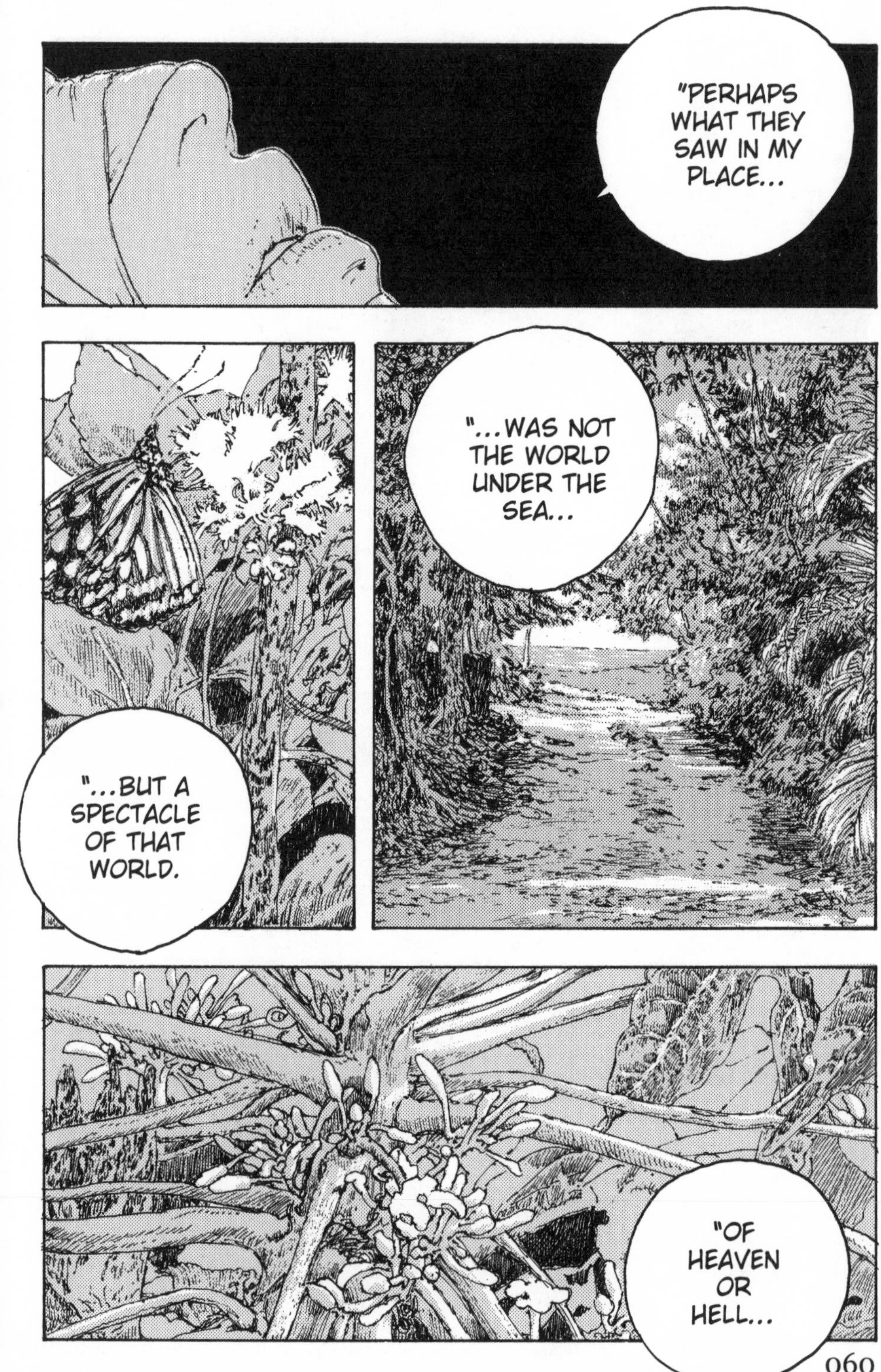
"PERHAPS WHAT THEY SAW IN MY PLACE...
"...WAS NOT THE WORLD UNDER THE SEA...
"...BUT A SPECTACLE OF THAT WORLD.
"OF HEAVEN OR HELL...

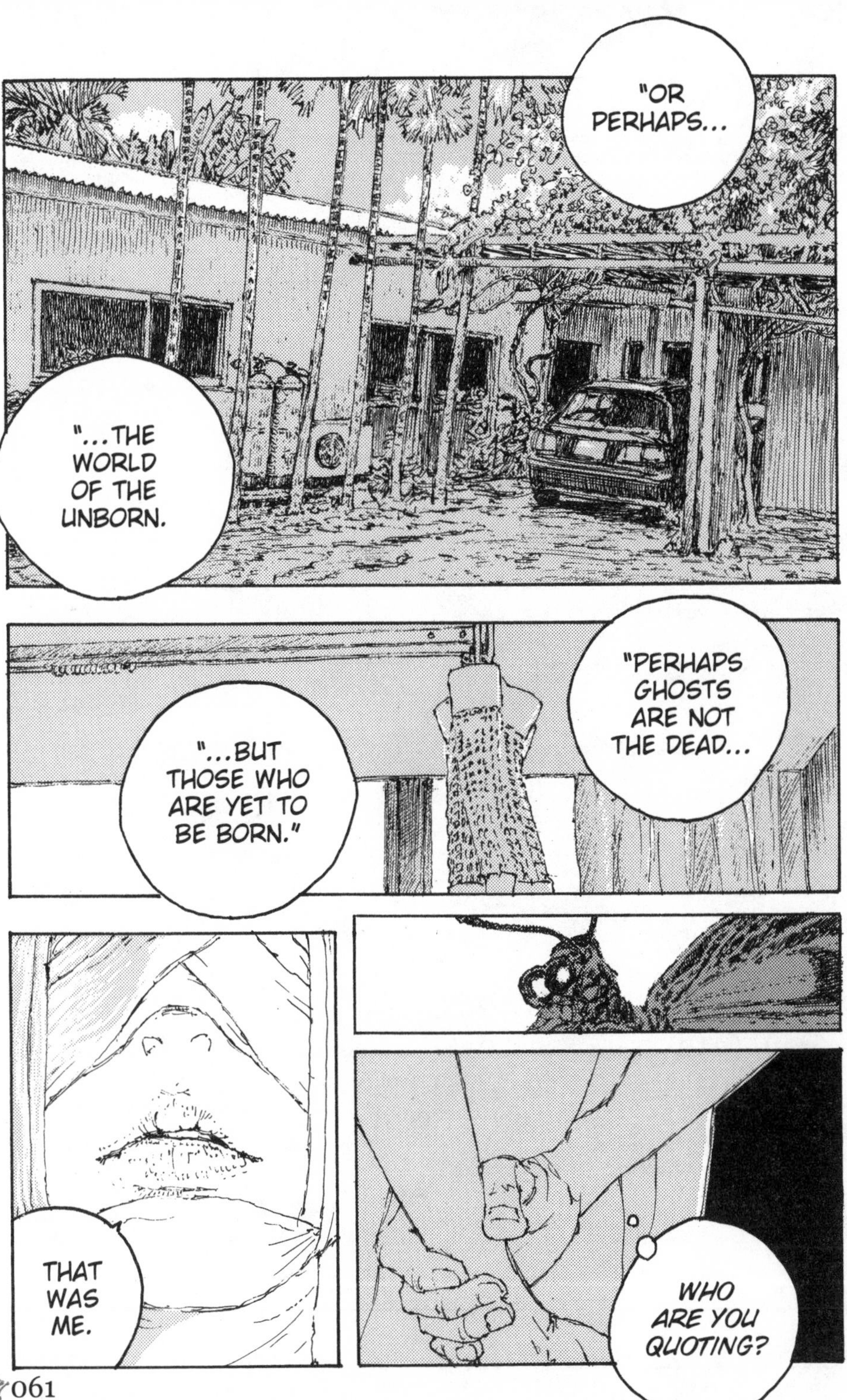
"OR PERHAPS...
"...THE WORLD OF THE UNBORN.
"PERHAPS GHOSTS ARE NOT THE DEAD...
"...BUT THOSE WHO ARE YET TO BE BORN."
WHO ARE YOU QUOTING?
THAT WAS ME.

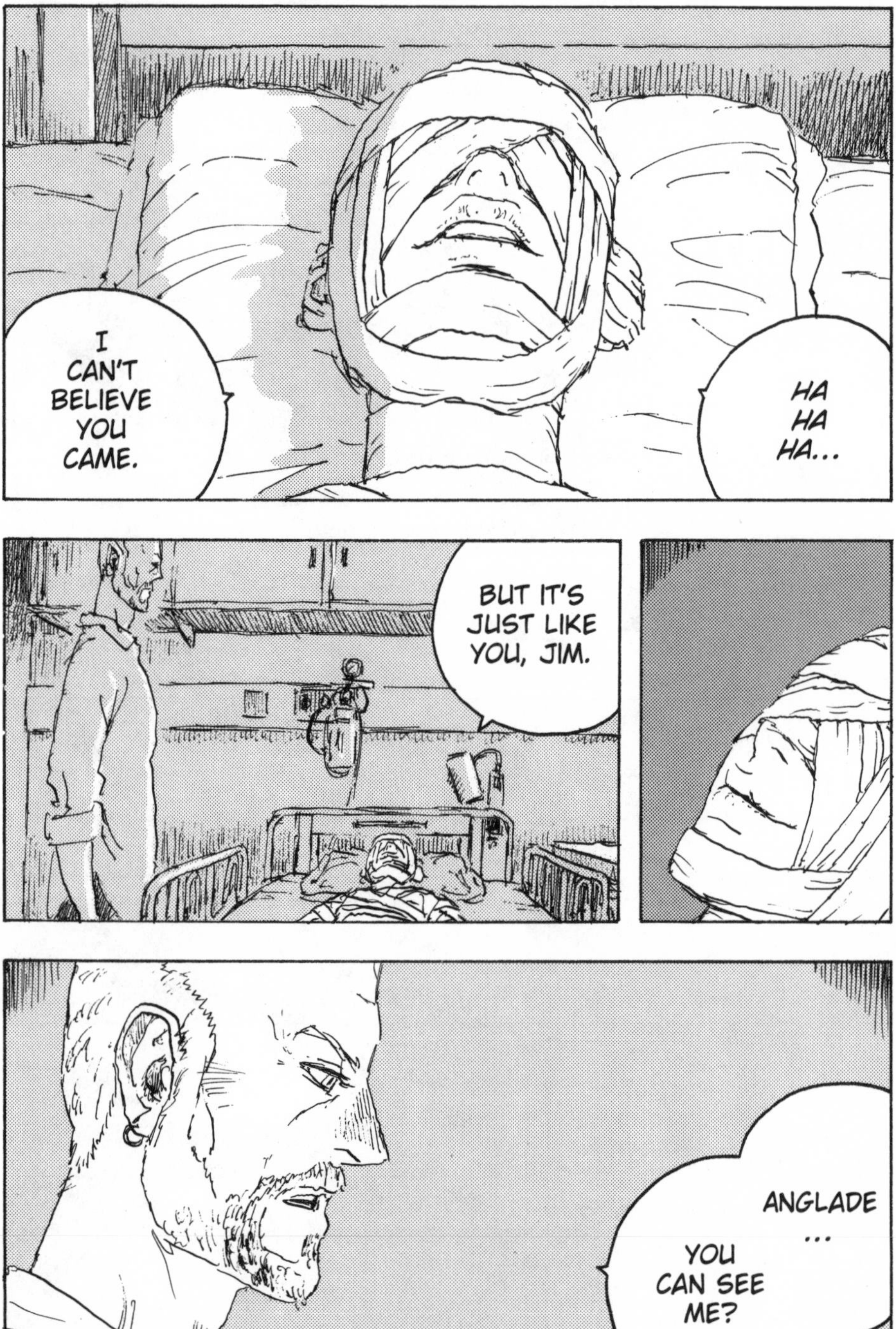
HA HA HA...
I CAN'T BELIEVE YOU CAME.
BUT IT'S JUST LIKE YOU, JIM.
ANGLADE ... YOU CAN SEE ME?

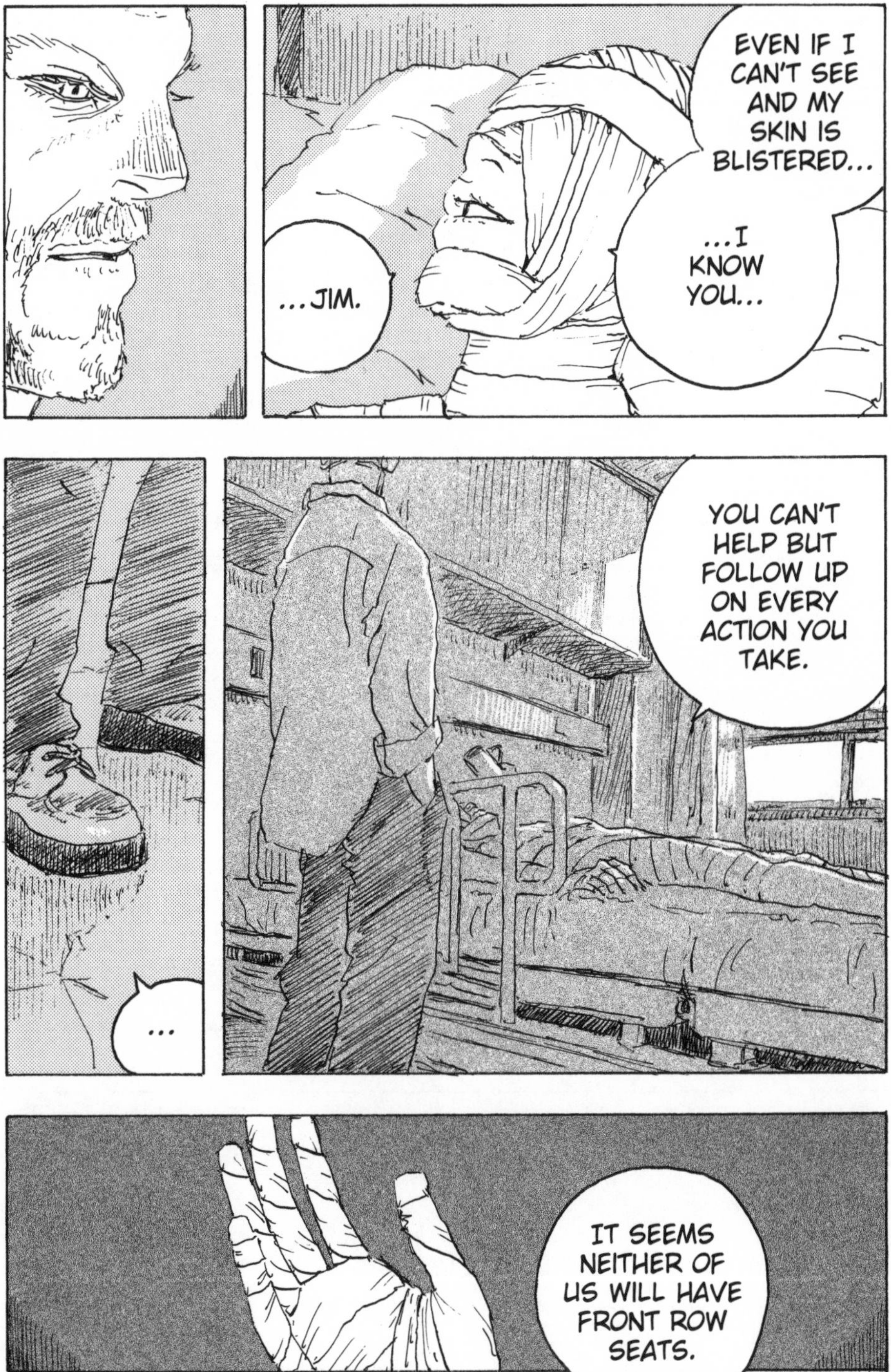
EVEN IF I CAN'T SEE AND MY SKIN IS BLISTERED...
...I KNOW YOU...
...JIM.
YOU CAN'T HELP BUT FOLLOW UP ON EVERY ACTION YOU TAKE.
...
IT SEEMS NEITHER OF US WILL HAVE FRONT ROW SEATS.

YOU WEREN'T CHOSEN.

...

WELL, NEITHER WAS I.

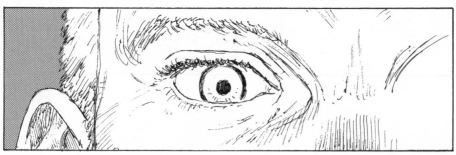

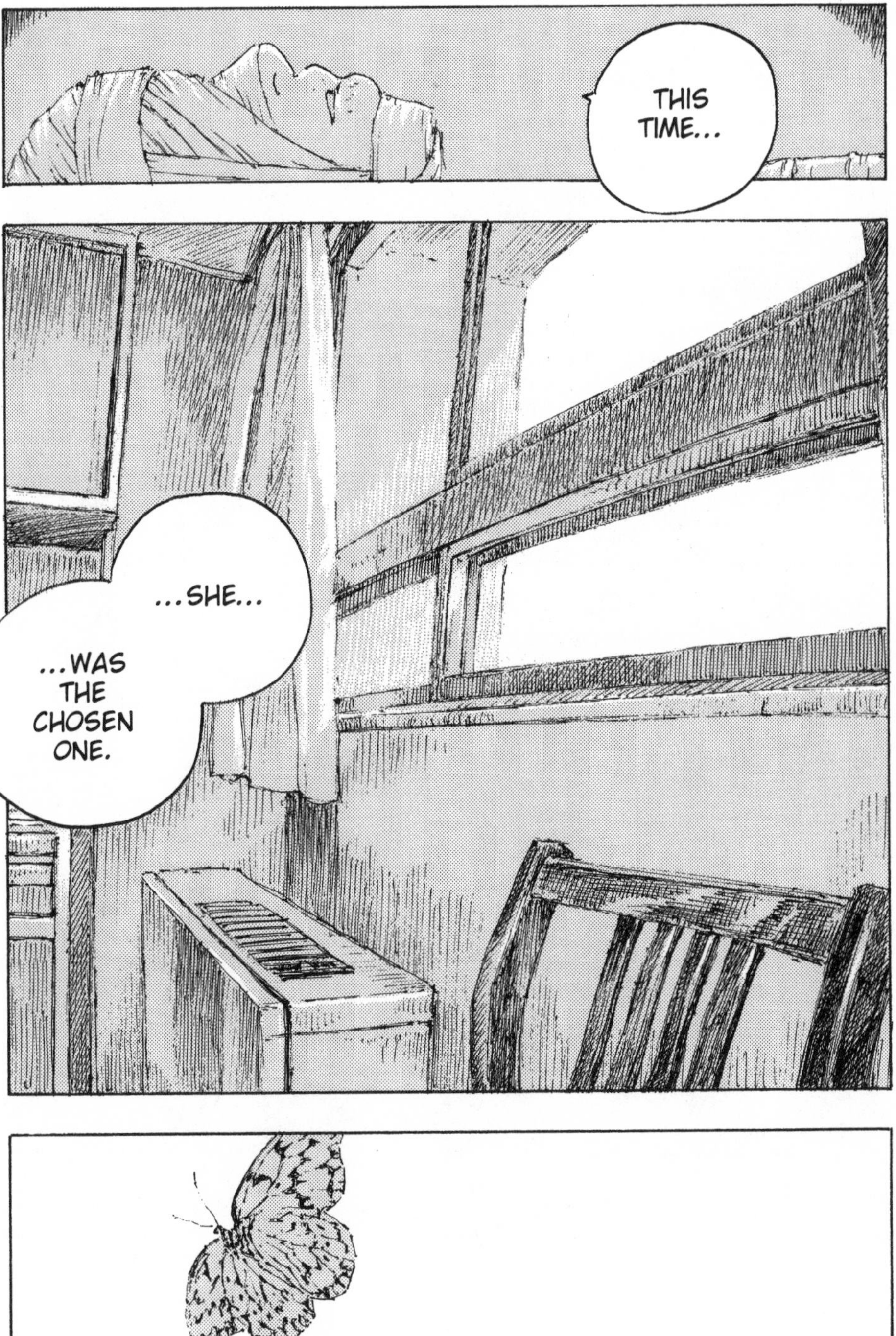
THIS TIME...
...SHE...
...WAS THE CHOSEN ONE.

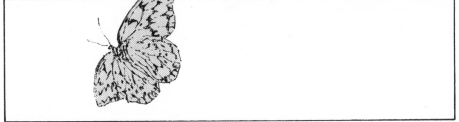

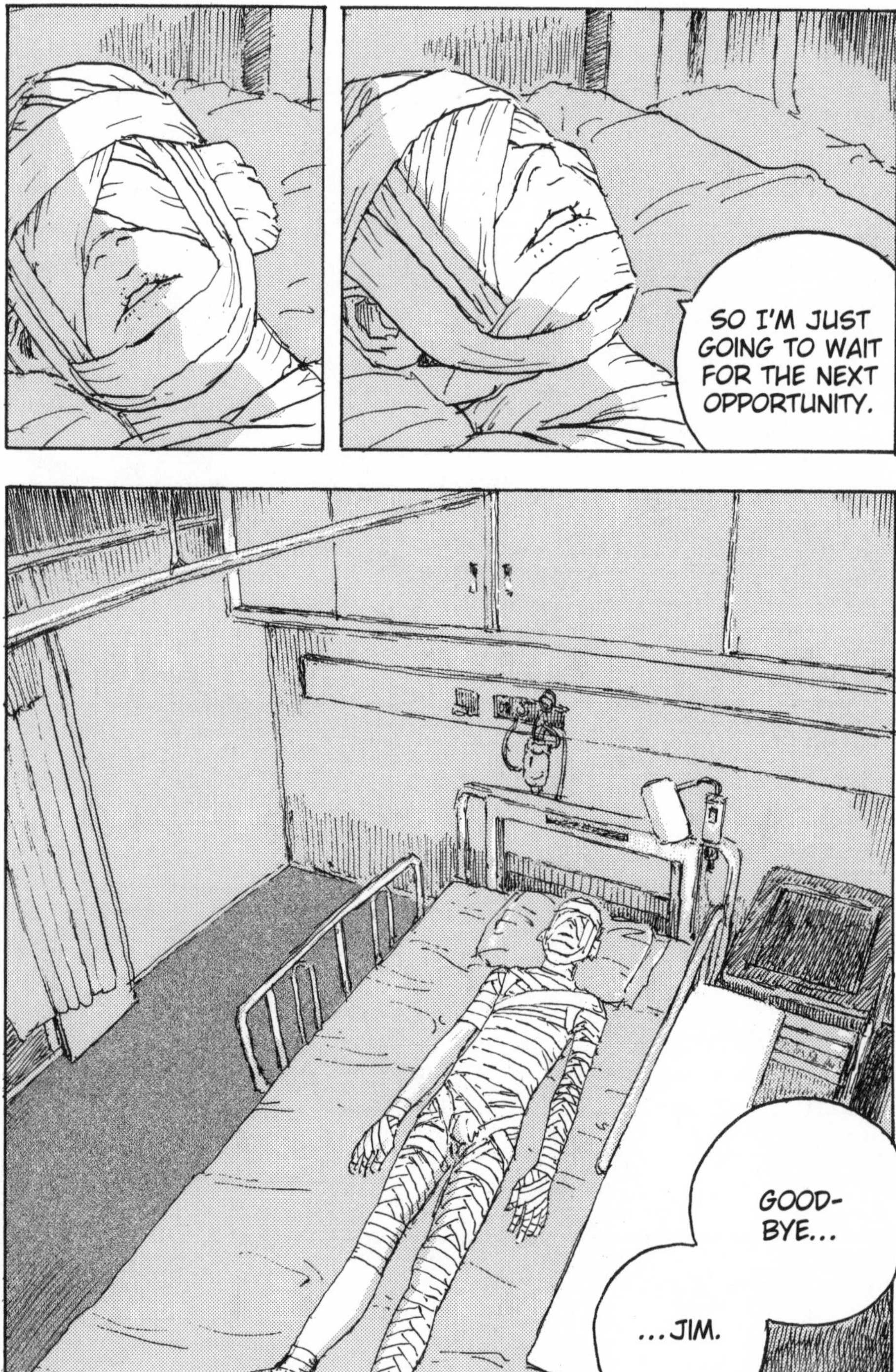
SO I'M JUST GOING TO WAIT FOR THE NEXT OPPORTUNITY.
GOOD-BYE...
...JIM.

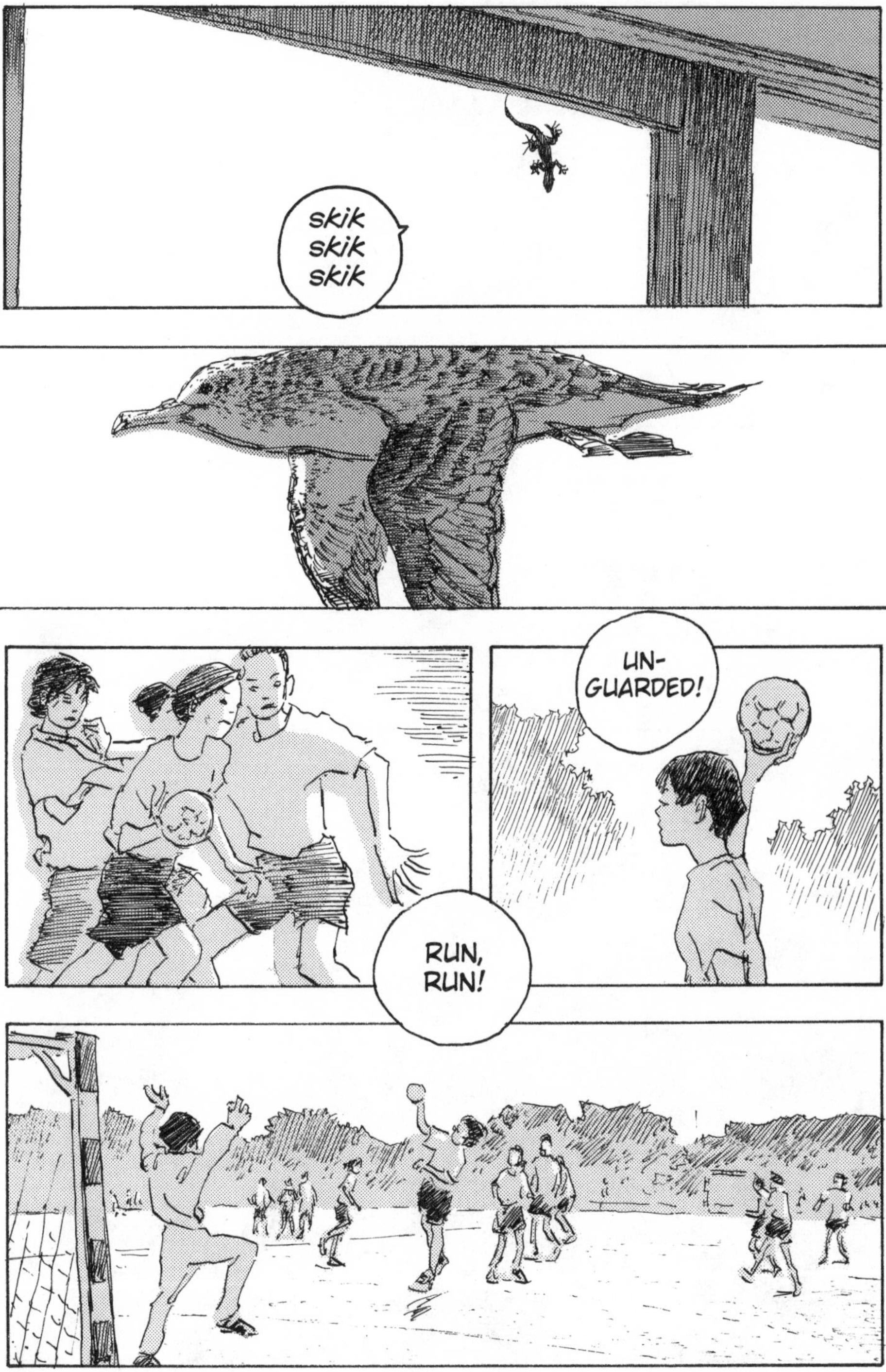
skik skik skik
UN-GUARDED!
RUN, RUN!

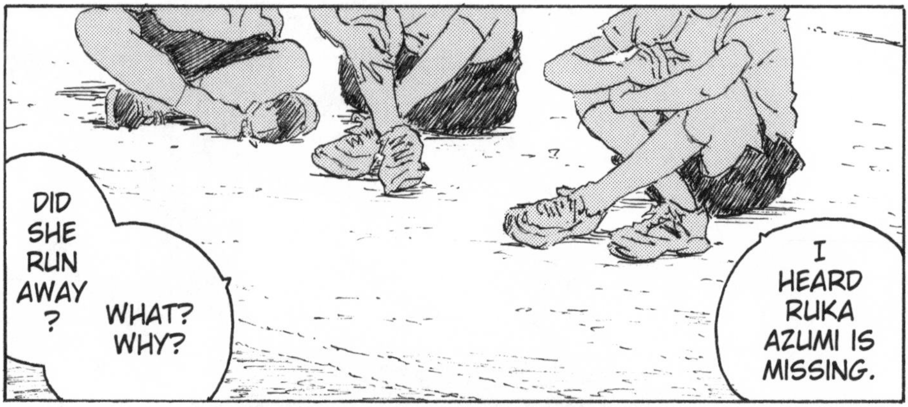
I HEARD RUKA AZUMI IS MISSING.
WHAT? WHY?
DID SHE RUN AWAY?

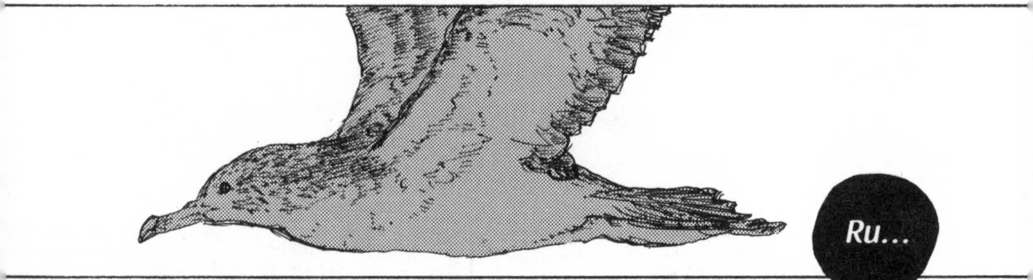
Ru...

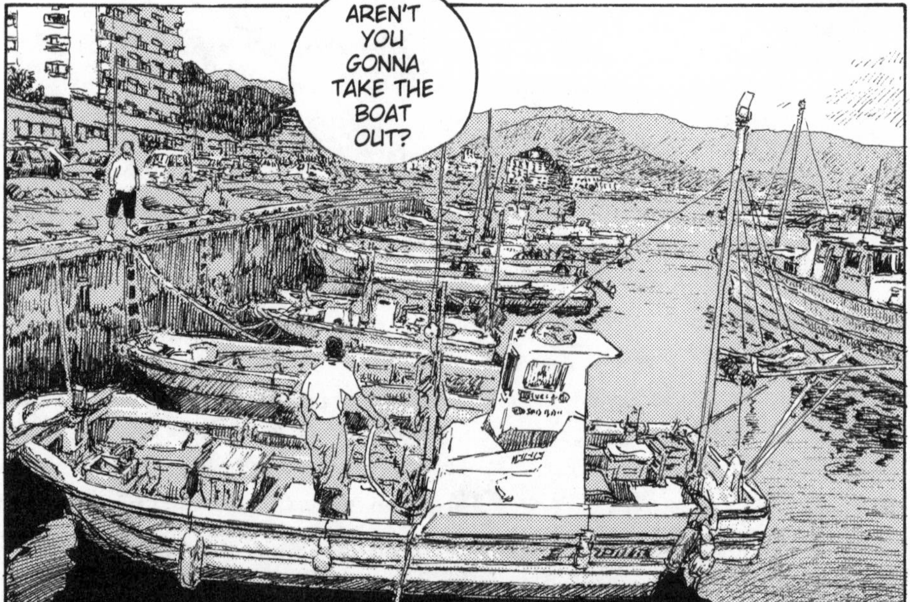
AREN'T YOU GONNA TAKE THE BOAT OUT?

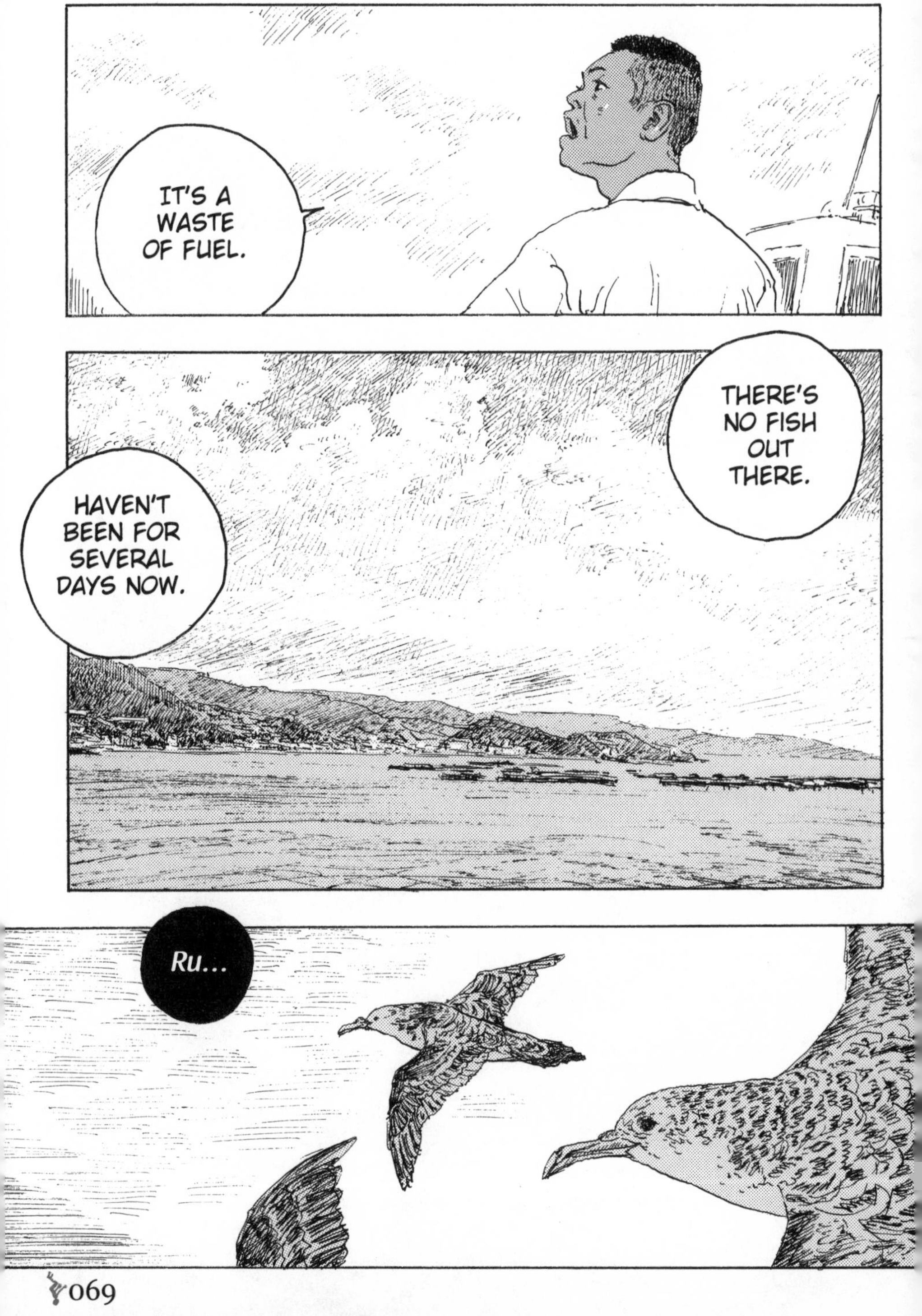
IT'S A WASTE OF FUEL.
THERE'S NO FISH OUT THERE.
HAVEN'T BEEN FOR SEVERAL DAYS NOW.
Ru...

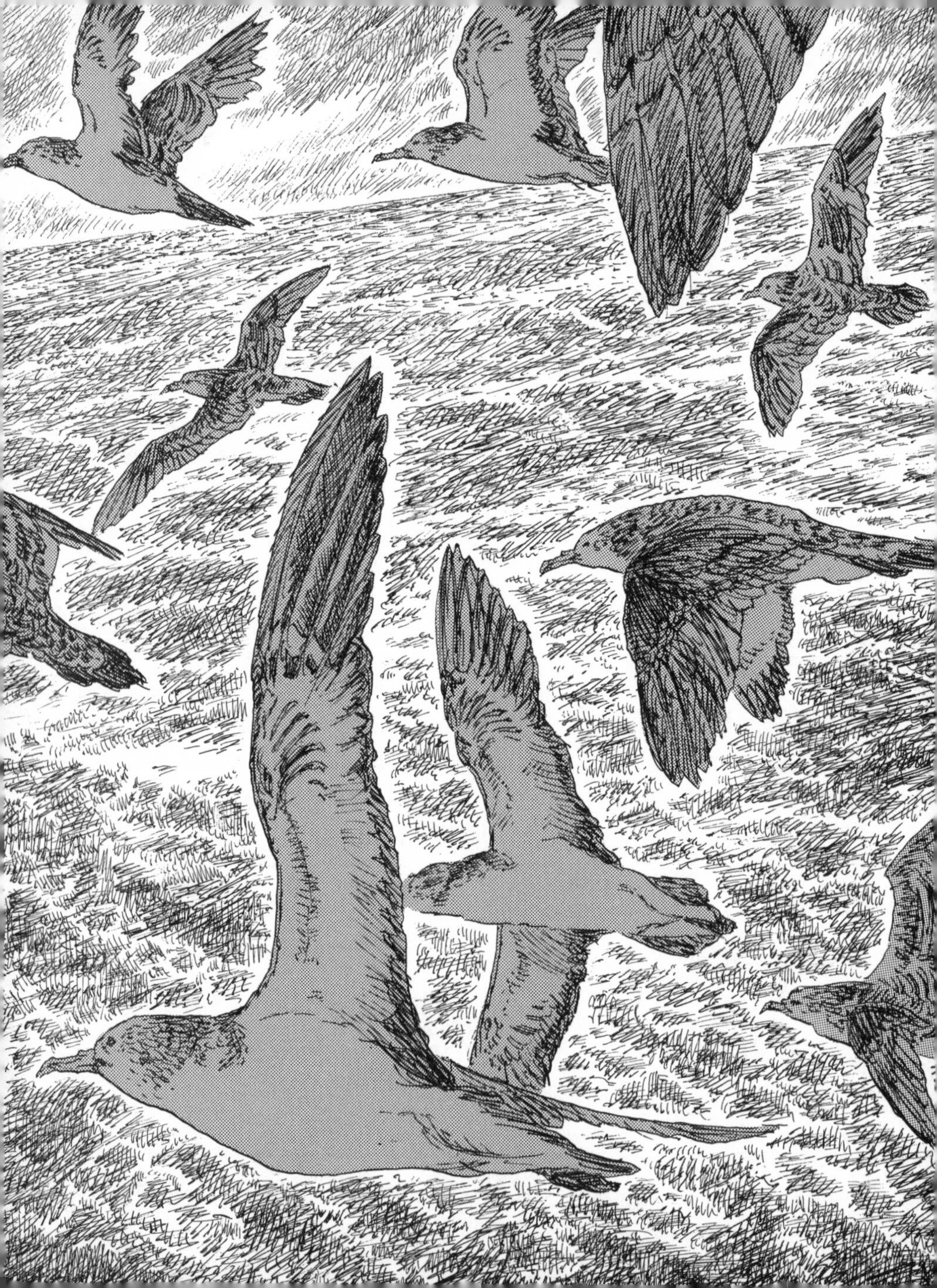

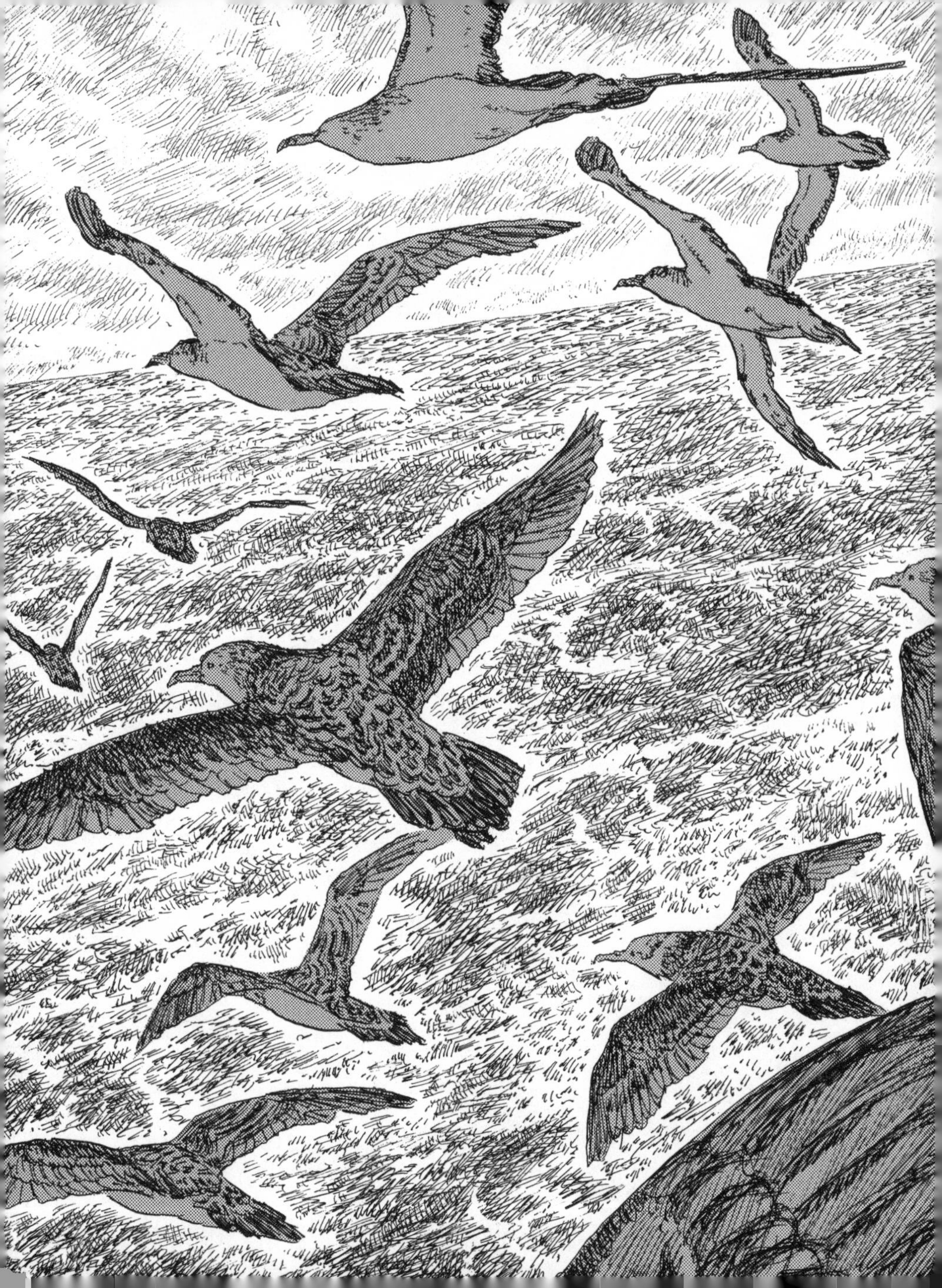

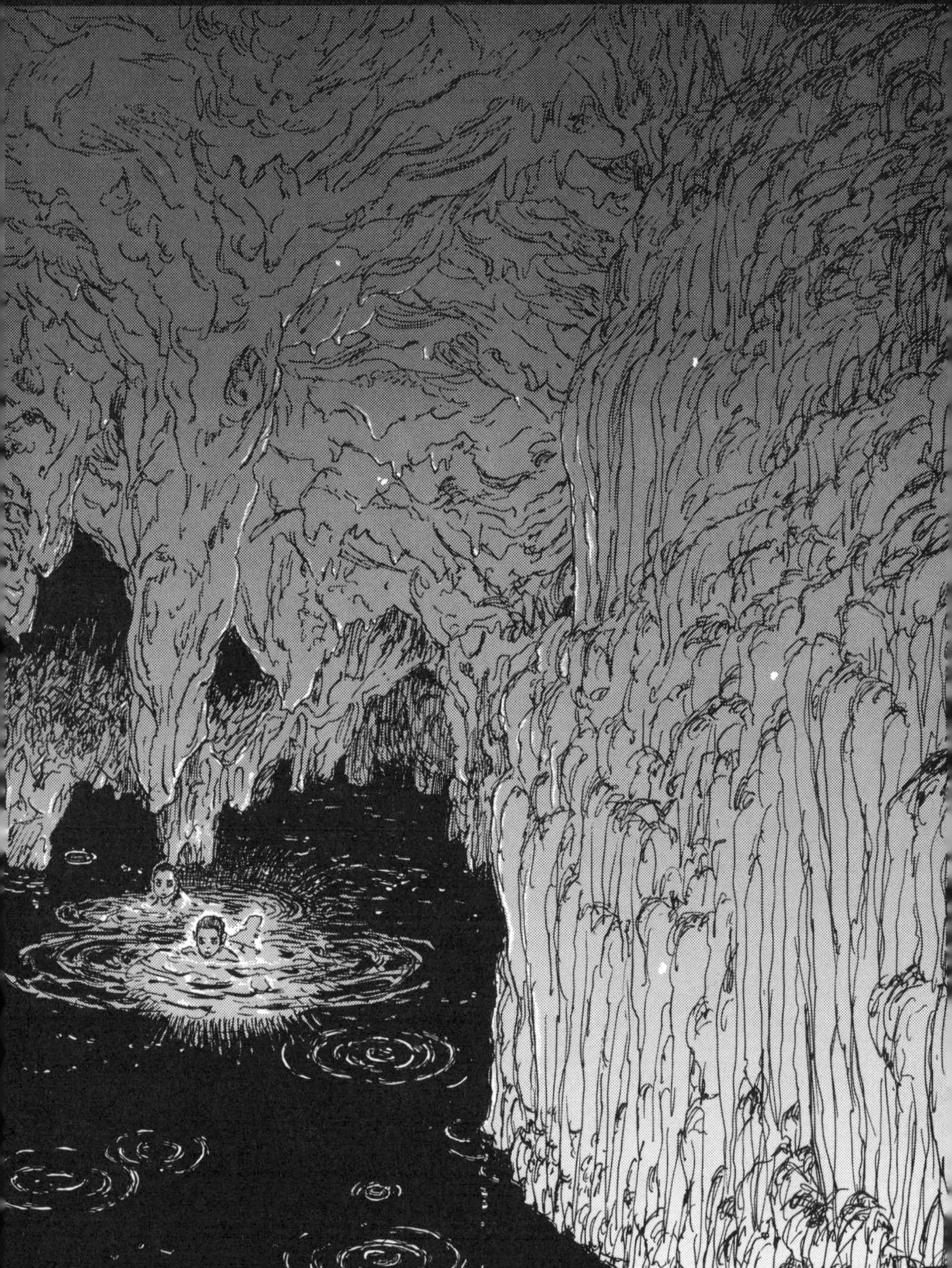

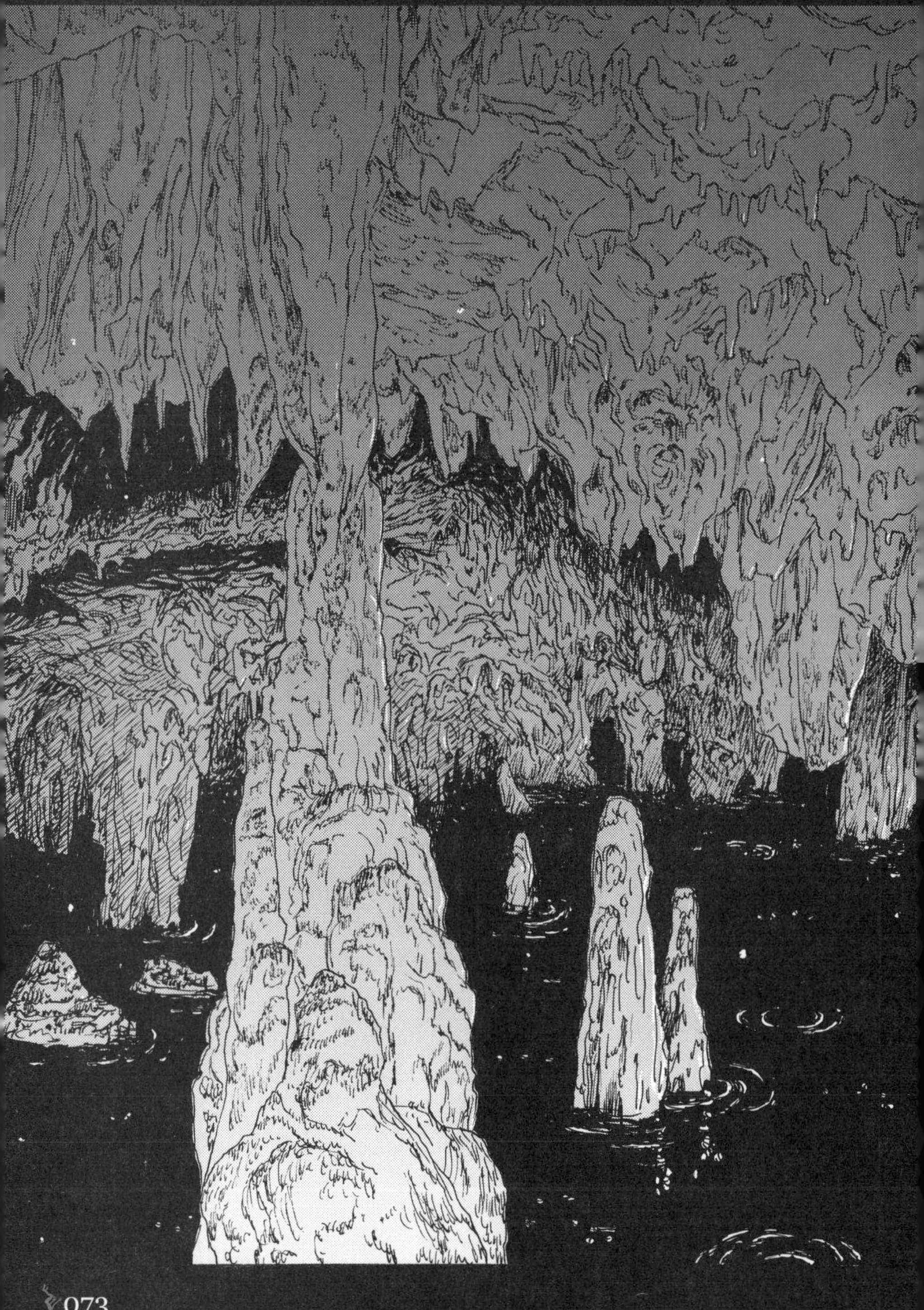

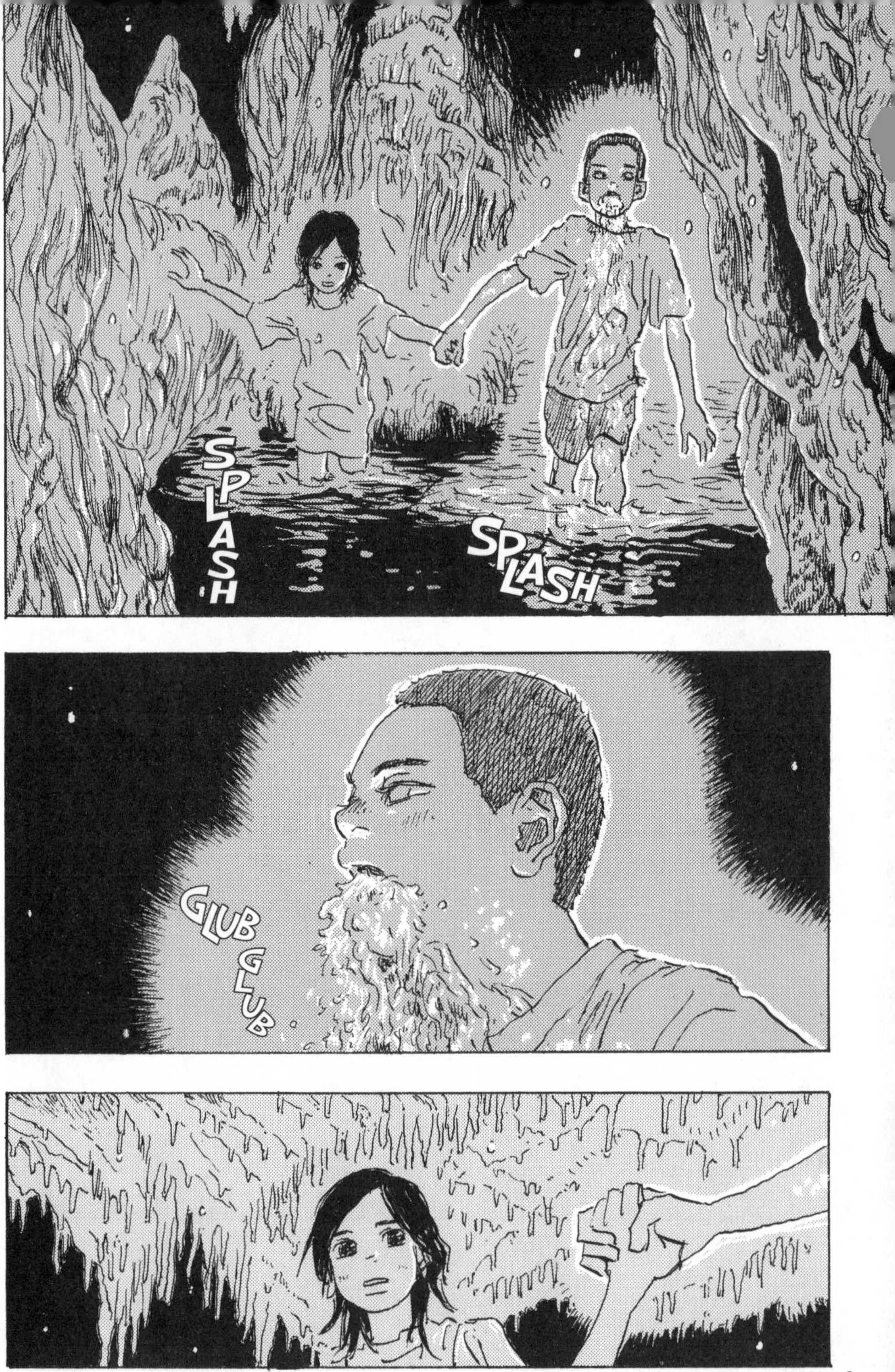
SPLASH
SPLASH
GLUB GLUB

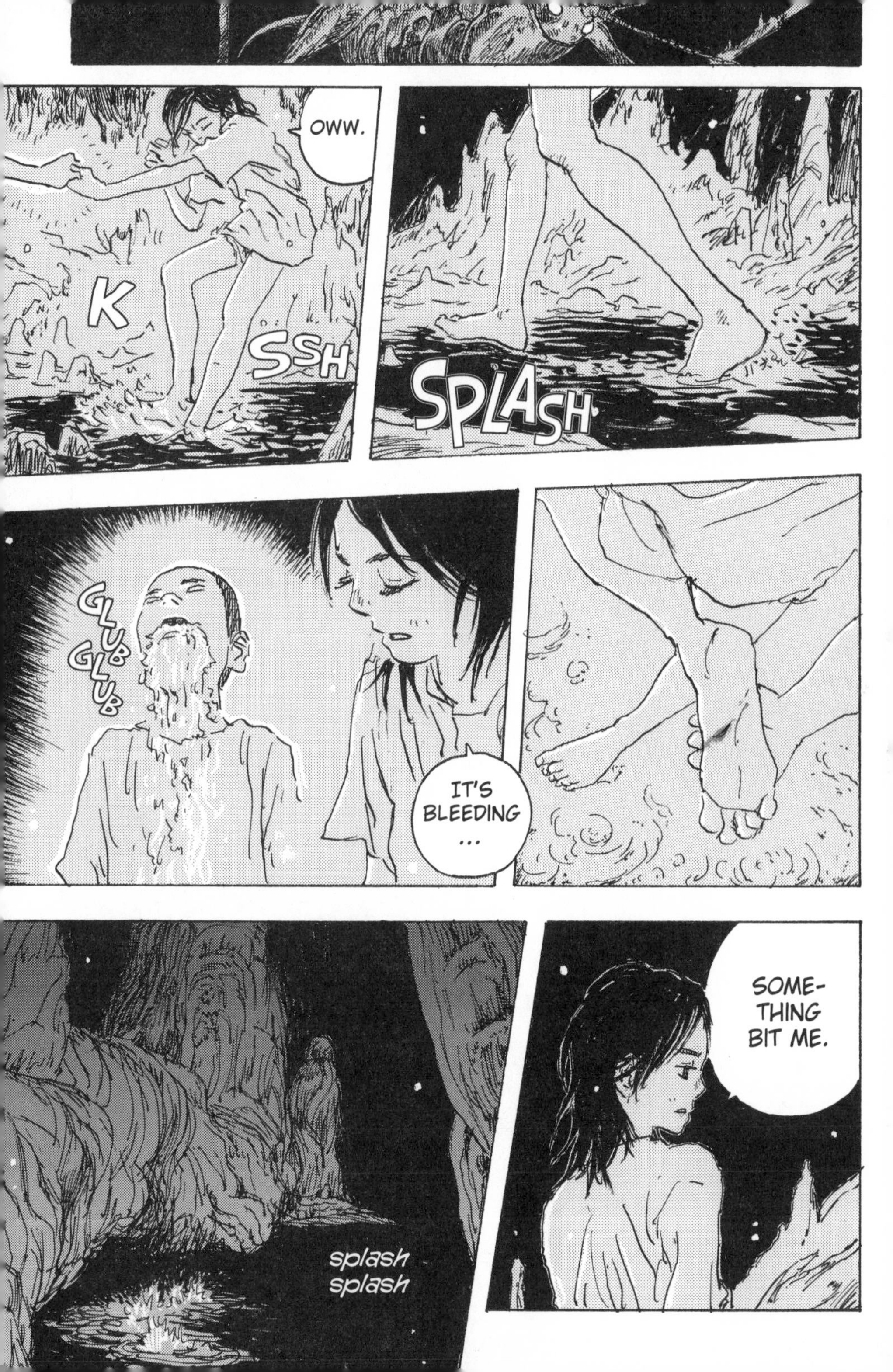
SPLASH
OWW.
K SSH
IT'S BLEEDING ...
GLUB GLUB
SOME-THING BIT ME.
splash splash

IT
HURTS...

!

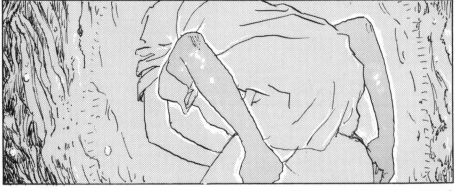

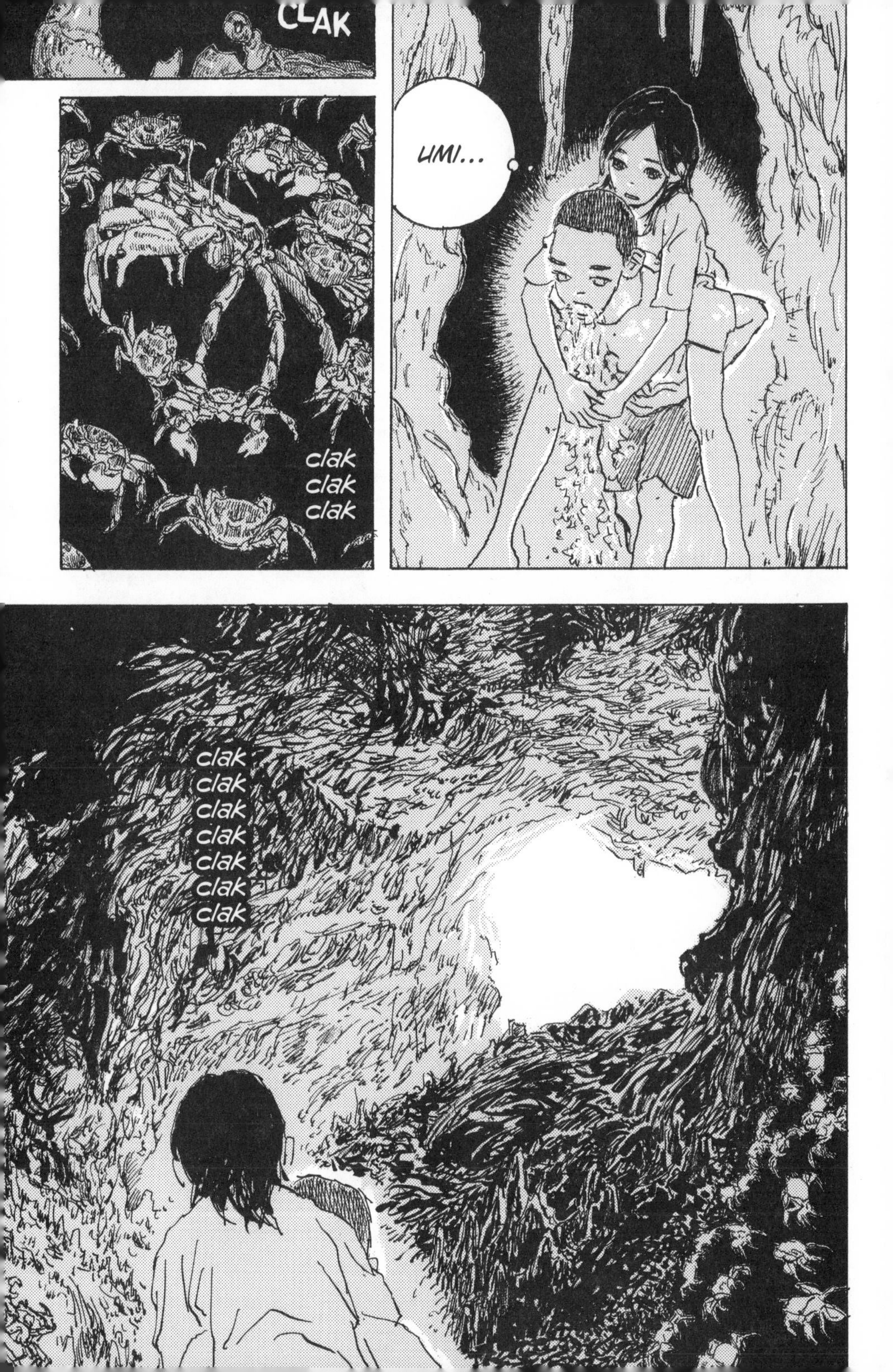
UMI...
CLAK
clak
clak
clak
clak
clak
clak
clak
clak
clak
clak

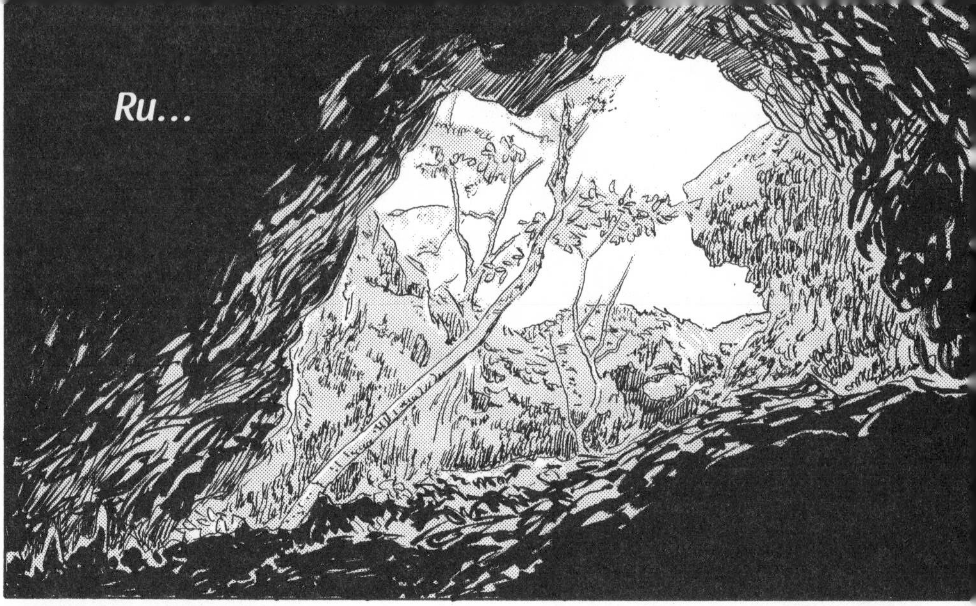
Ru...

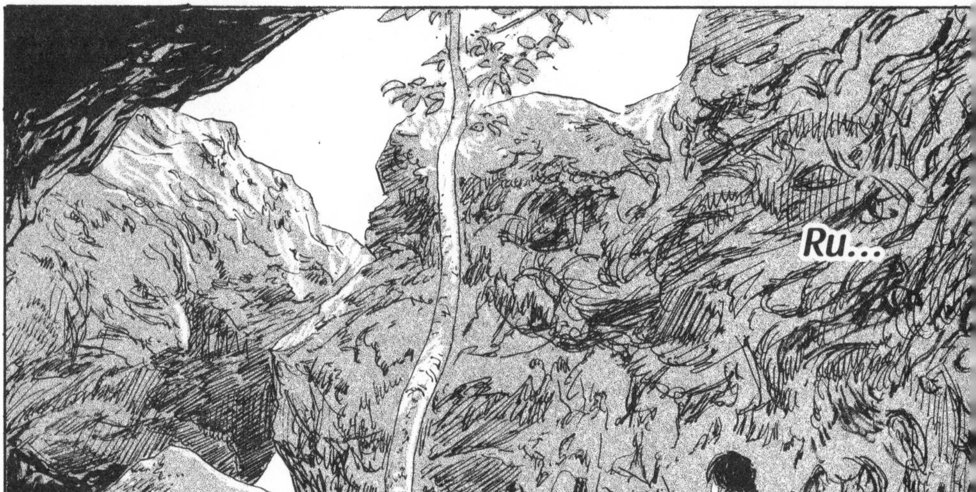
Ru...

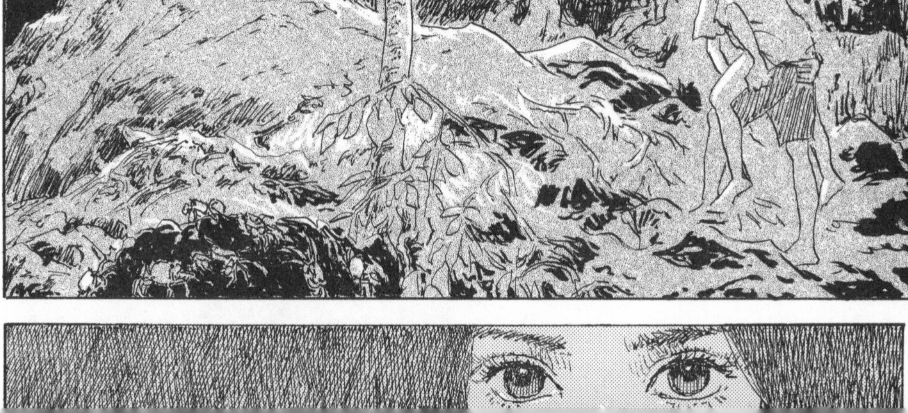

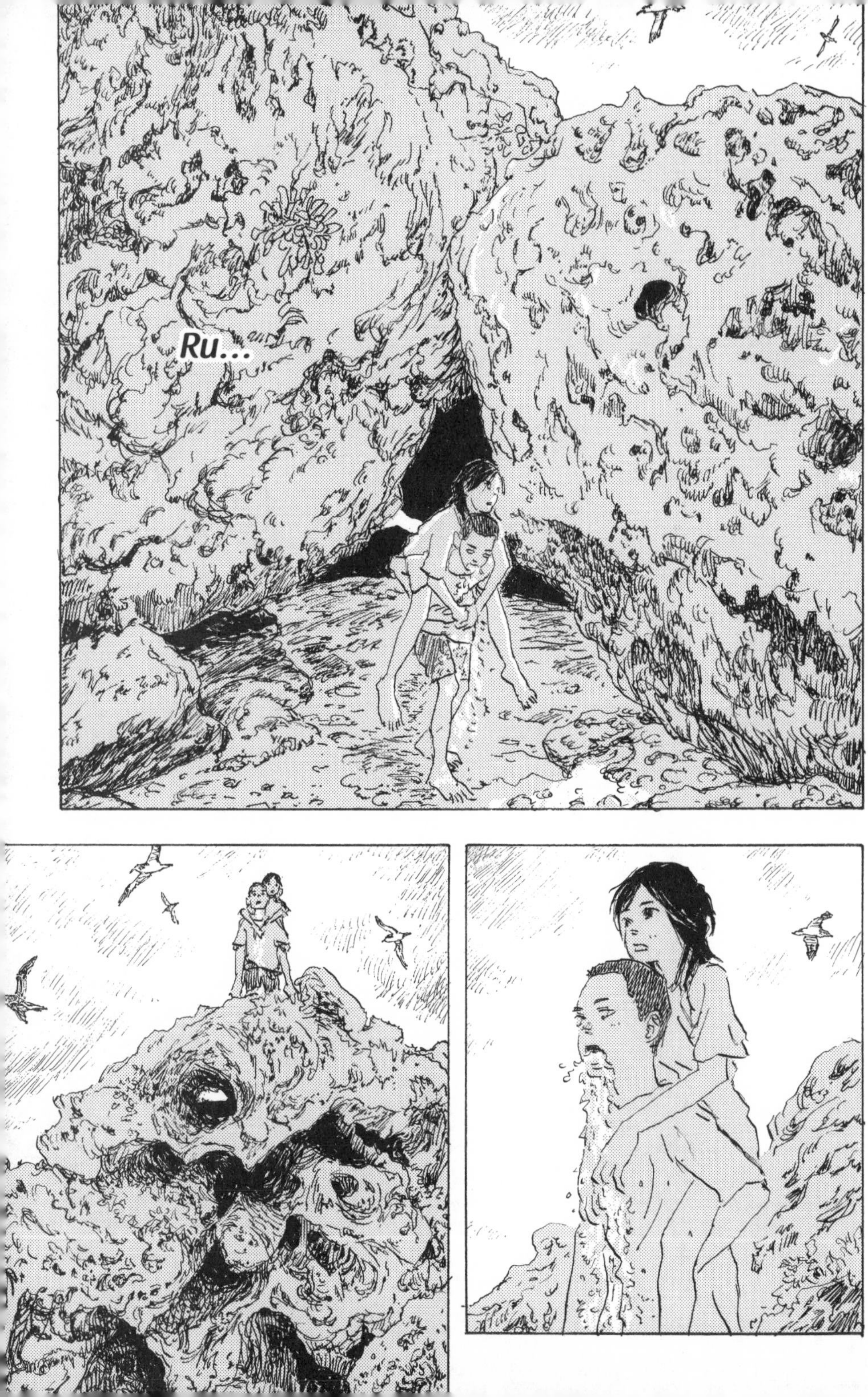
Ru…

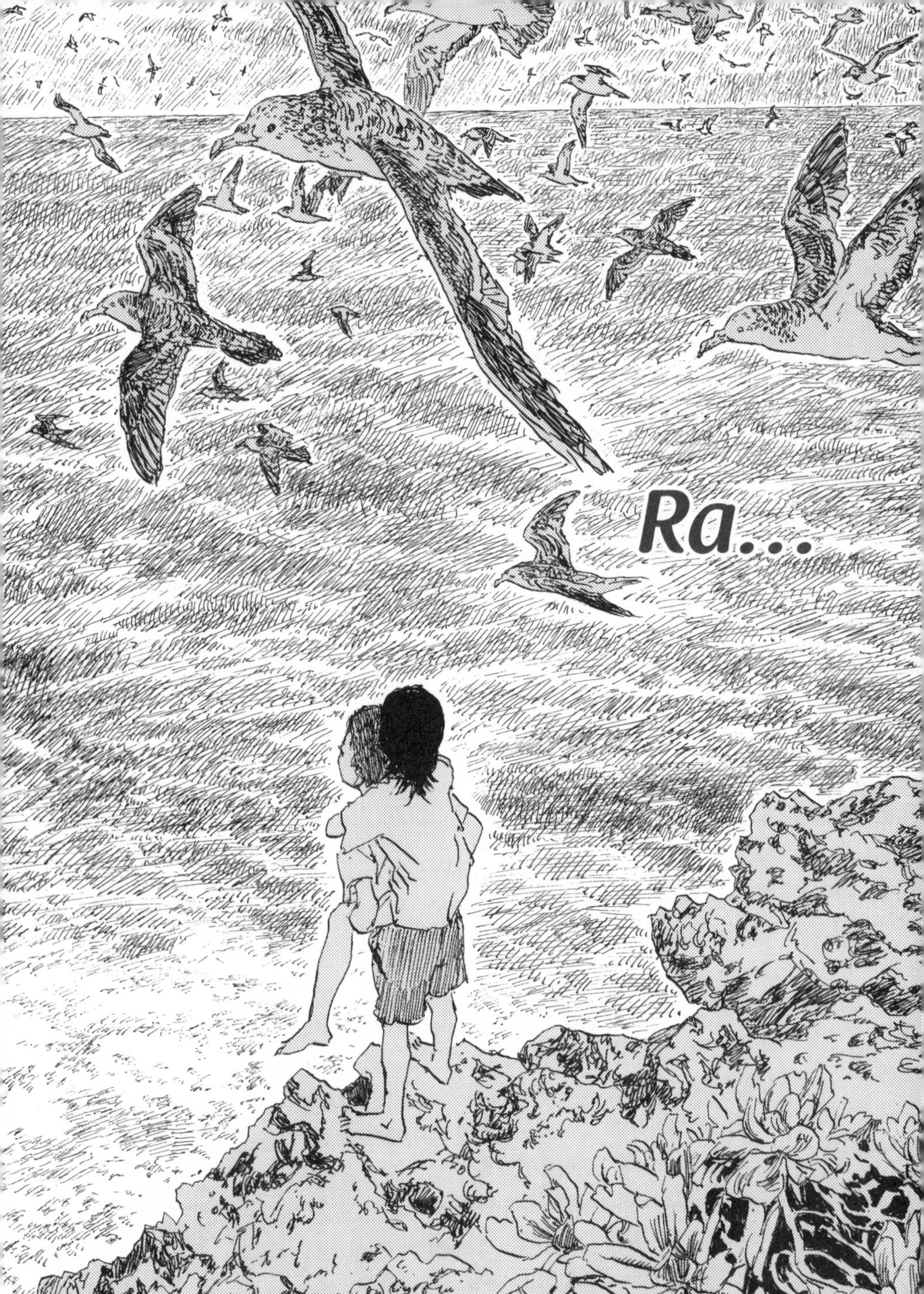
Ra...

KOOOSH

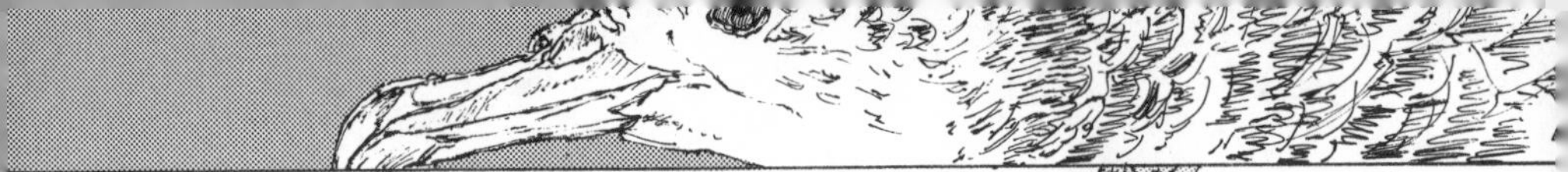
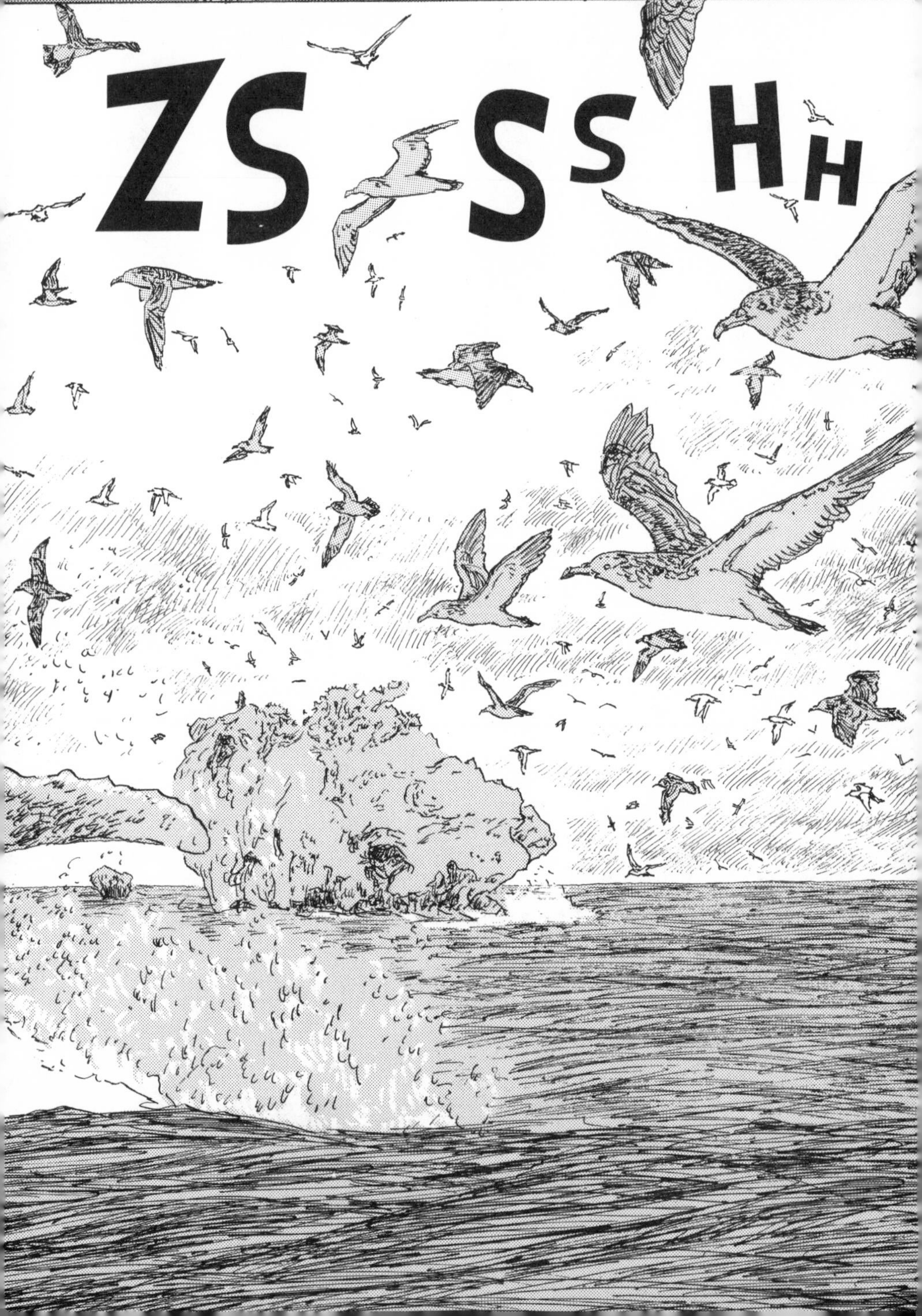
ZSSSHH

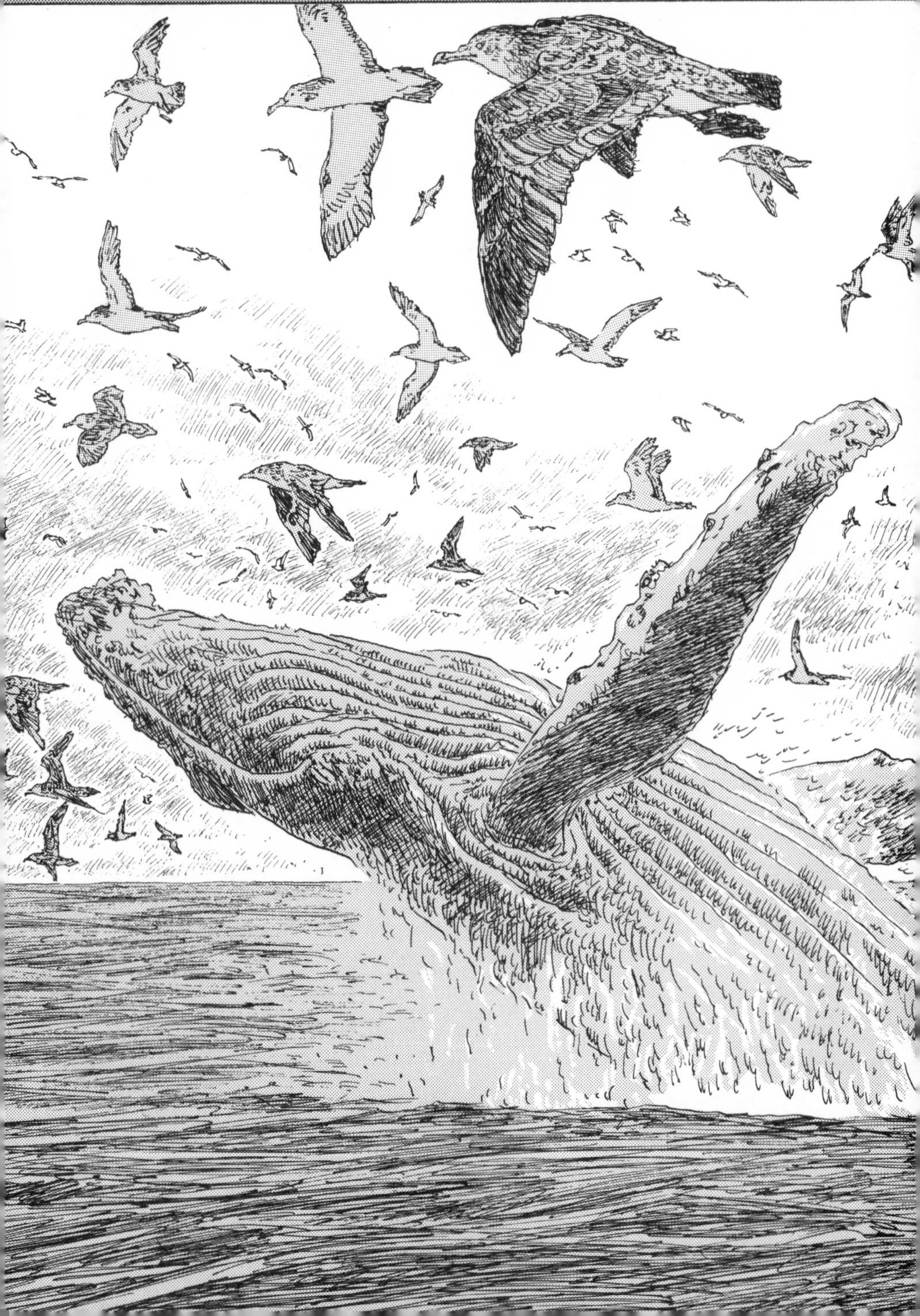

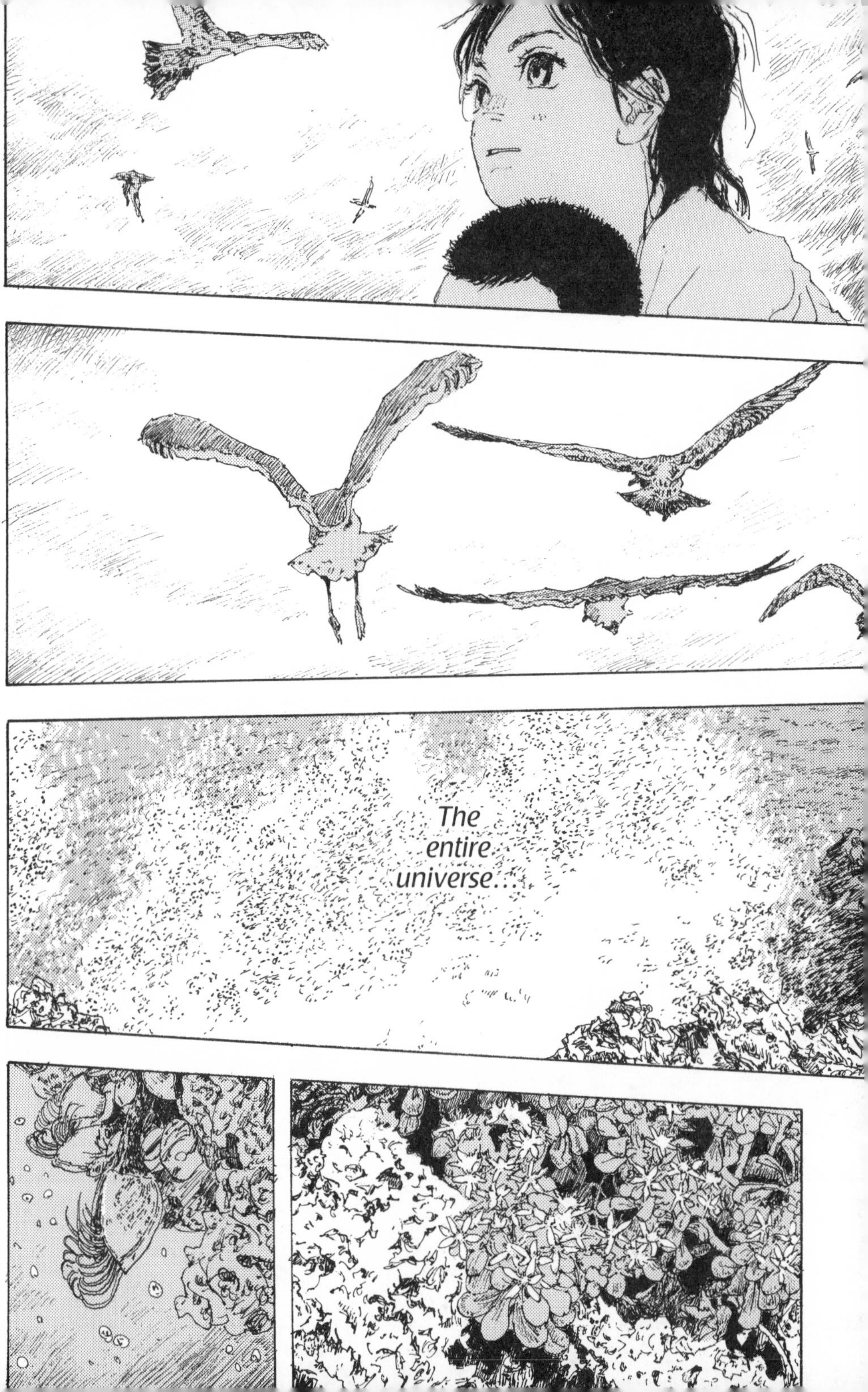
The entire universe...

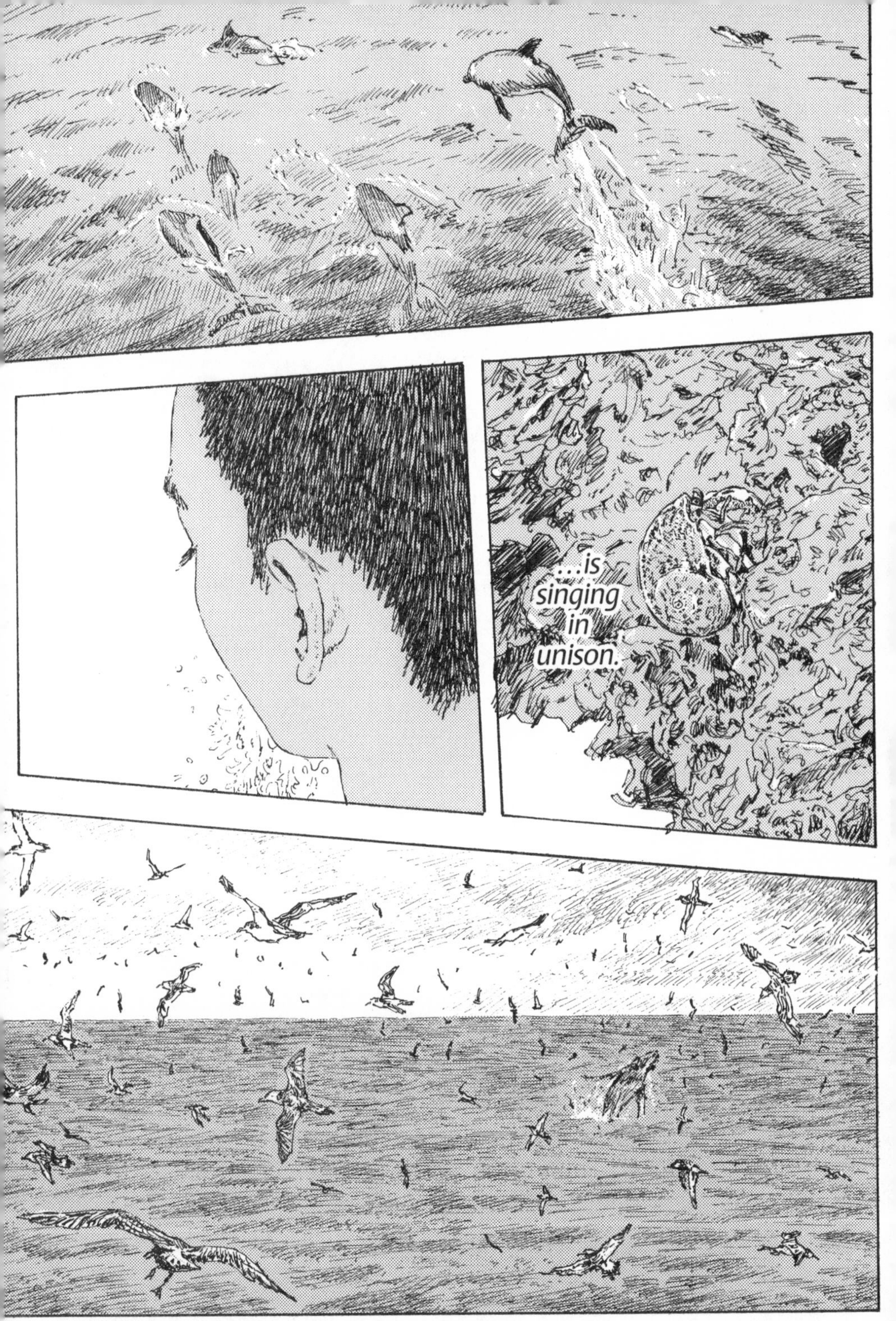
...is singing in unison.

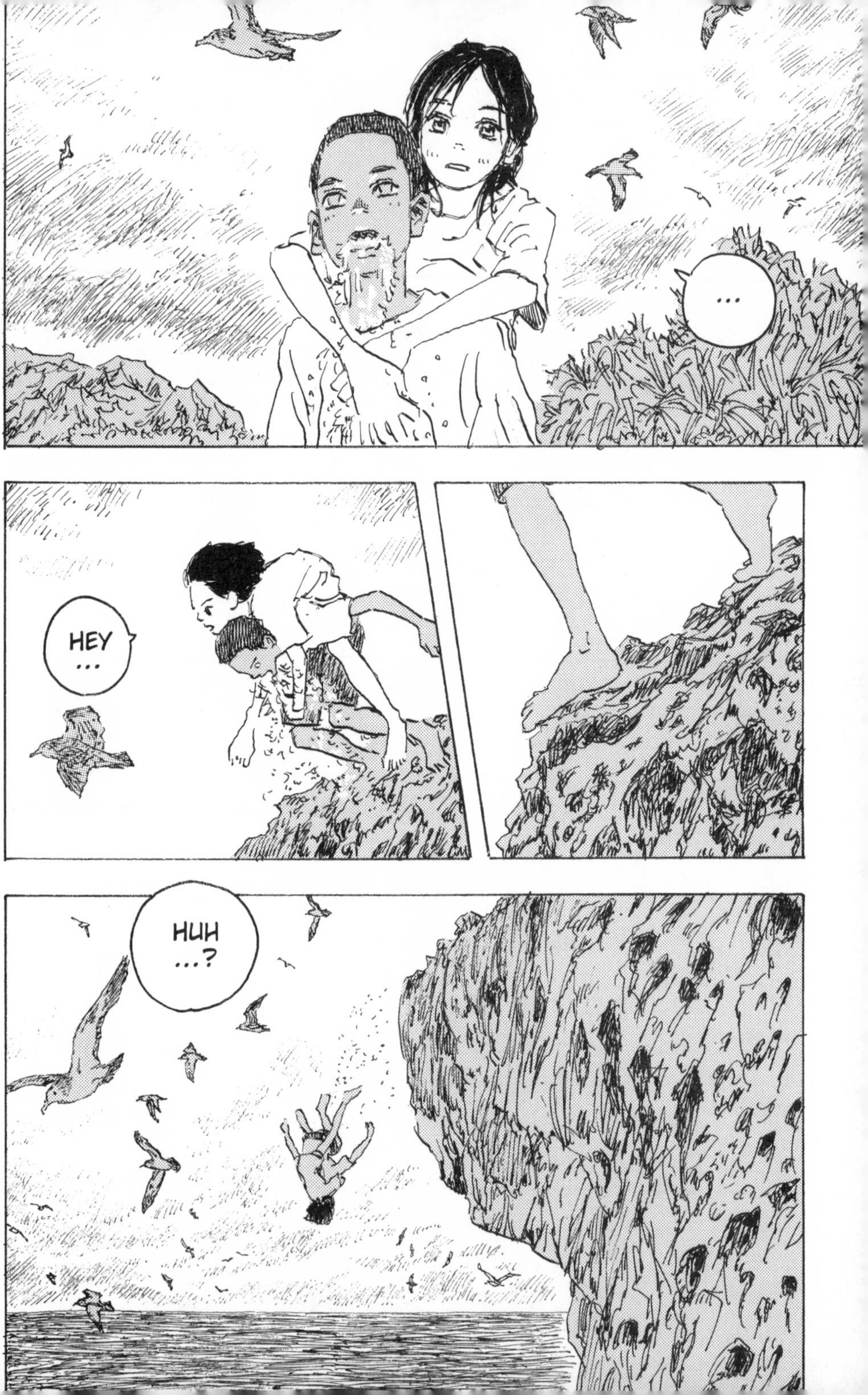
…
HEY …
HUH …?

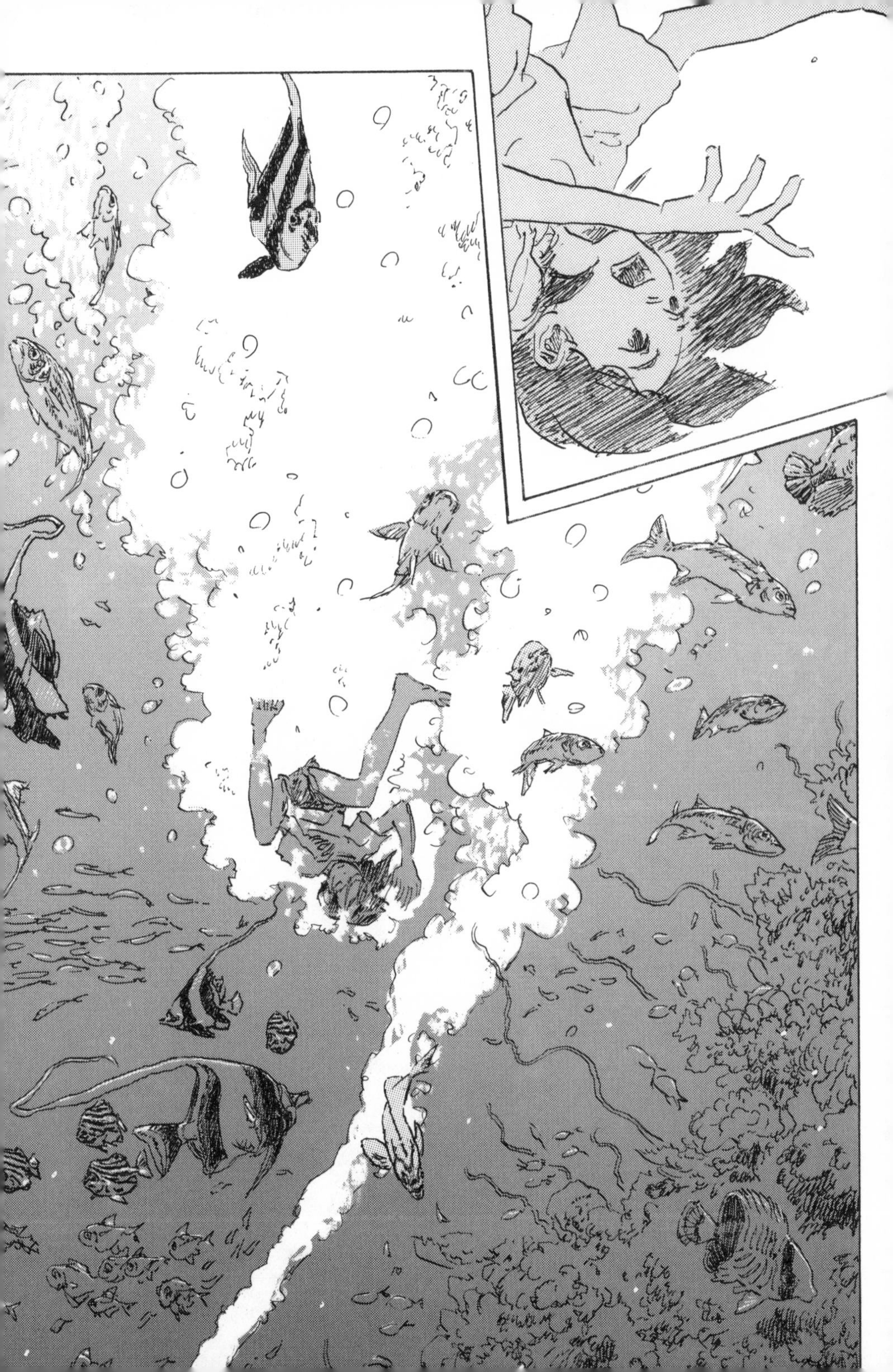

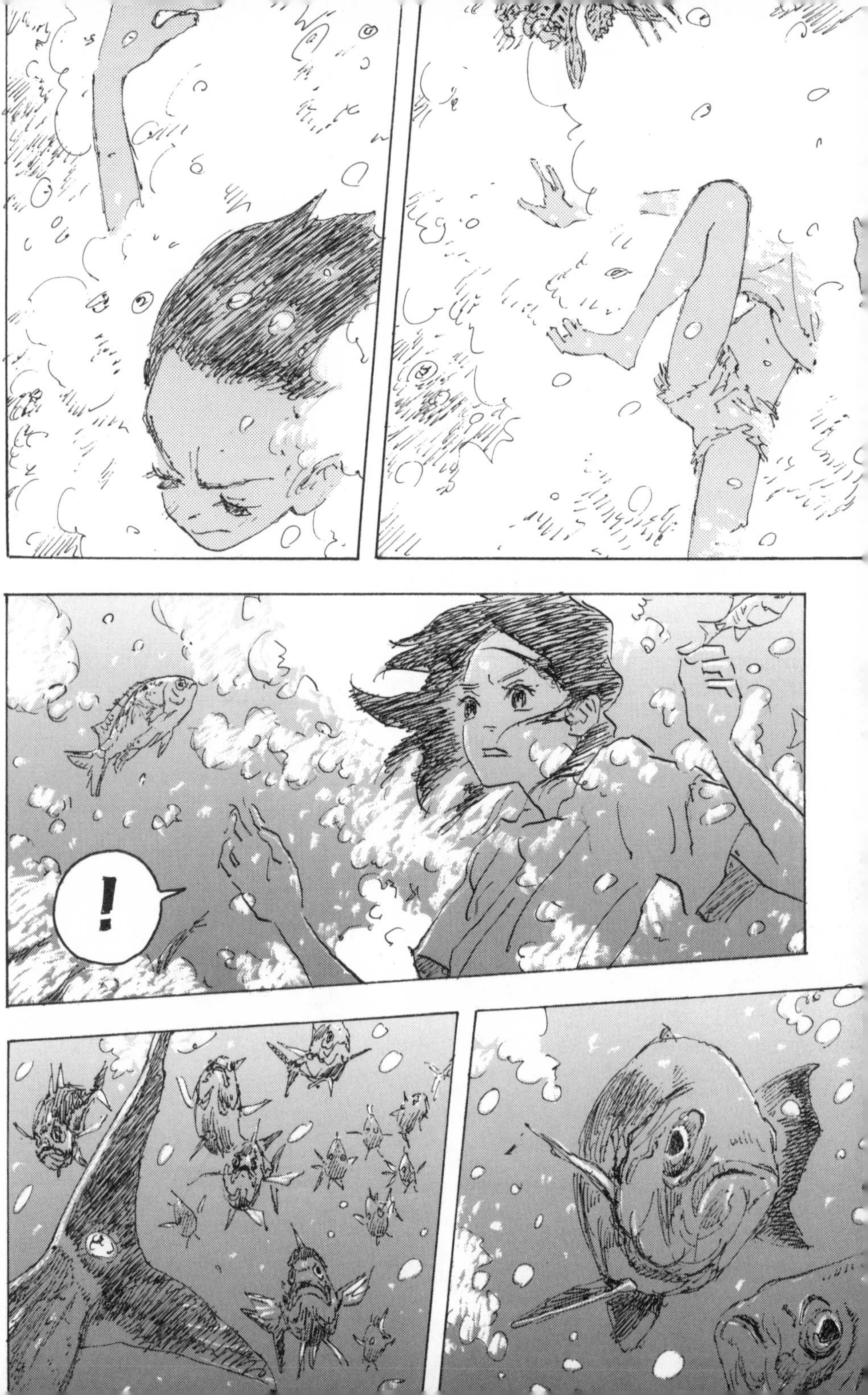
!

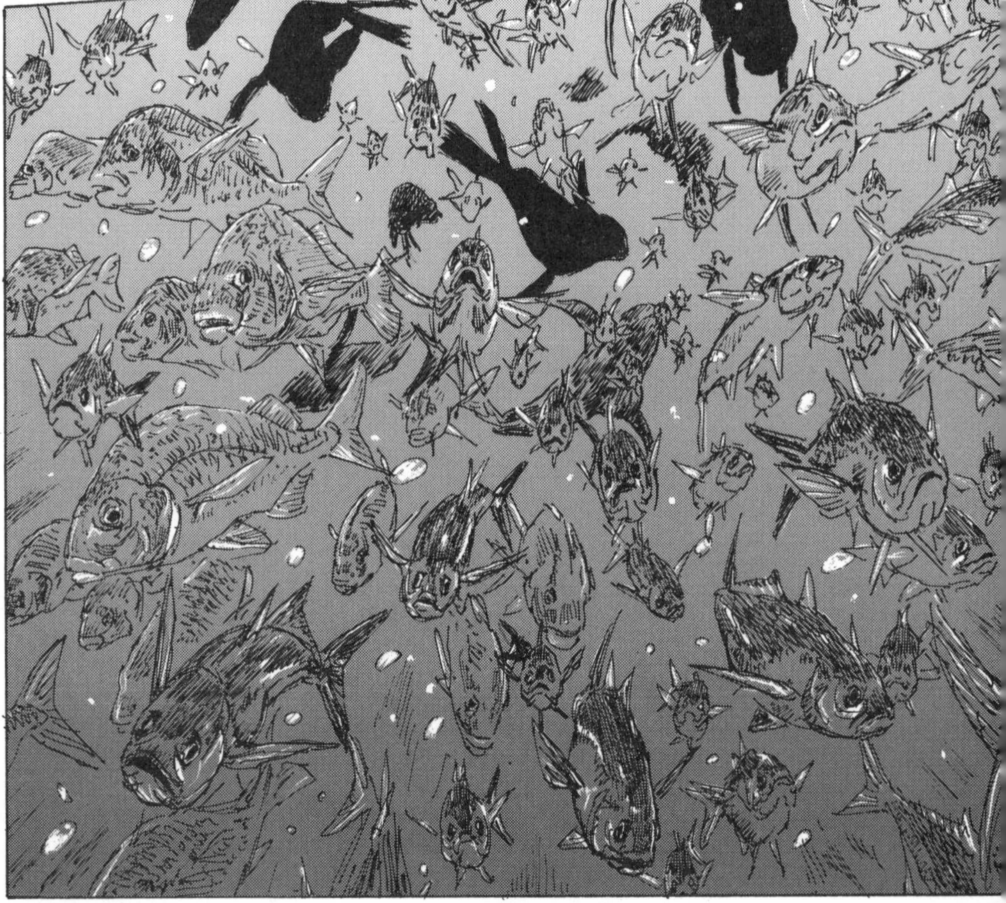
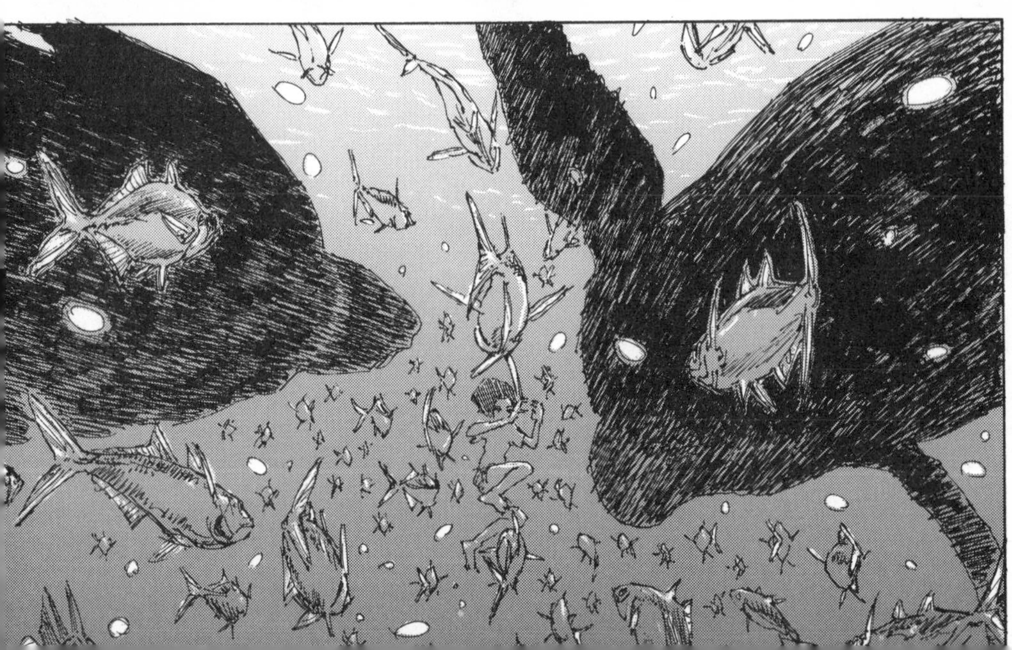

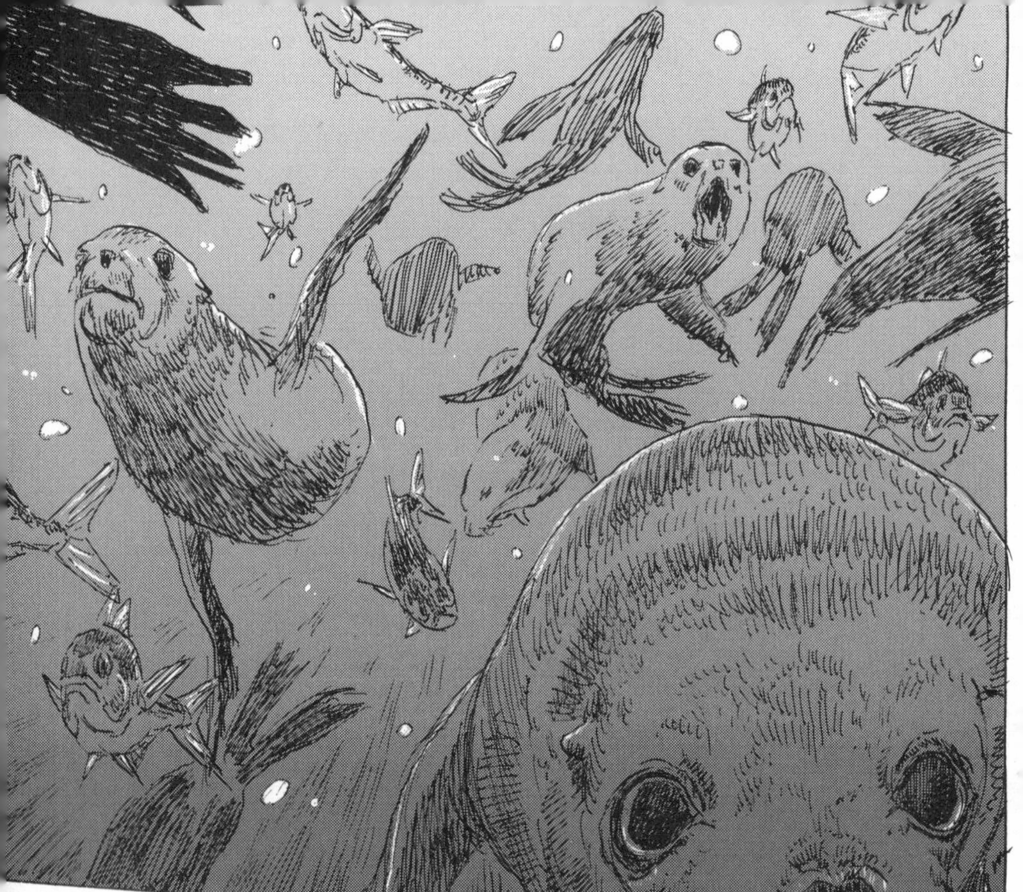
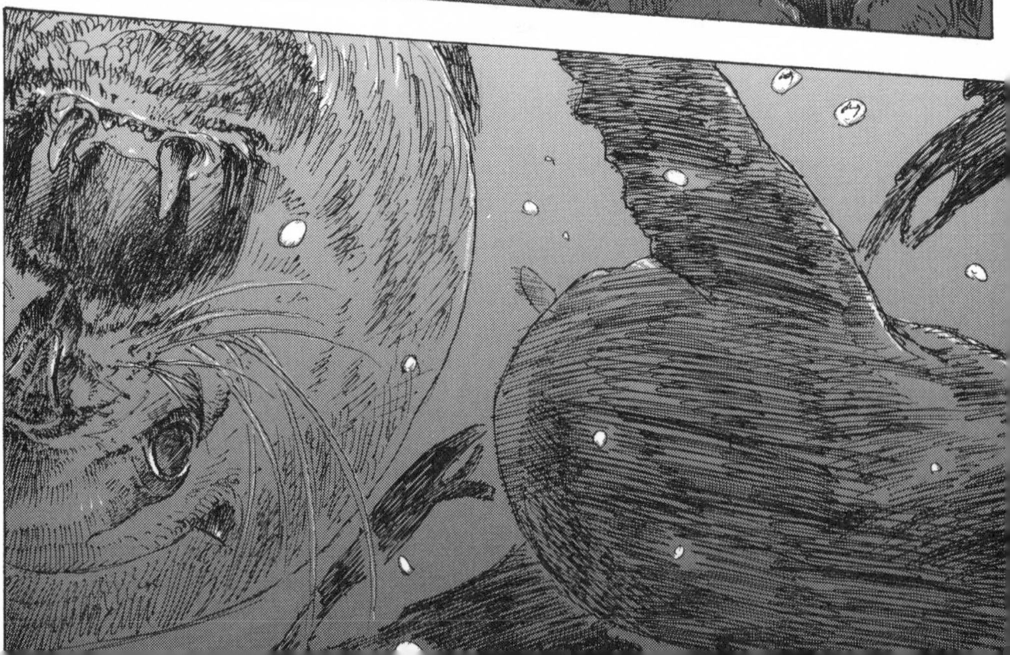

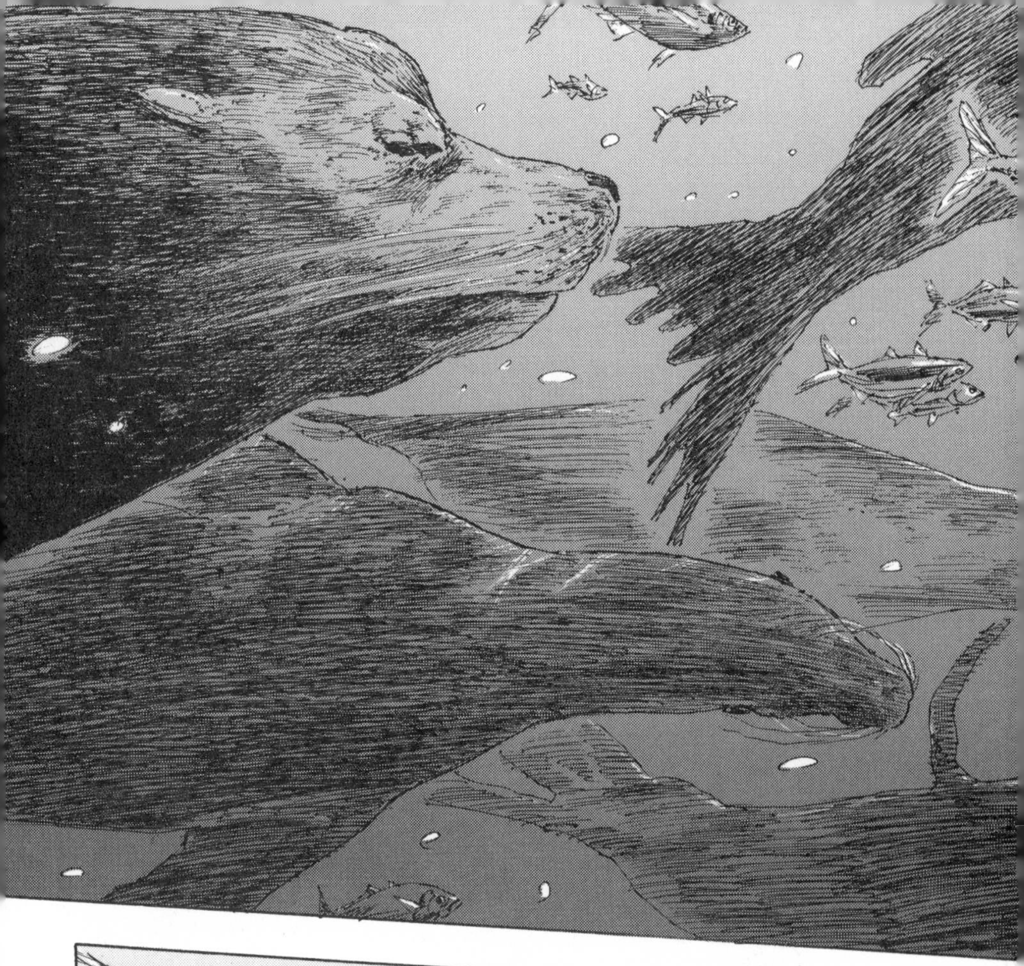
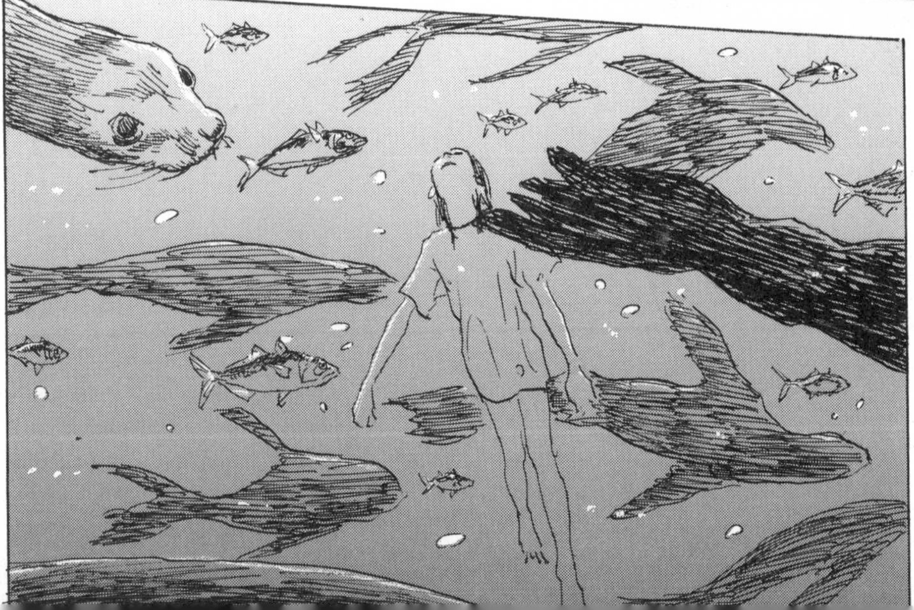

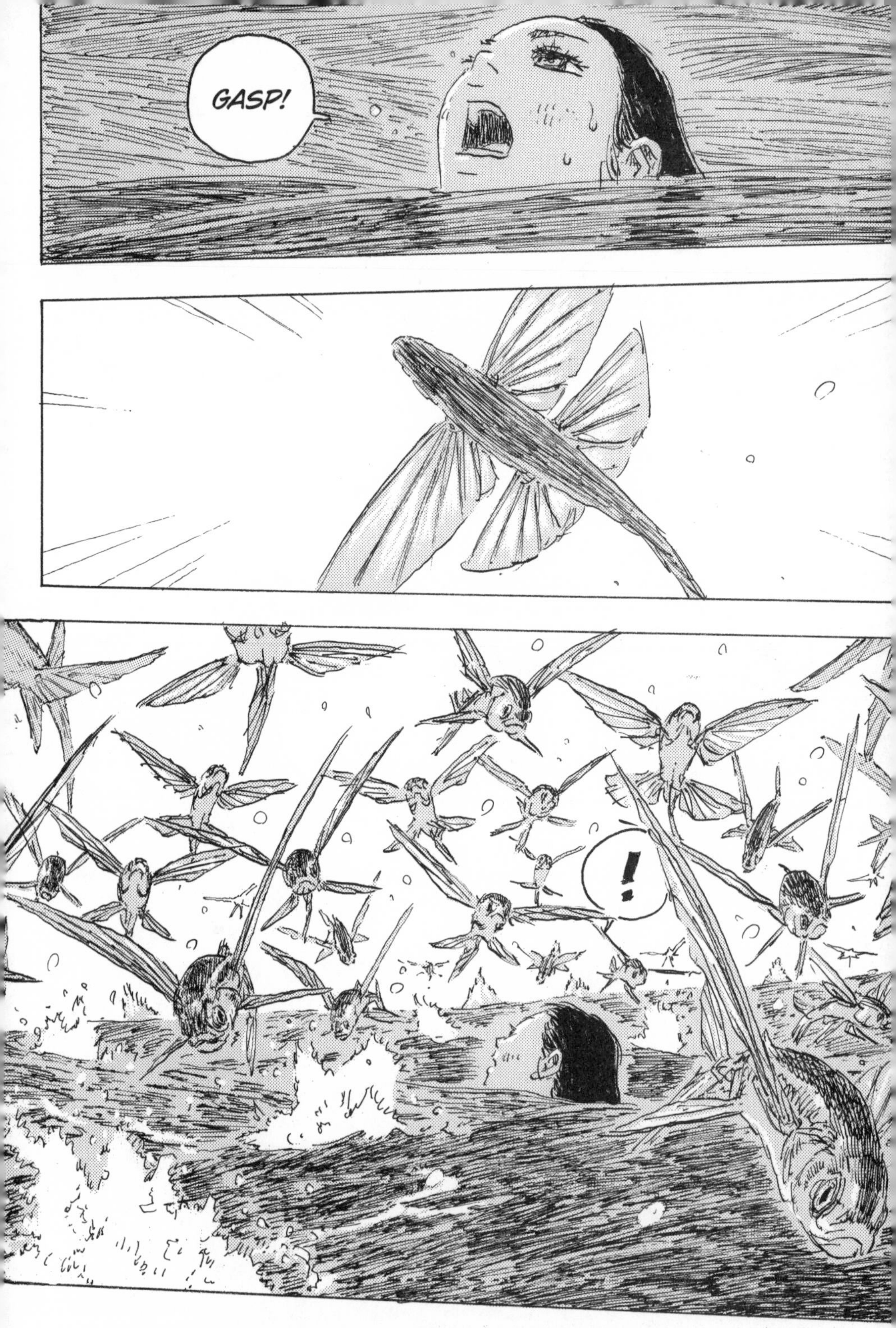
GASP!
!

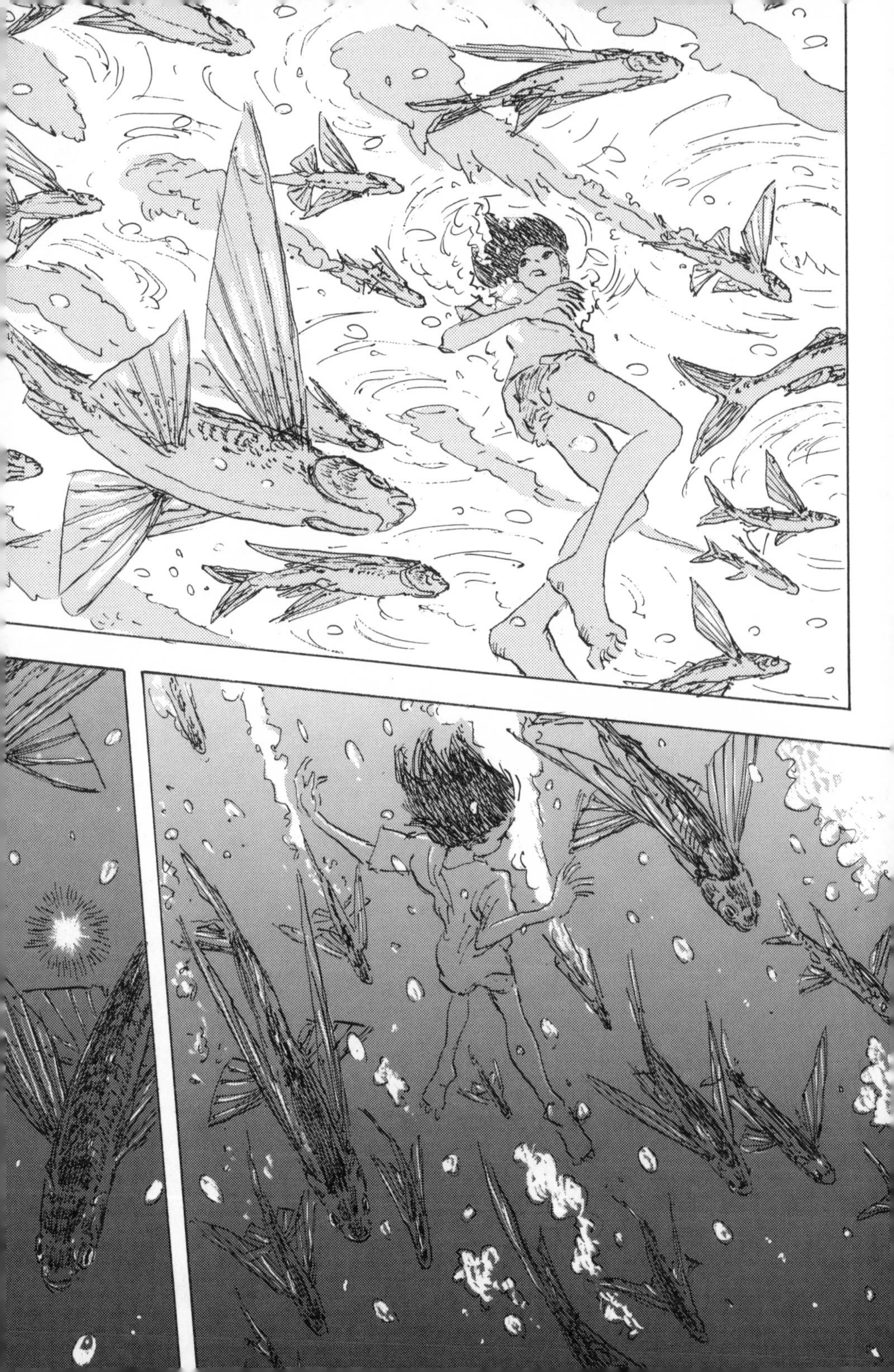

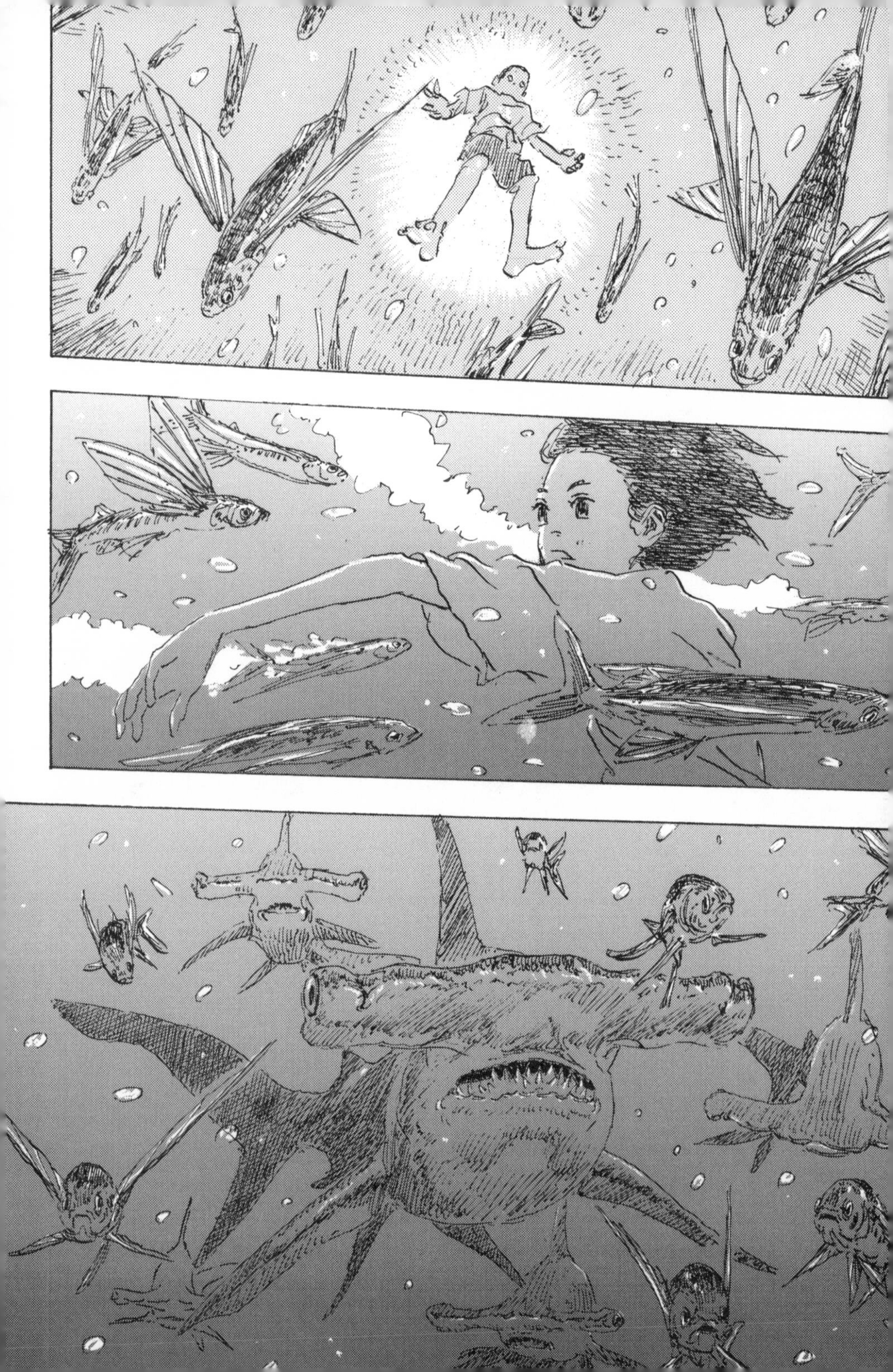

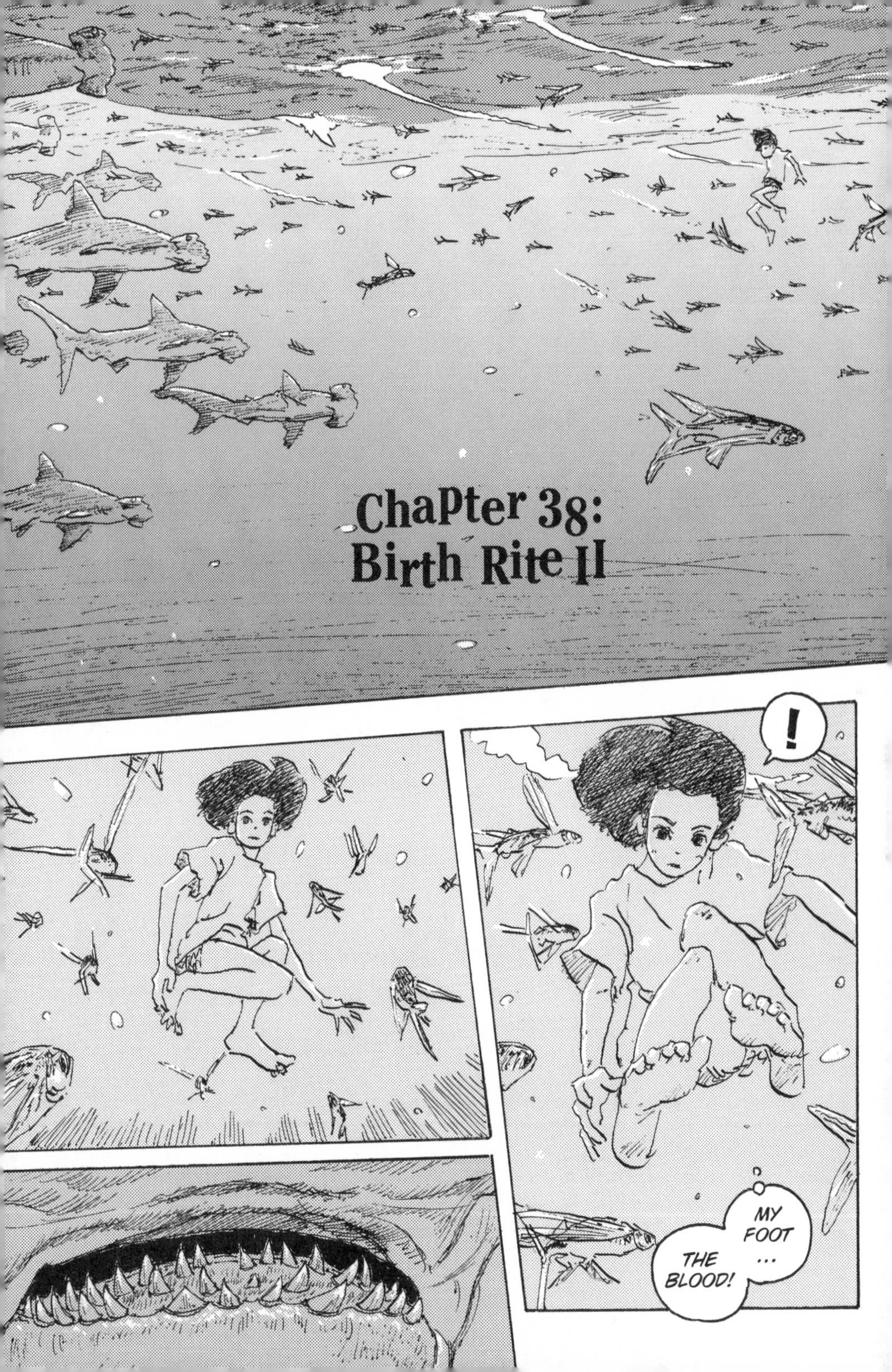
Chapter 38:
Birth Rite II
!
MY FOOT ...
THE BLOOD!

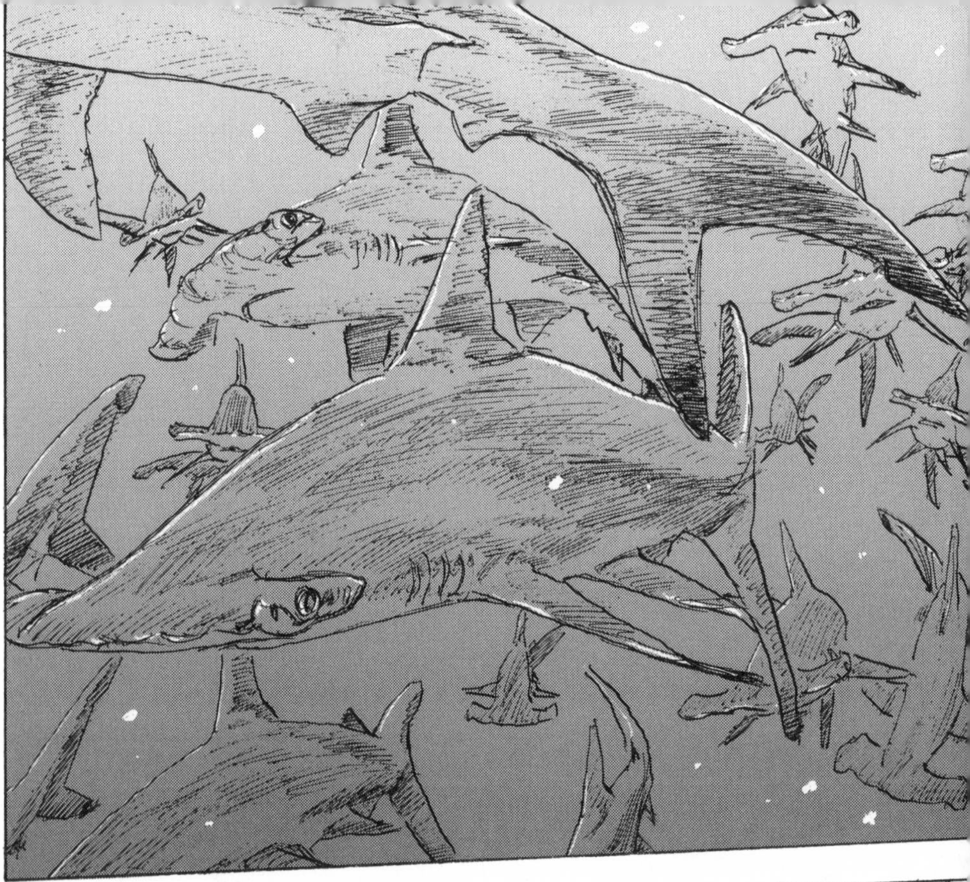

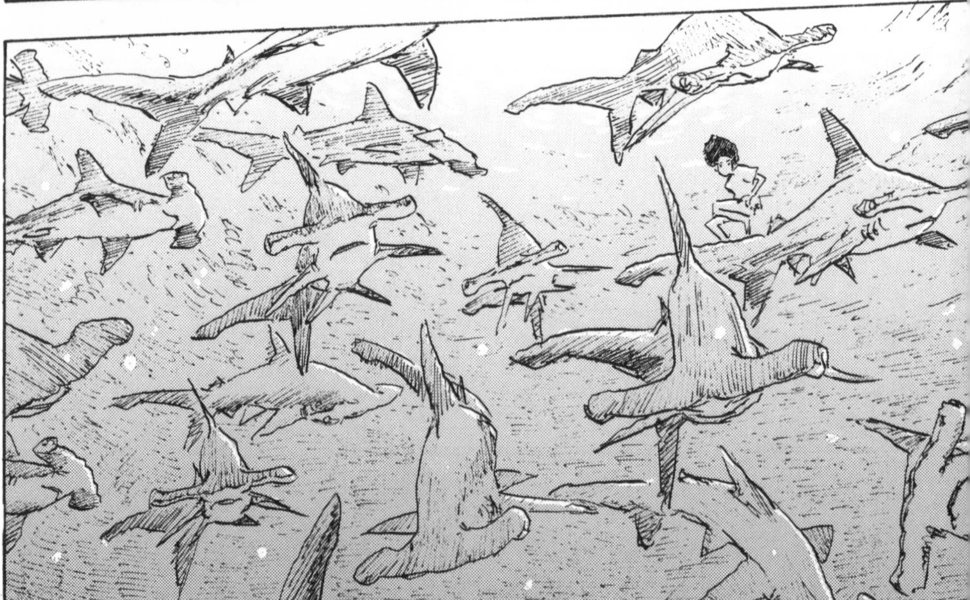

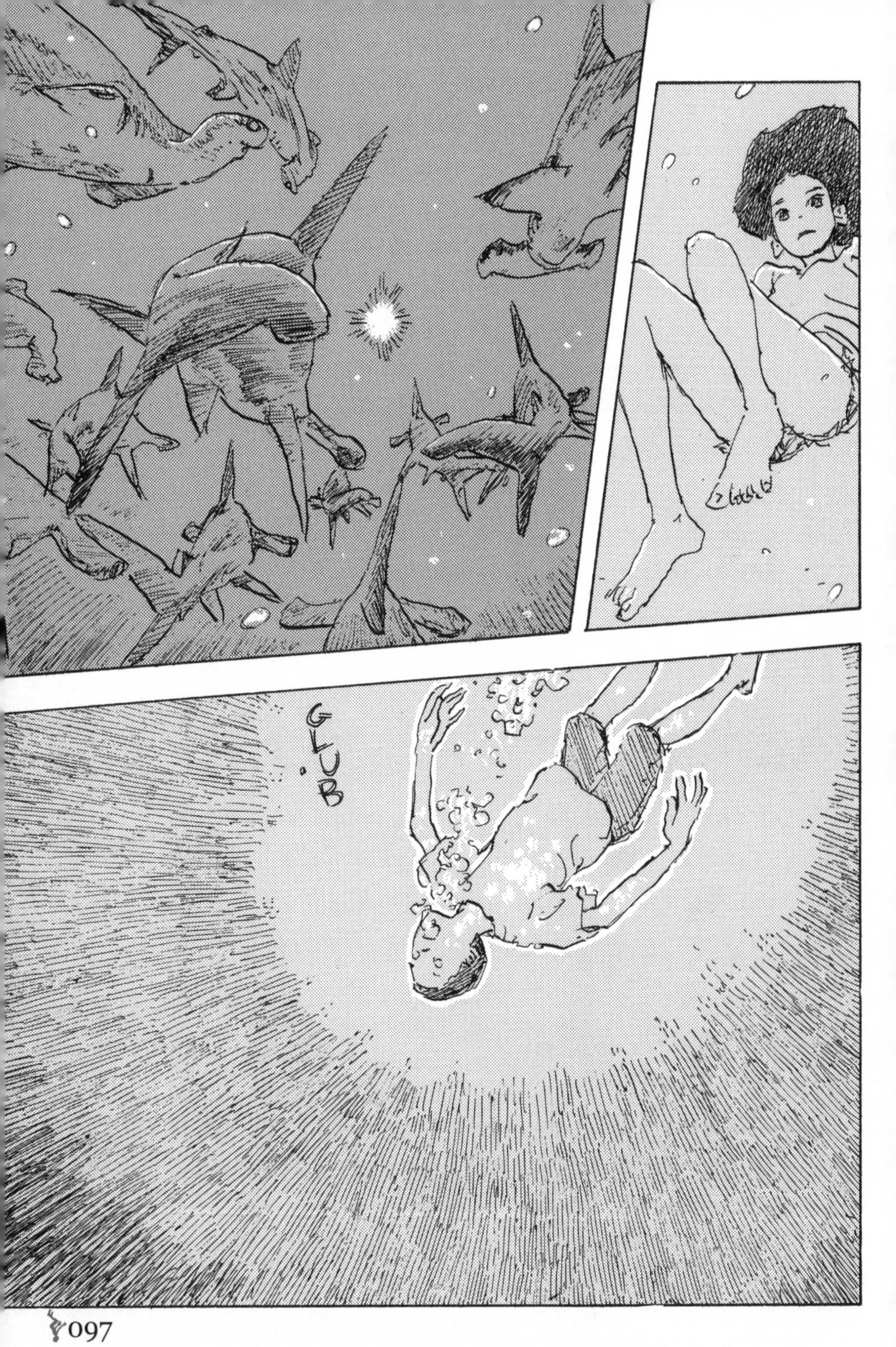
GLUB

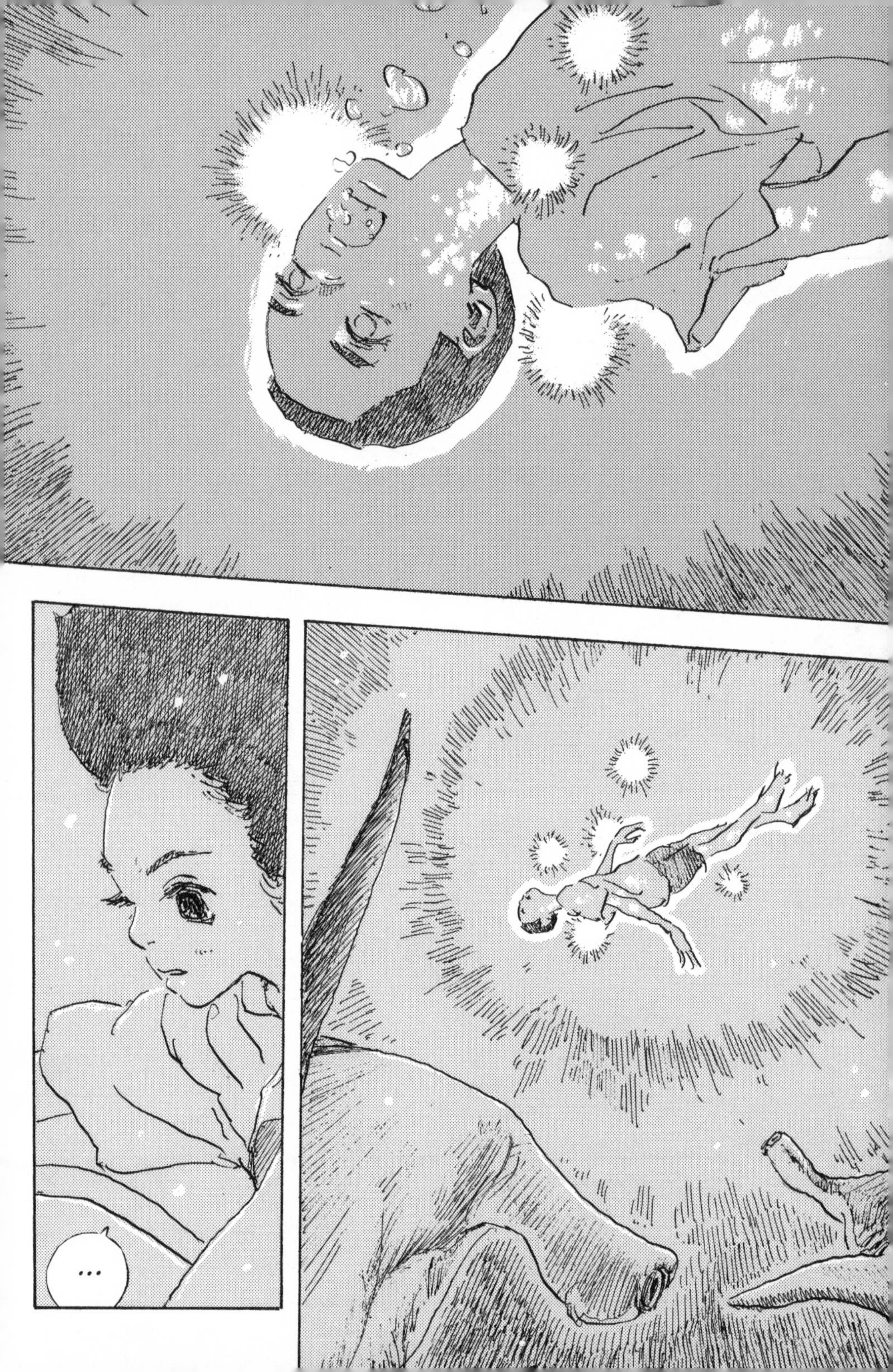
...

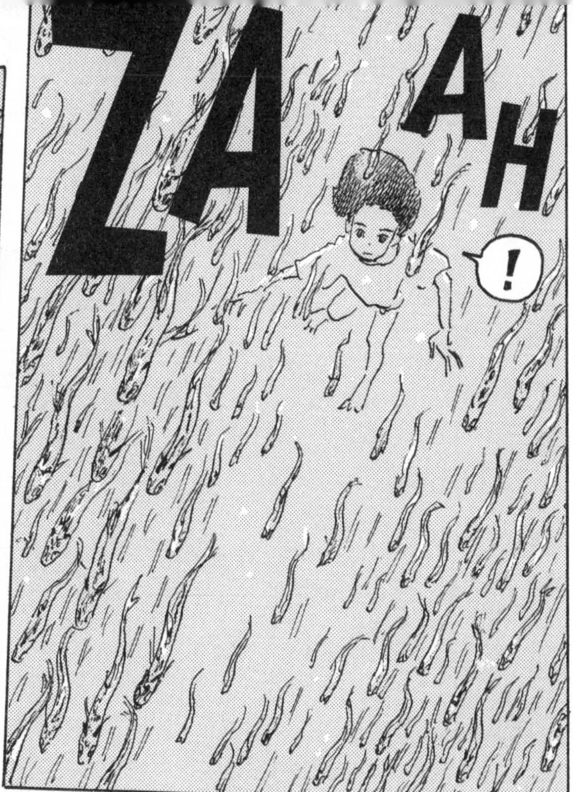
ZAAH
!
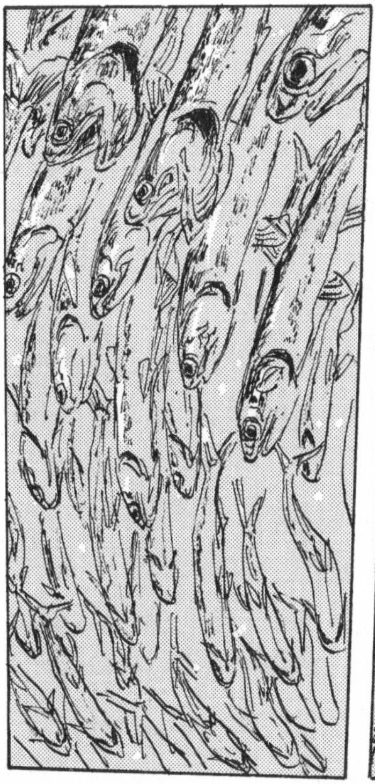
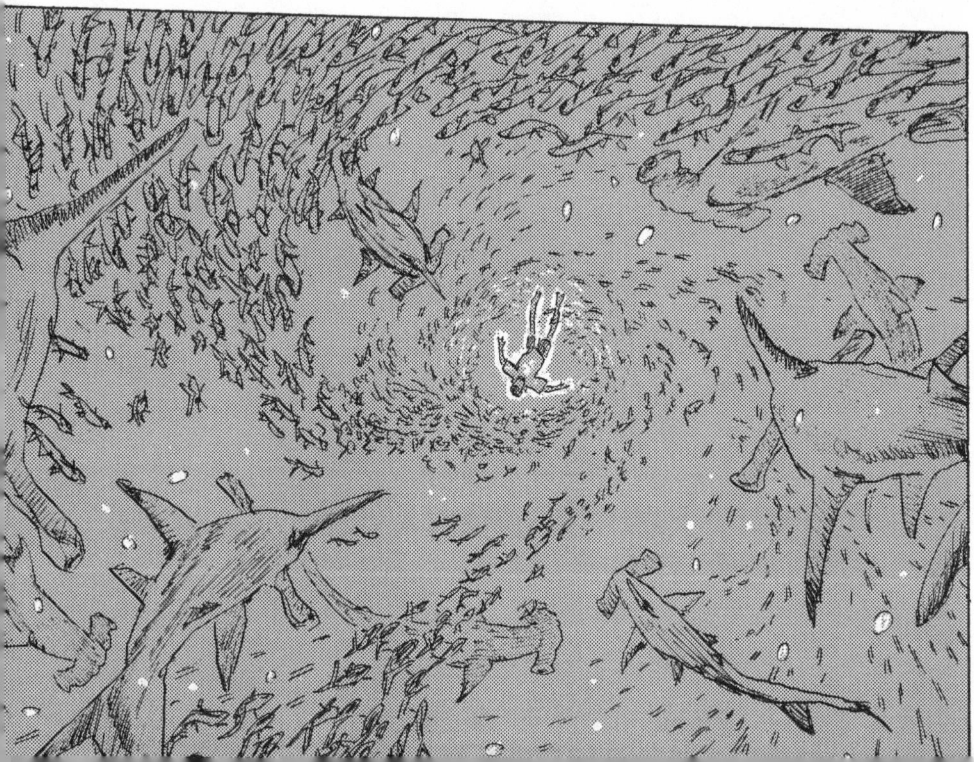

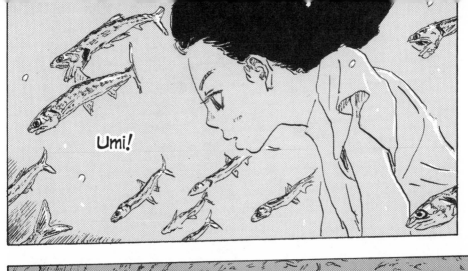

Umi!

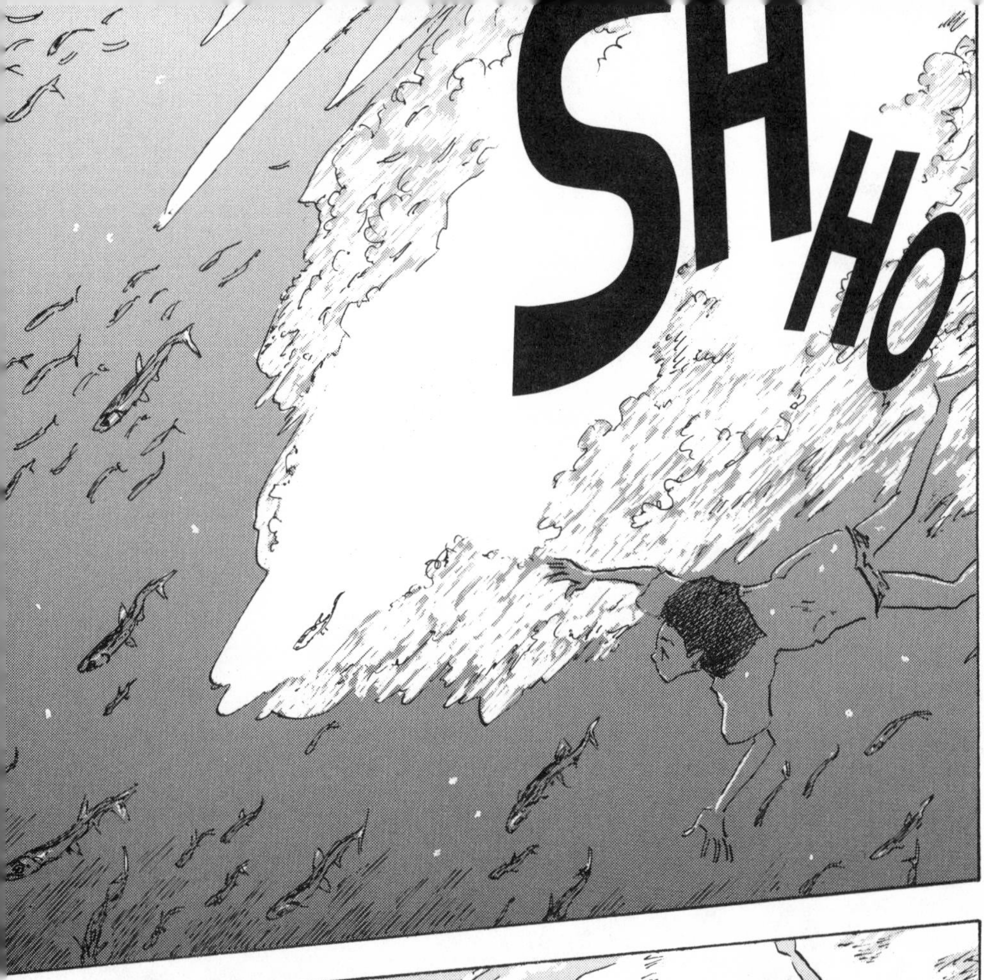
SHHO
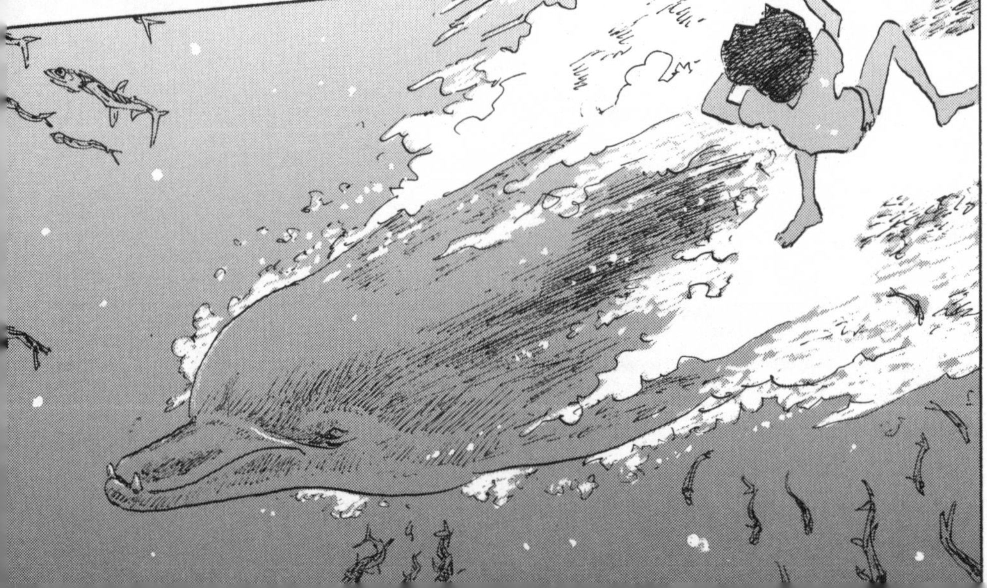

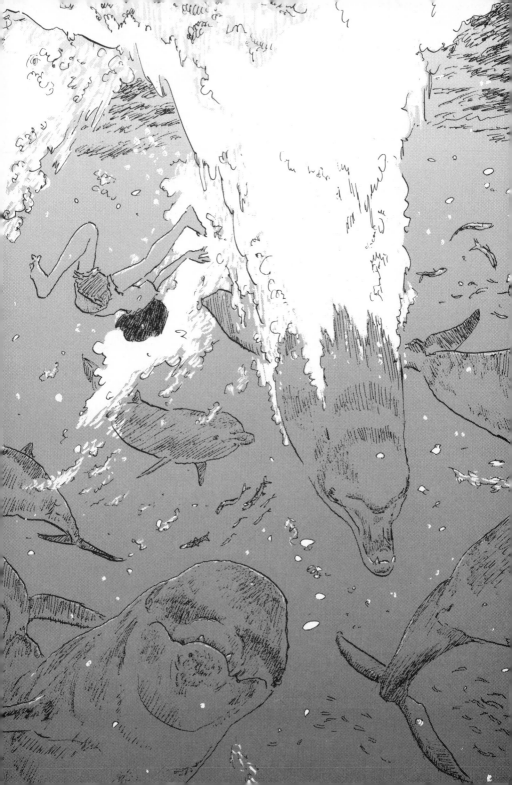

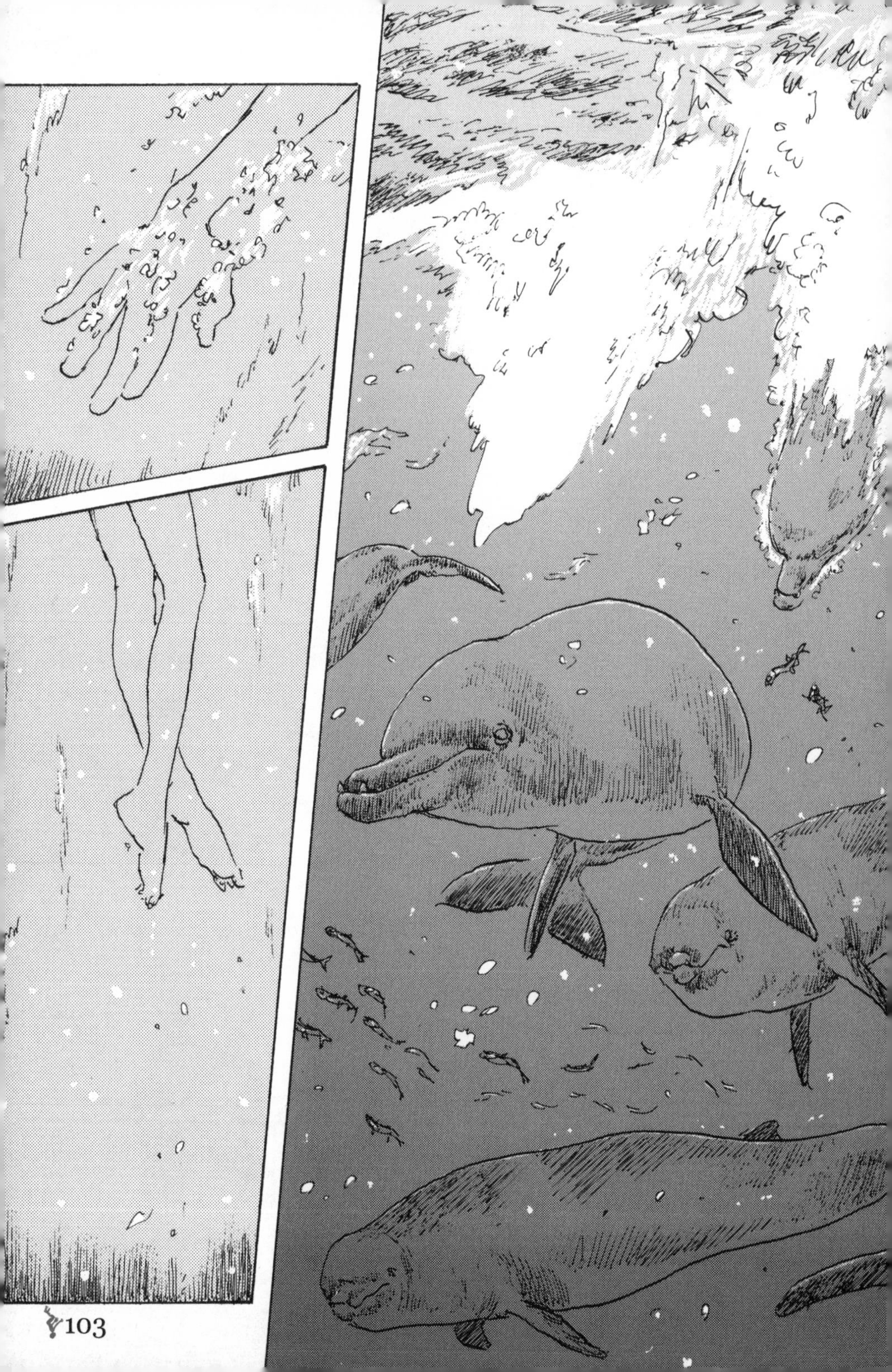

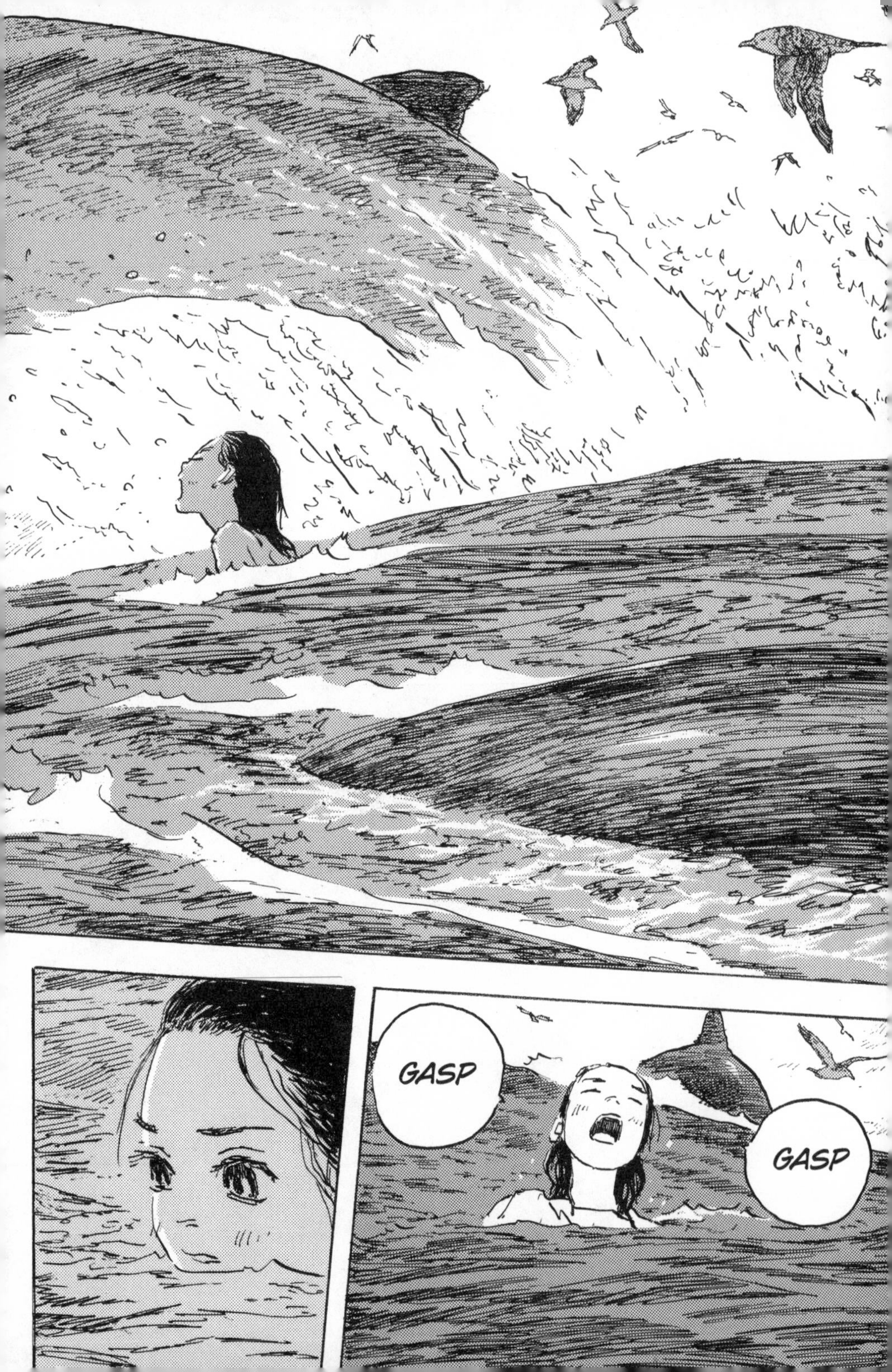
GASP
GASP

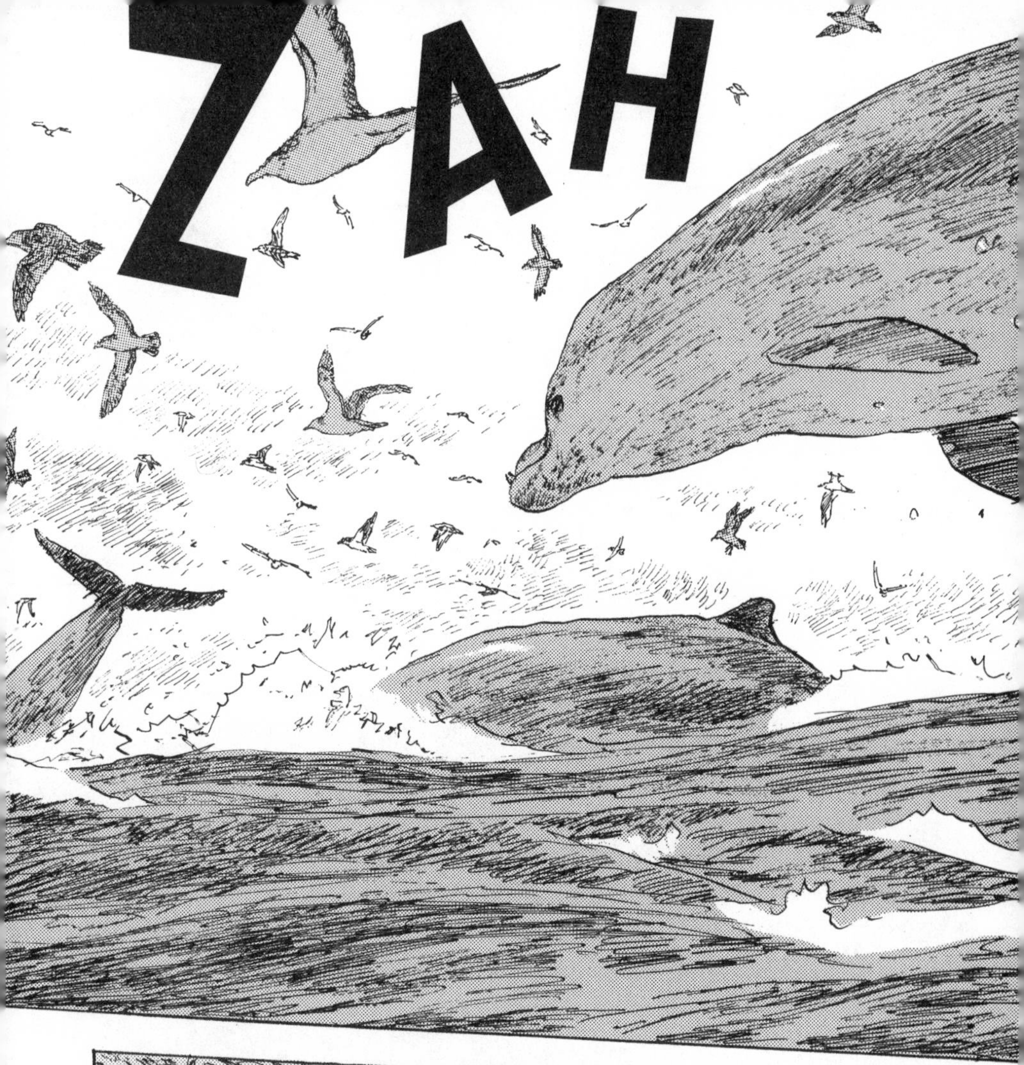
ZAH
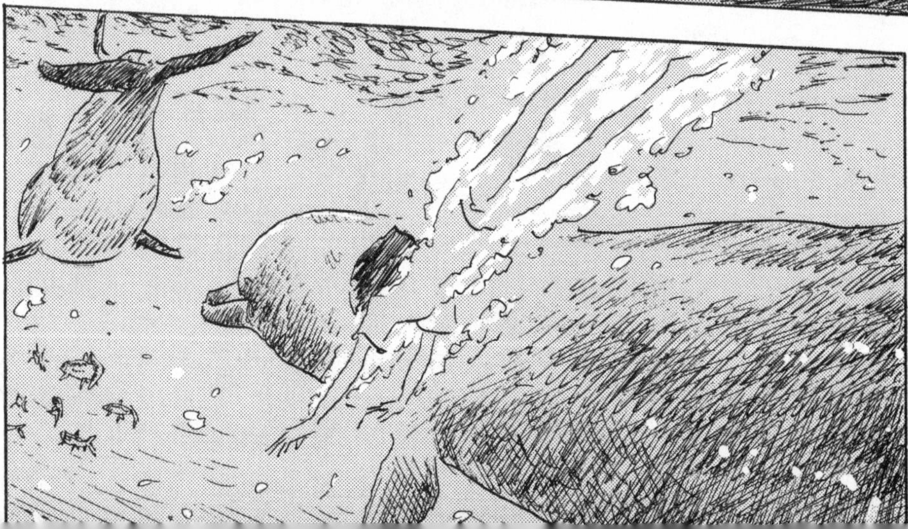

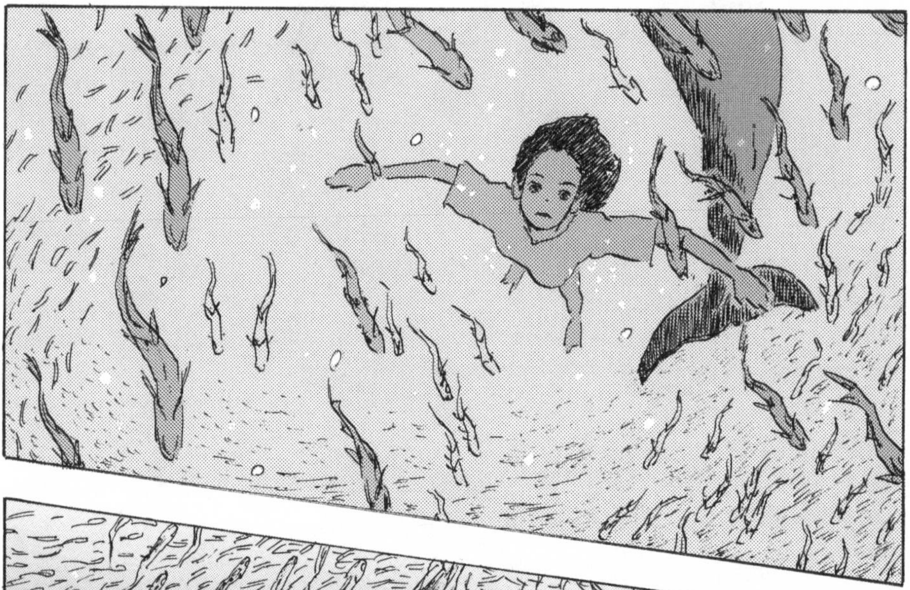
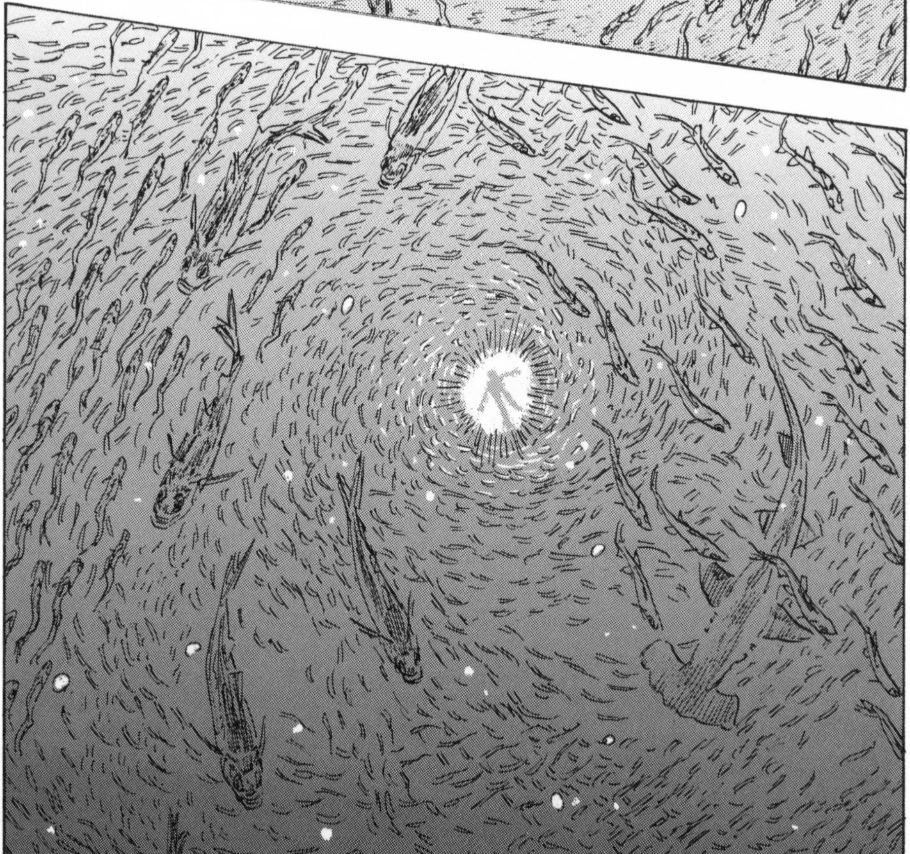

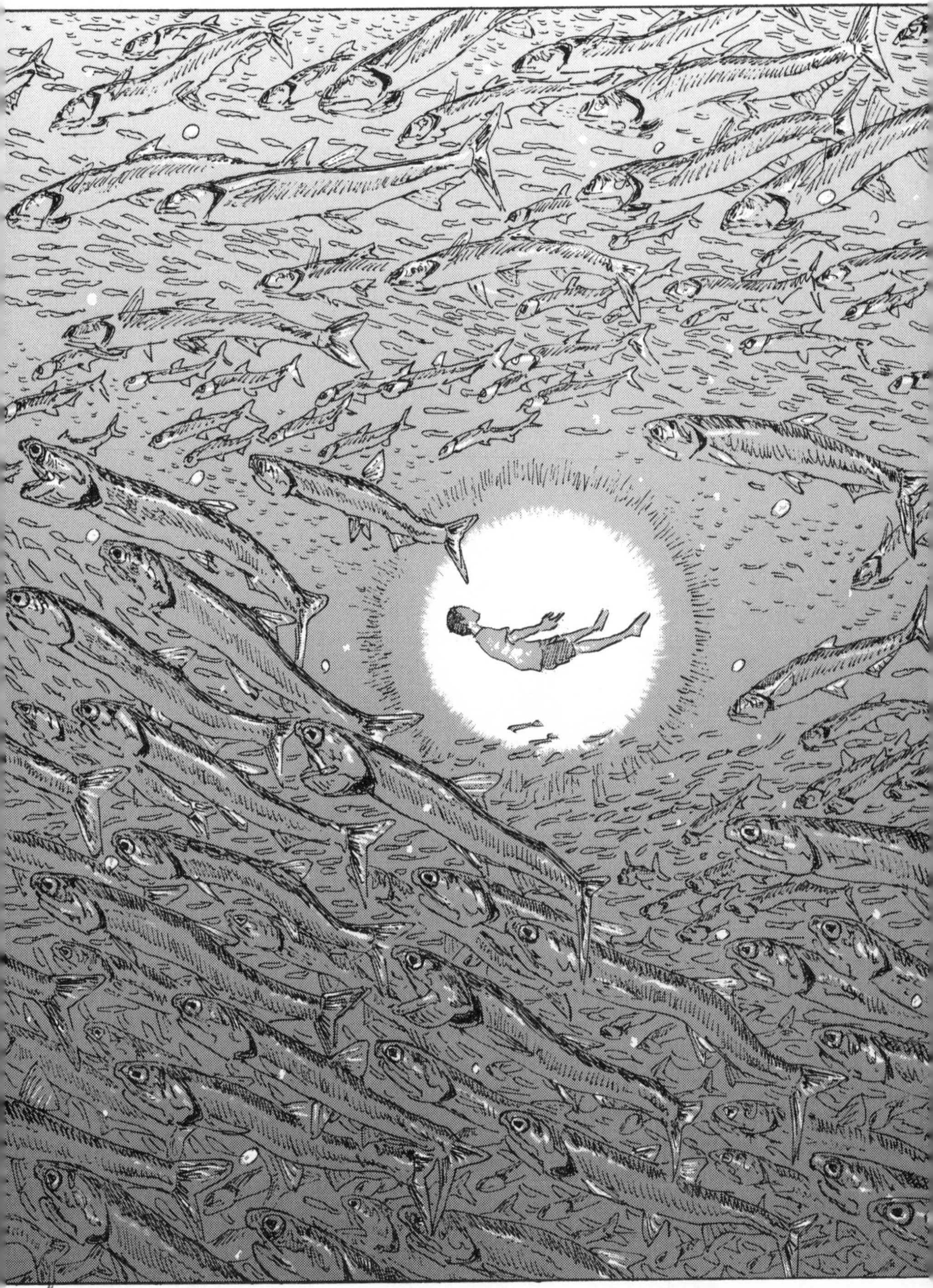

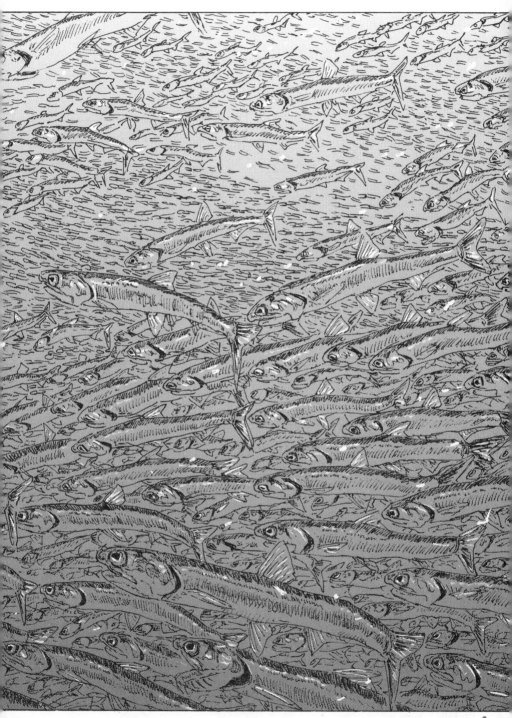

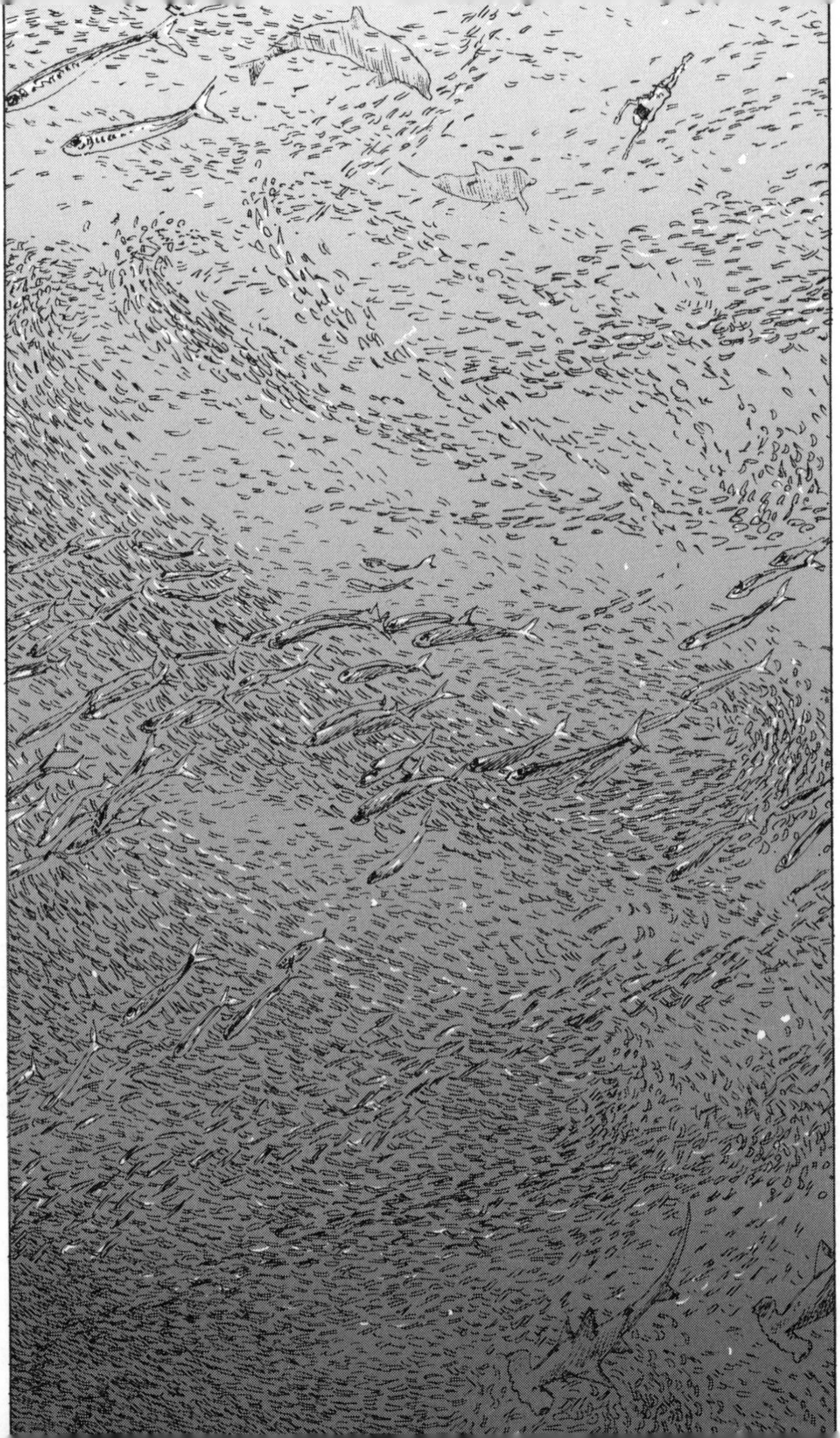

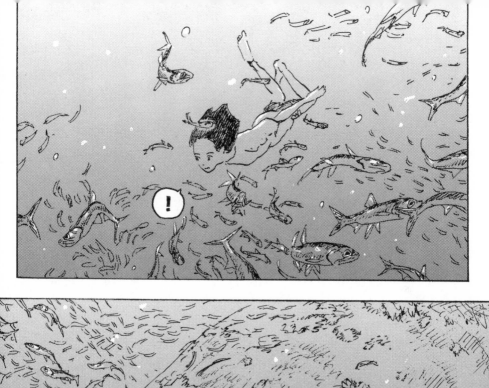

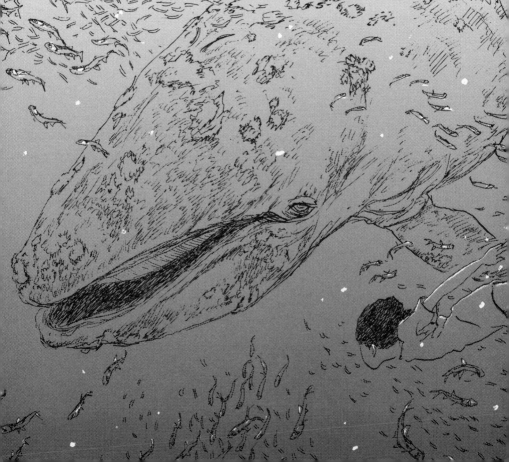

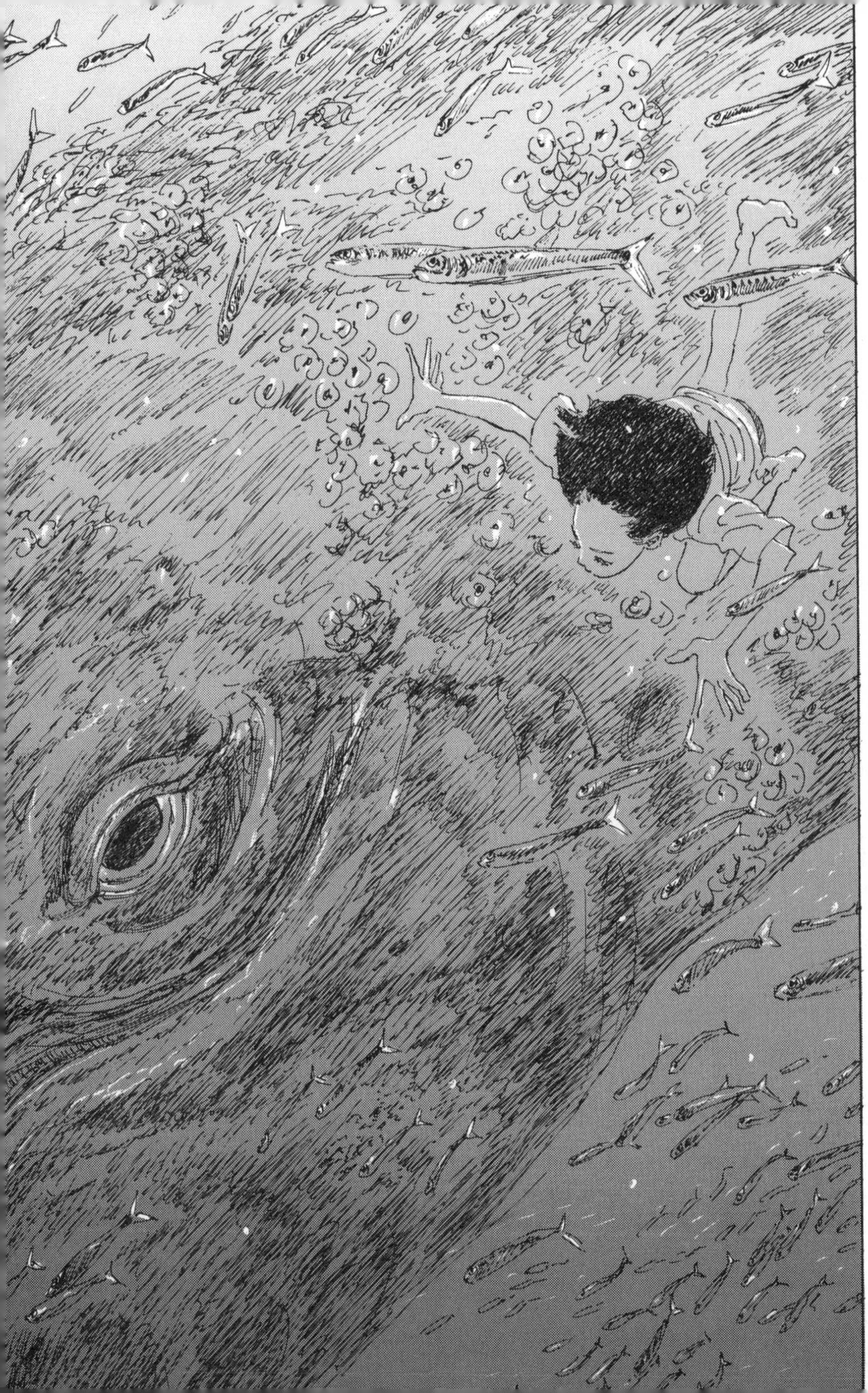

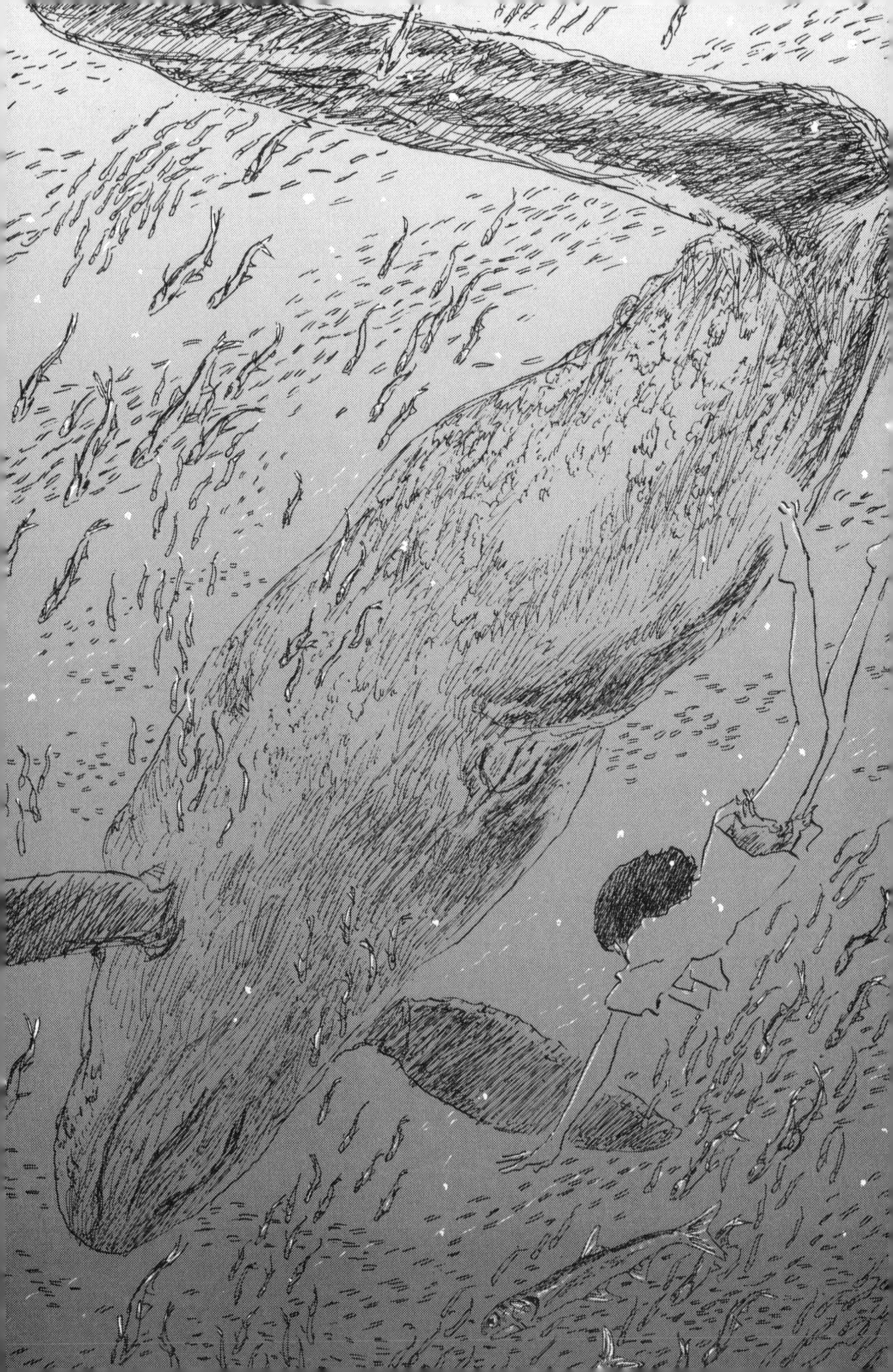

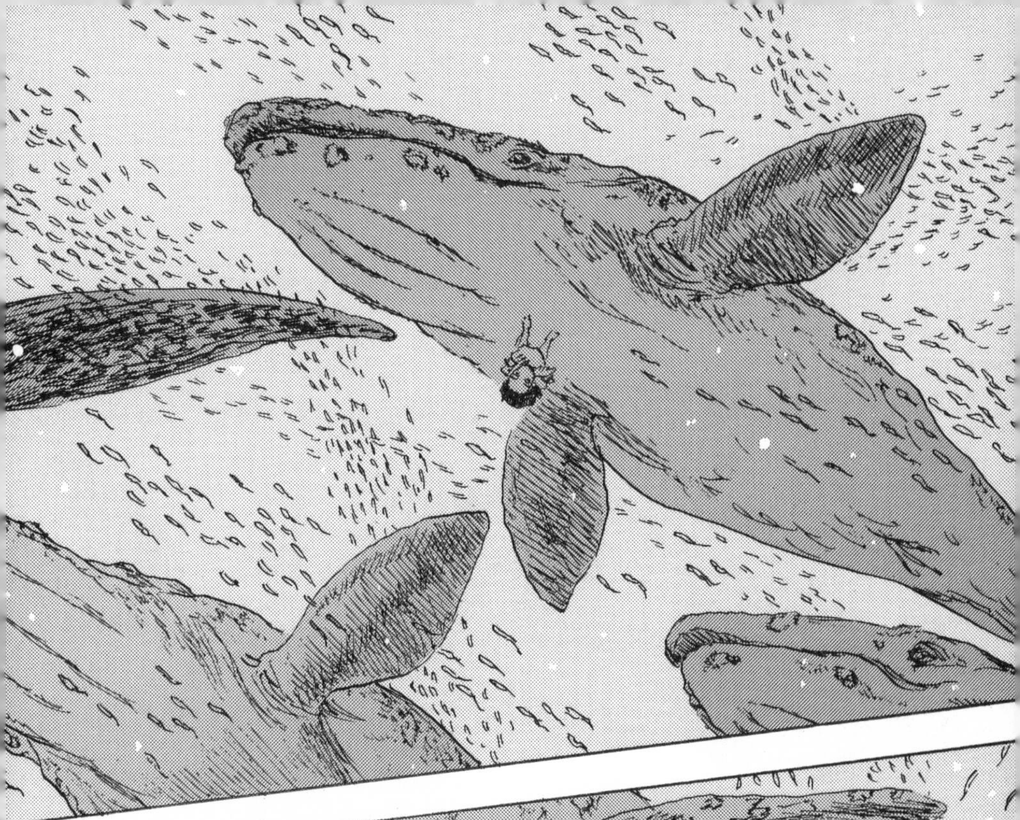
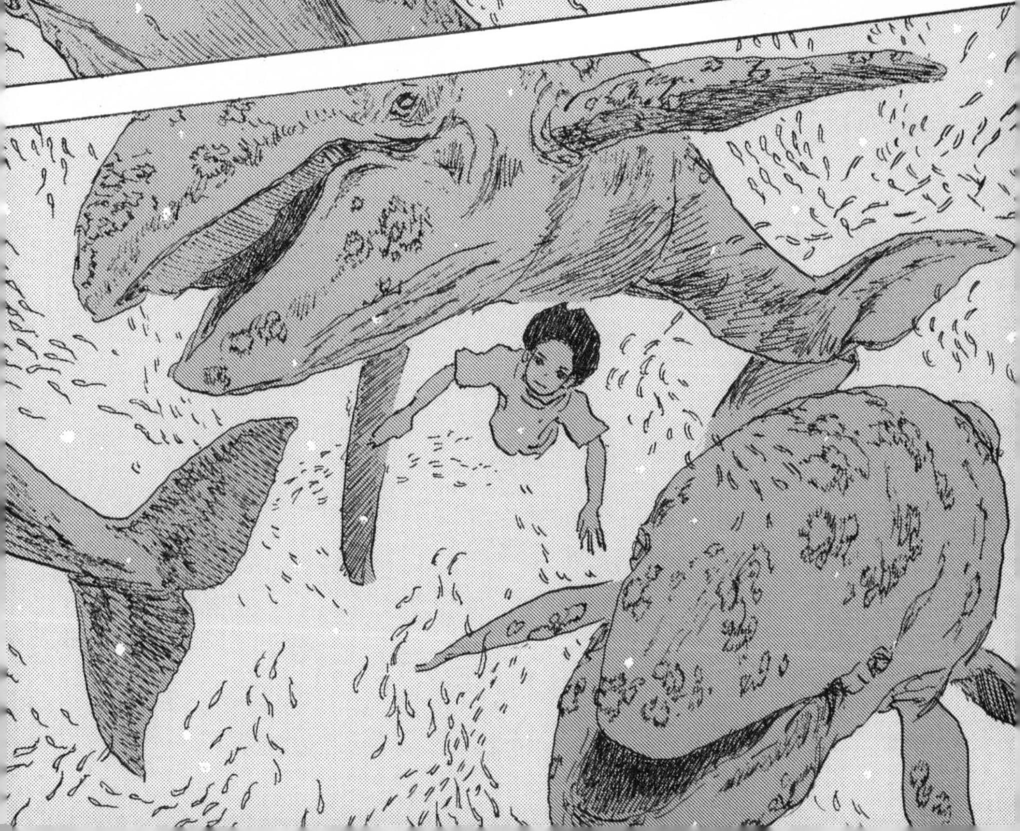

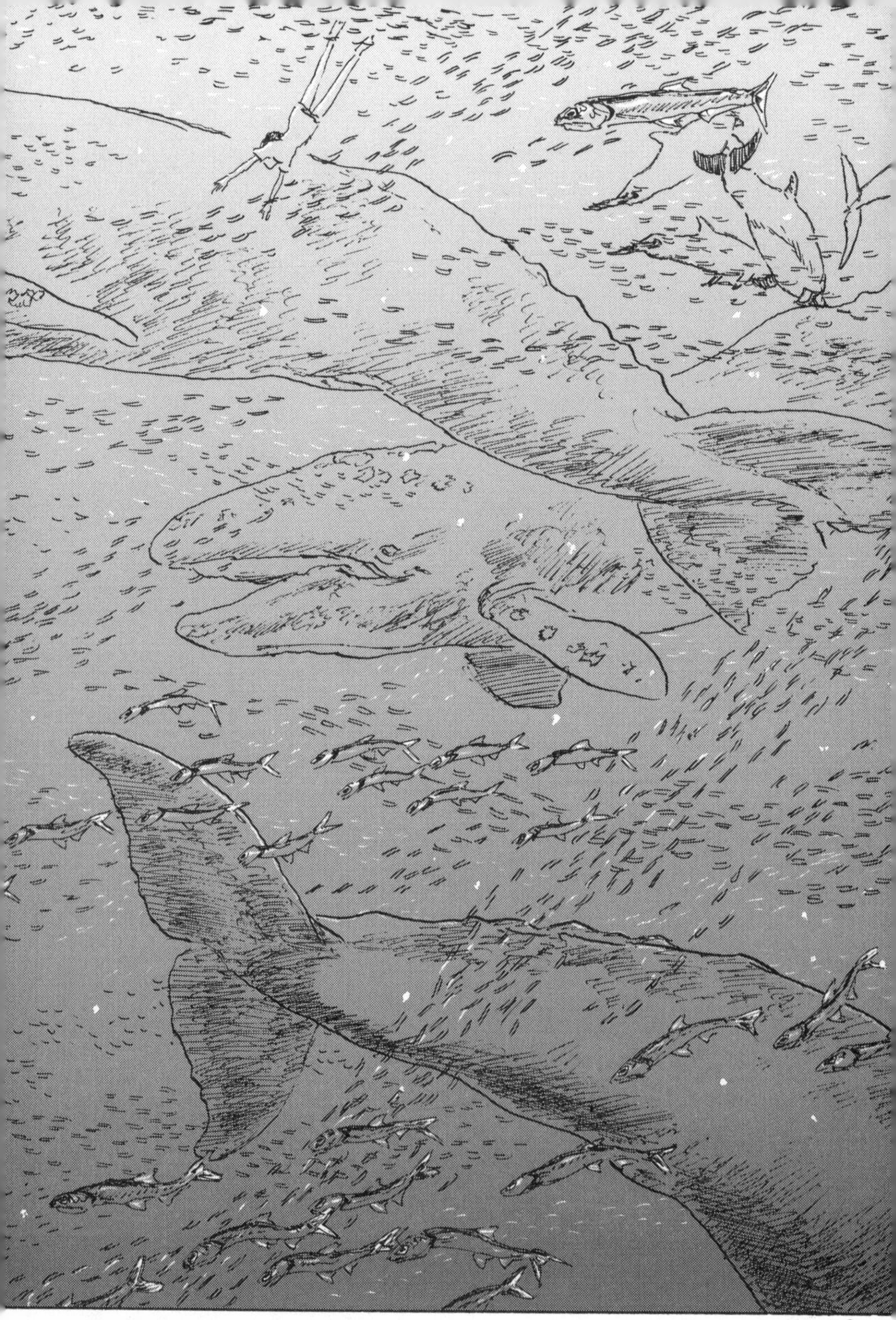

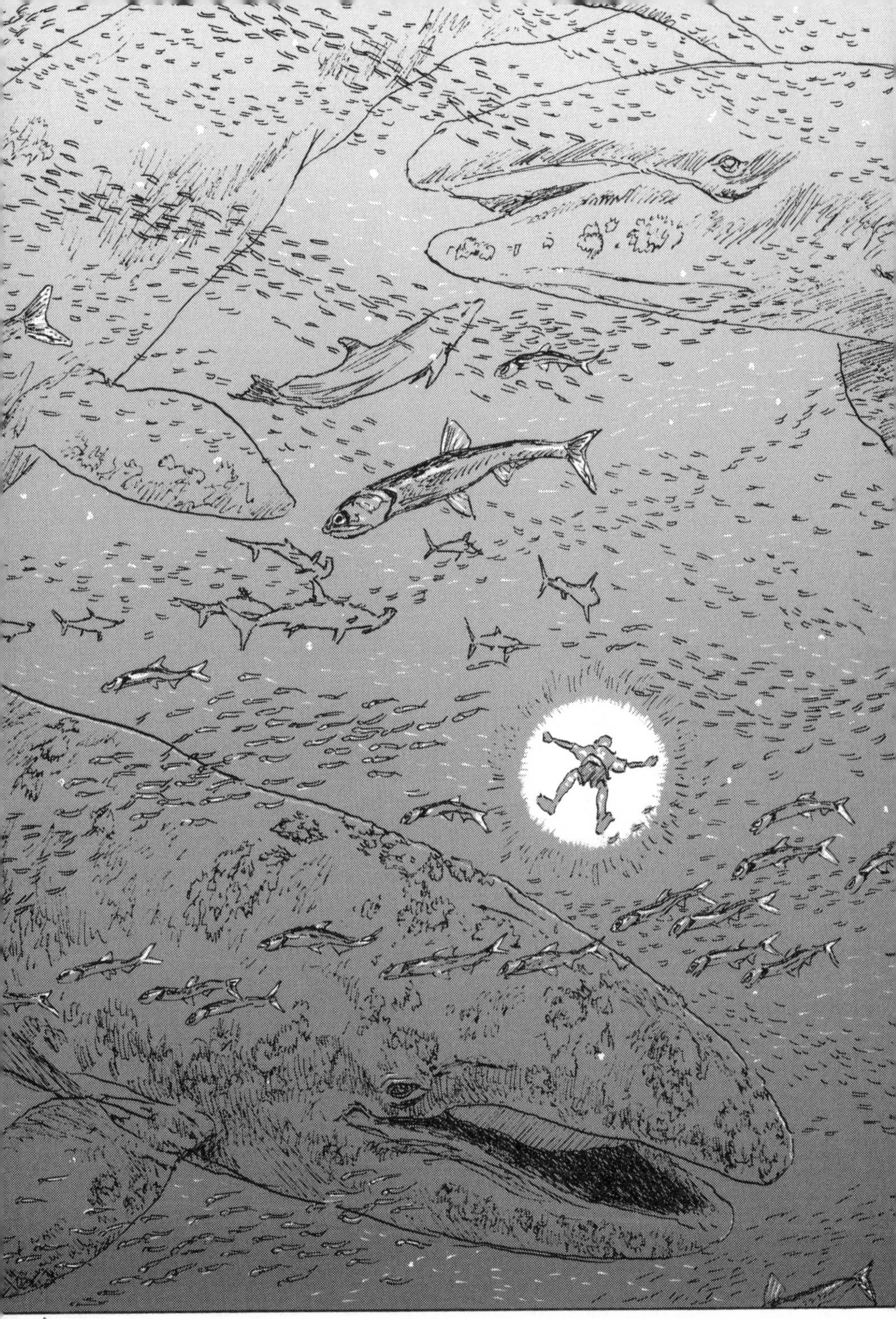

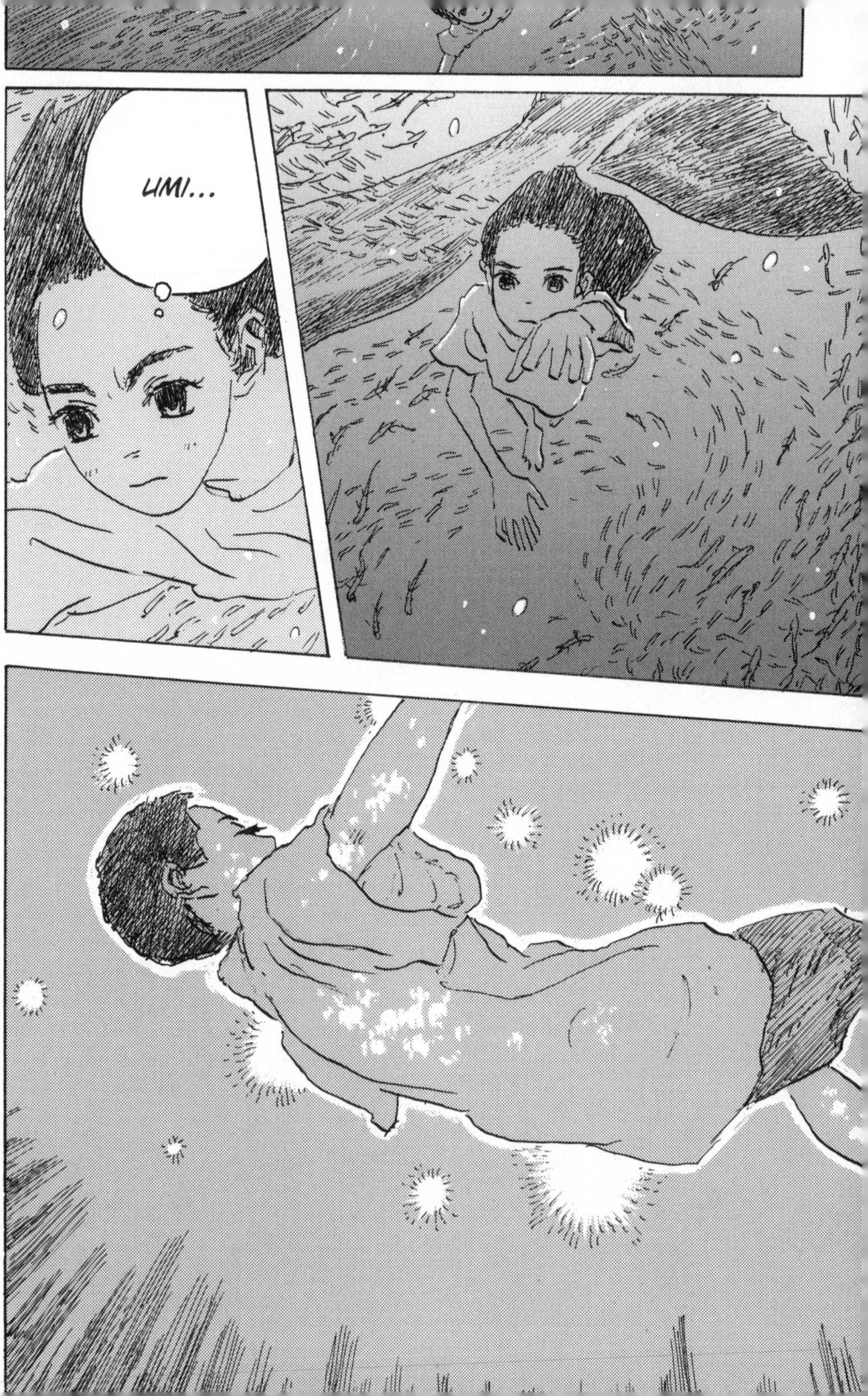
UMI...

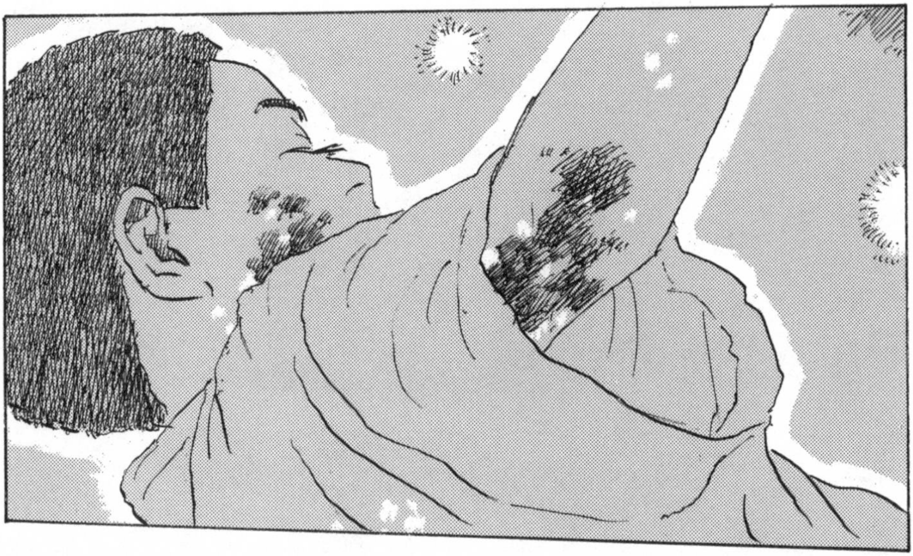
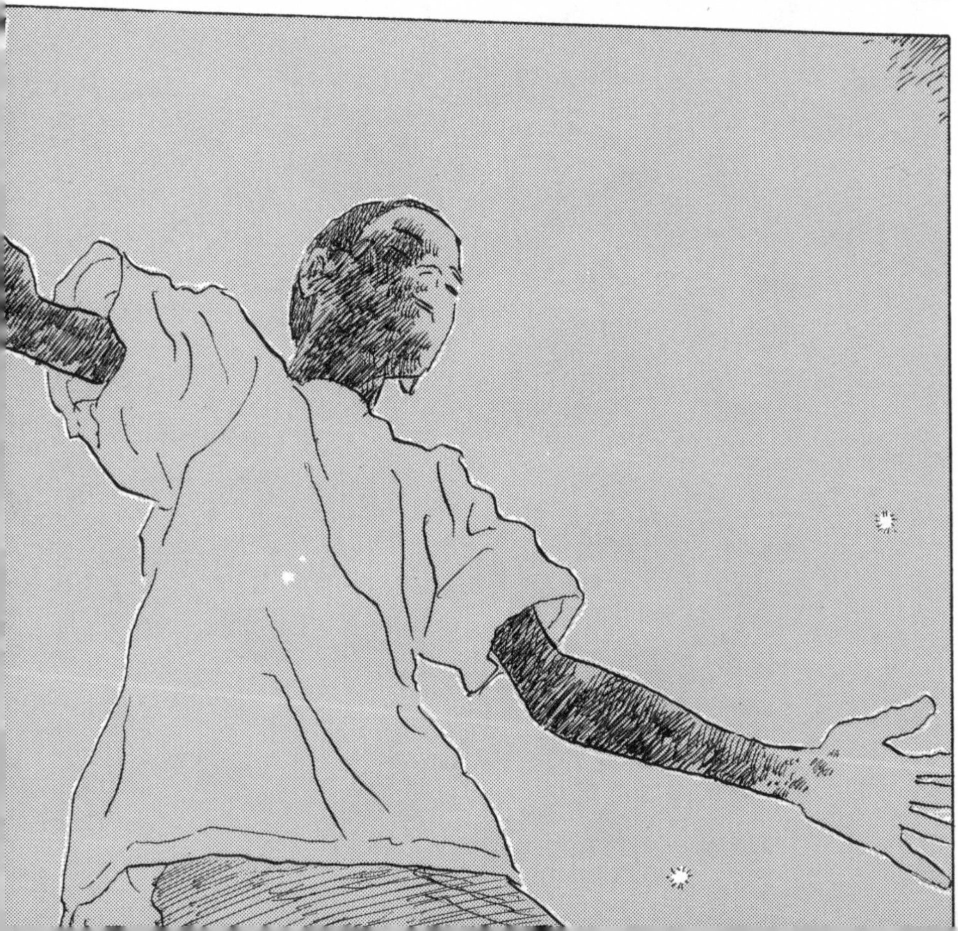

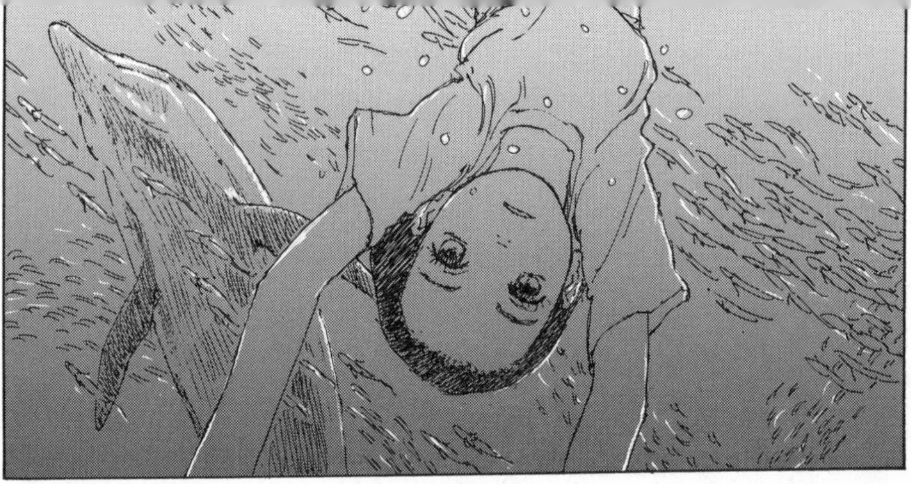
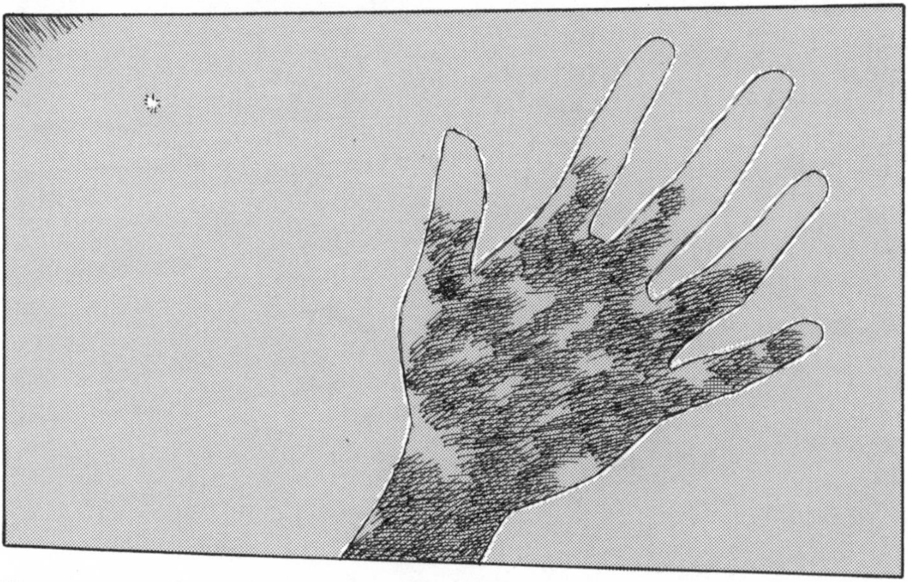
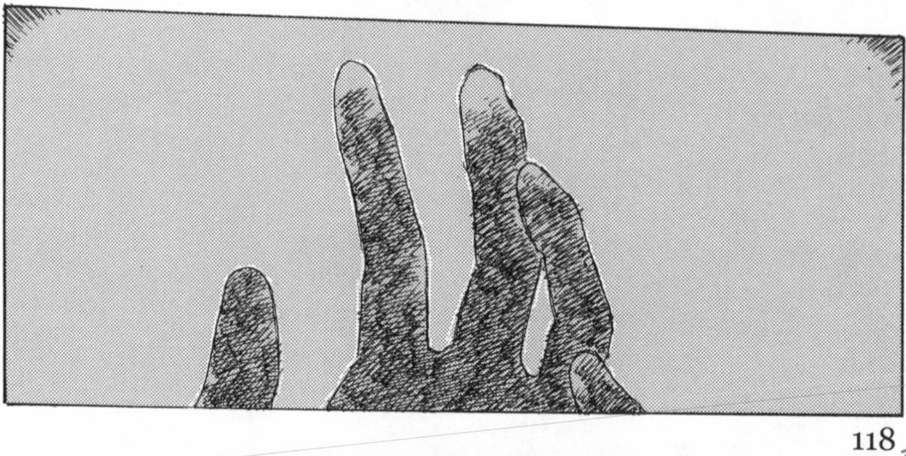

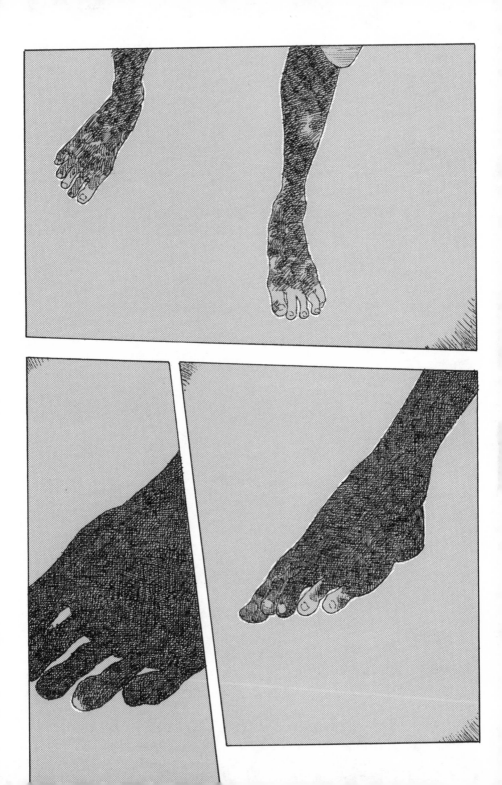

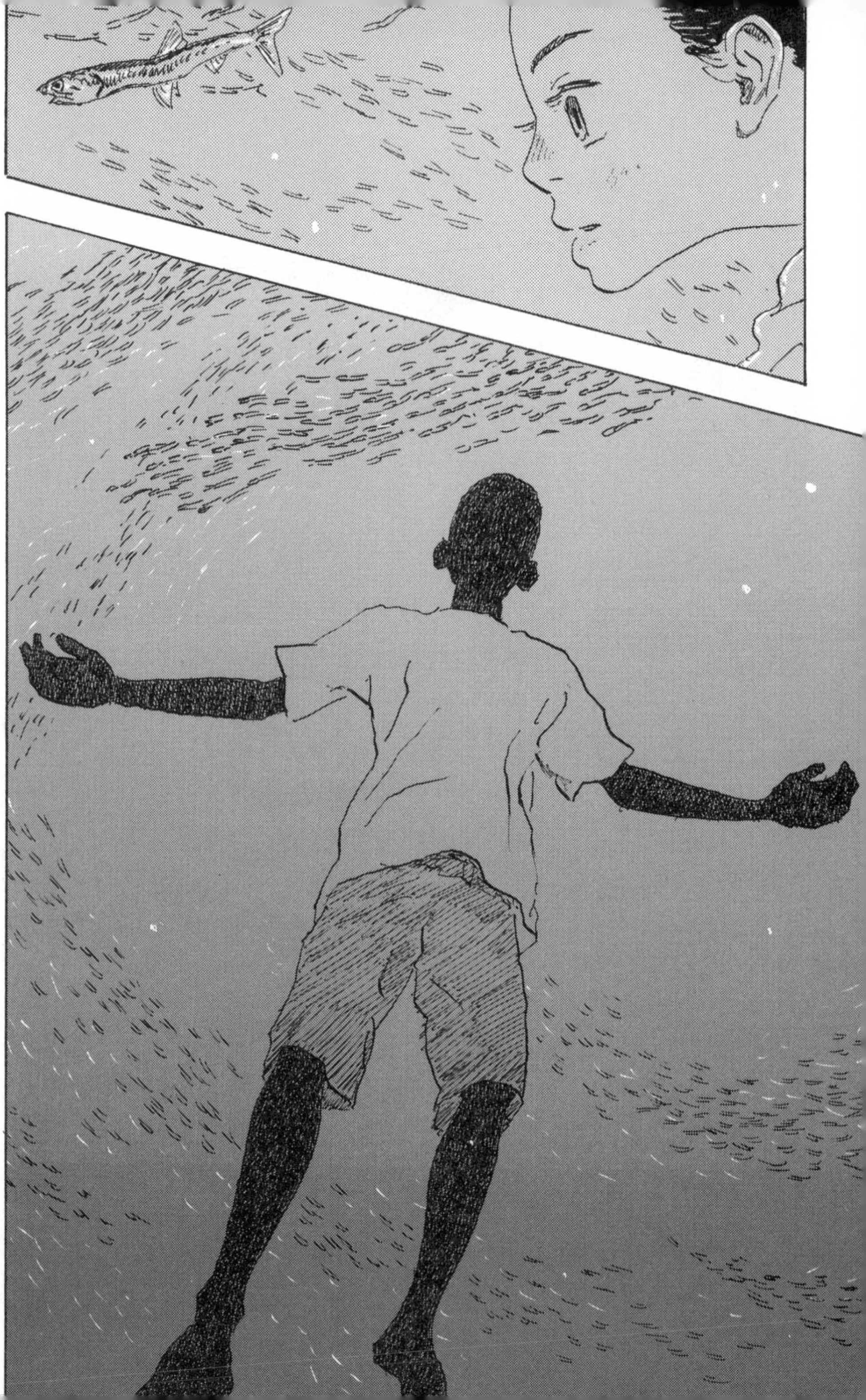

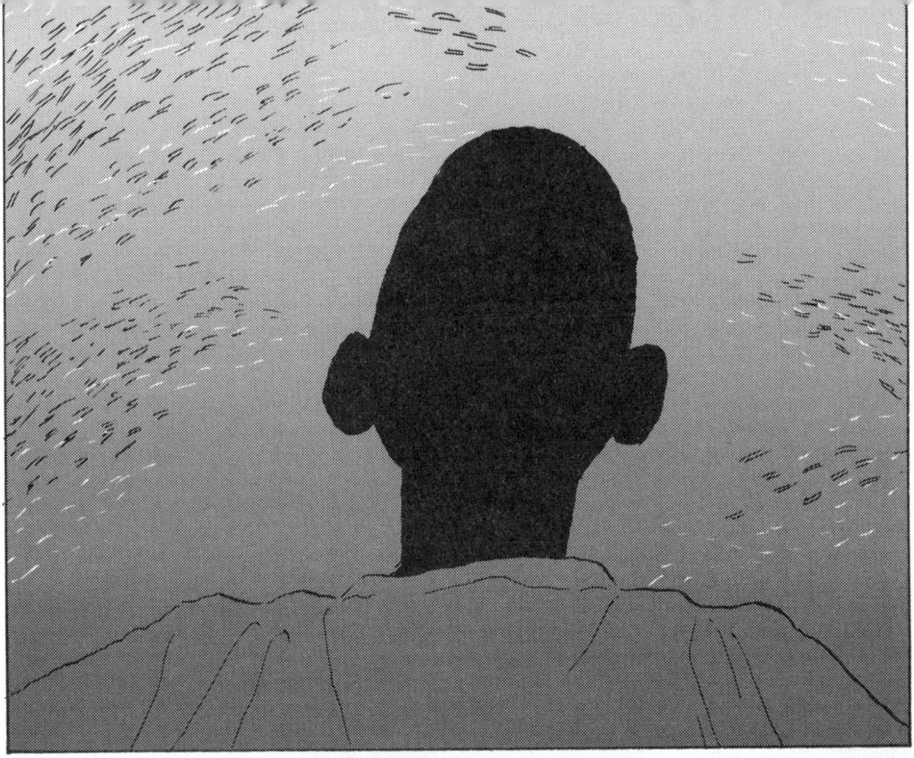
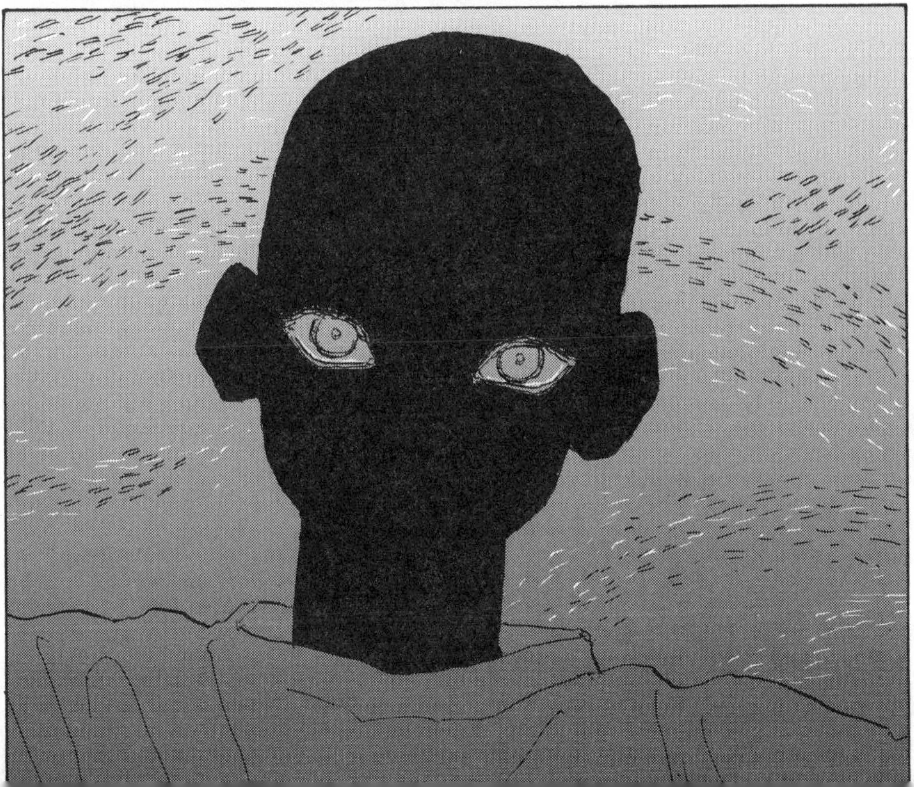

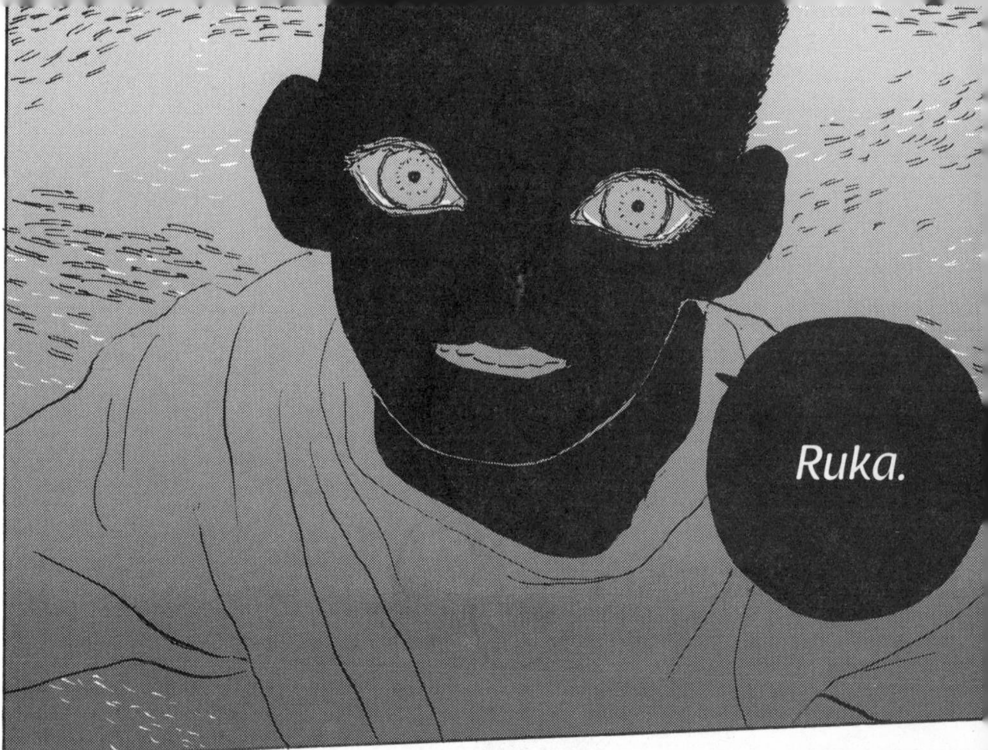
Ruka.
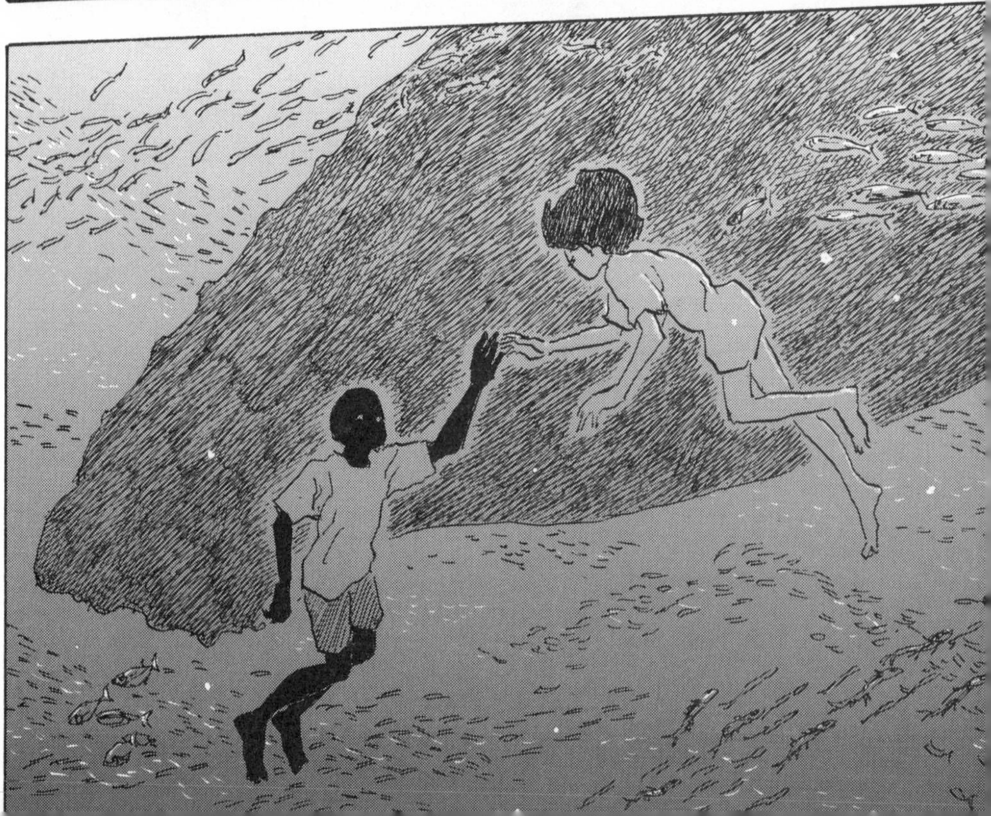

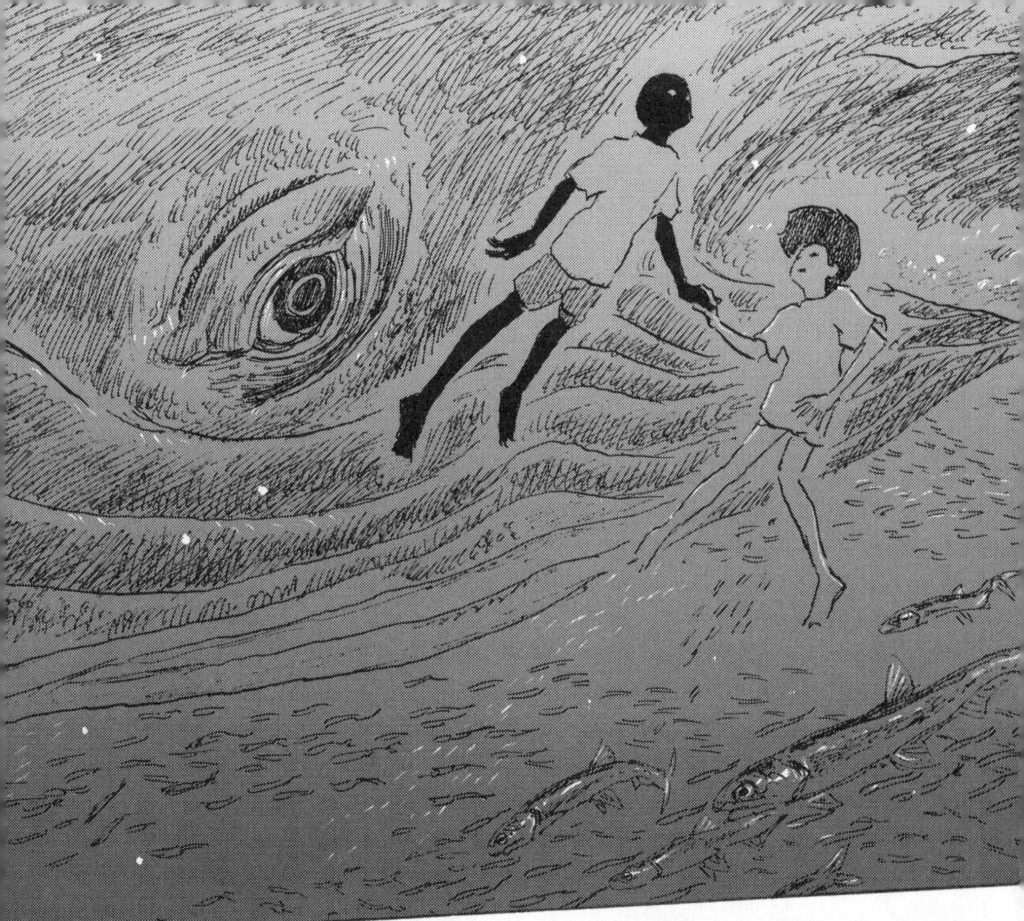
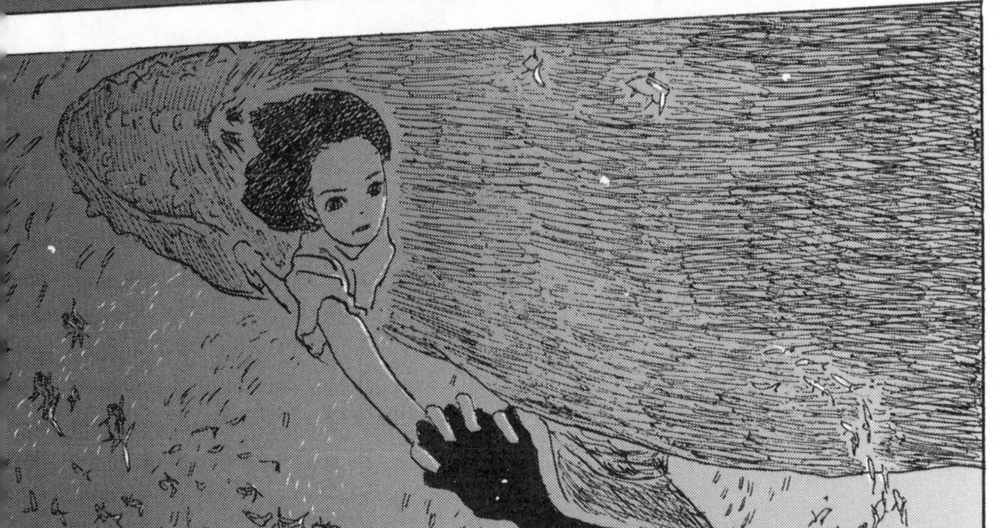

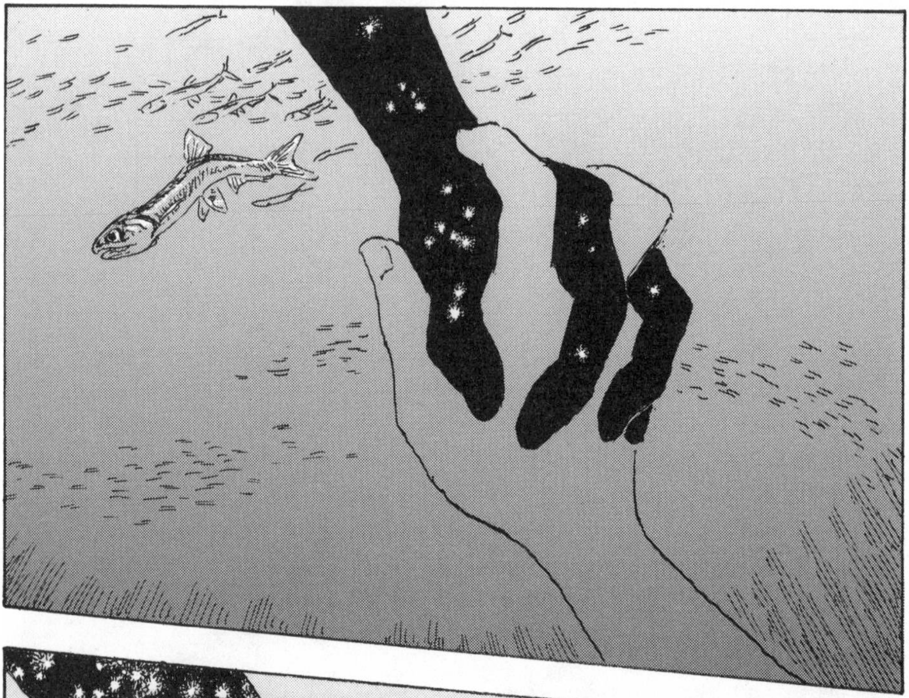
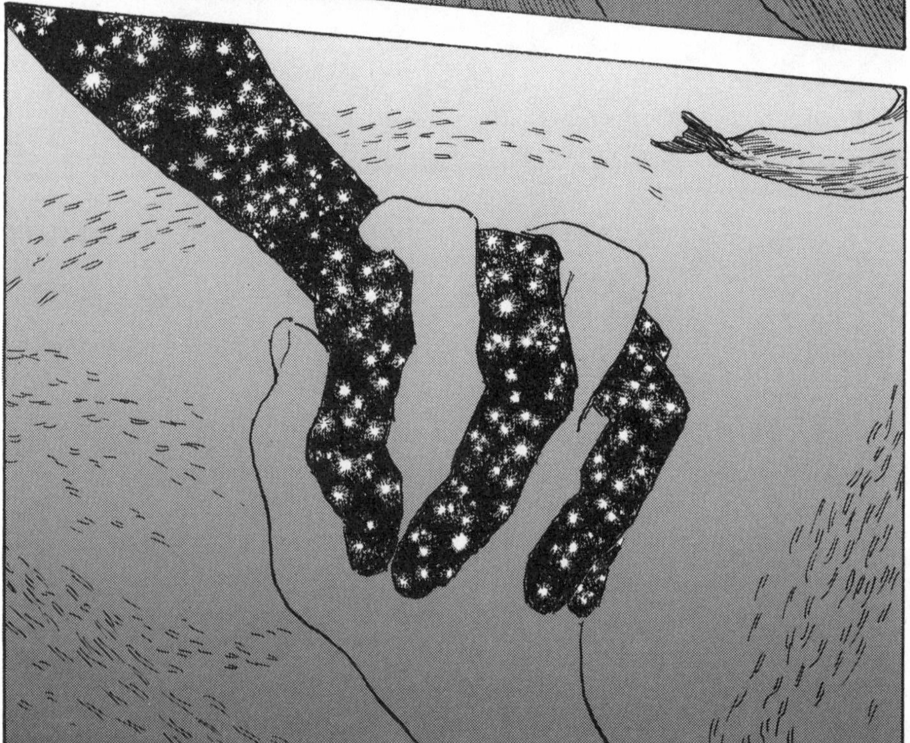

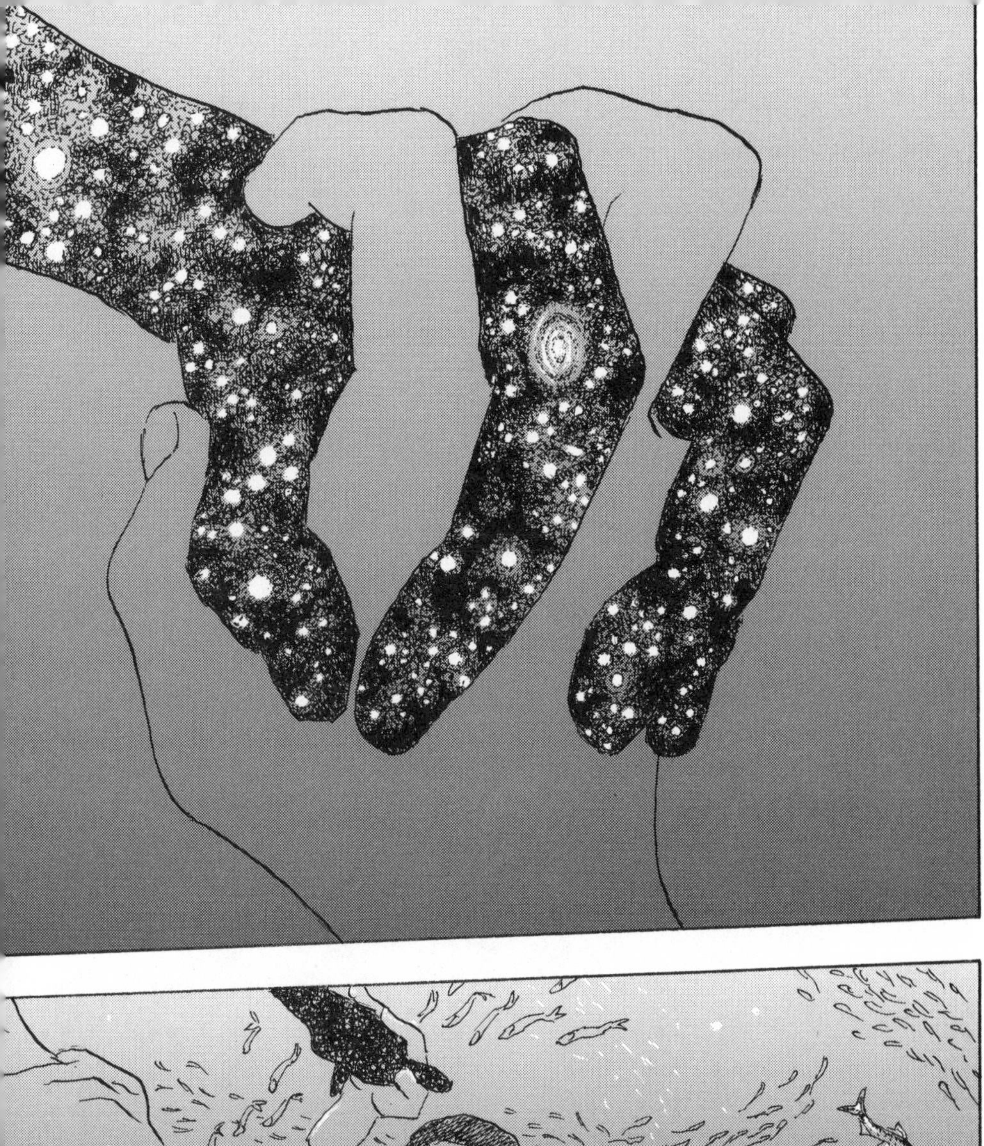

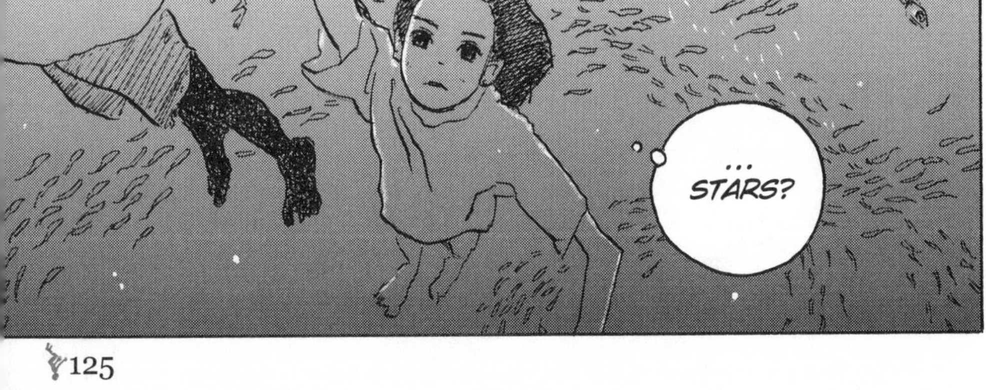
... STARS?

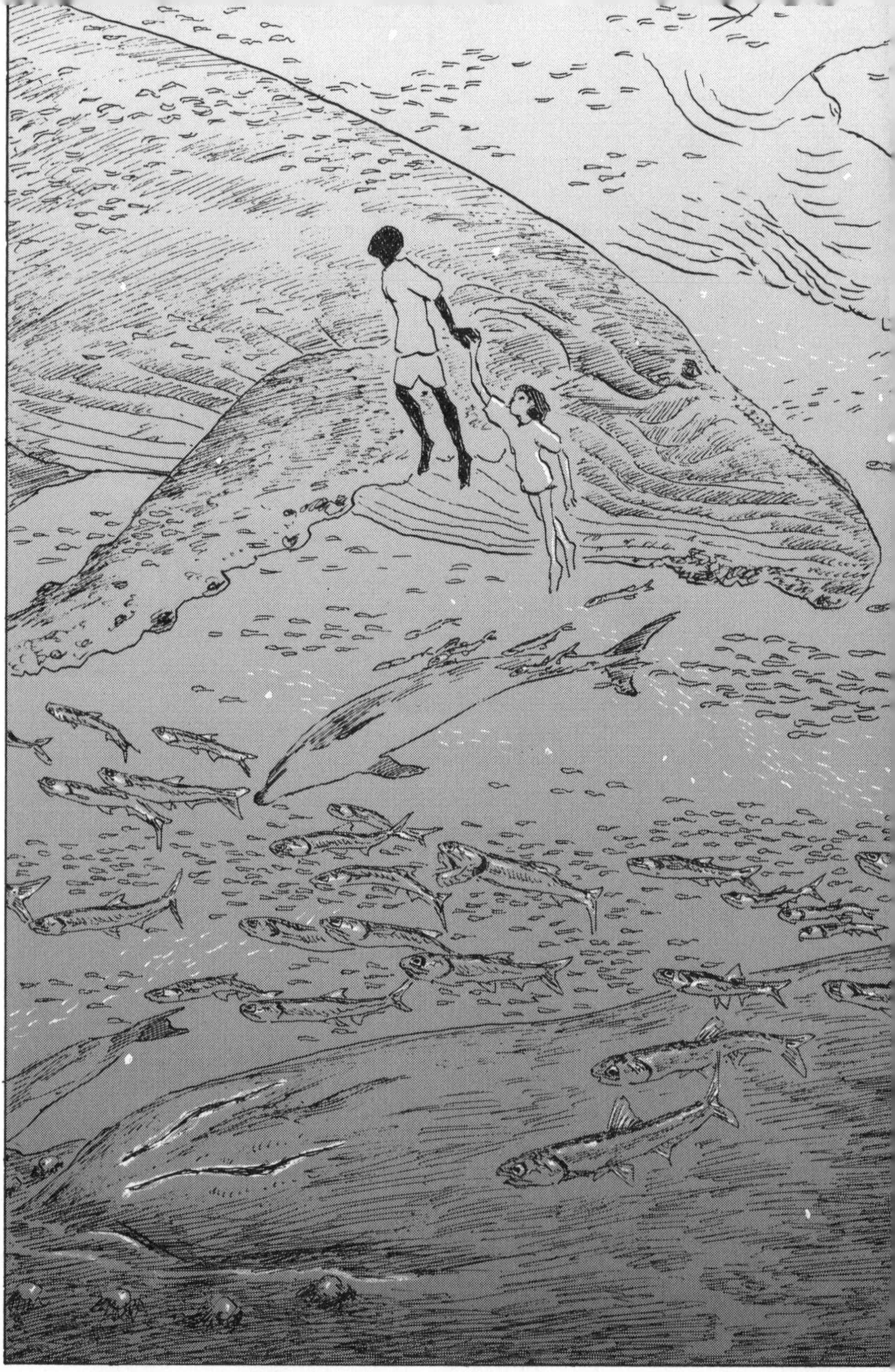

Chapter 39: Birth Rite III

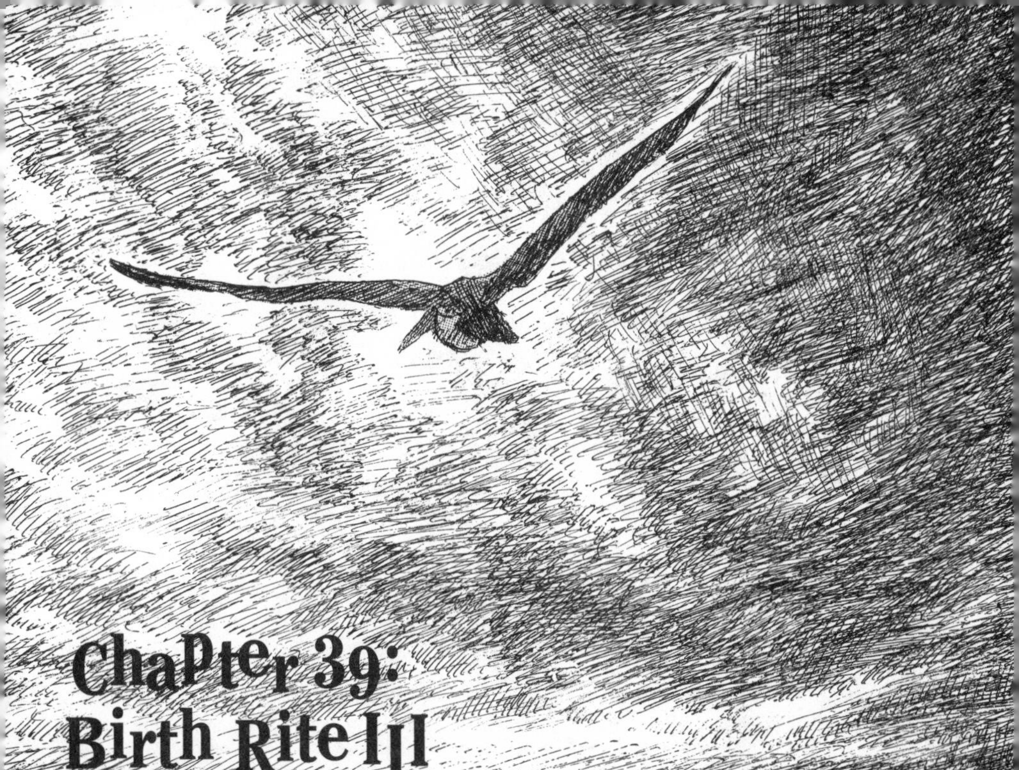

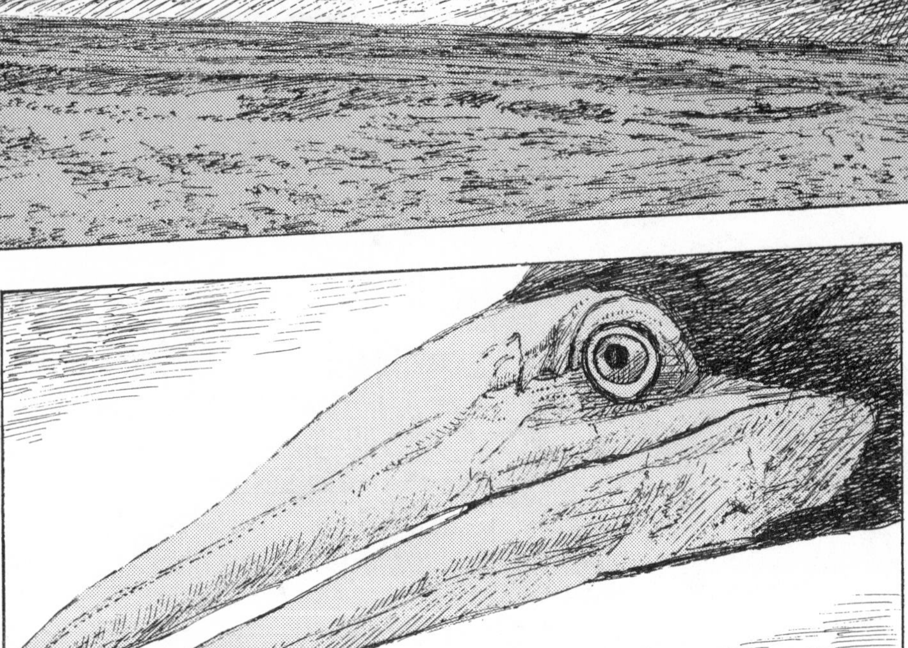

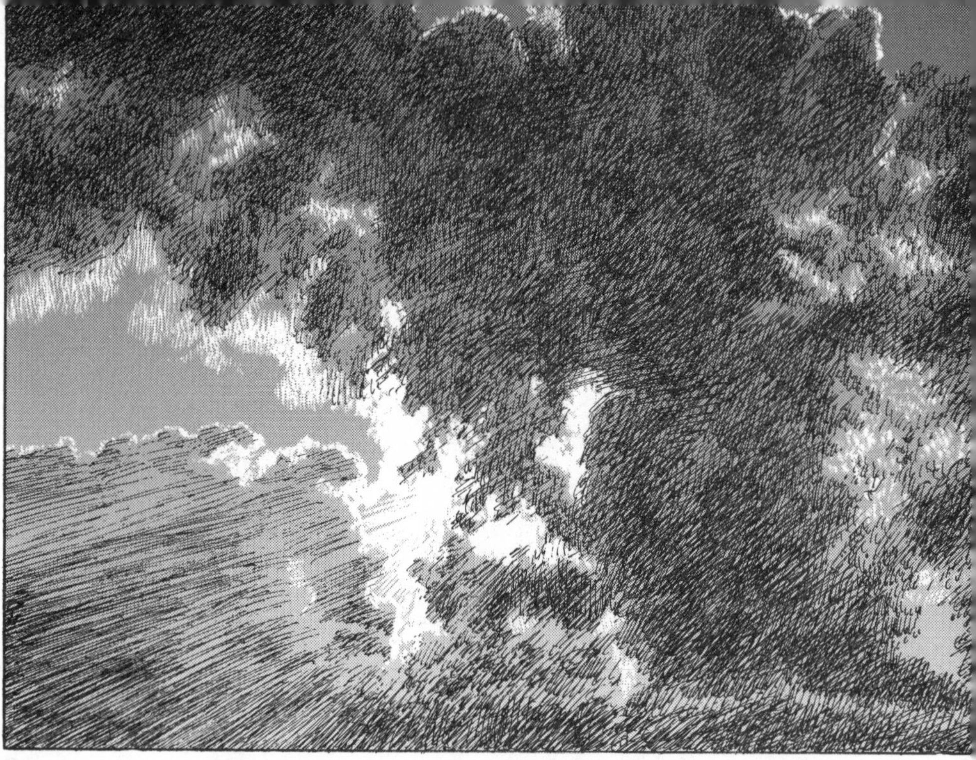
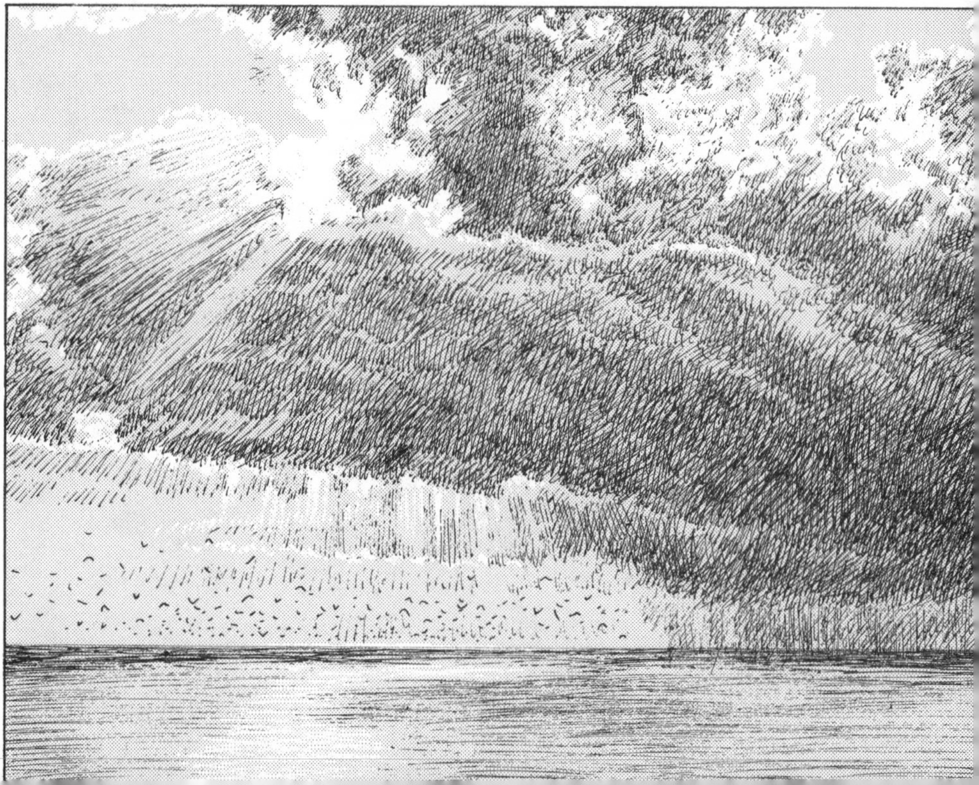

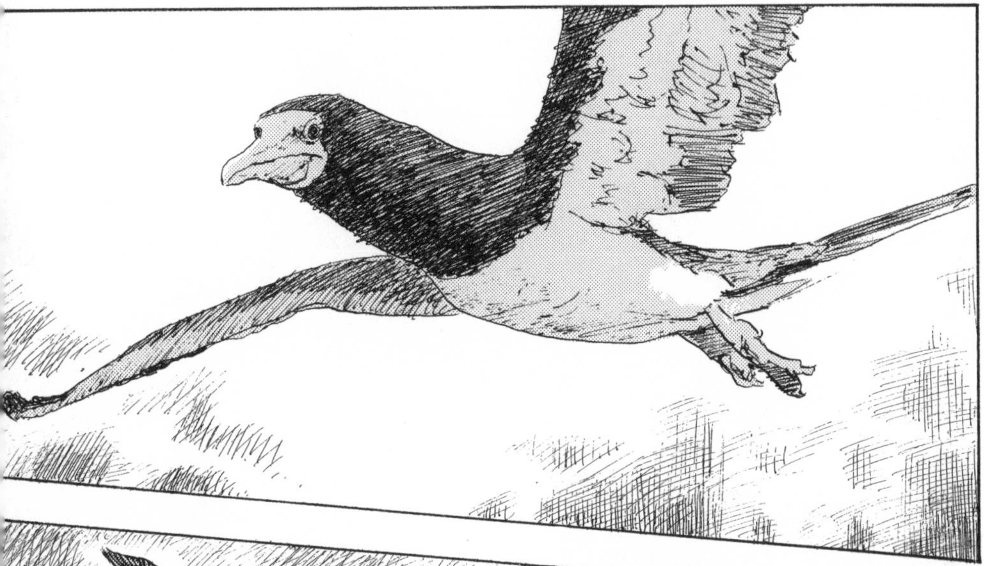
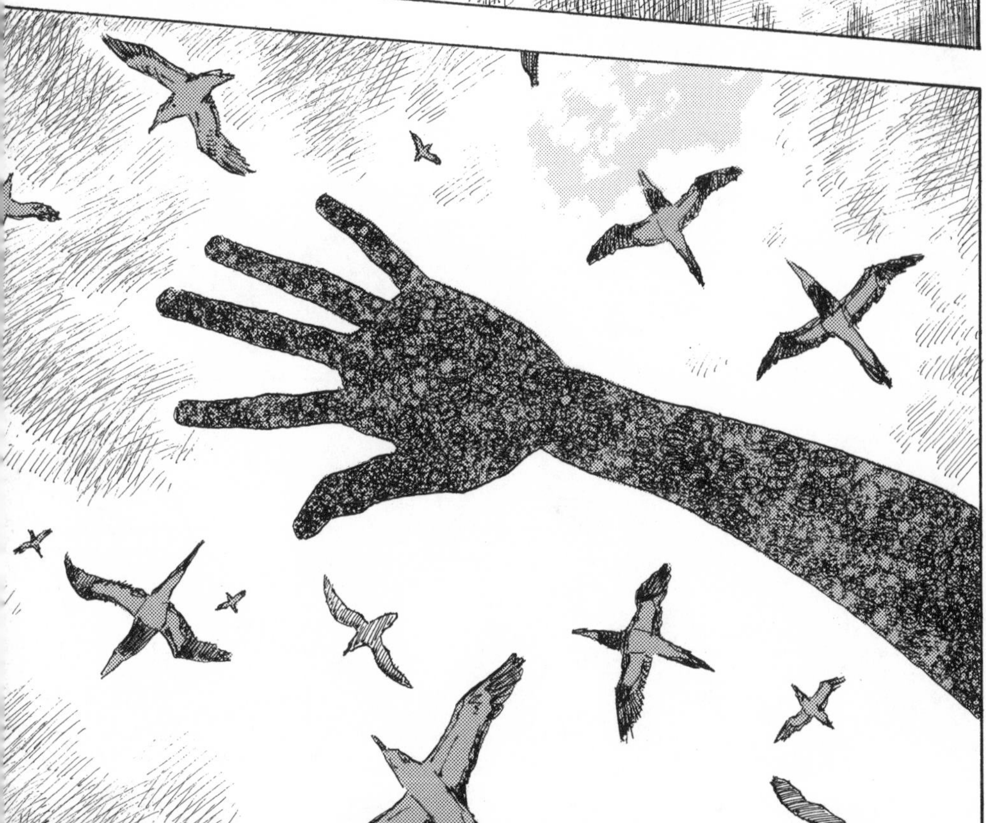

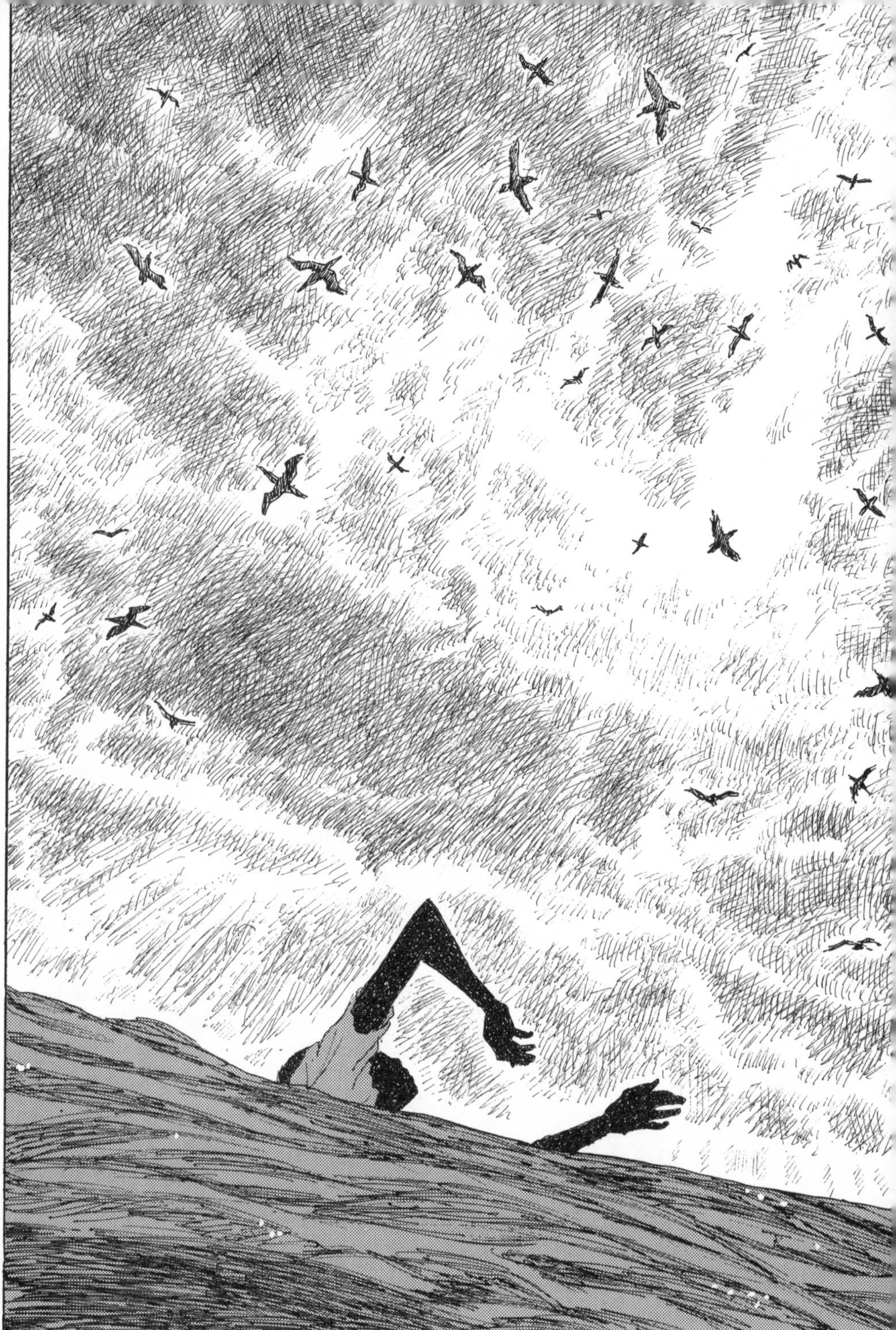

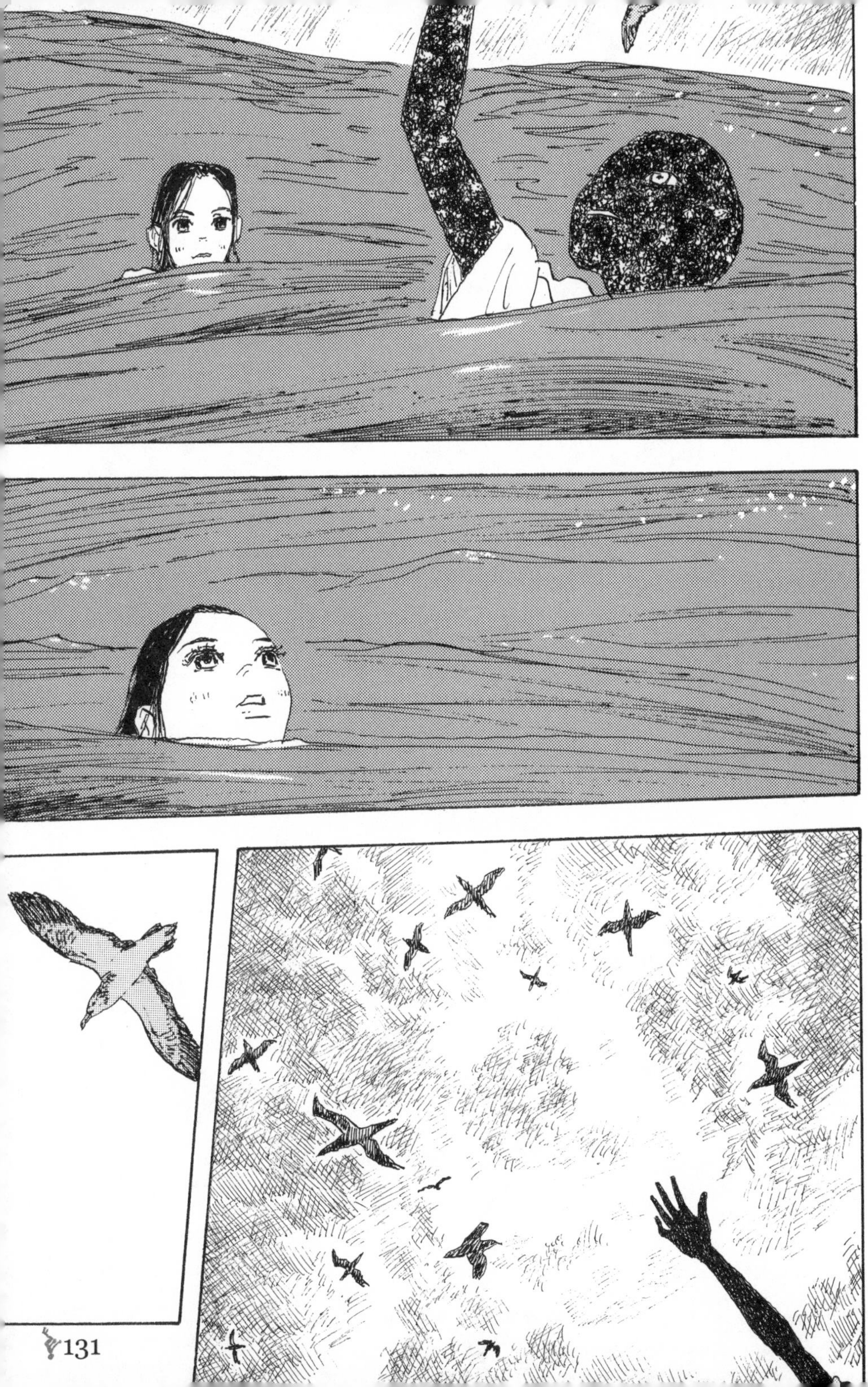

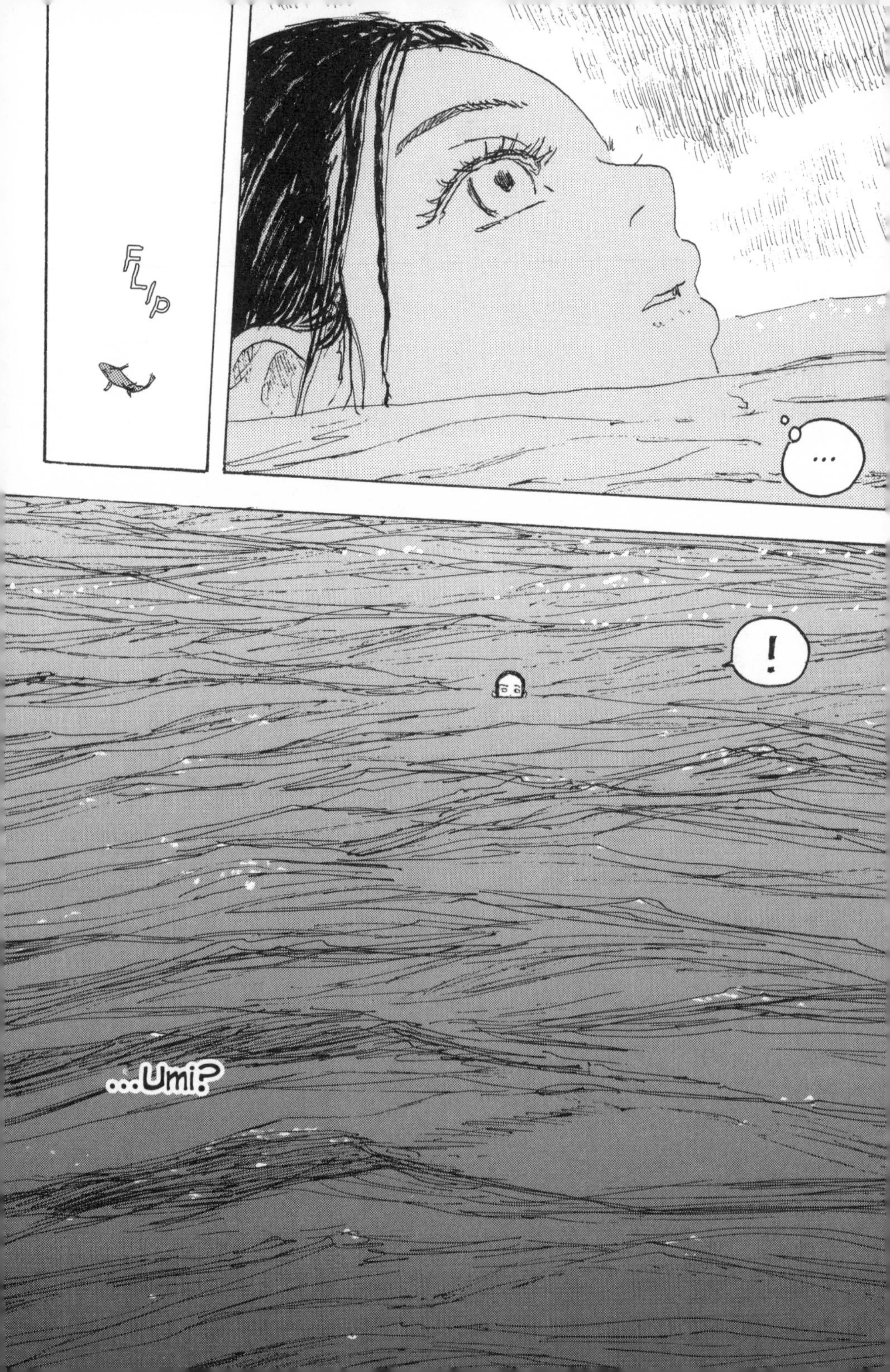
FLIP
...
!
...Umi?

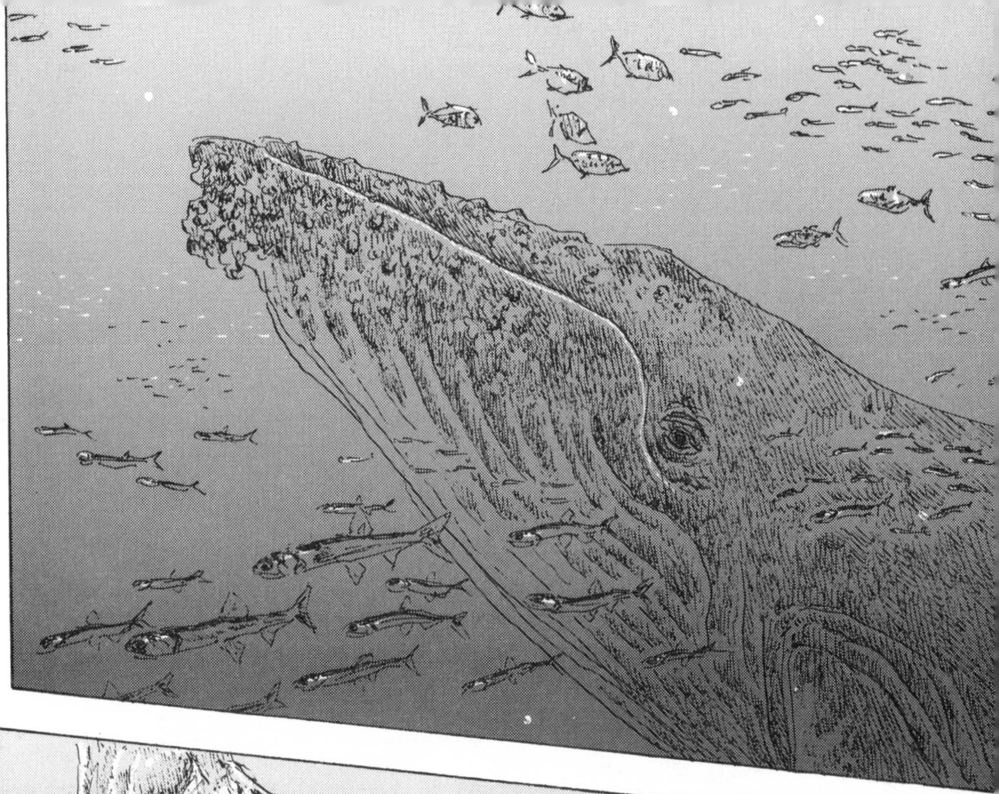
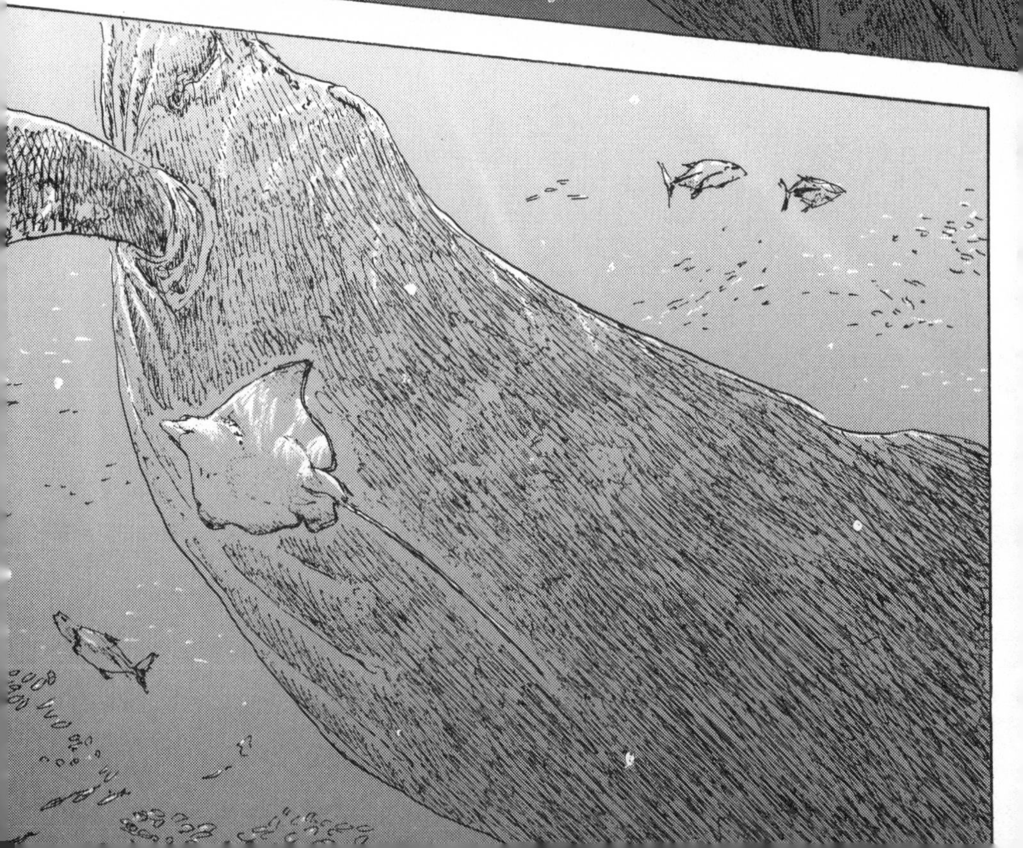

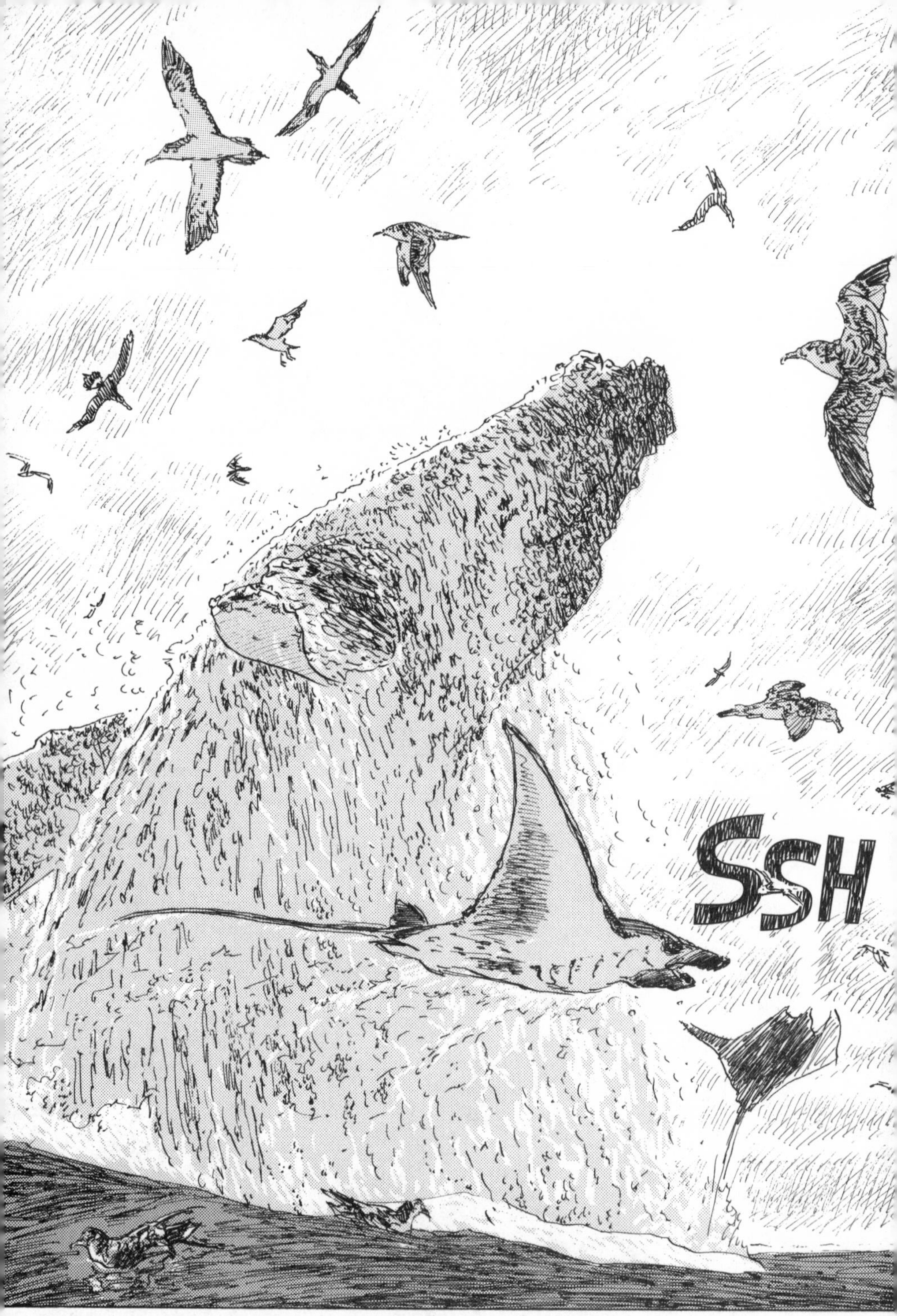
SSH

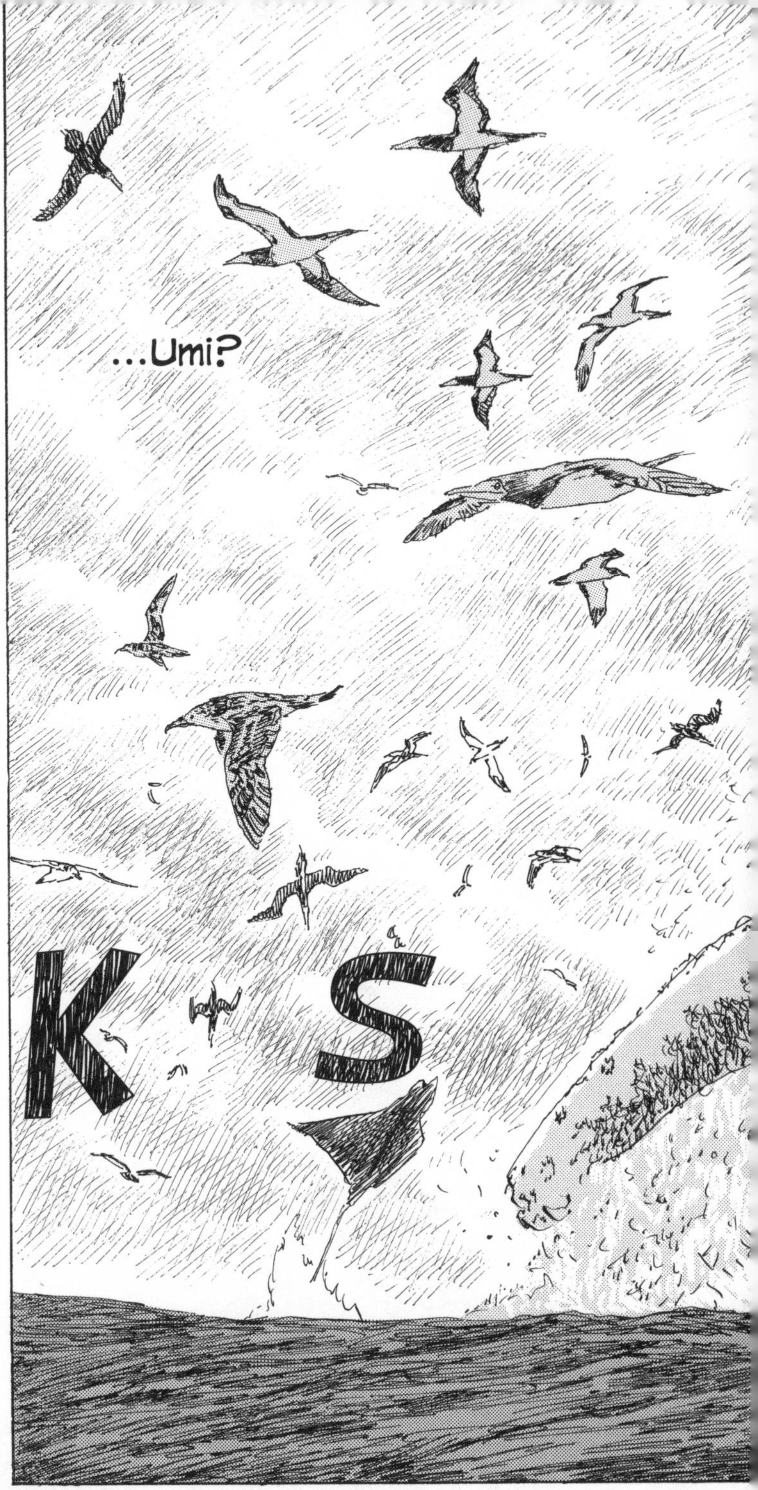
...Umi?
K S
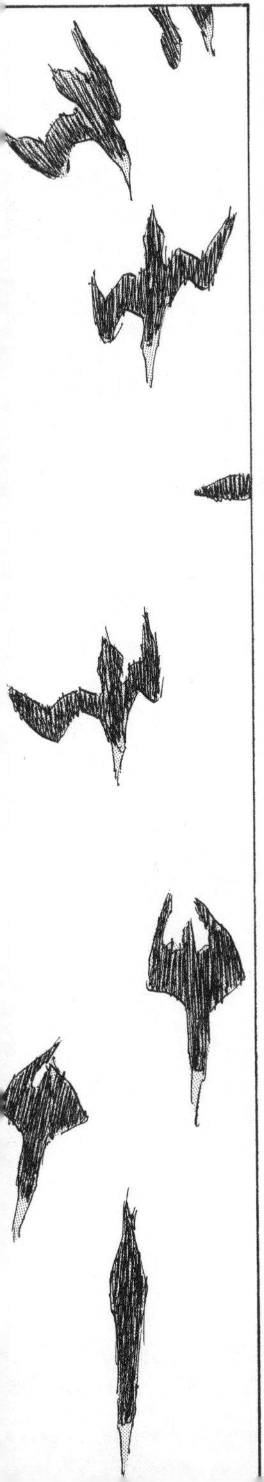

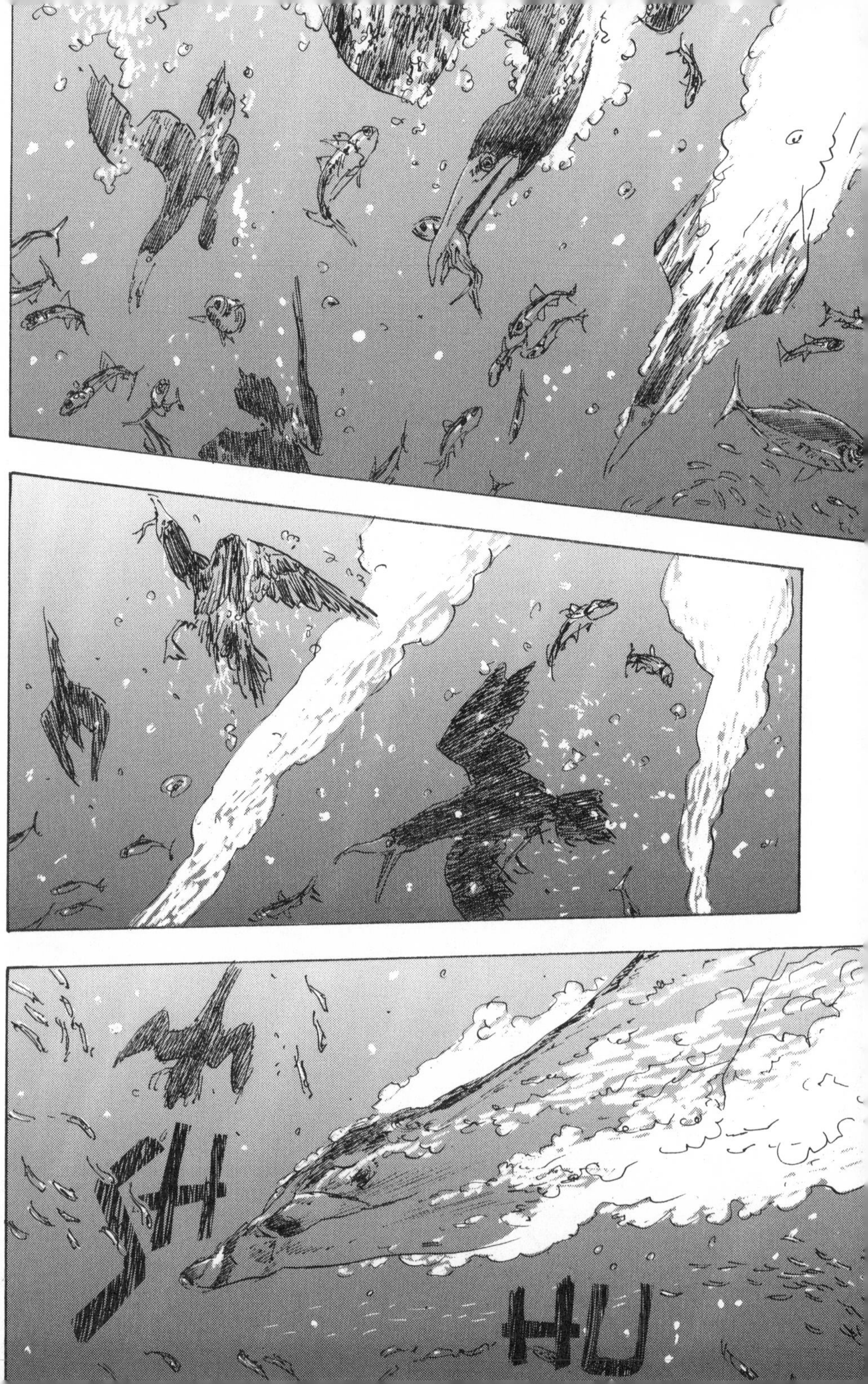
SH
HU

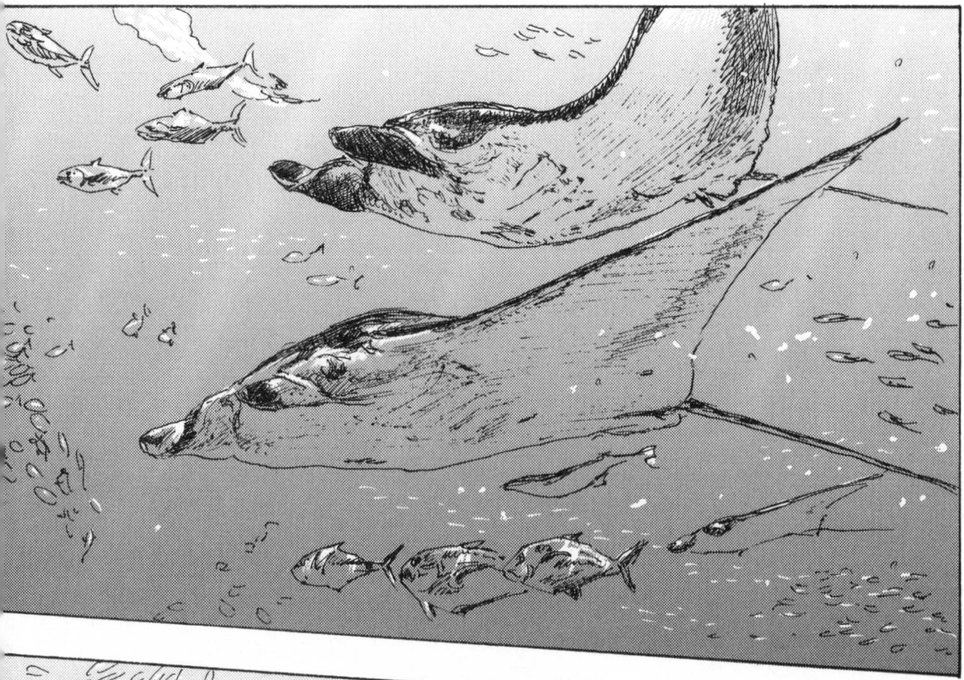
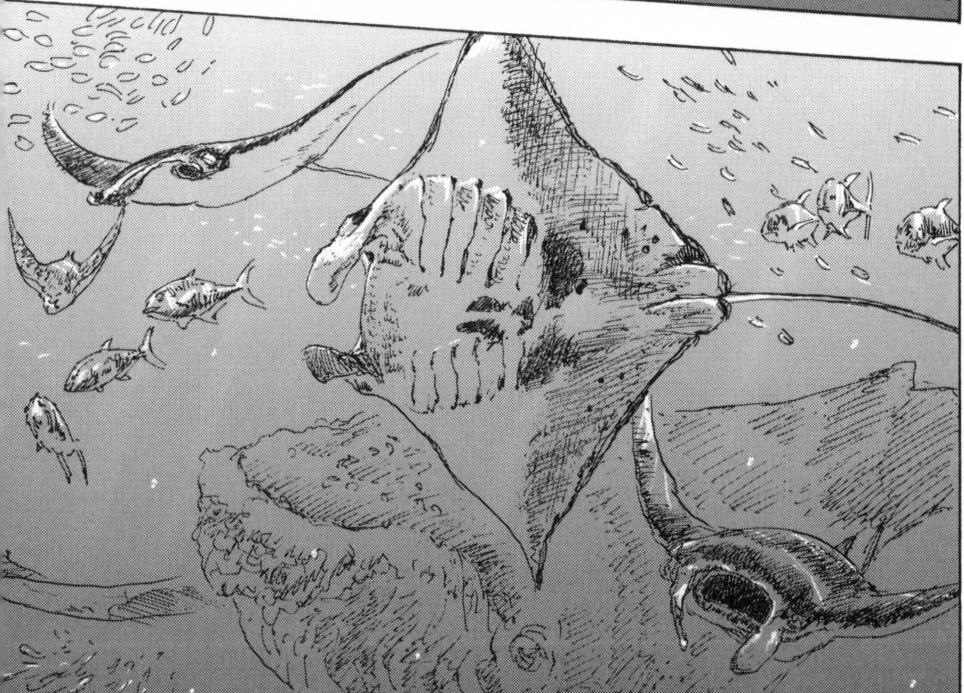

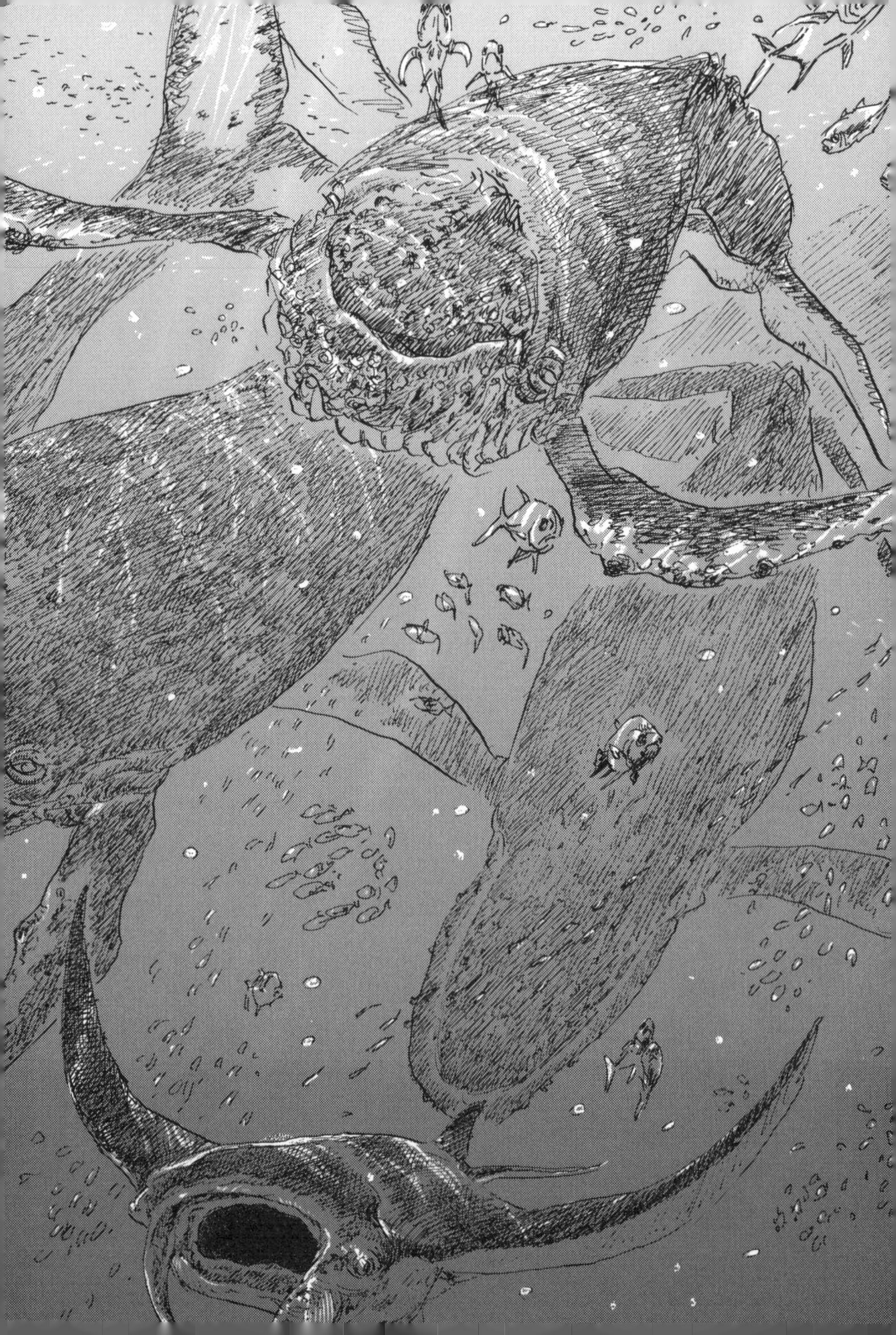

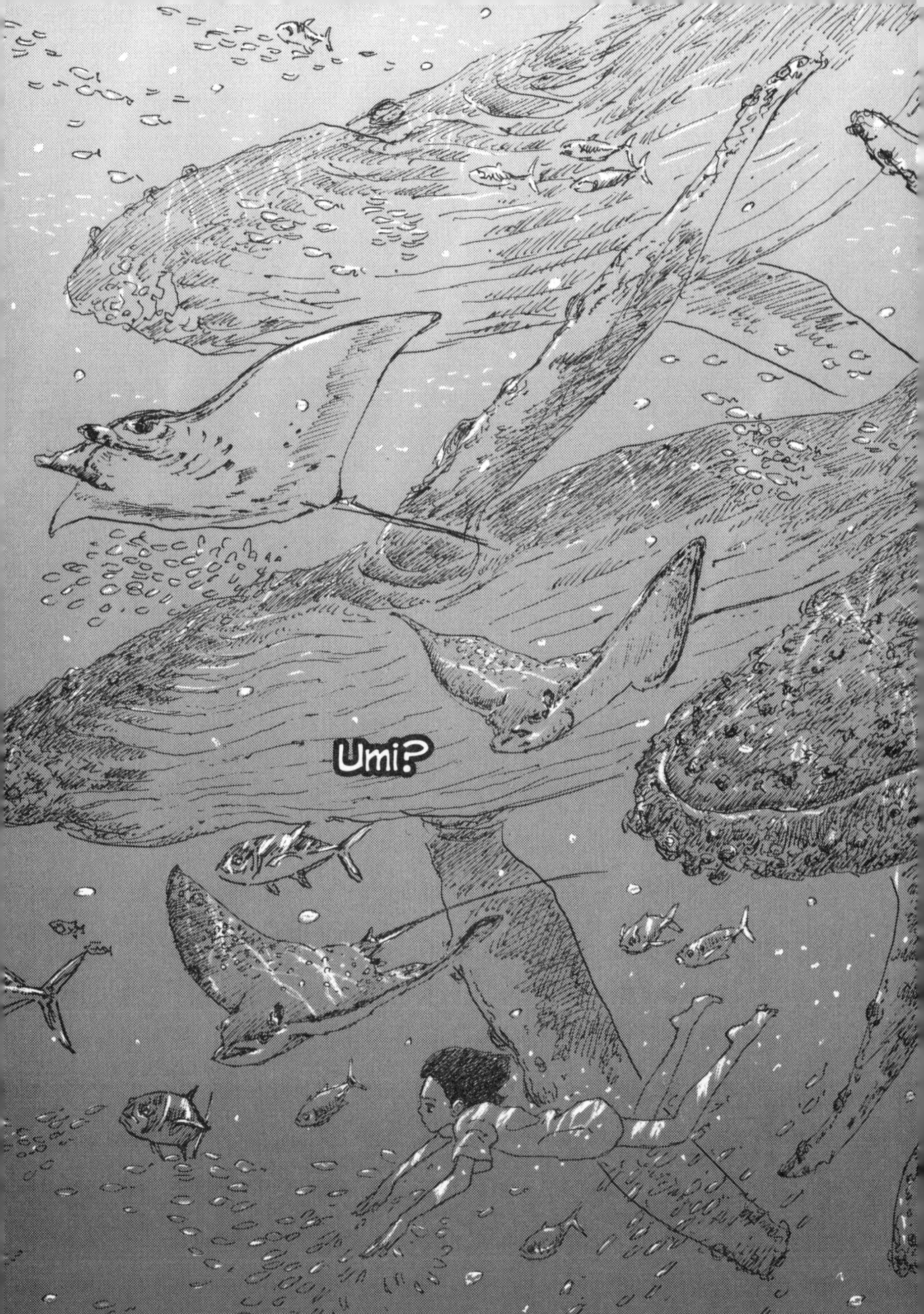
Umi?

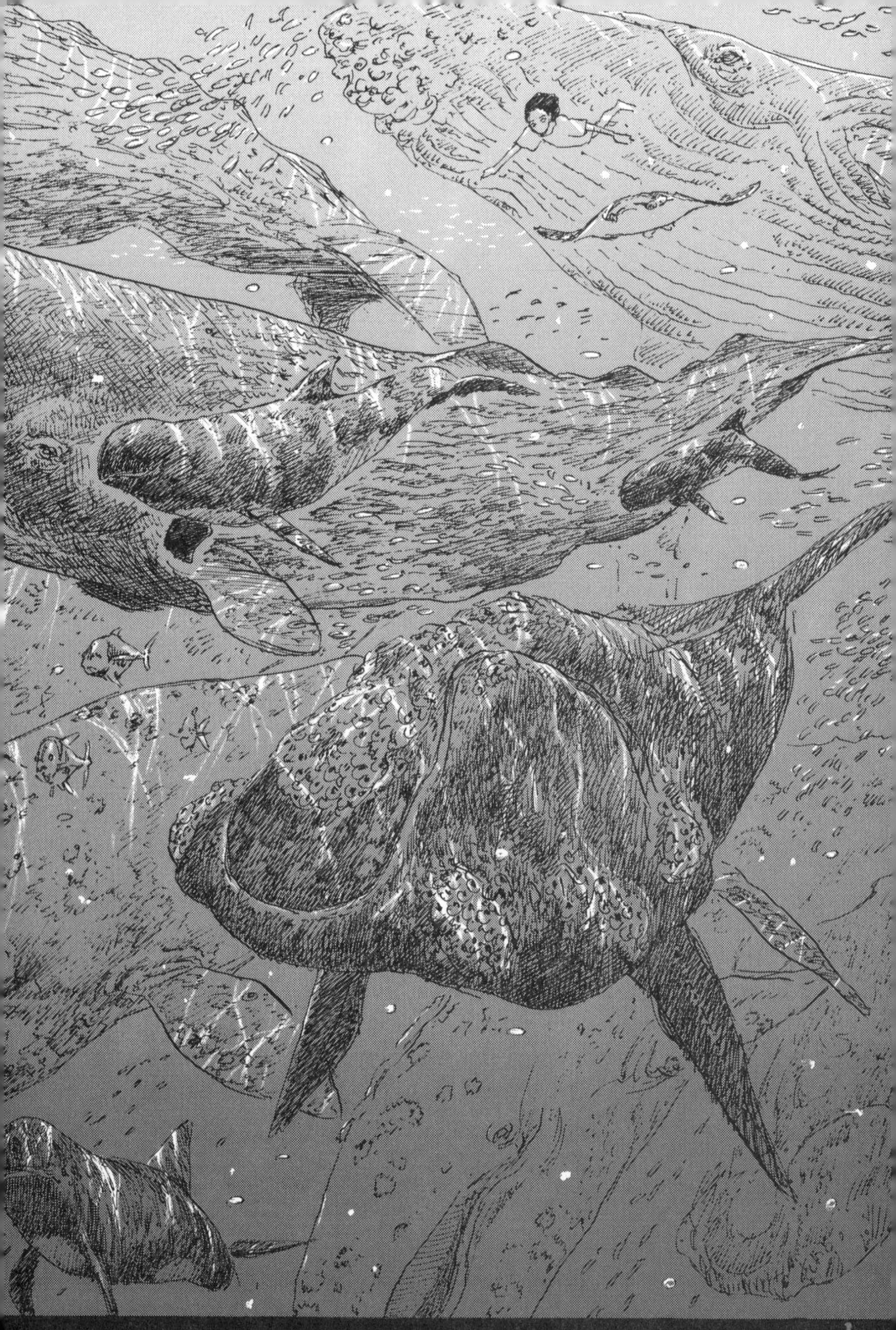

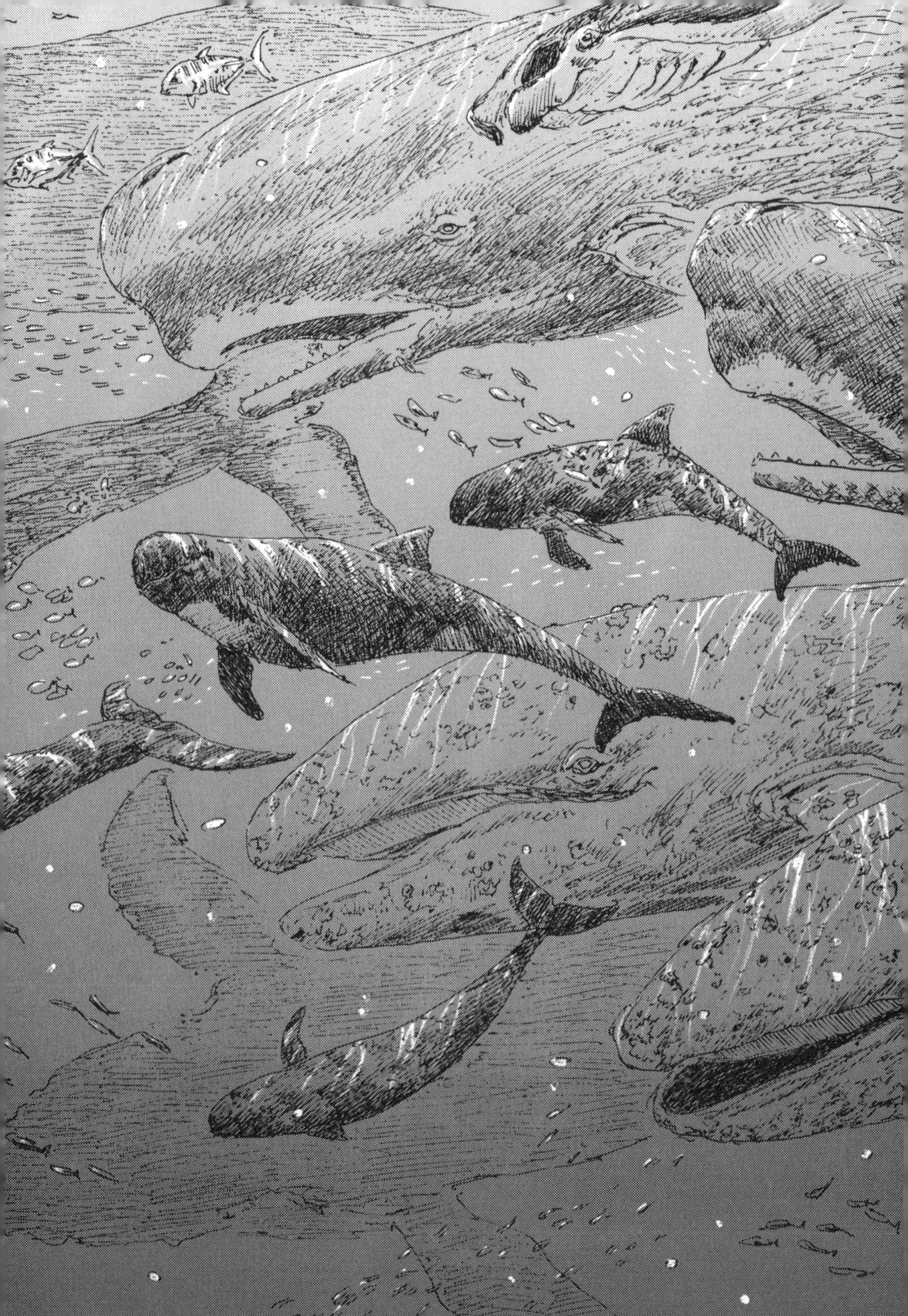

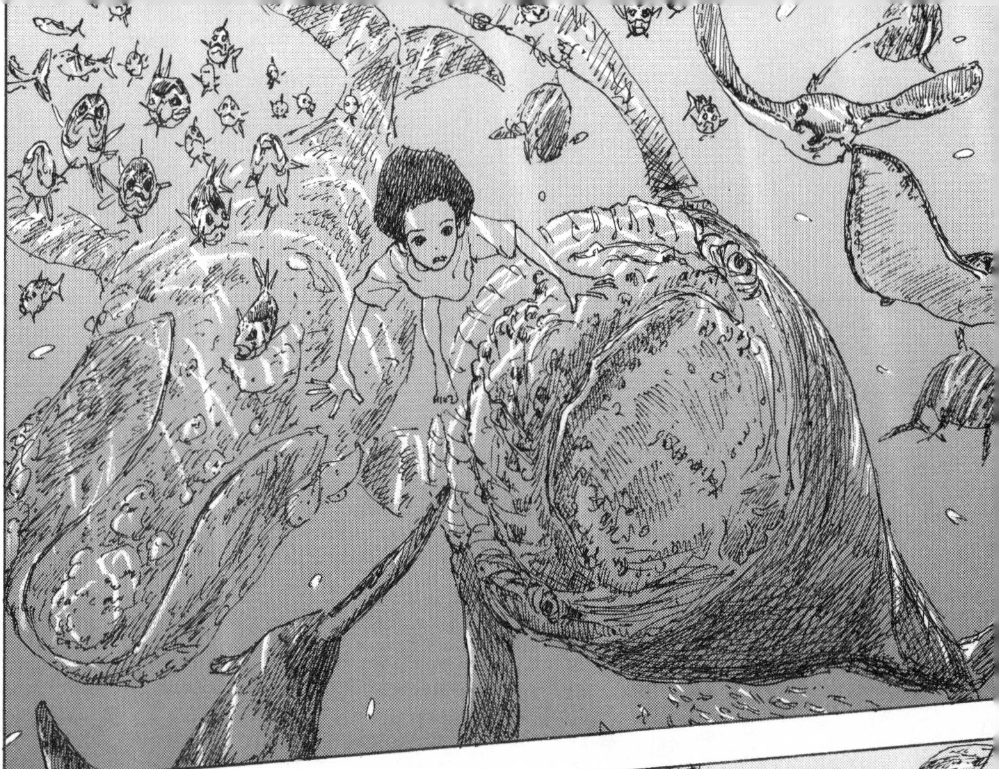
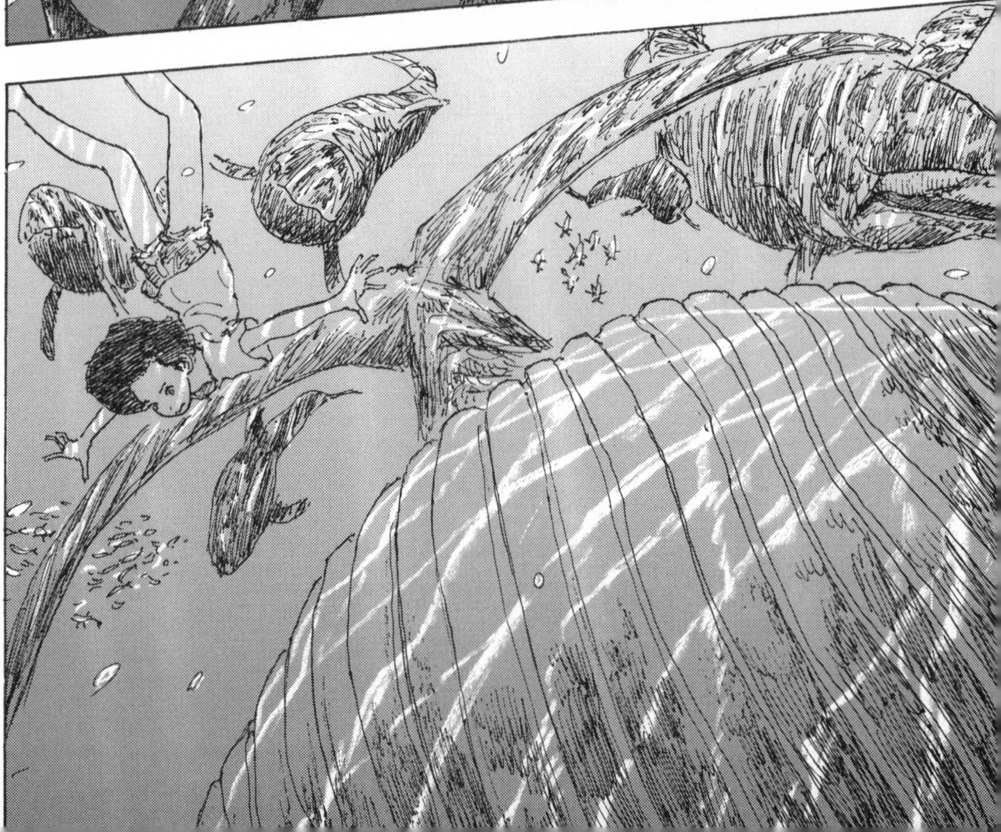

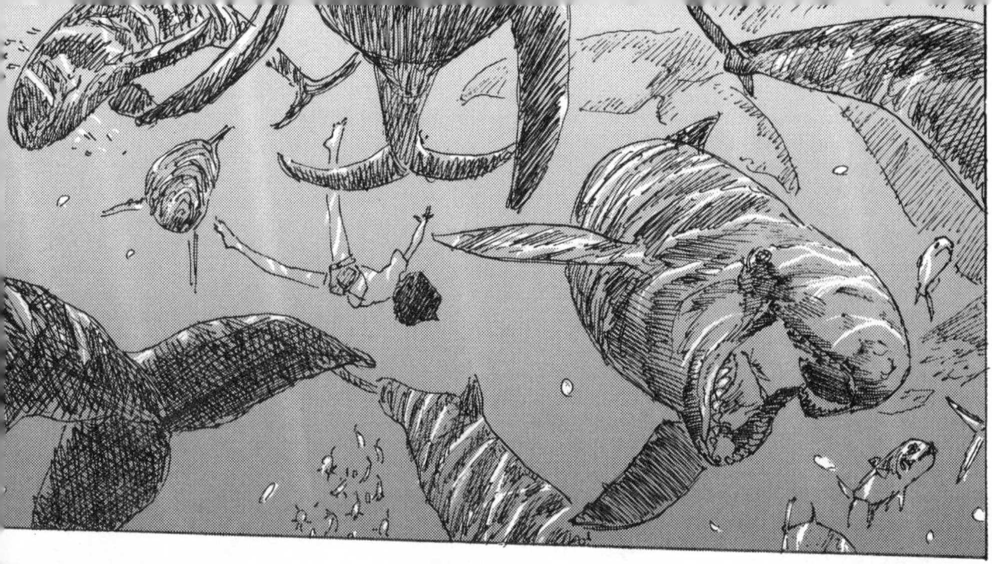
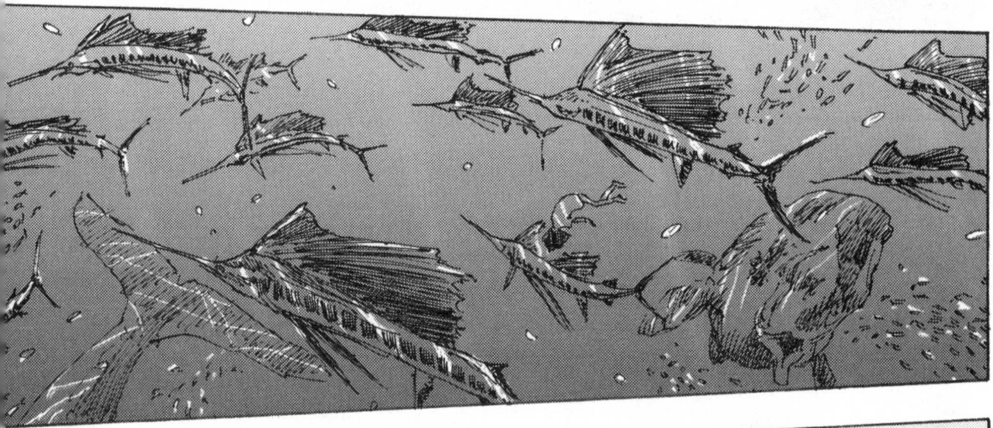
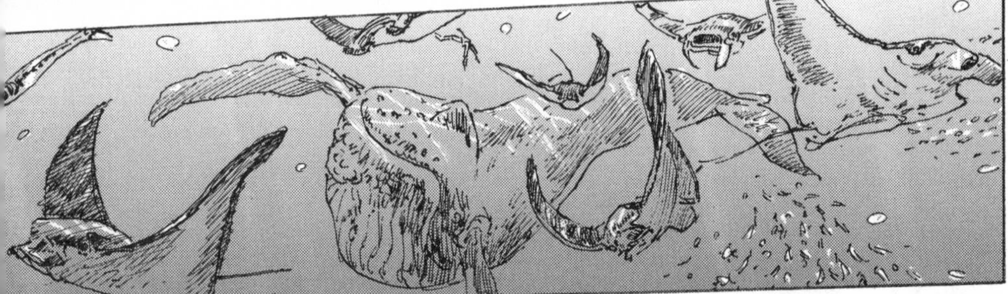
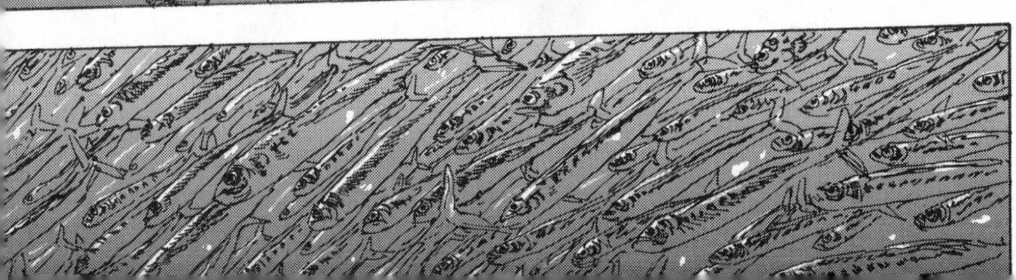

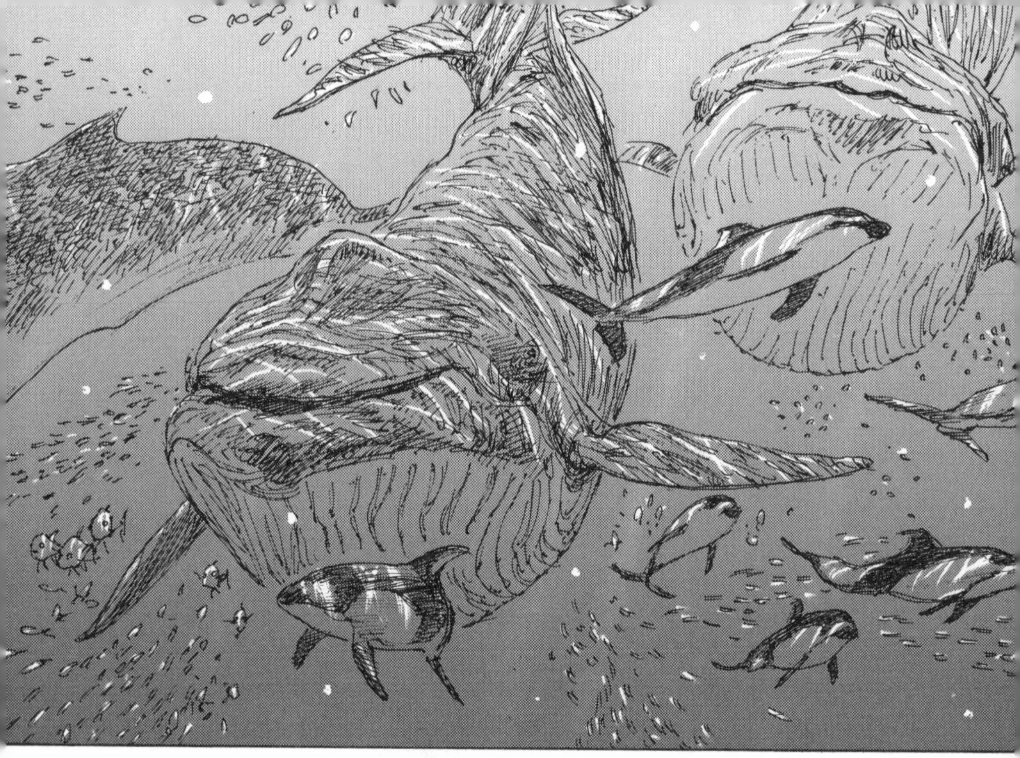
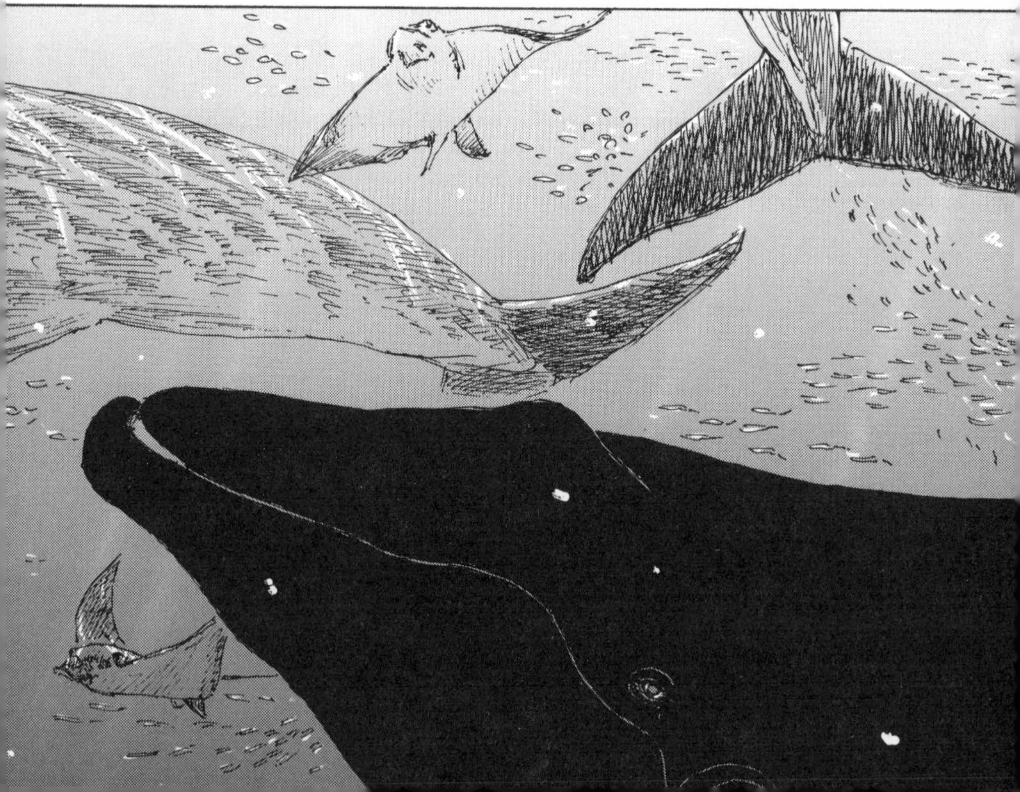

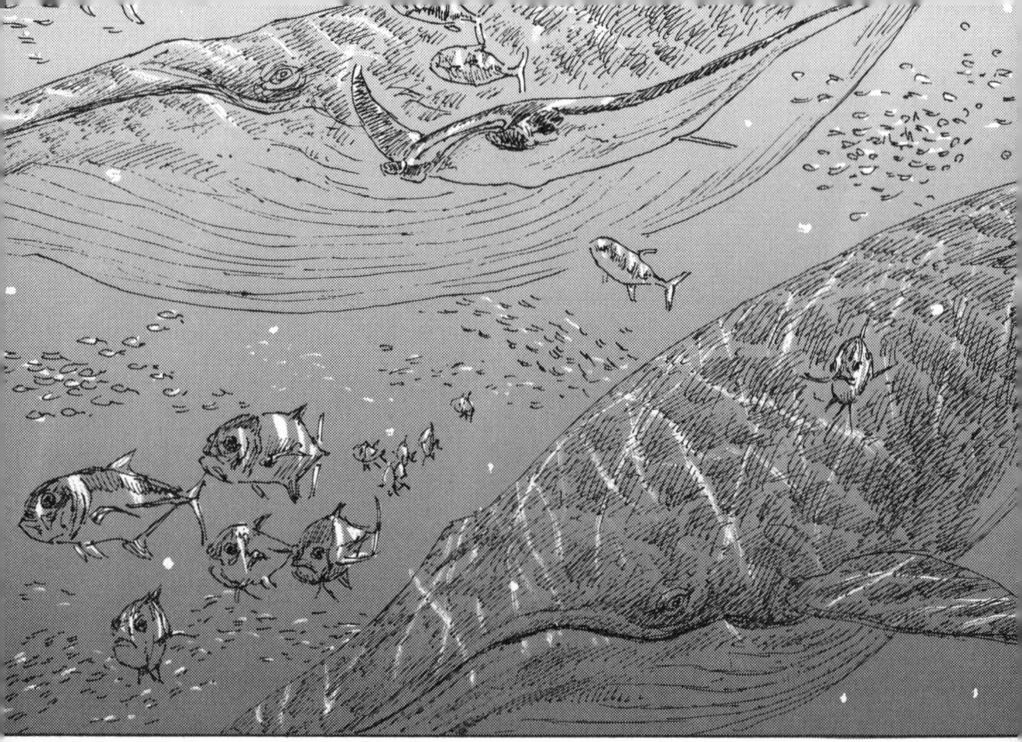
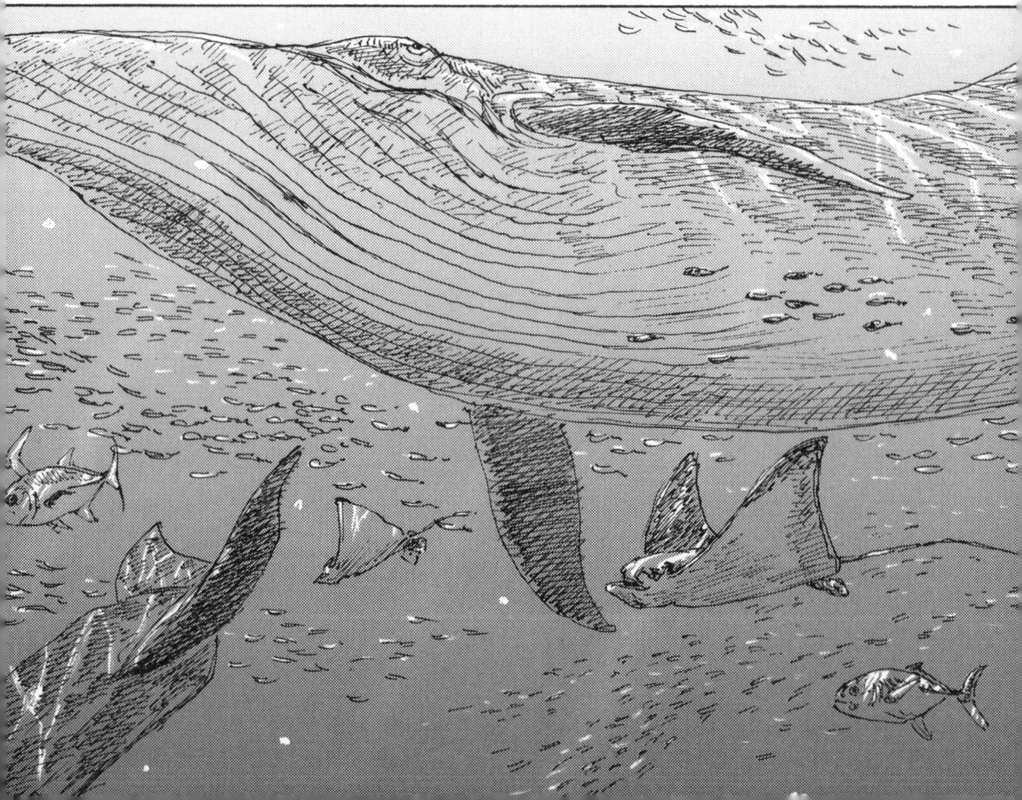

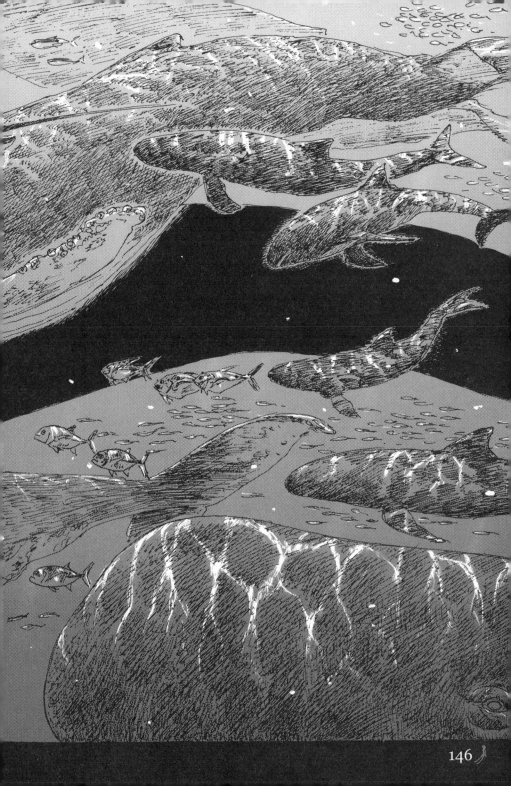

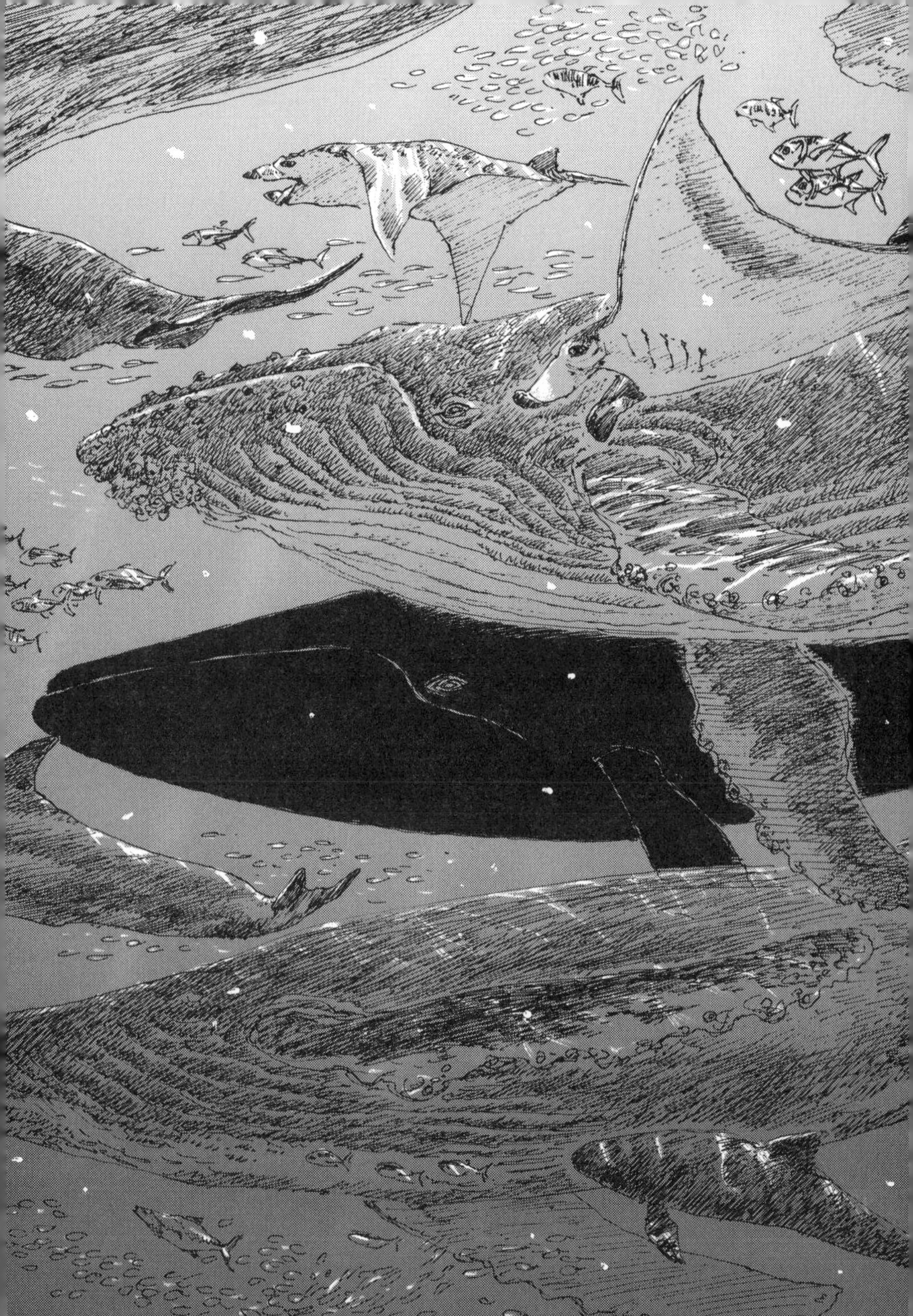

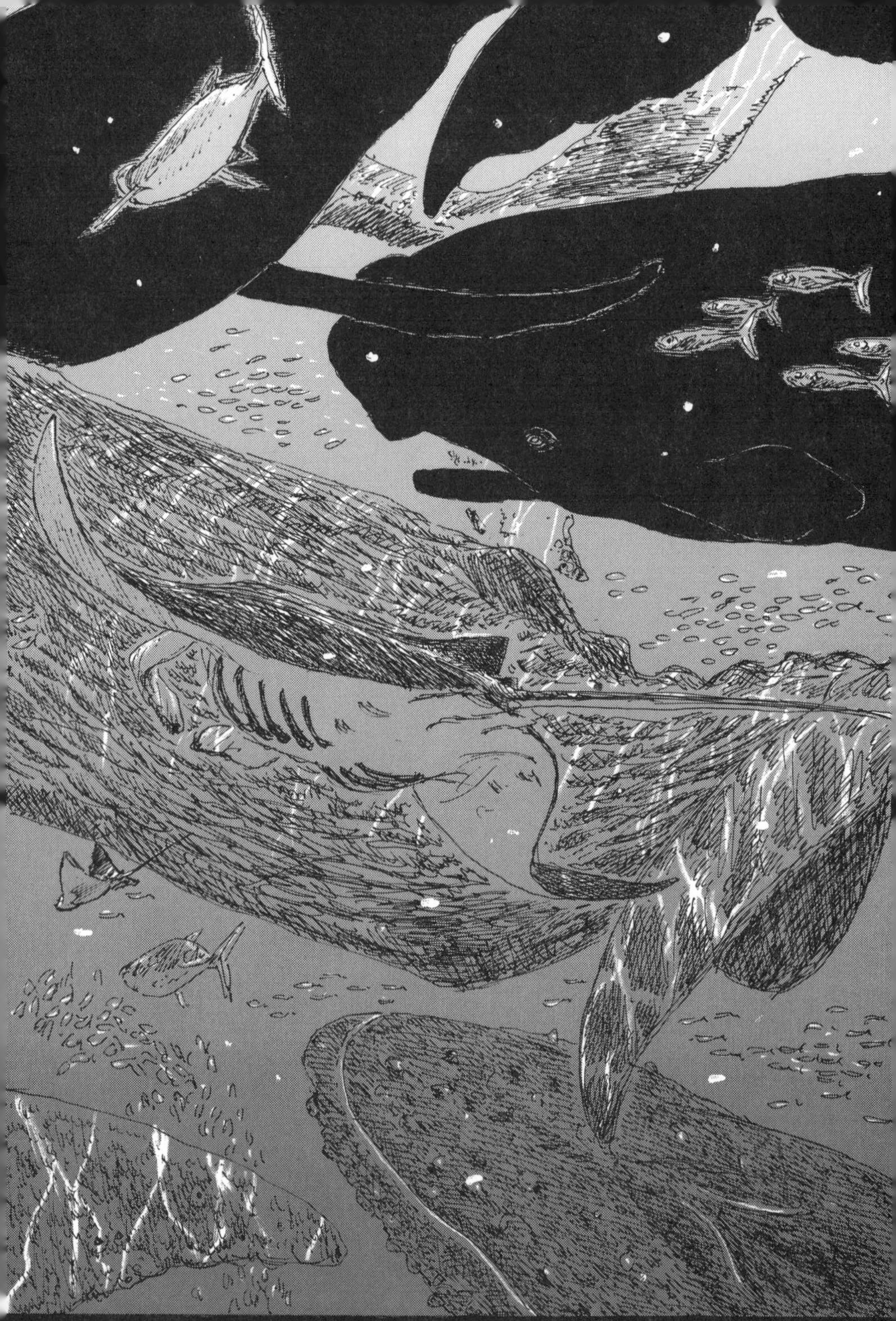

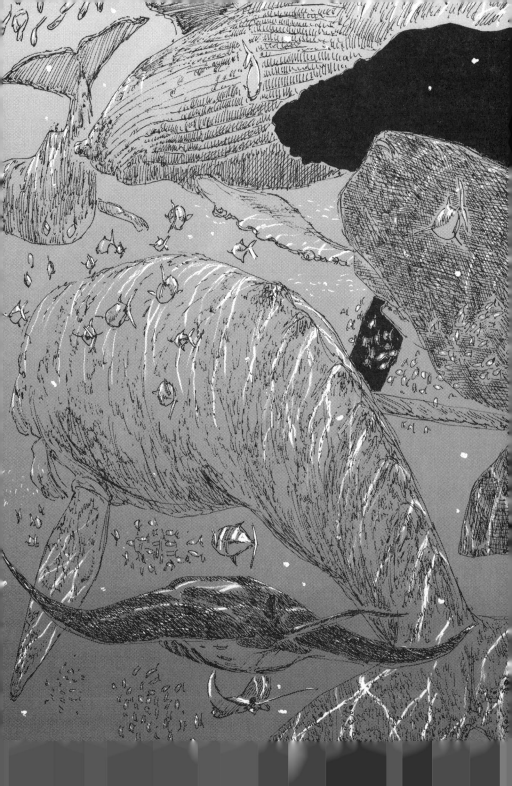

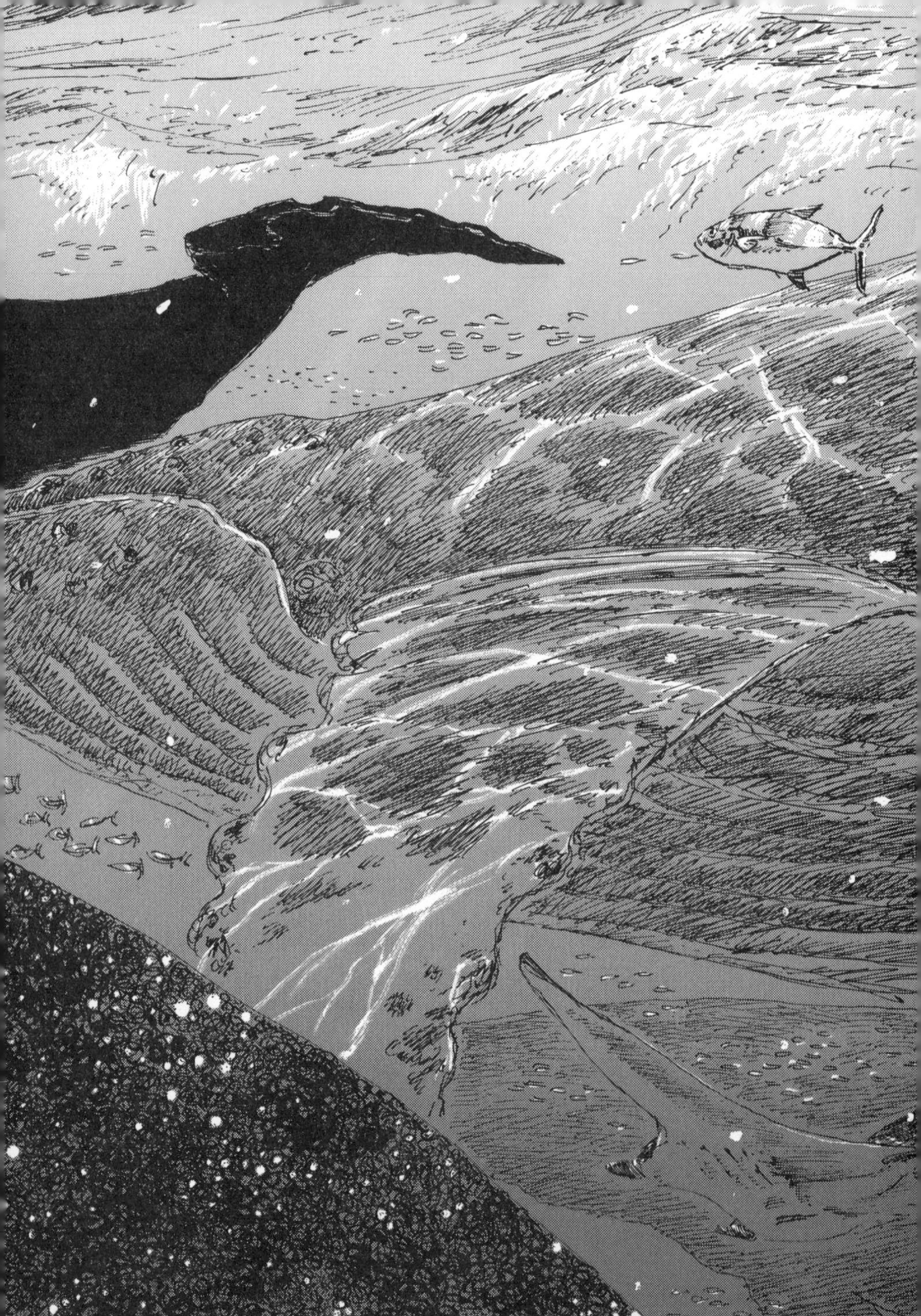

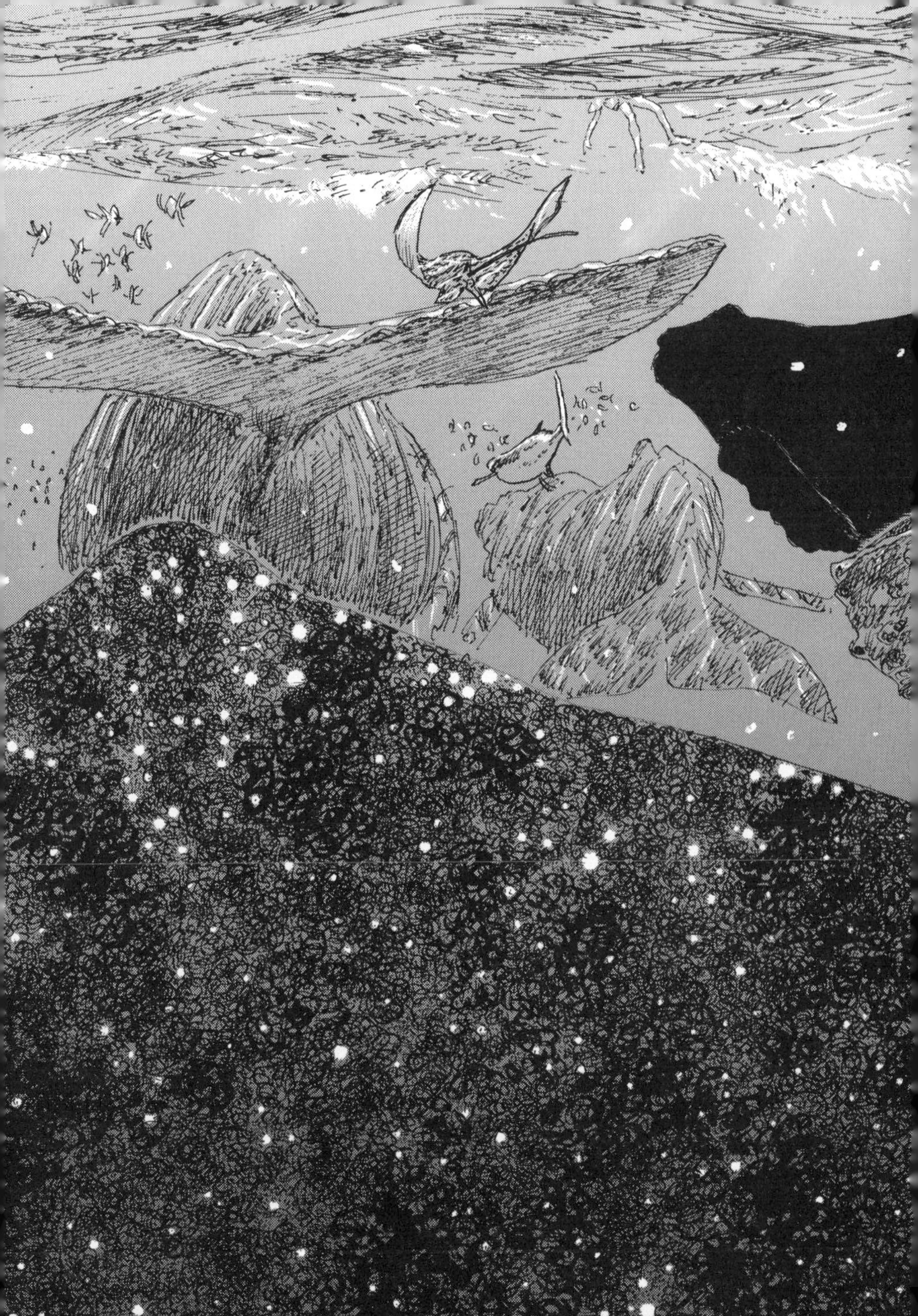

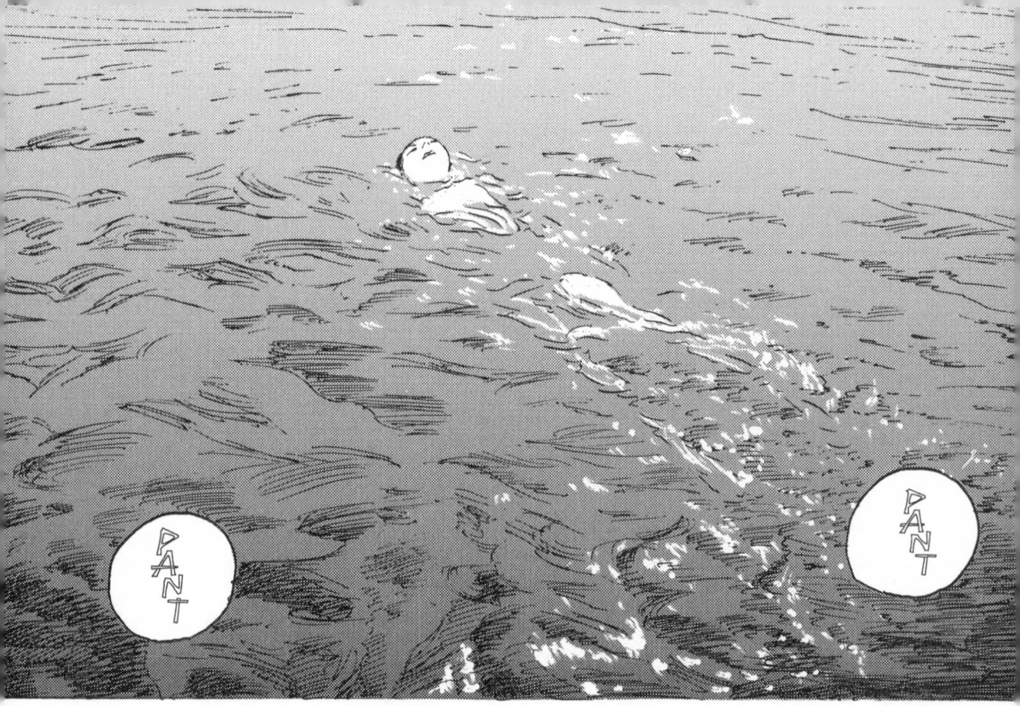
PANT
PANT
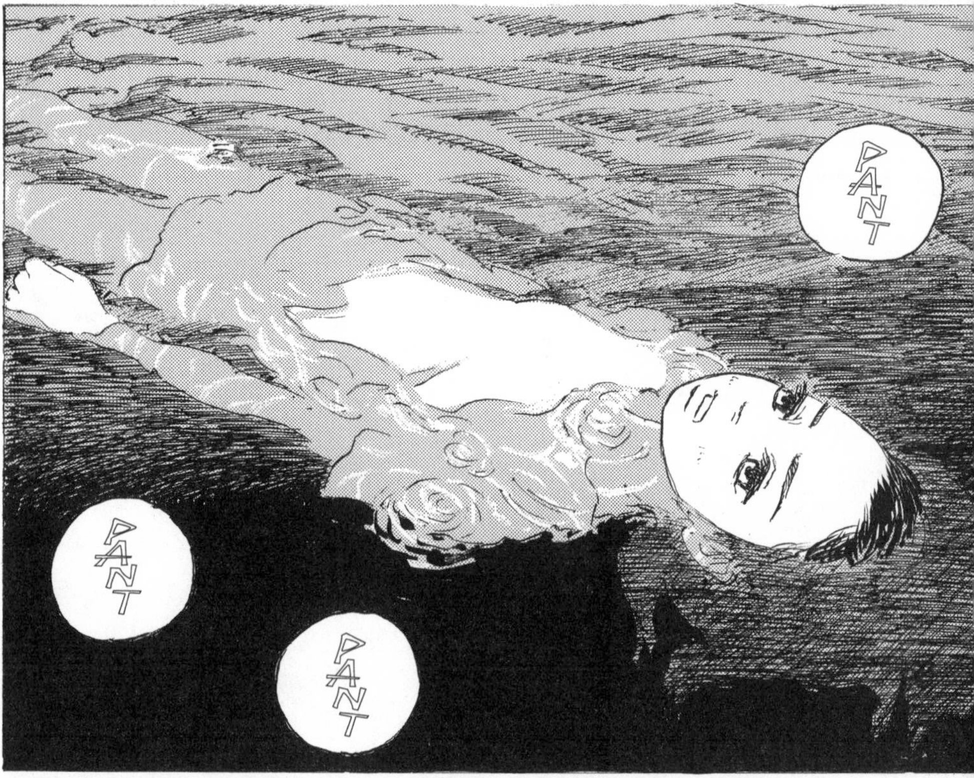
PANT
PANT
PANT

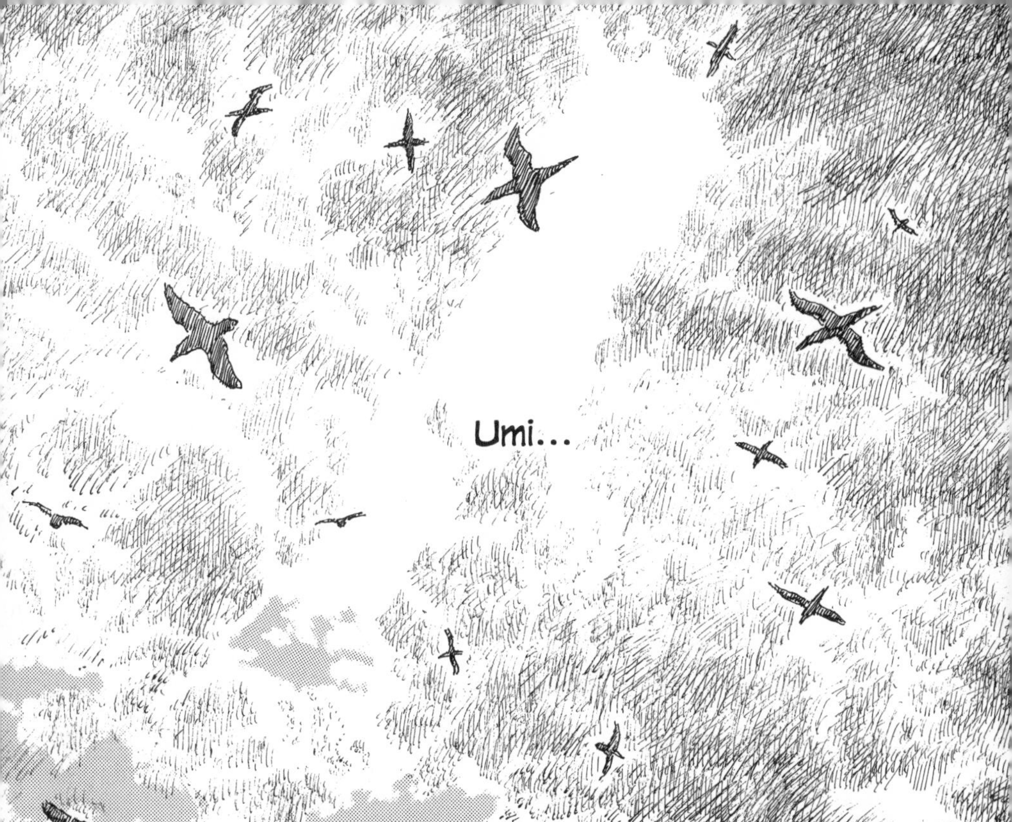
Umi...
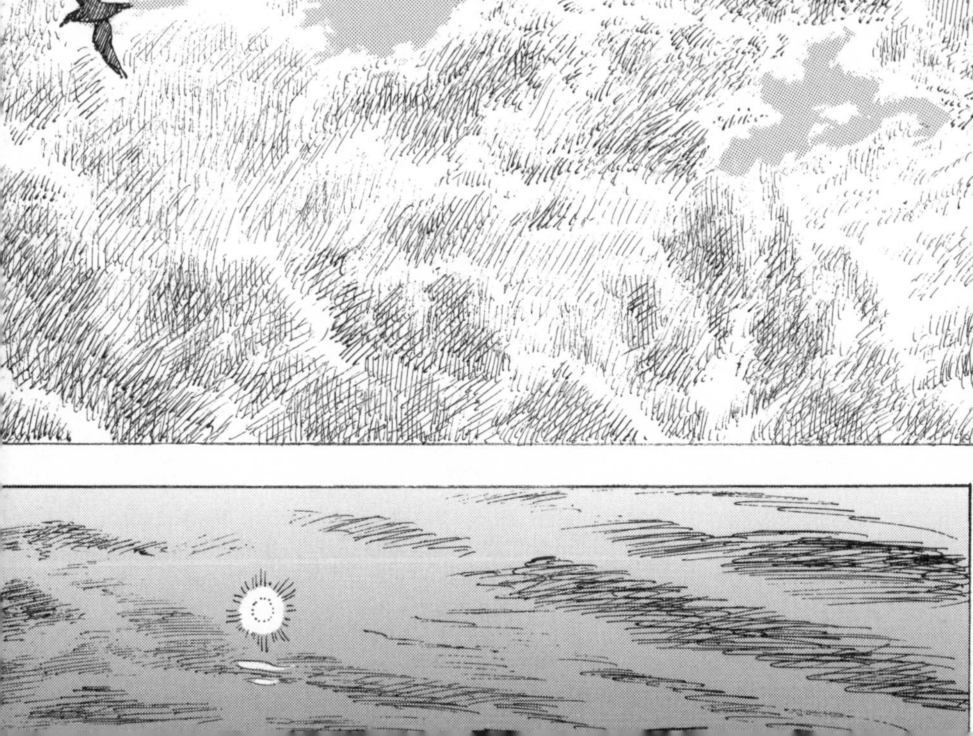

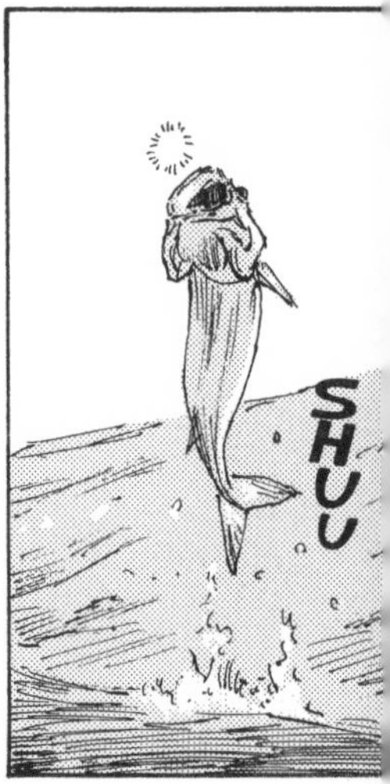
SHUU
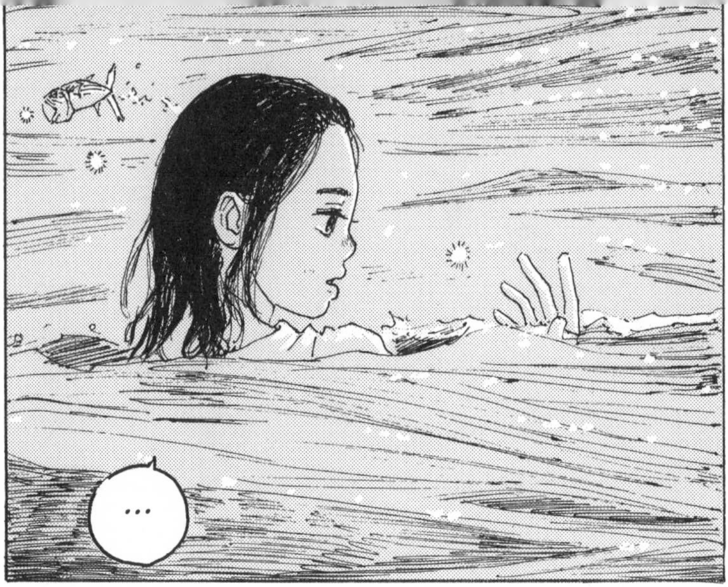
...
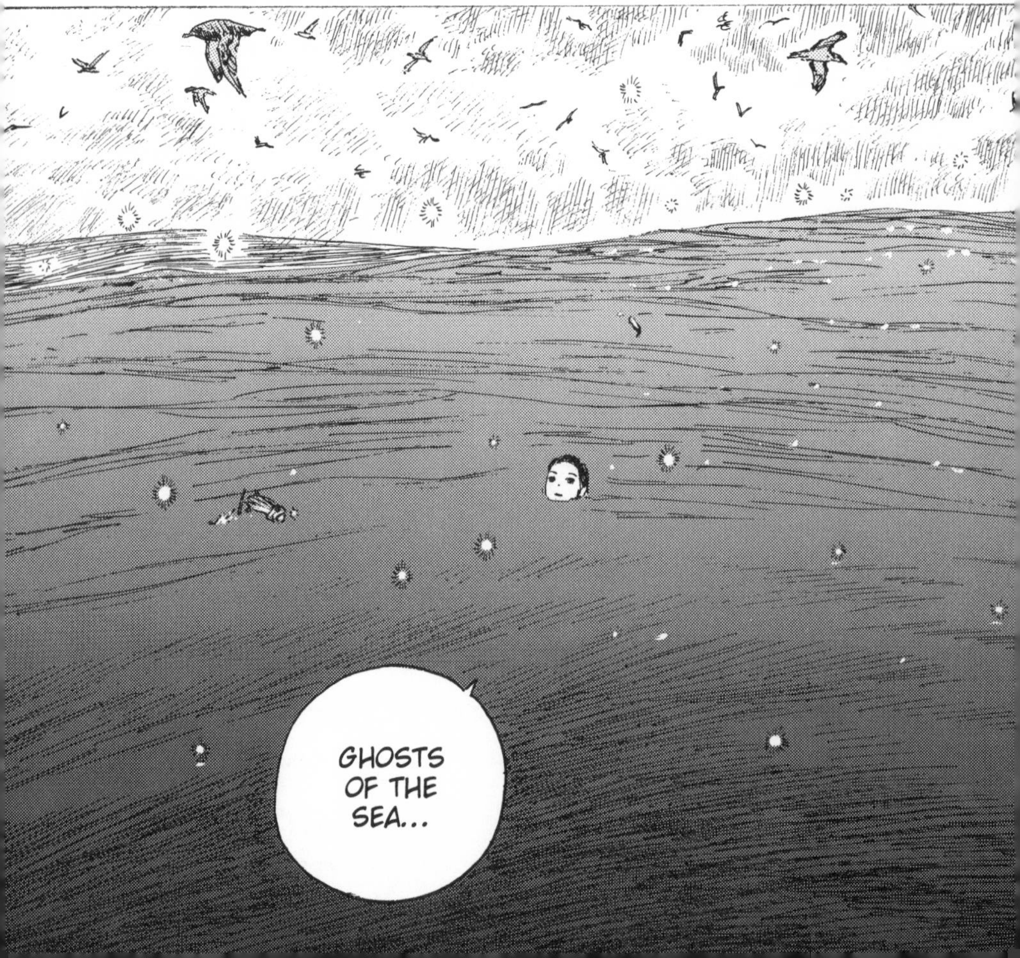
GHOSTS OF THE SEA...

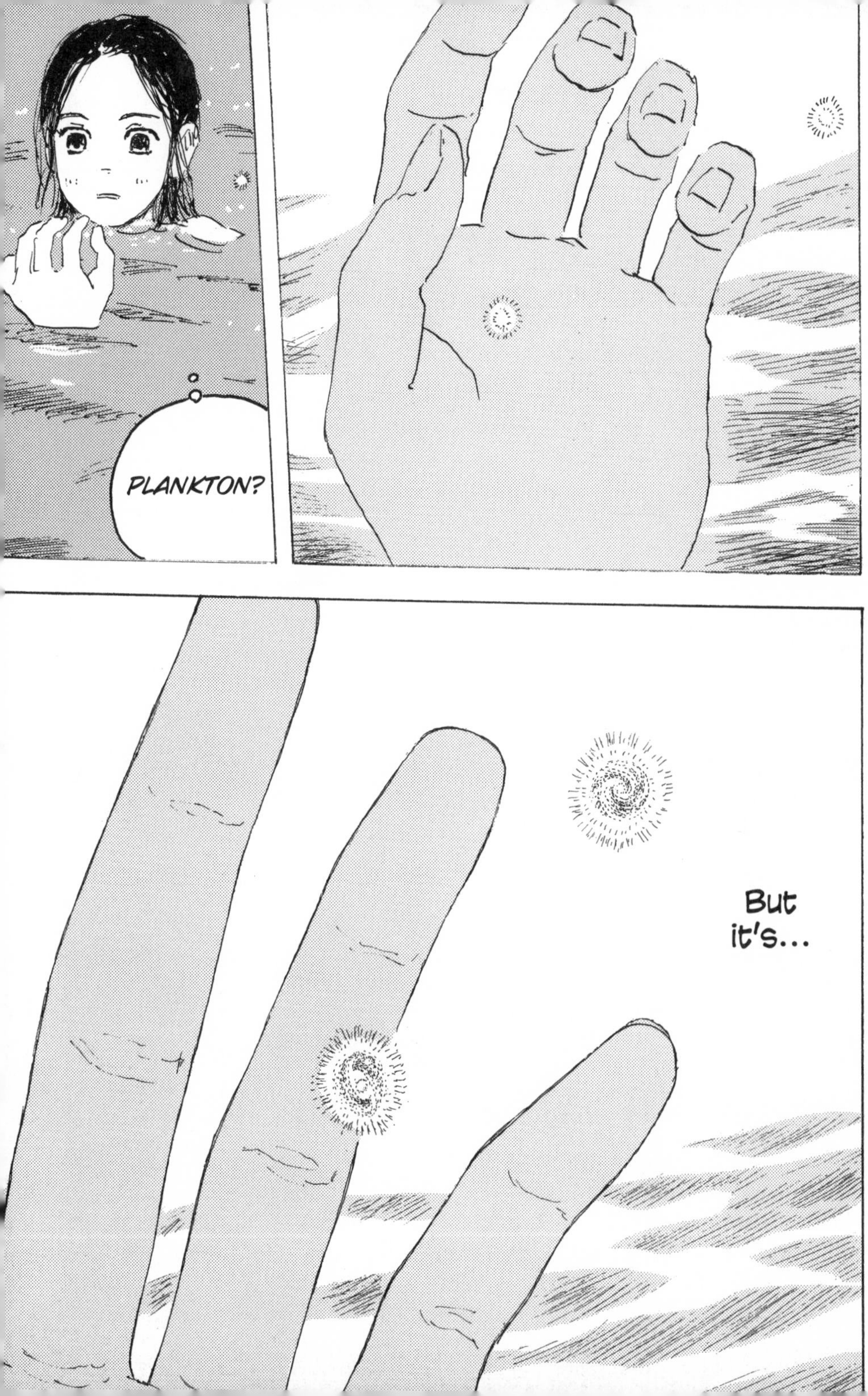
PLANKTON?
But it's...

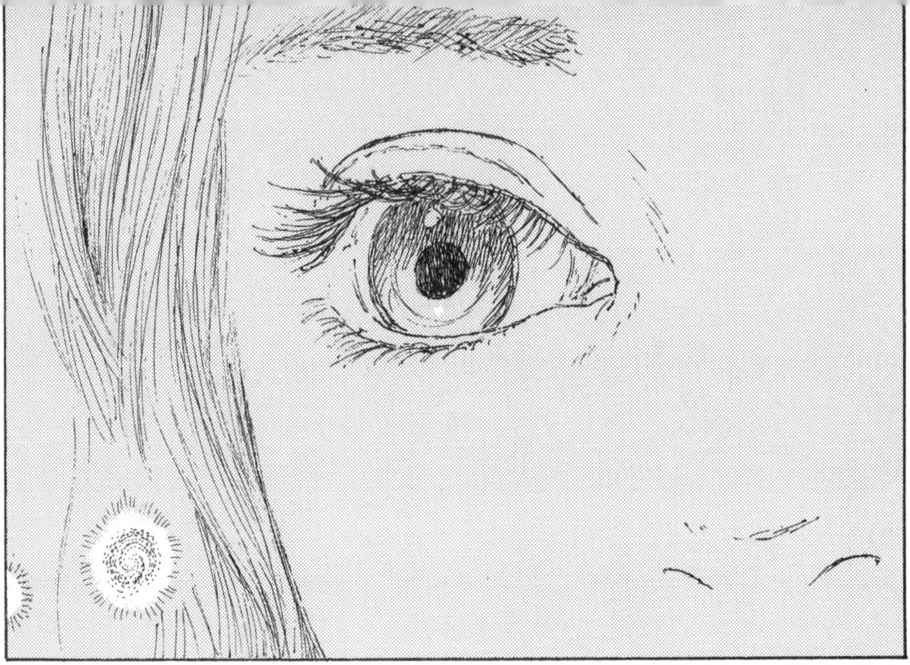

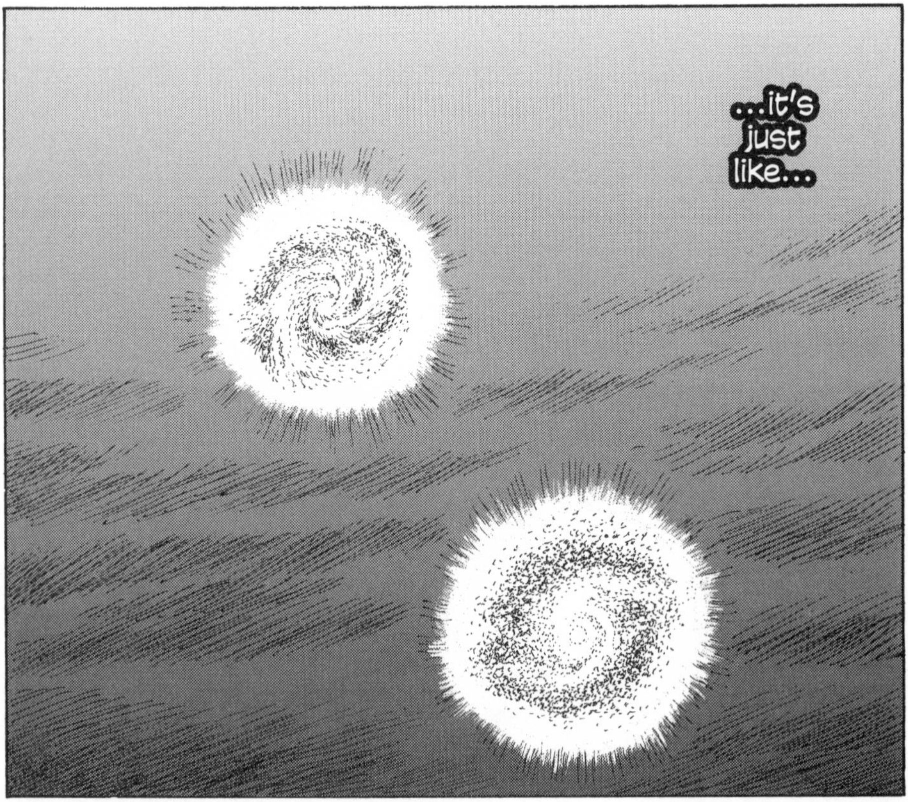
...it's just like...

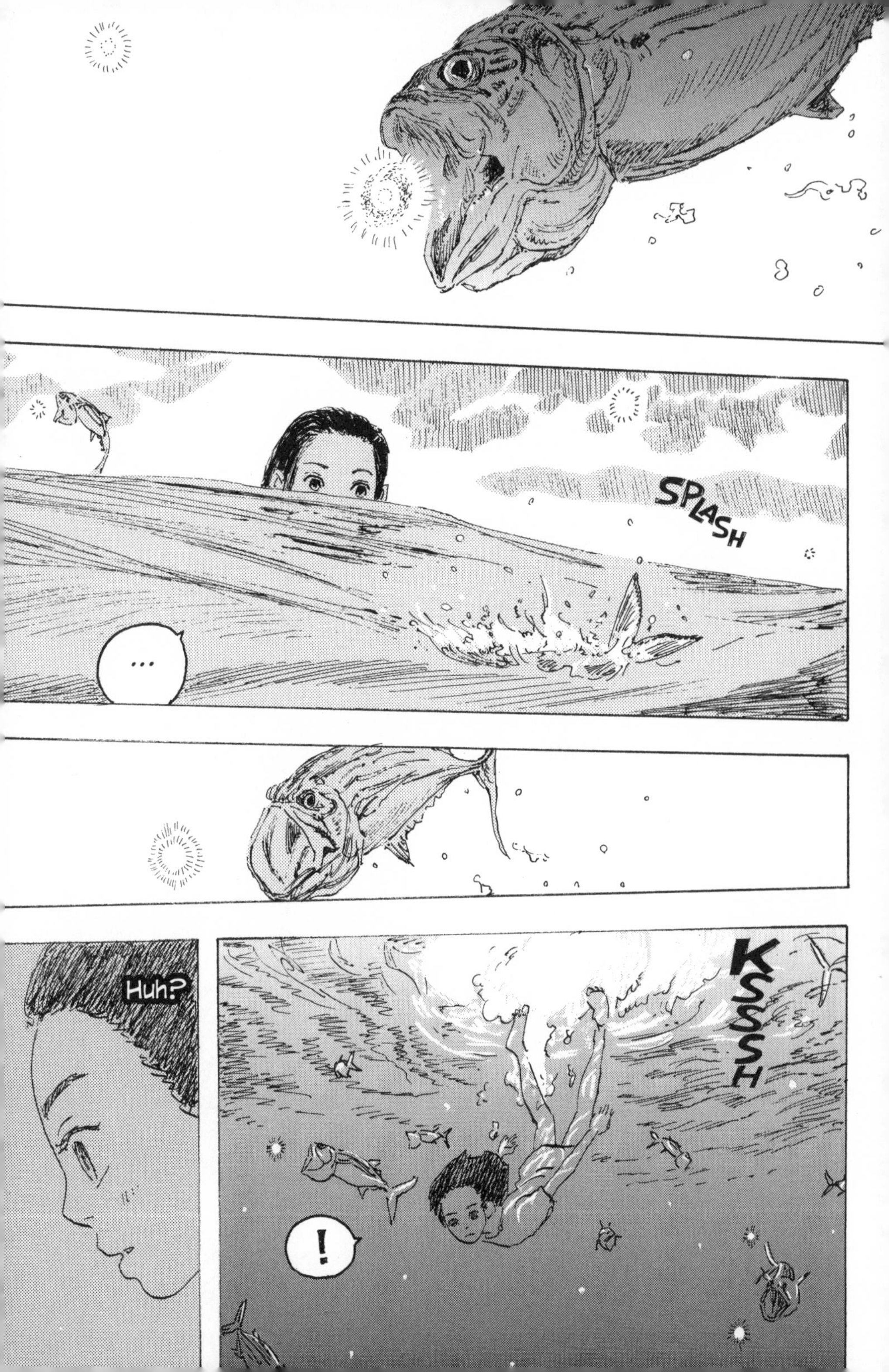
SPLASH
...
KSSSH
Huh?
!

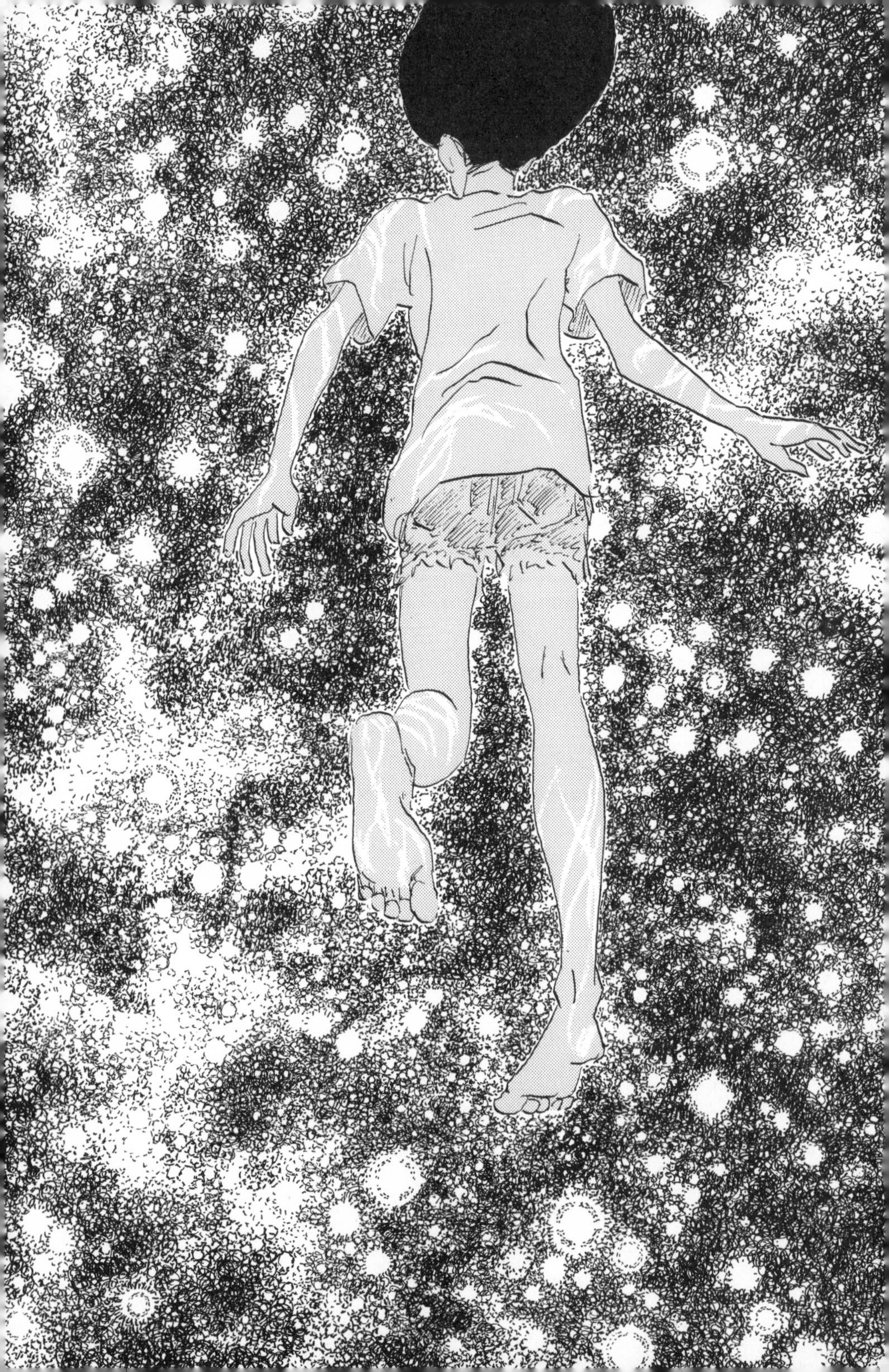

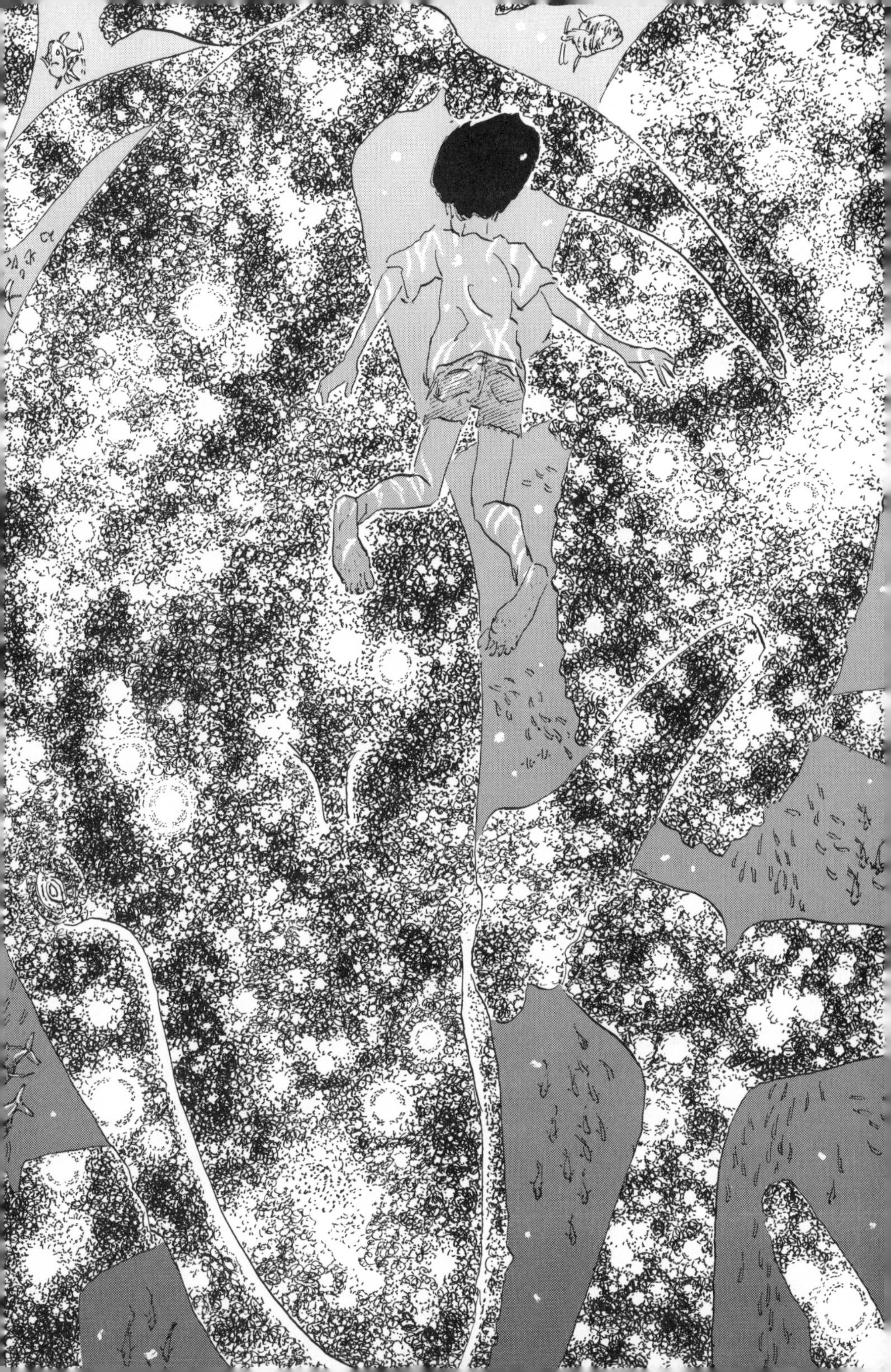

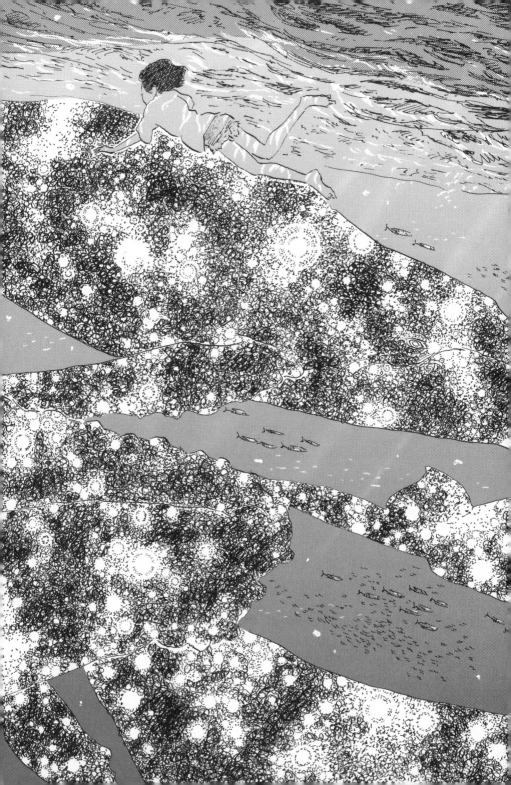

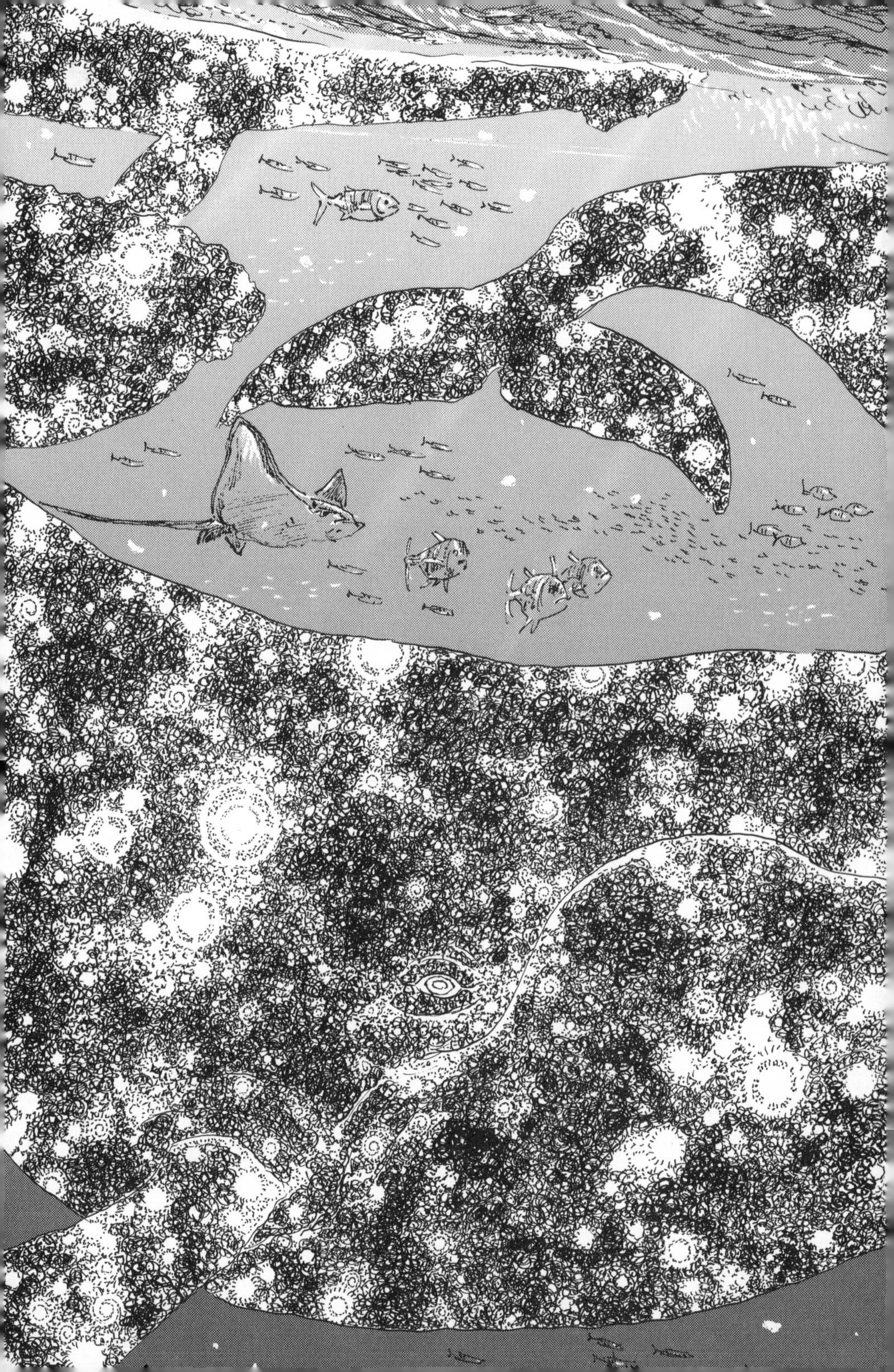

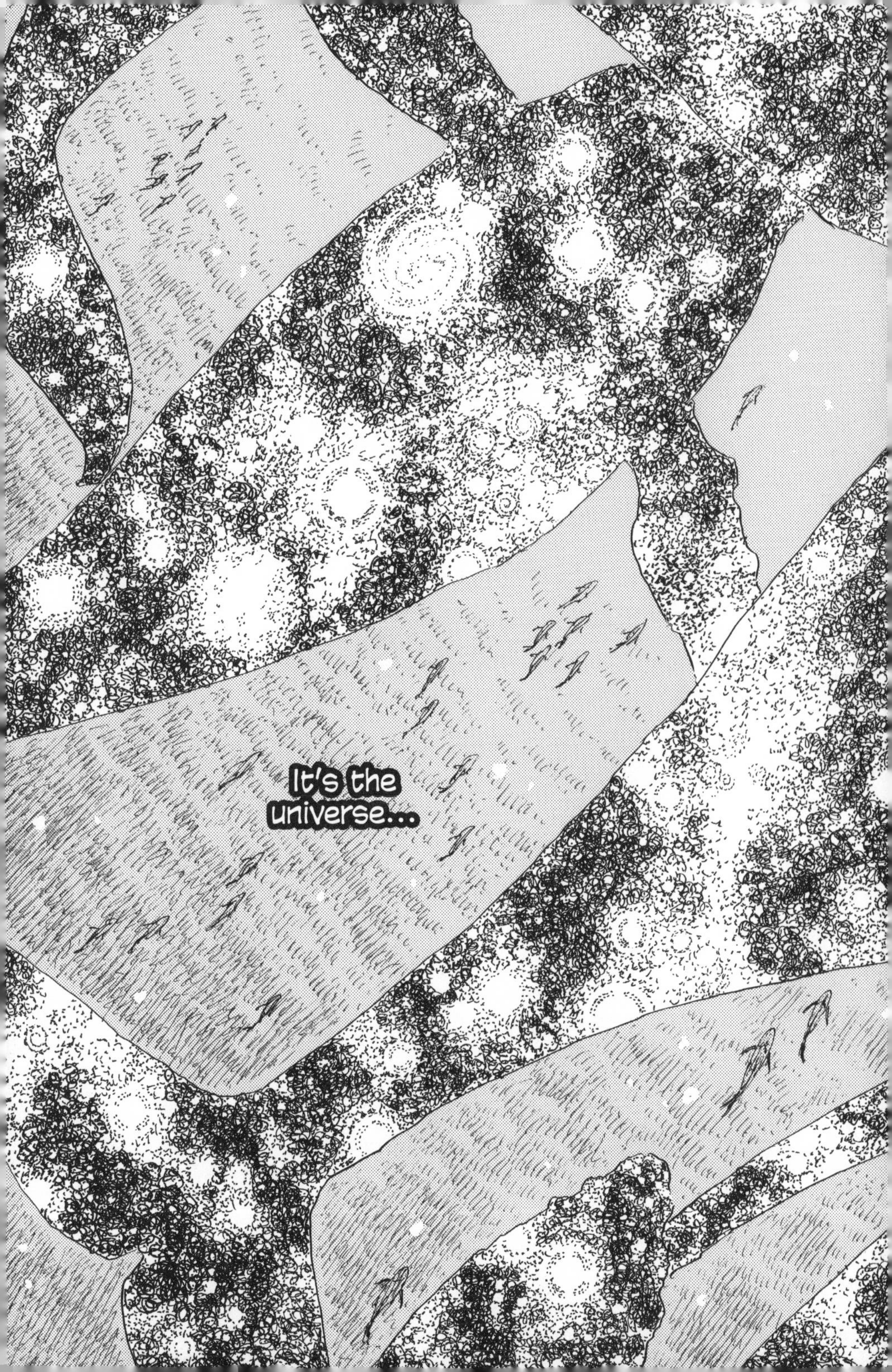
It's the universe...

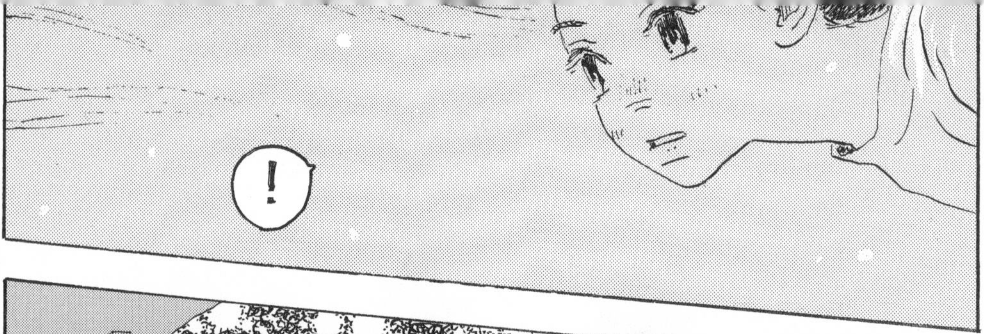
!
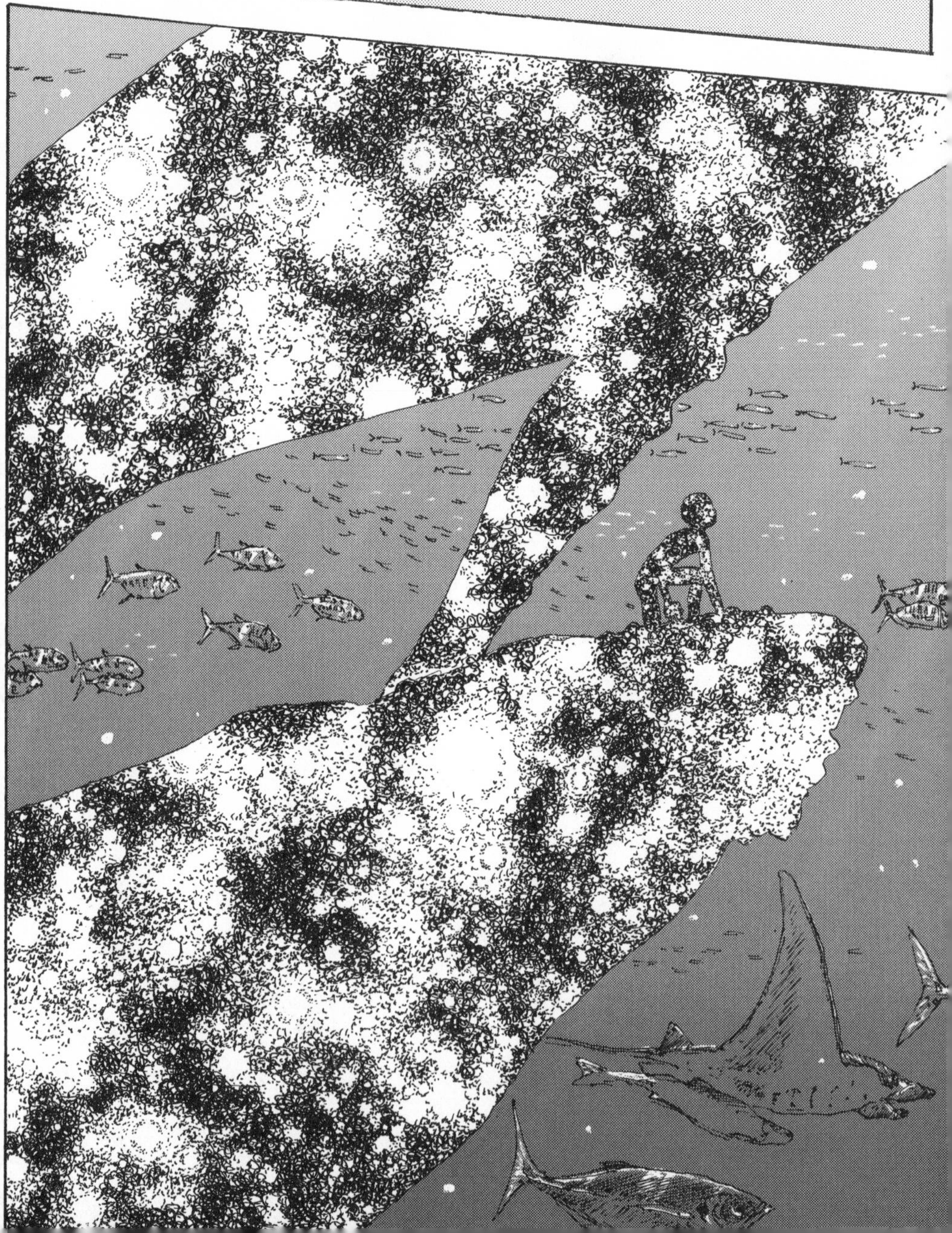

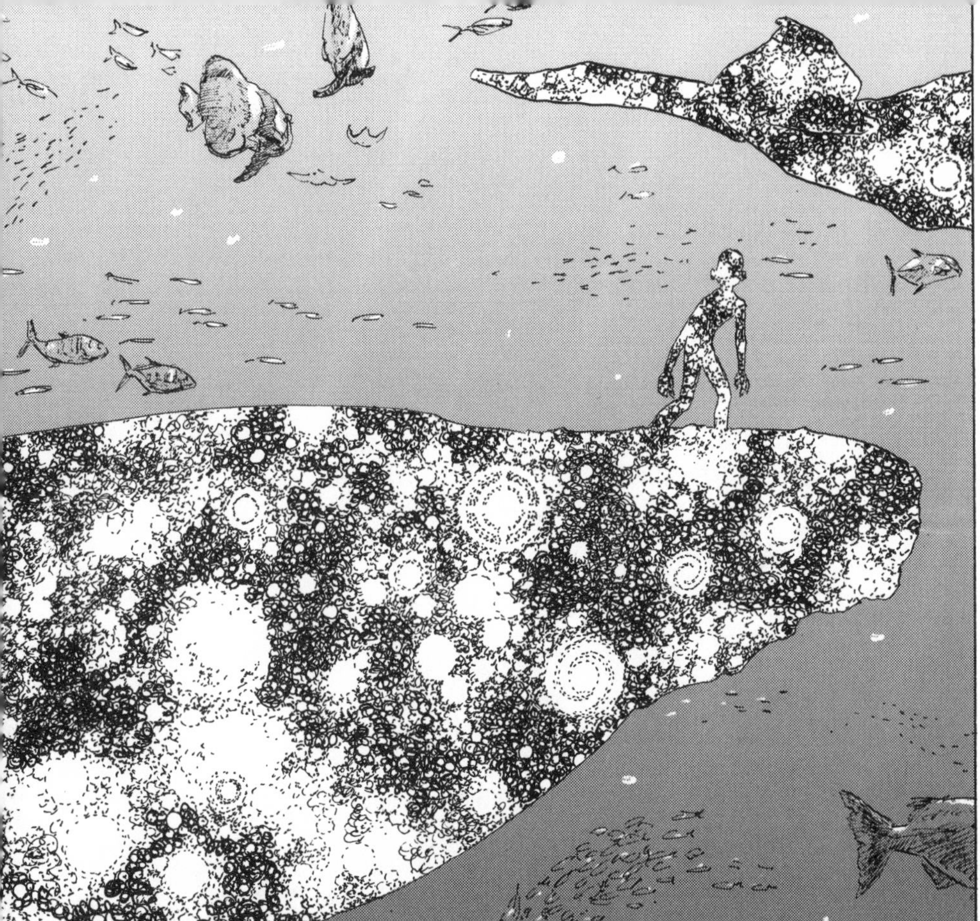

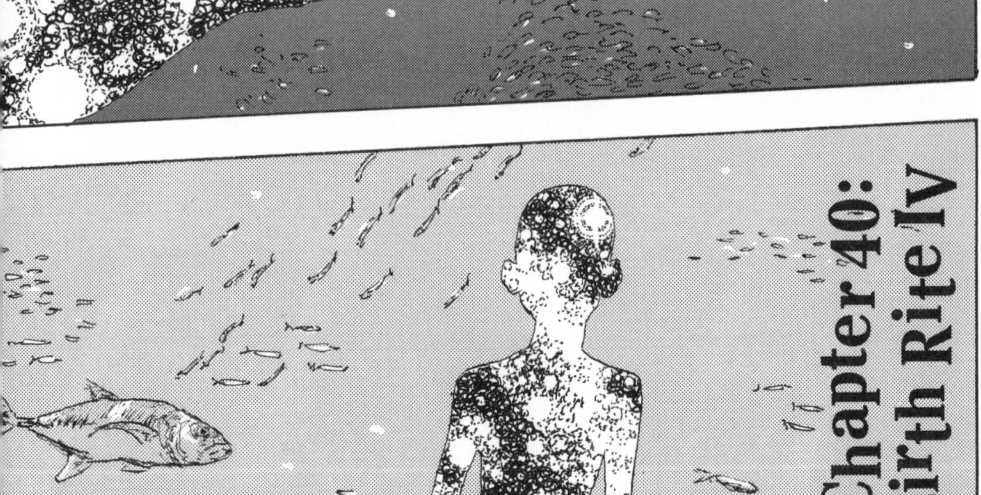
Chapter 40:
Birth Rite IV

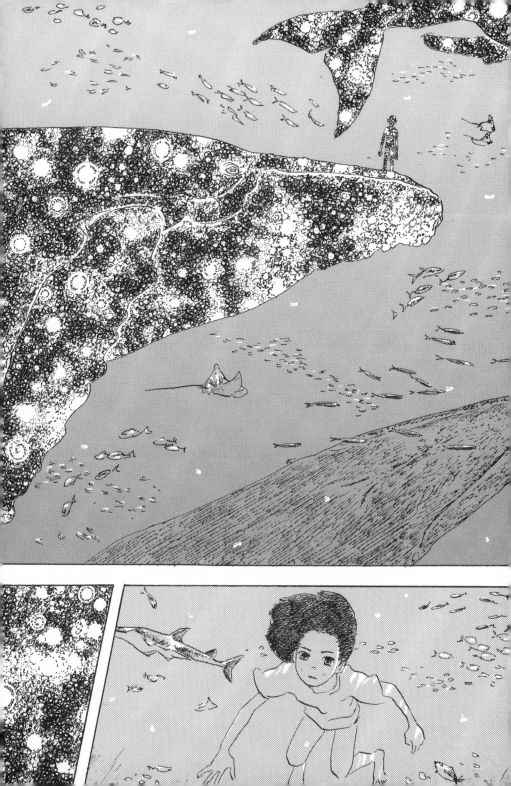

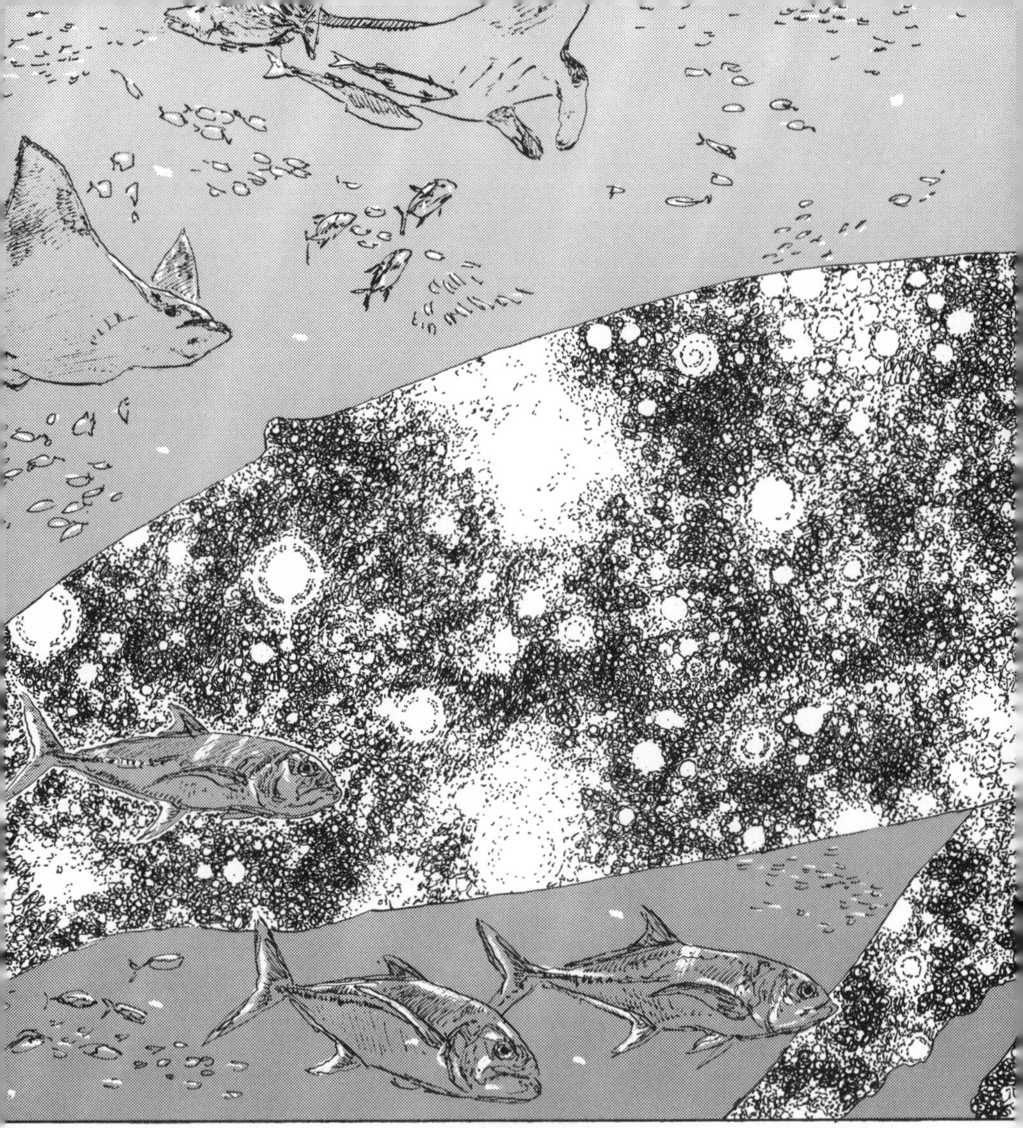
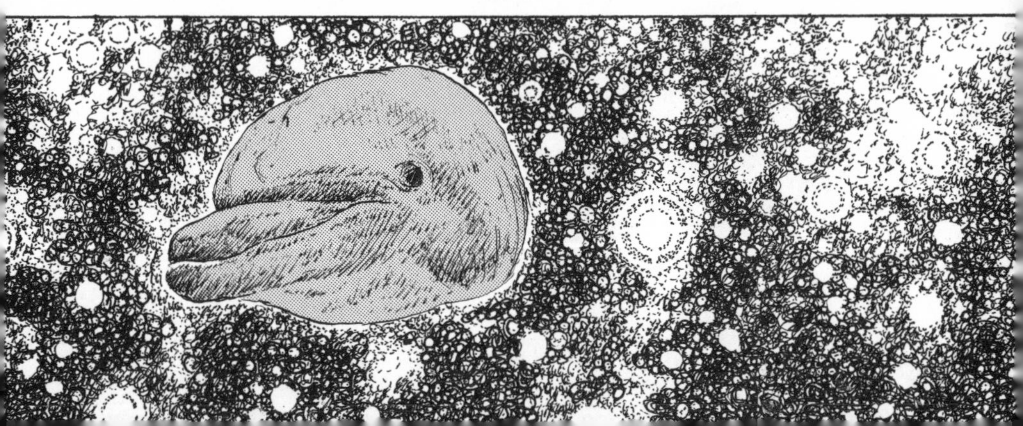

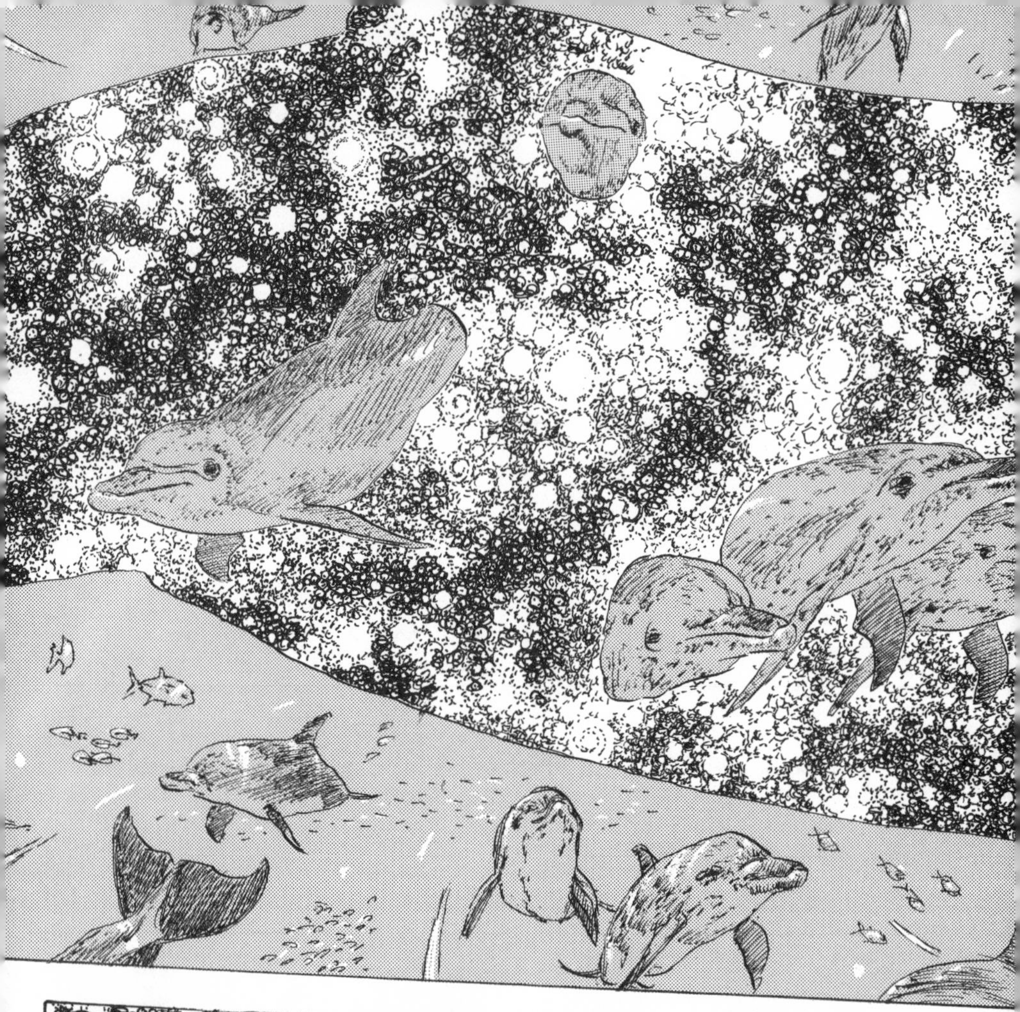
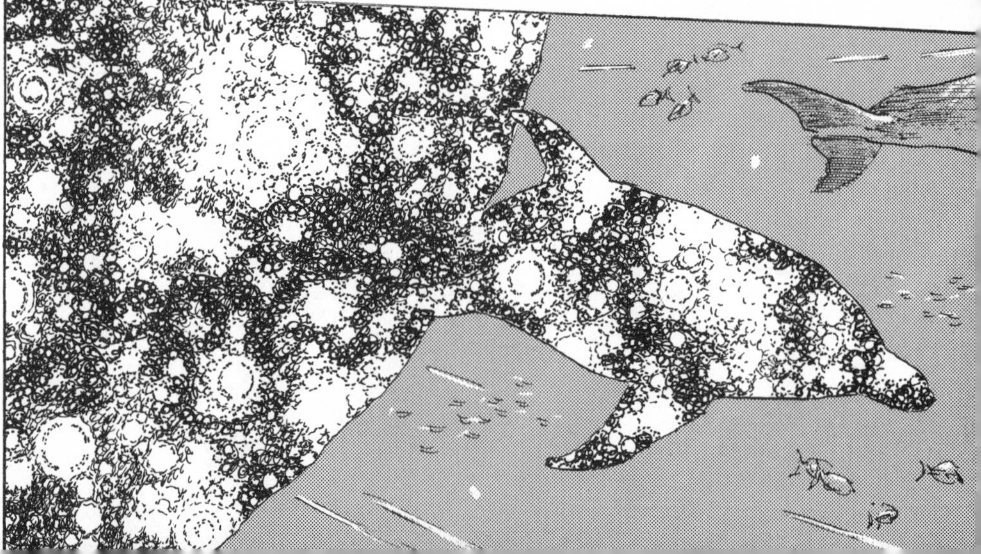

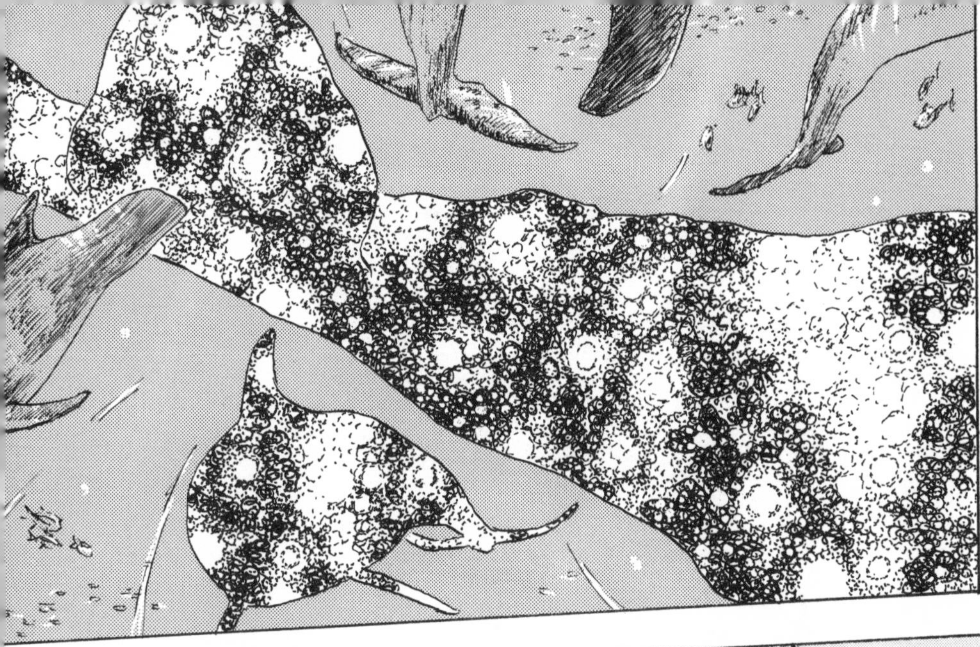
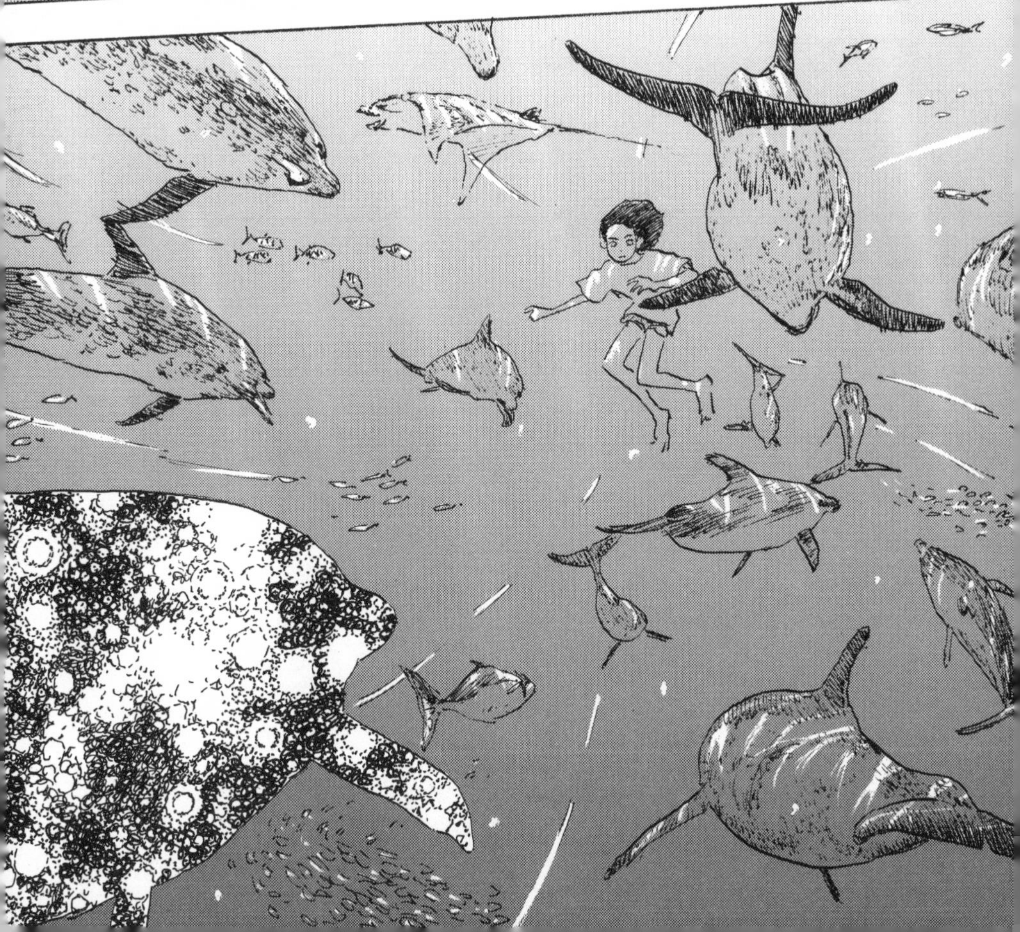

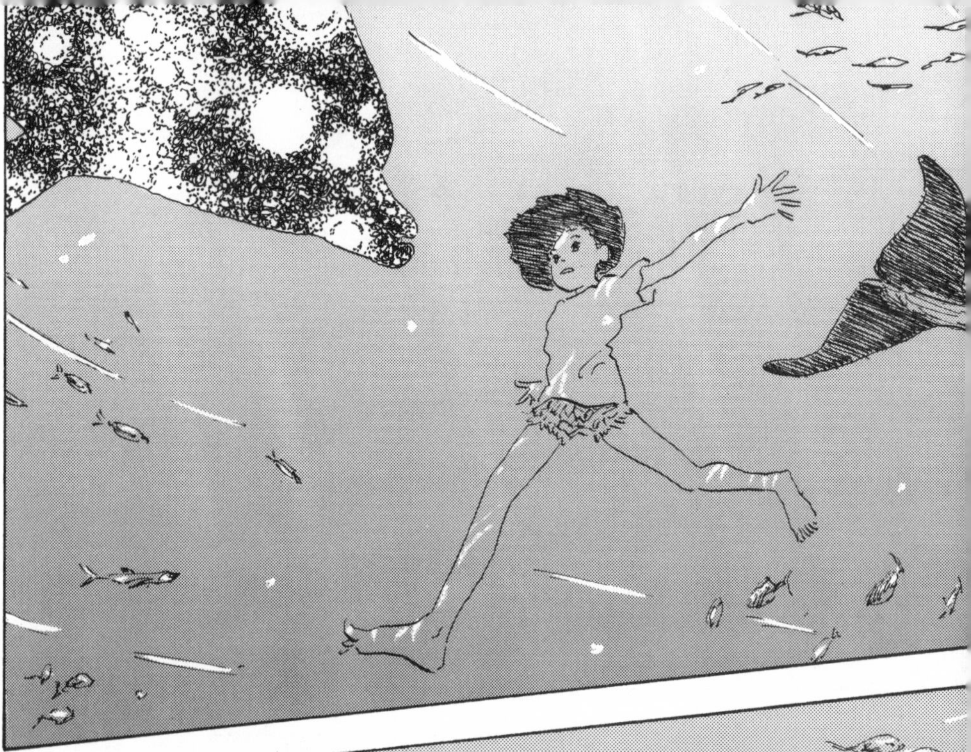
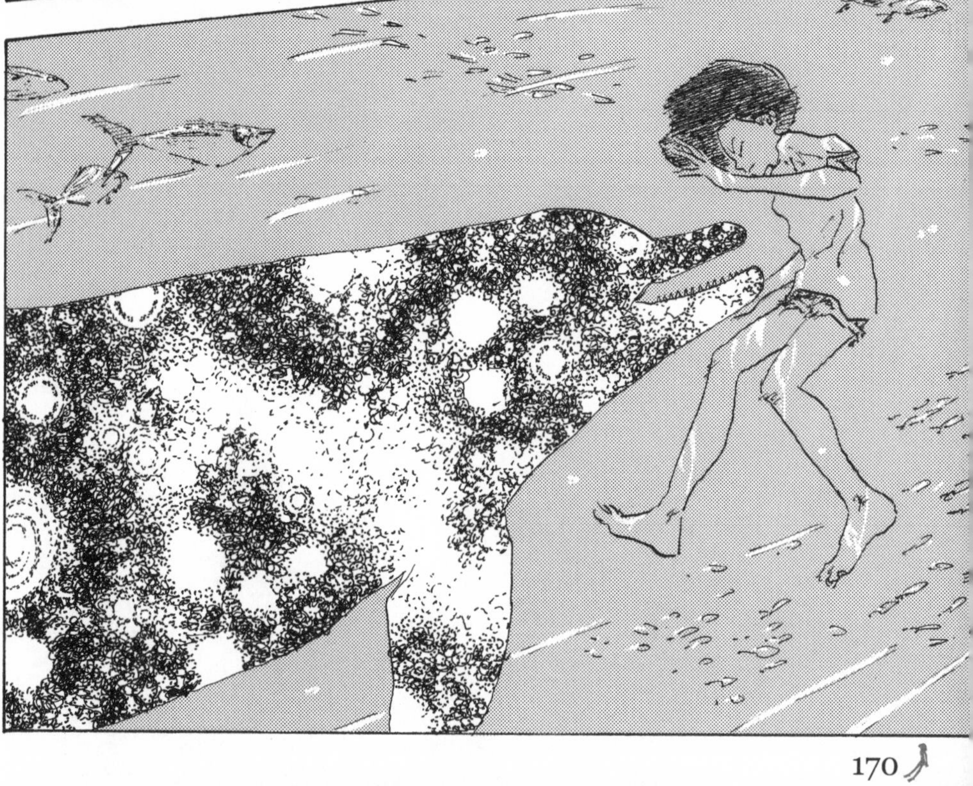

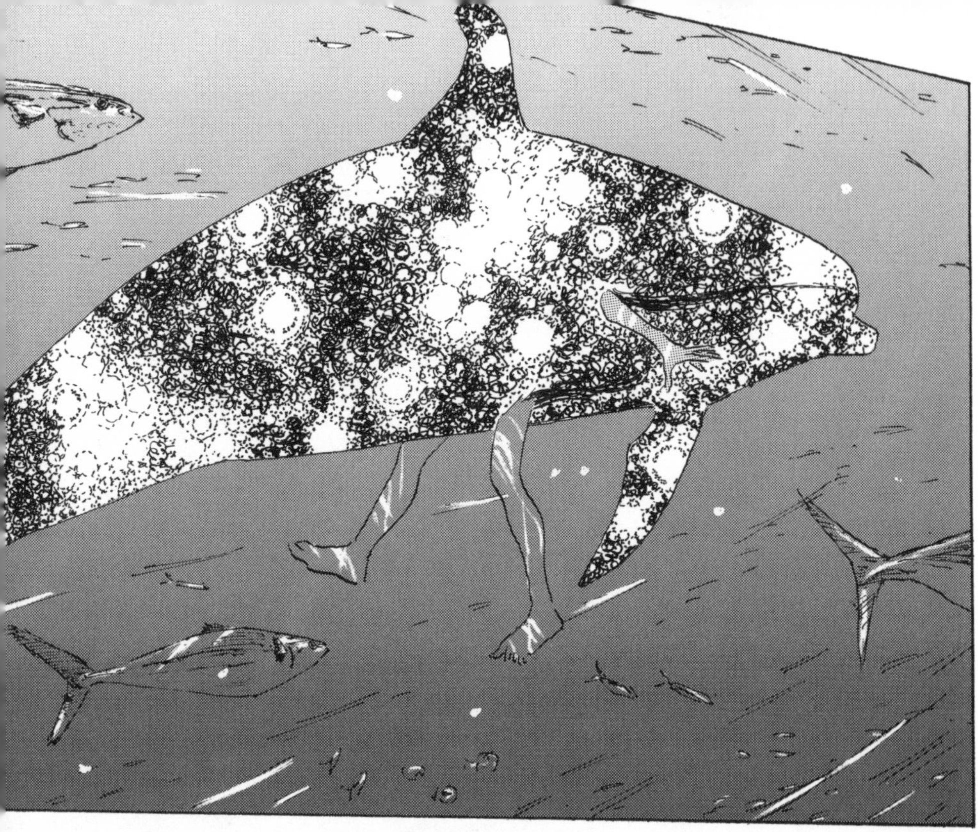
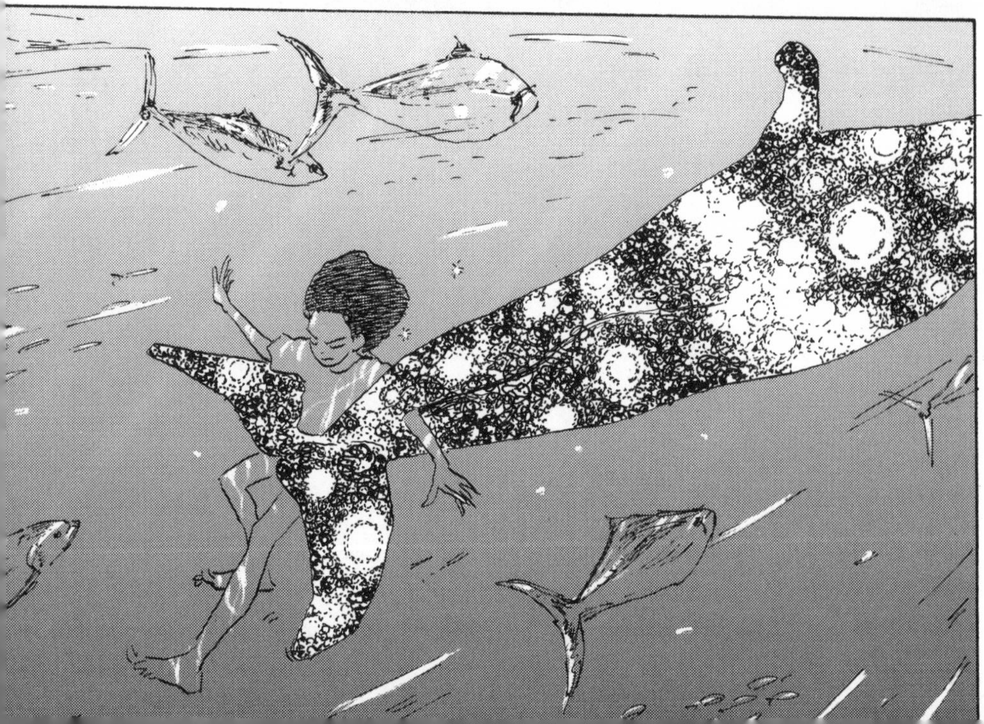

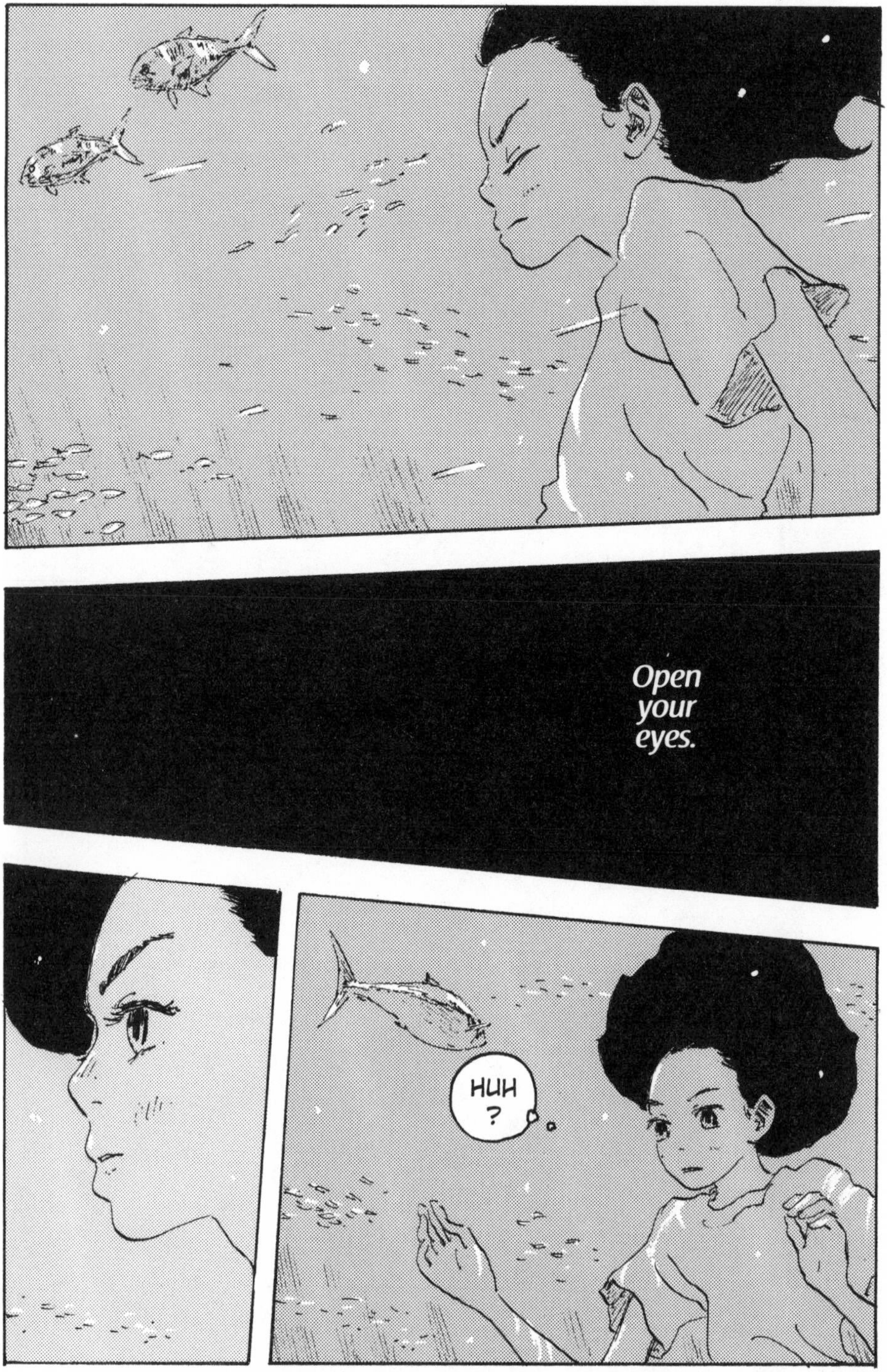
Open your eyes.
HUH?

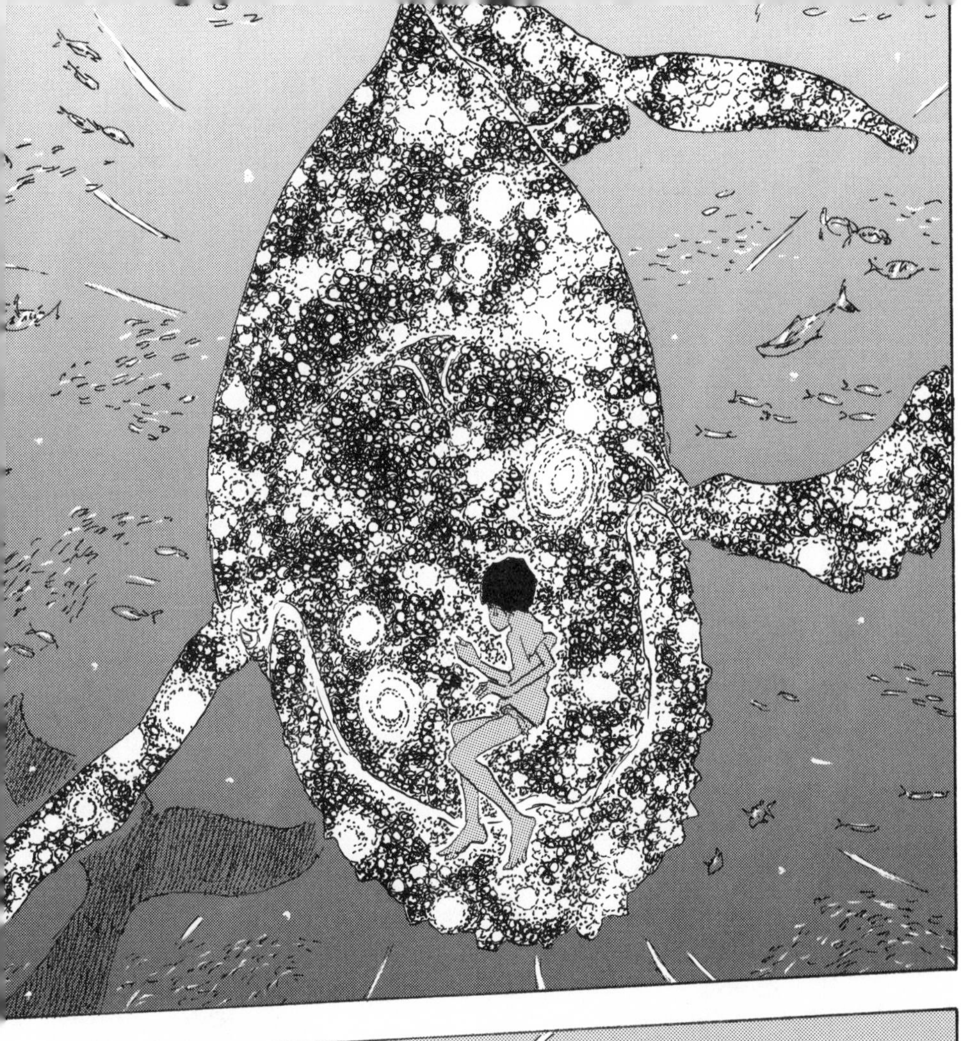
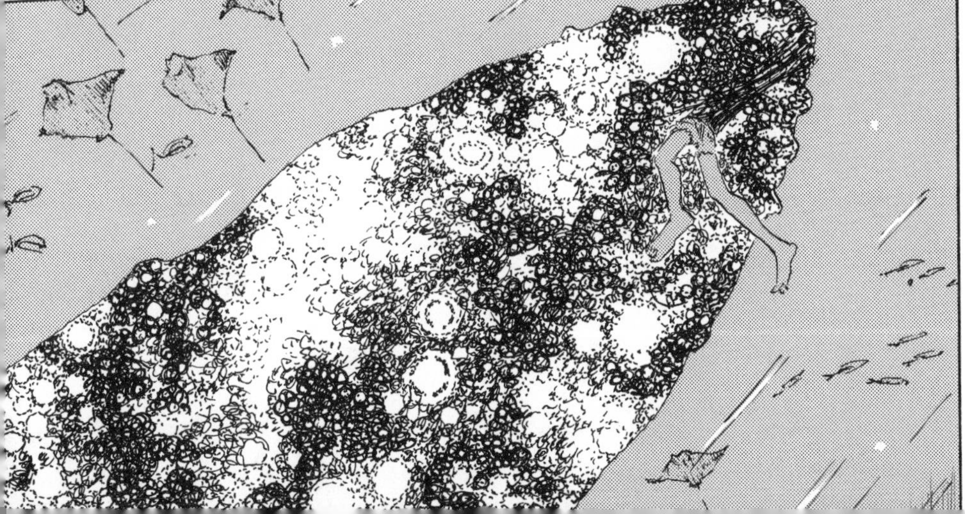

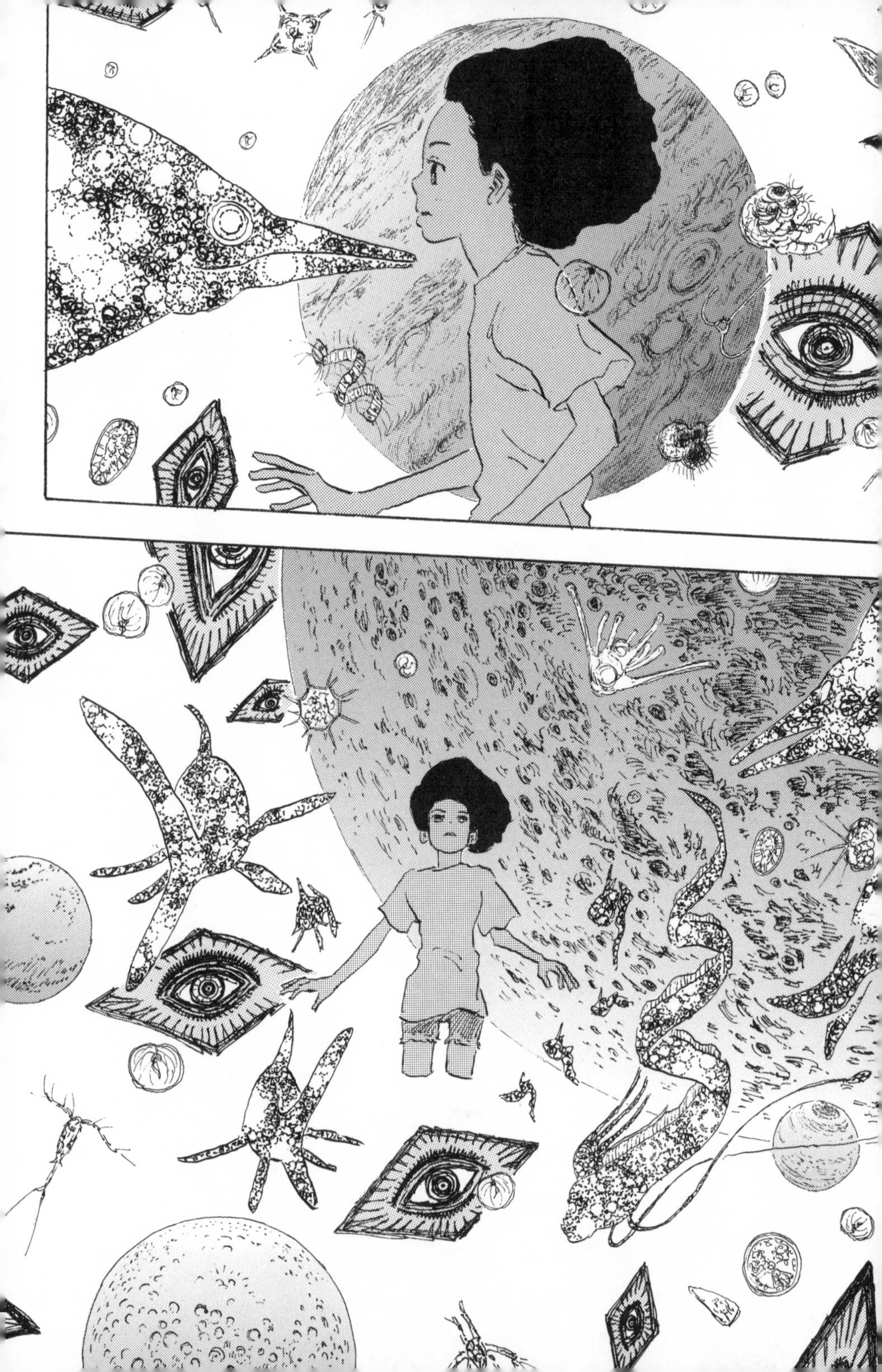

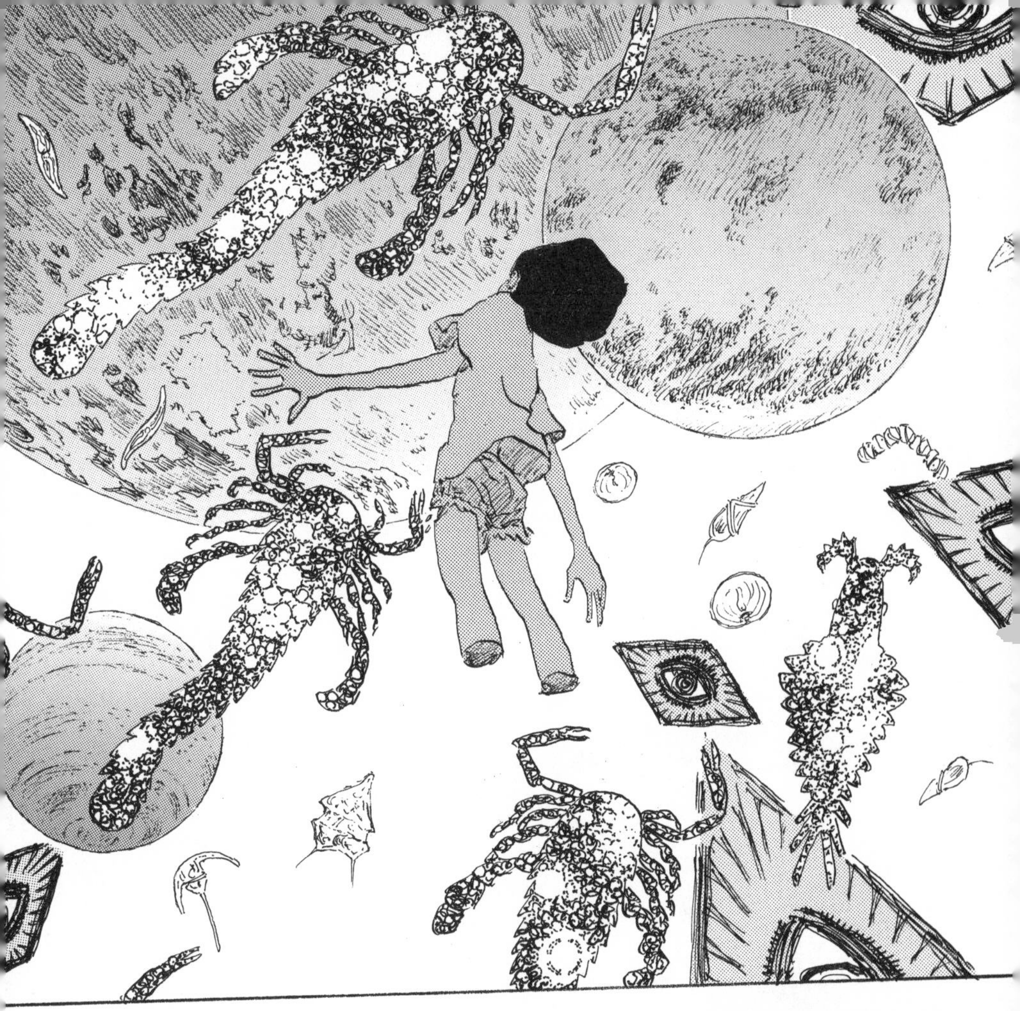
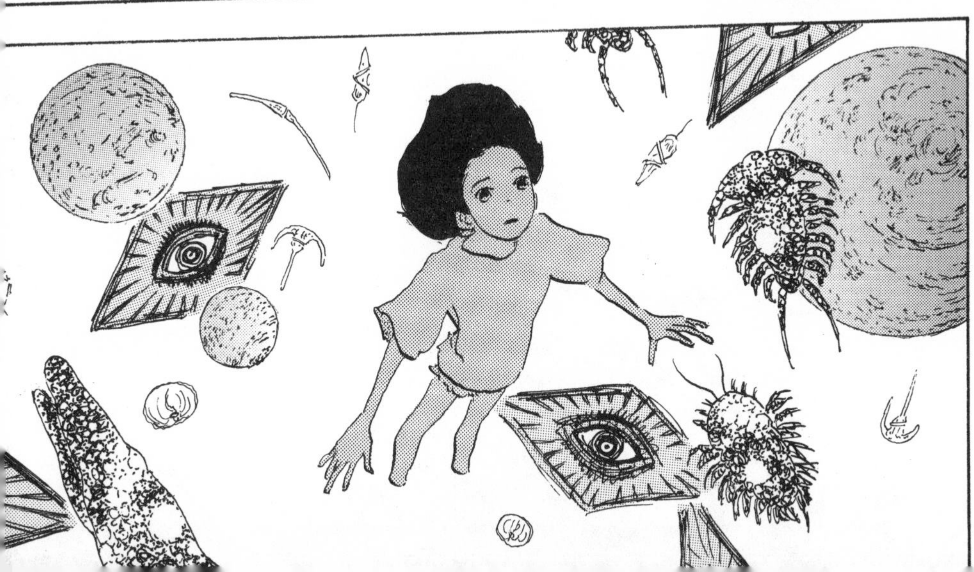

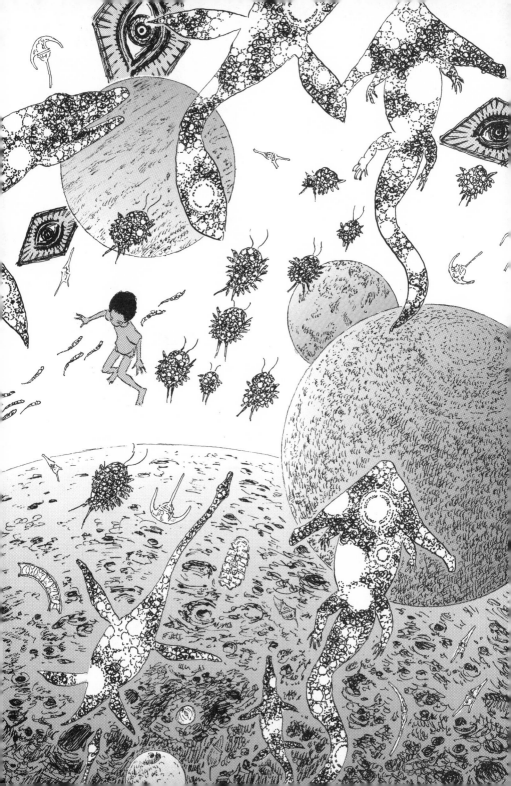

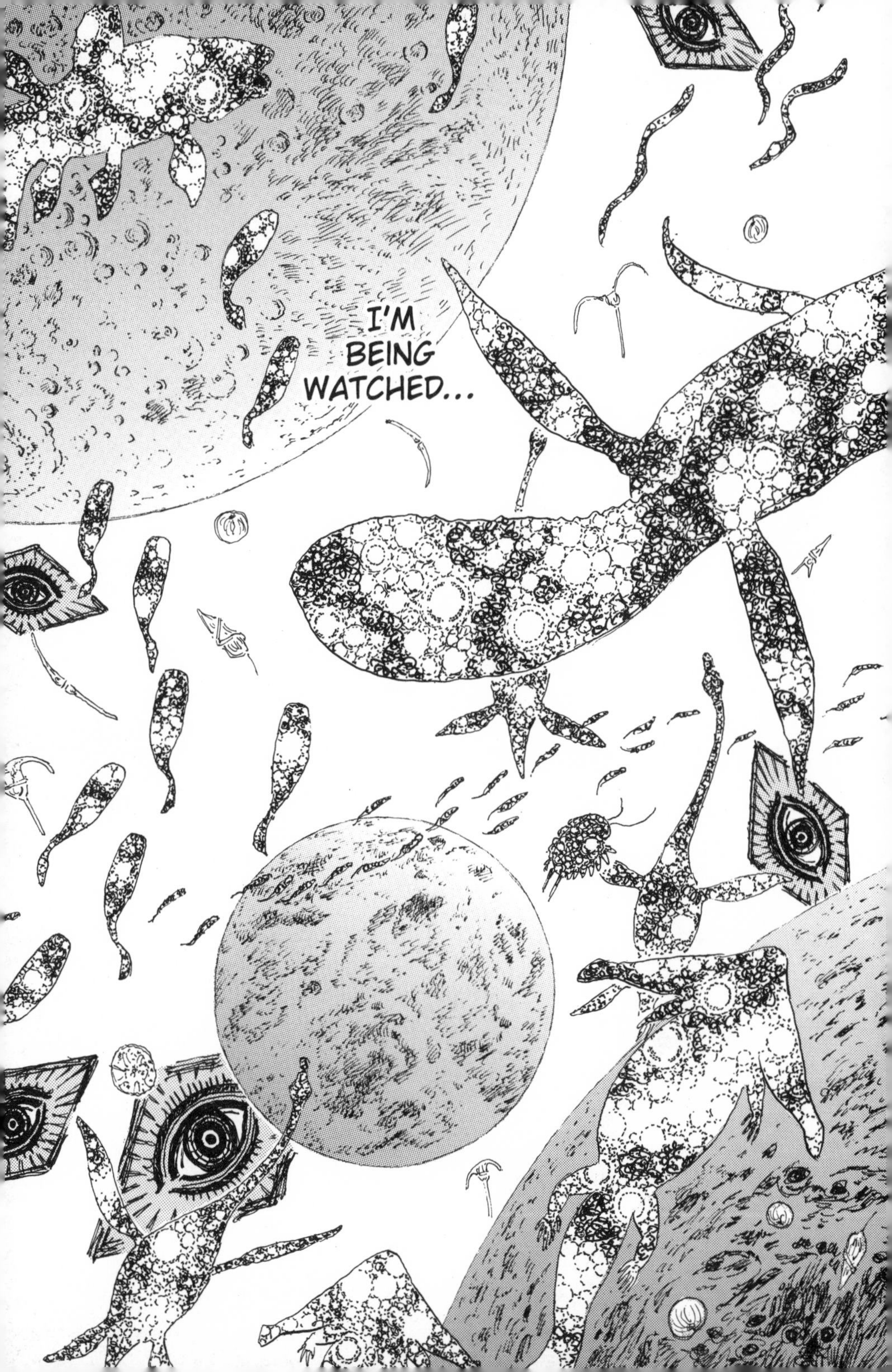
I'M BEING WATCHED...

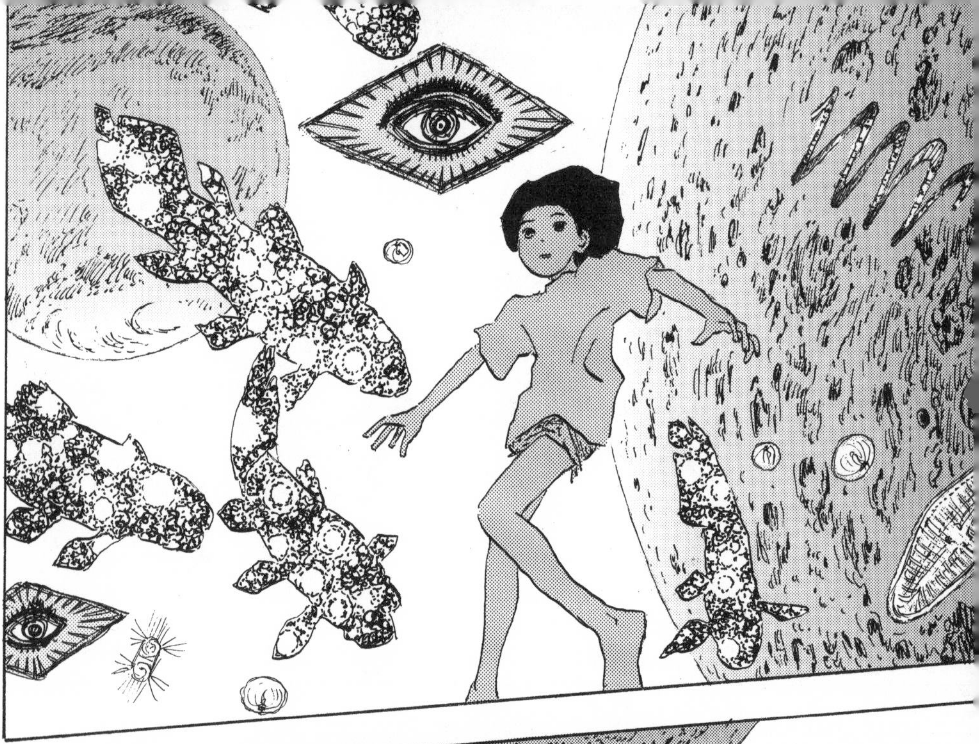
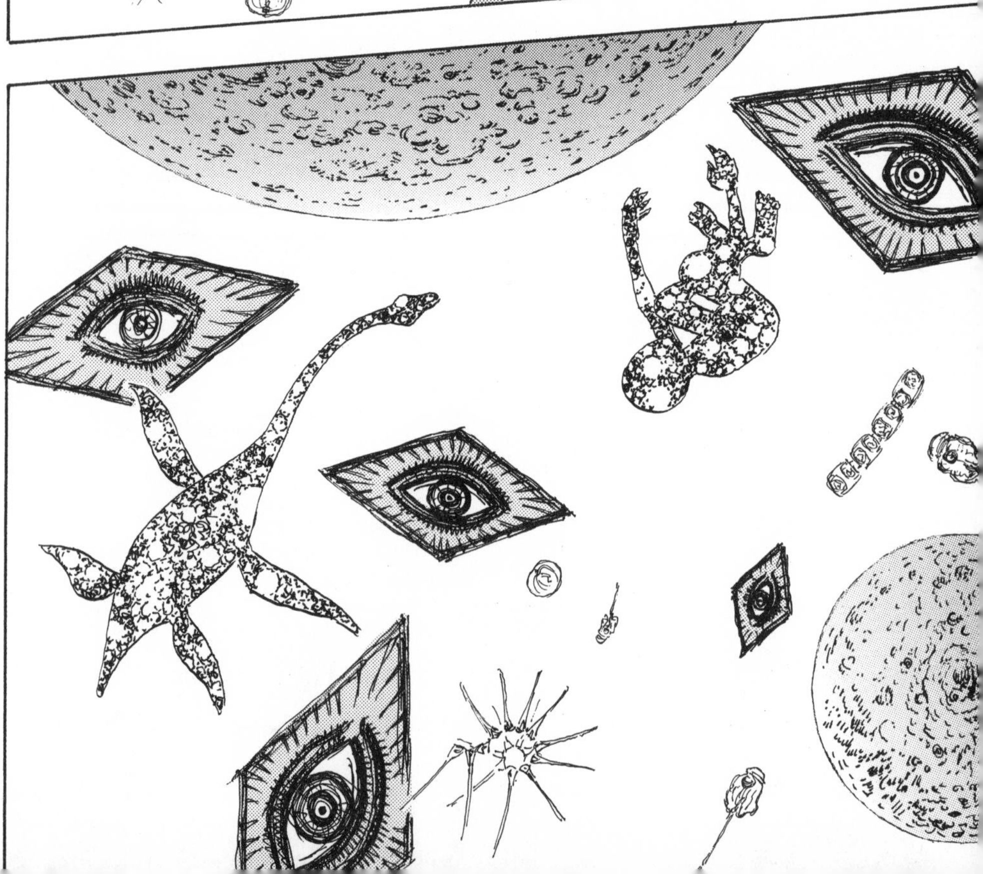

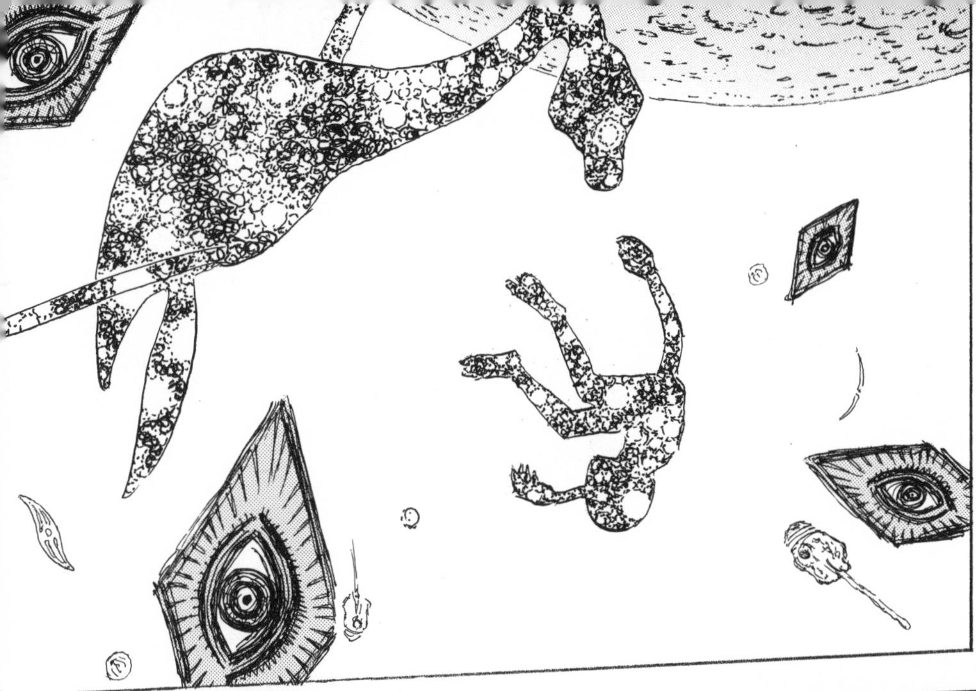

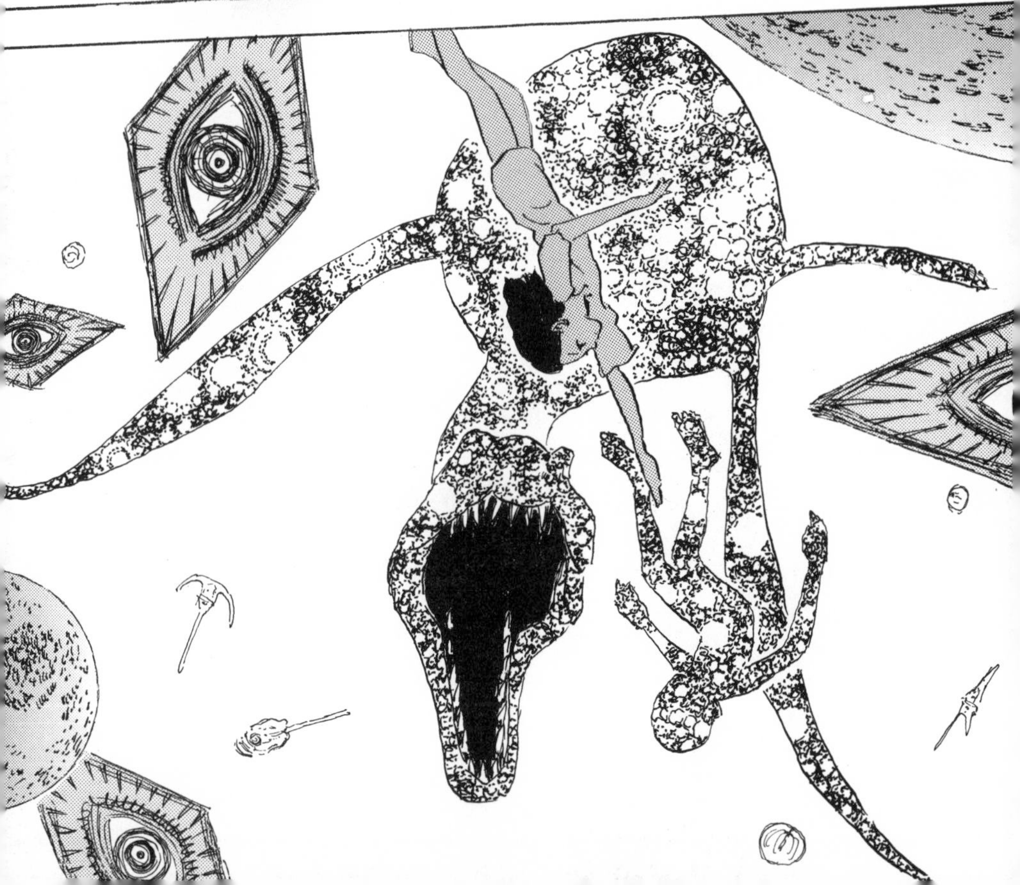

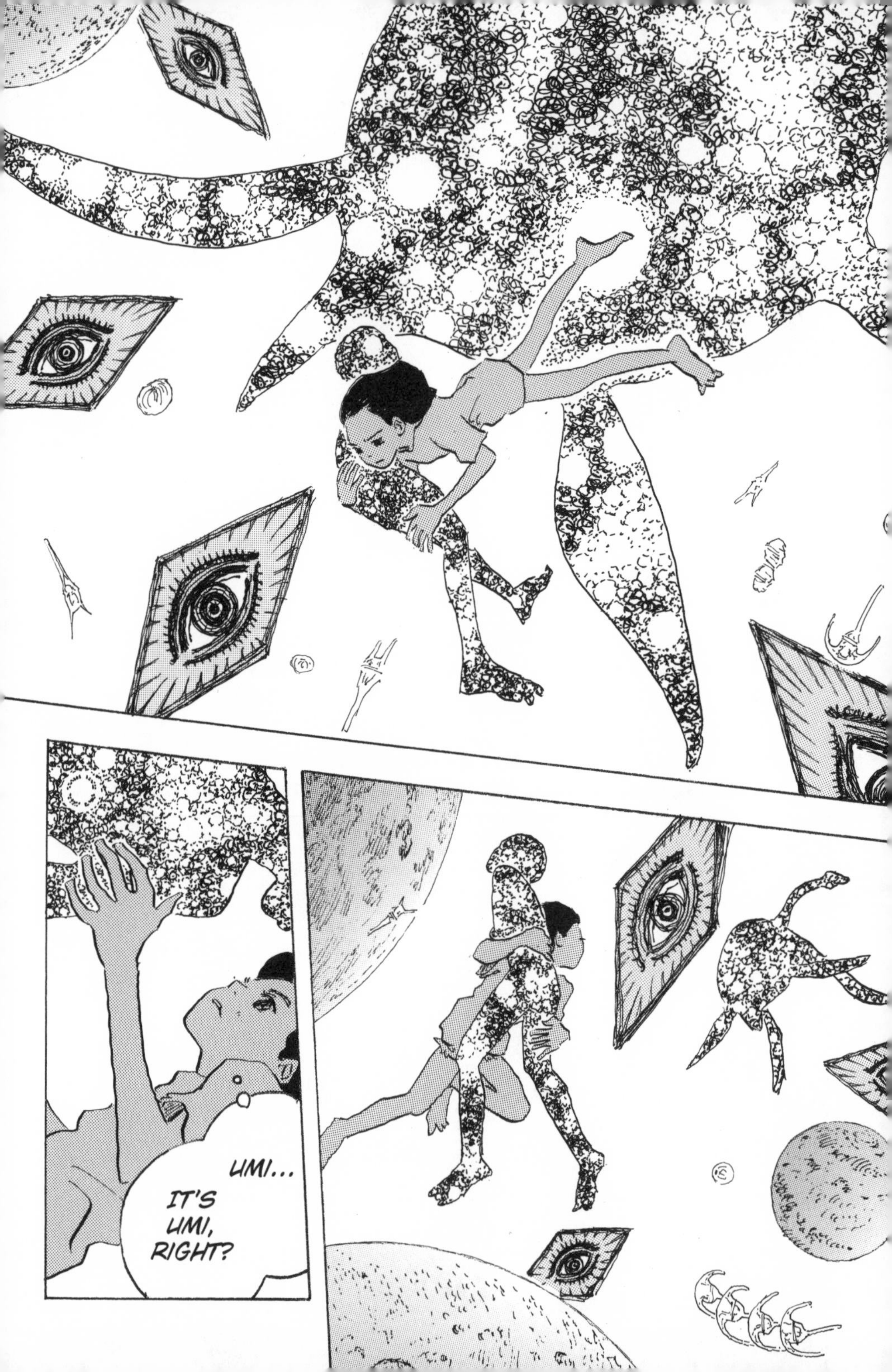
UMI...
IT'S UMI, RIGHT?

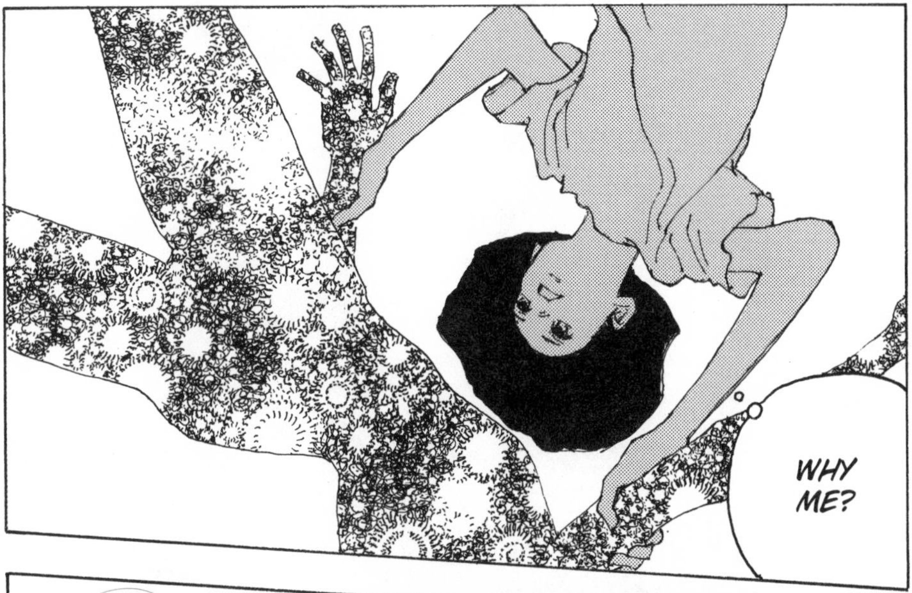
WHY ME?

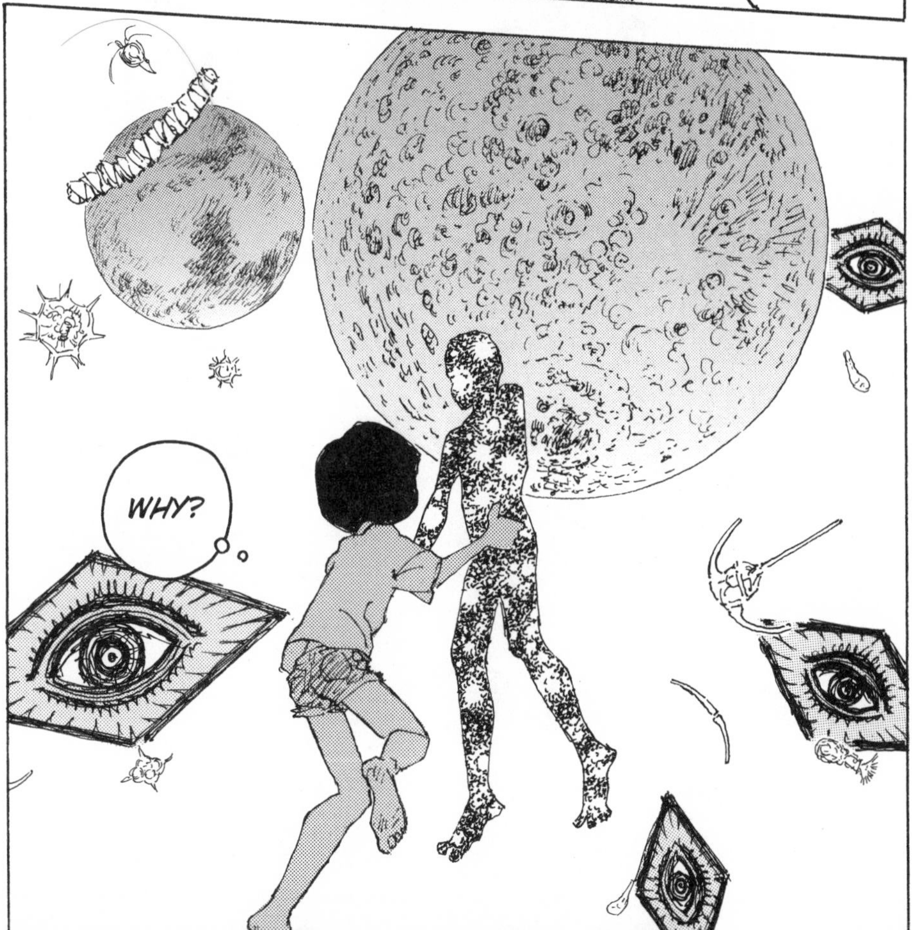
WHY?

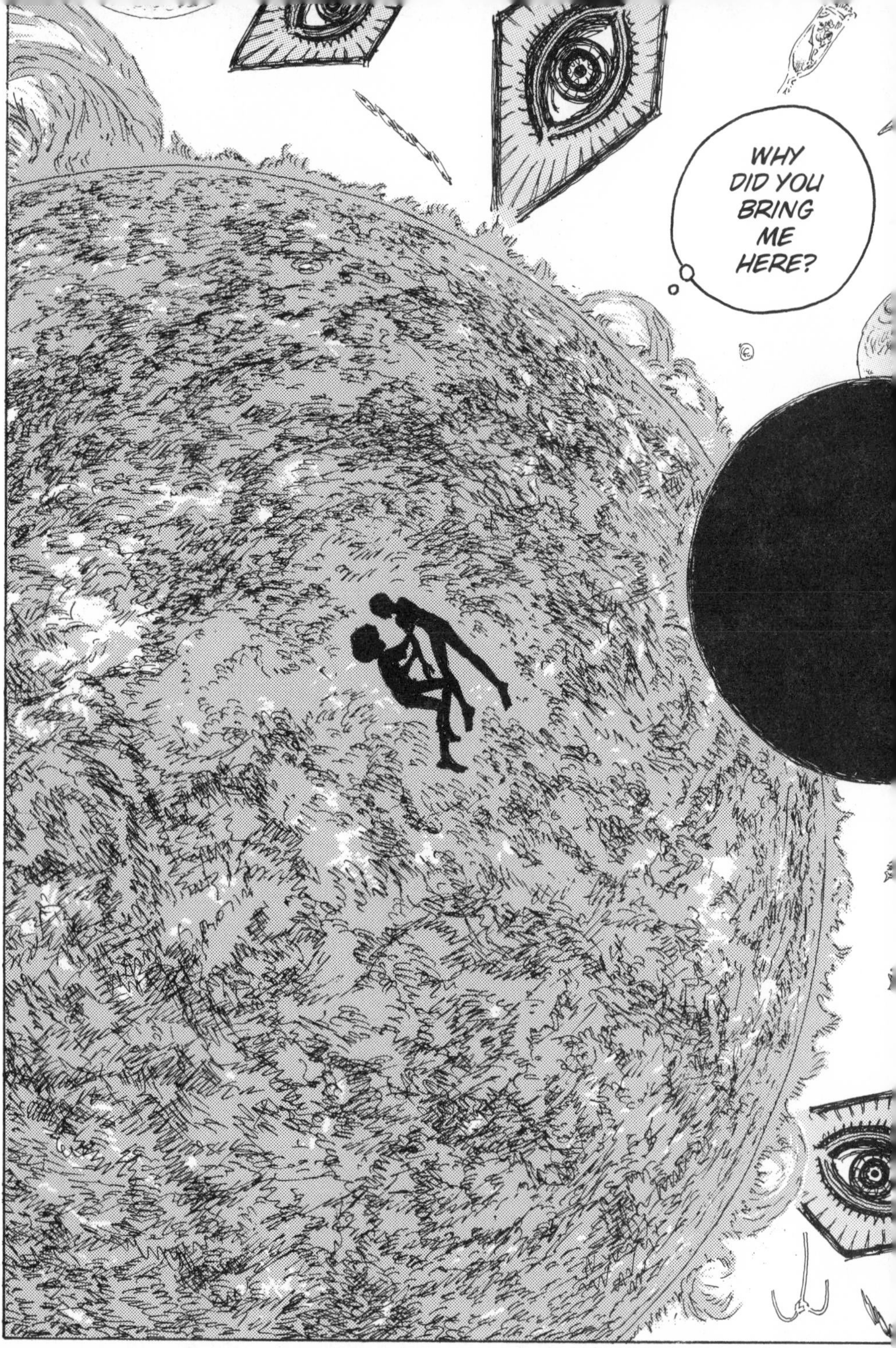
WHY DID YOU BRING ME HERE?

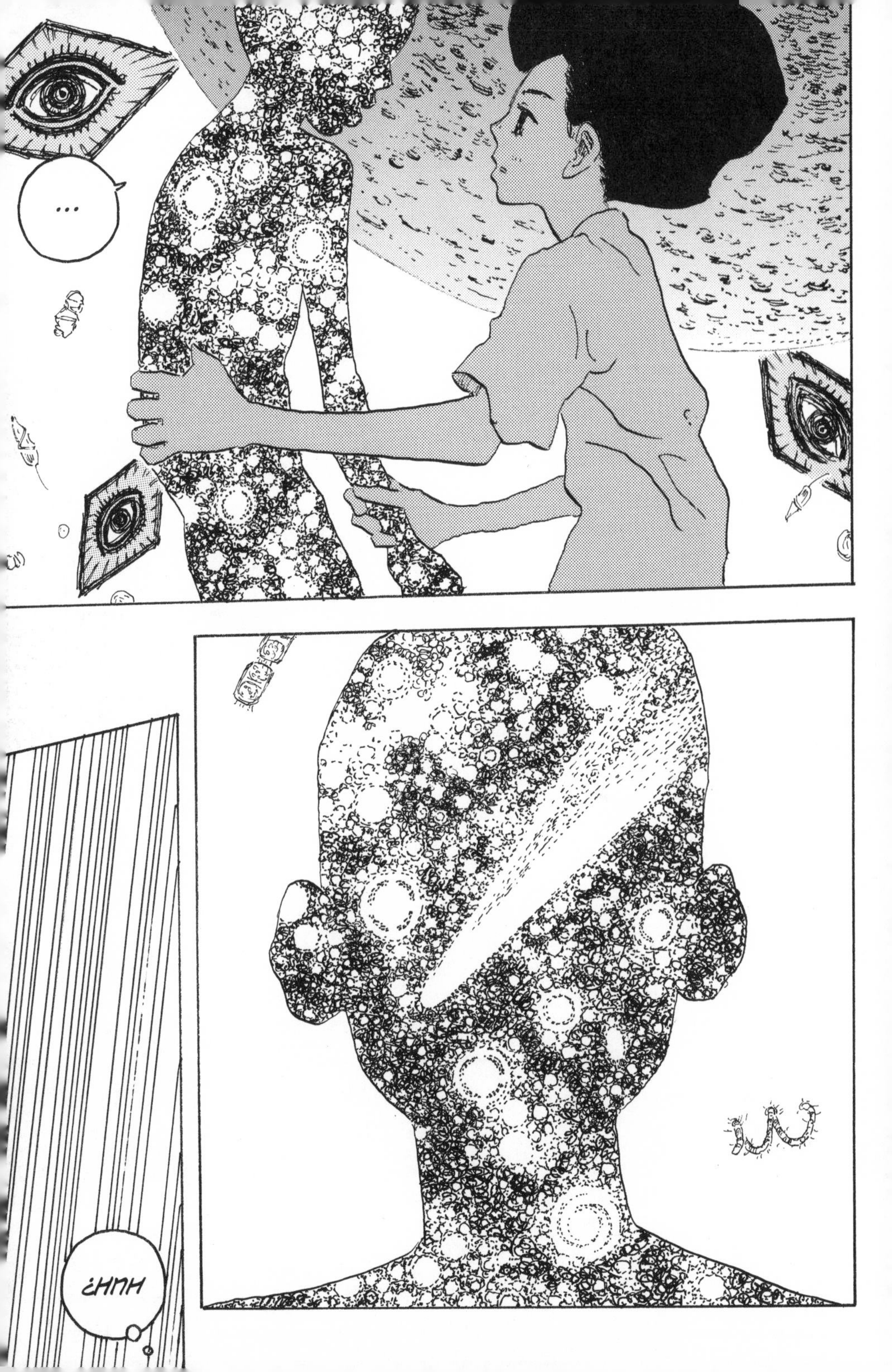
...
HUH?

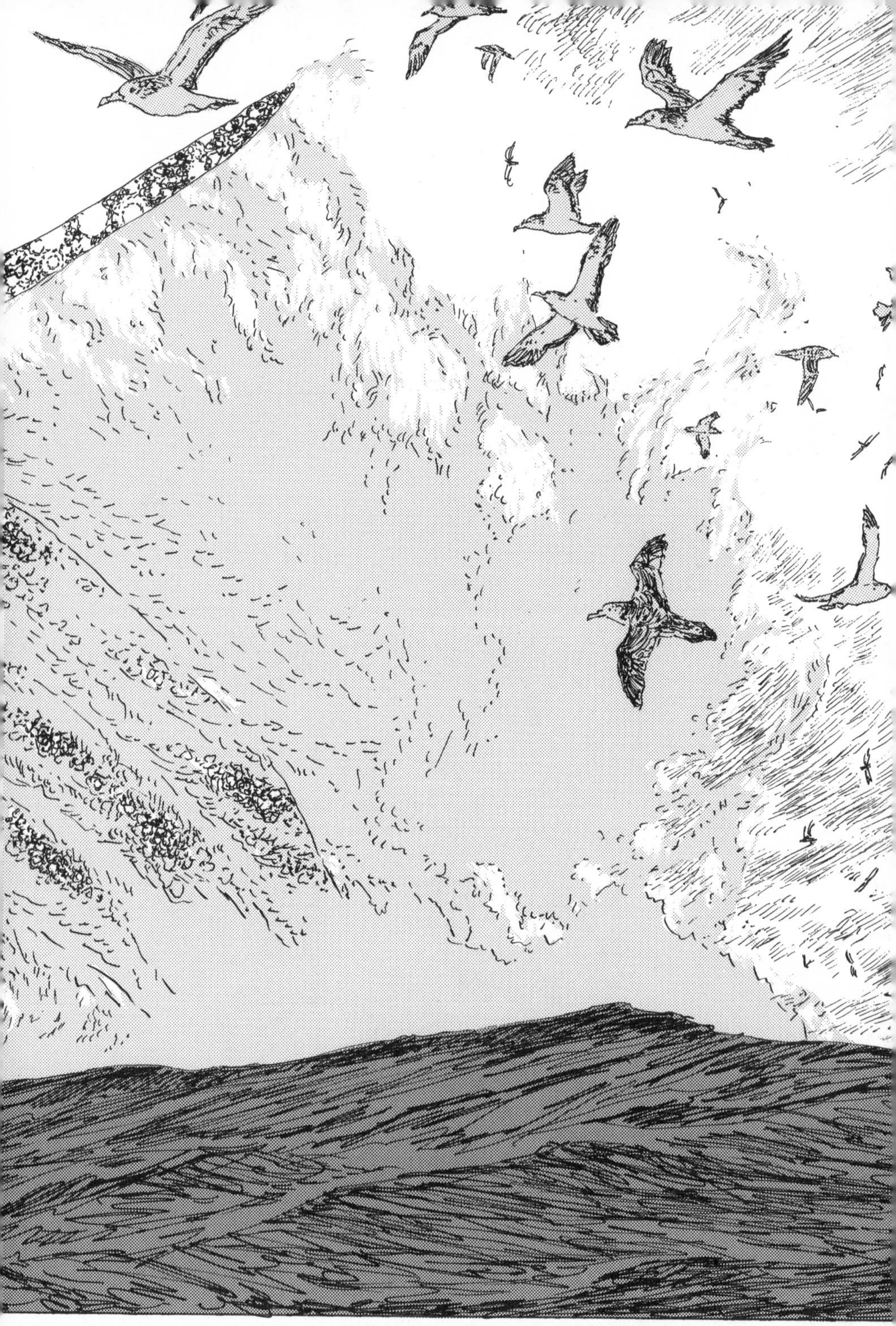

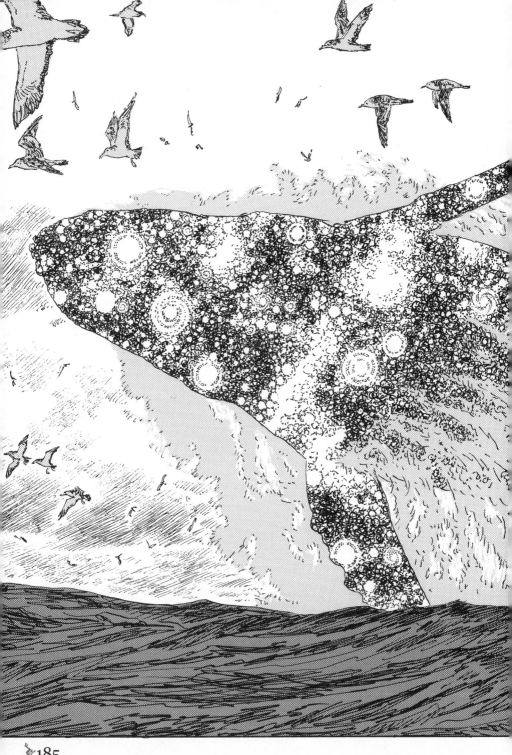

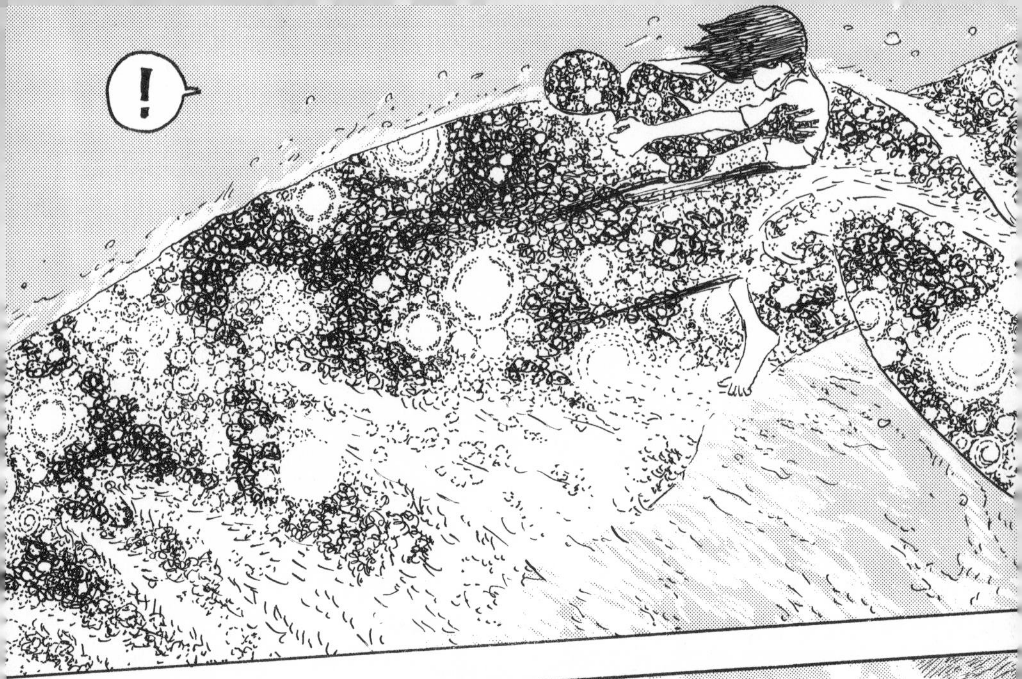
!
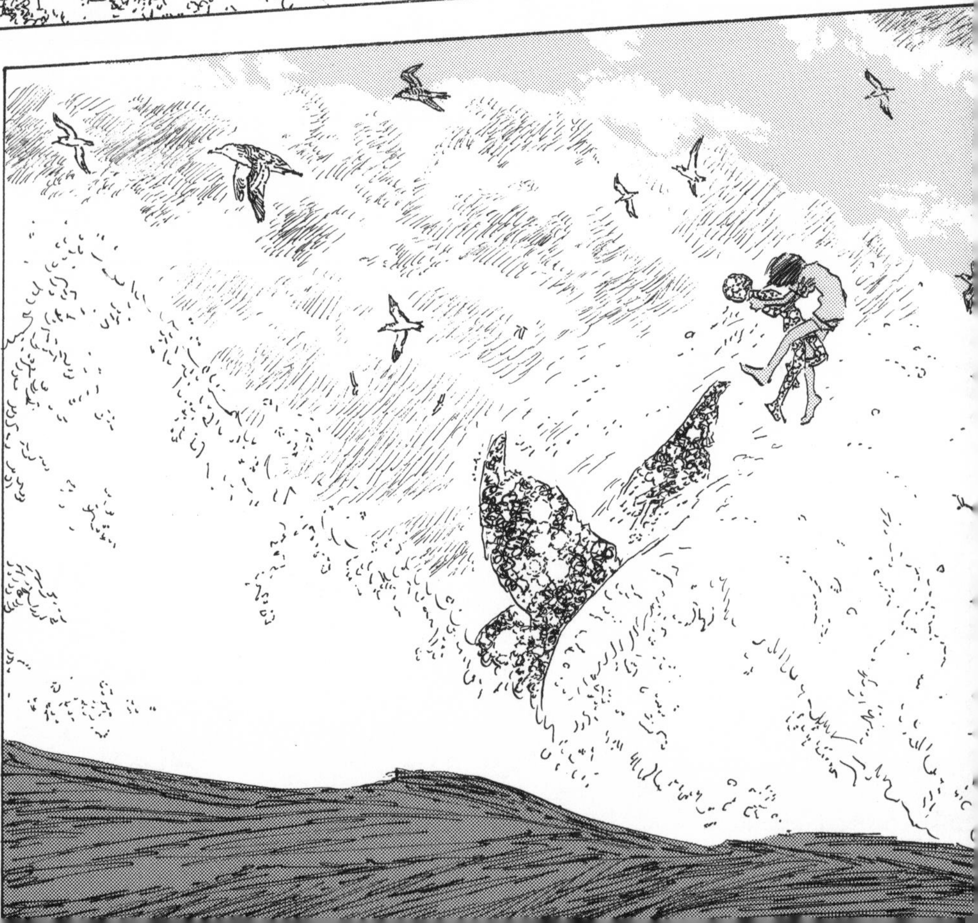

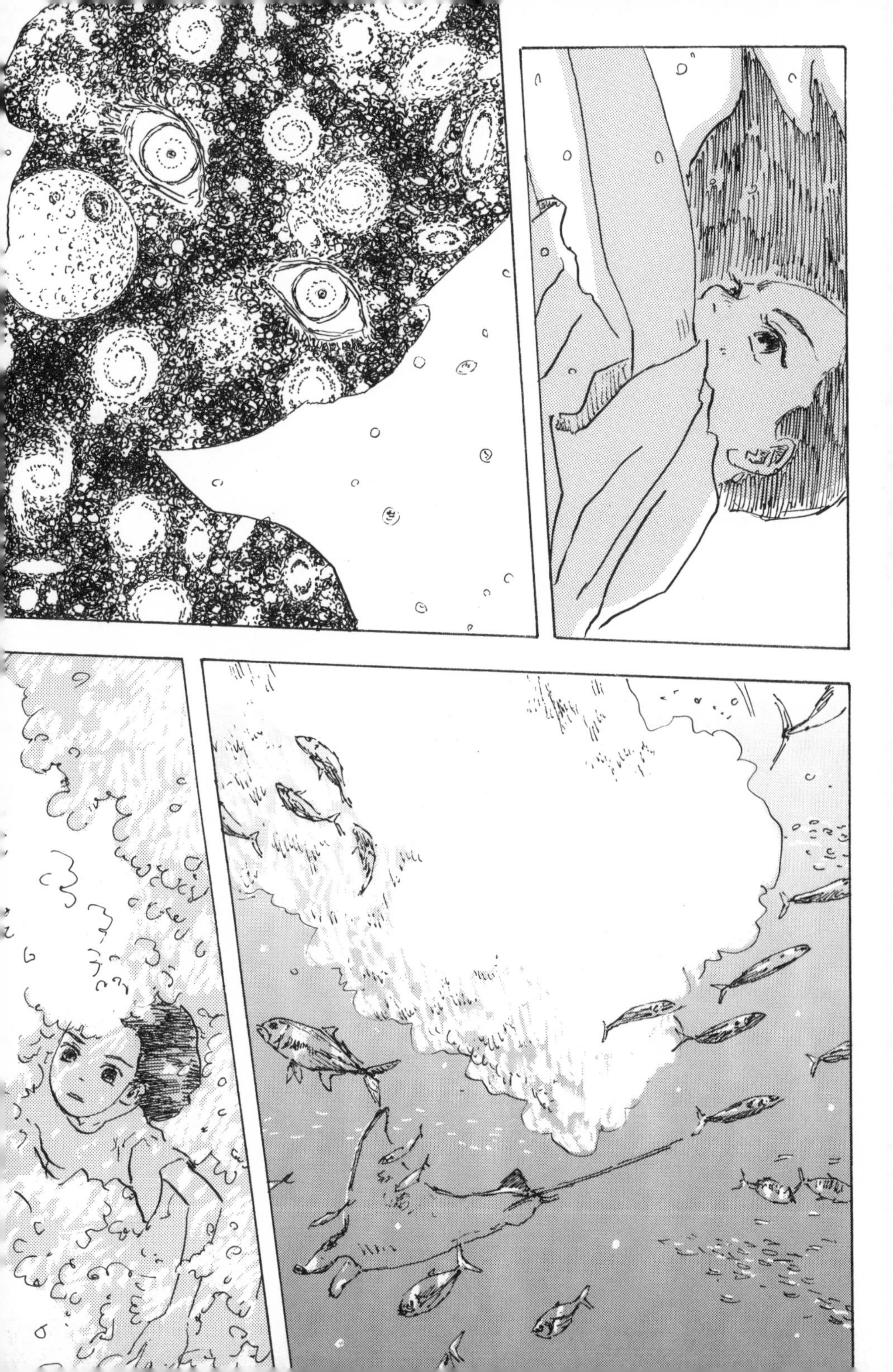

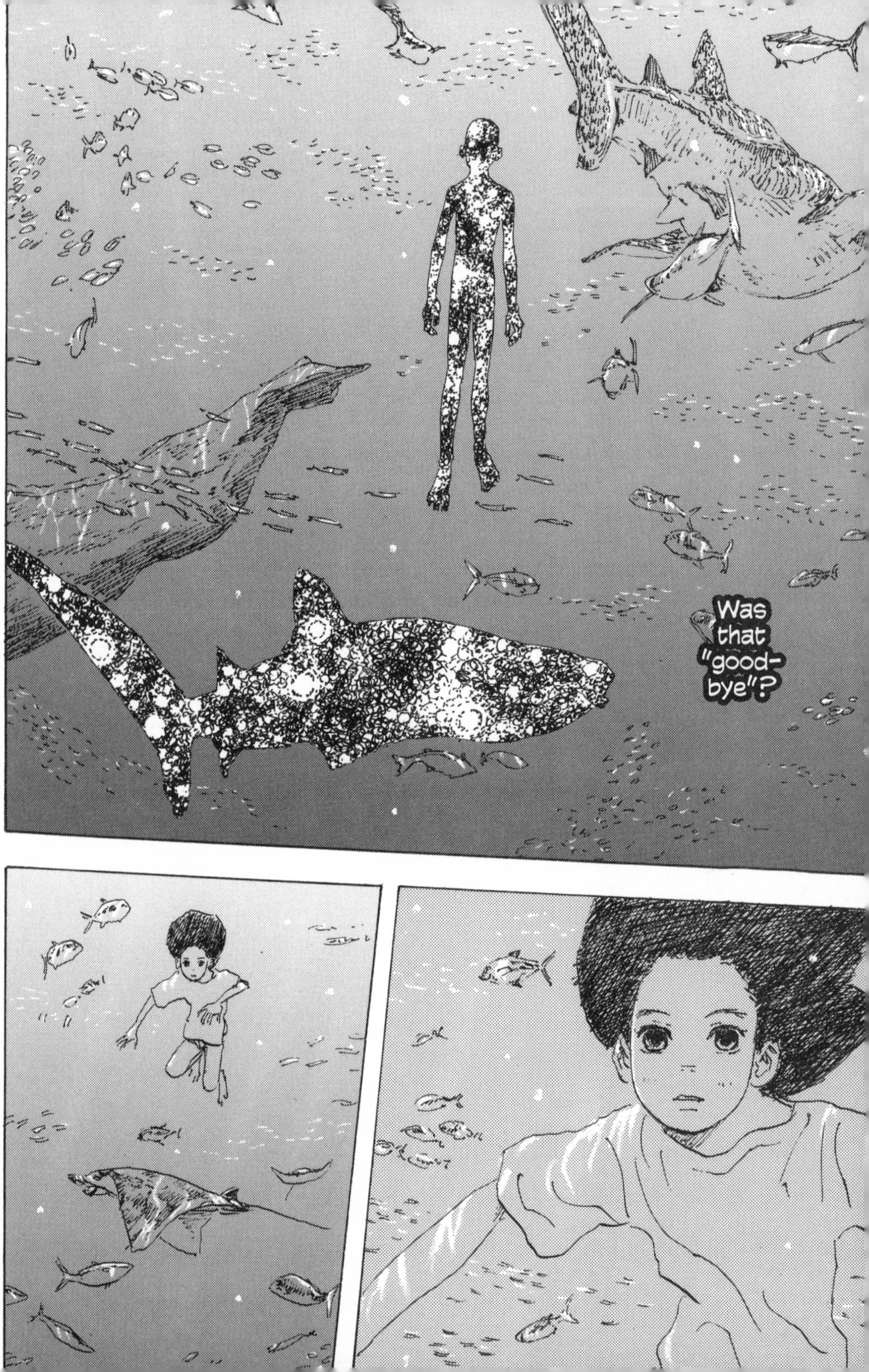
Was that "good-bye"?

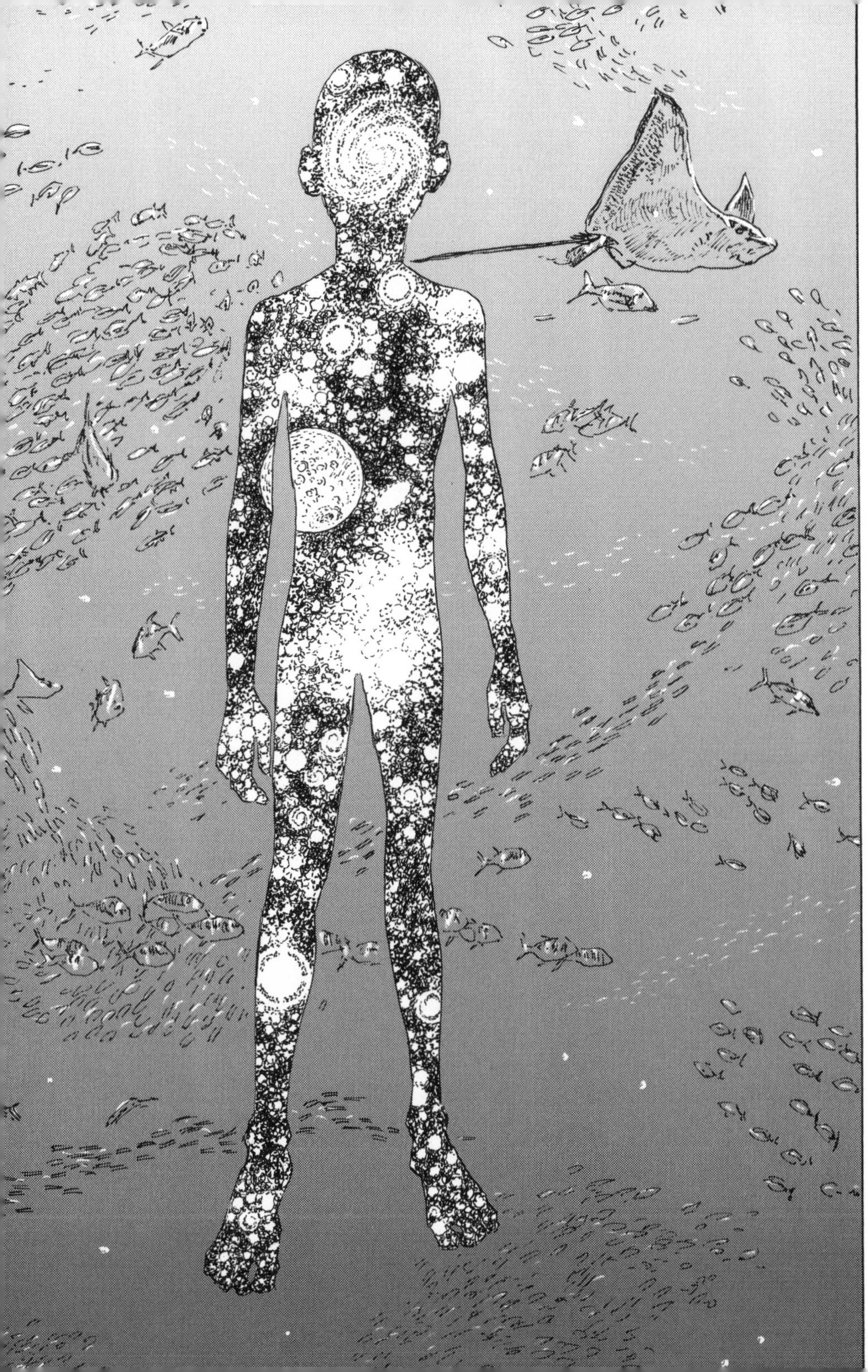

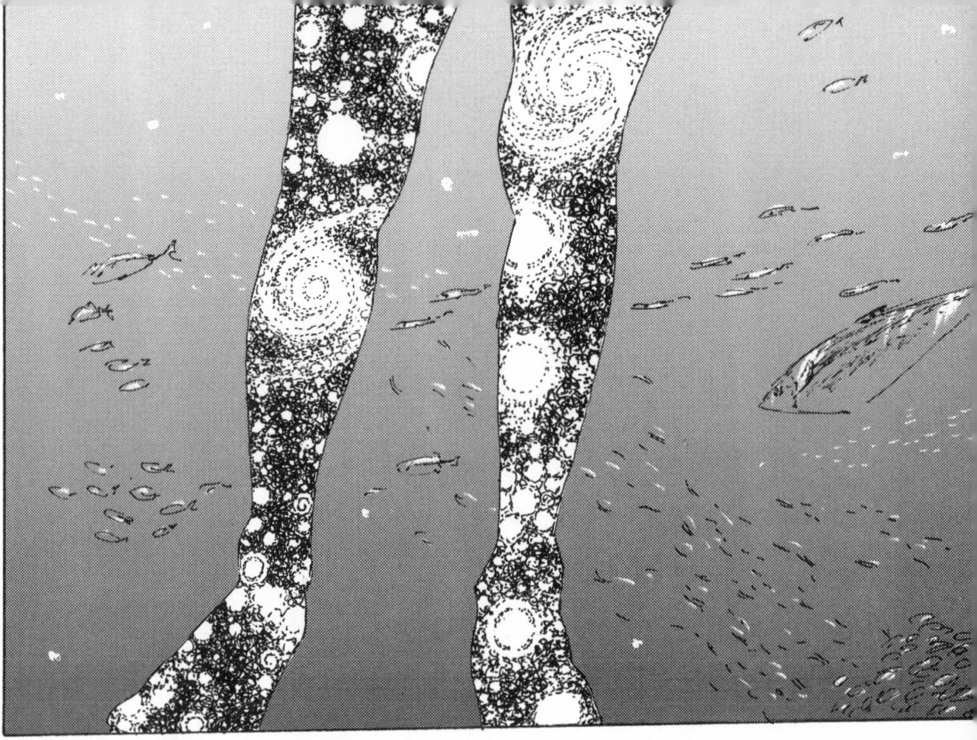
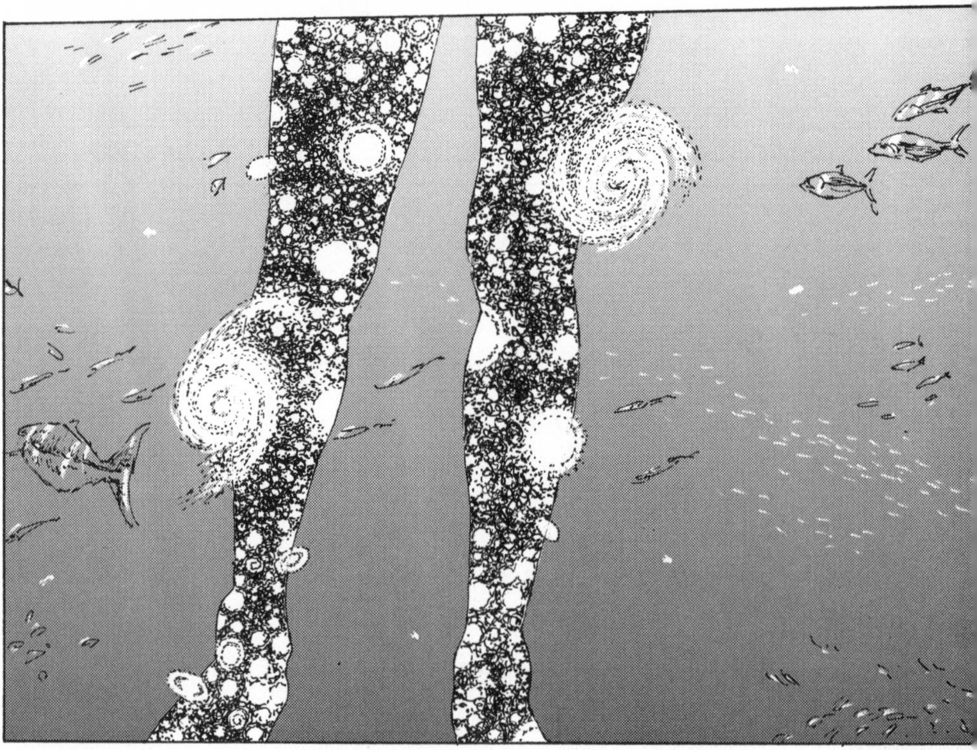

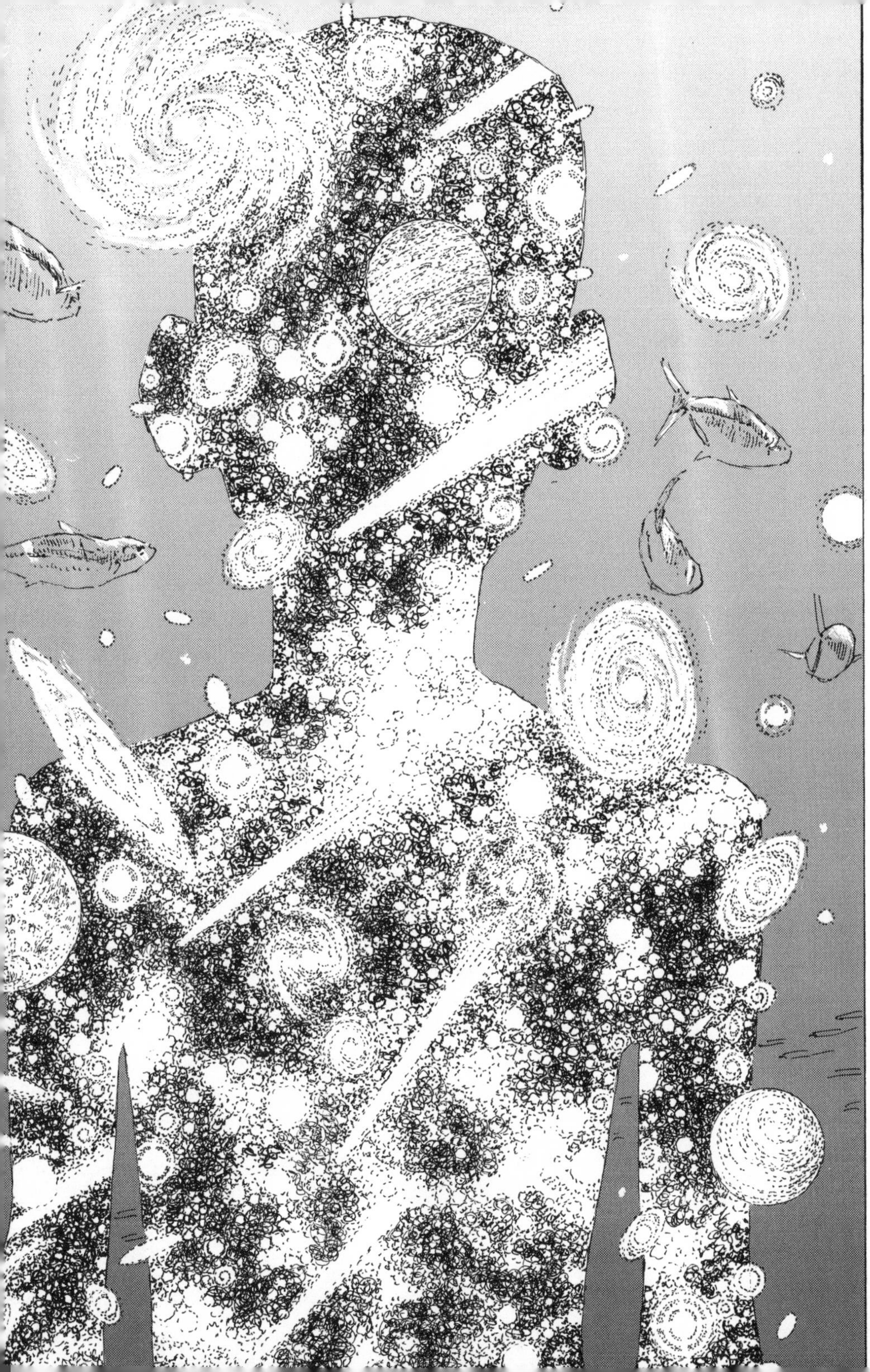

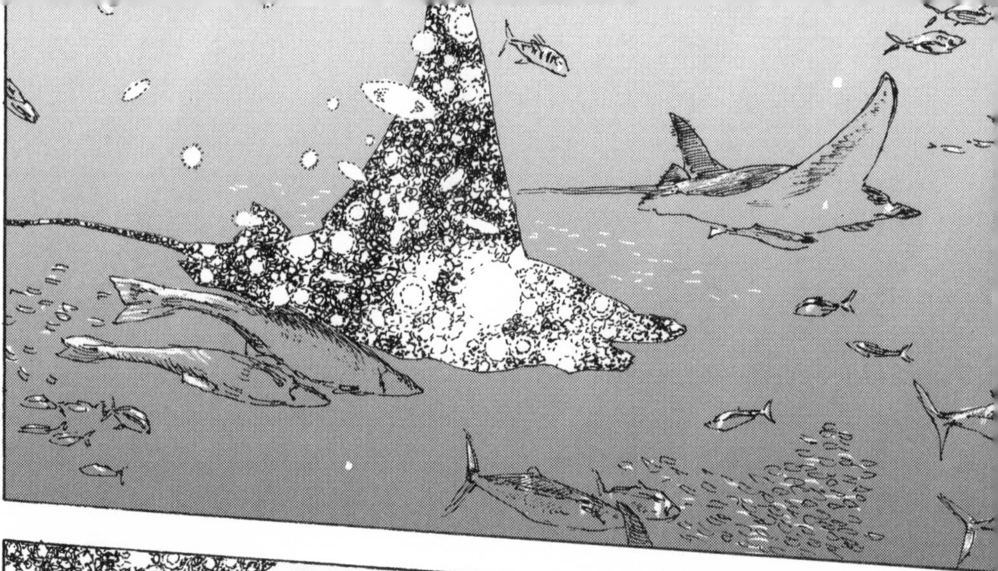
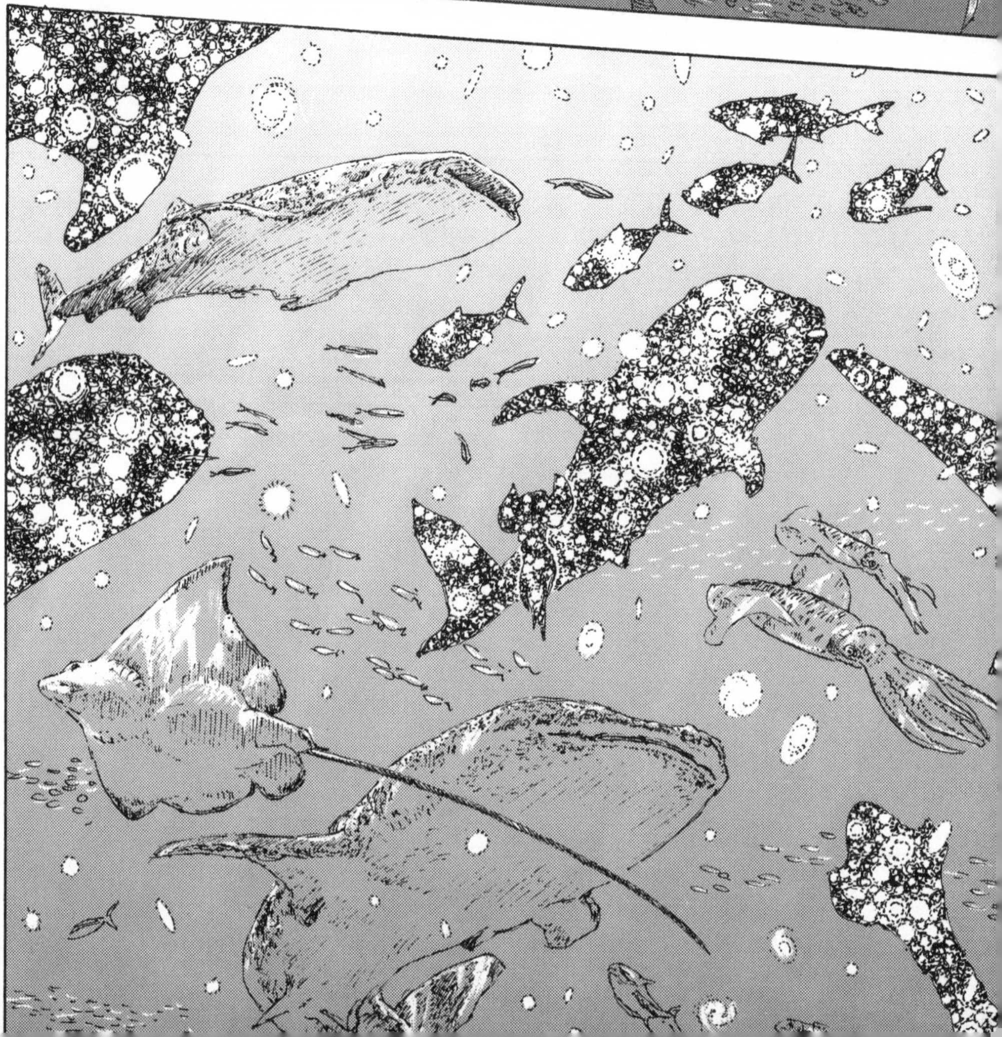

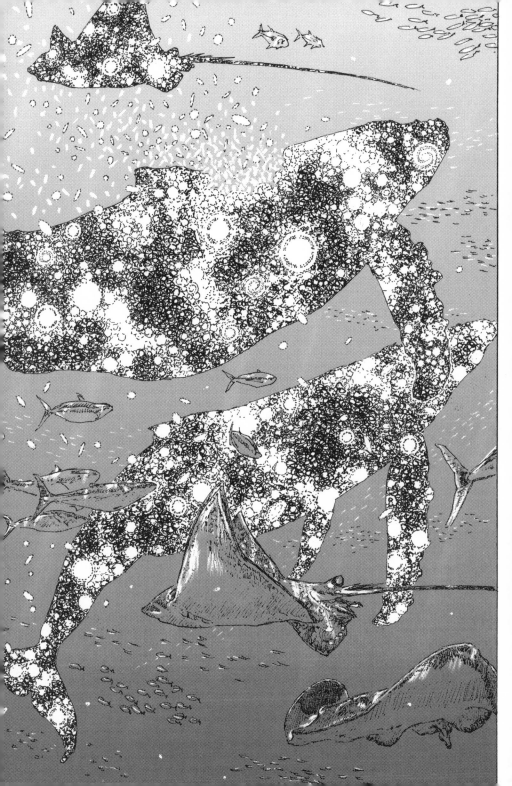

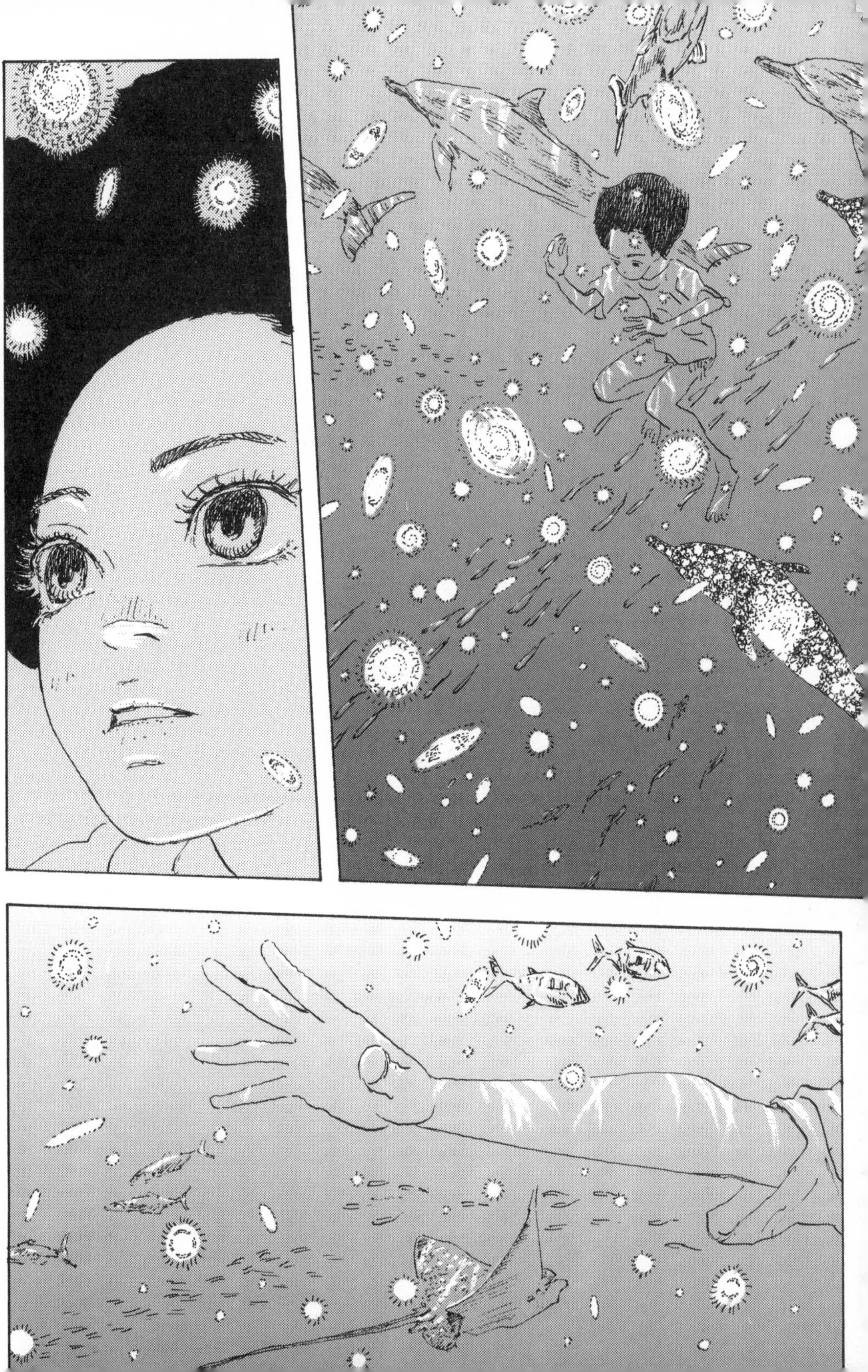

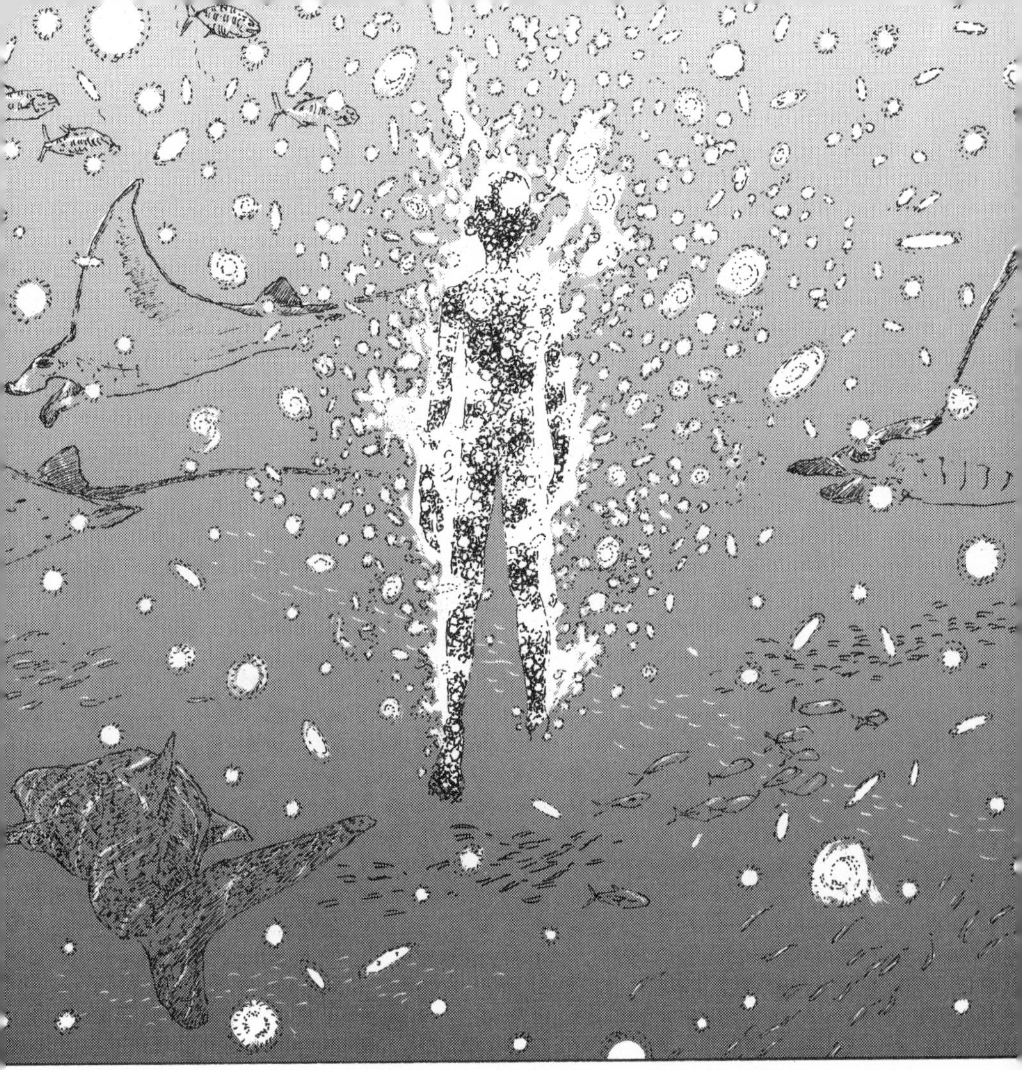
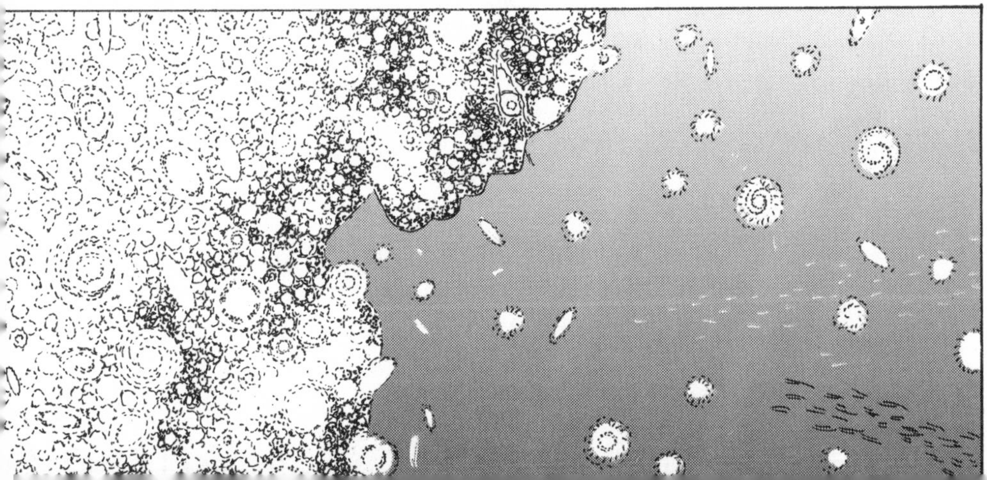

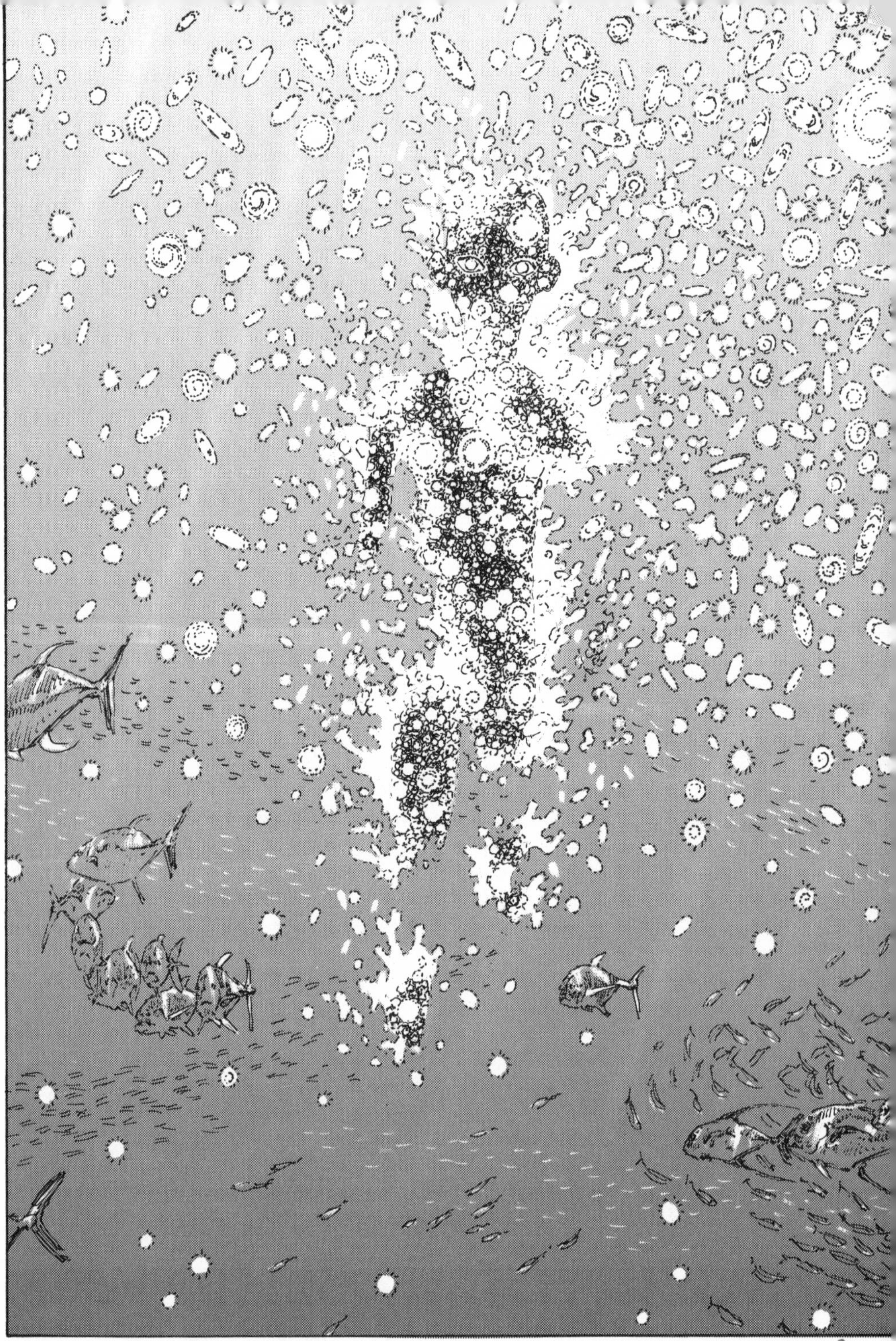

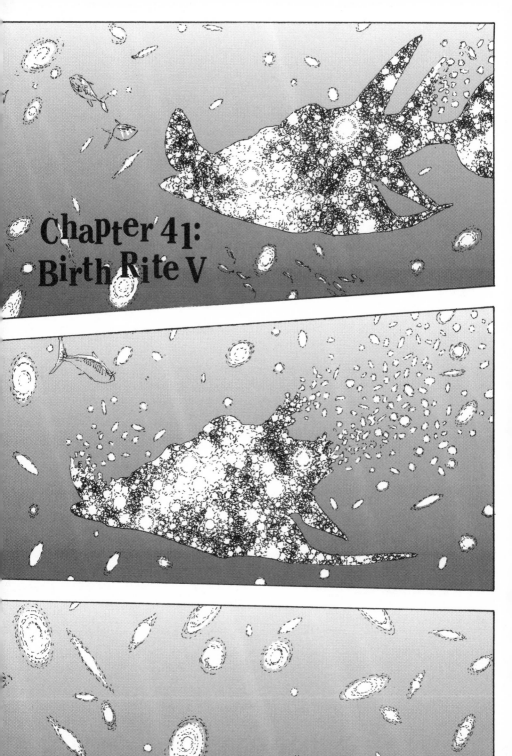

Chapter 41:
Birth Rite V

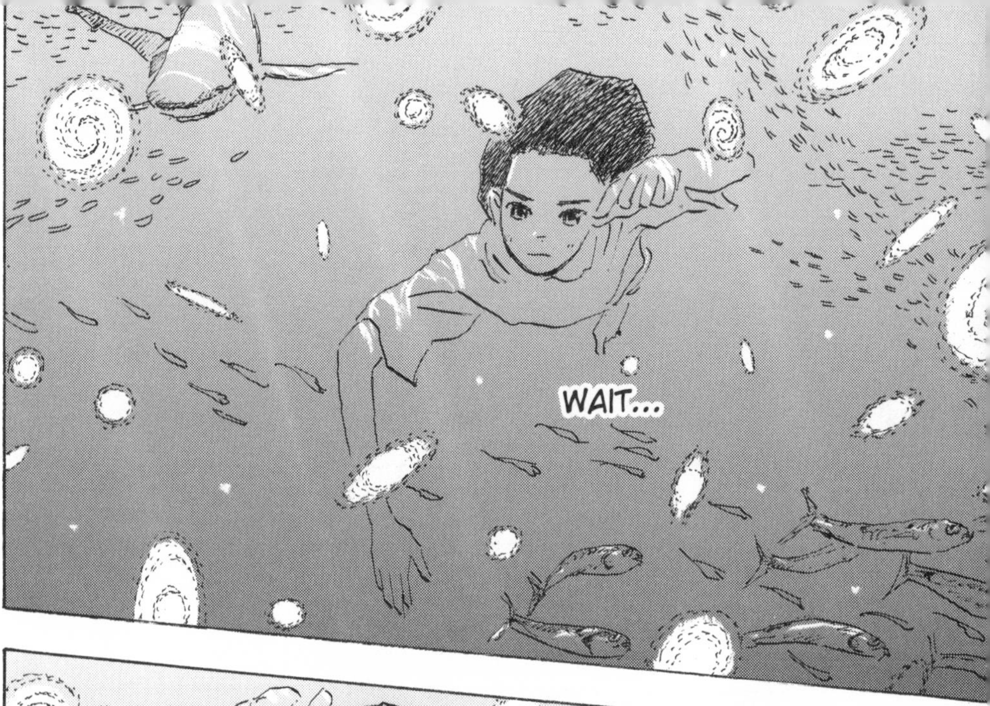
WAIT...
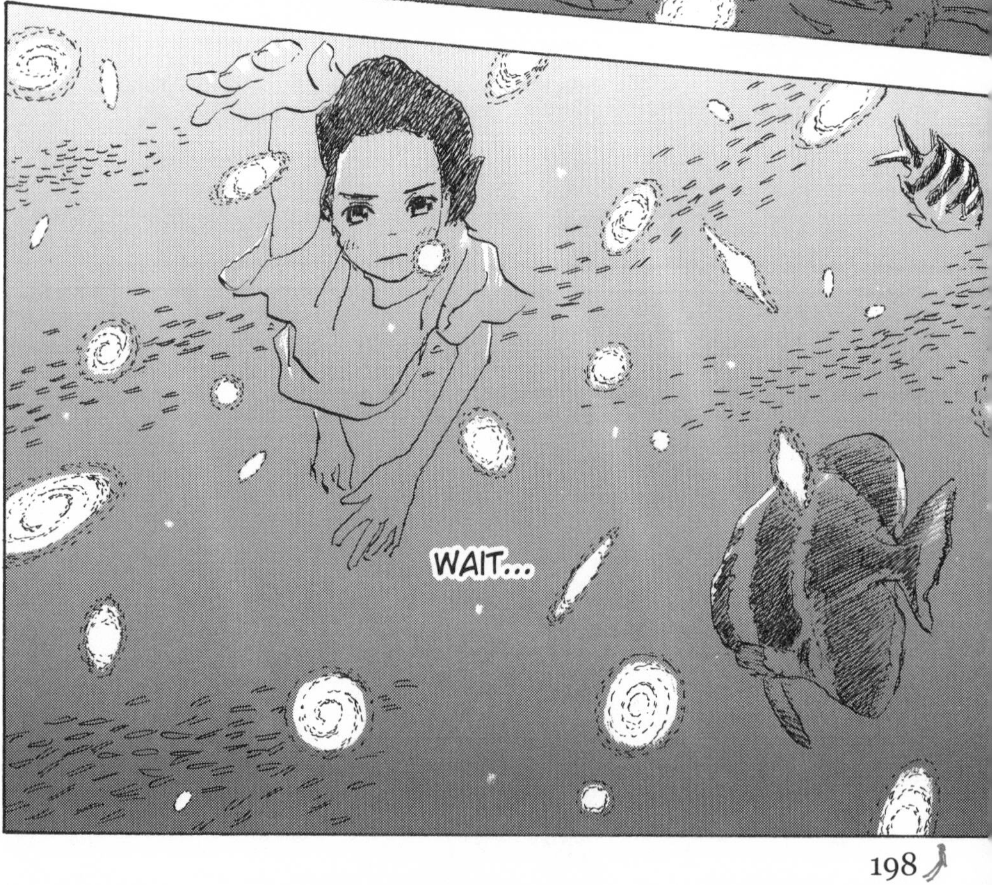
WAIT...

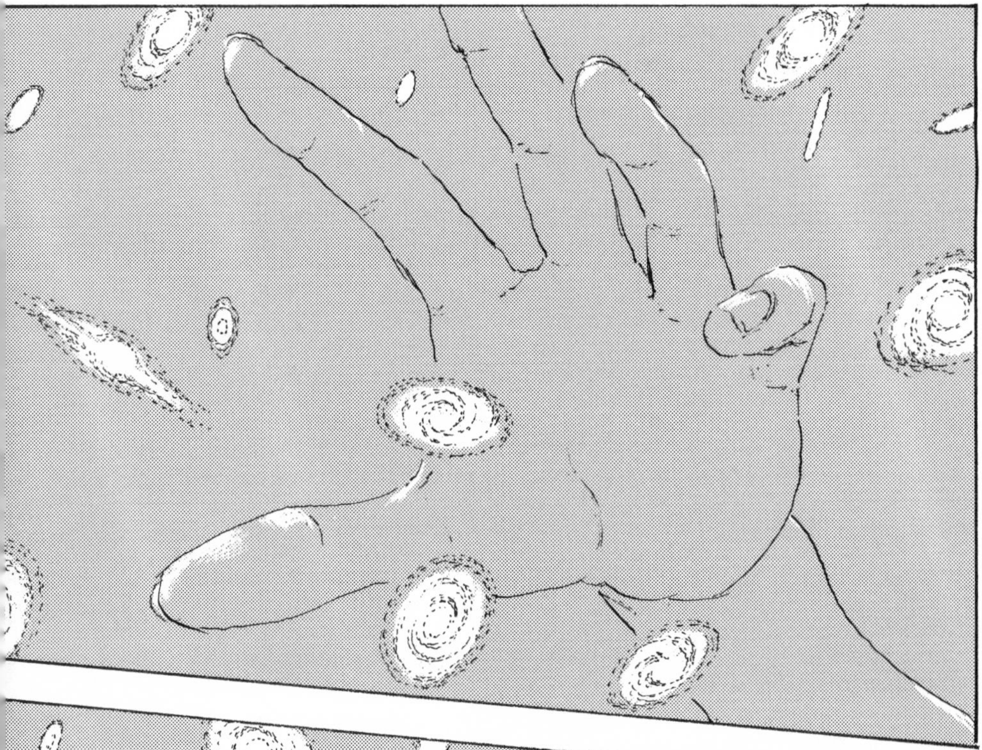

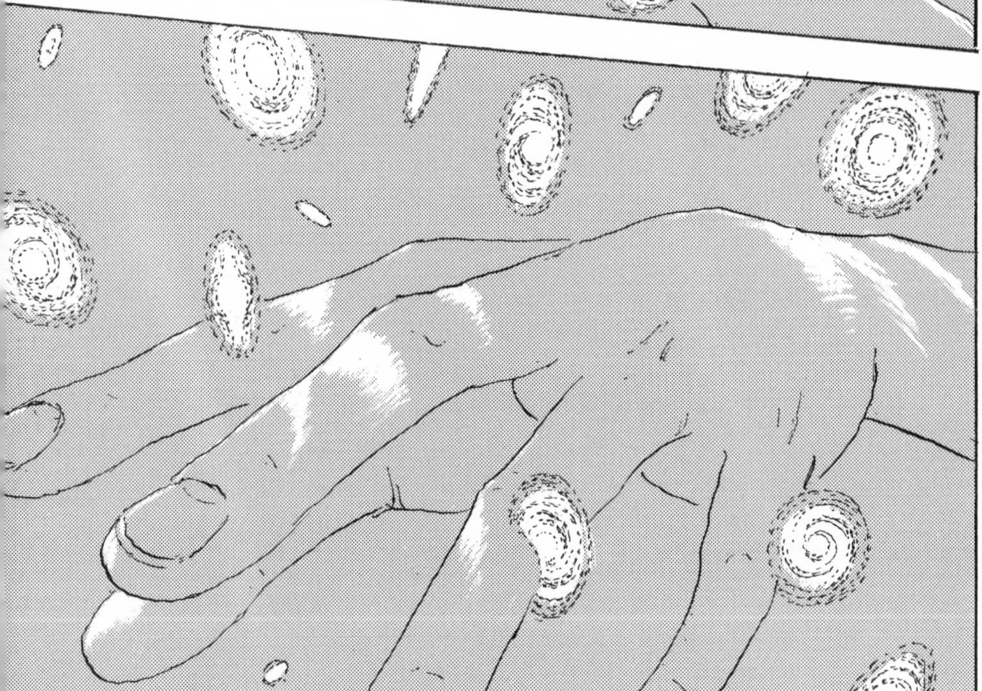

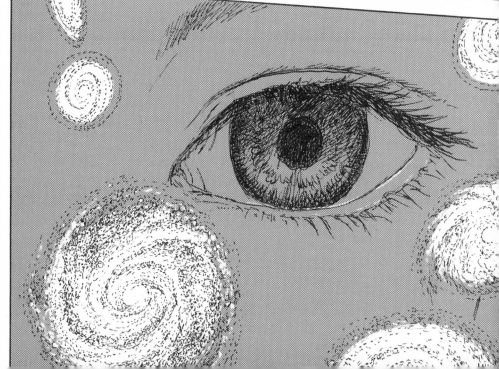

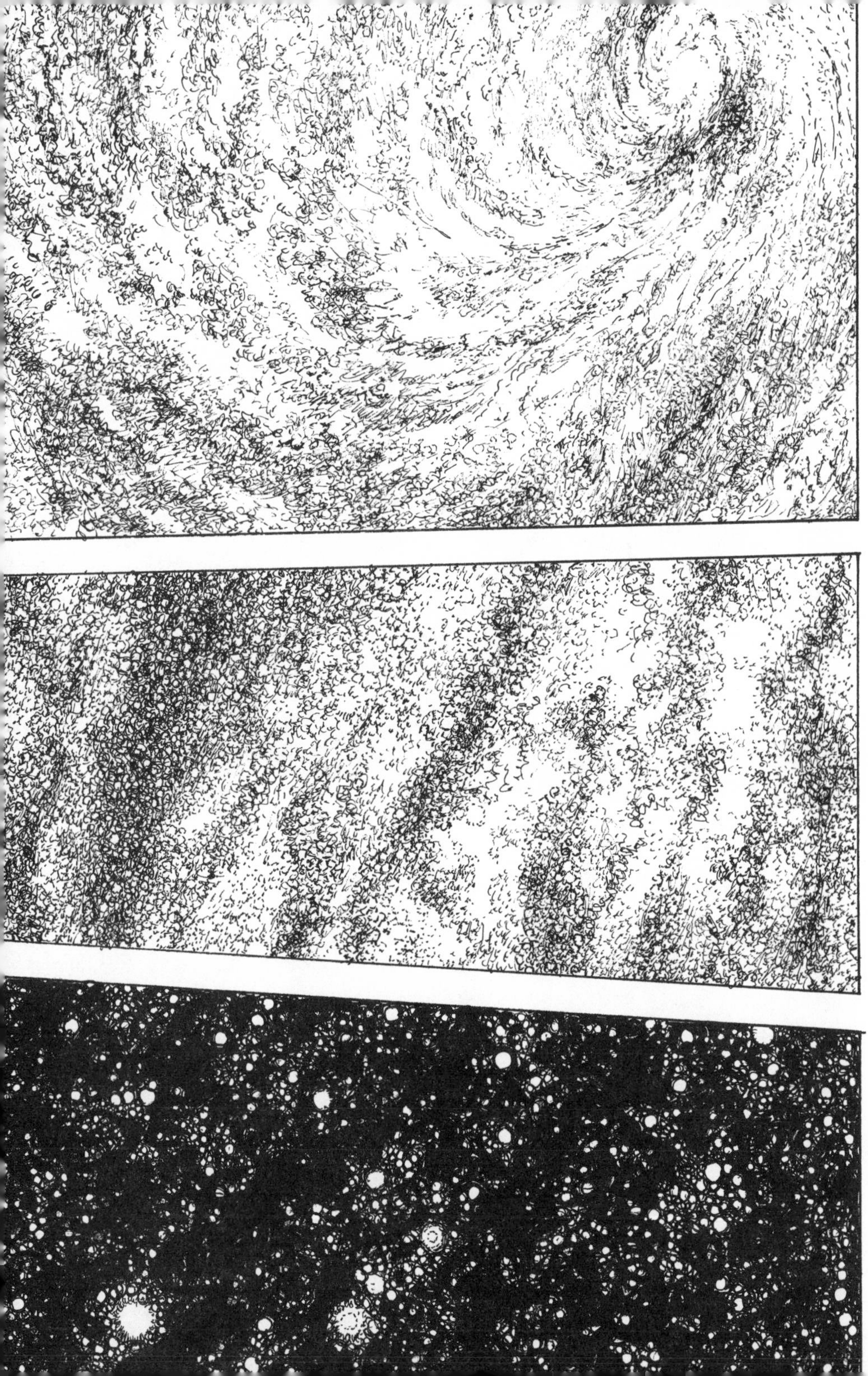

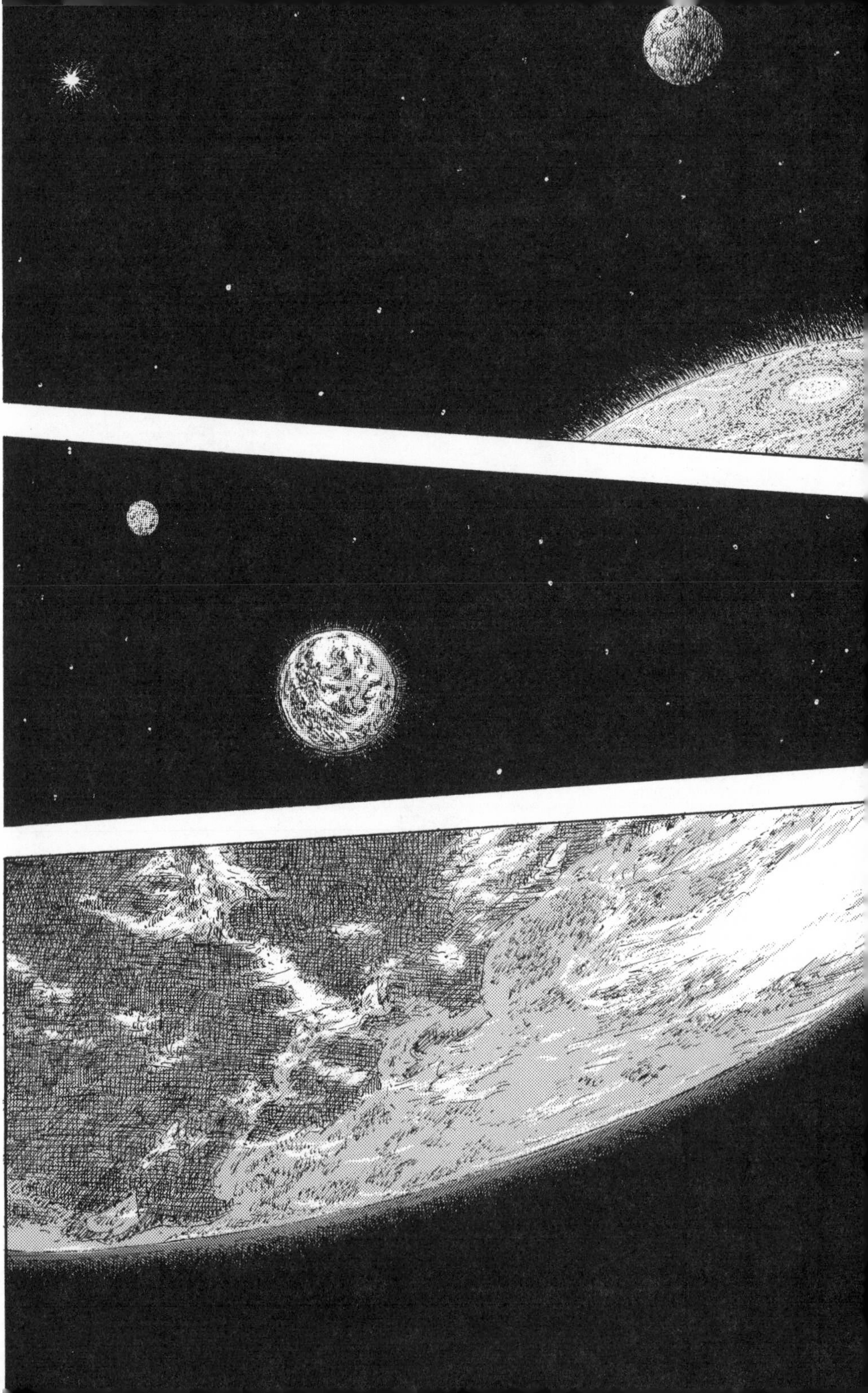

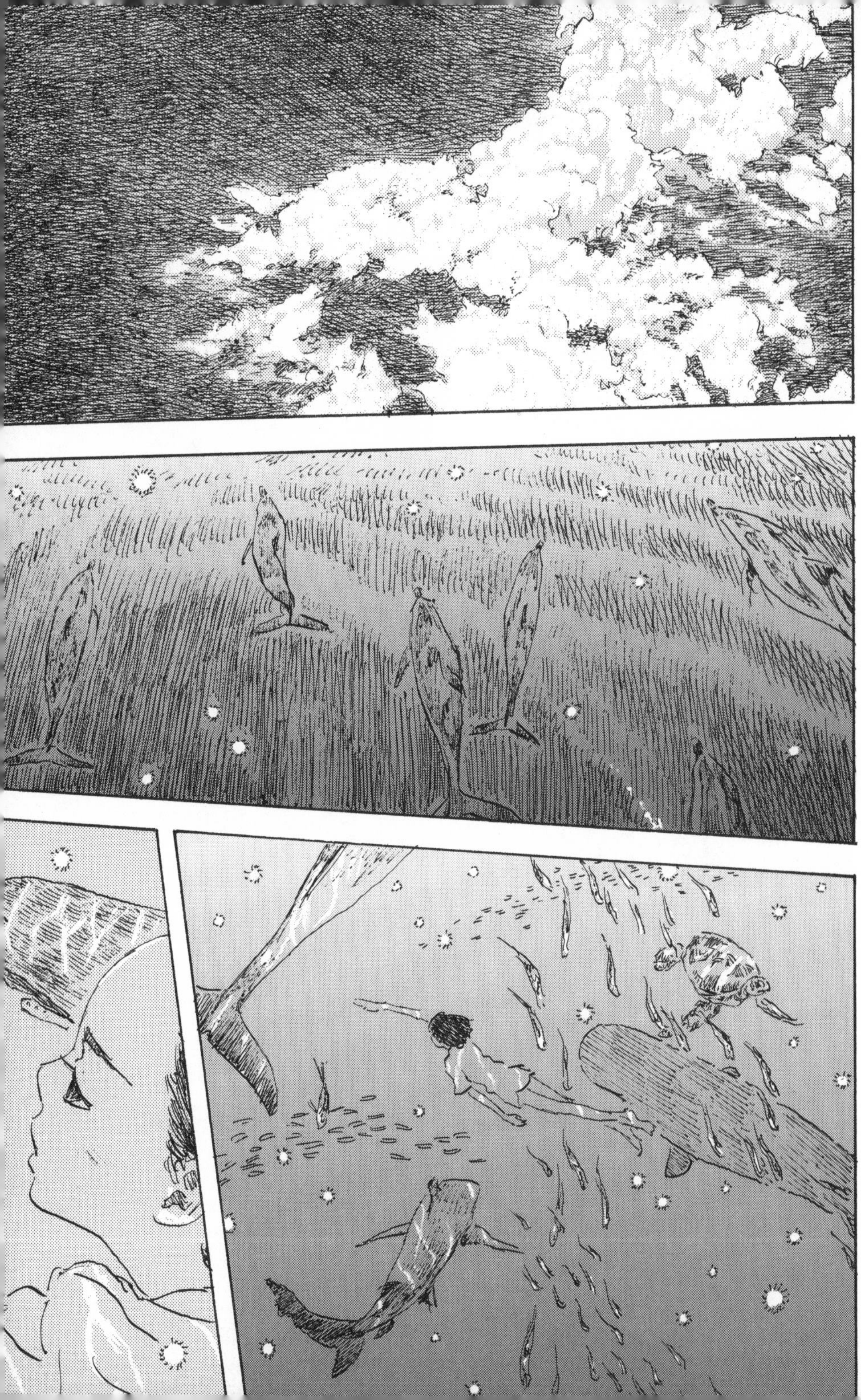

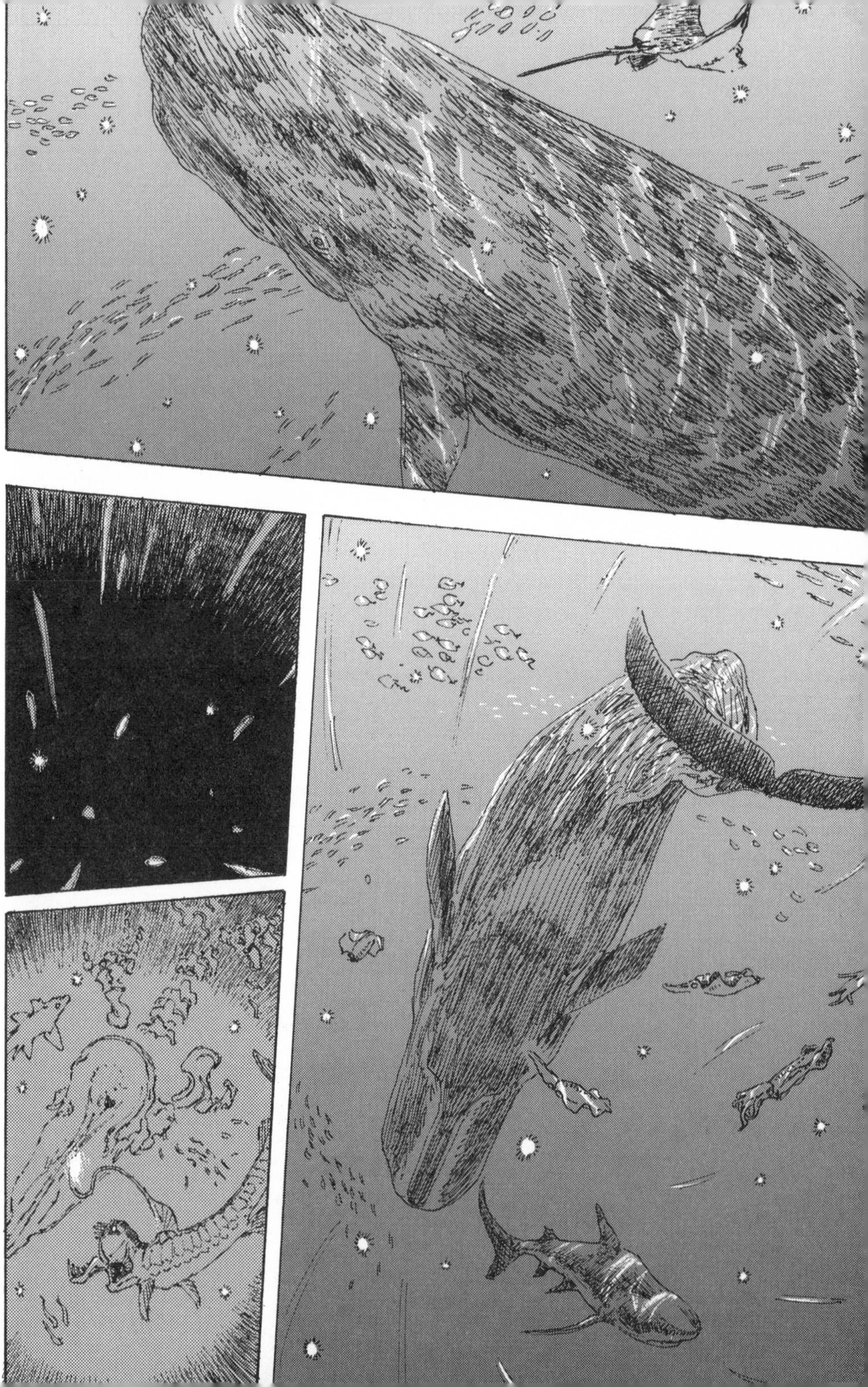

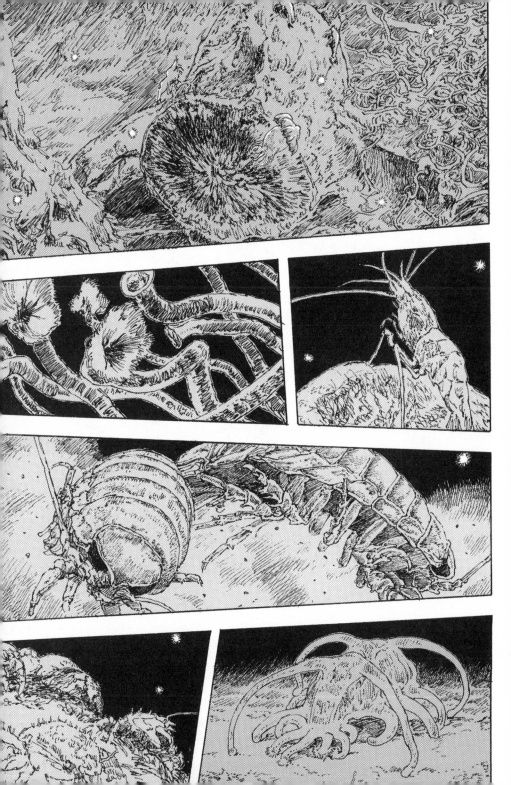

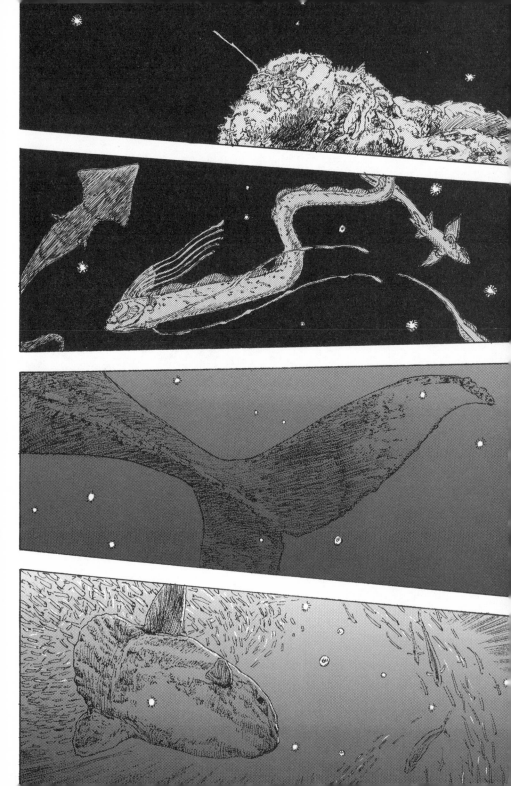

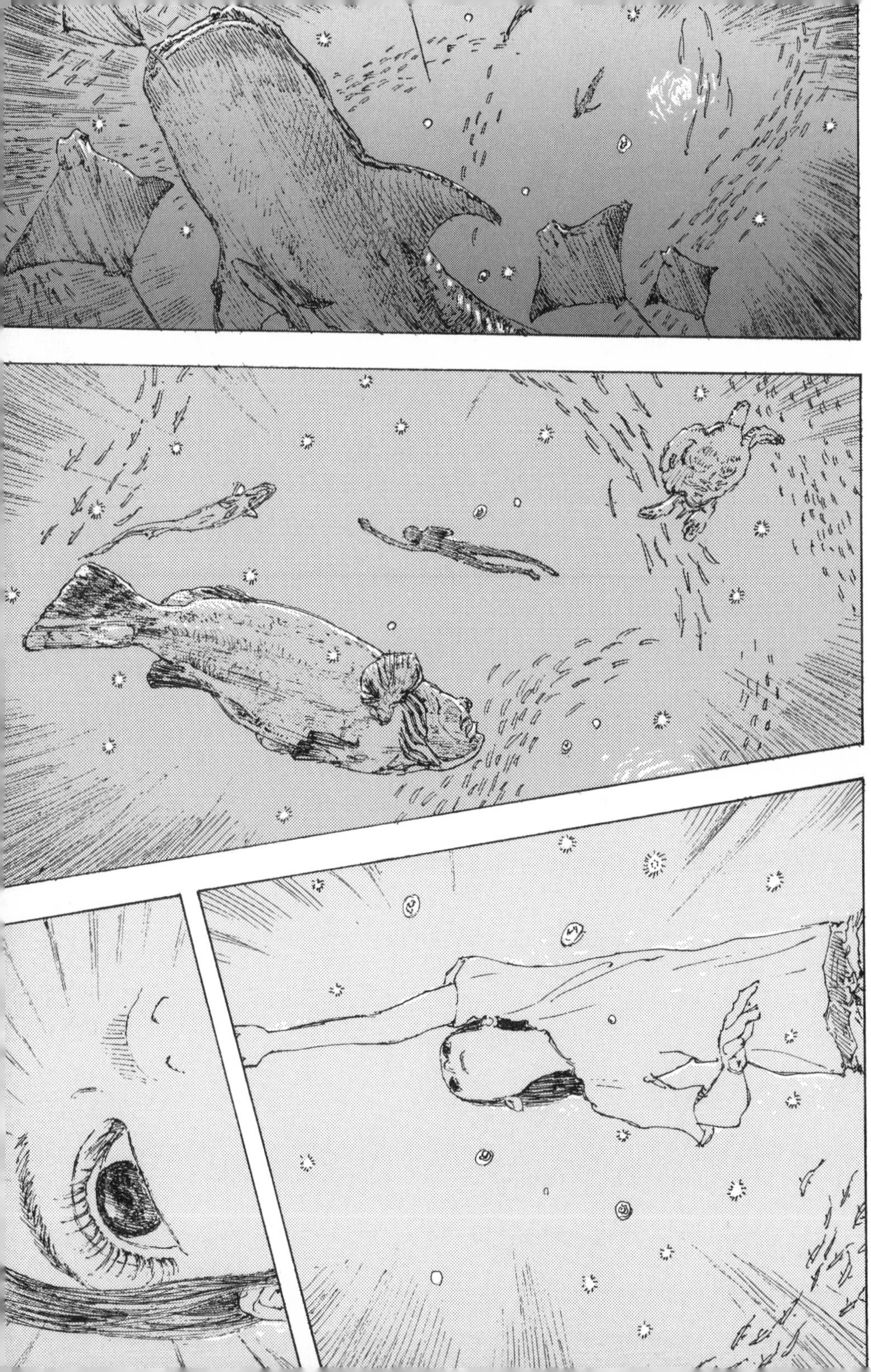

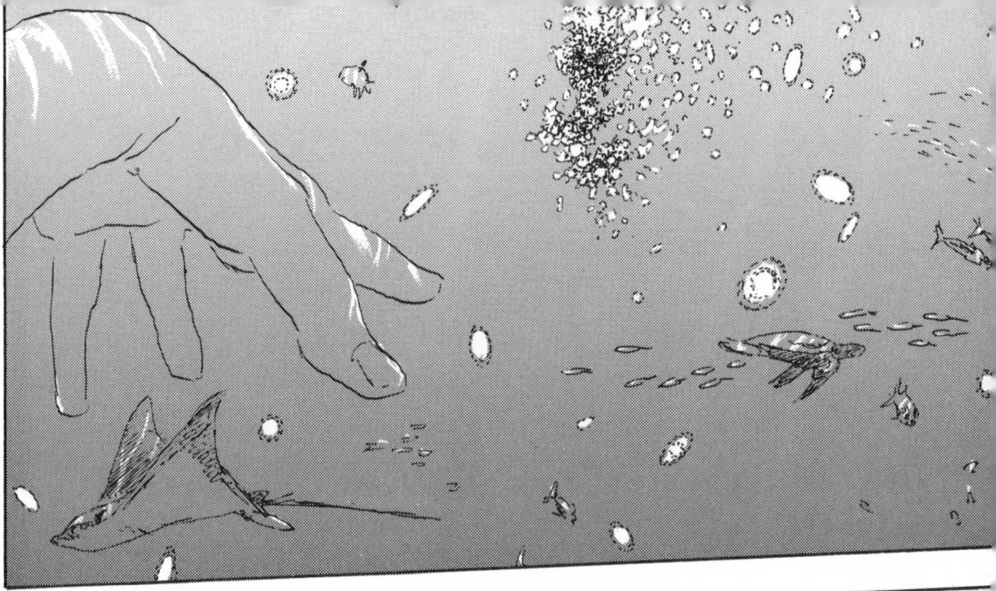
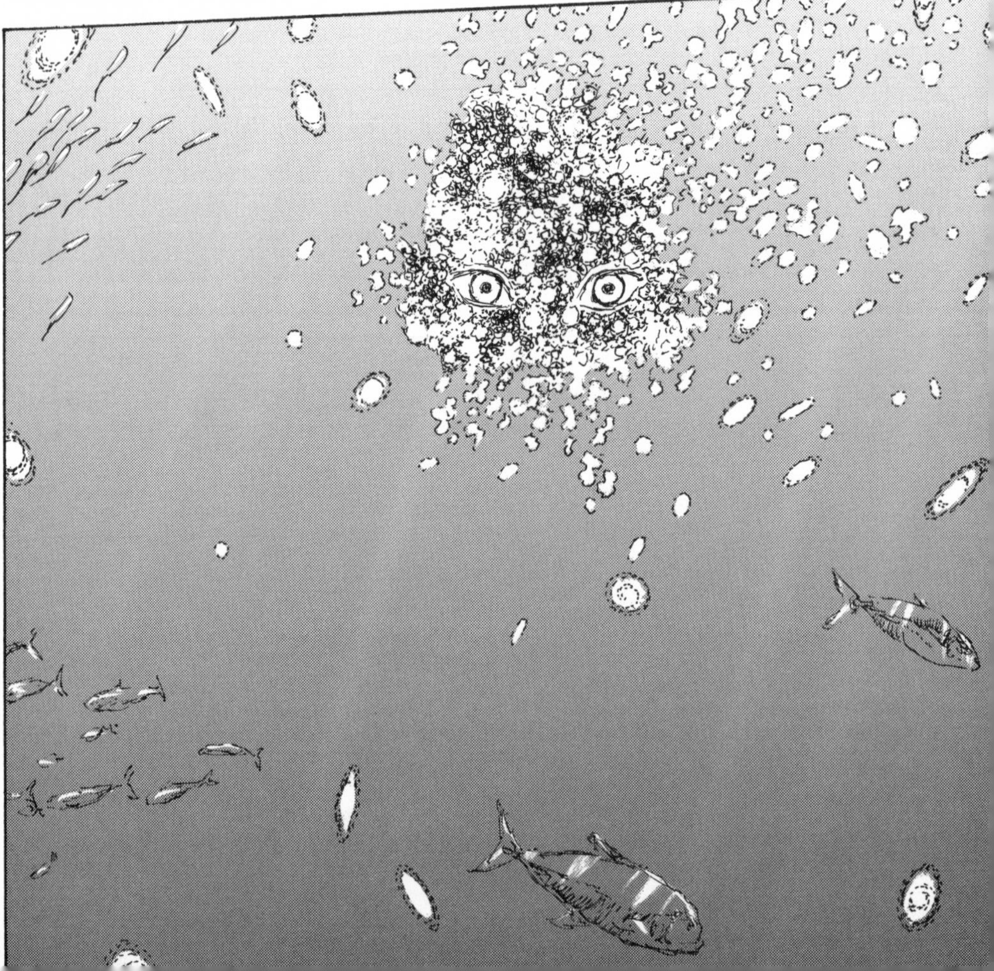

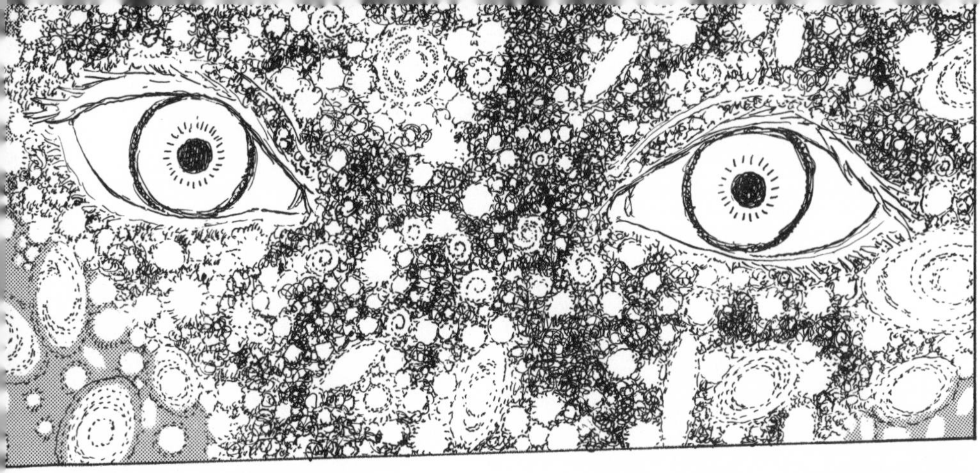
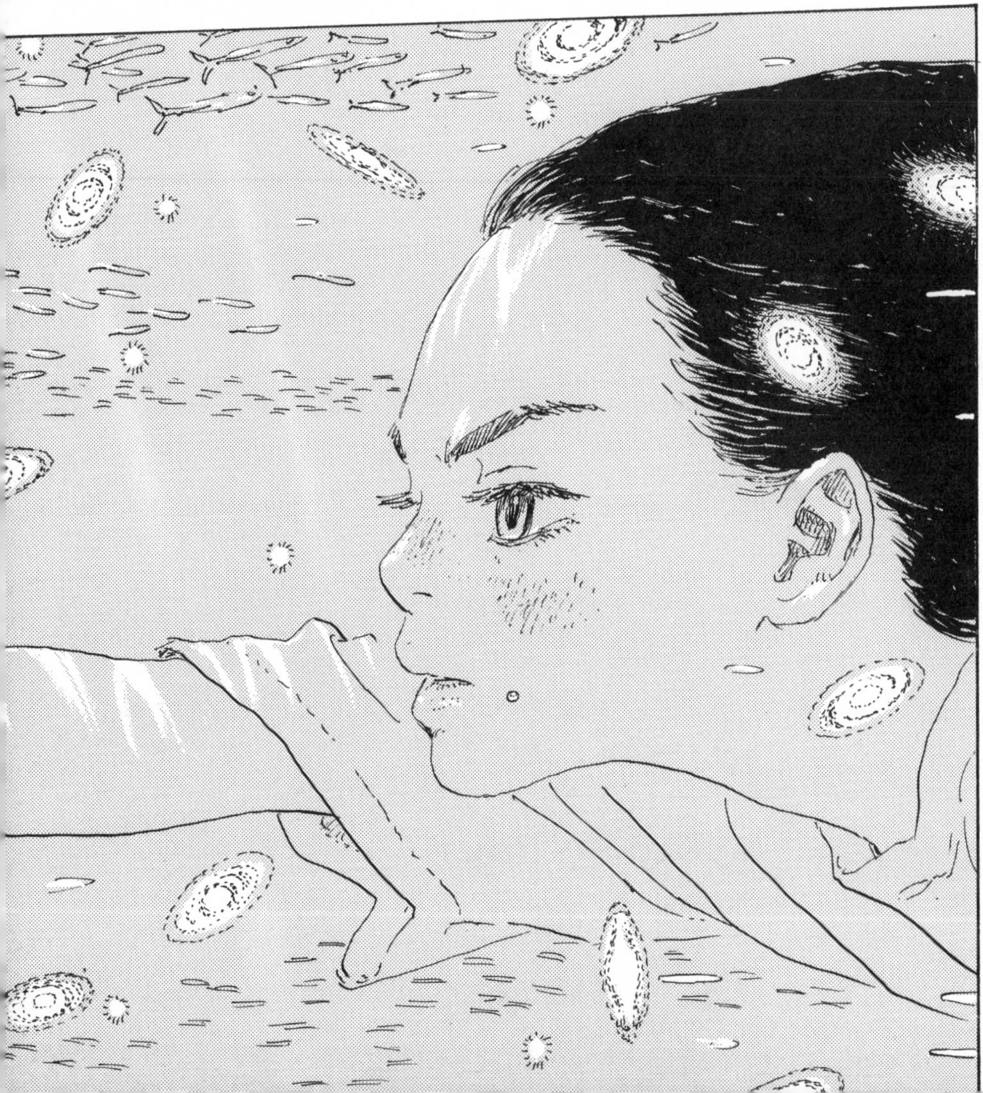

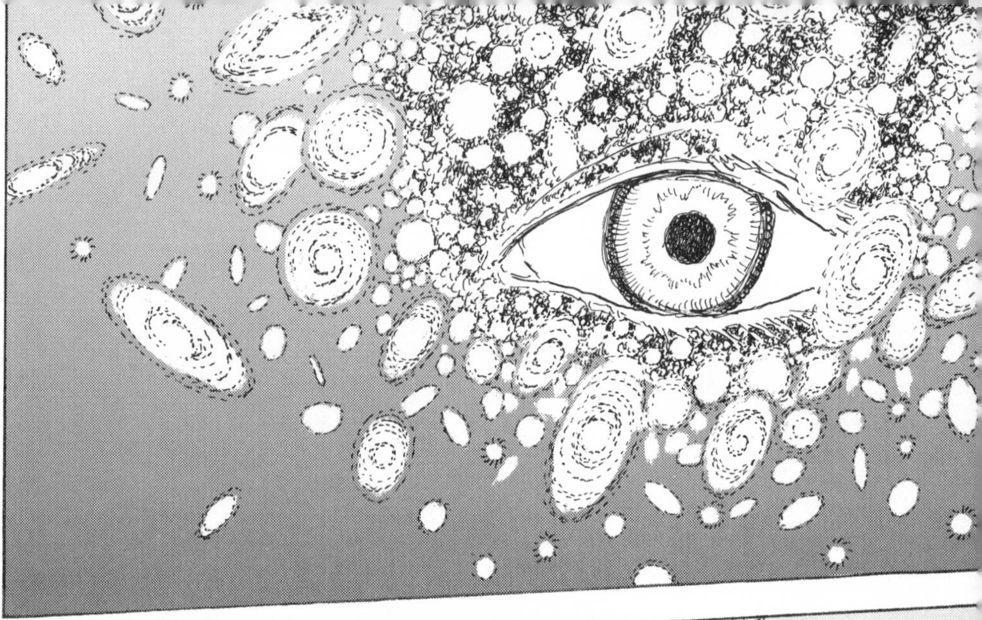

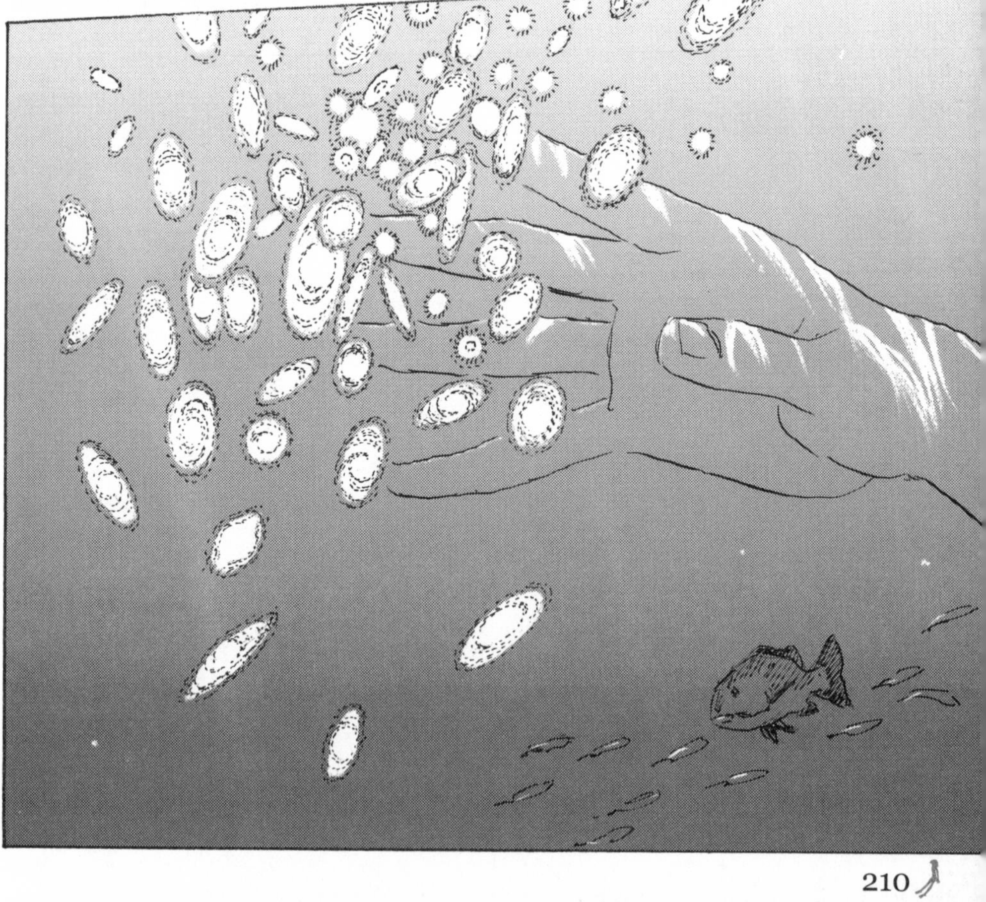

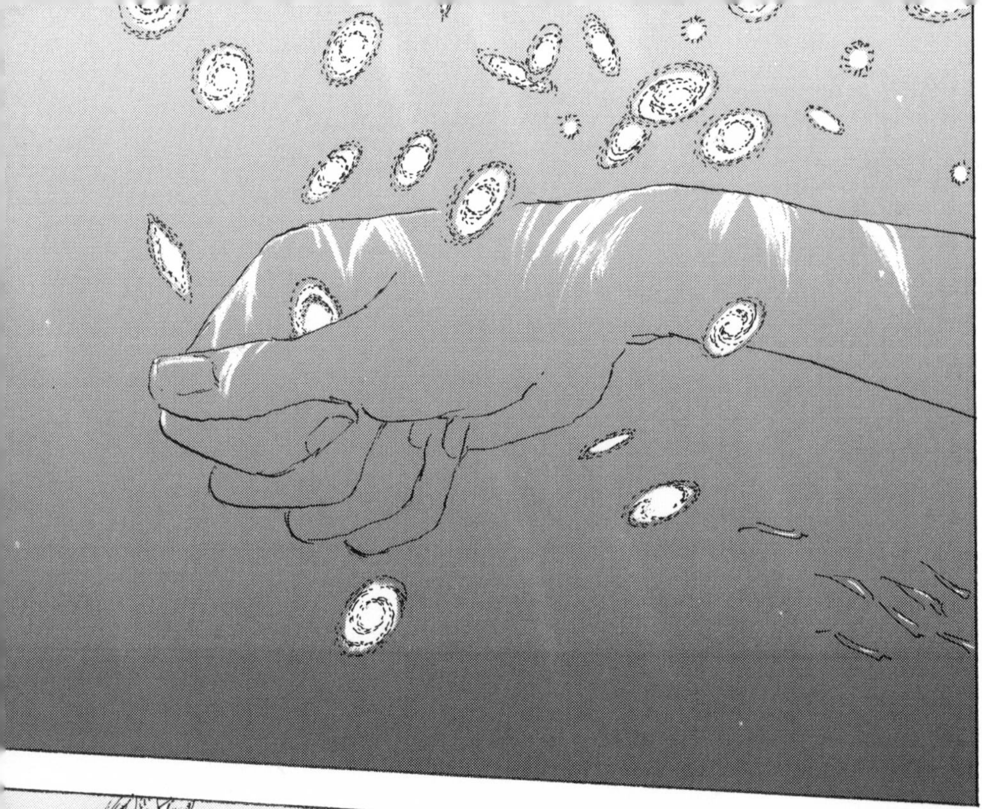
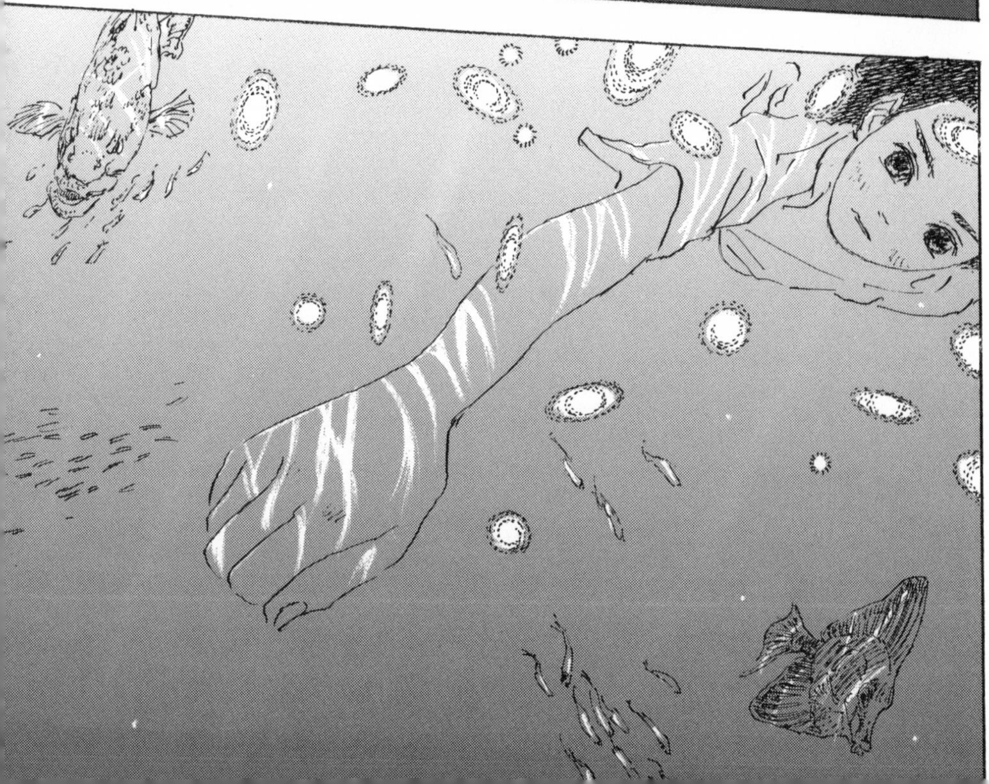

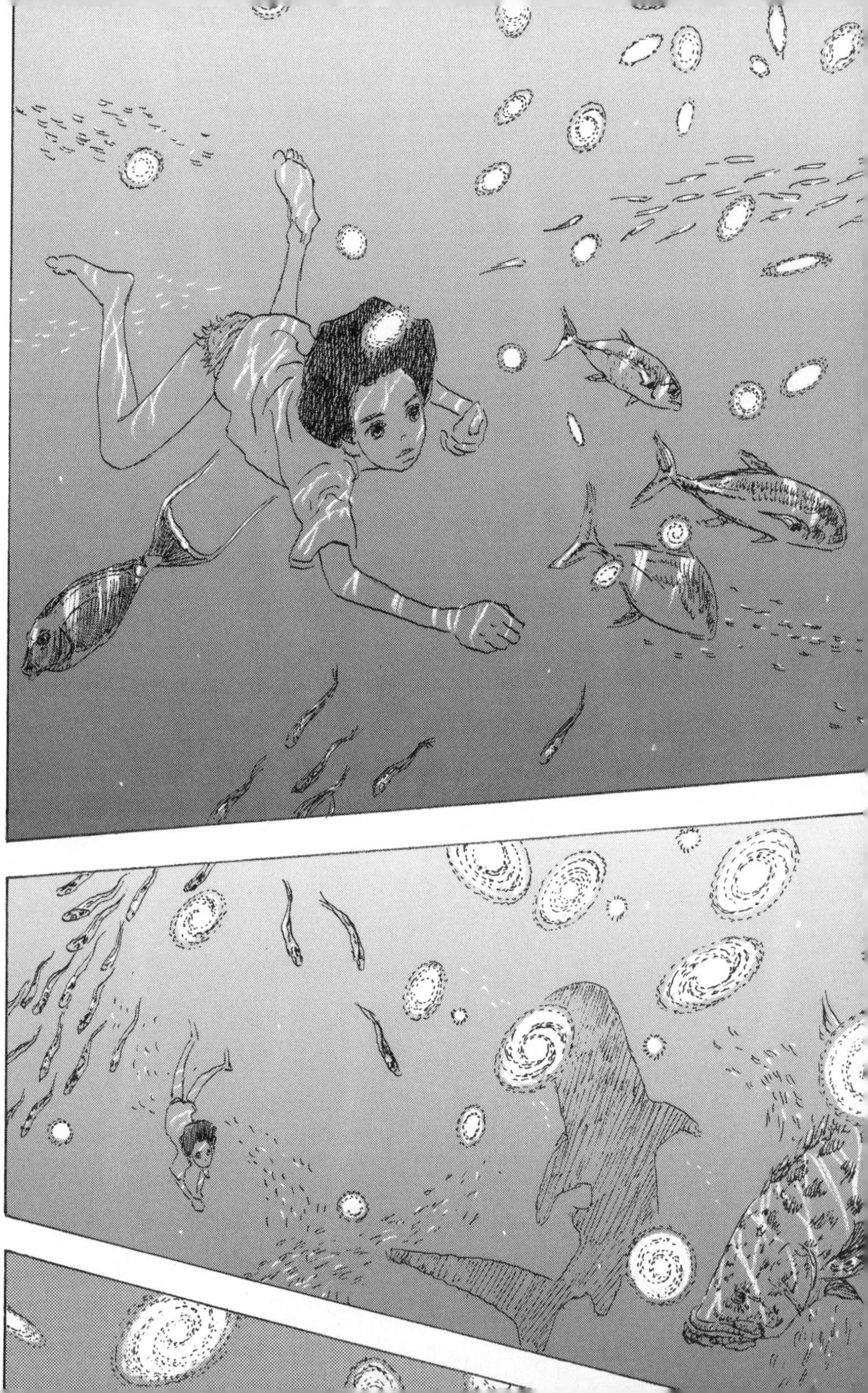

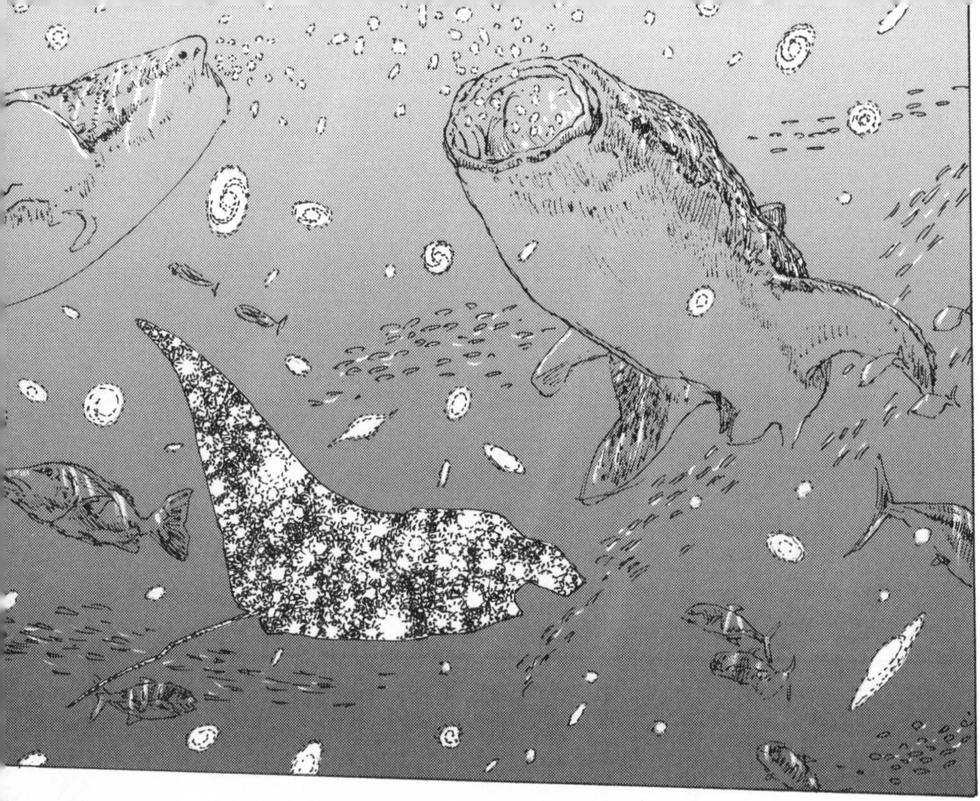
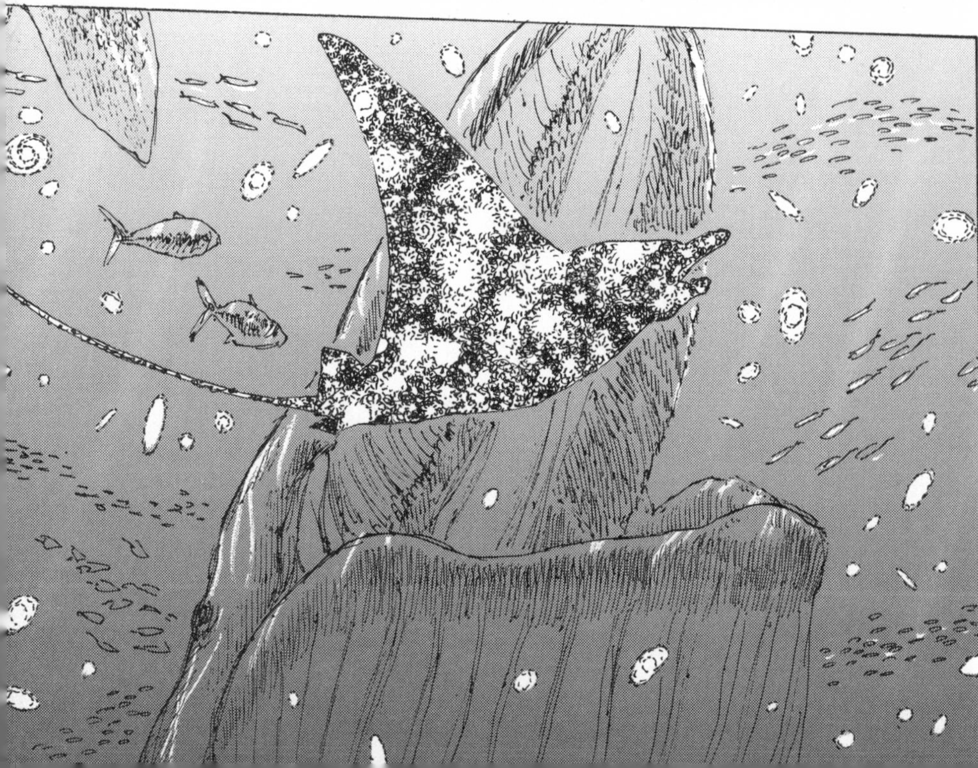

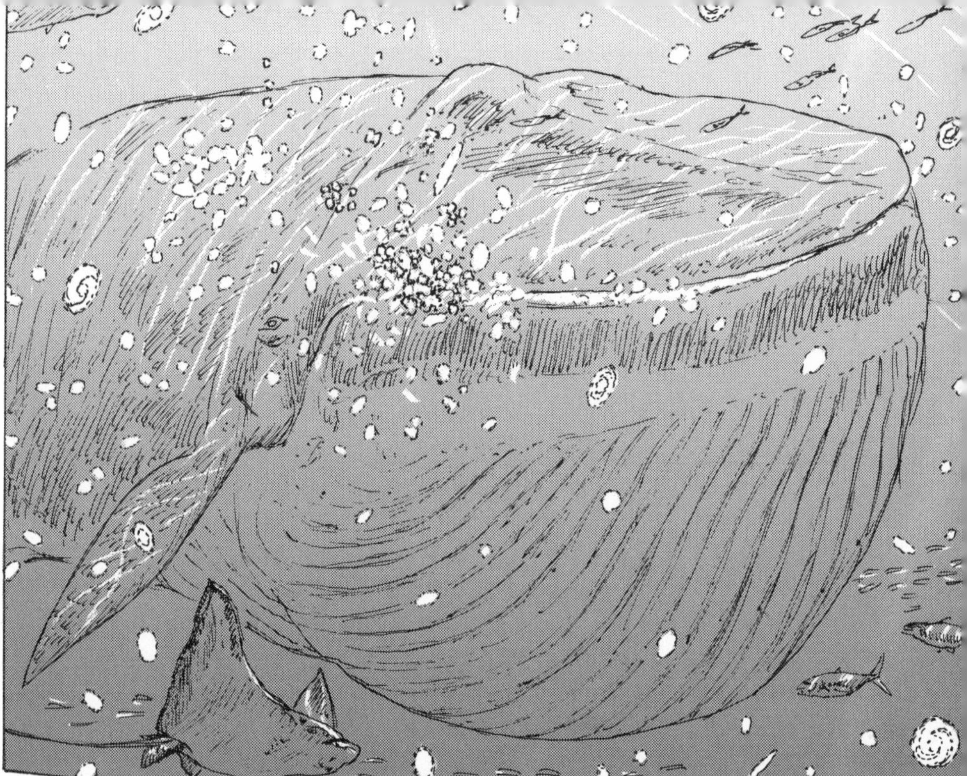
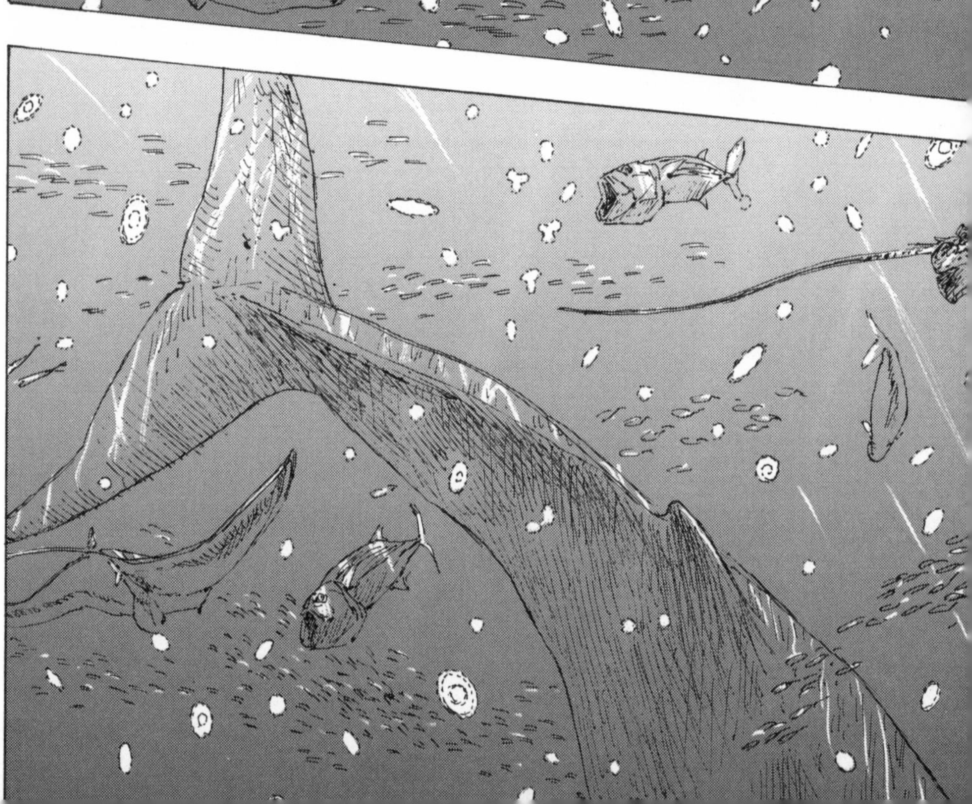

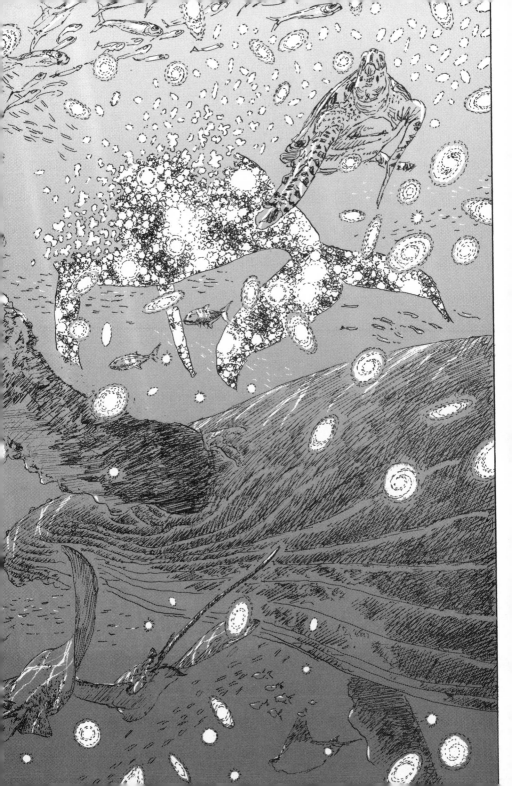

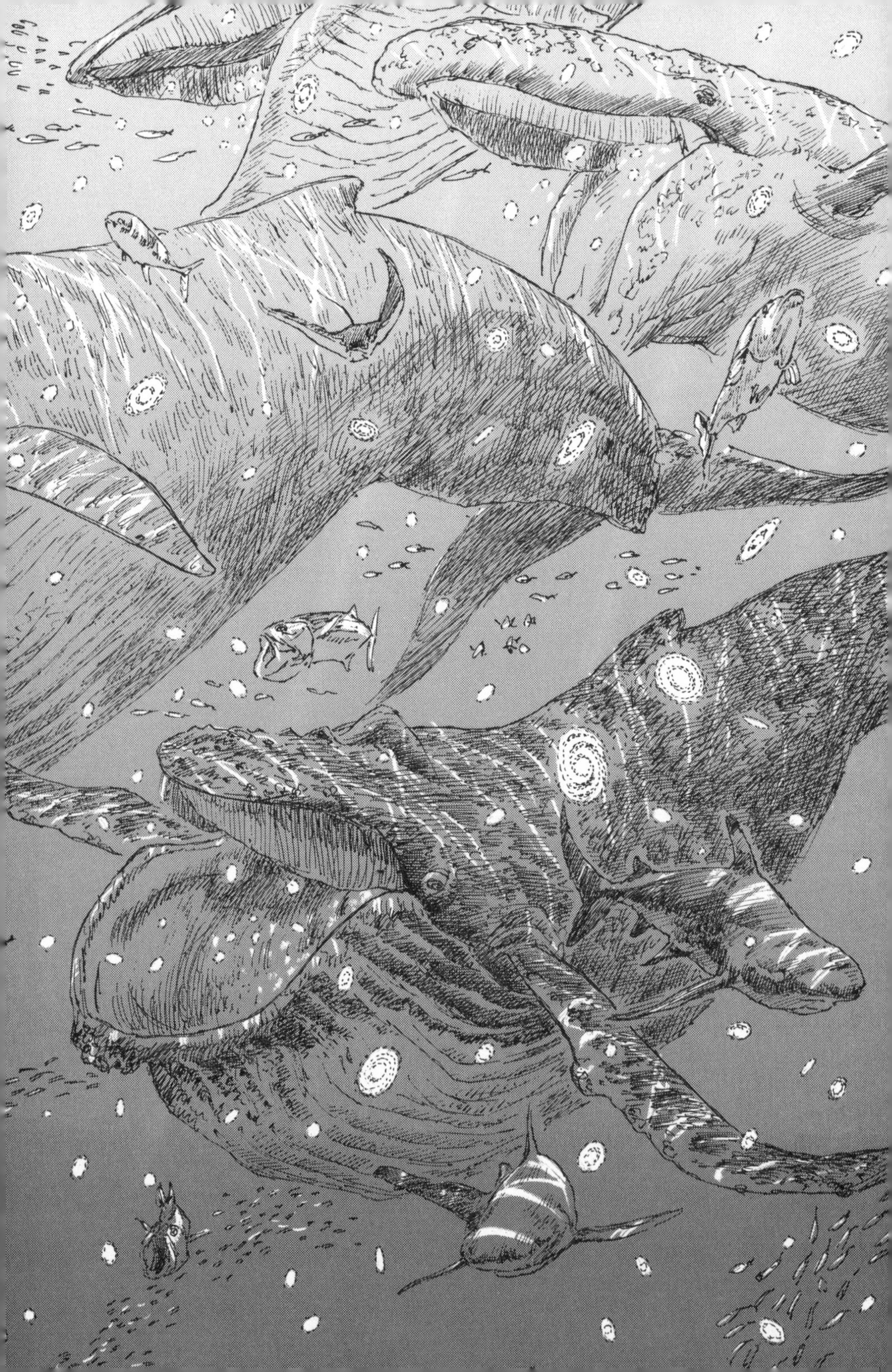

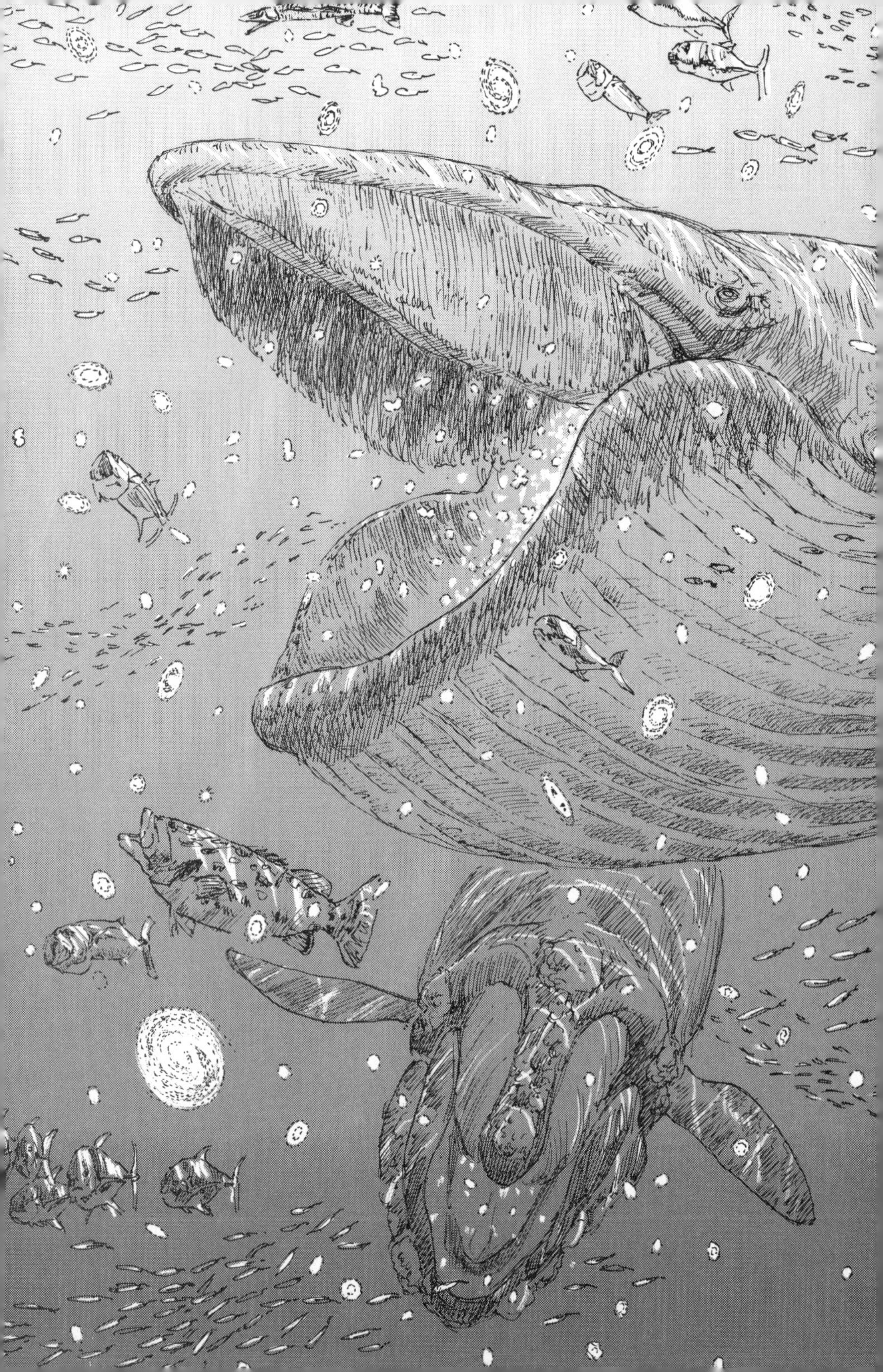

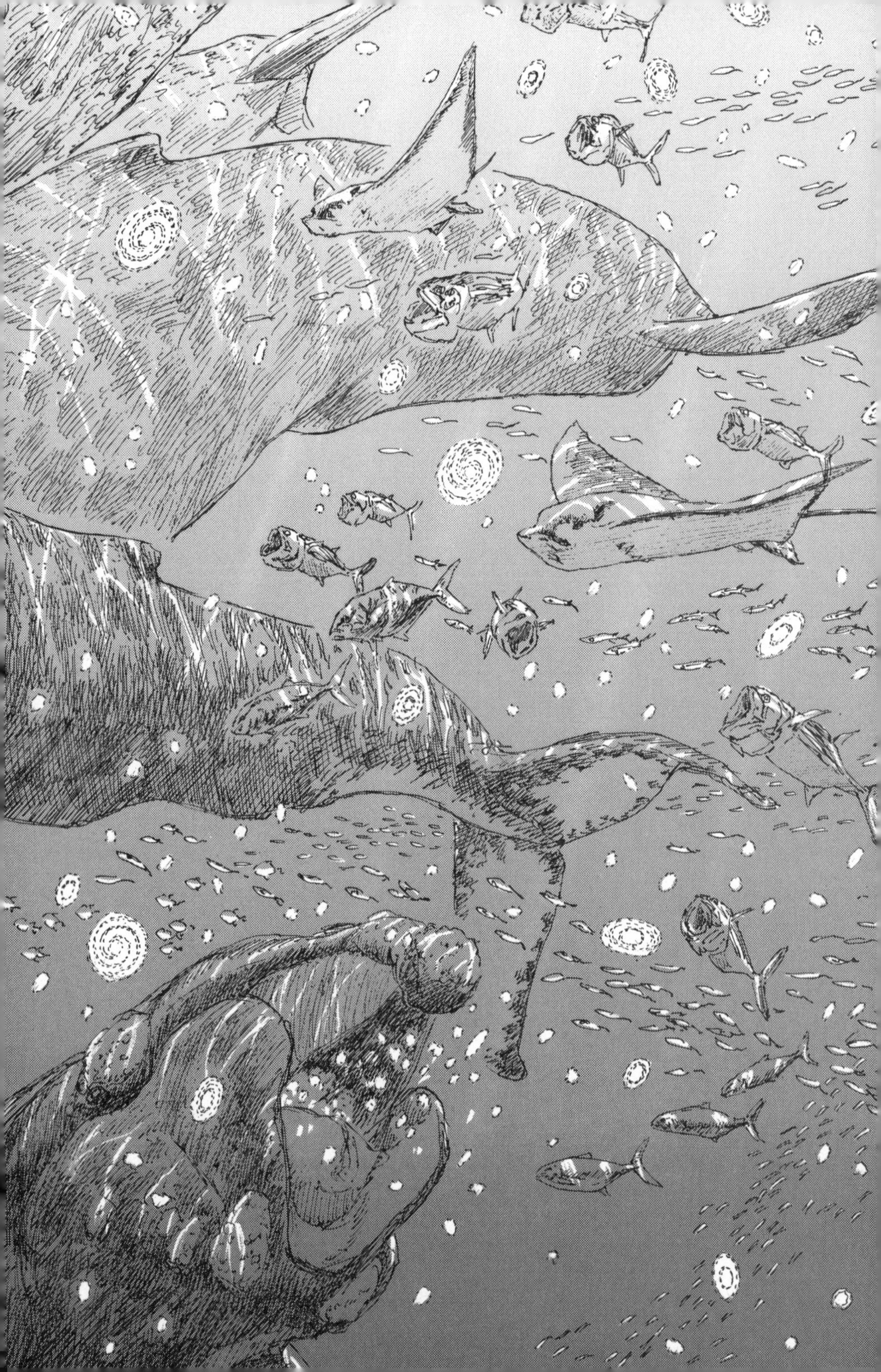

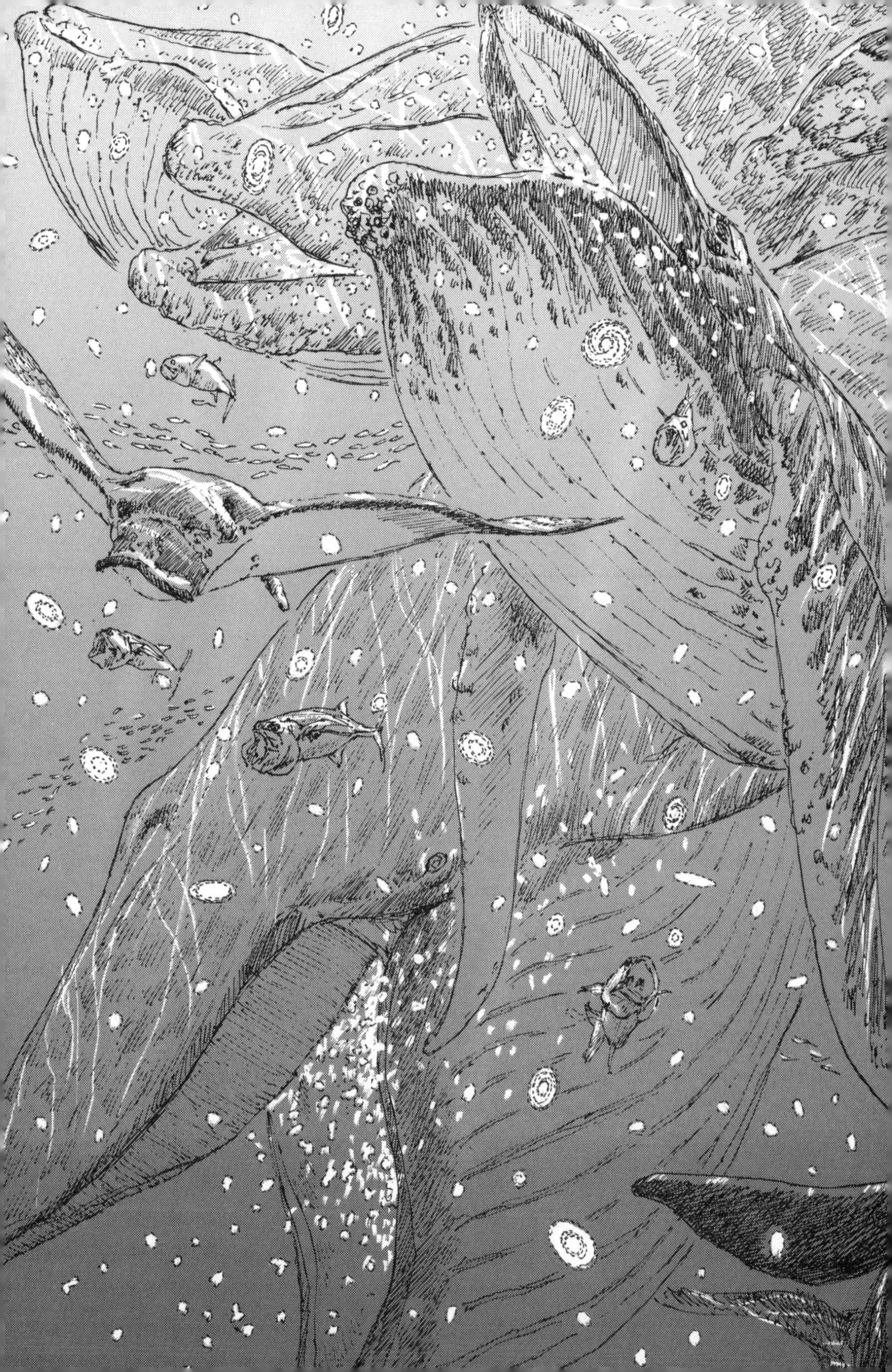

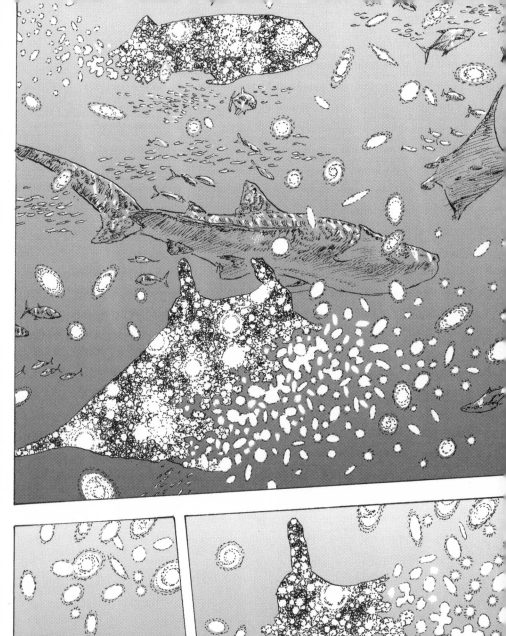
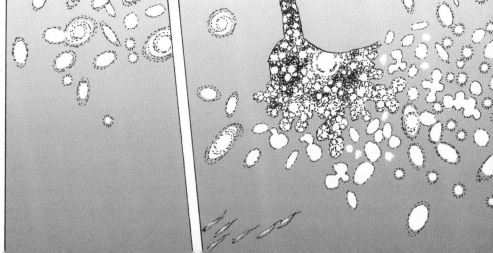

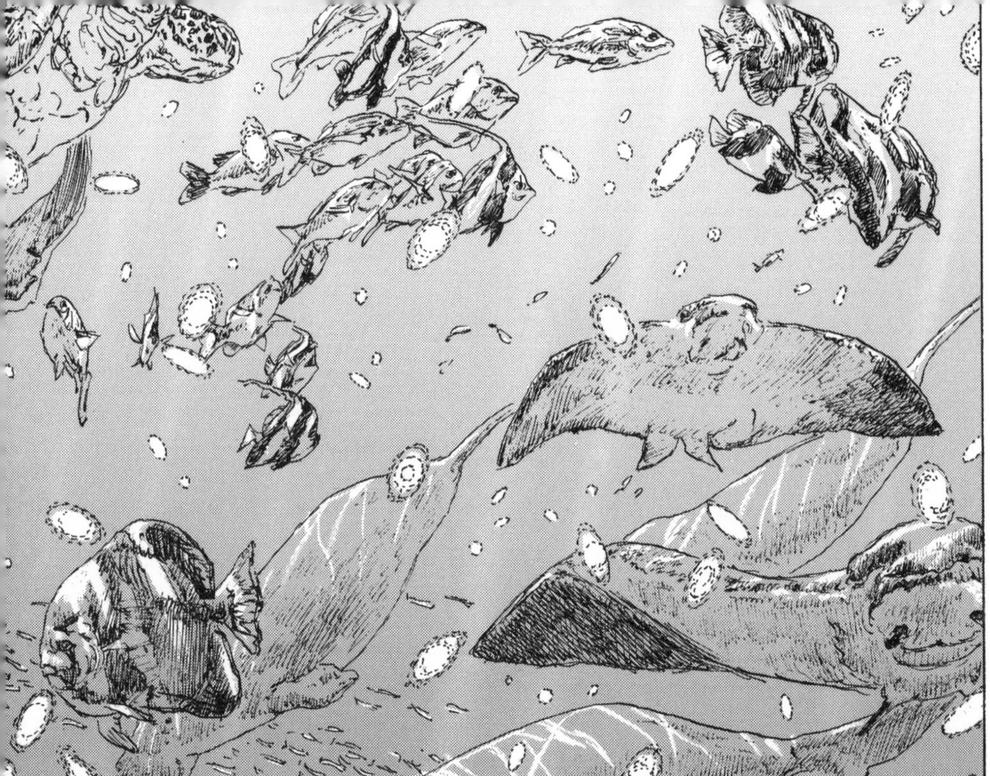
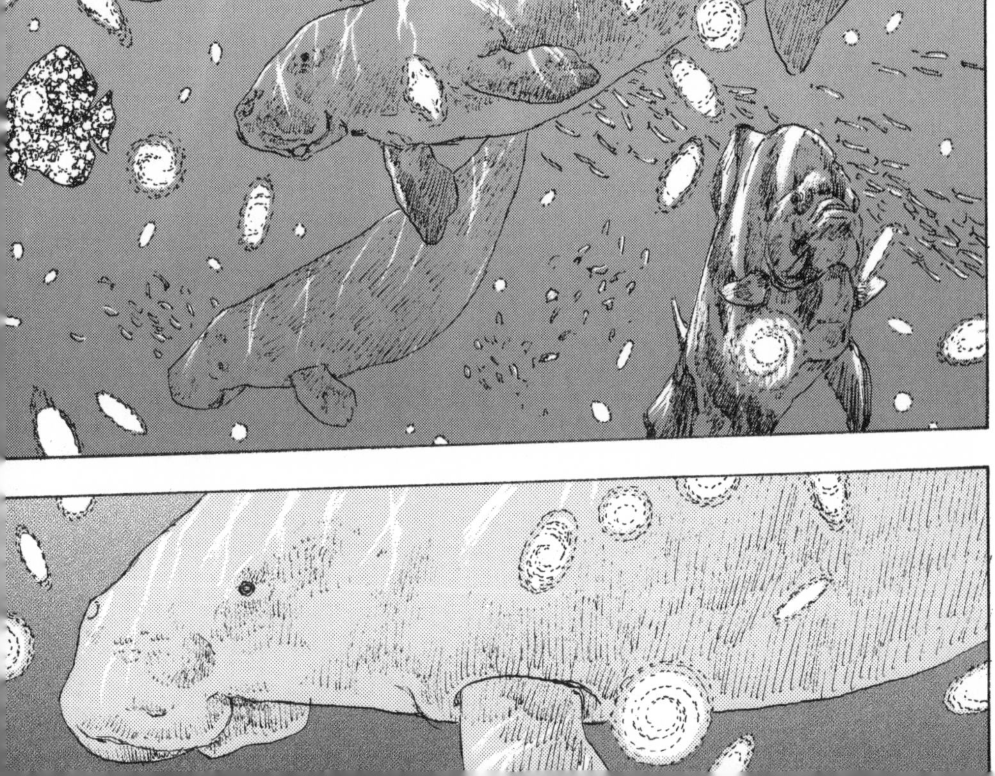

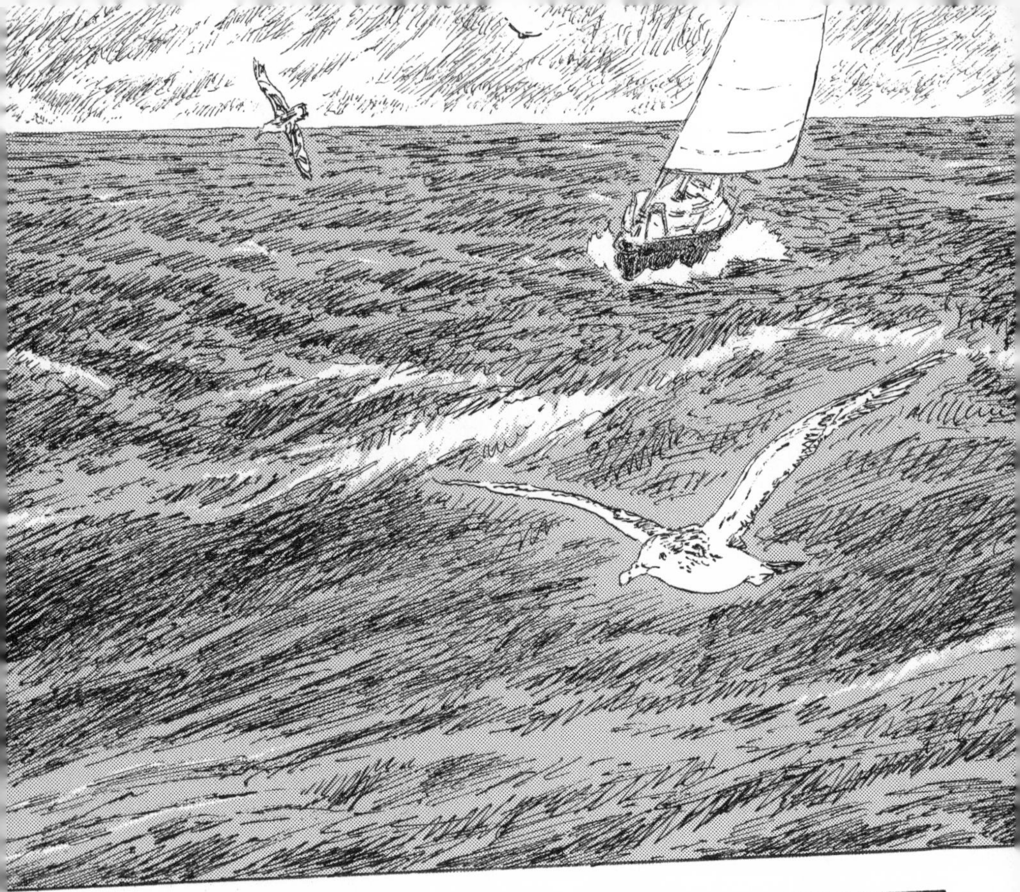

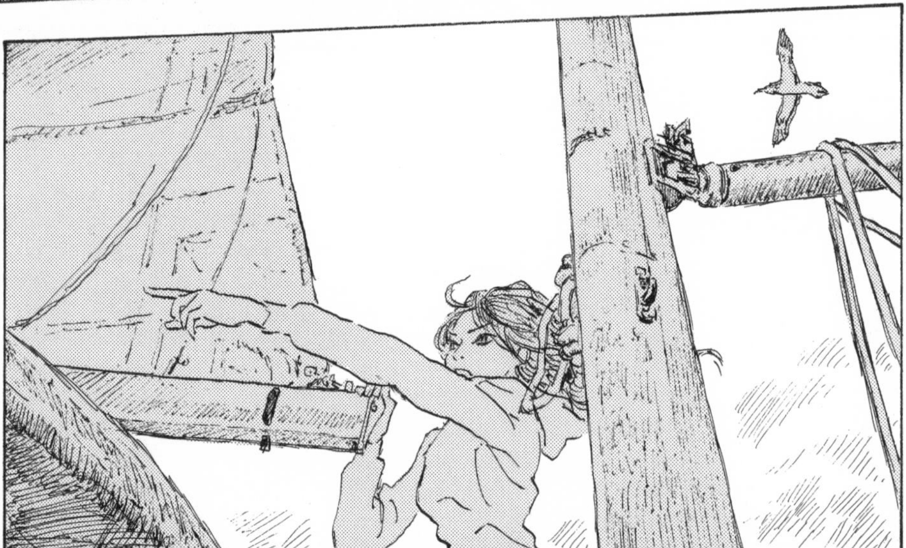

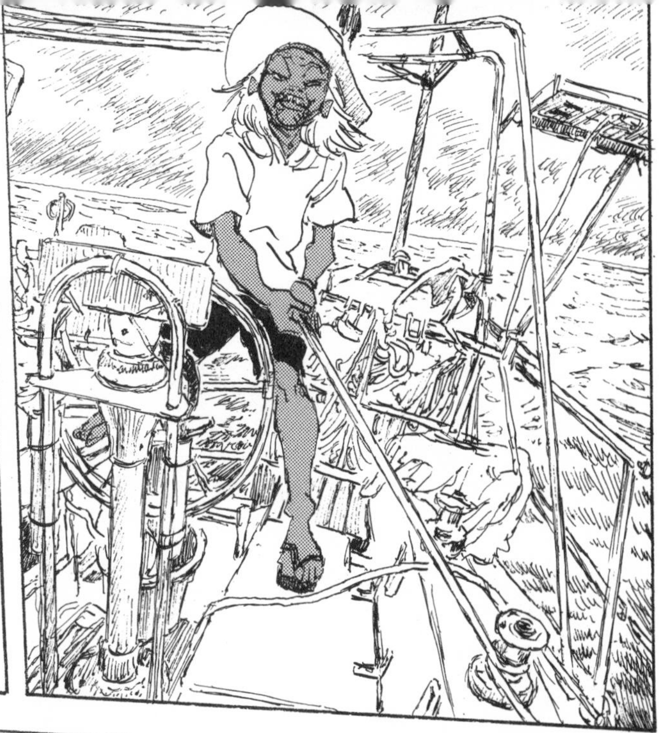
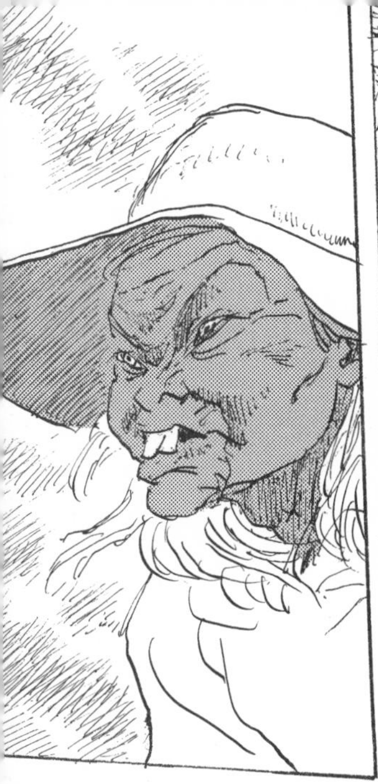
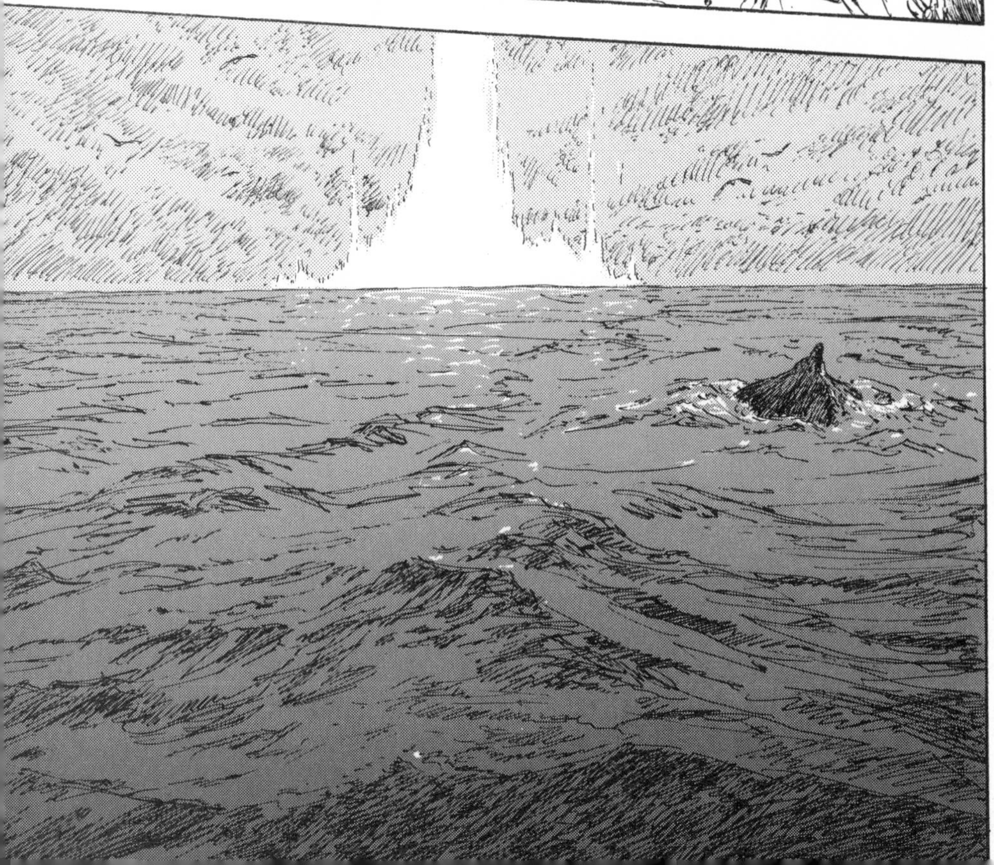

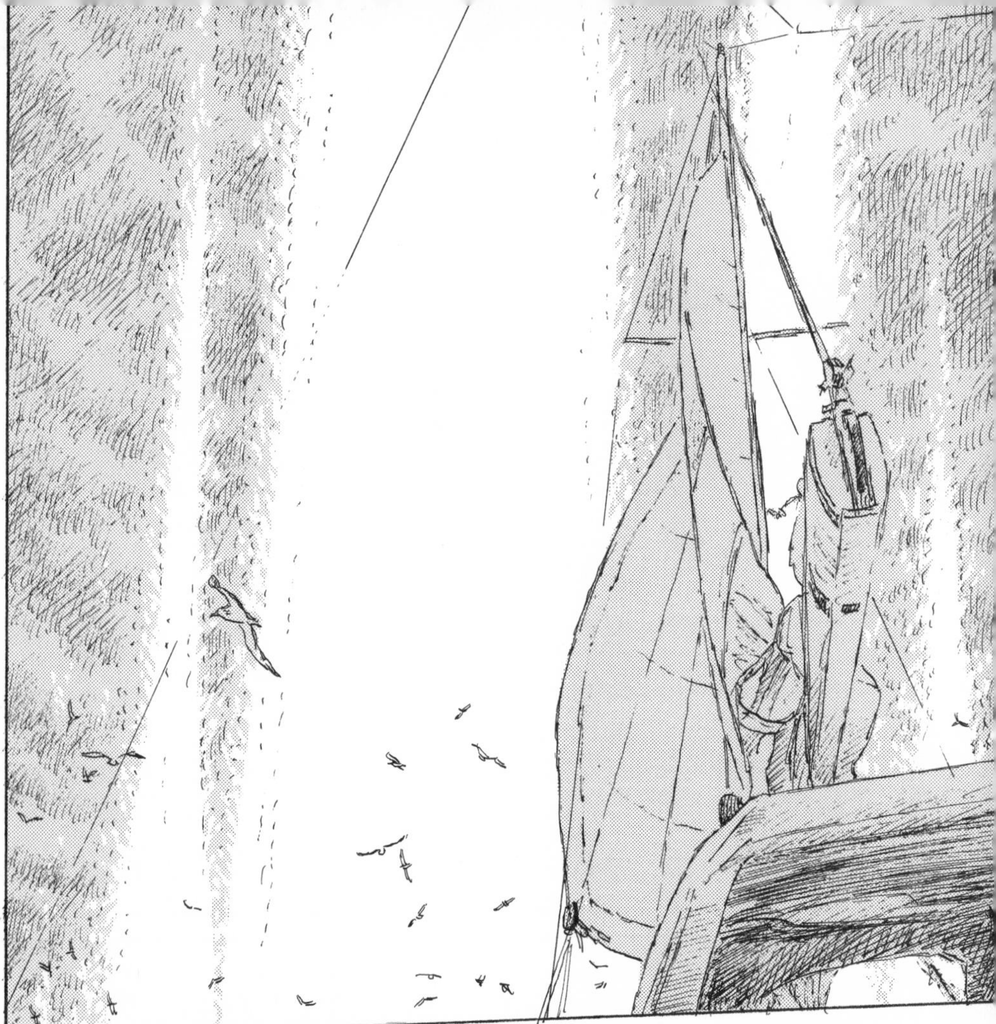
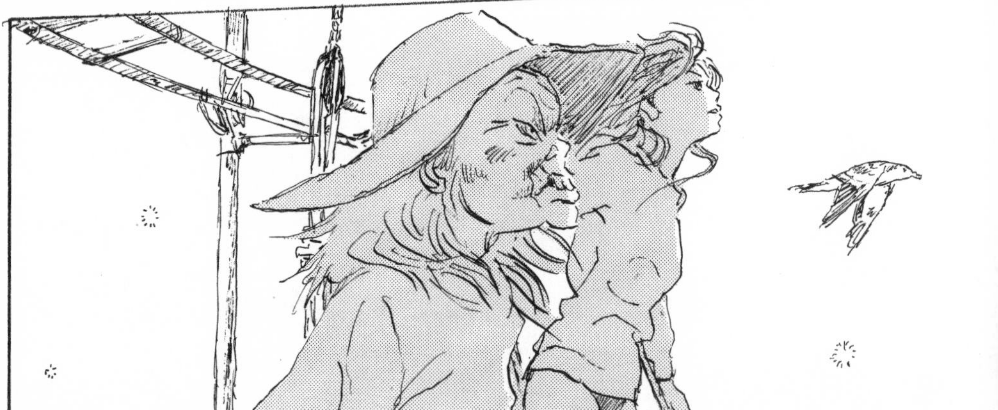

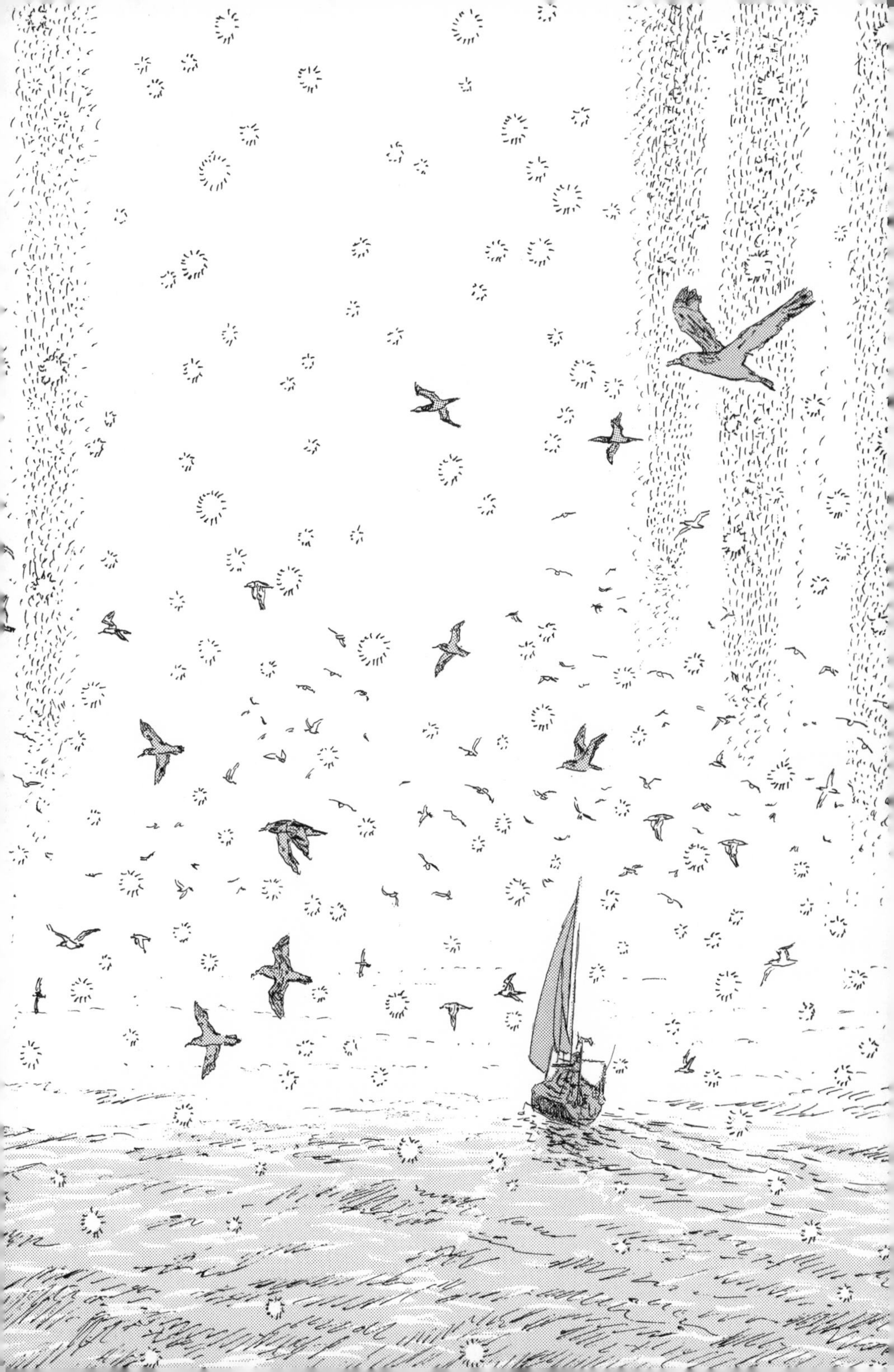

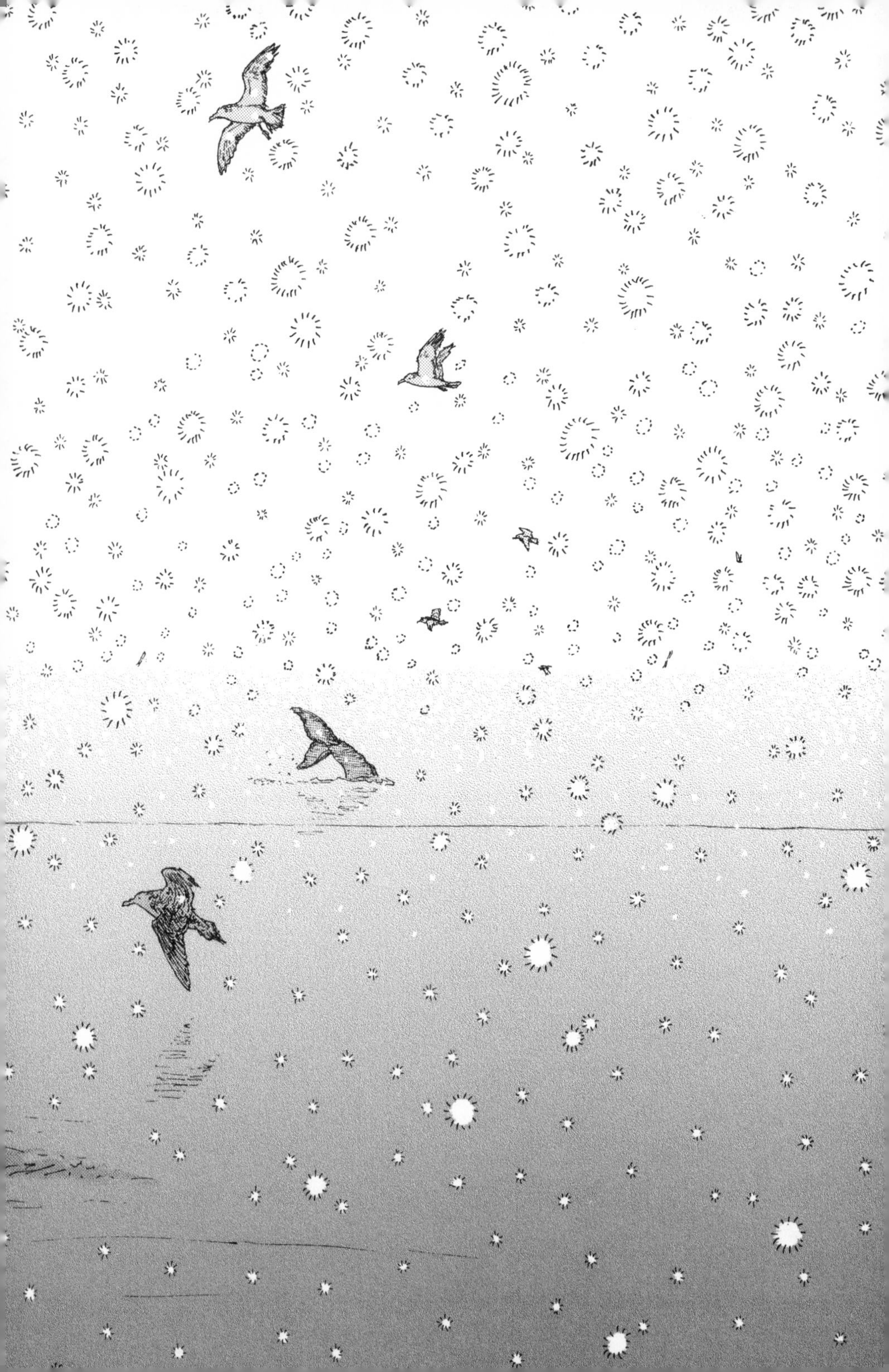

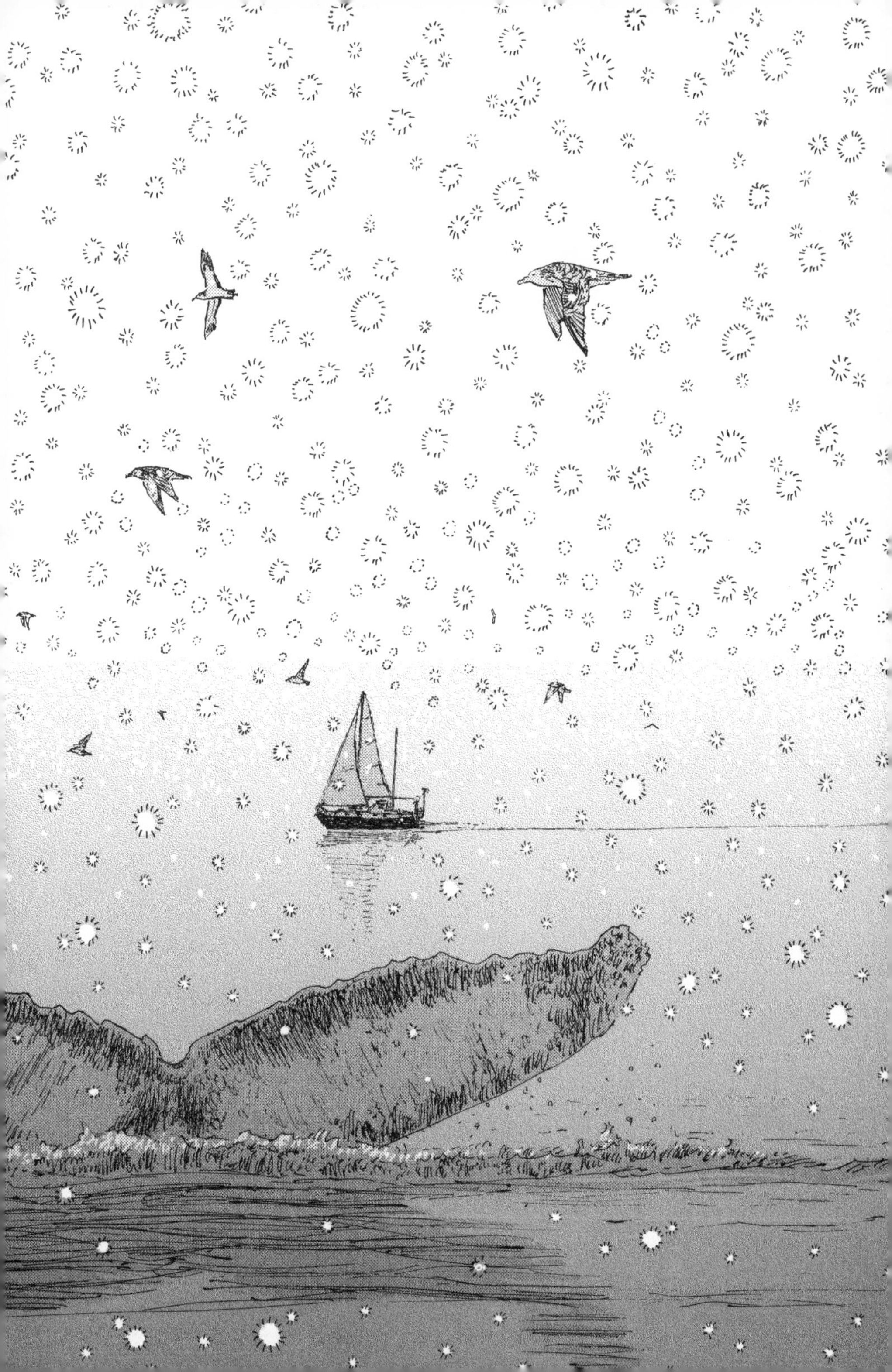

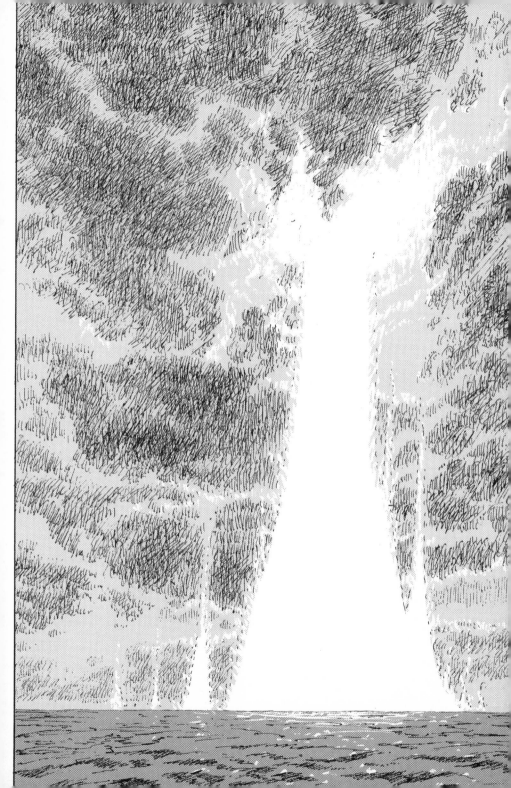

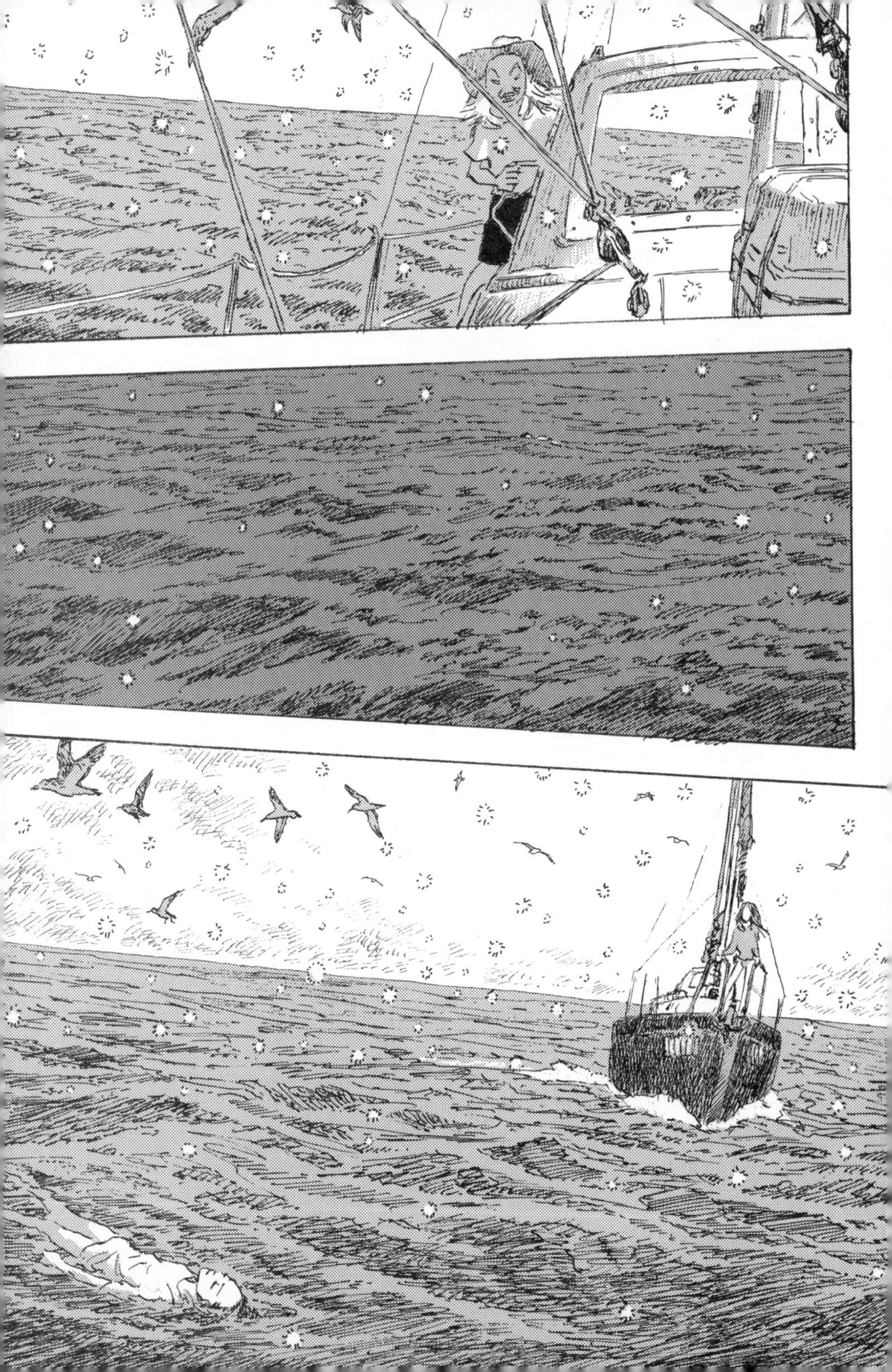

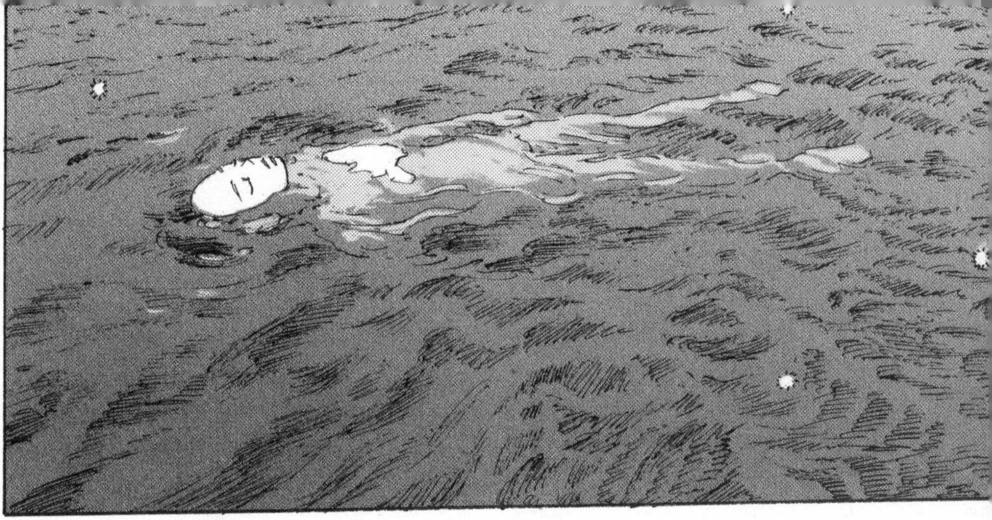
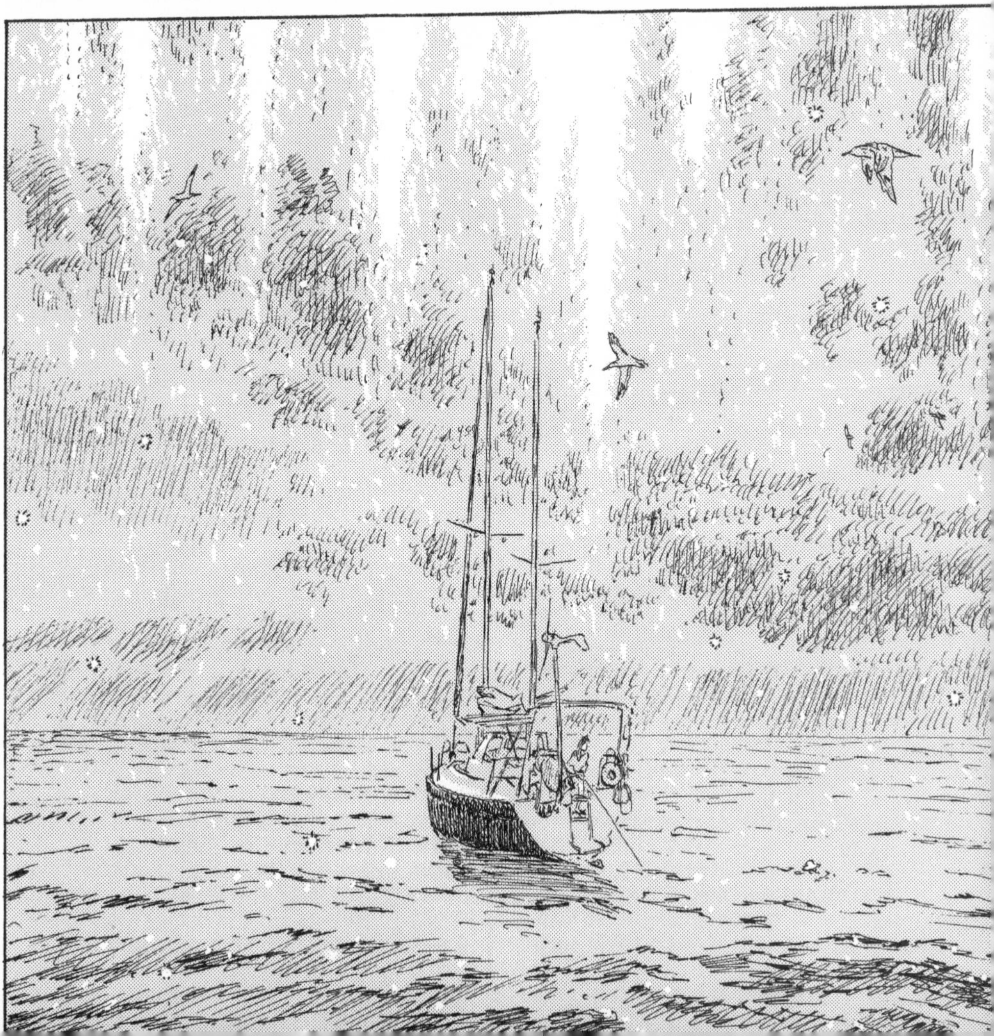

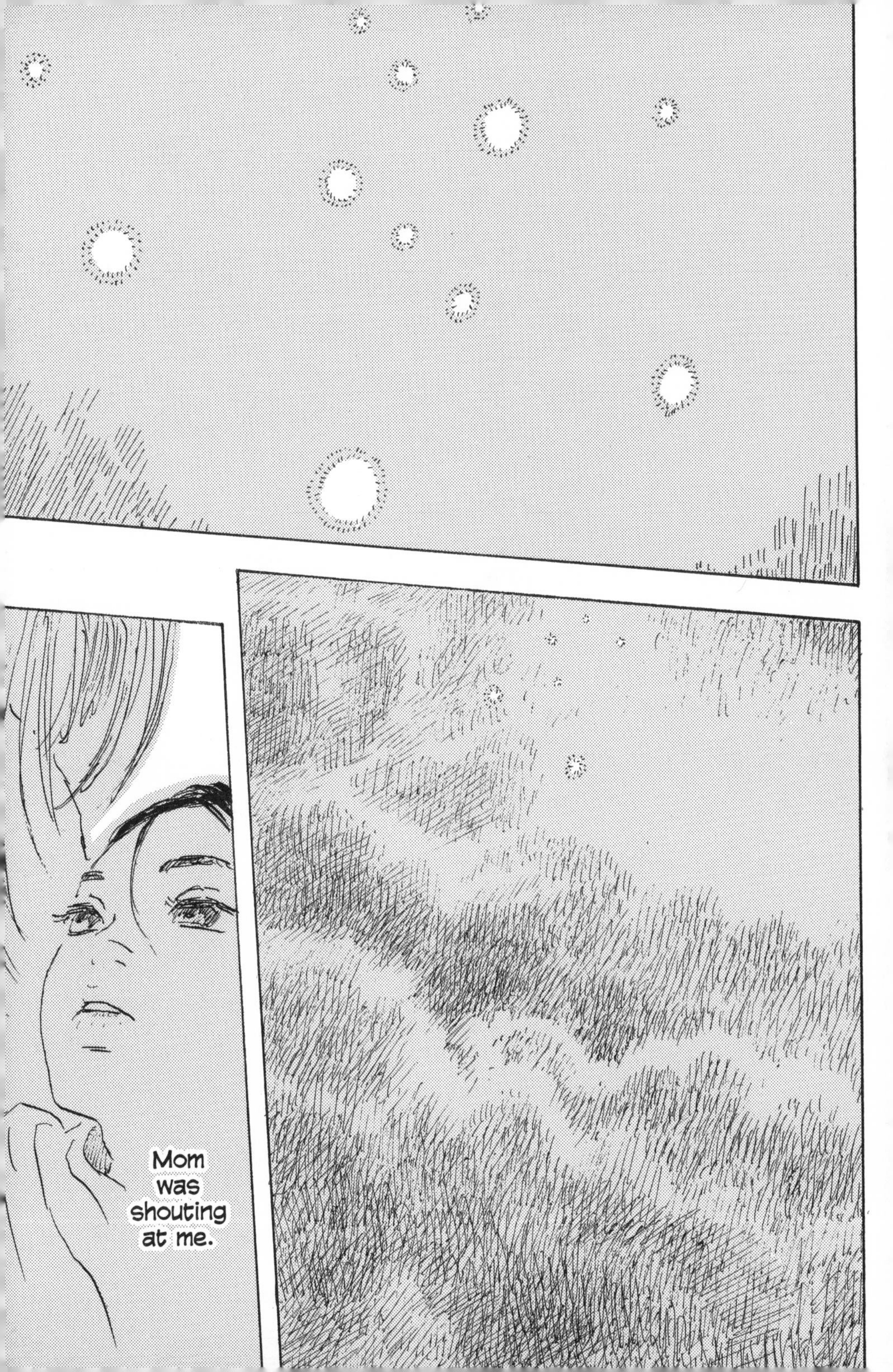
Mom was shouting at me.

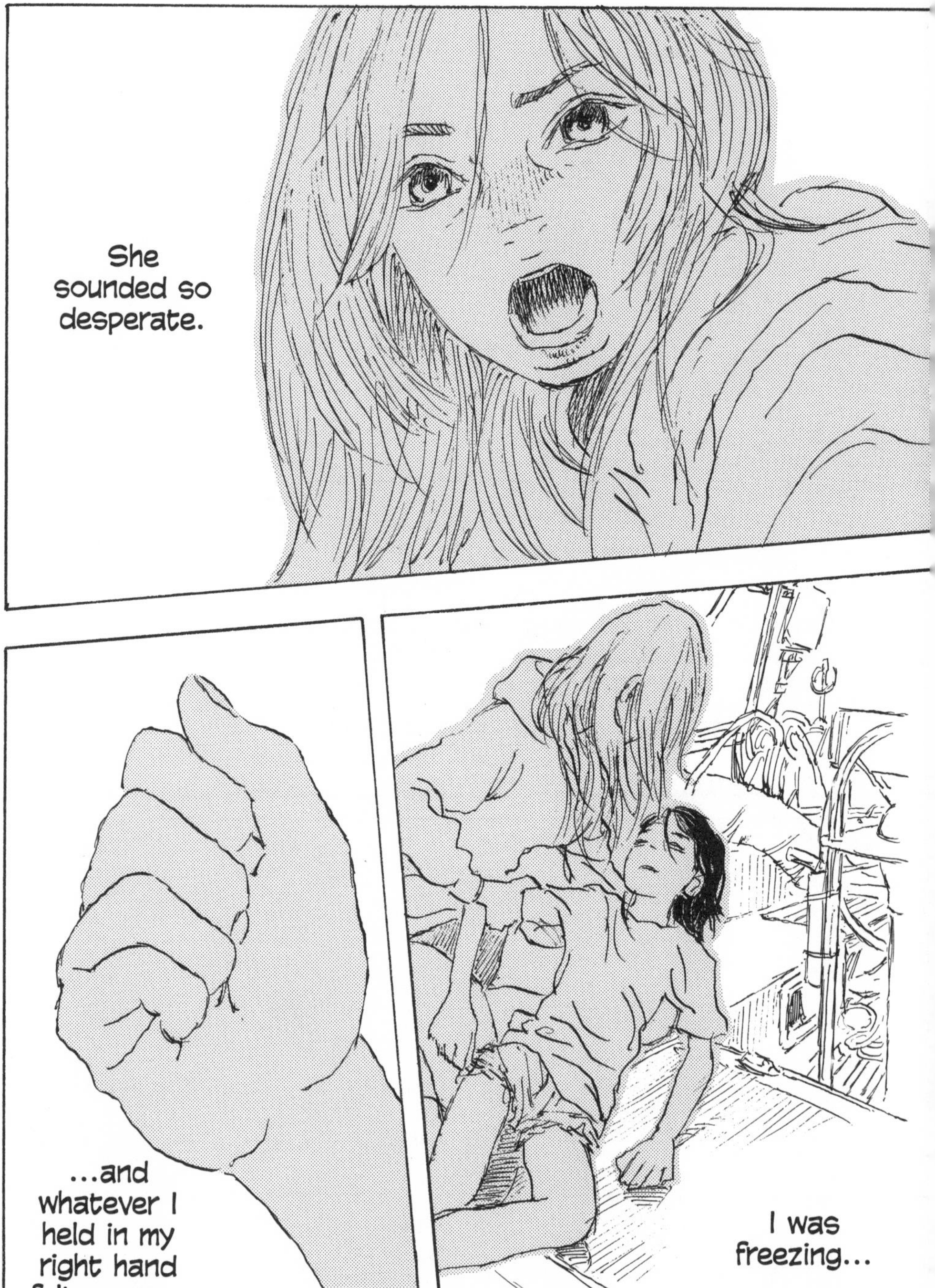
She sounded so desperate.
I was freezing...
...and whatever I held in my right hand felt warm...

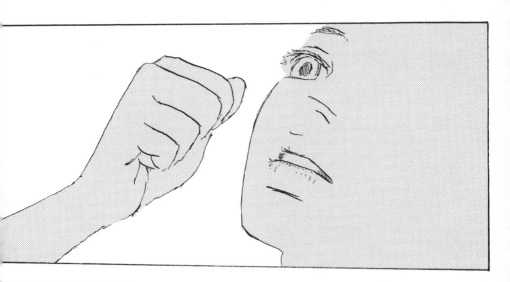

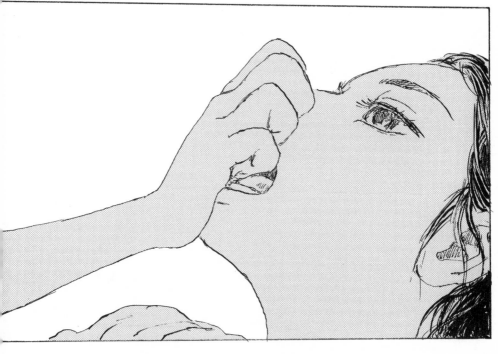

...so I
swallowed
it.

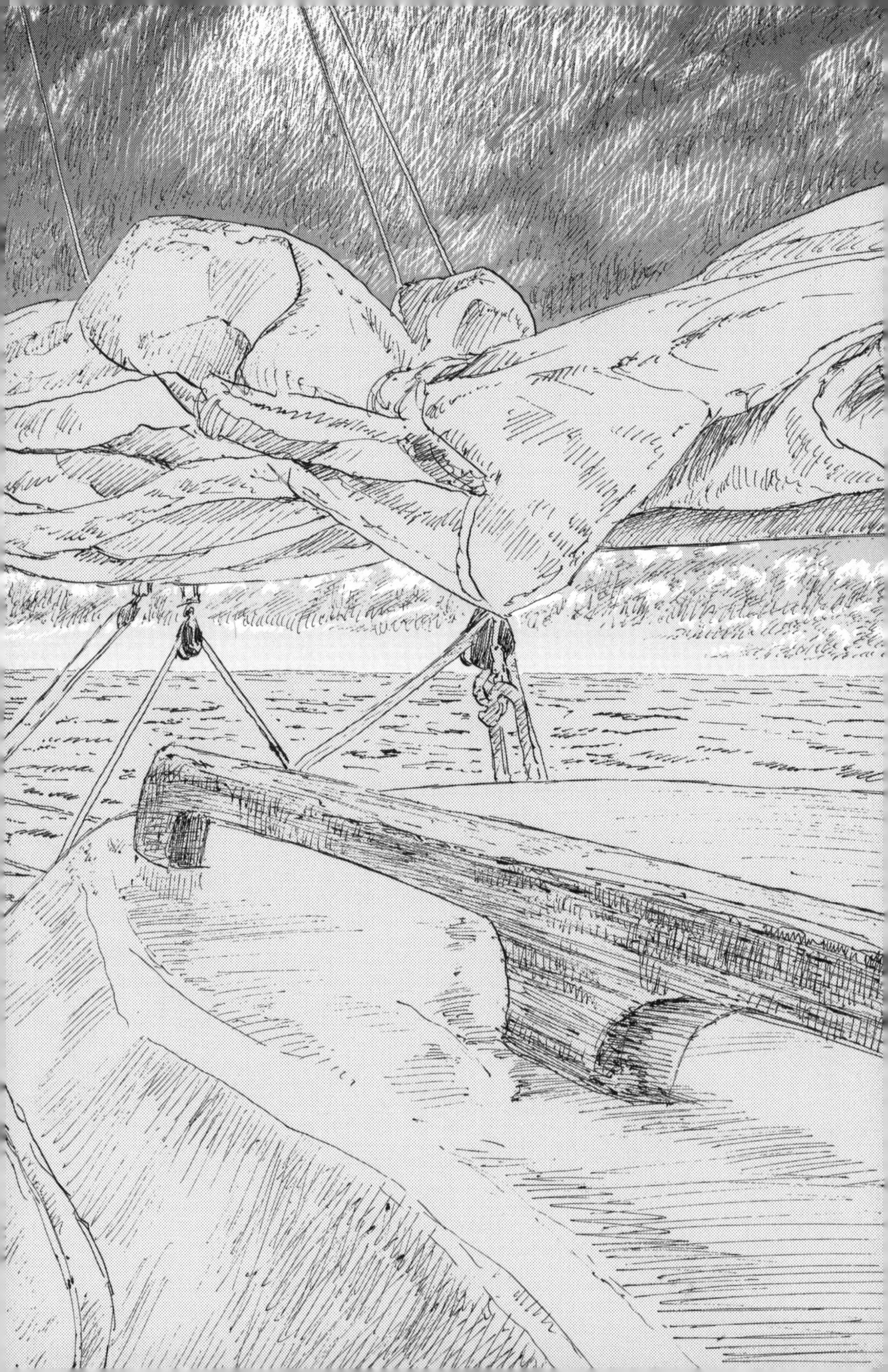

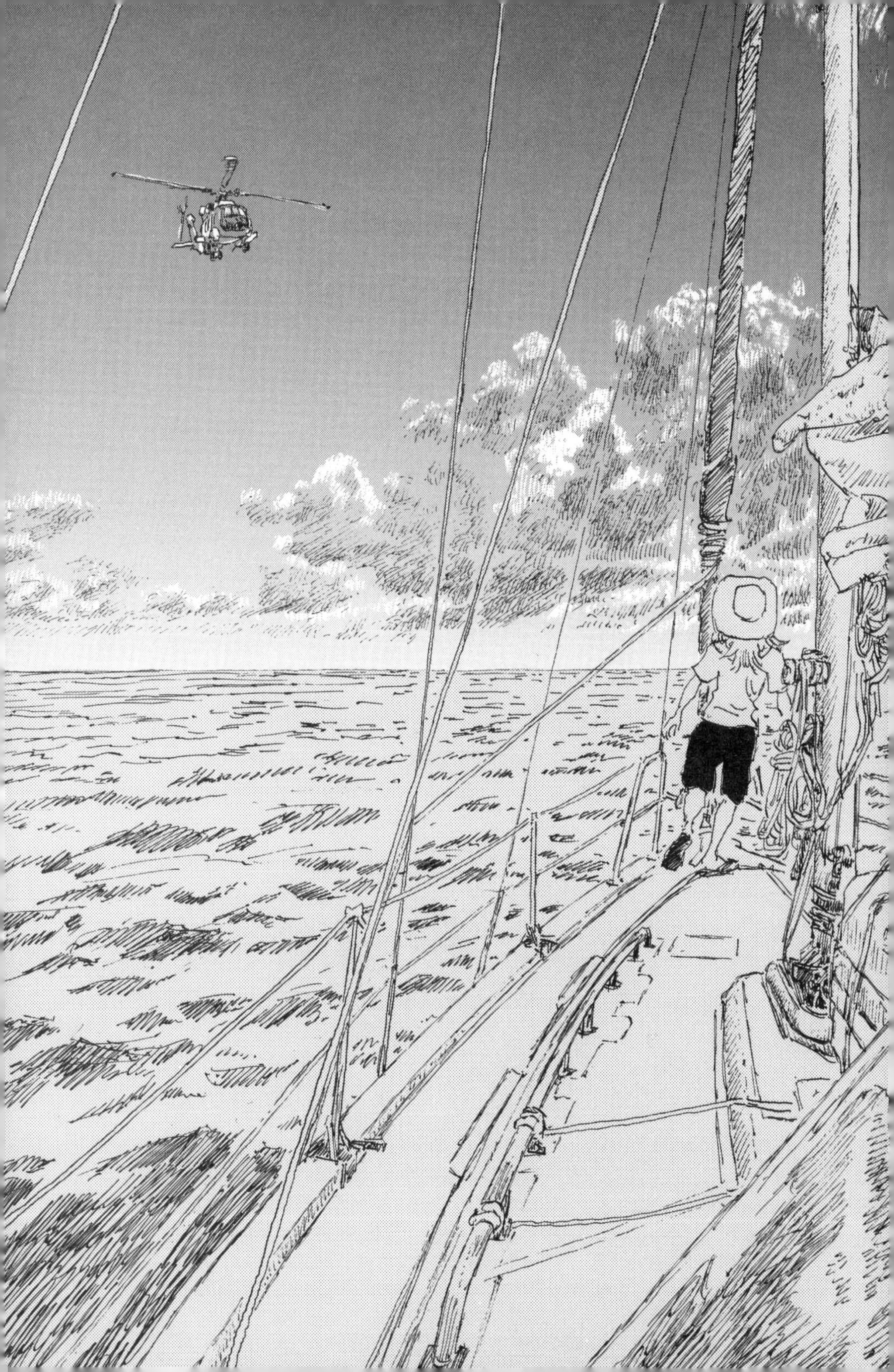

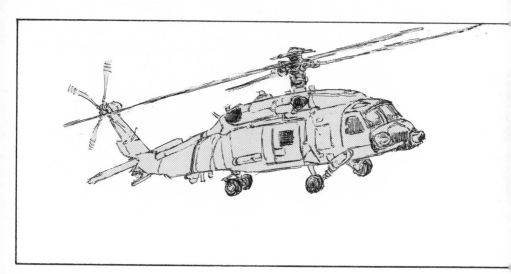

I was hospitalized for a week due to hypothermia and dehydration.

All I remember about that time is how sleepy I was.

By autumn,
all the
people I'd
met during
summer had
gone.

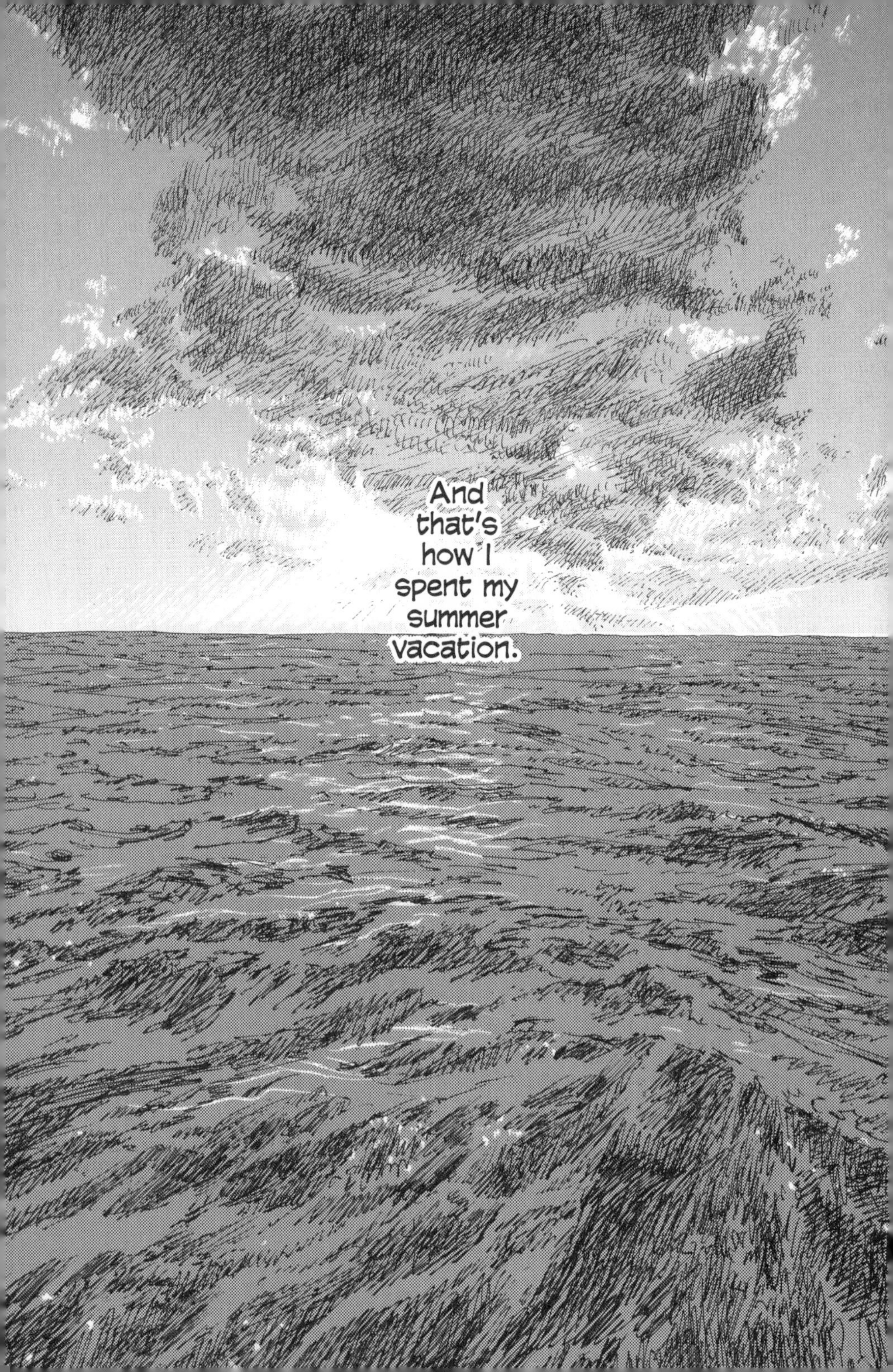
And that's how I spent my summer vacation.

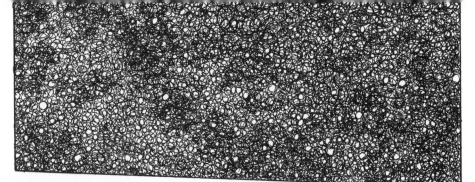

KSSSH

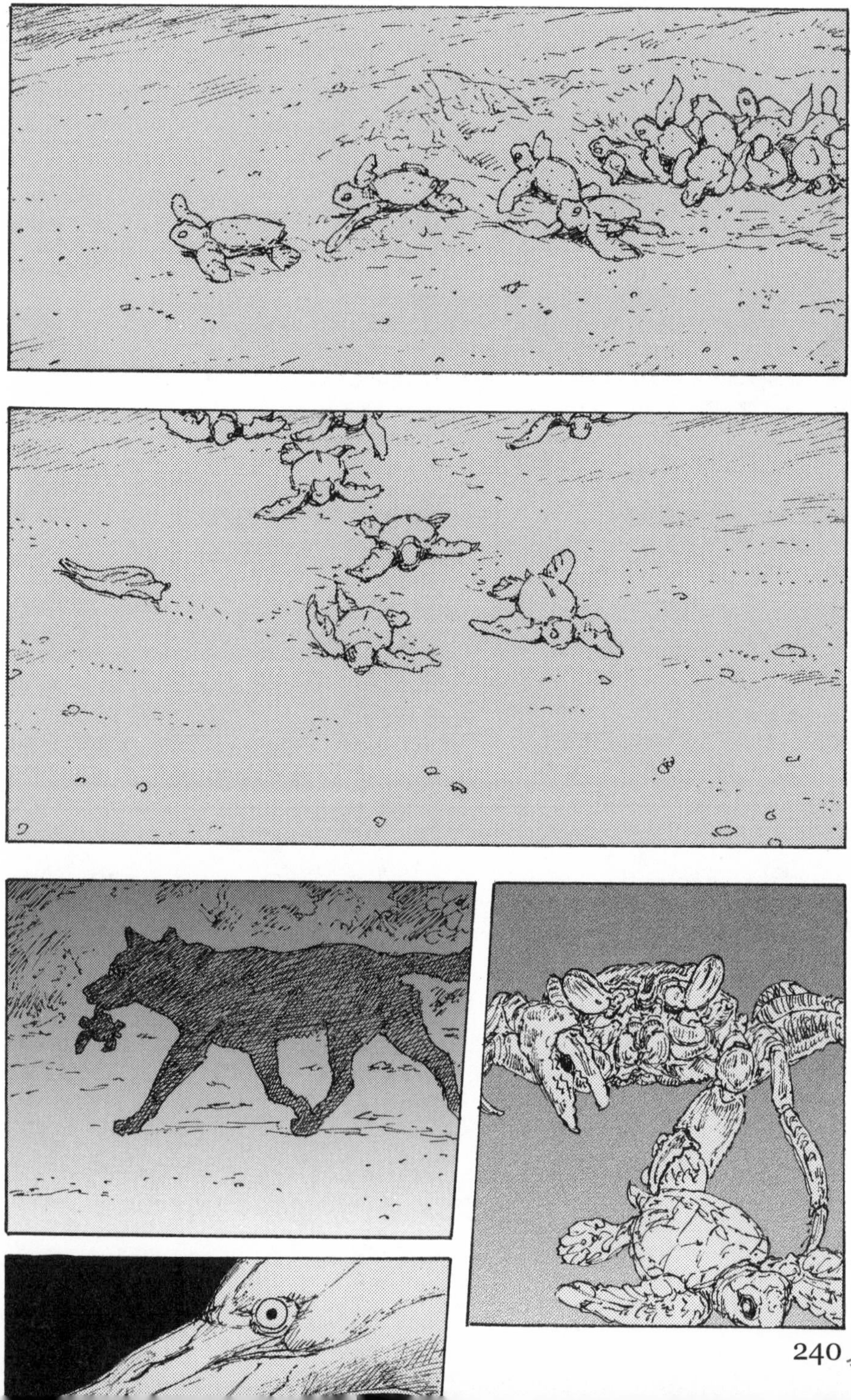

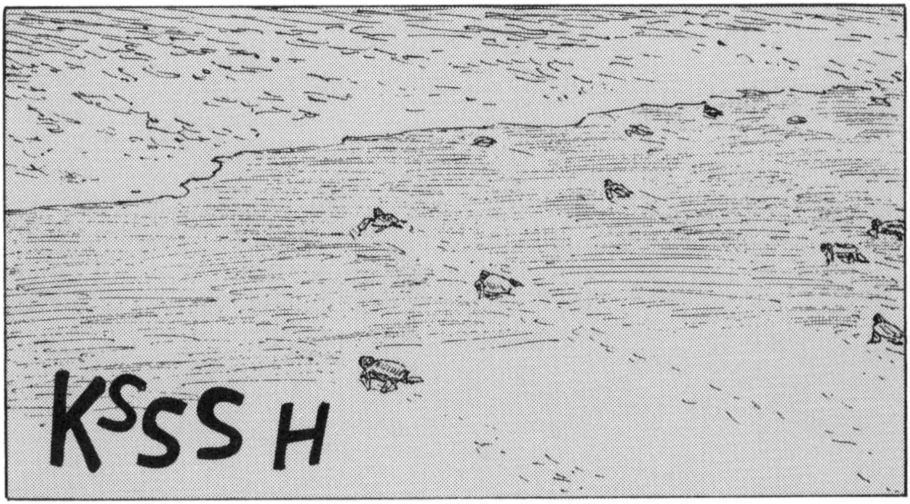
KSSSH
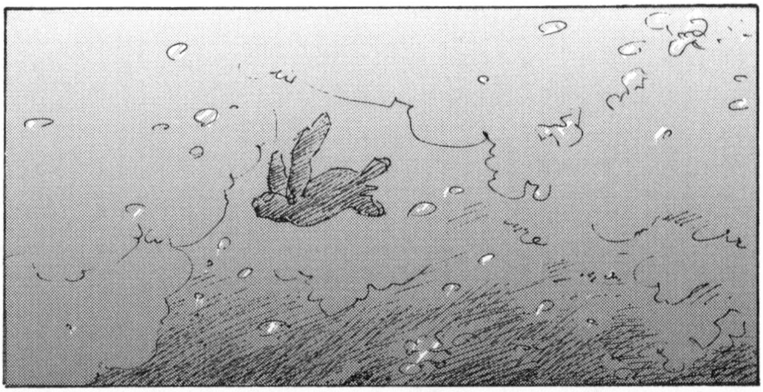
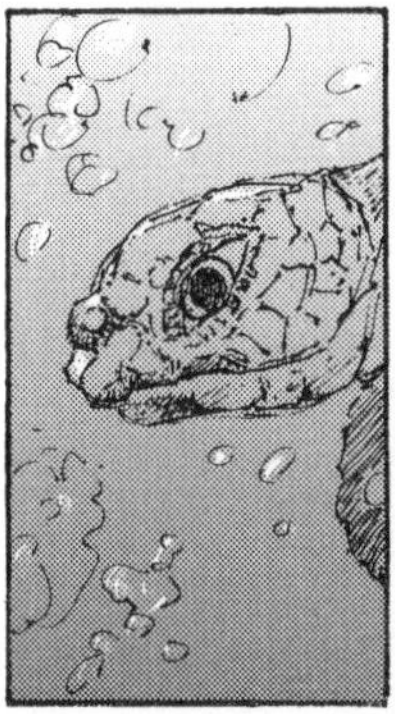
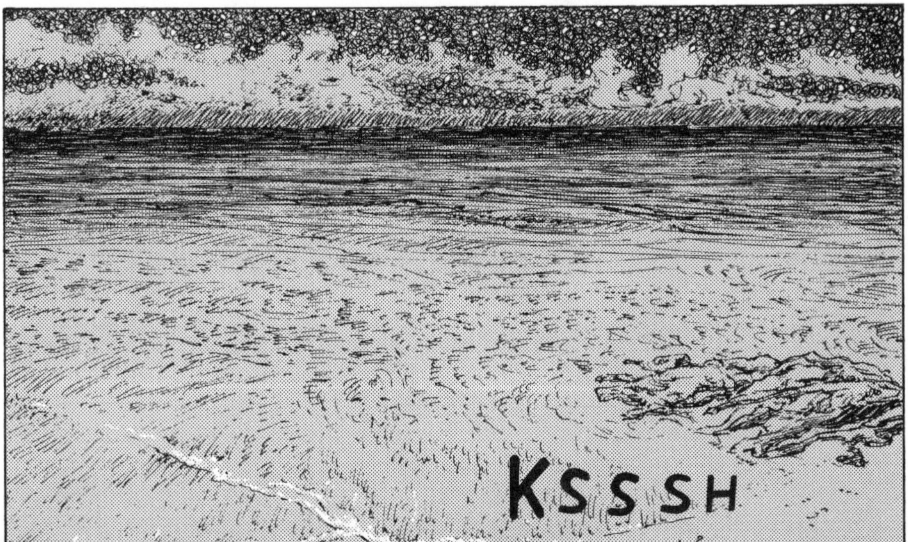
KSSSH

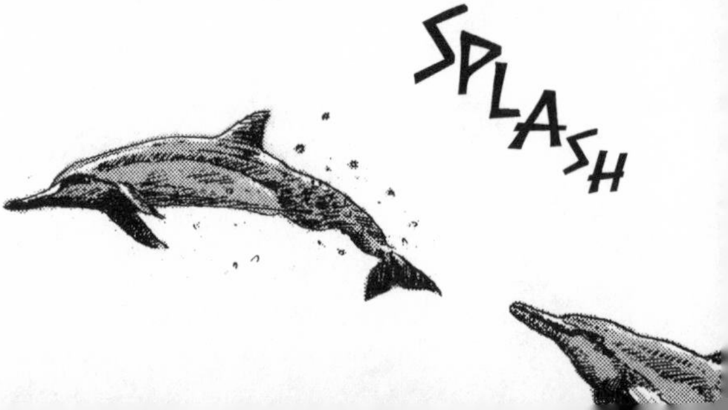
SPLASH

Chapter 42: Iruka

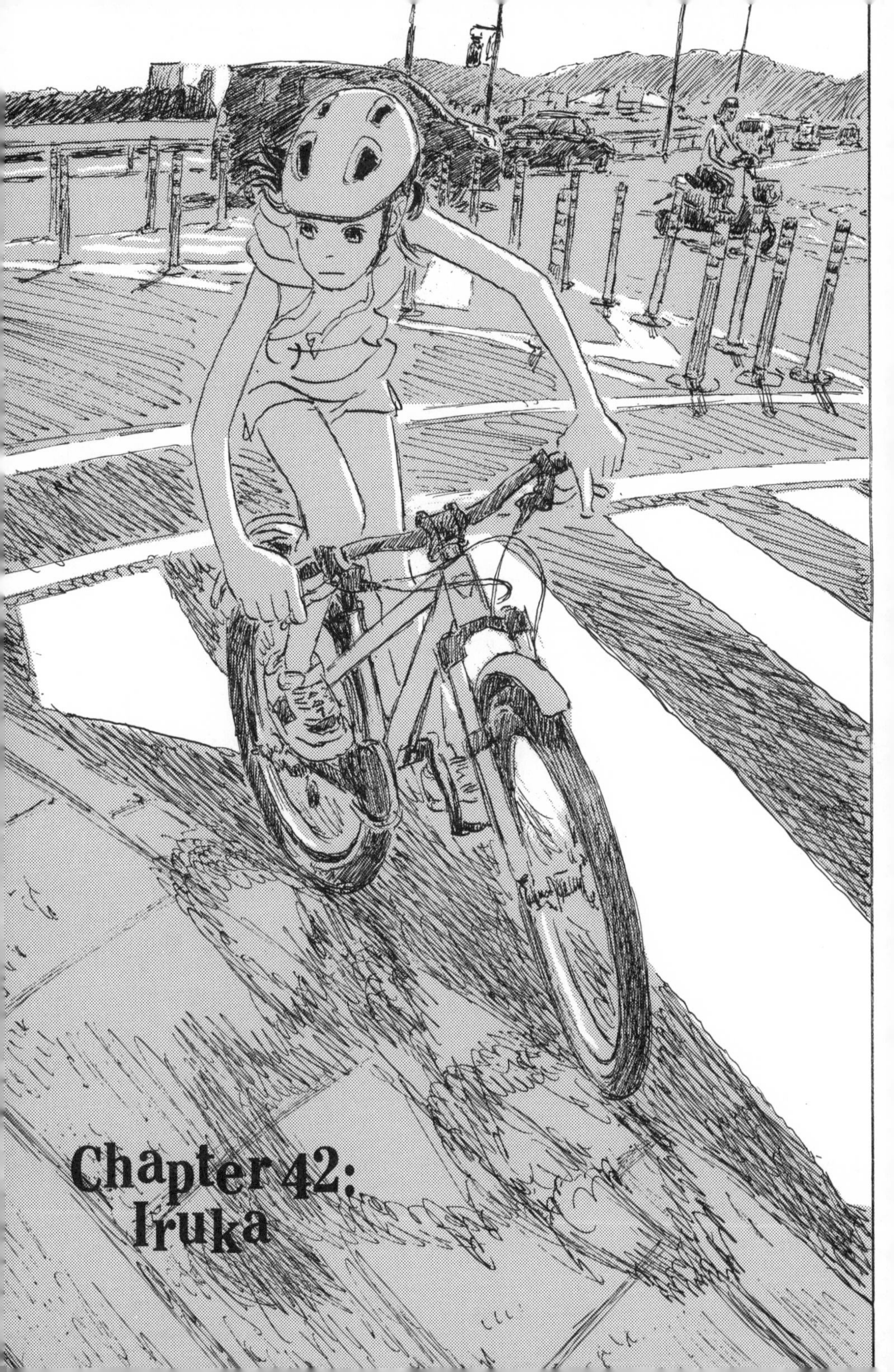

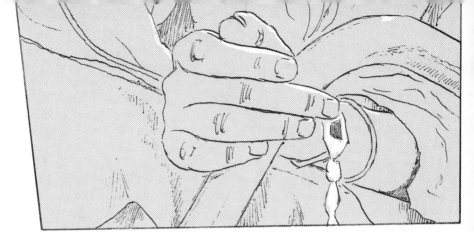

RUKA...

HOLD...

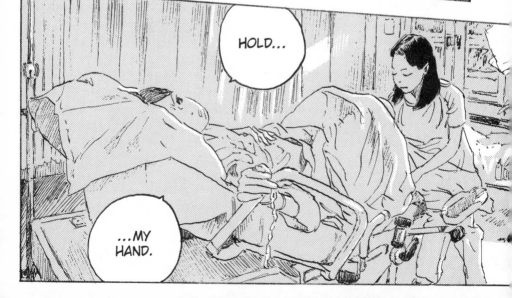

...MY HAND.

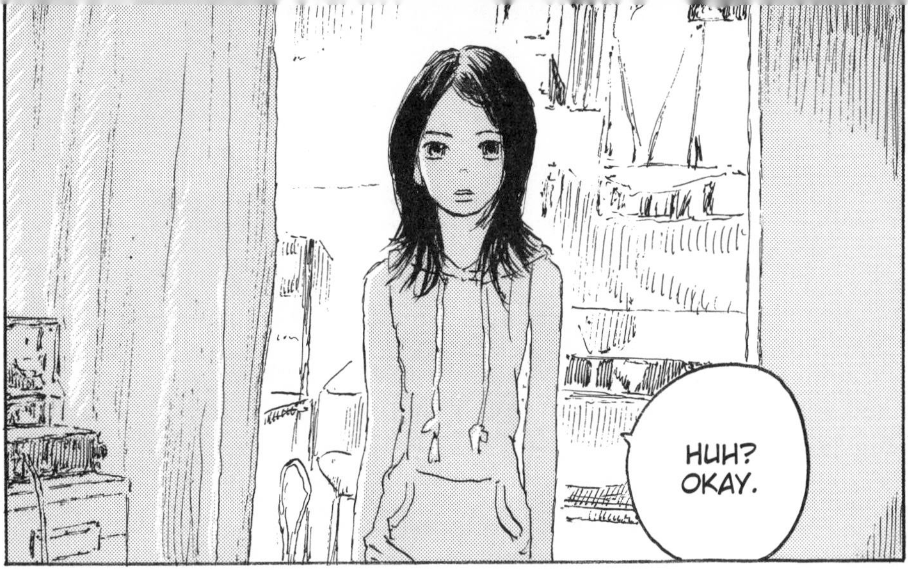
HUH? OKAY.
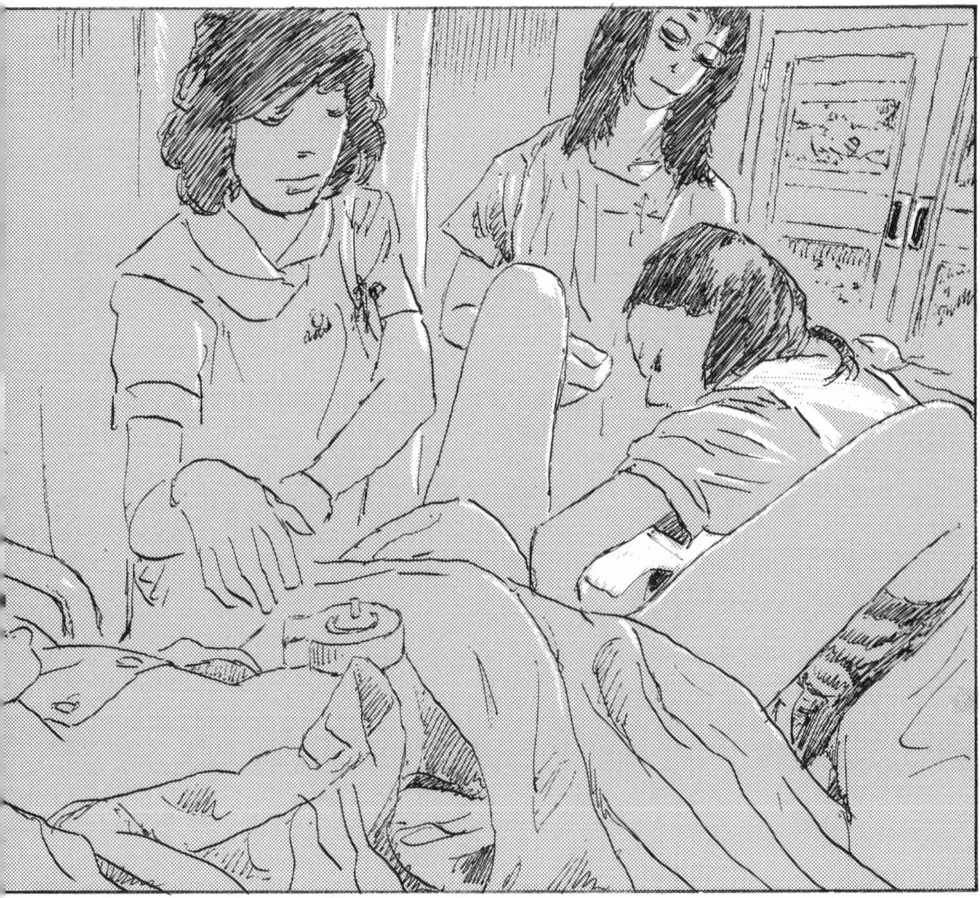

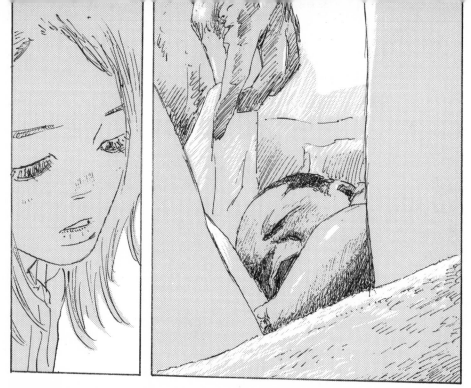

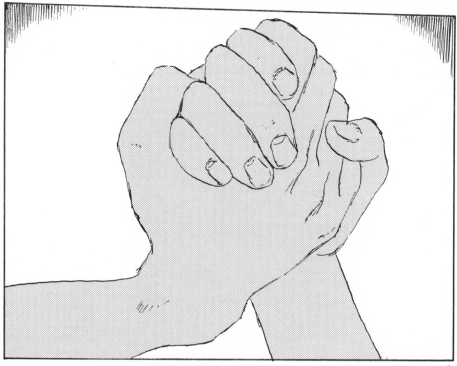

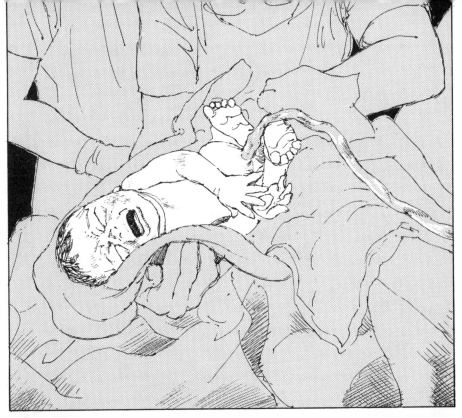

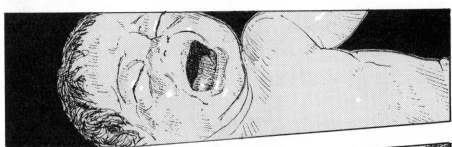

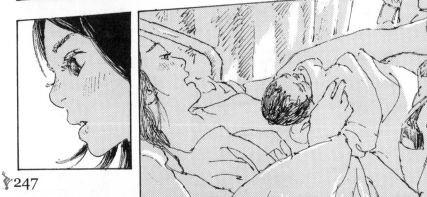

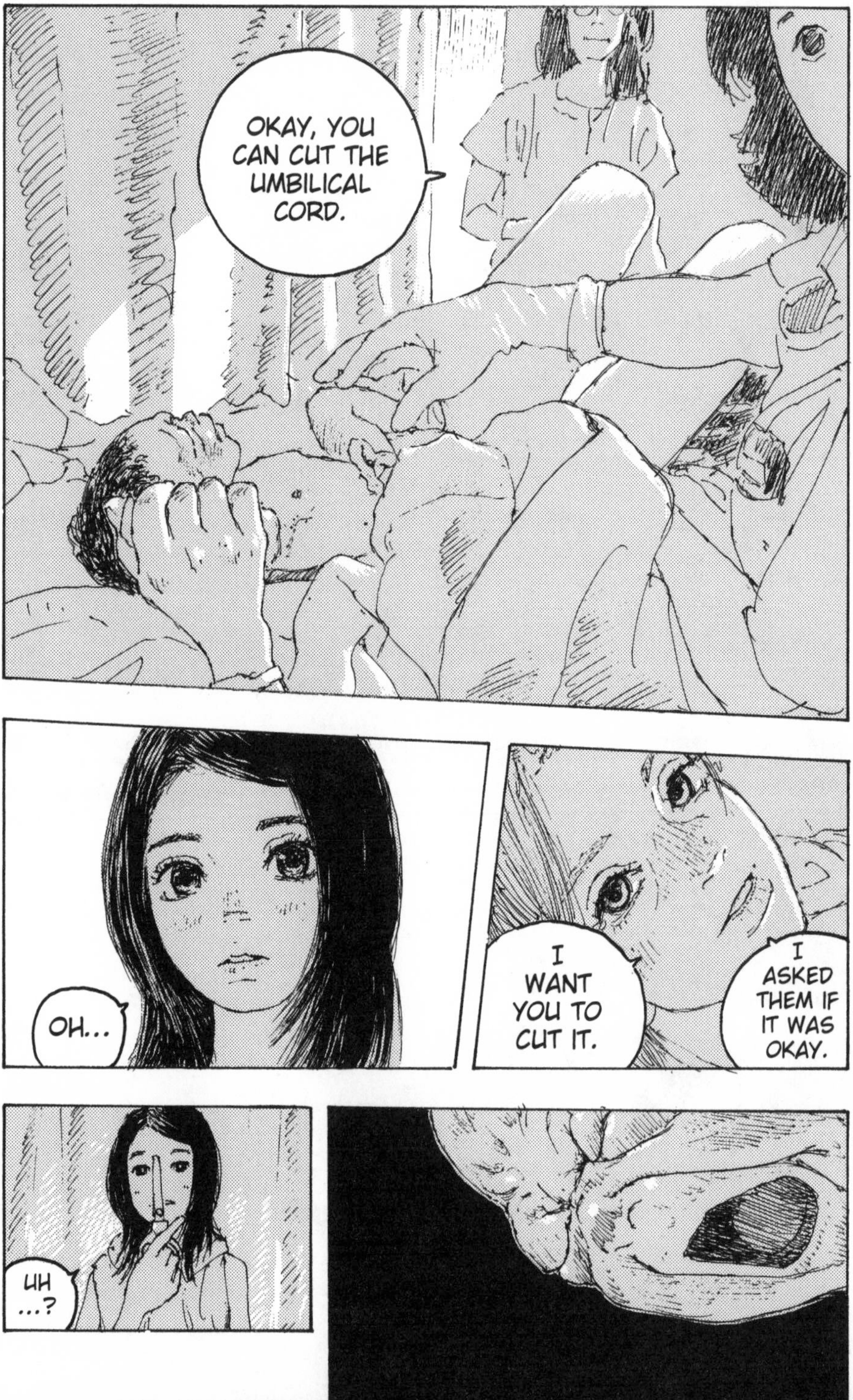
OKAY, YOU CAN CUT THE UMBILICAL CORD.
I ASKED THEM IF IT WAS OKAY.
I WANT YOU TO CUT IT.
OH...
UH ...?

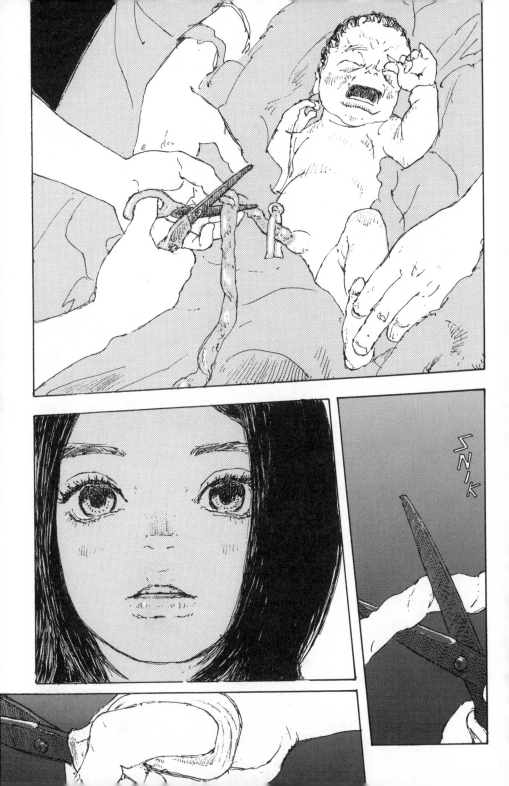

SNIK

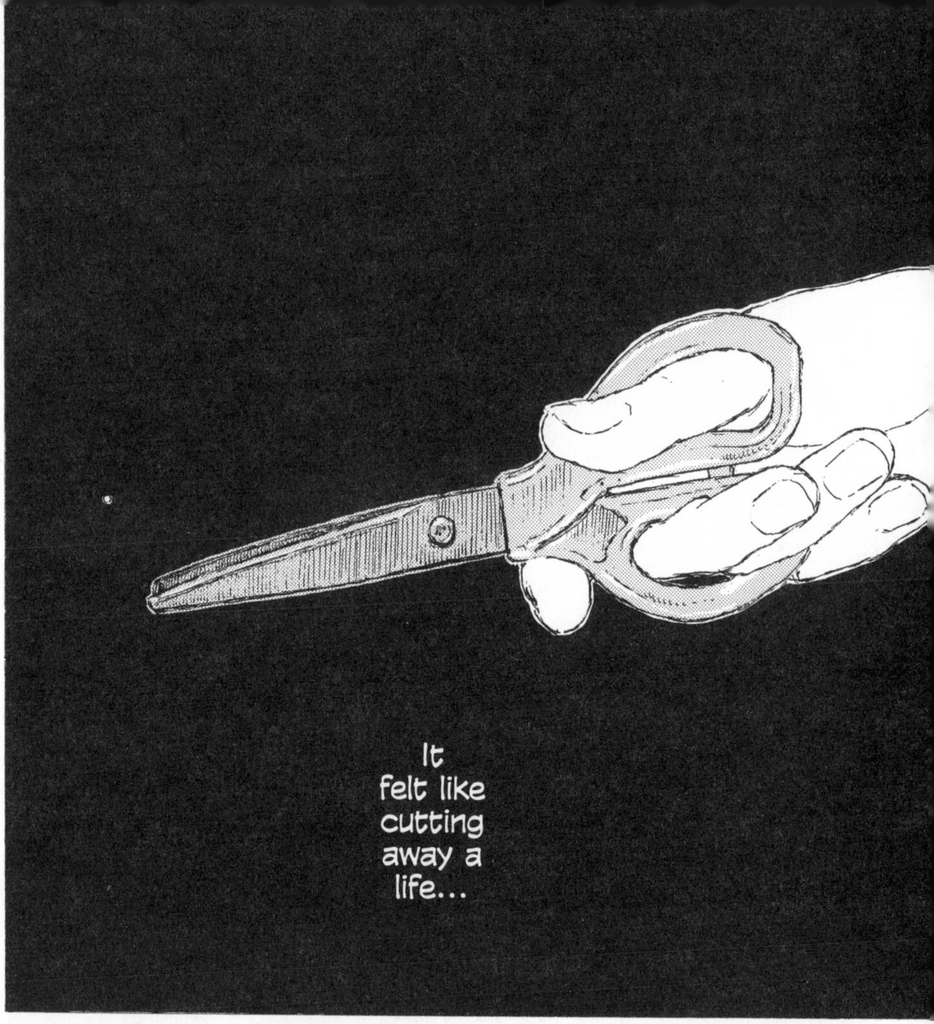
It felt like cutting away a life...
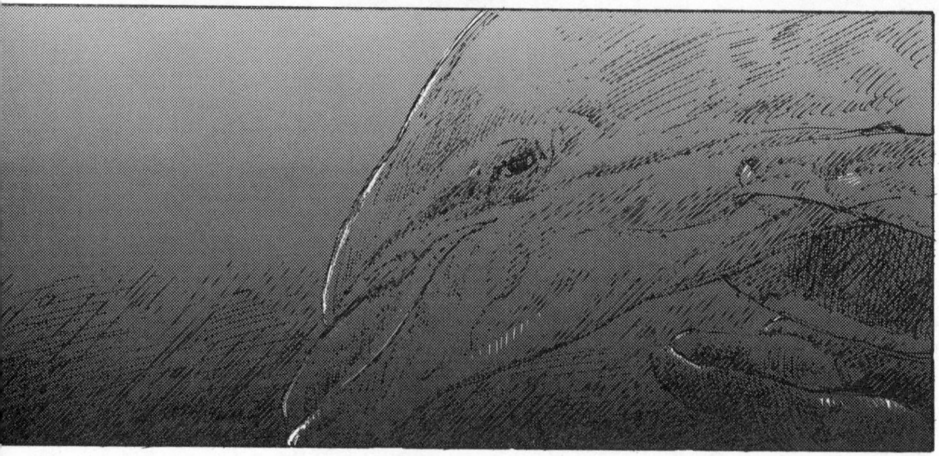

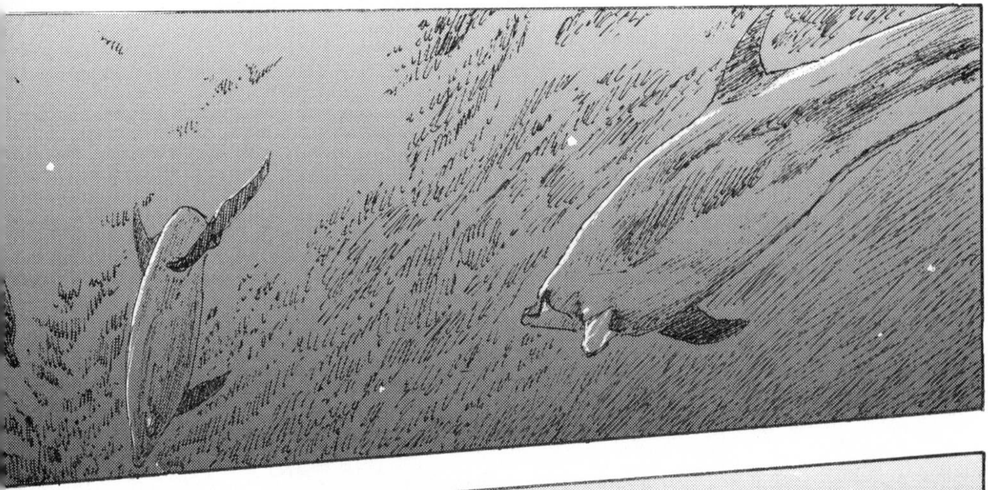
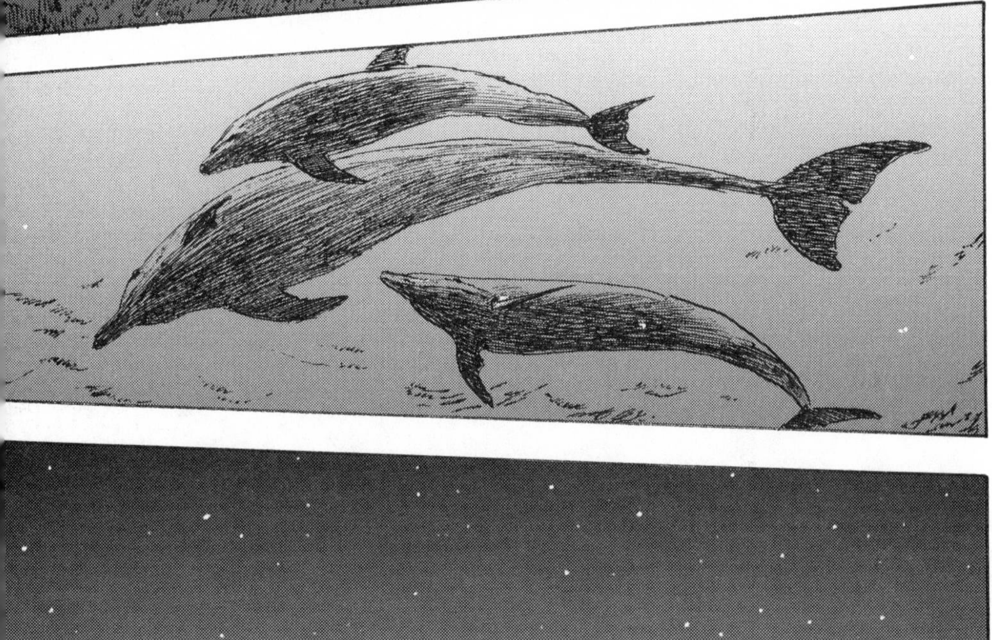
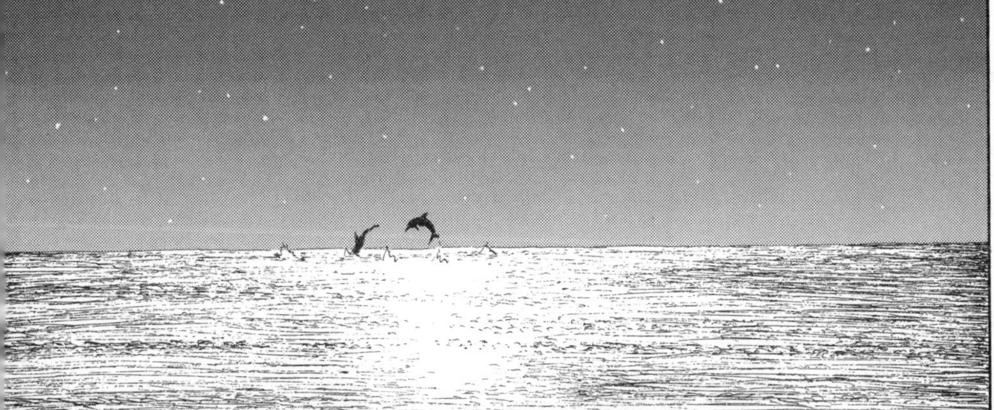

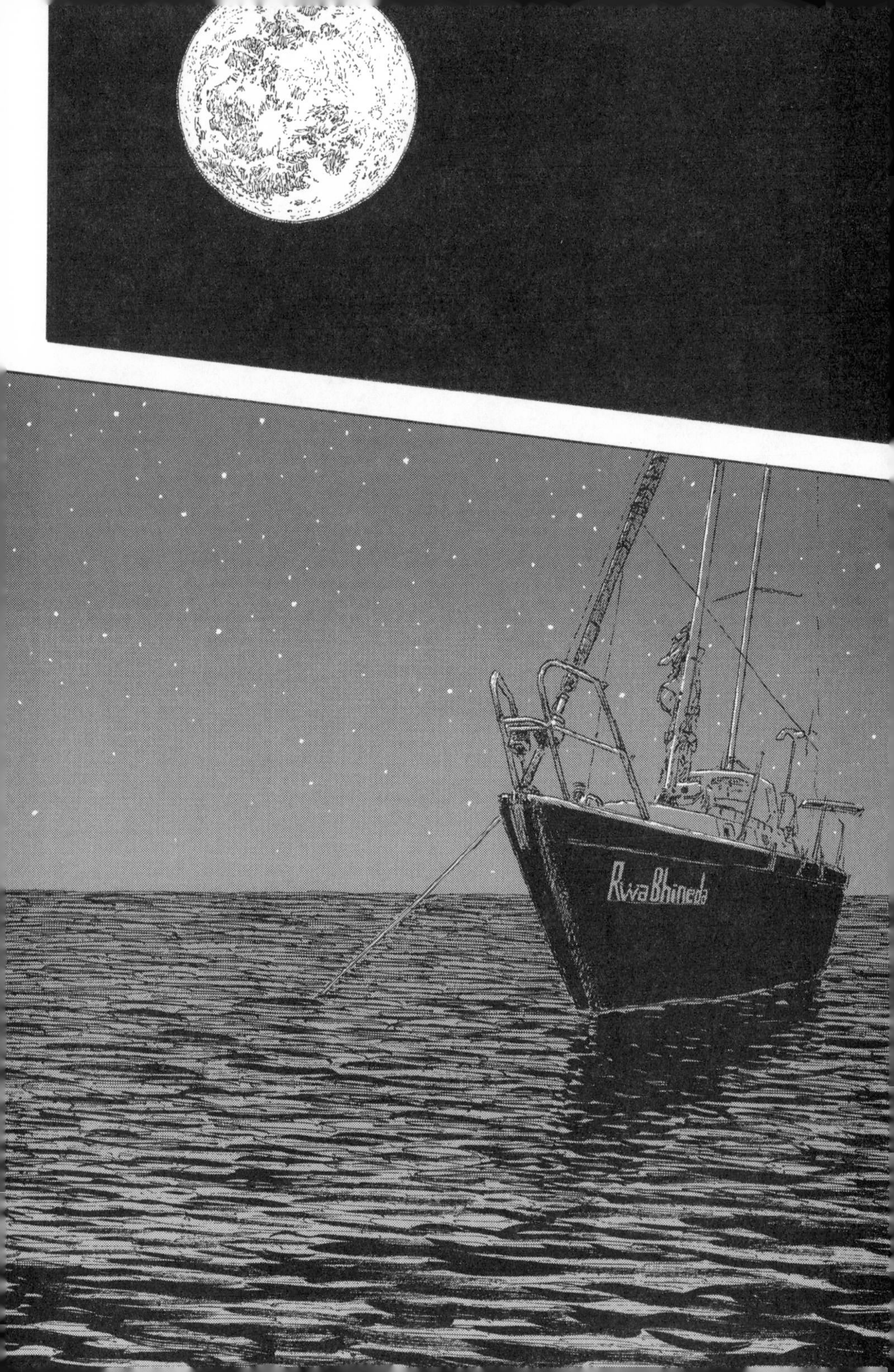
RwaBhineda

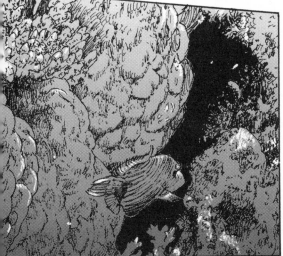

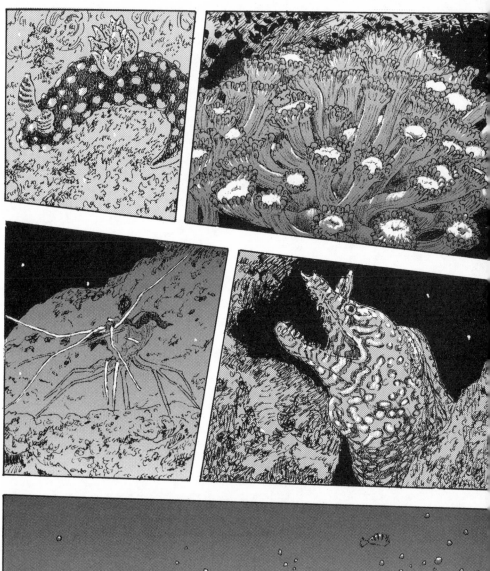

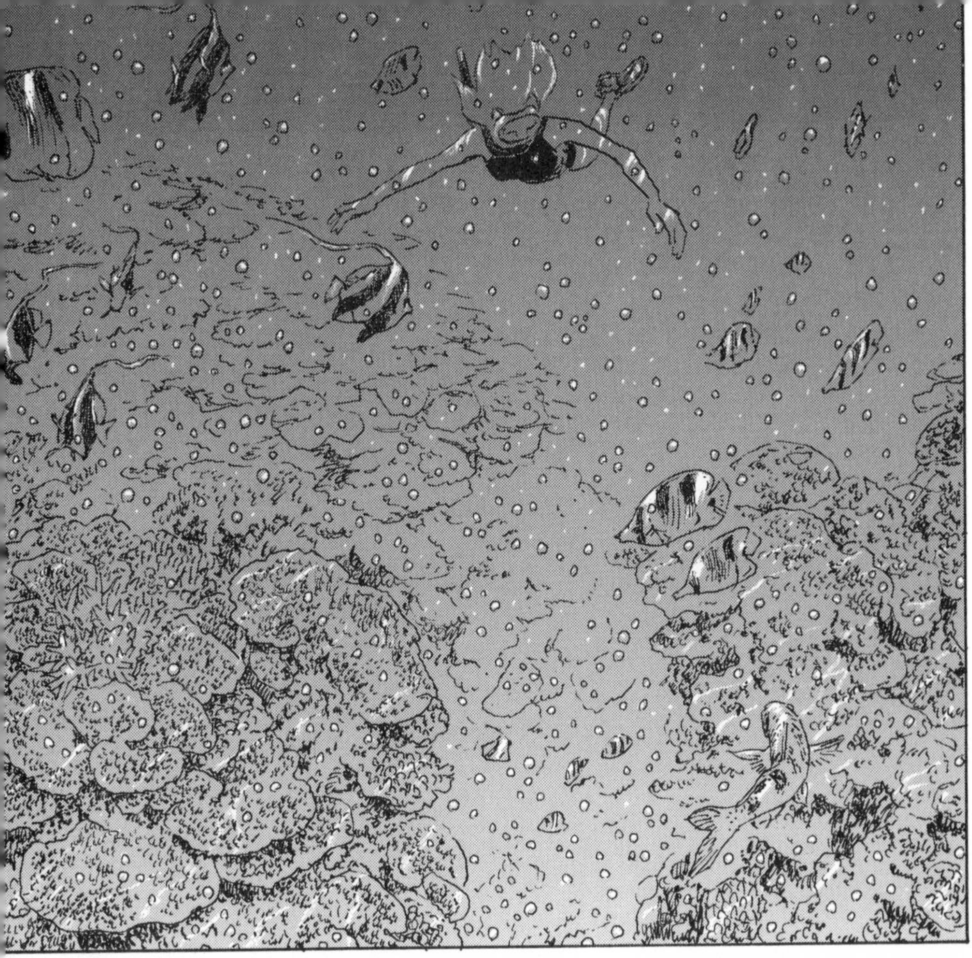

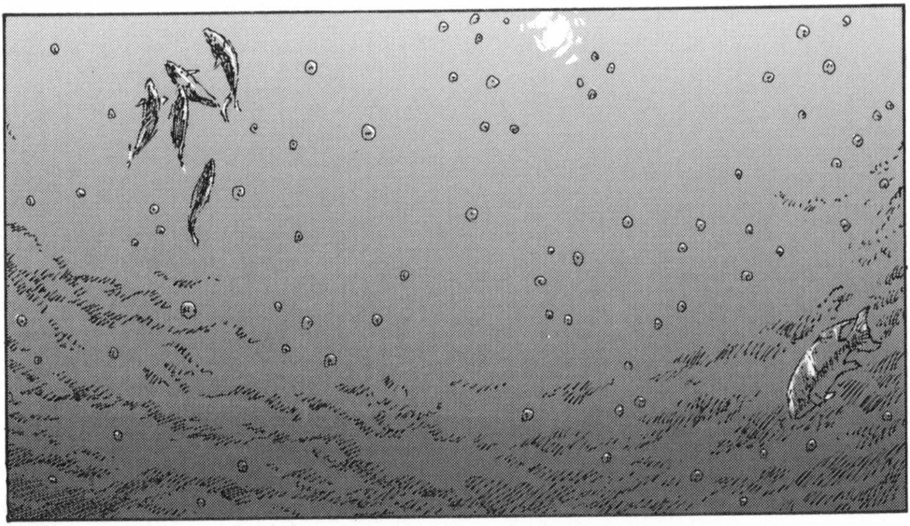

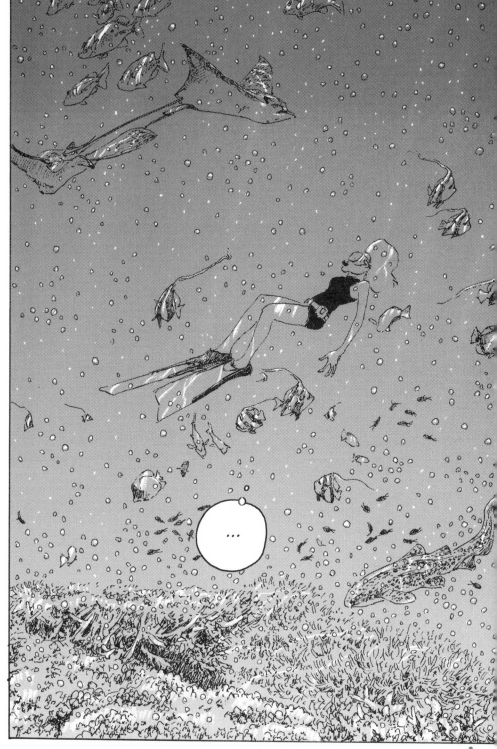

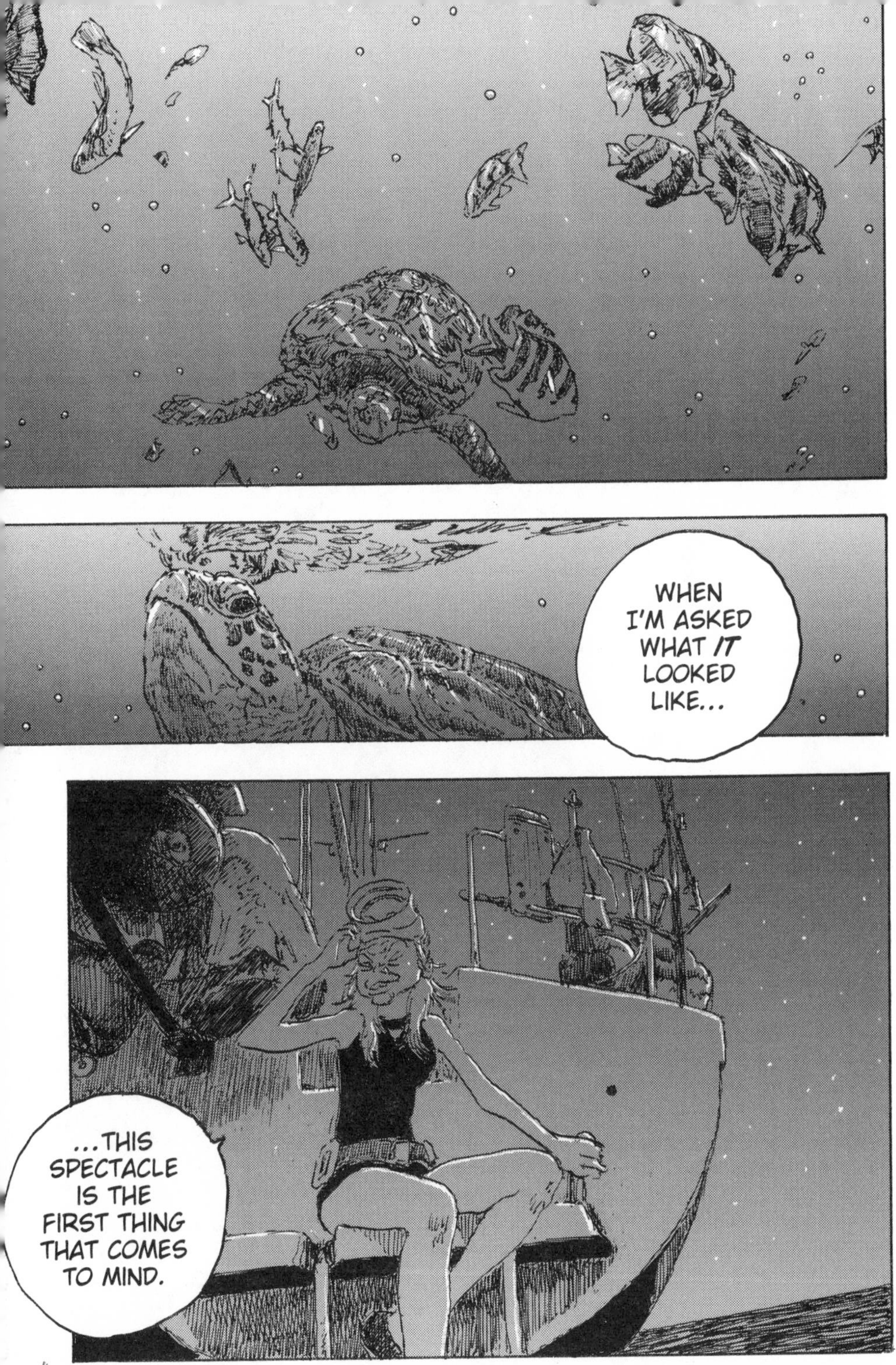
WHEN I'M ASKED WHAT *IT* LOOKED LIKE...
...THIS SPECTACLE IS THE FIRST THING THAT COMES TO MIND.

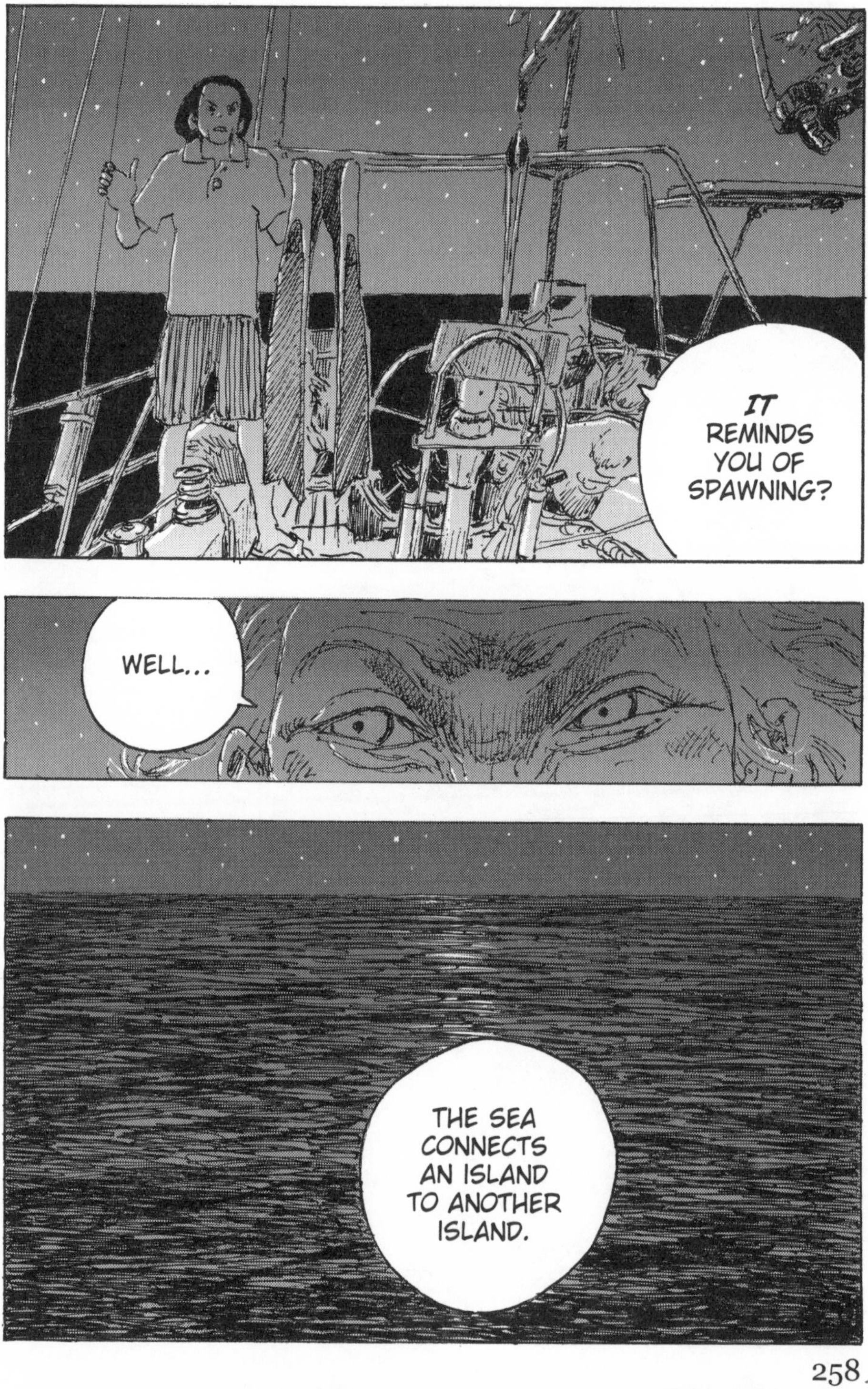
IT REMINDS YOU OF SPAWNING?
WELL...
THE SEA CONNECTS AN ISLAND TO ANOTHER ISLAND.

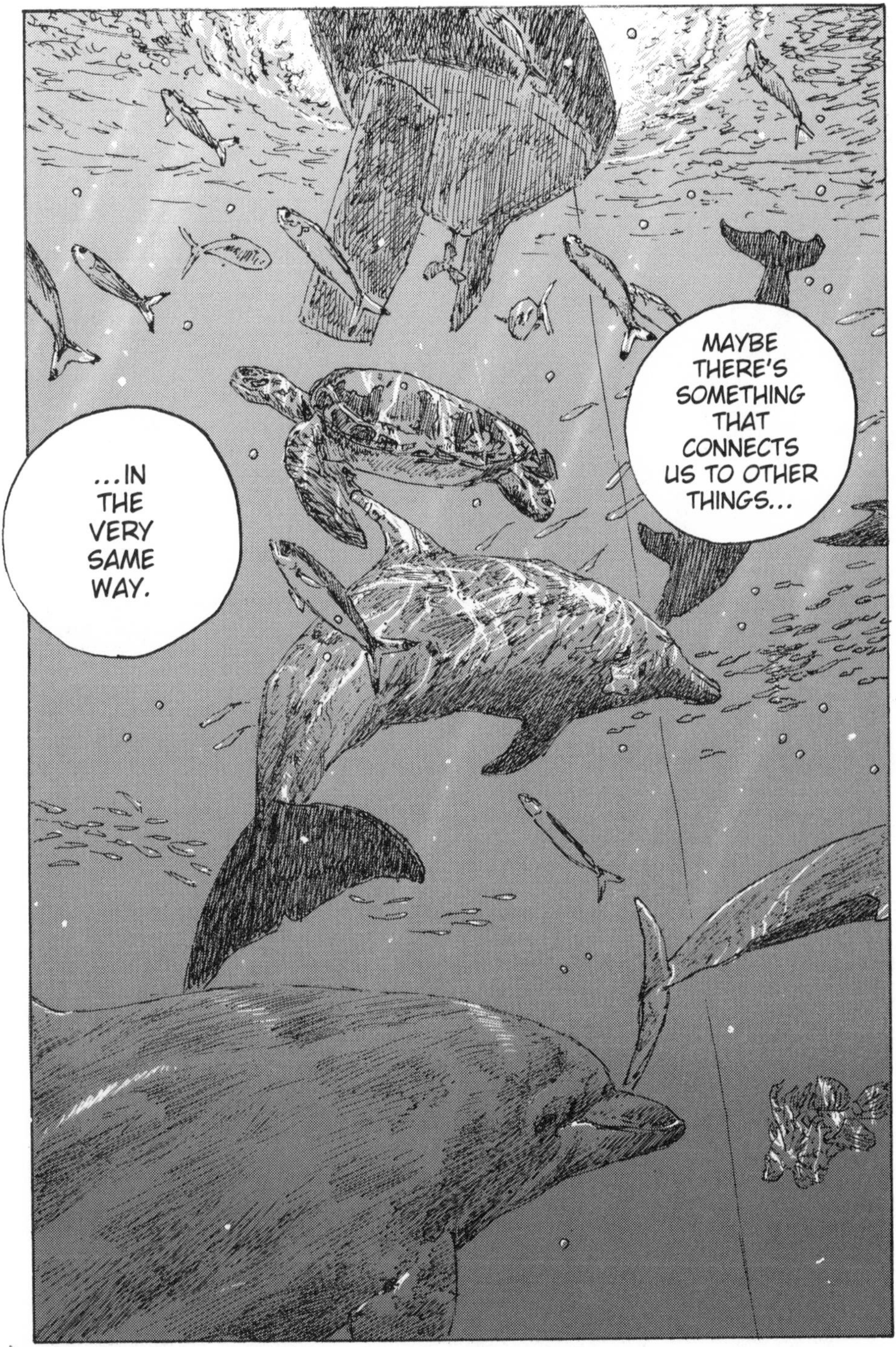
MAYBE THERE'S SOMETHING THAT CONNECTS US TO OTHER THINGS...
...IN THE VERY SAME WAY.

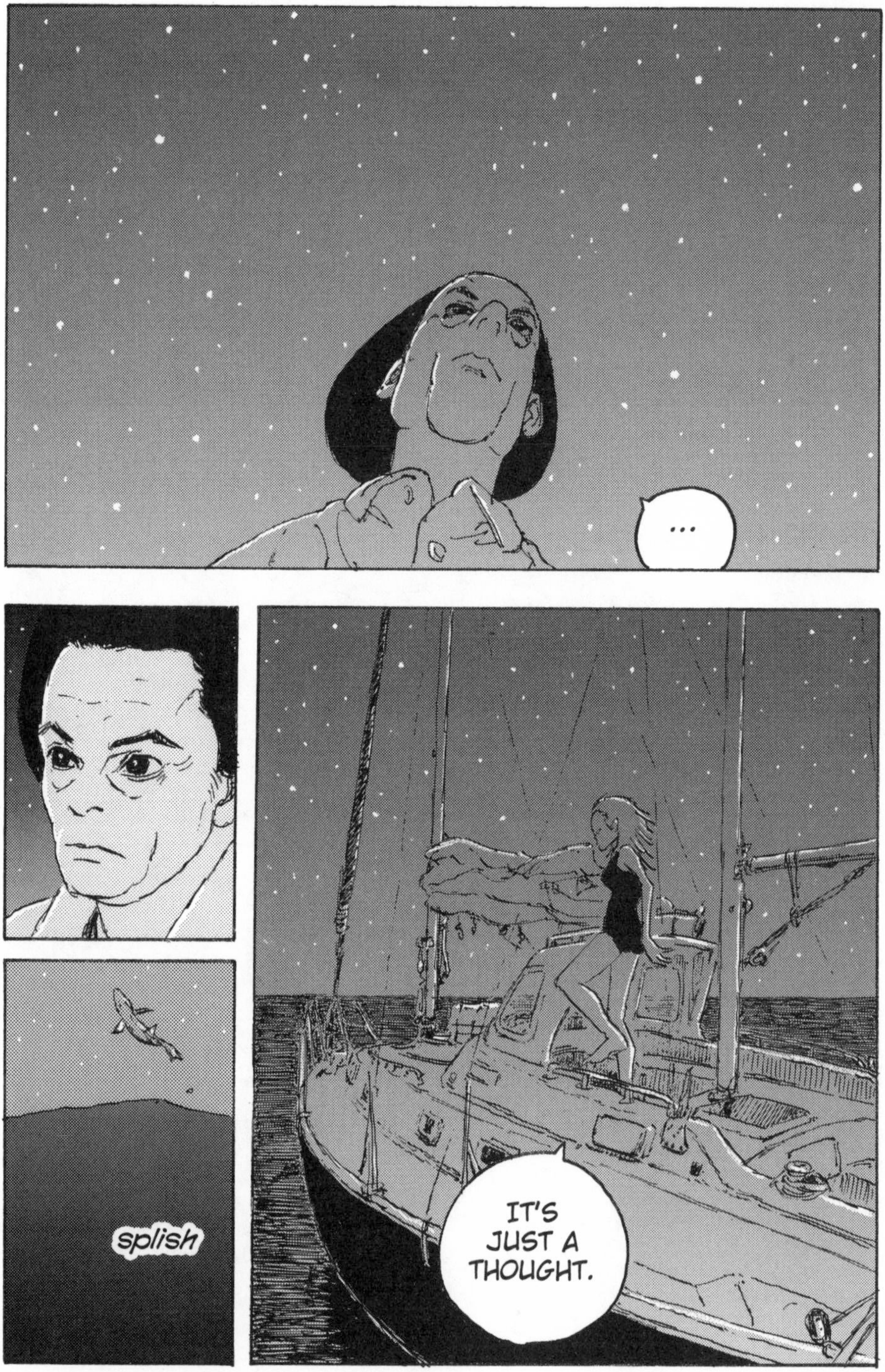
...
IT'S JUST A THOUGHT.
splish

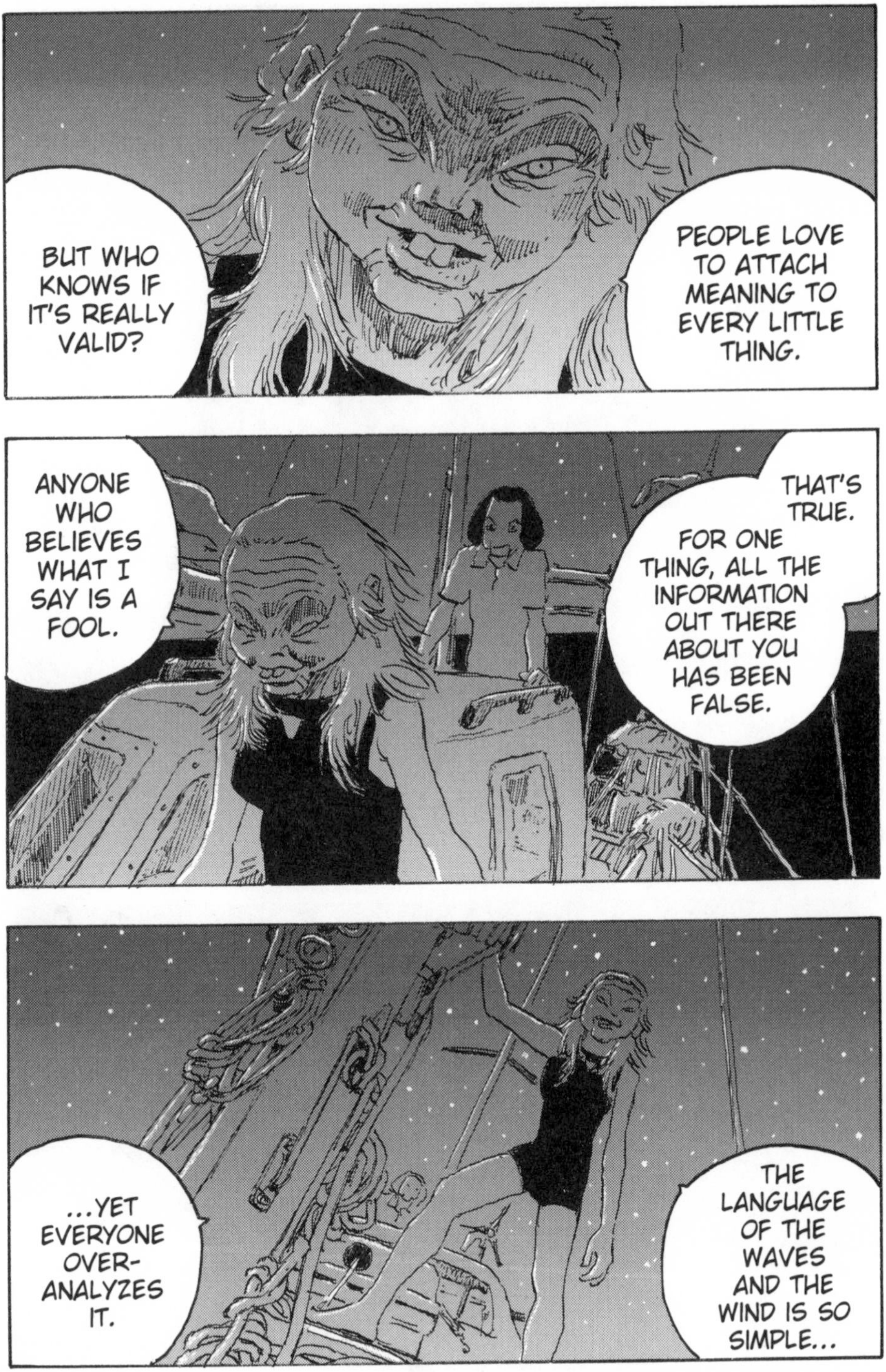
PEOPLE LOVE TO ATTACH MEANING TO EVERY LITTLE THING.
BUT WHO KNOWS IF IT'S REALLY VALID?
THAT'S TRUE. FOR ONE THING, ALL THE INFORMATION OUT THERE ABOUT YOU HAS BEEN FALSE.
ANYONE WHO BELIEVES WHAT I SAY IS A FOOL.
THE LANGUAGE OF THE WAVES AND THE WIND IS SO SIMPLE...
...YET EVERYONE OVER-ANALYZES IT.

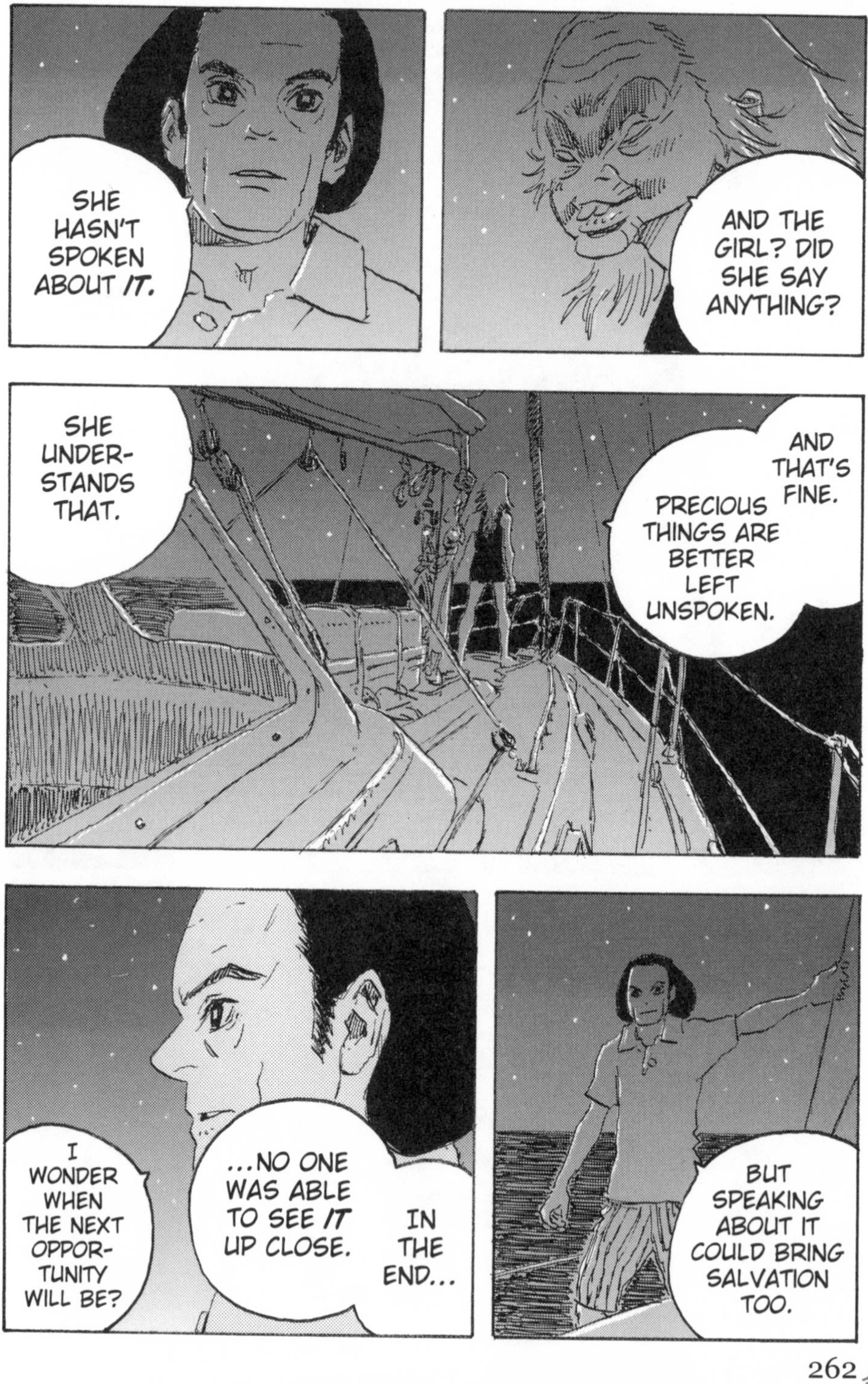
AND THE GIRL? DID SHE SAY ANYTHING?
SHE HASN'T SPOKEN ABOUT *IT.*
AND THAT'S FINE.
PRECIOUS THINGS ARE BETTER LEFT UNSPOKEN.
SHE UNDER-STANDS THAT.
BUT SPEAKING ABOUT IT COULD BRING SALVATION TOO.
IN THE END...
...NO ONE WAS ABLE TO SEE *IT* UP CLOSE.
I WONDER WHEN THE NEXT OPPOR-TUNITY WILL BE?

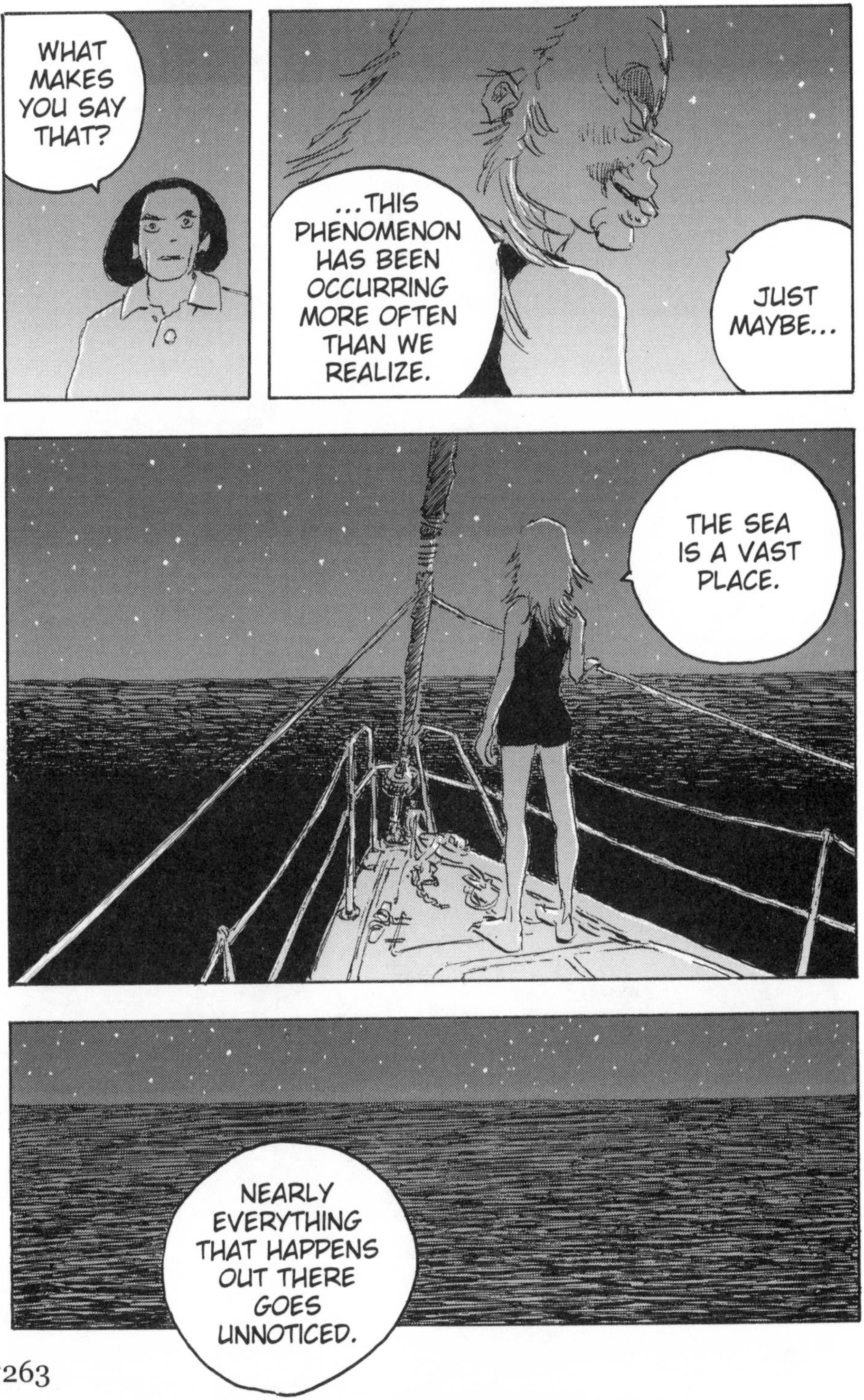
JUST MAYBE...
...THIS PHENOMENON HAS BEEN OCCURRING MORE OFTEN THAN WE REALIZE.
WHAT MAKES YOU SAY THAT?
THE SEA IS A VAST PLACE.
NEARLY EVERYTHING THAT HAPPENS OUT THERE GOES UNNOTICED.

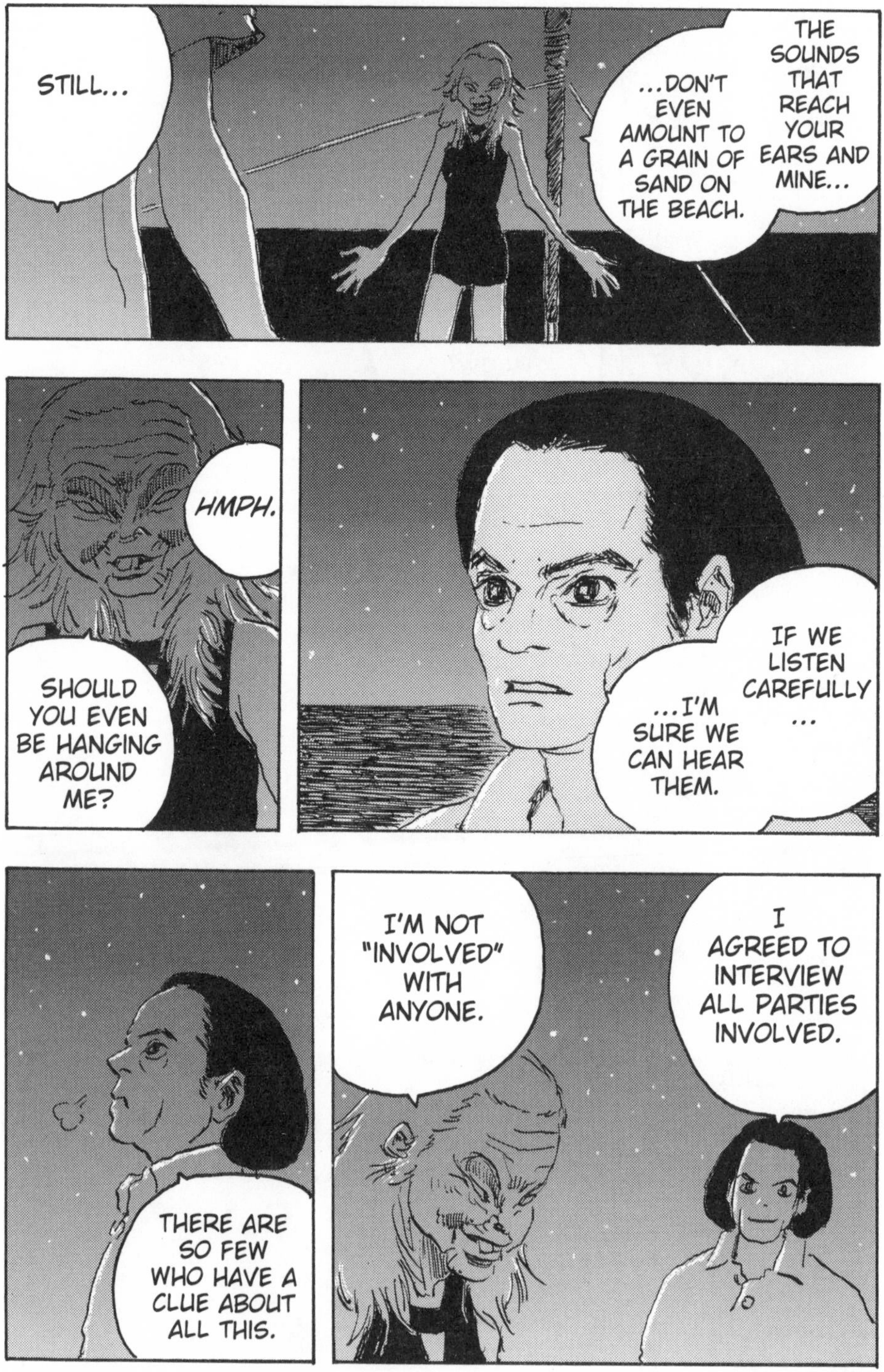
THE SOUNDS THAT REACH YOUR EARS AND MINE...
...DON'T EVEN AMOUNT TO A GRAIN OF SAND ON THE BEACH.
STILL...
IF WE LISTEN CAREFULLY...
...I'M SURE WE CAN HEAR THEM.
HMPH.
SHOULD YOU EVEN BE HANGING AROUND ME?
I AGREED TO INTERVIEW ALL PARTIES INVOLVED.
I'M NOT "INVOLVED" WITH ANYONE.
THERE ARE SO FEW WHO HAVE A CLUE ABOUT ALL THIS.

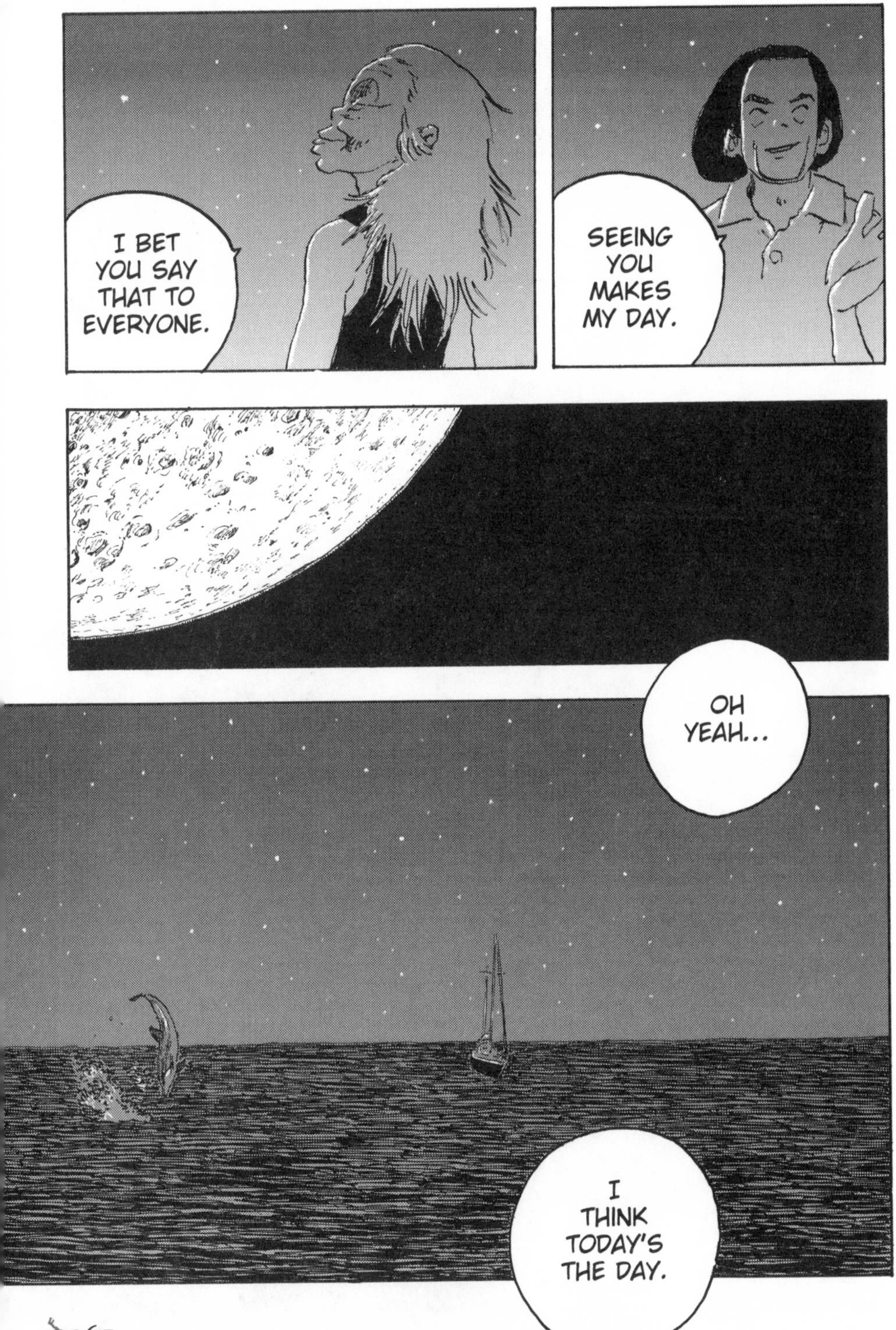

SEEING YOU MAKES MY DAY.
I BET YOU SAY THAT TO EVERYONE.
OH YEAH...
I THINK TODAY'S THE DAY.

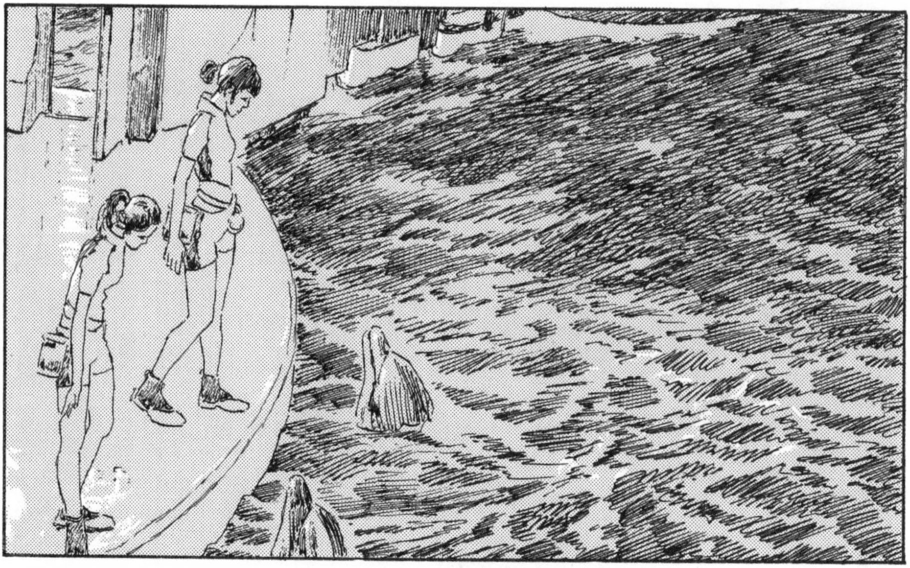
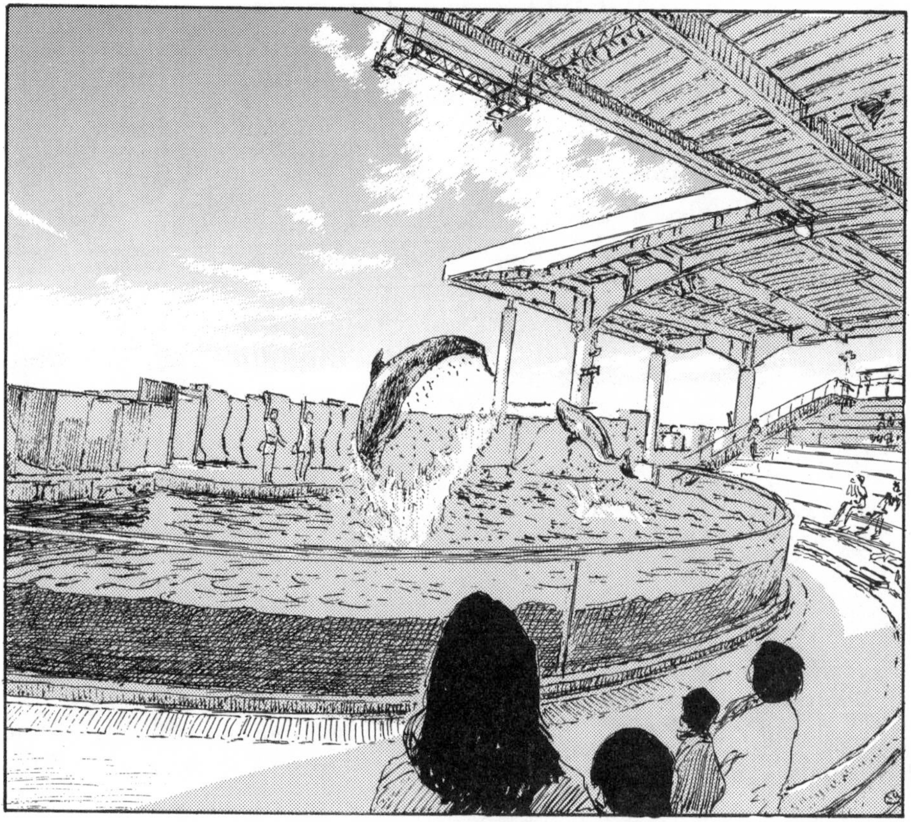

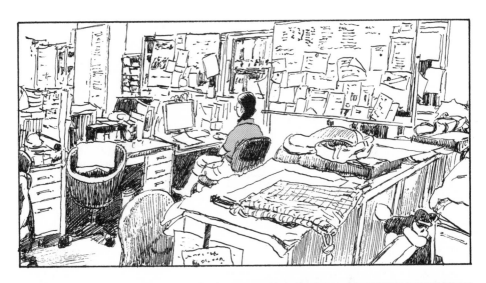

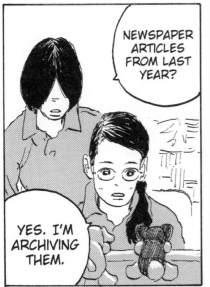

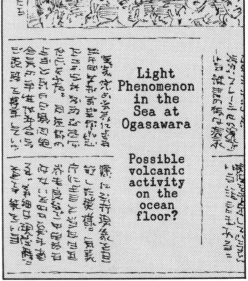

Light Phenomenon in the Sea at Ogasawara
Possible volcanic activity on the ocean floor?
NEWSPAPER ARTICLES FROM LAST YEAR?
YES. I'M ARCHIVING THEM.
OH, THIS ONE...
THERE WAS A HUGE CONFLUENCE OF SEA-FIREFLIES AROUND THAT TIME...
...AND SOME PEOPLE SPECULATE THAT THEY WERE THE CAUSE.

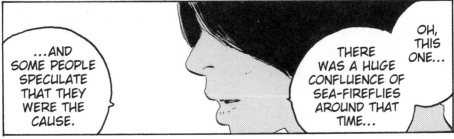

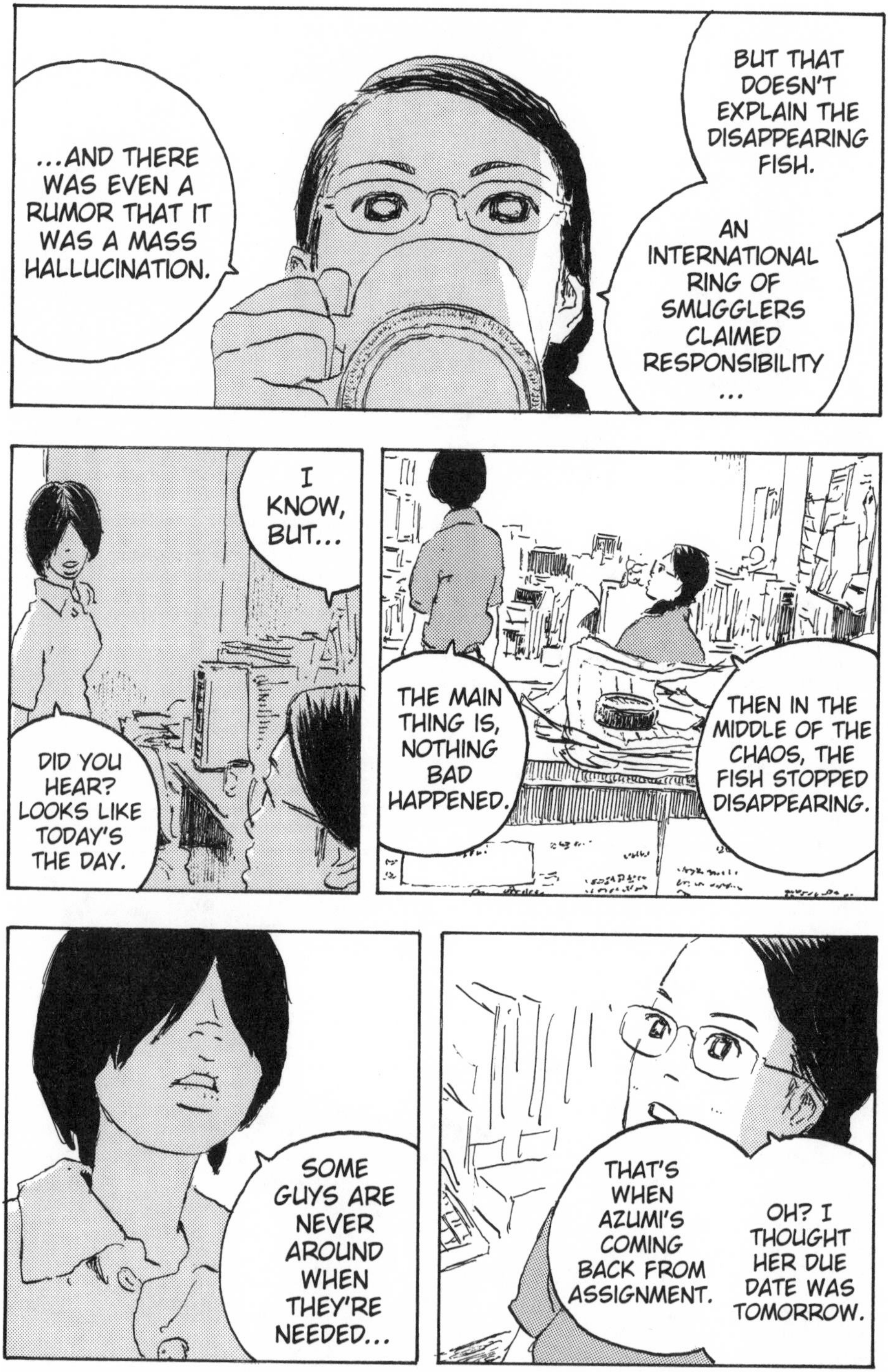
BUT THAT DOESN'T EXPLAIN THE DISAPPEARING FISH.
AN INTERNATIONAL RING OF SMUGGLERS CLAIMED RESPONSIBILITY ...
...AND THERE WAS EVEN A RUMOR THAT IT WAS A MASS HALLUCINATION.
THEN IN THE MIDDLE OF THE CHAOS, THE FISH STOPPED DISAPPEARING.
THE MAIN THING IS, NOTHING BAD HAPPENED.
I KNOW, BUT...
DID YOU HEAR? LOOKS LIKE TODAY'S THE DAY.
OH? I THOUGHT HER DUE DATE WAS TOMORROW.
THAT'S WHEN AZUMI'S COMING BACK FROM ASSIGNMENT.
SOME GUYS ARE NEVER AROUND WHEN THEY'RE NEEDED...

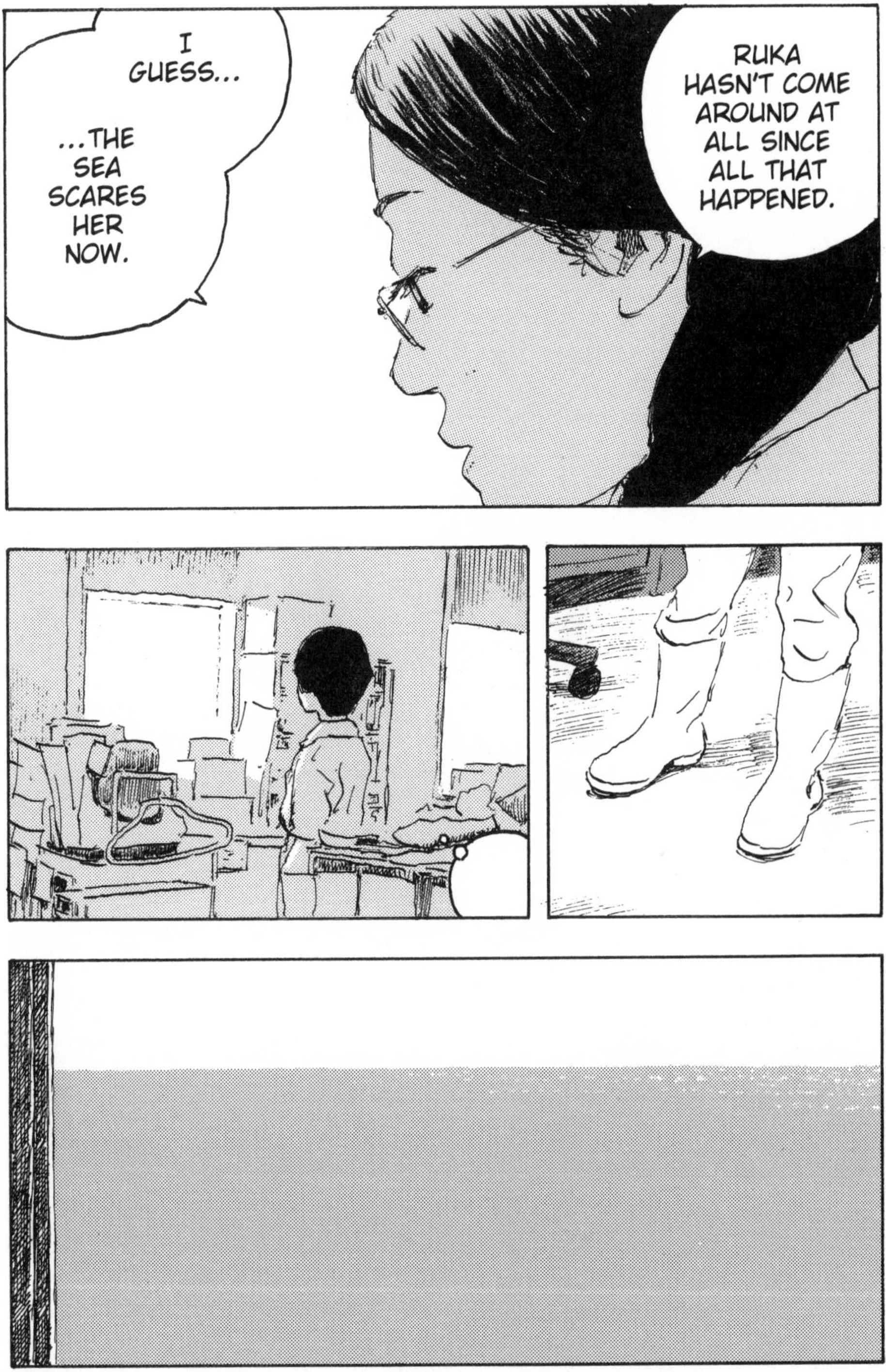
RUKA HASN'T COME AROUND AT ALL SINCE ALL THAT HAPPENED.
I GUESS...
...THE SEA SCARES HER NOW.

SEE HOW POINTED HIS HEAD IS?

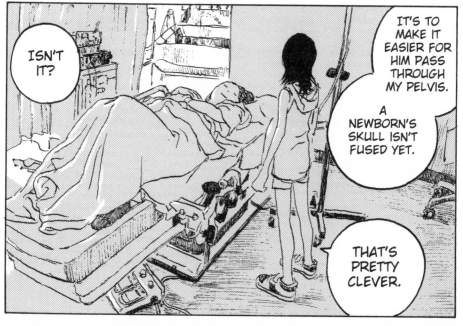

IT'S TO MAKE IT EASIER FOR HIM PASS THROUGH MY PELVIS.

A NEWBORN'S SKULL ISN'T FUSED YET.

ISN'T IT?

THAT'S PRETTY CLEVER.

In the womb, babies breathe amniotic fluid.

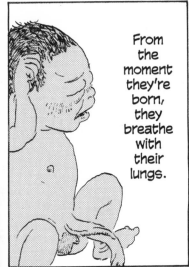

From the moment they're born, they breathe with their lungs.
IT'S LIKE A SEA CREATURE BEING REBORN INTO A LAND CREATURE.
IS DYING LIKE BEING REBORN INTO A DIFFERENT WORLD?

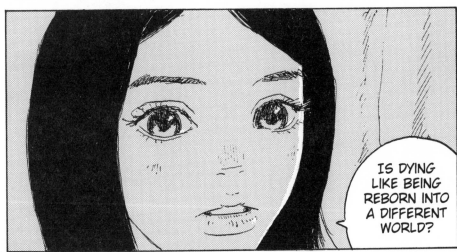

...LIKE OPPOSITE SIDES...
...OF THE SAME THING?
I USED TO THINK THAT YOU AND I COULDN'T GET CLOSE.
JUST LIKE MY MOM AND ME.

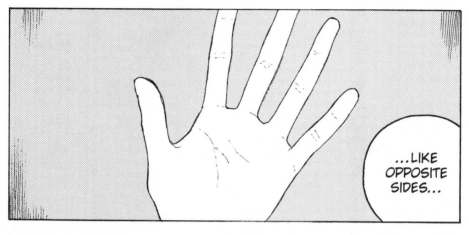

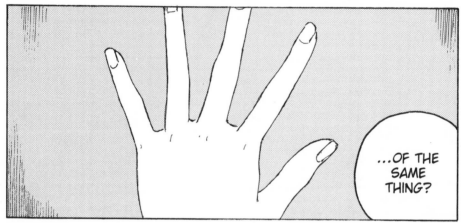

...WHAT MADE ME SET OUT TO RESCUE YOU...?

SO I WONDER..

...AND THIS CHILD WILL GET ALONG.

PERHAPS YOU ...

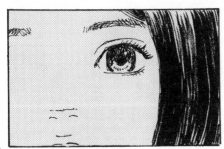

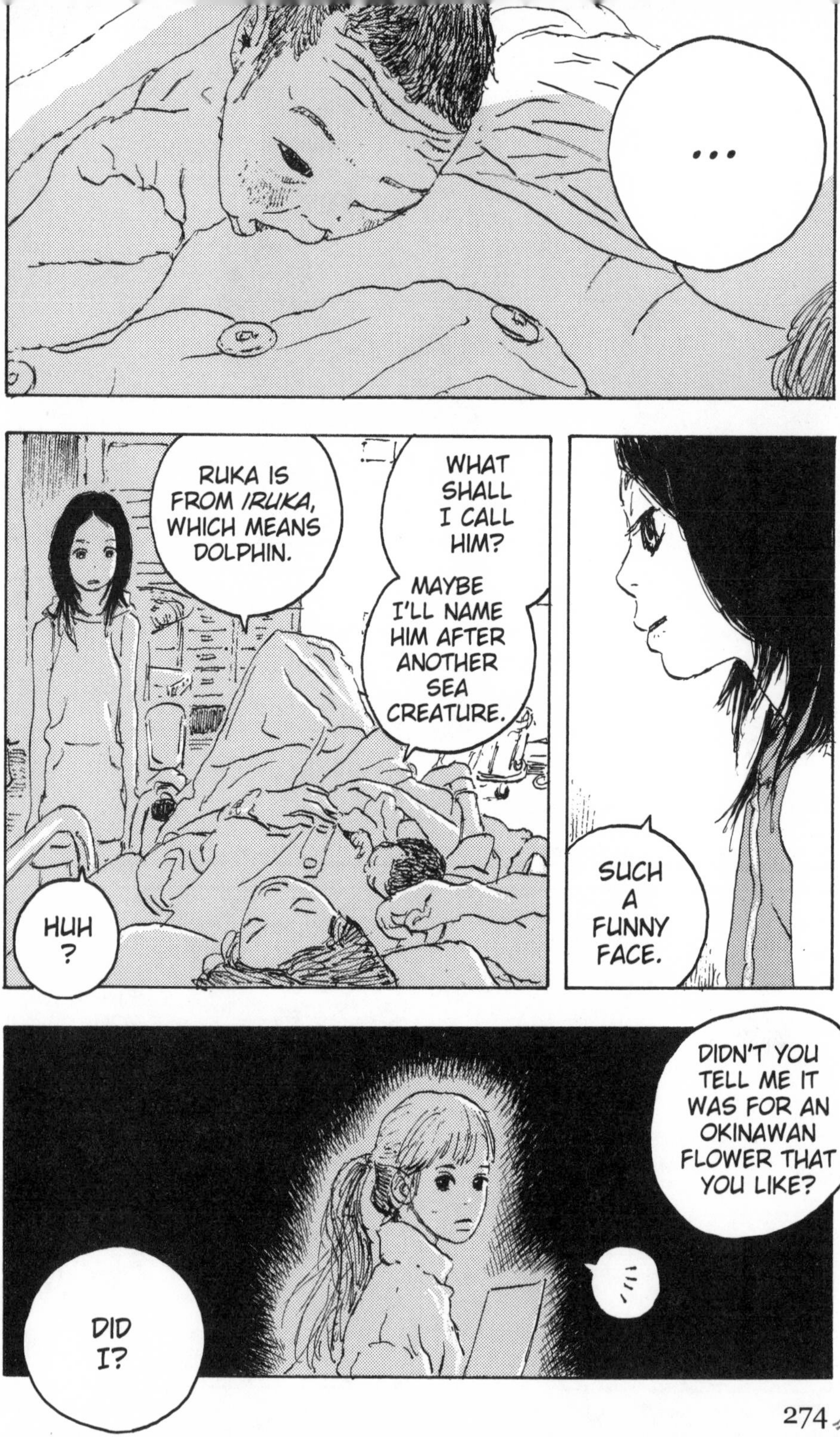
...
SUCH A FUNNY FACE.
WHAT SHALL I CALL HIM?
MAYBE I'LL NAME HIM AFTER ANOTHER SEA CREATURE.
RUKA IS FROM *IRUKA*, WHICH MEANS DOLPHIN.
HUH?
DIDN'T YOU TELL ME IT WAS FOR AN OKINAWAN FLOWER THAT YOU LIKE?
DID I?

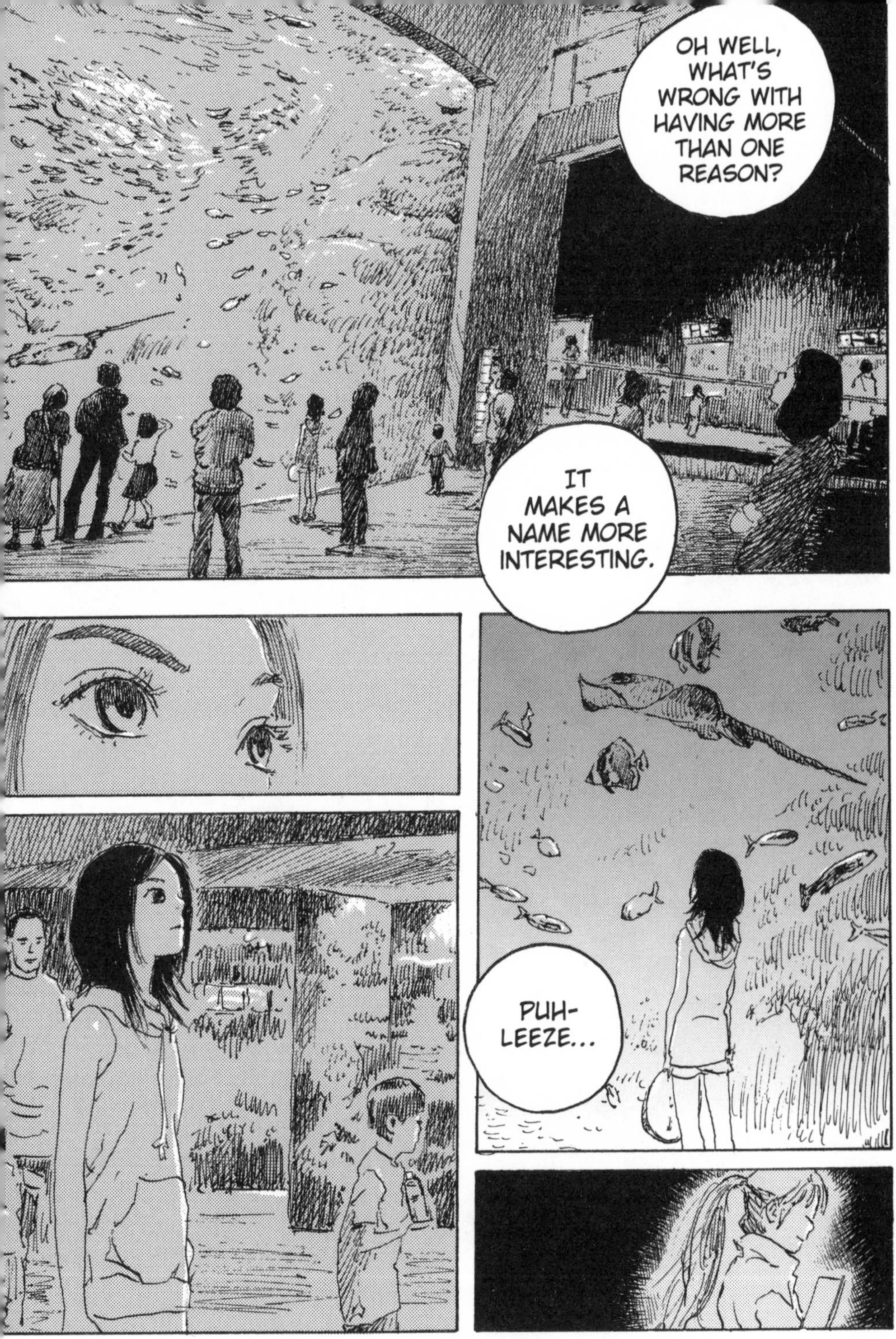
OH WELL, WHAT'S WRONG WITH HAVING MORE THAN ONE REASON?
IT MAKES A NAME MORE INTERESTING.
PUH-LEEZE...

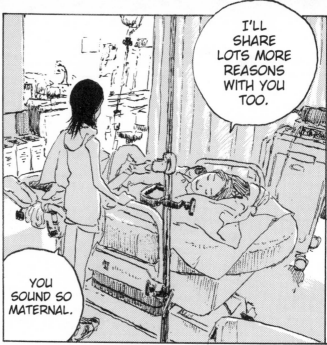

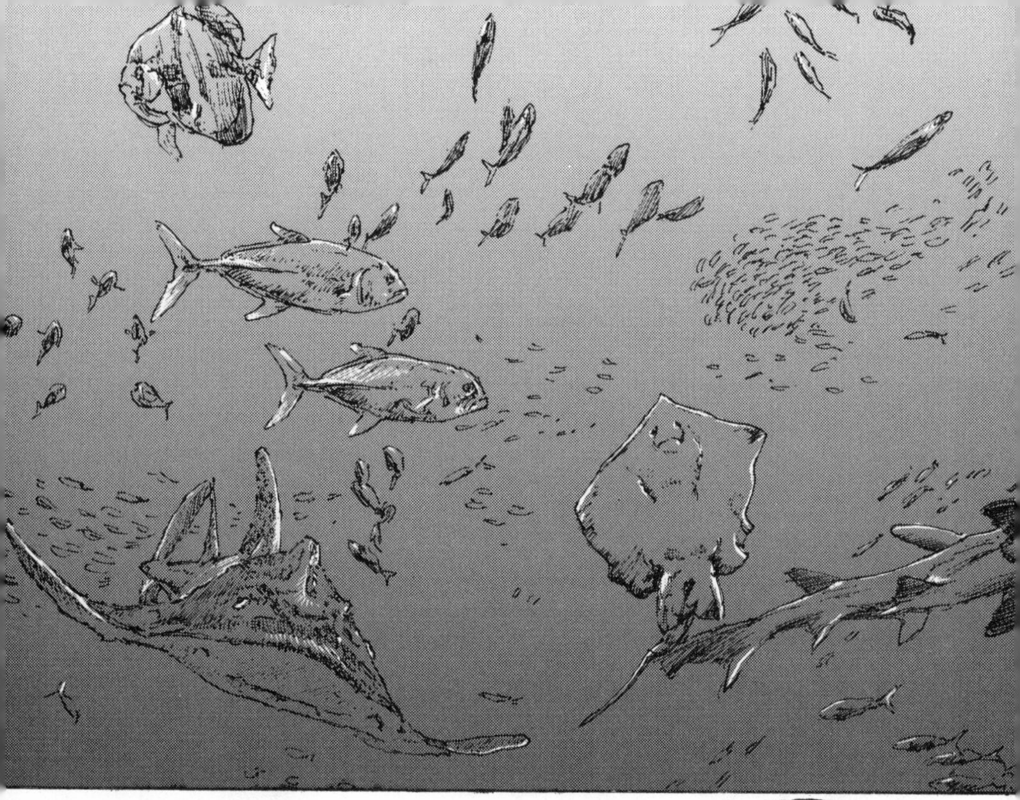
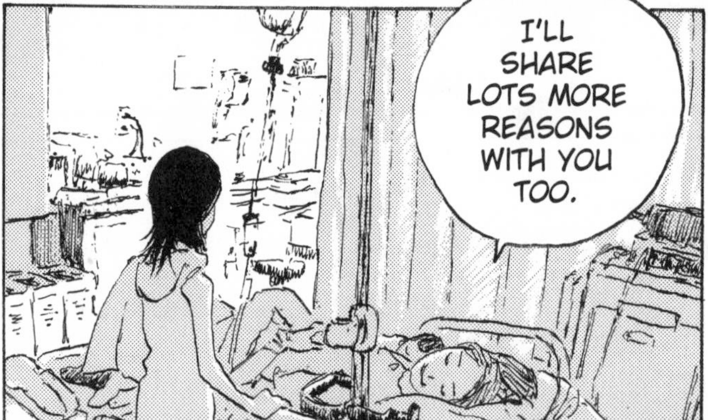
I'LL SHARE LOTS MORE REASONS WITH YOU TOO.
YOU SOUND SO MATERNAL.
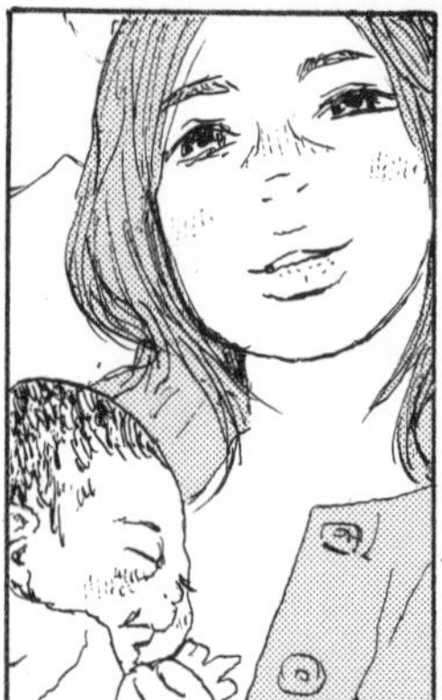
RELAX.
IT WON'T LAST.

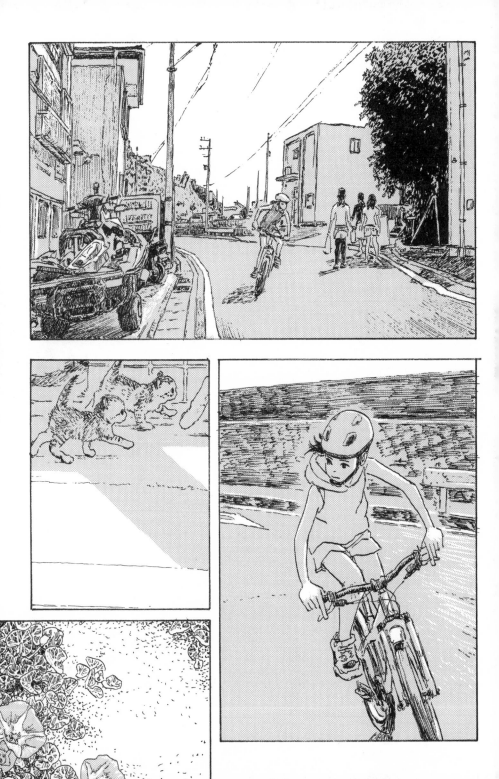

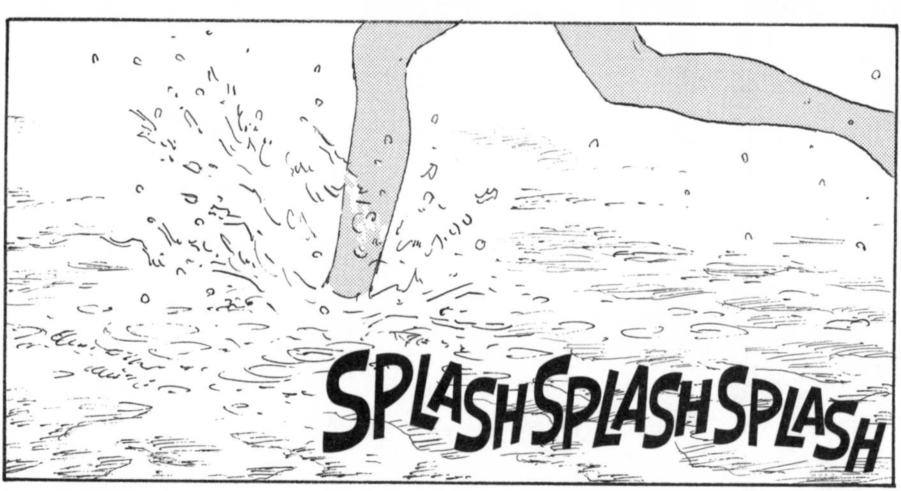
SPLASH SPLASH SPLASH
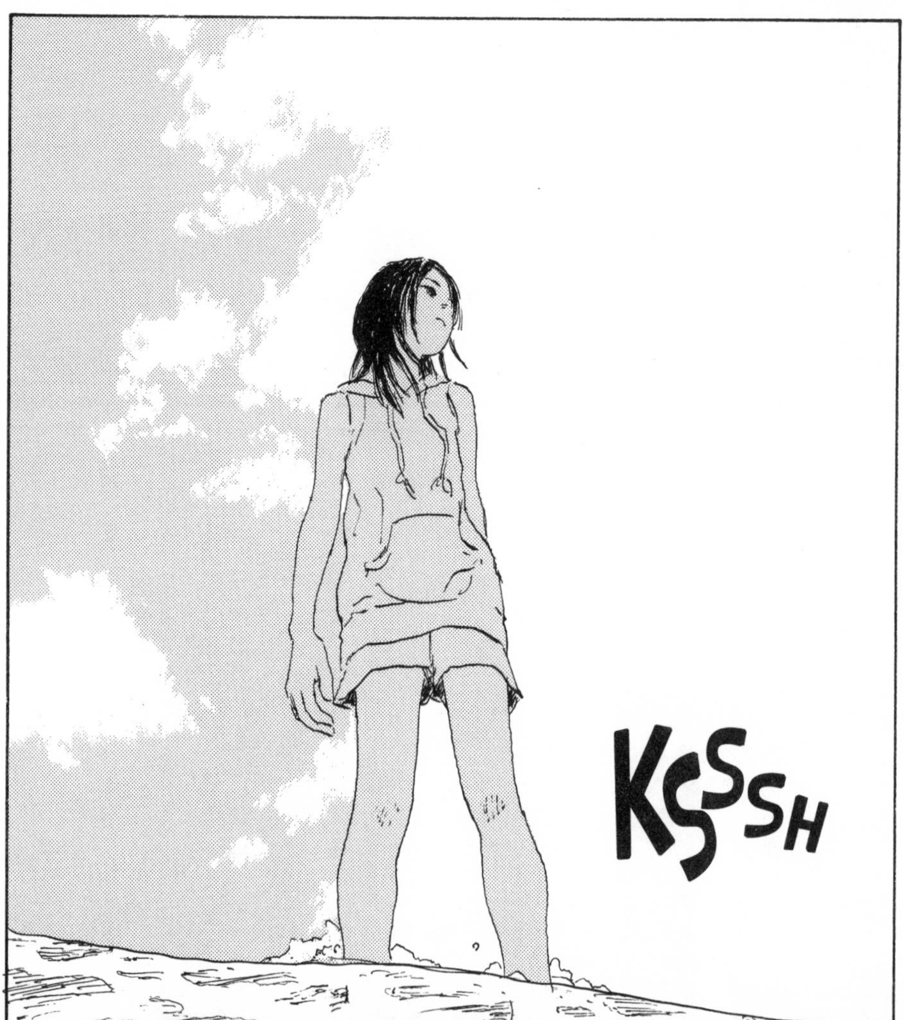
KSSSH

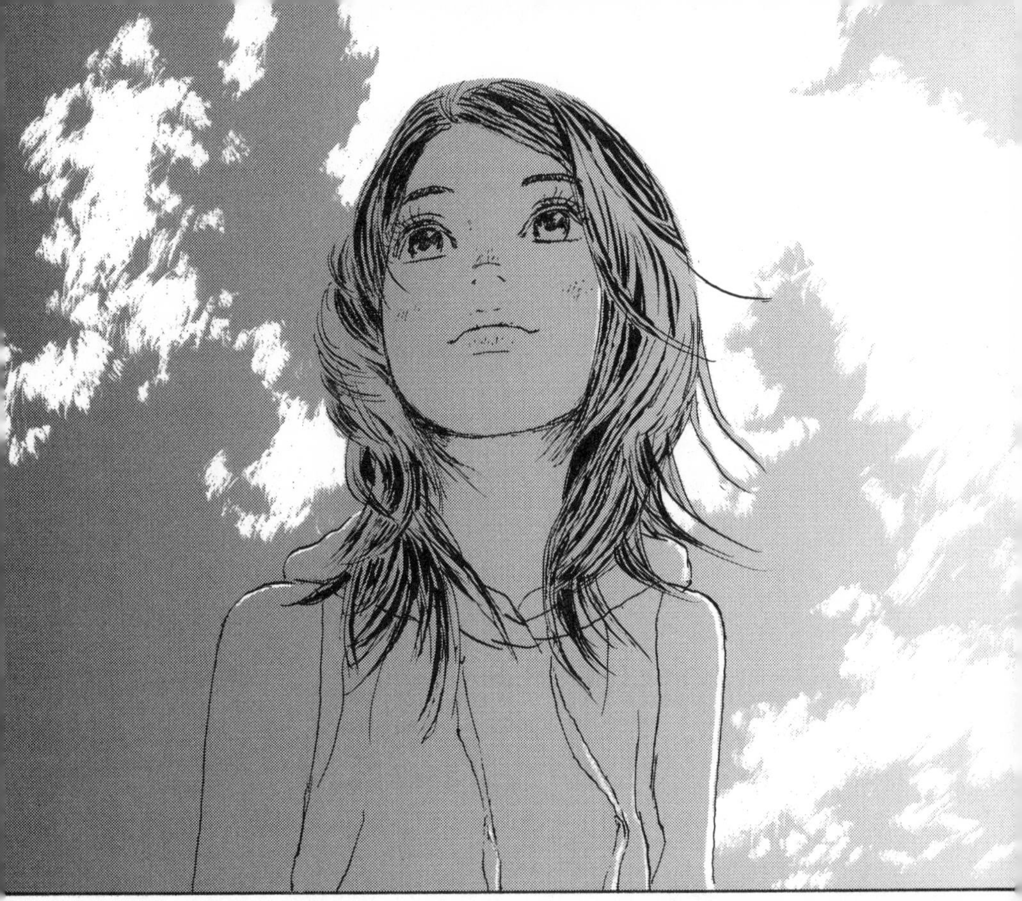

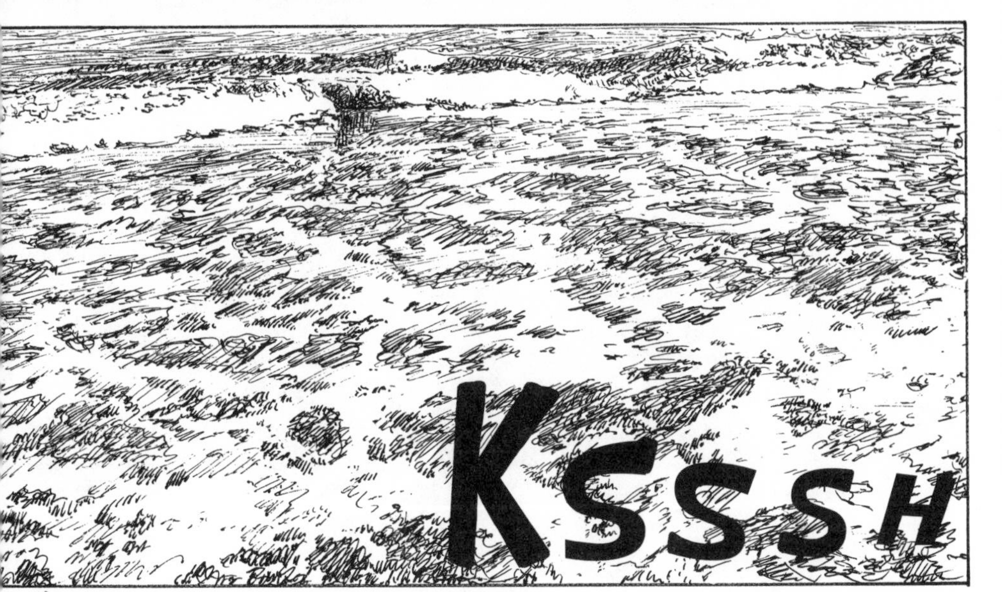
KSSSH

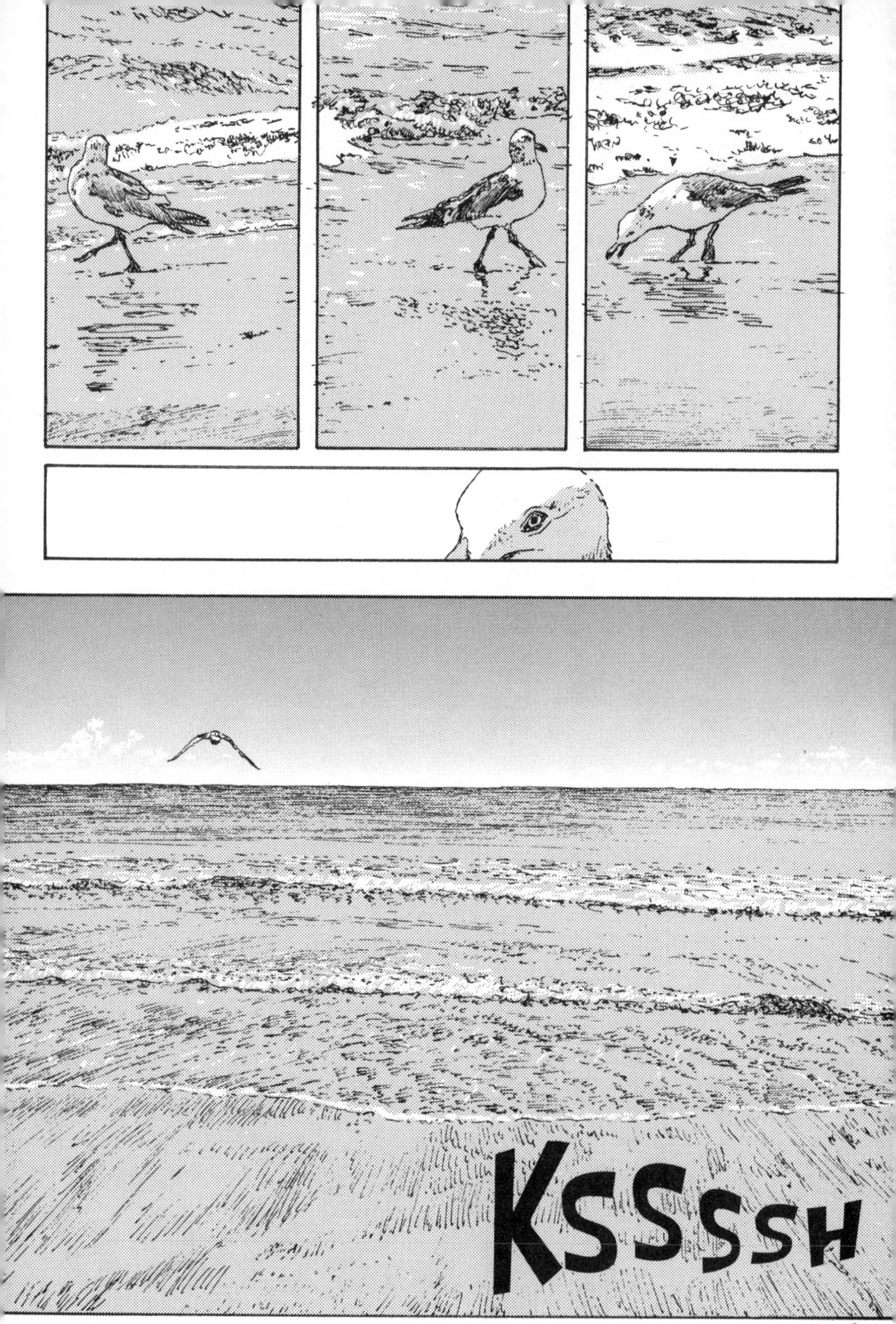
KSSSSH

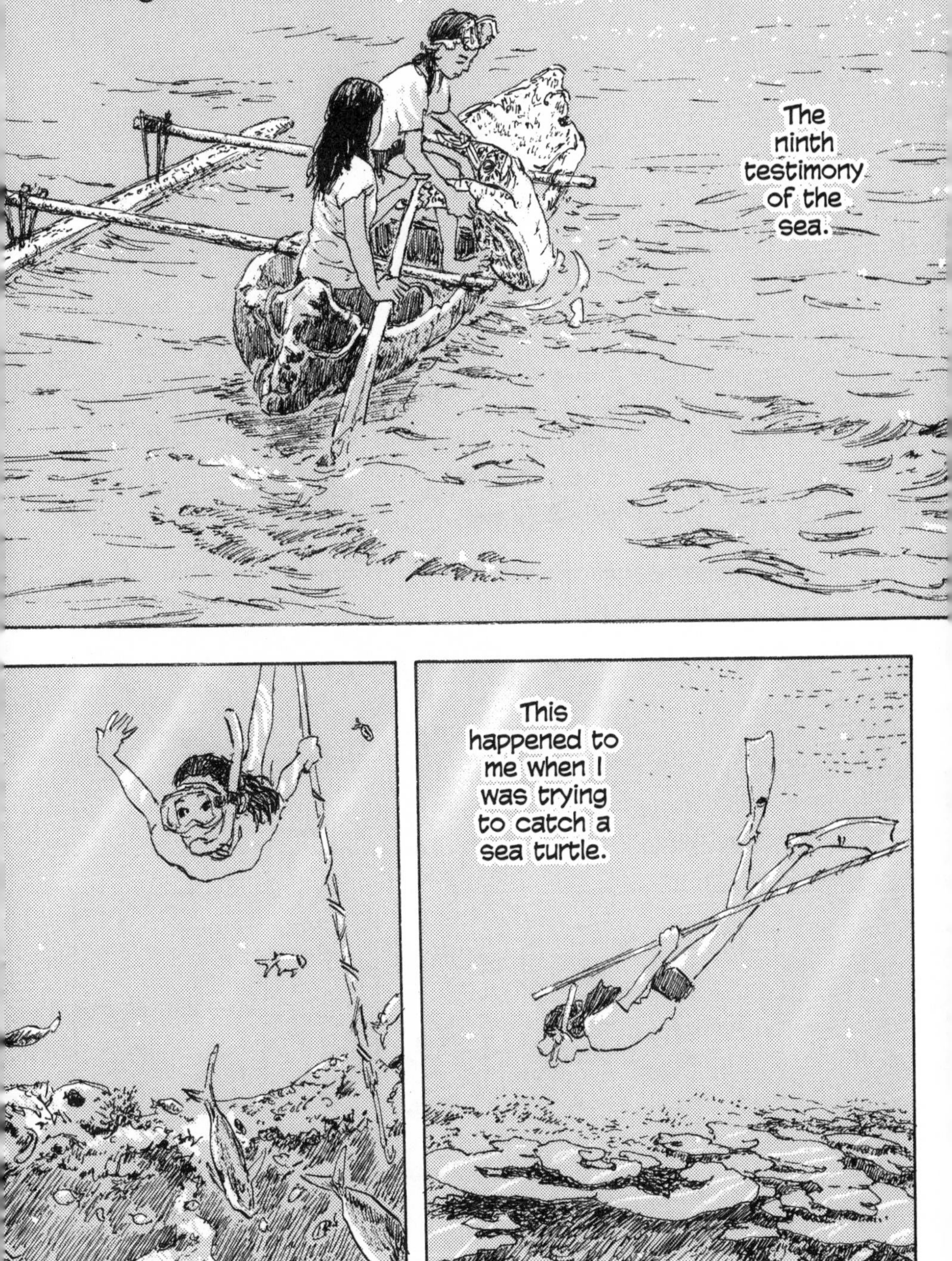
The ninth testimony of the sea.
This happened to me when I was trying to catch a sea turtle.

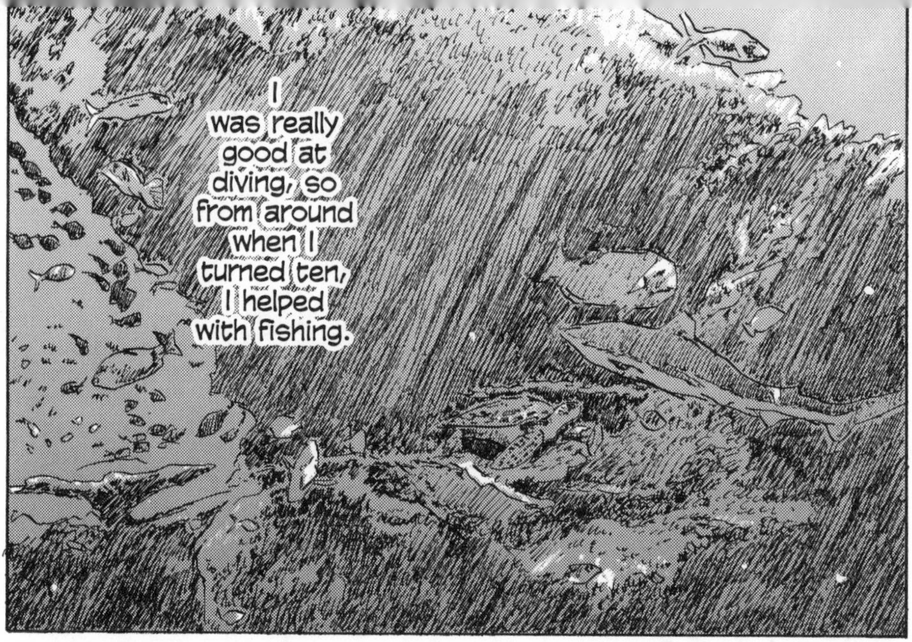
I was really good at diving, so from around when I turned ten, I helped with fishing.

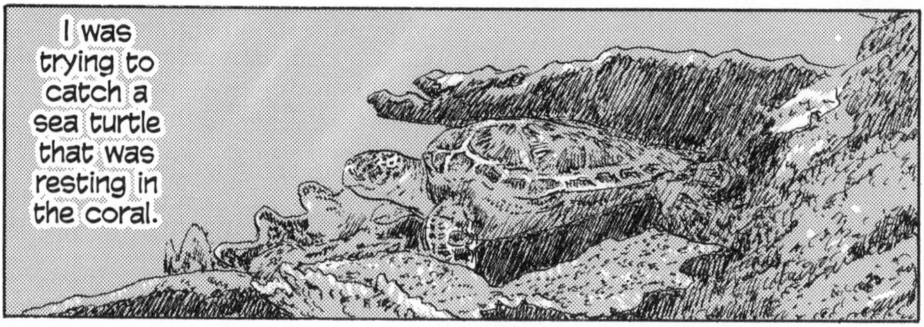
I was trying to catch a sea turtle that was resting in the coral.

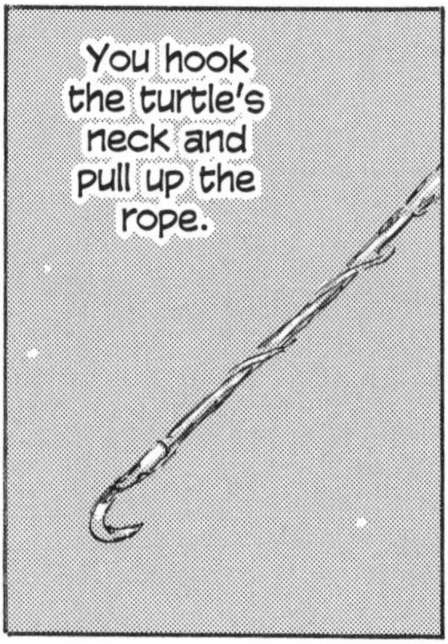
You hook the turtle's neck and pull up the rope.

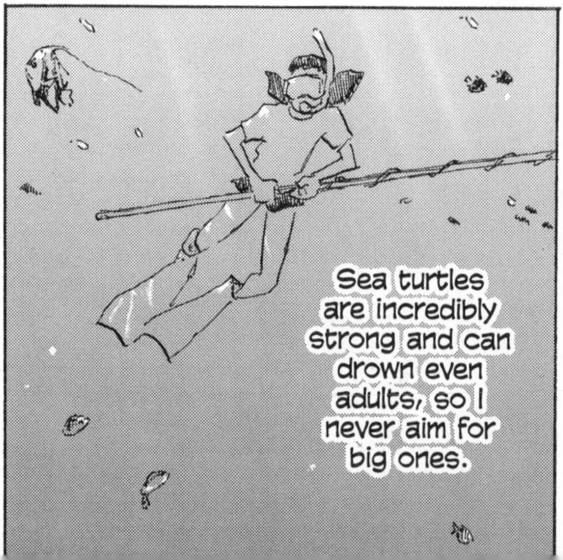
Sea turtles are incredibly strong and can drown even adults, so I never aim for big ones.

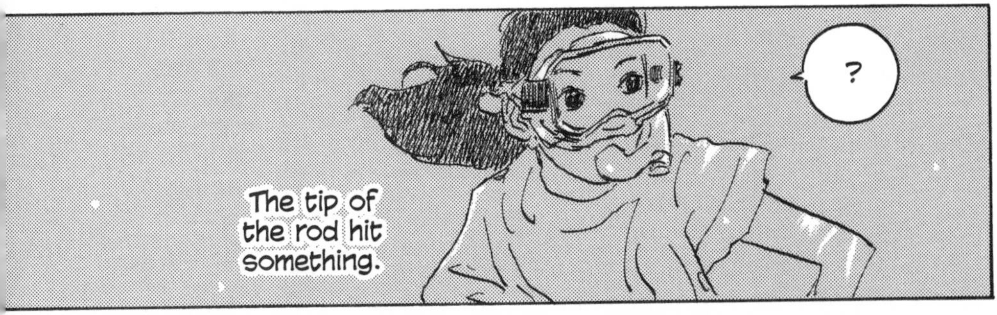
?
The tip of the rod hit something.
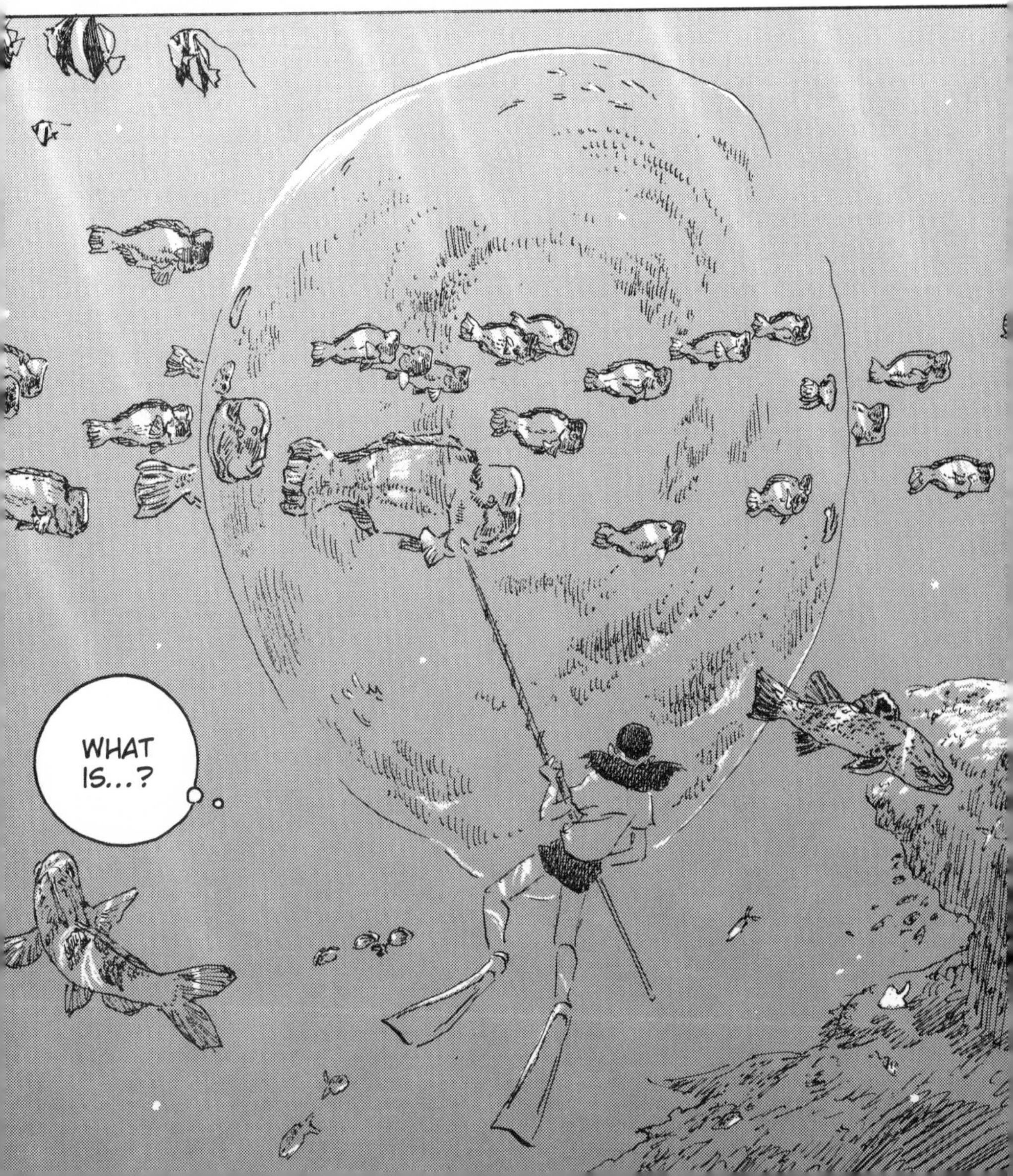
WHAT IS...?

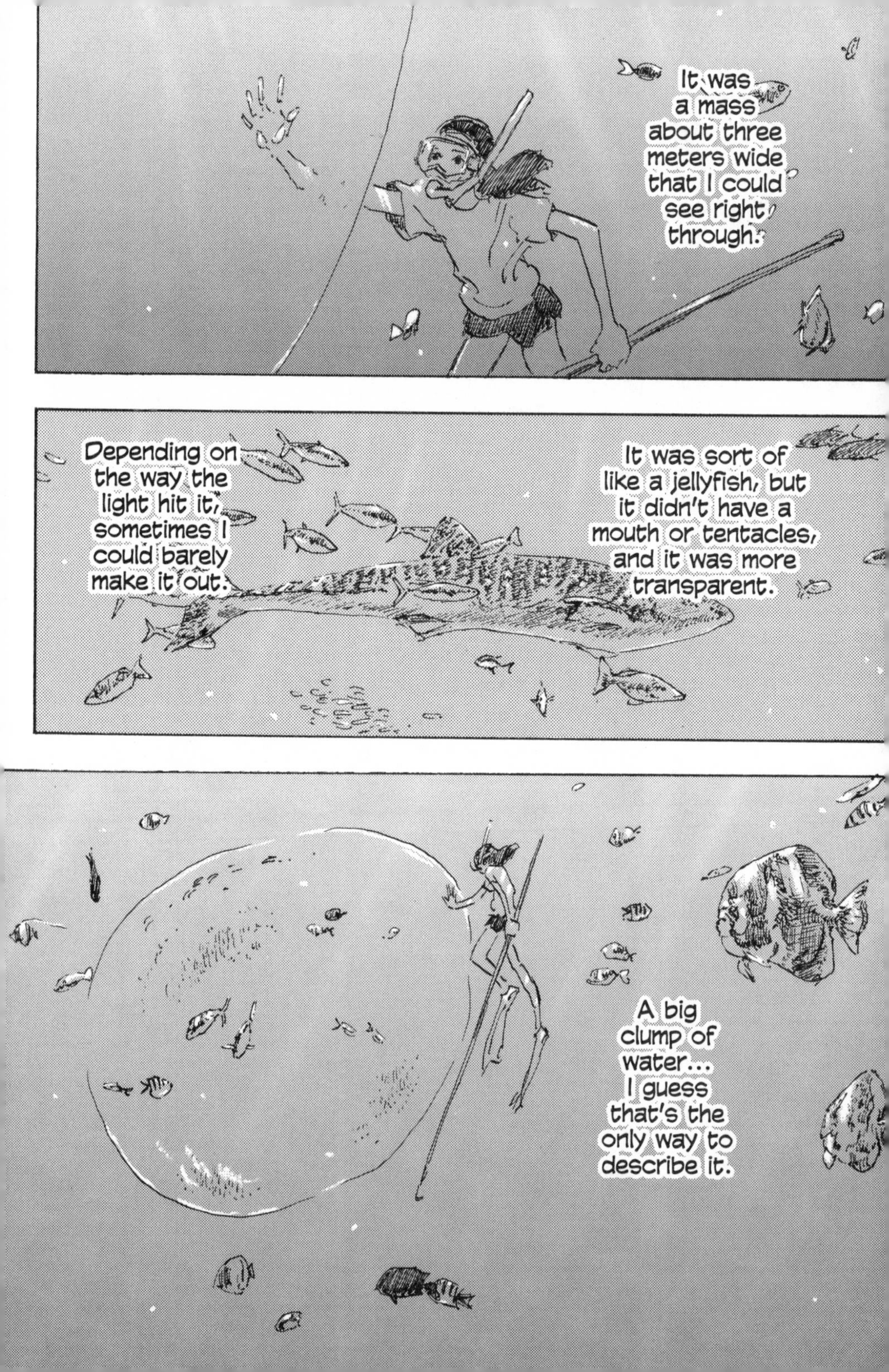
It was a mass about three meters wide that I could see right through.
It was sort of like a jellyfish, but it didn't have a mouth or tentacles, and it was more transparent.
Depending on the way the light hit it, sometimes I could barely make it out.
A big clump of water... I guess that's the only way to describe it.

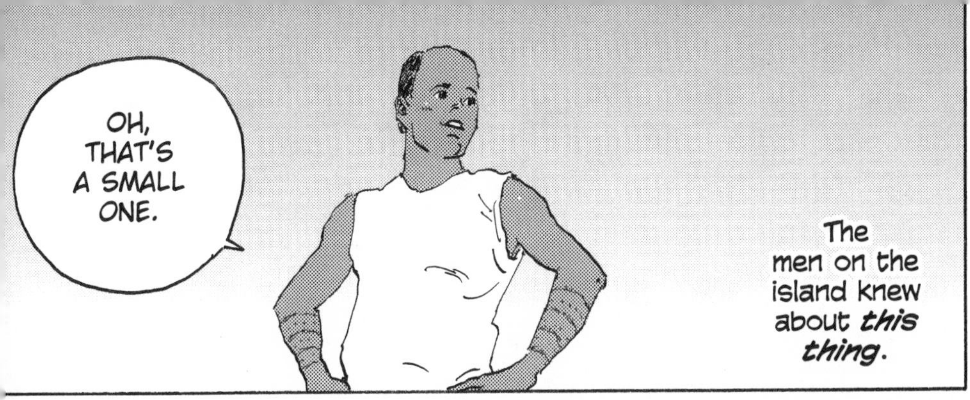
The men on the island knew about *this thing*.
OH, THAT'S A SMALL ONE.

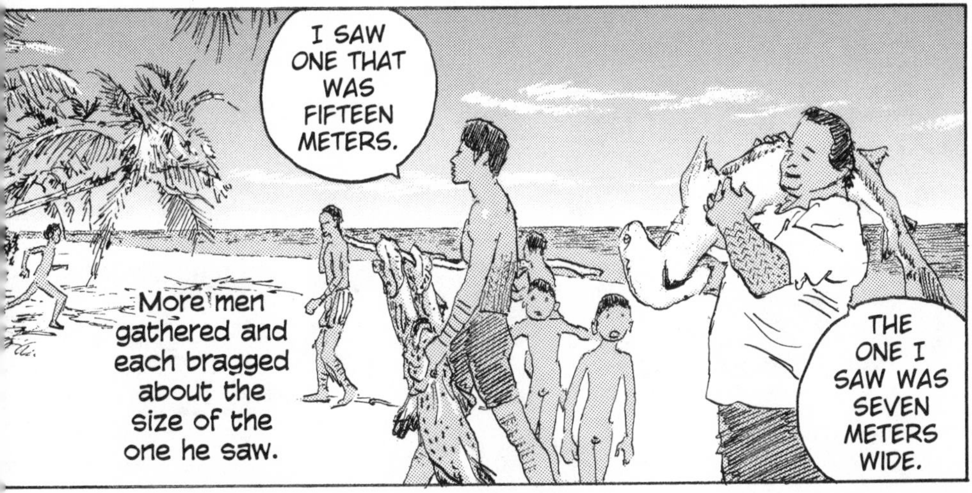
I SAW ONE THAT WAS FIFTEEN METERS.
THE ONE I SAW WAS SEVEN METERS WIDE.
More men gathered and each bragged about the size of the one he saw.

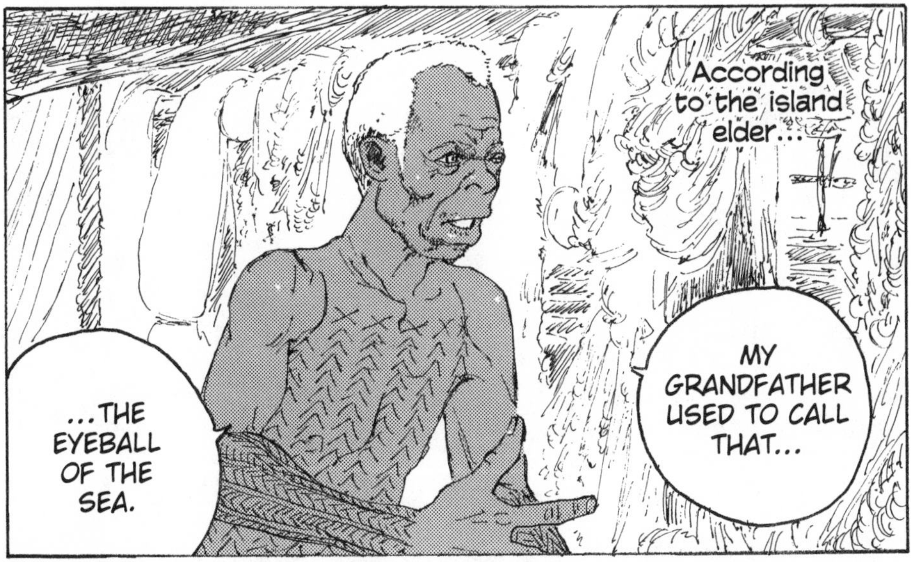
According to the island elder...
MY GRANDFATHER USED TO CALL THAT...
...THE EYEBALL OF THE SEA.

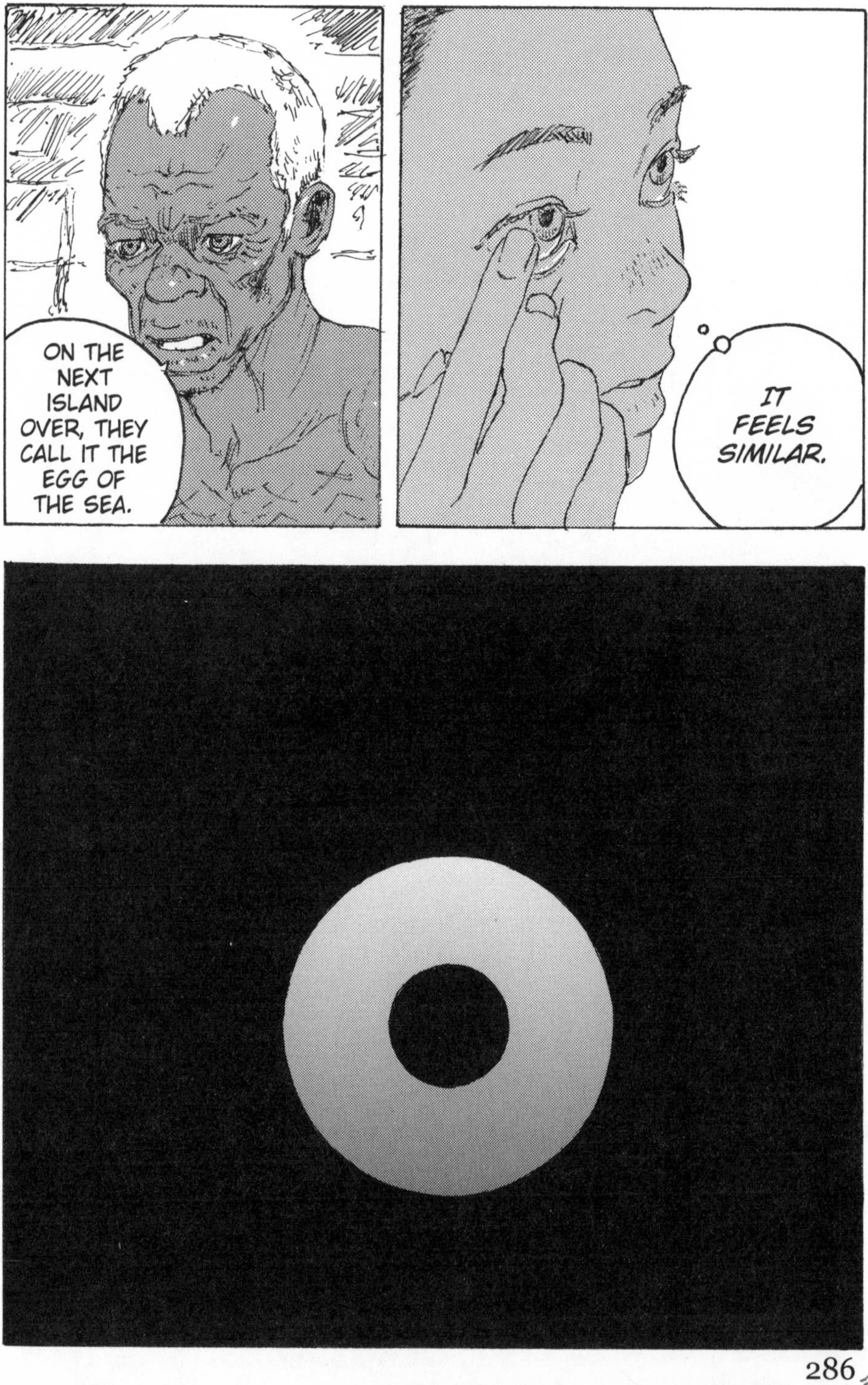
IT FEELS SIMILAR.
ON THE NEXT ISLAND OVER, THEY CALL IT THE EGG OF THE SEA.

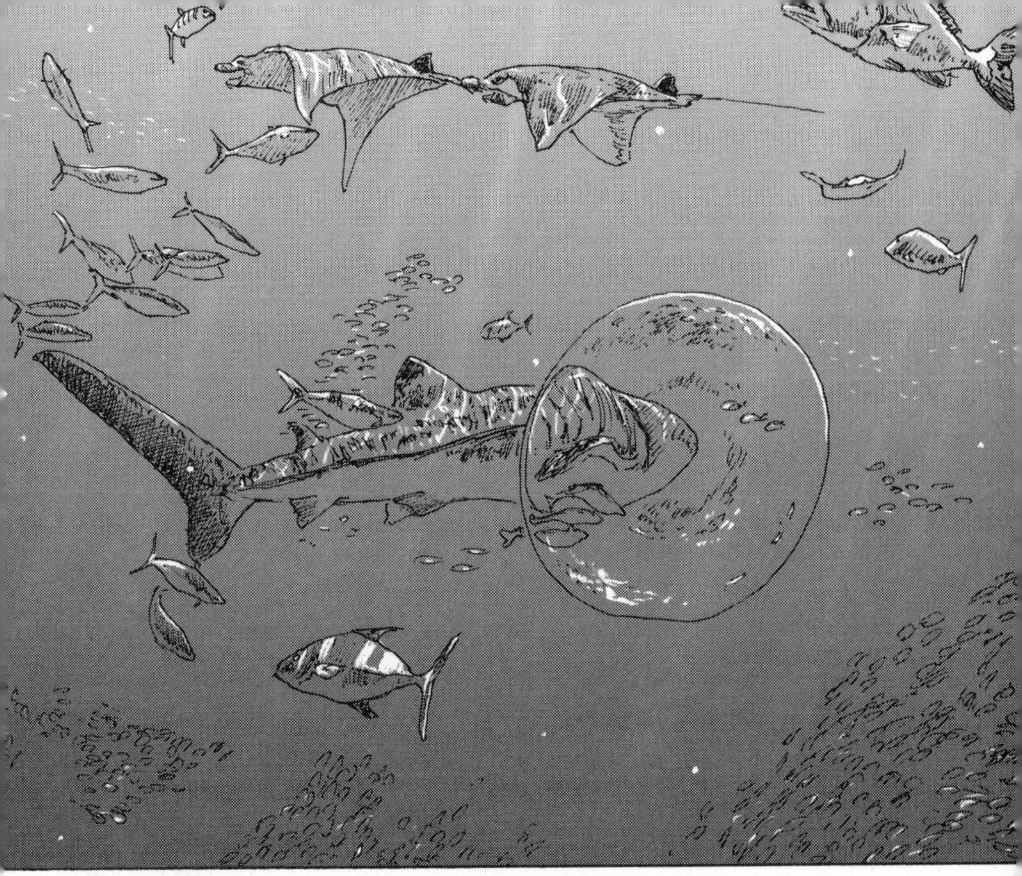

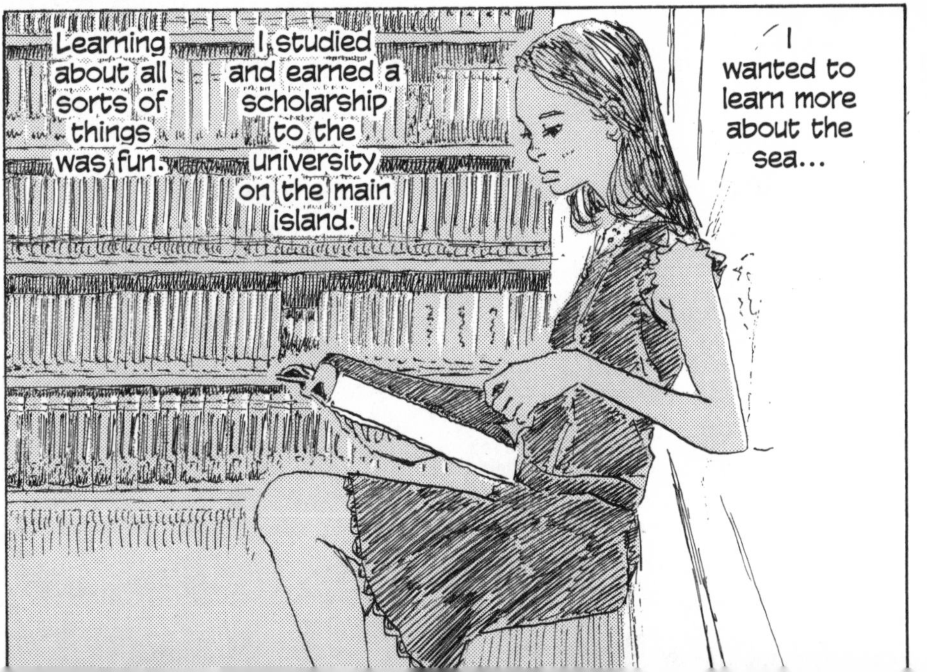
I wanted to learn more about the sea...
I studied and earned a scholarship to the university on the main island.
Learning about all sorts of things was fun.

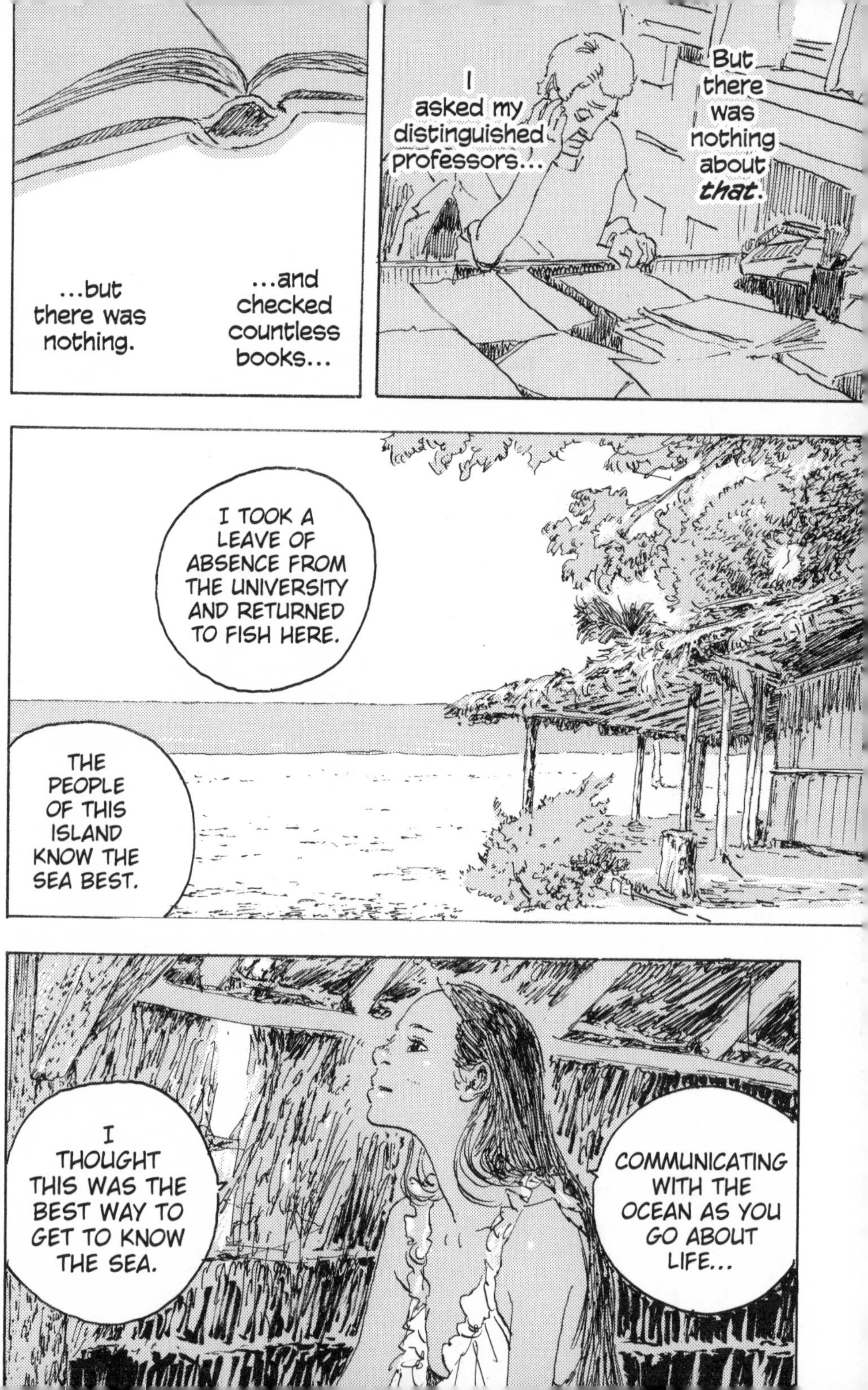
I asked my distinguished professors...
But there was nothing about *that*.
...and checked countless books...
...but there was nothing.
I TOOK A LEAVE OF ABSENCE FROM THE UNIVERSITY AND RETURNED TO FISH HERE.
THE PEOPLE OF THIS ISLAND KNOW THE SEA BEST.
COMMUNICATING WITH THE OCEAN AS YOU GO ABOUT LIFE...
I THOUGHT THIS WAS THE BEST WAY TO GET TO KNOW THE SEA.

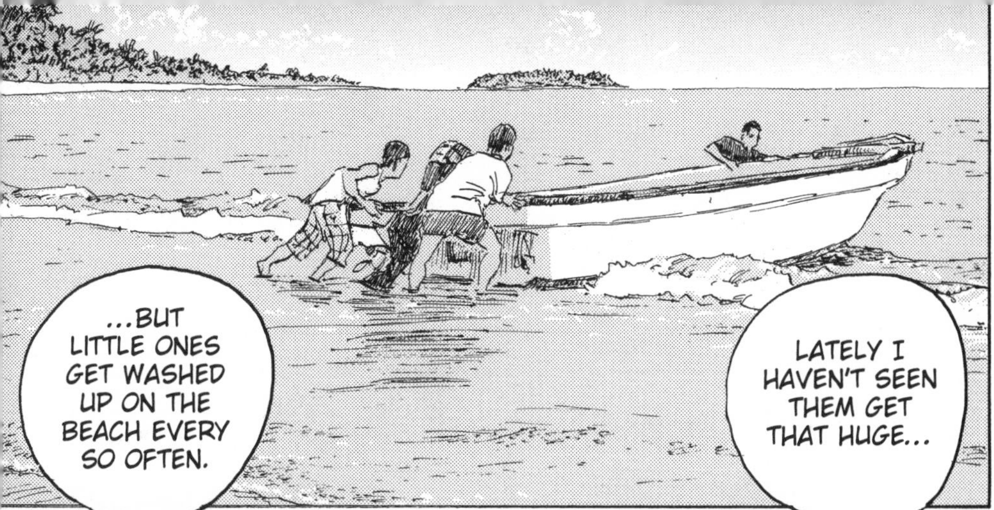
LATELY I HAVEN'T SEEN THEM GET THAT HUGE...
...BUT LITTLE ONES GET WASHED UP ON THE BEACH EVERY SO OFTEN.

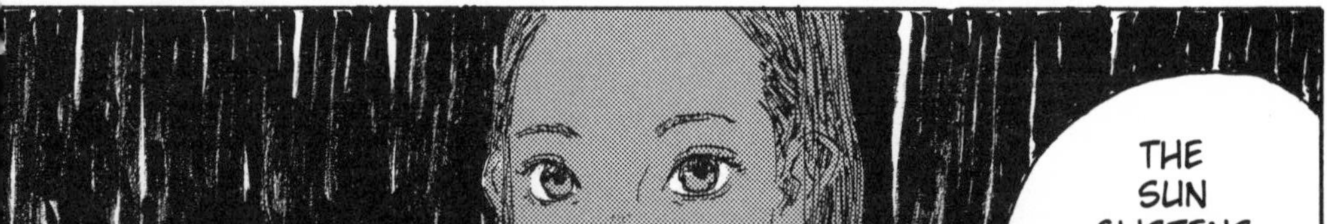
THE SUN GLISTENS ON THEM AND THEY'RE VERY PRETTY.
Testimony from La La Piairugu, college student and fisherwoman.

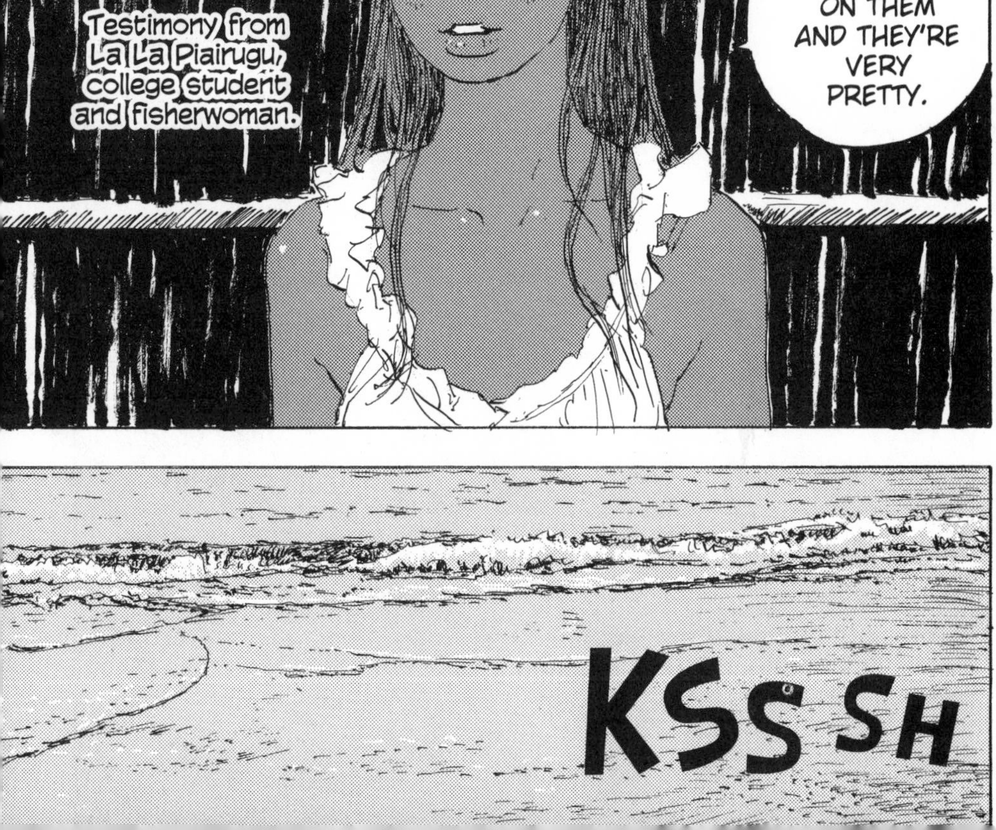
KSSSH

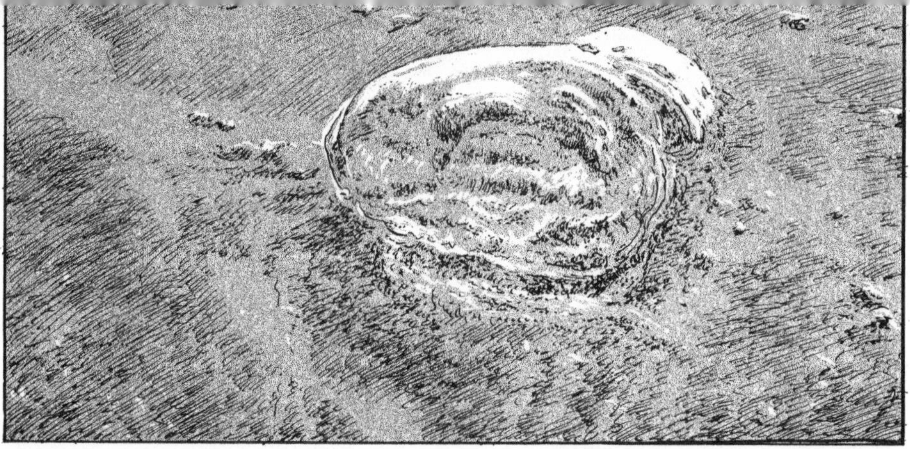

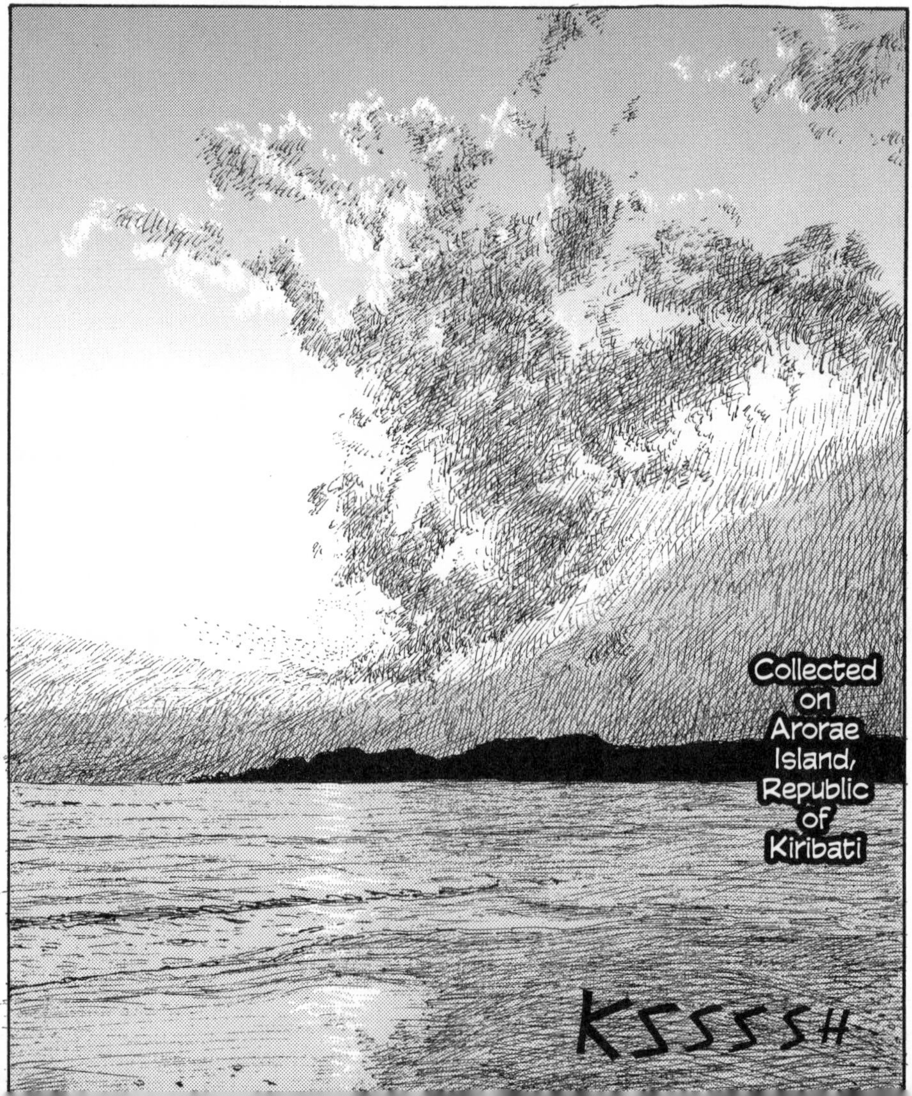
Collected on Arorae Island, Republic of Kiribati
KSSSSH

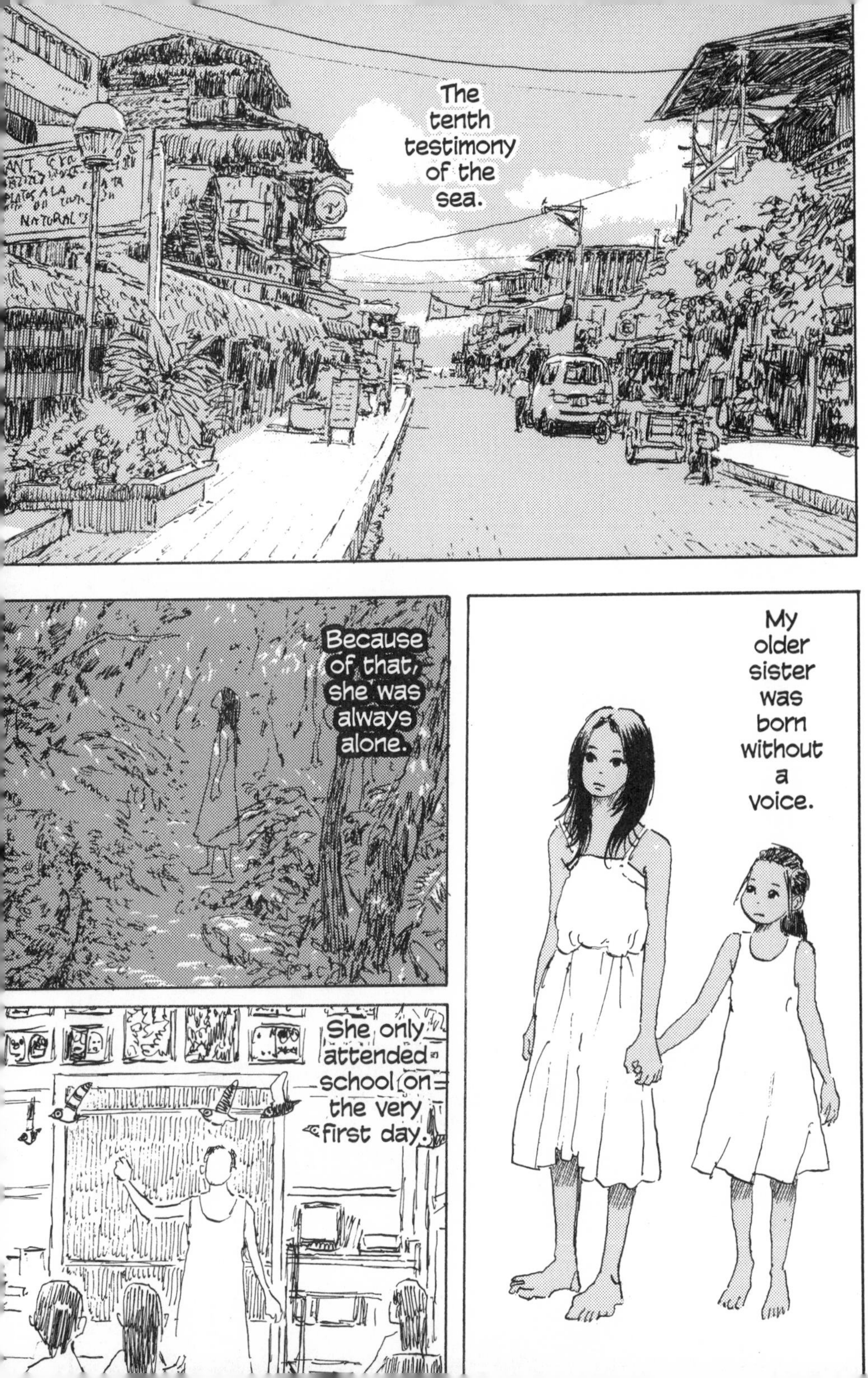
The tenth testimony of the sea.
My older sister was born without a voice.
Because of that, she was always alone.
She only attended school on the very first day.

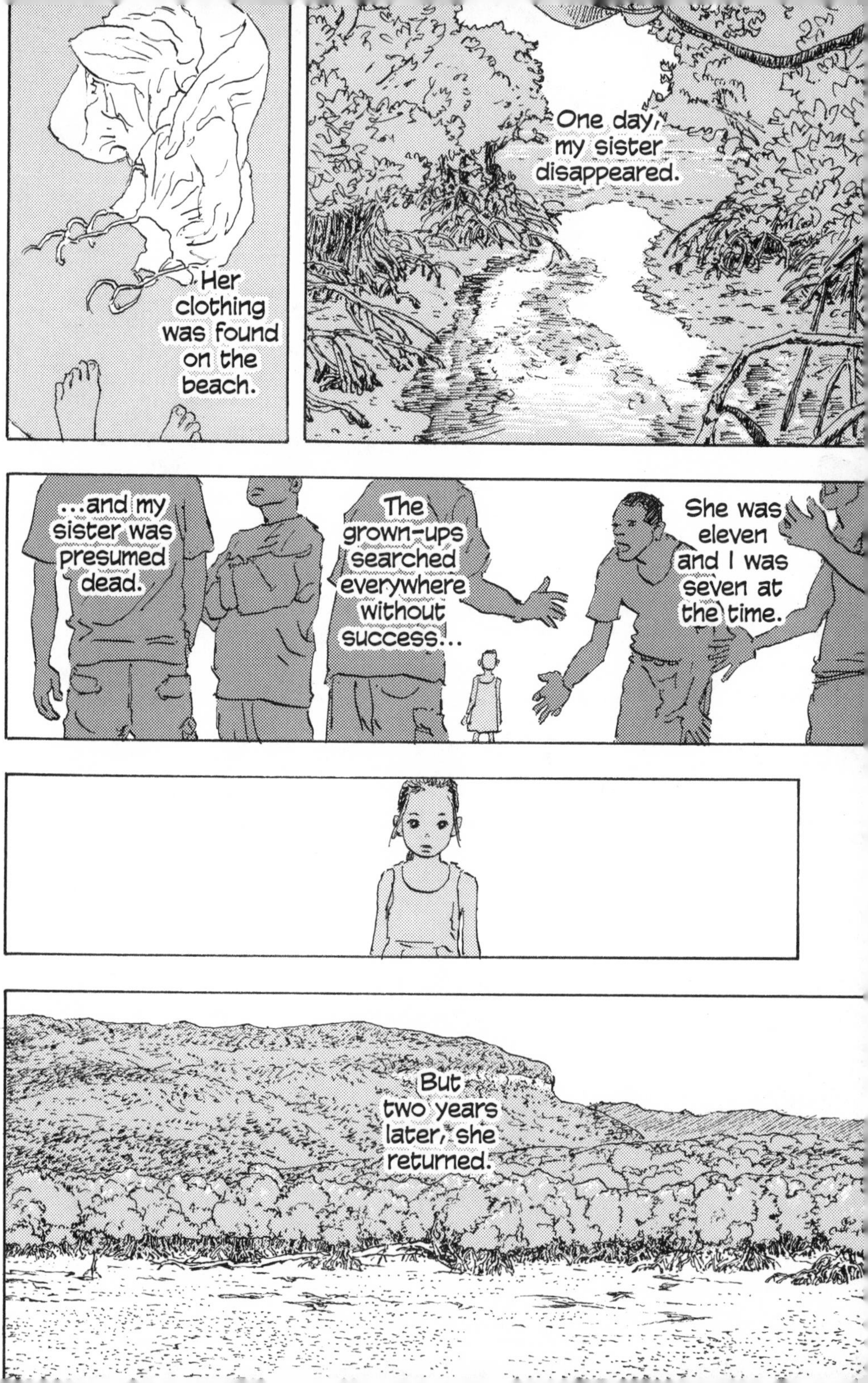
One day, my sister disappeared.
Her clothing was found on the beach.
She was eleven and I was seven at the time.
The grown-ups searched everywhere without success...
...and my sister was presumed dead.
But two years later, she returned.

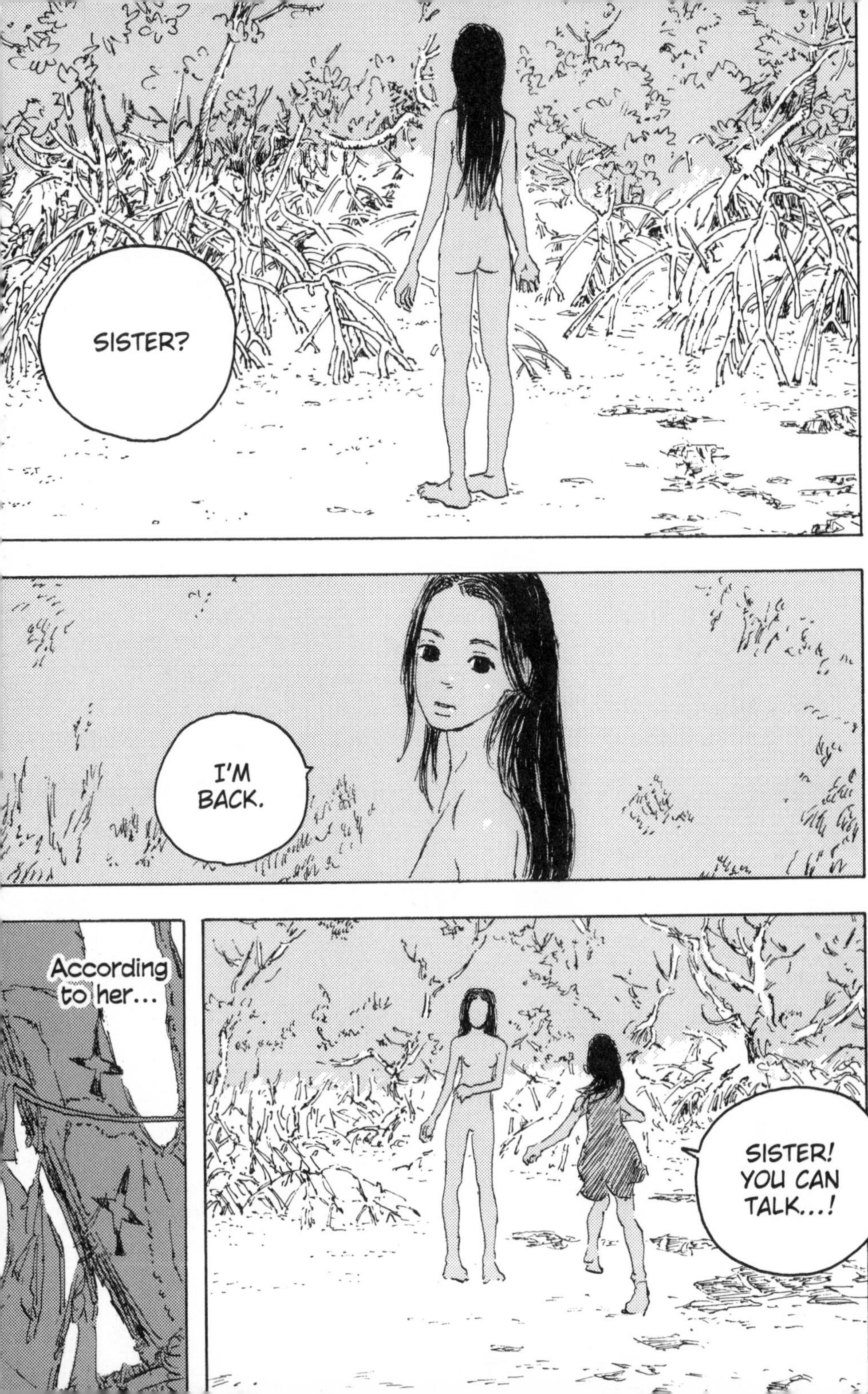
SISTER?
I'M BACK.
SISTER! YOU CAN TALK...!
According to her...

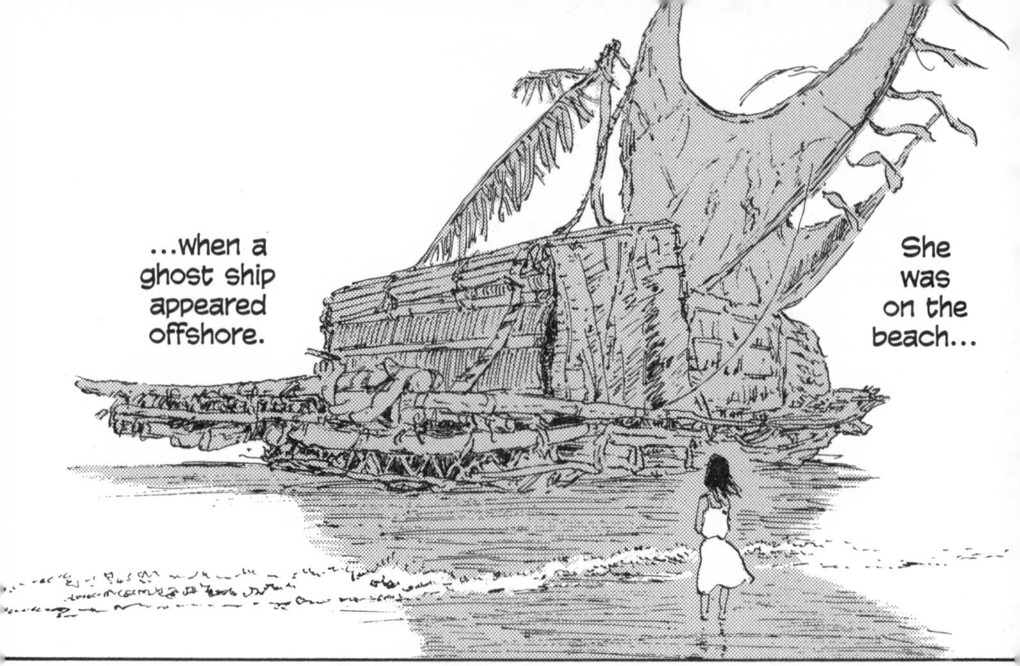
She was on the beach...
...when a ghost ship appeared offshore.
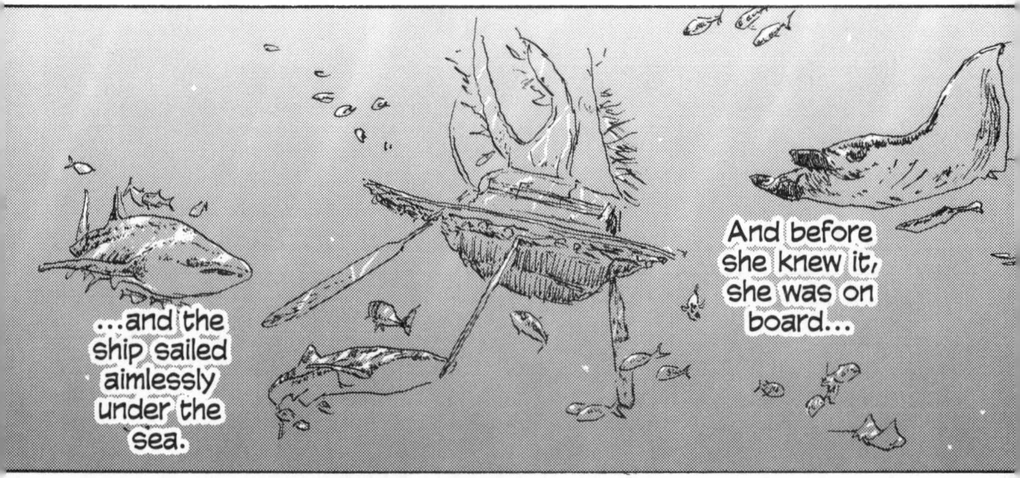
And before she knew it, she was on board...
...and the ship sailed aimlessly under the sea.
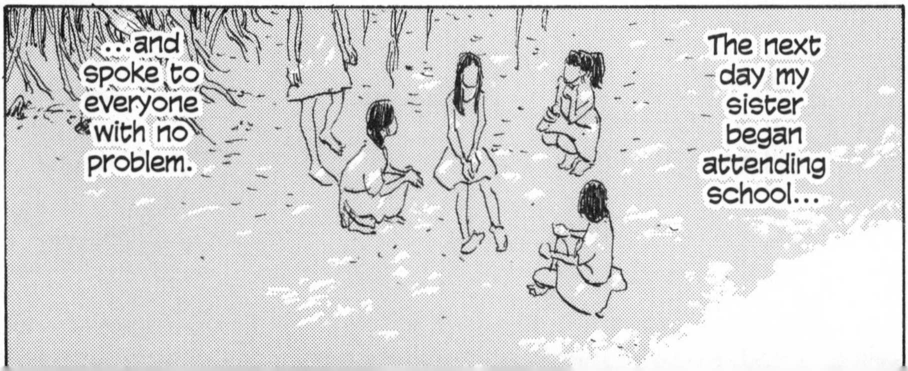
The next day my sister began attending school...
...and spoke to everyone with no problem.

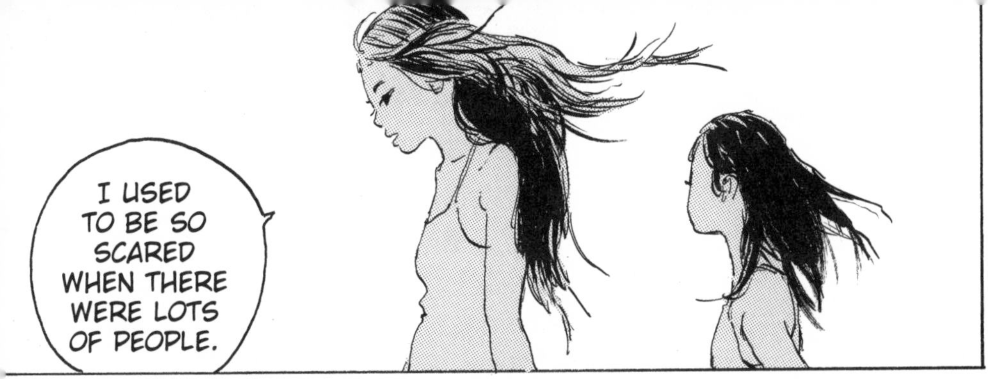
I USED TO BE SO SCARED WHEN THERE WERE LOTS OF PEOPLE.

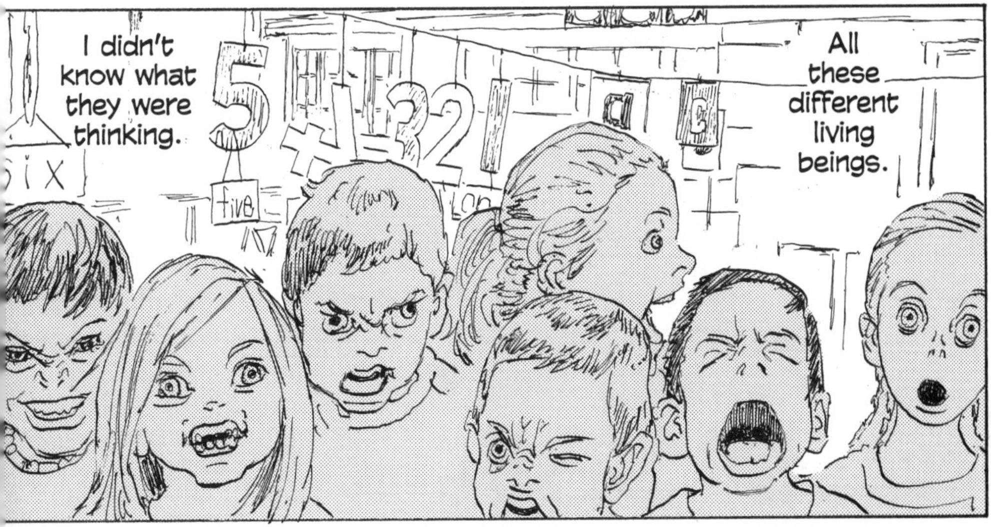
All these different living beings.
I didn't know what they were thinking.

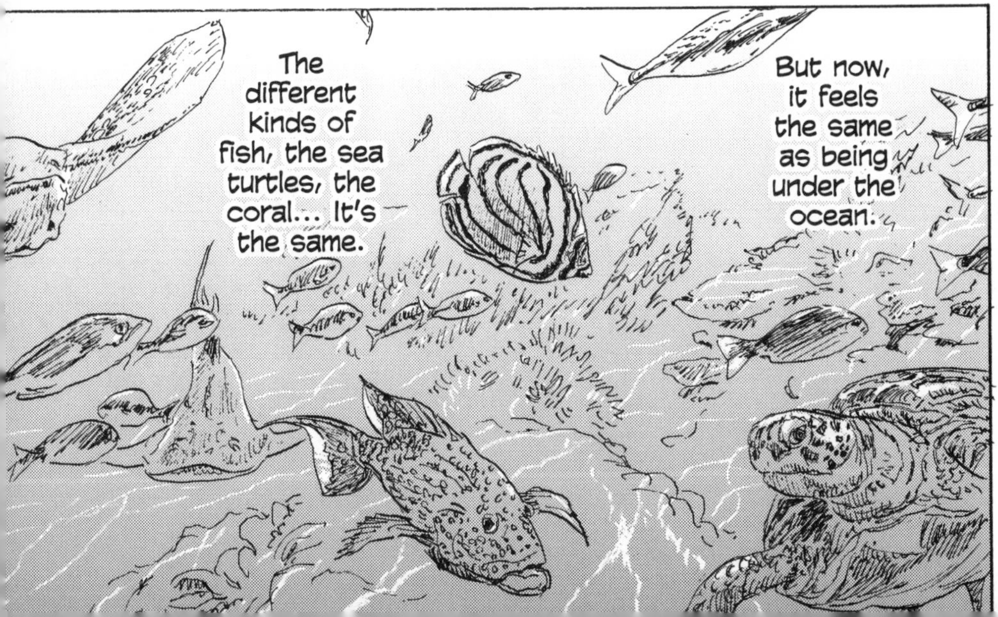
But now, it feels the same as being under the ocean.
The different kinds of fish, the sea turtles, the coral... It's the same.

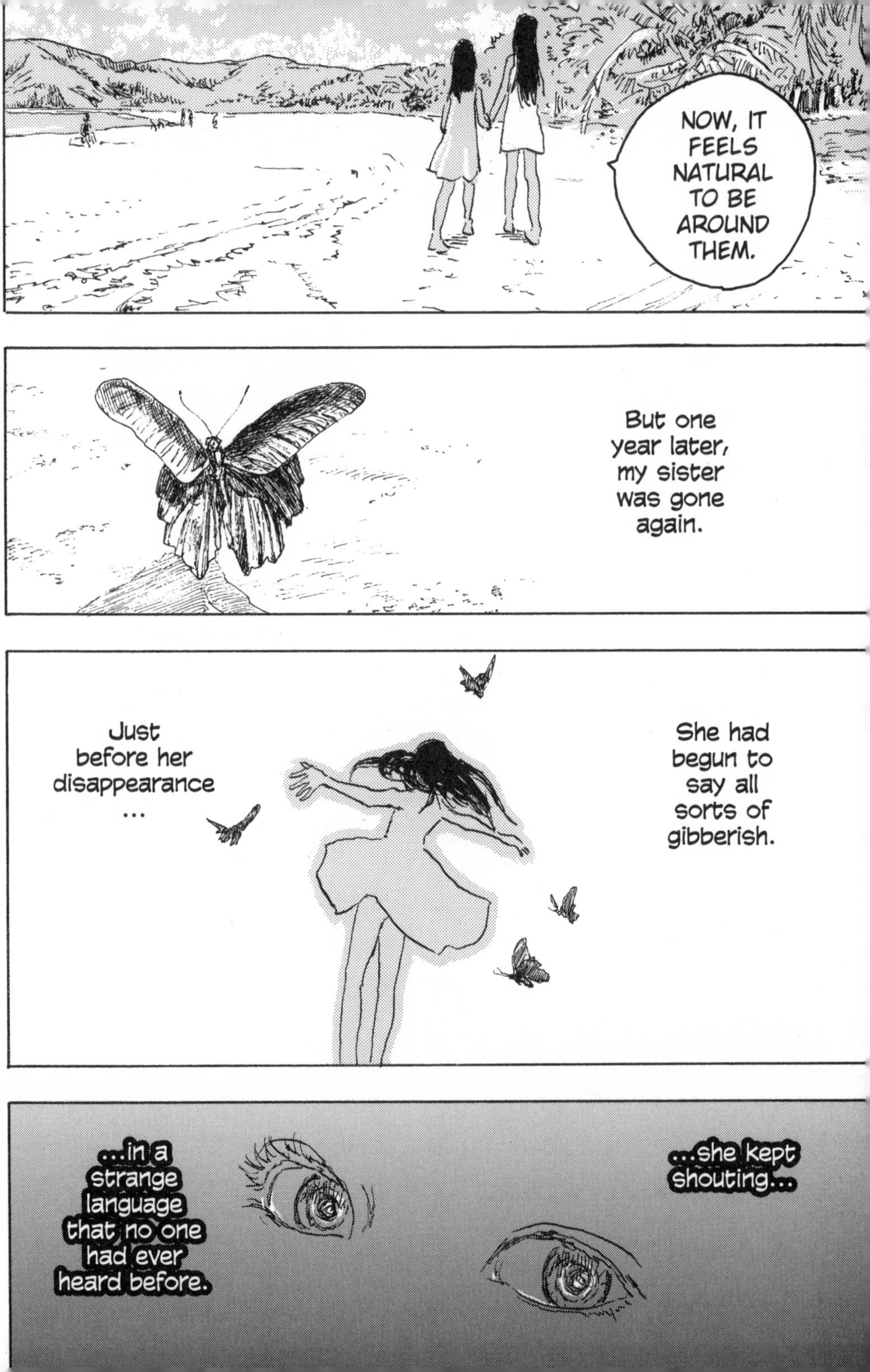
NOW, IT FEELS NATURAL TO BE AROUND THEM.
But one year later, my sister was gone again.
She had begun to say all sorts of gibberish.
Just before her disappearance ...
...she kept shouting...
...in a strange language that no one had ever heard before.

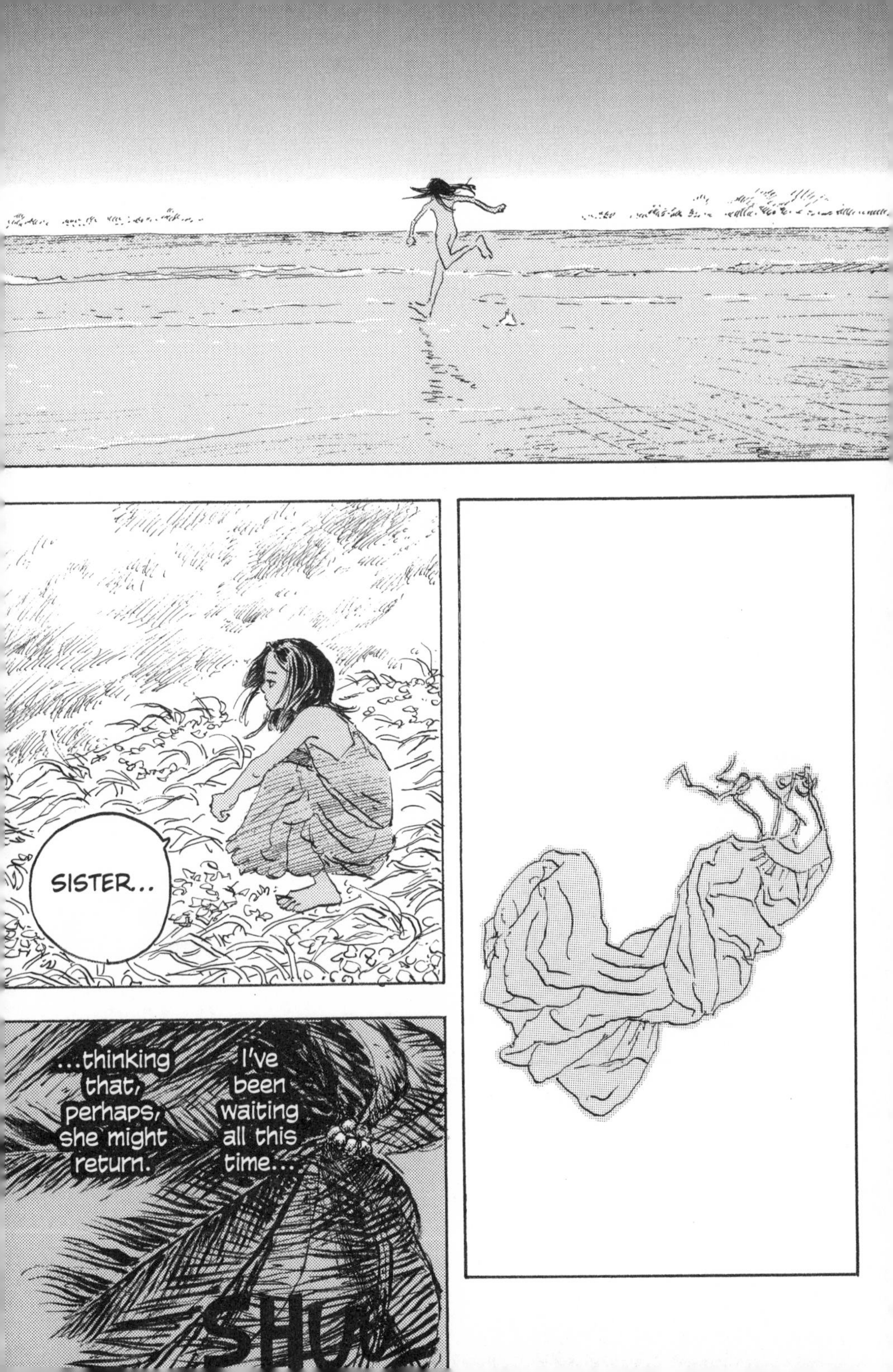
SISTER...
I've been waiting all this time...
...thinking that, perhaps, she might return.
SHU

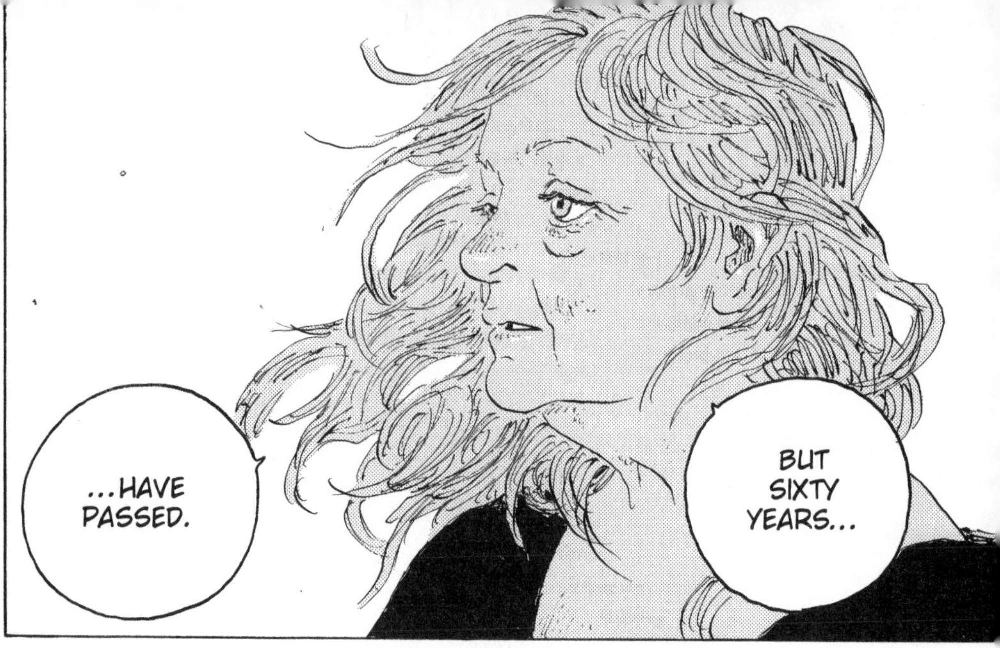
BUT SIXTY YEARS...
...HAVE PASSED.

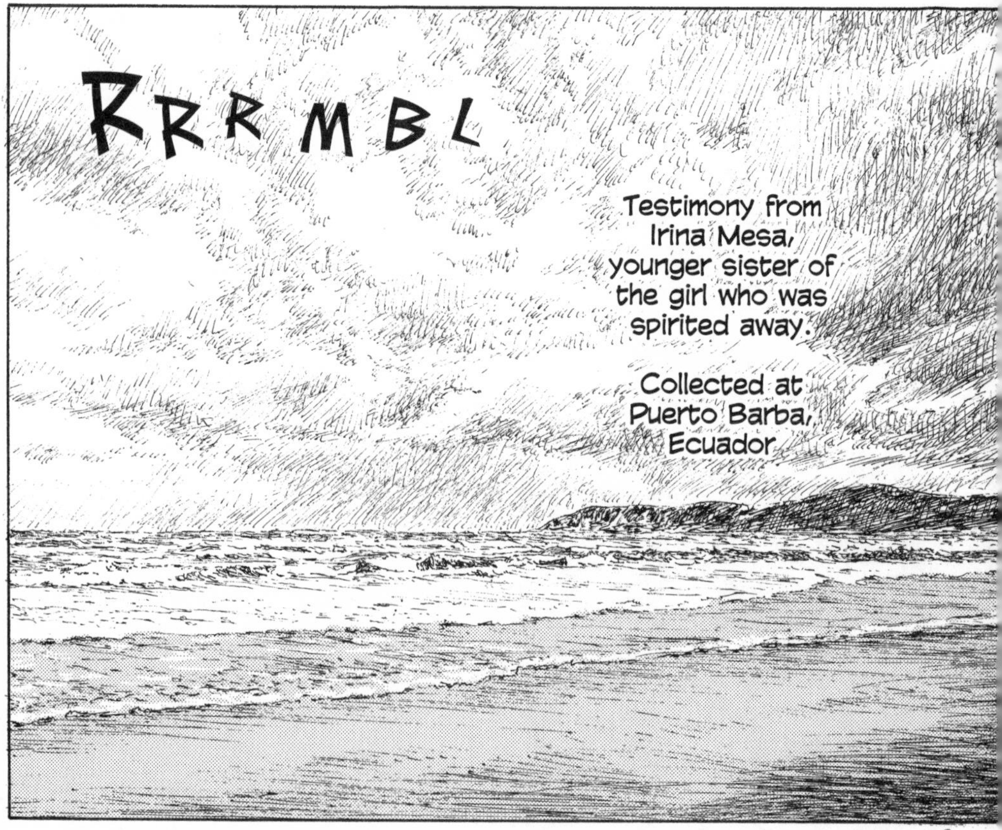
RRRMBL
Testimony from Irina Mesa, younger sister of the girl who was spirited away.
Collected at Puerto Barba, Ecuador

Final Chapter
Children of the Sea

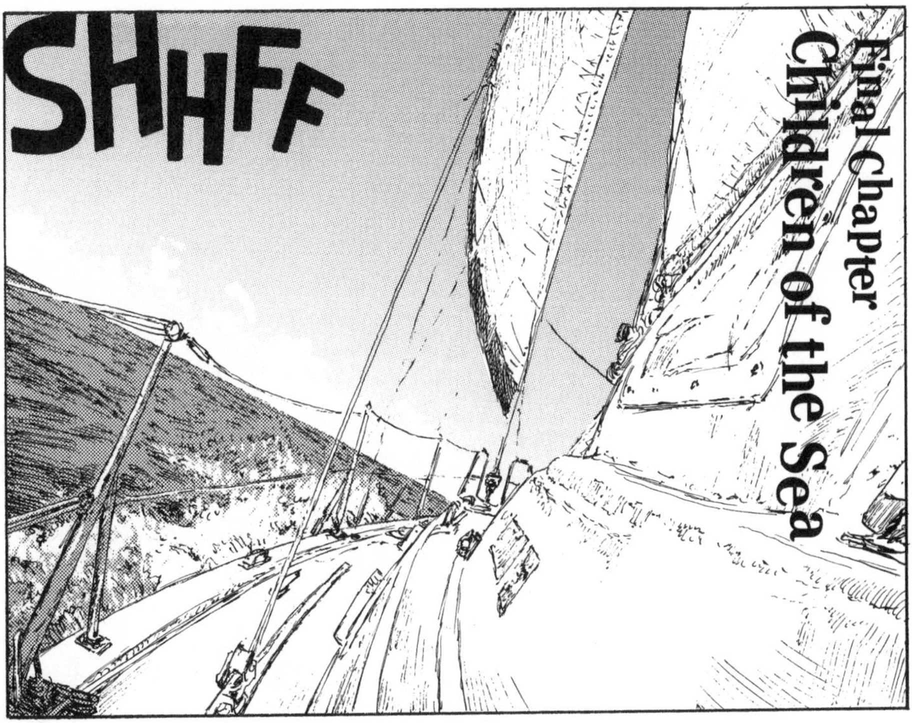
SHHFF

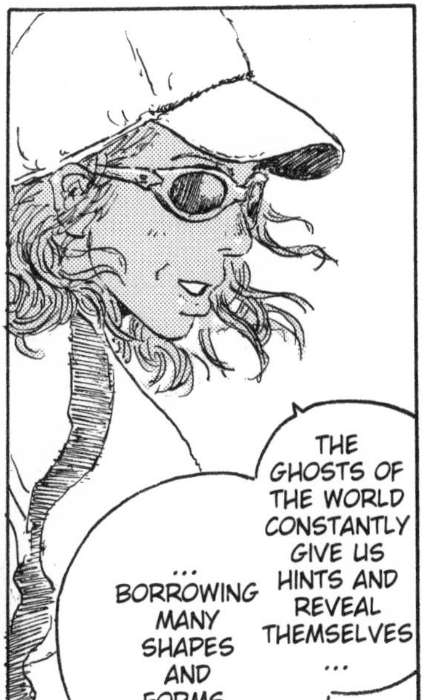
THE GHOSTS OF THE WORLD CONSTANTLY GIVE US HINTS AND REVEAL THEMSELVES...
...BORROWING MANY SHAPES AND FORMS.

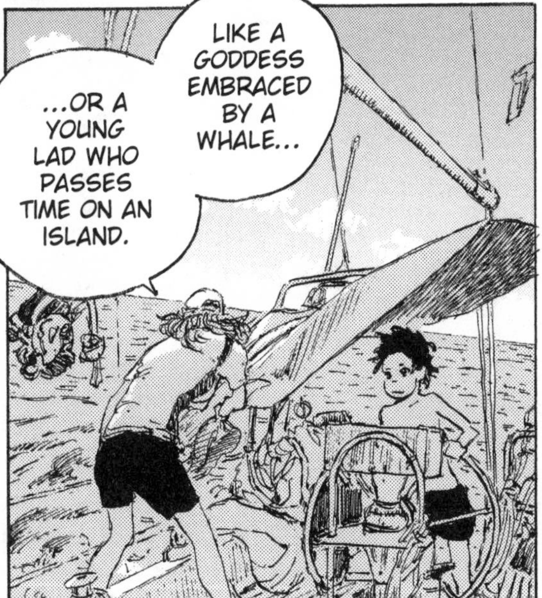
LIKE A GODDESS EMBRACED BY A WHALE...
...OR A YOUNG LAD WHO PASSES TIME ON AN ISLAND.

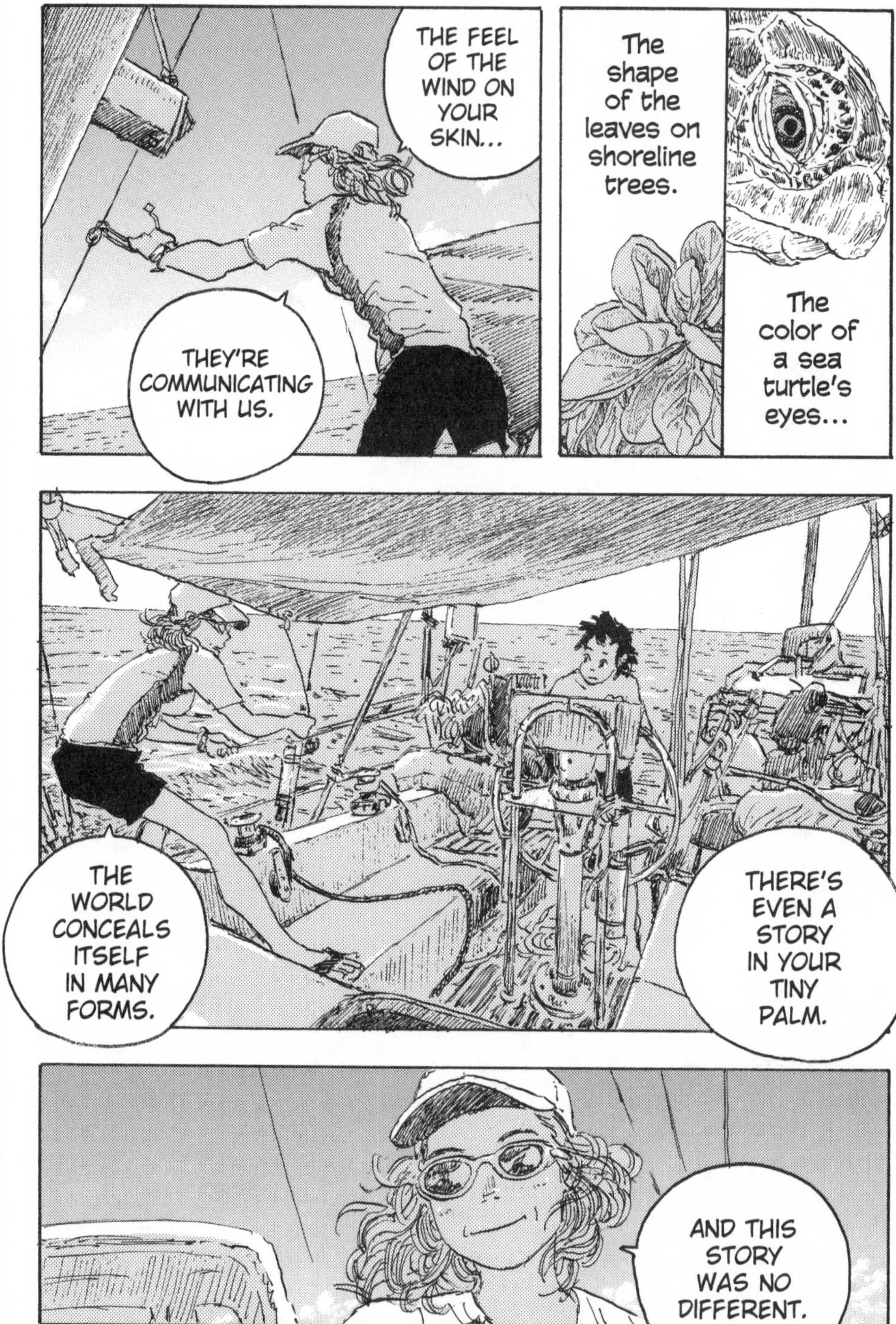
THE FEEL OF THE WIND ON YOUR SKIN...
The shape of the leaves on shoreline trees.
The color of a sea turtle's eyes...
THEY'RE COMMUNICATING WITH US.
THE WORLD CONCEALS ITSELF IN MANY FORMS.
THERE'S EVEN A STORY IN YOUR TINY PALM.
AND THIS STORY WAS NO DIFFERENT.

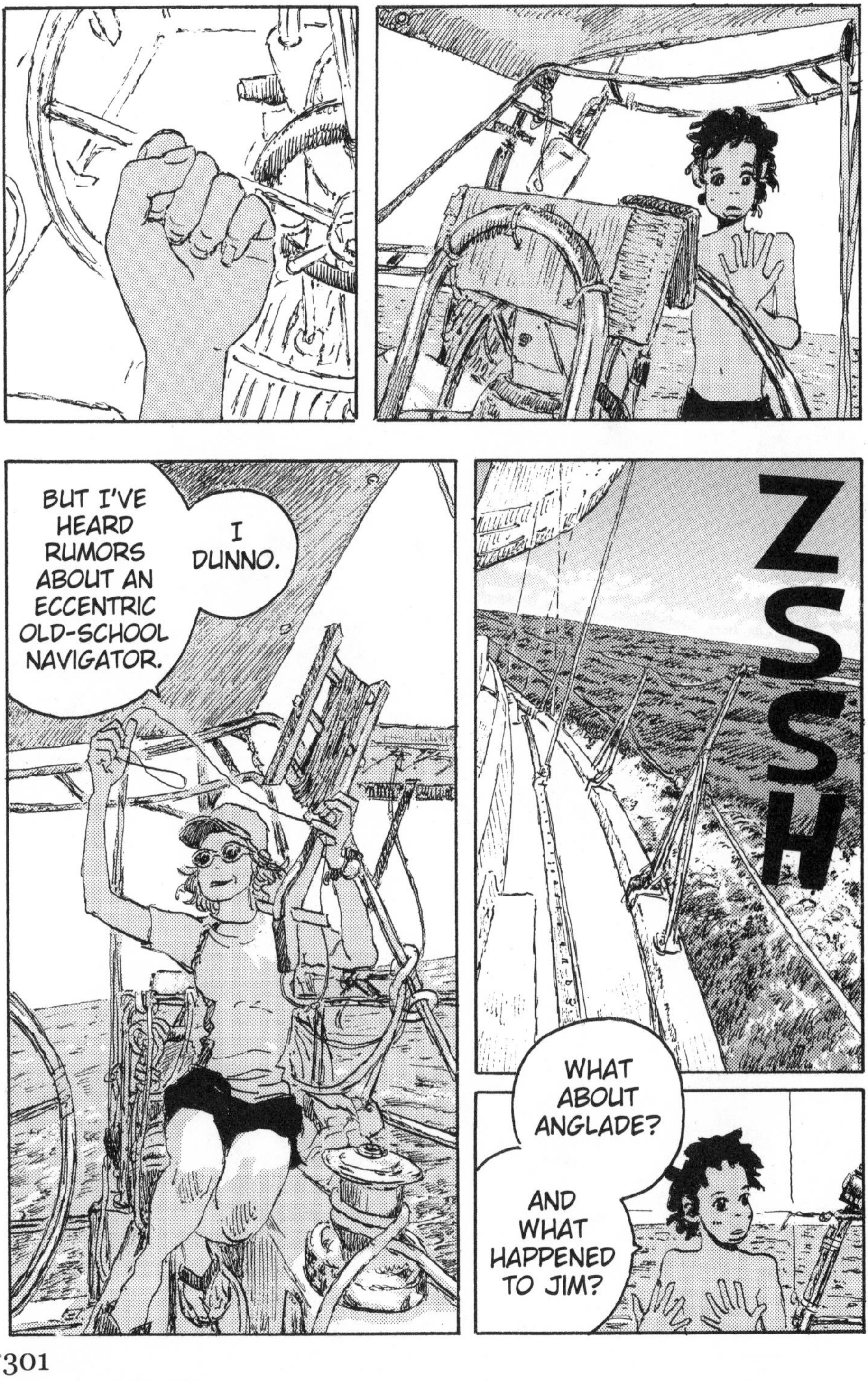
ZSSH
WHAT ABOUT ANGLADE?
AND WHAT HAPPENED TO JIM?
I DUNNO.
BUT I'VE HEARD RUMORS ABOUT AN ECCENTRIC OLD-SCHOOL NAVIGATOR.

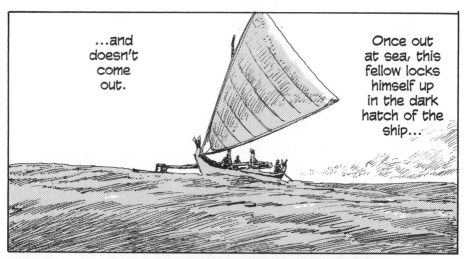

Once out at sea, this fellow locks himself up in the dark hatch of the ship...
...and doesn't come out.
He doesn't look at the stars and he doesn't feel the wind.
All he pays attention to is the undulation of the waves.
That's how he calculates his position and which direction to sail.
Even on land, he shies away from people.

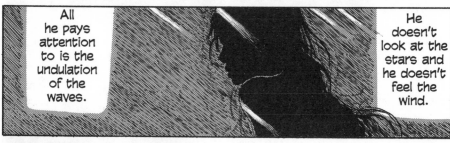

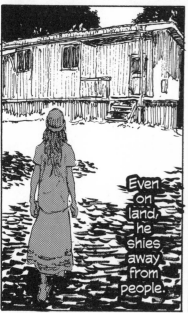

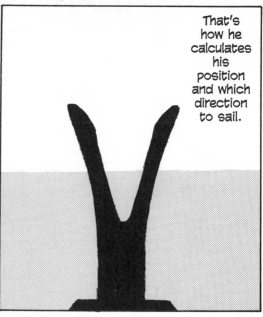

OTHER THAN THE FACT THAT HE SEEMS TO BE A WESTERNER, NO ONE KNOWS ANYTHING ABOUT HIM.

Half his body is covered with burn scars.

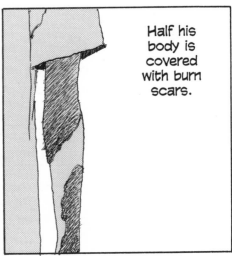

BUT HE ONLY CHOOSES LONG JOURNEYS.

I'VE HEARD OF ANOTHER MAN...

...WHO GOES FROM SHIP TO SHIP AS A COOK.

He's an average cook.

IT DOESN'T MATTER IF IT'S A FISHING BOAT OR A TANKER.

HE'S POPULAR AND GETS LOTS OF OFFERS.
BUT HE ALWAYS CHOOSES THE ONE THAT'LL BE OUT AT SEA THE LONGEST.

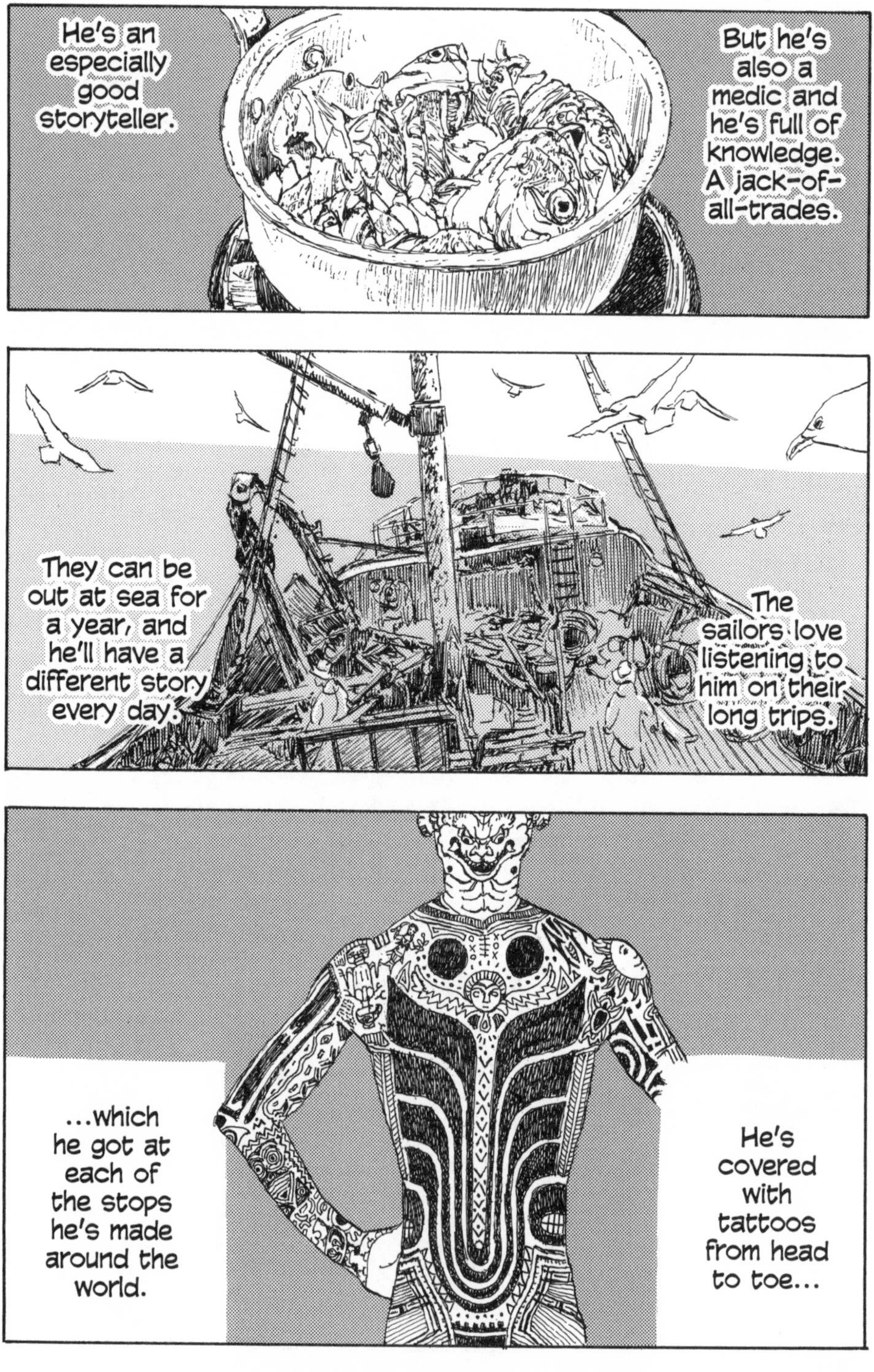
But he's also a medic and he's full of knowledge. A jack-of-all-trades.
He's an especially good storyteller.
The sailors love listening to him on their long trips.
They can be out at sea for a year, and he'll have a different story every day.
He's covered with tattoos from head to toe...
...which he got at each of the stops he's made around the world.

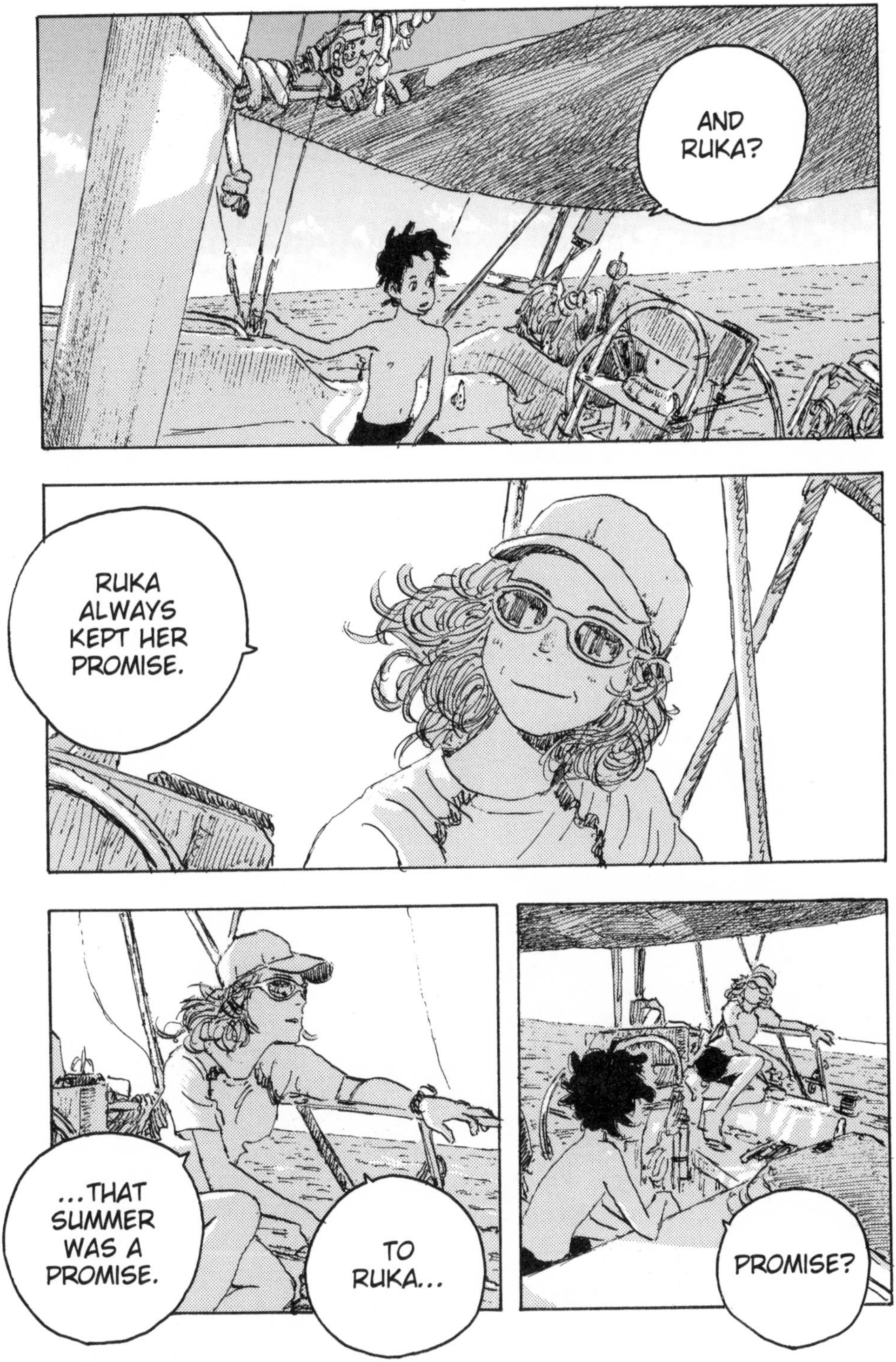
AND RUKA?
RUKA ALWAYS KEPT HER PROMISE.
TO RUKA...
...THAT SUMMER WAS A PROMISE.
PROMISE?

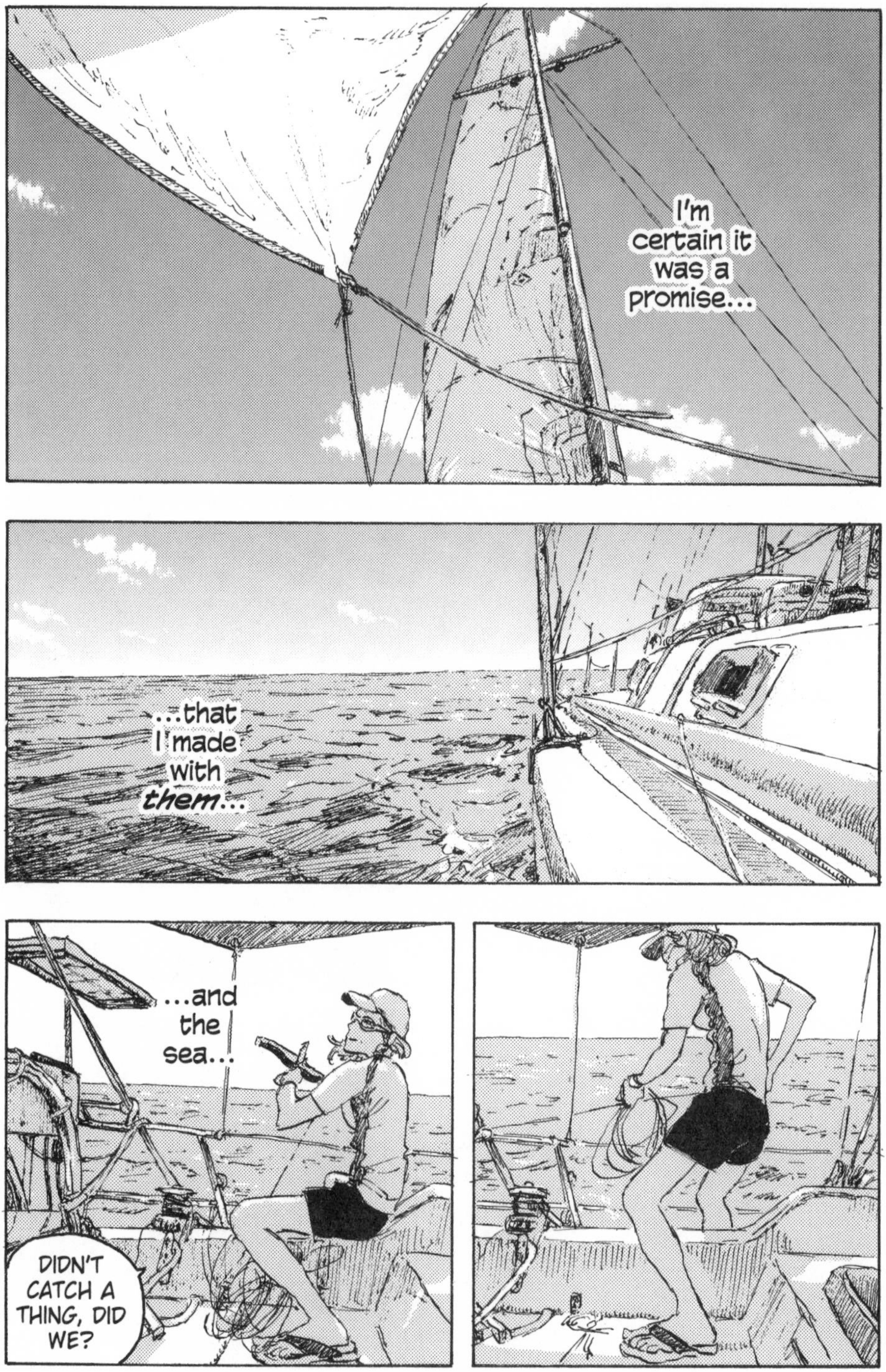
I'm certain it was a promise...
...that I made with *them*...
...and the sea...
DIDN'T CATCH A THING, DID WE?

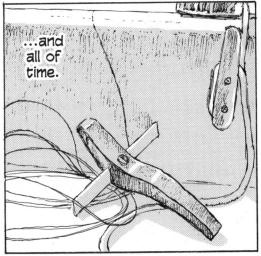

...and all of time.

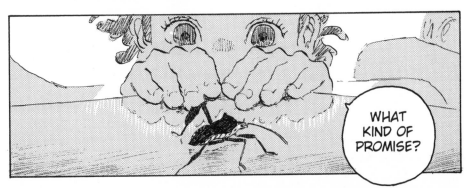

WHAT KIND OF PROMISE?

THE MOST CHERISHED KIND OF PROMISE ...

...IS NEVER MADE WITH WORDS.

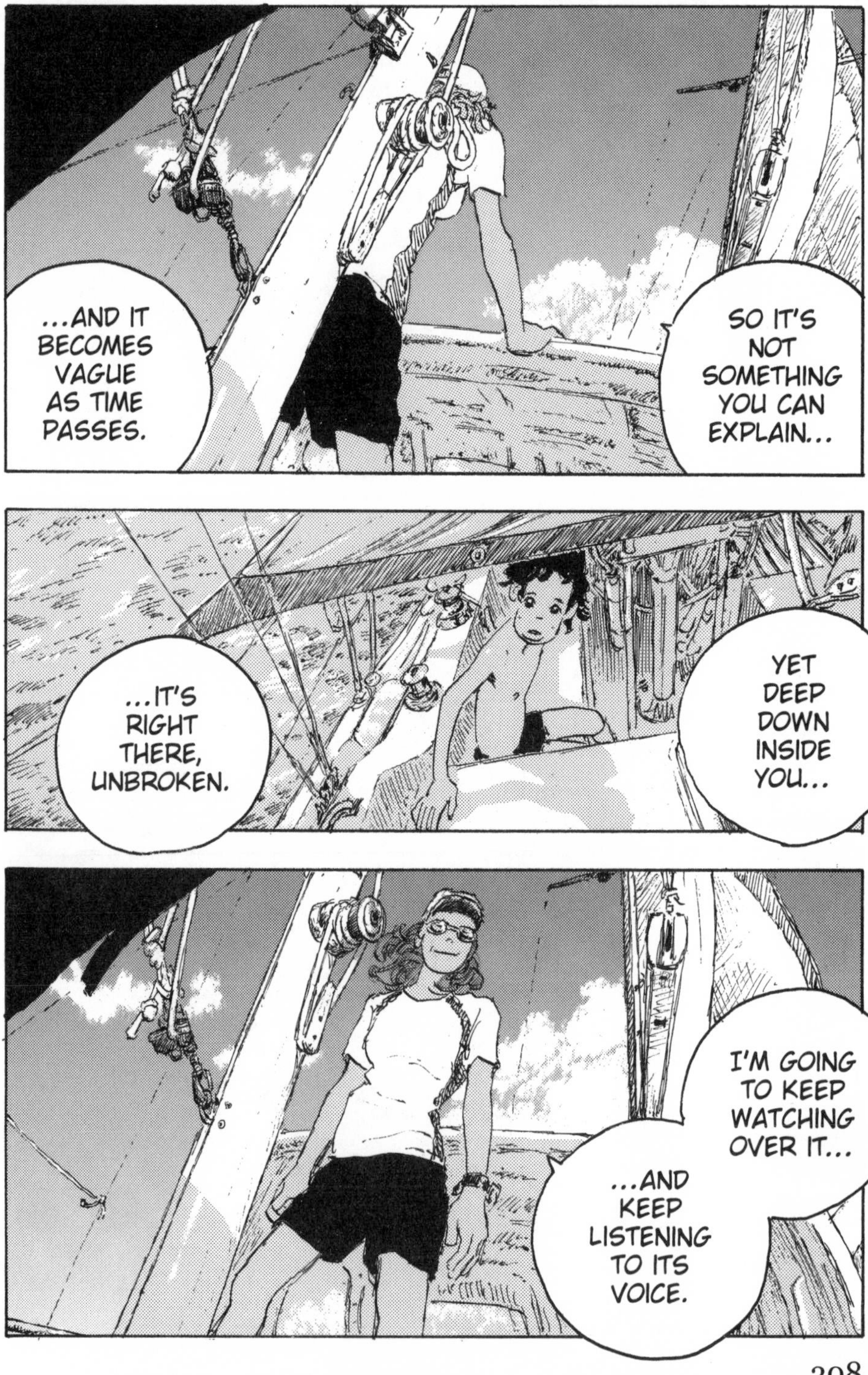
SO IT'S NOT SOMETHING YOU CAN EXPLAIN...
...AND IT BECOMES VAGUE AS TIME PASSES.
YET DEEP DOWN INSIDE YOU...
...IT'S RIGHT THERE, UNBROKEN.
I'M GOING TO KEEP WATCHING OVER IT...
...AND KEEP LISTENING TO ITS VOICE.

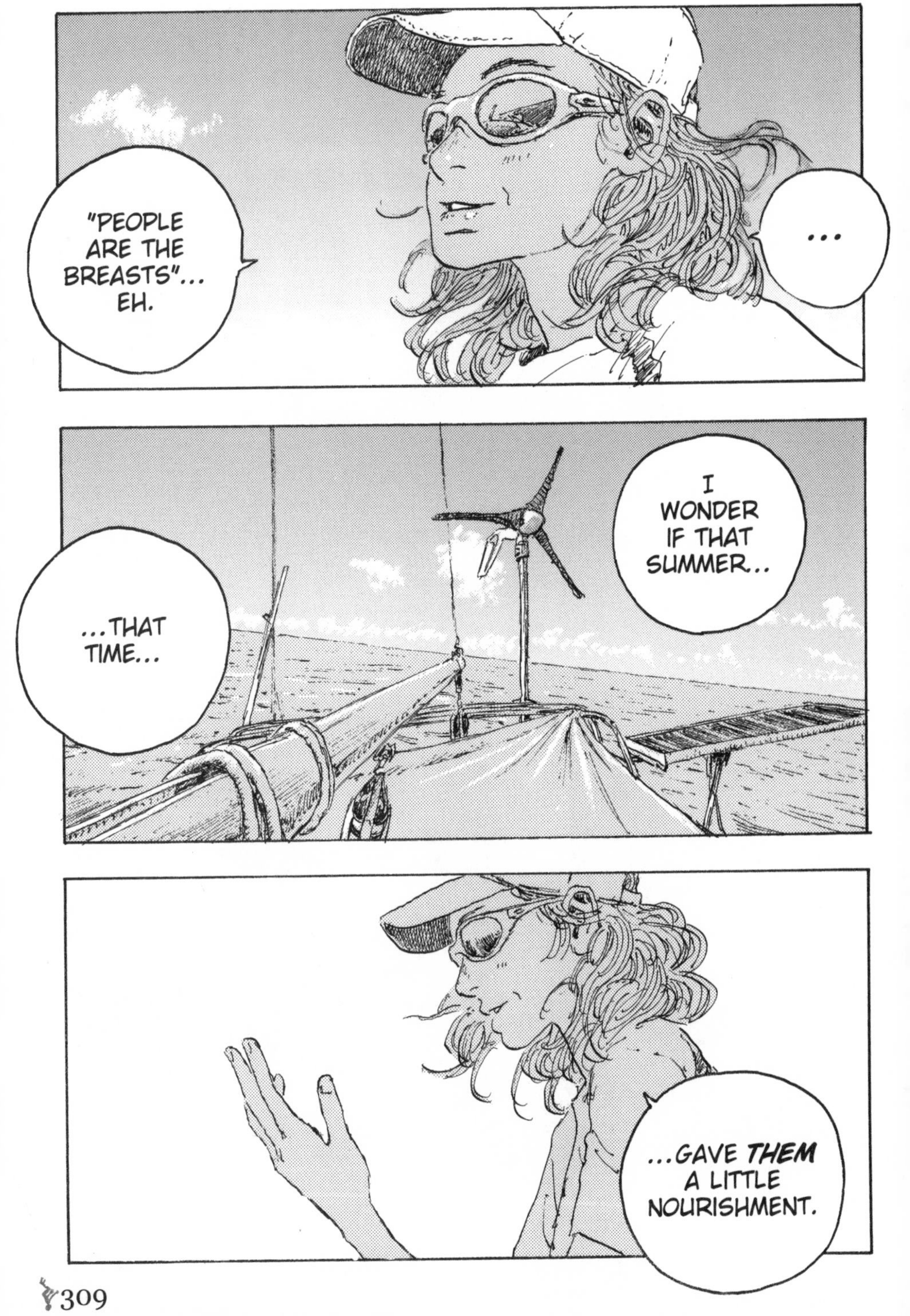
...
"PEOPLE ARE THE BREASTS"... EH.
I WONDER IF THAT SUMMER...
...THAT TIME...
...GAVE *THEM* A LITTLE NOURISHMENT.

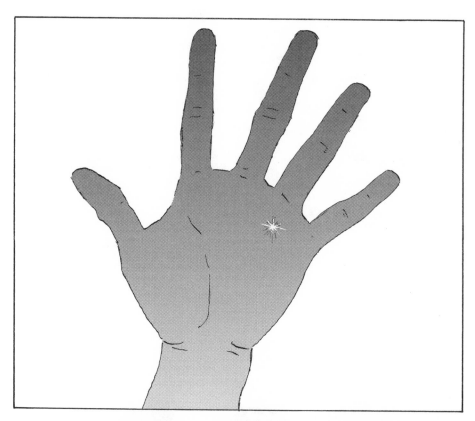

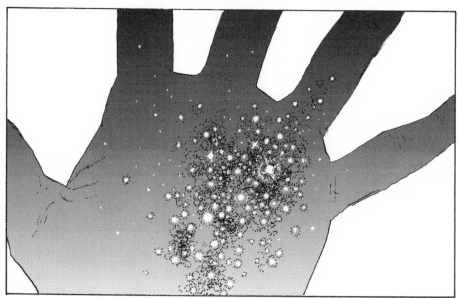

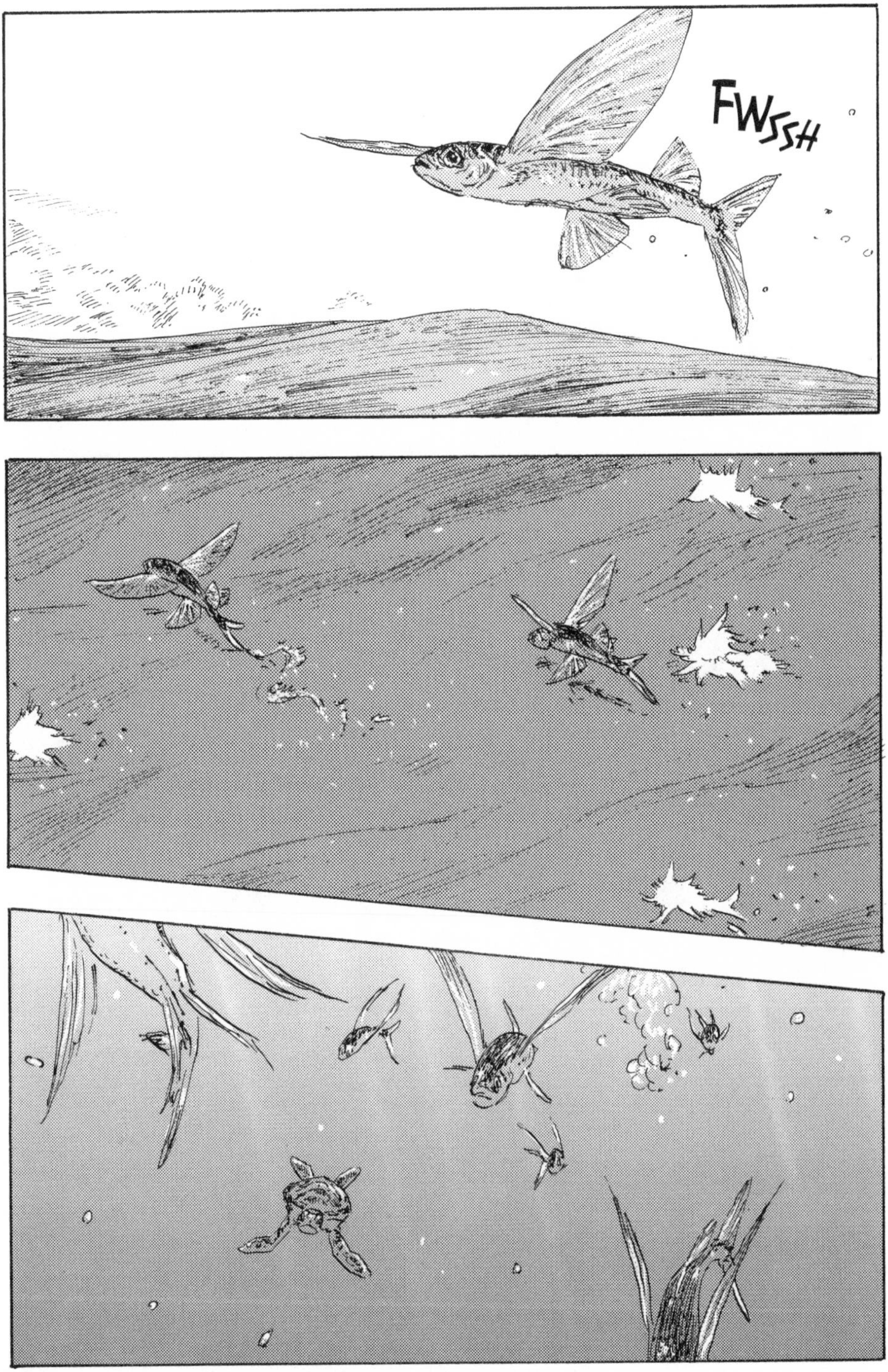
FWSSH

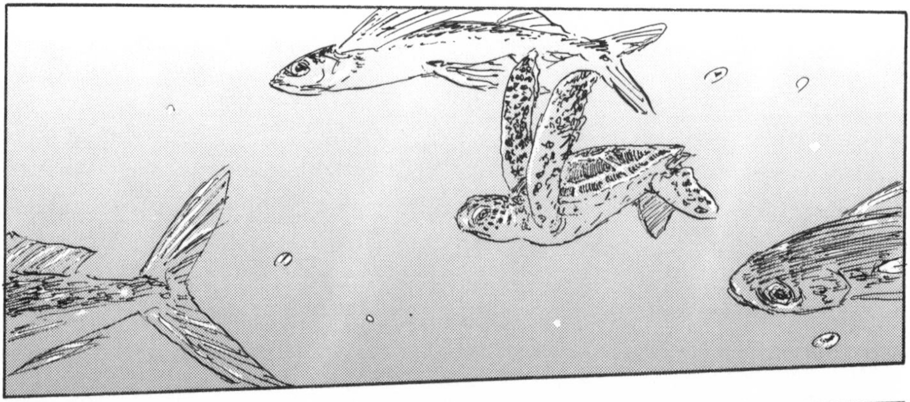
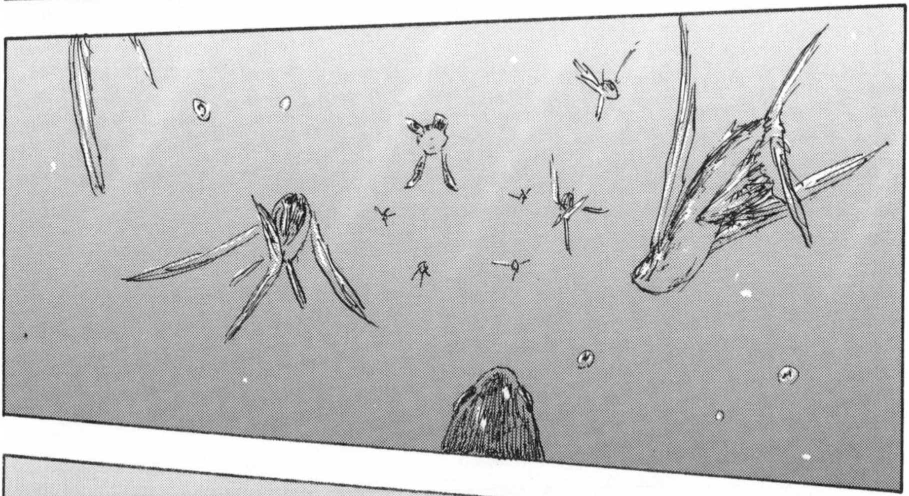
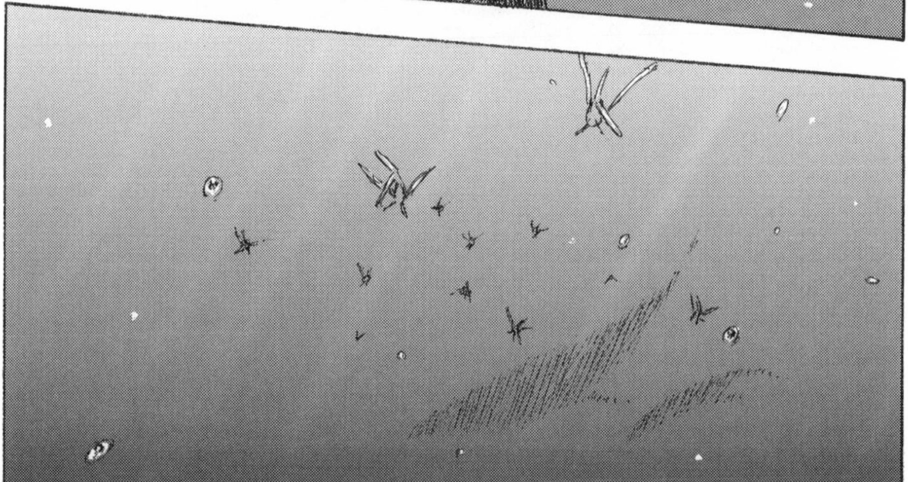

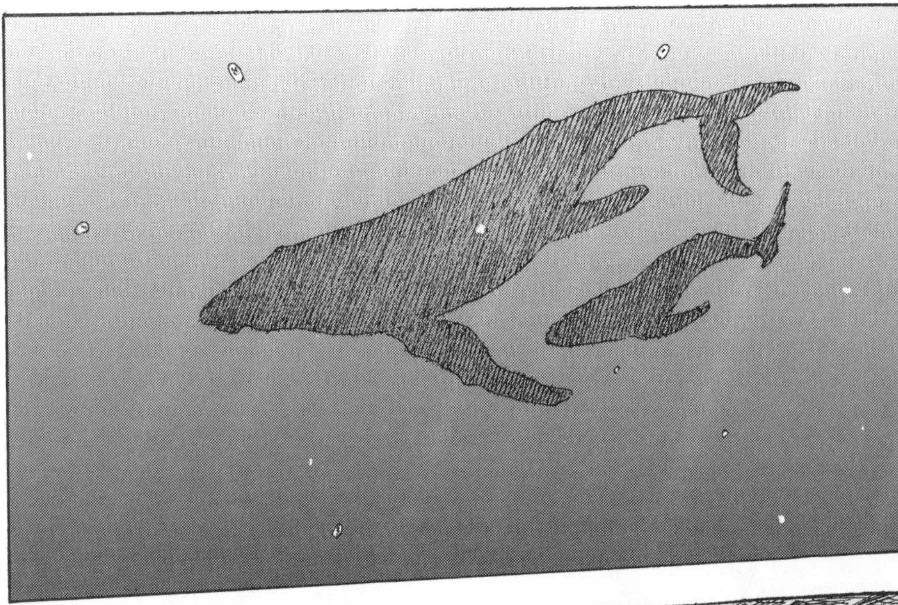

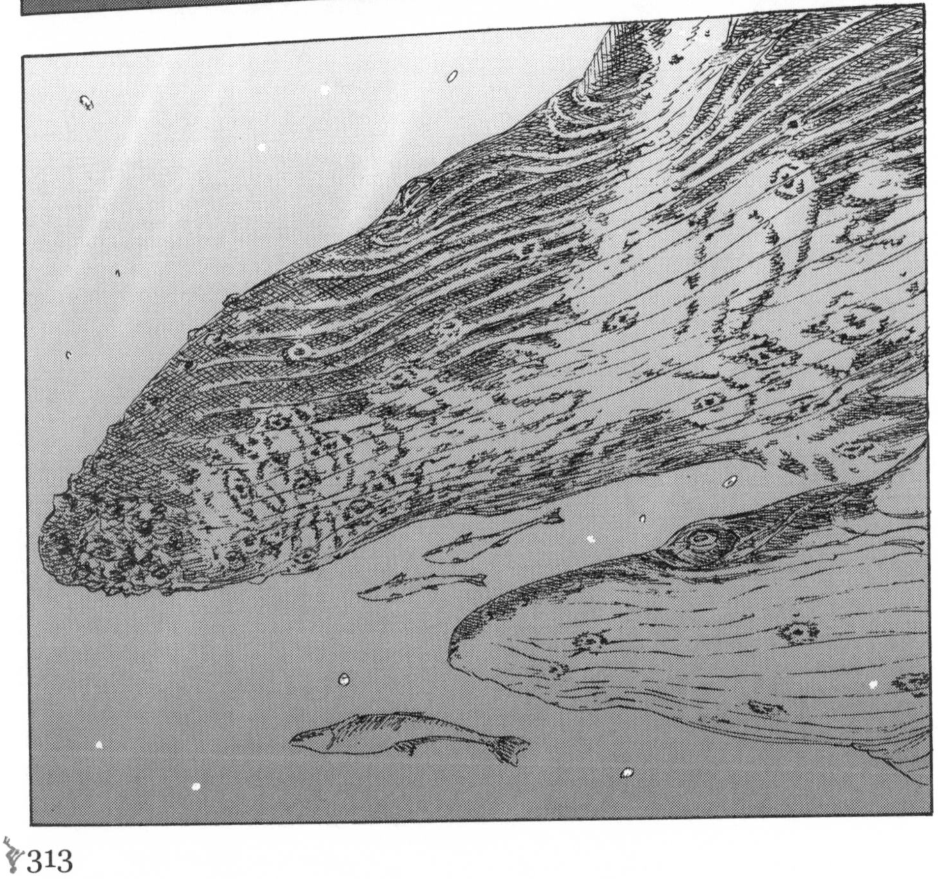

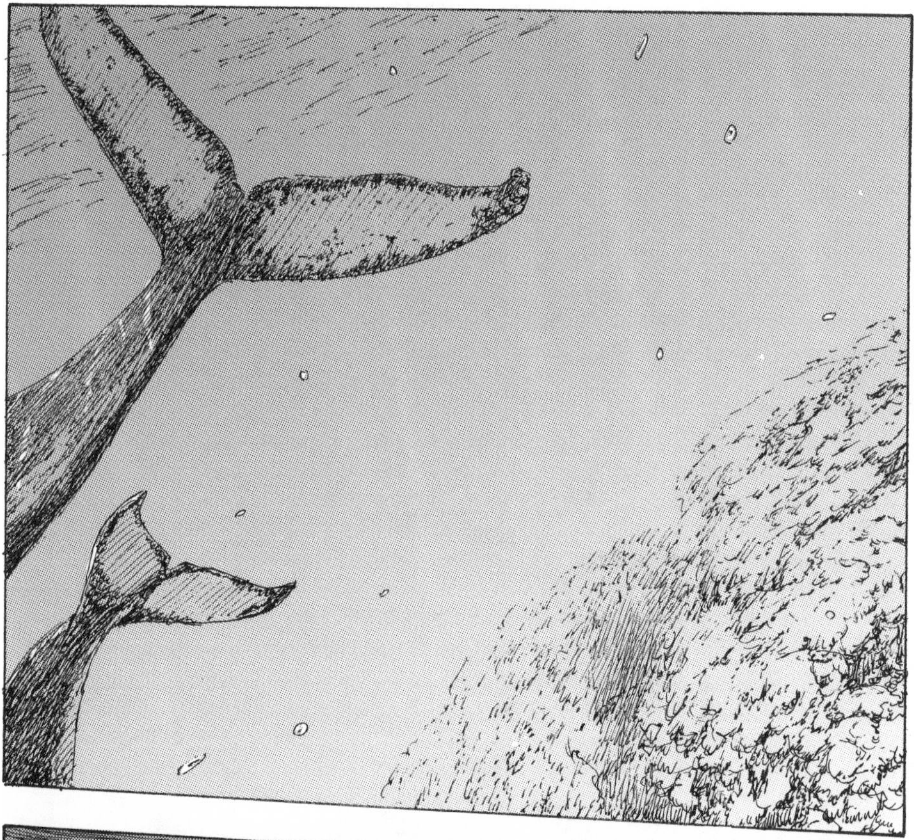
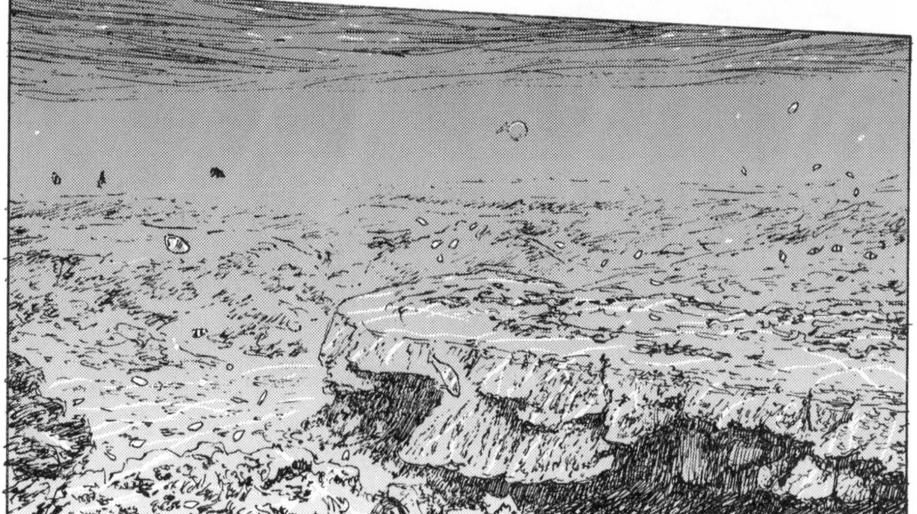

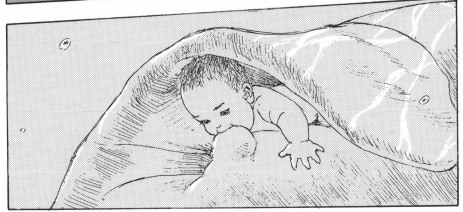

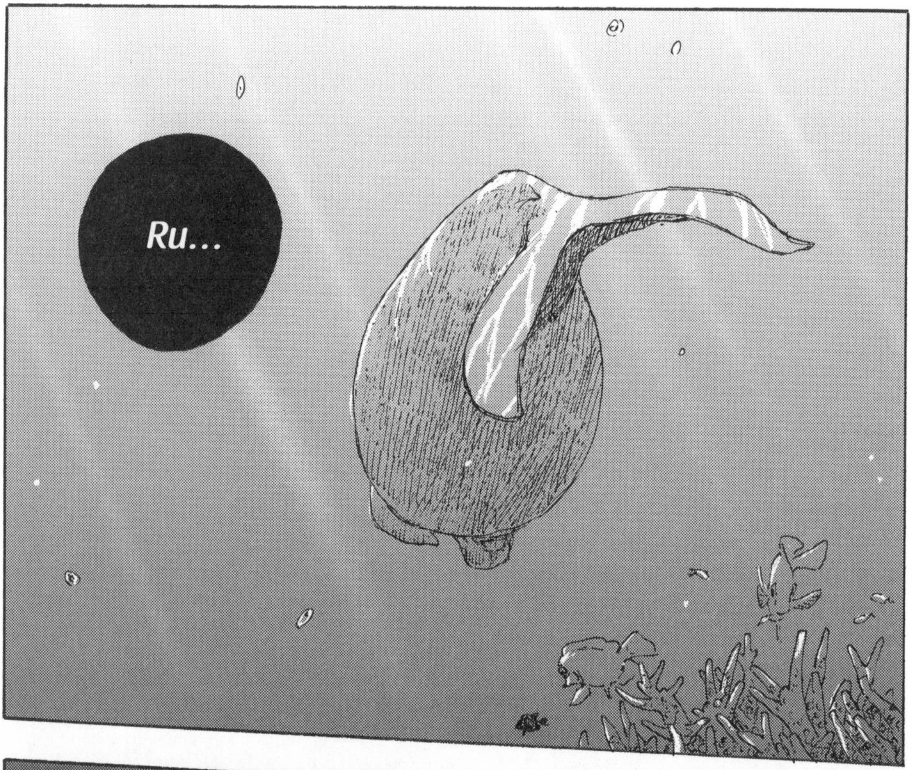
Ru...
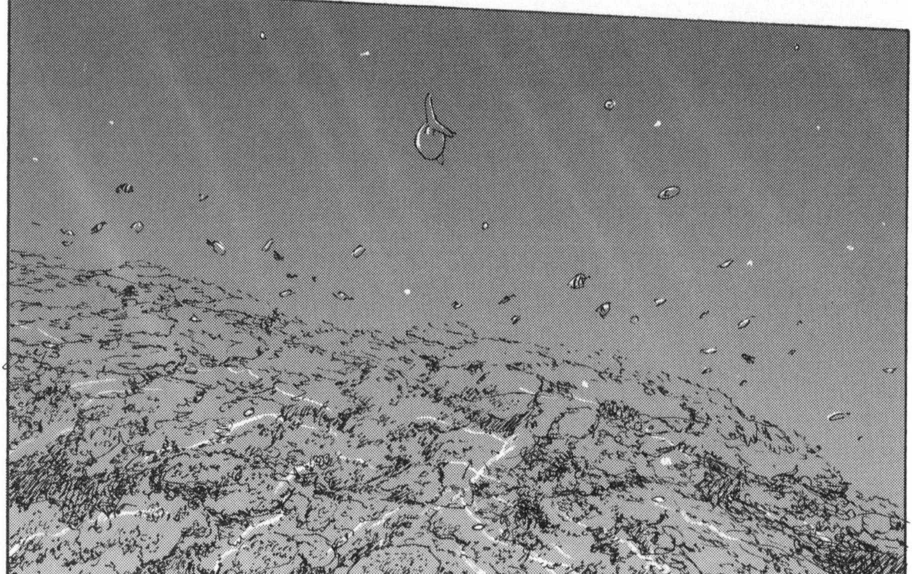

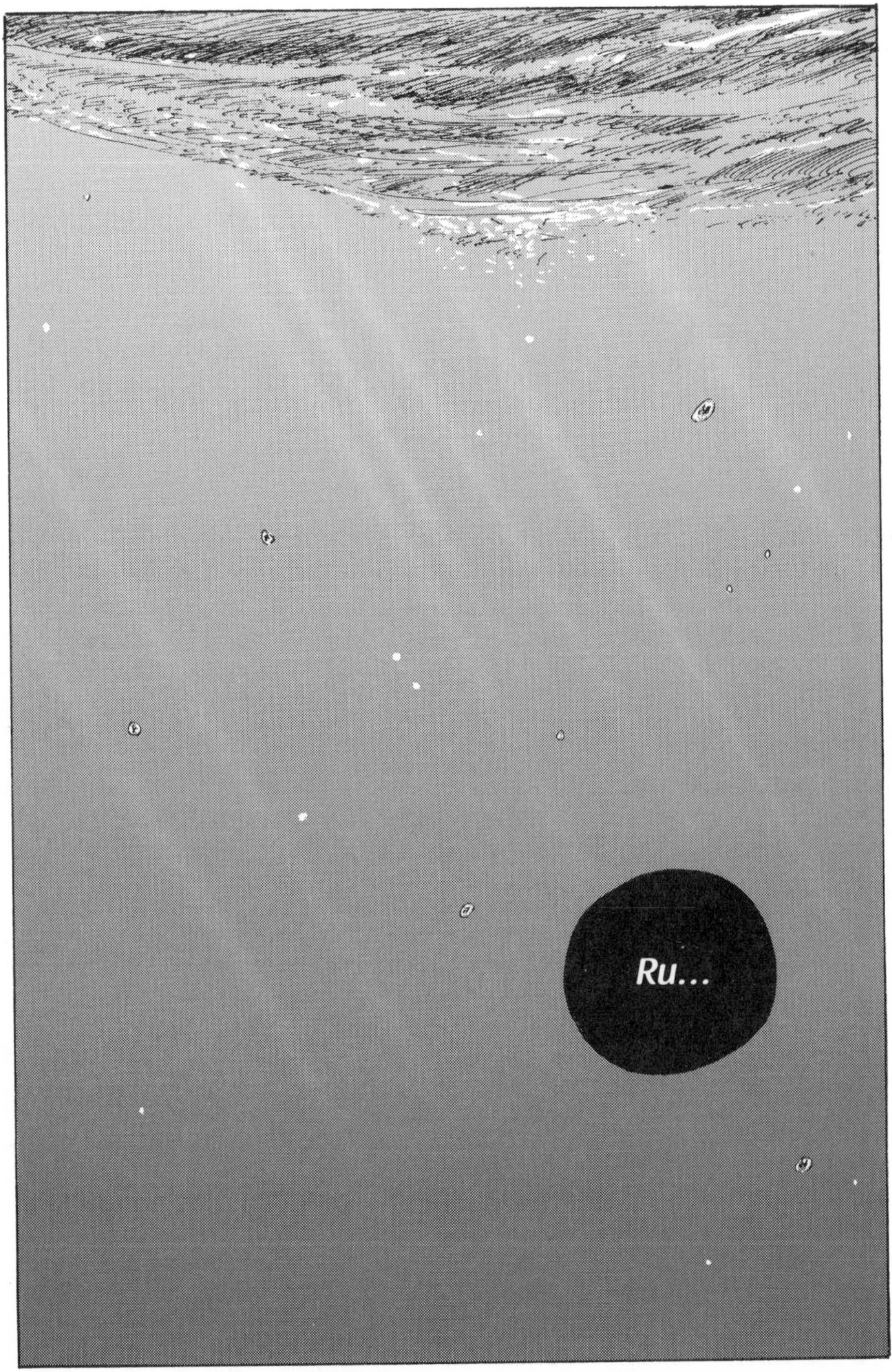
Ru...

Children of the Sea

The
End

First appeared in *Gekkan IKKI*
April - November 2011
In collaboration with Enoshima Aquarium

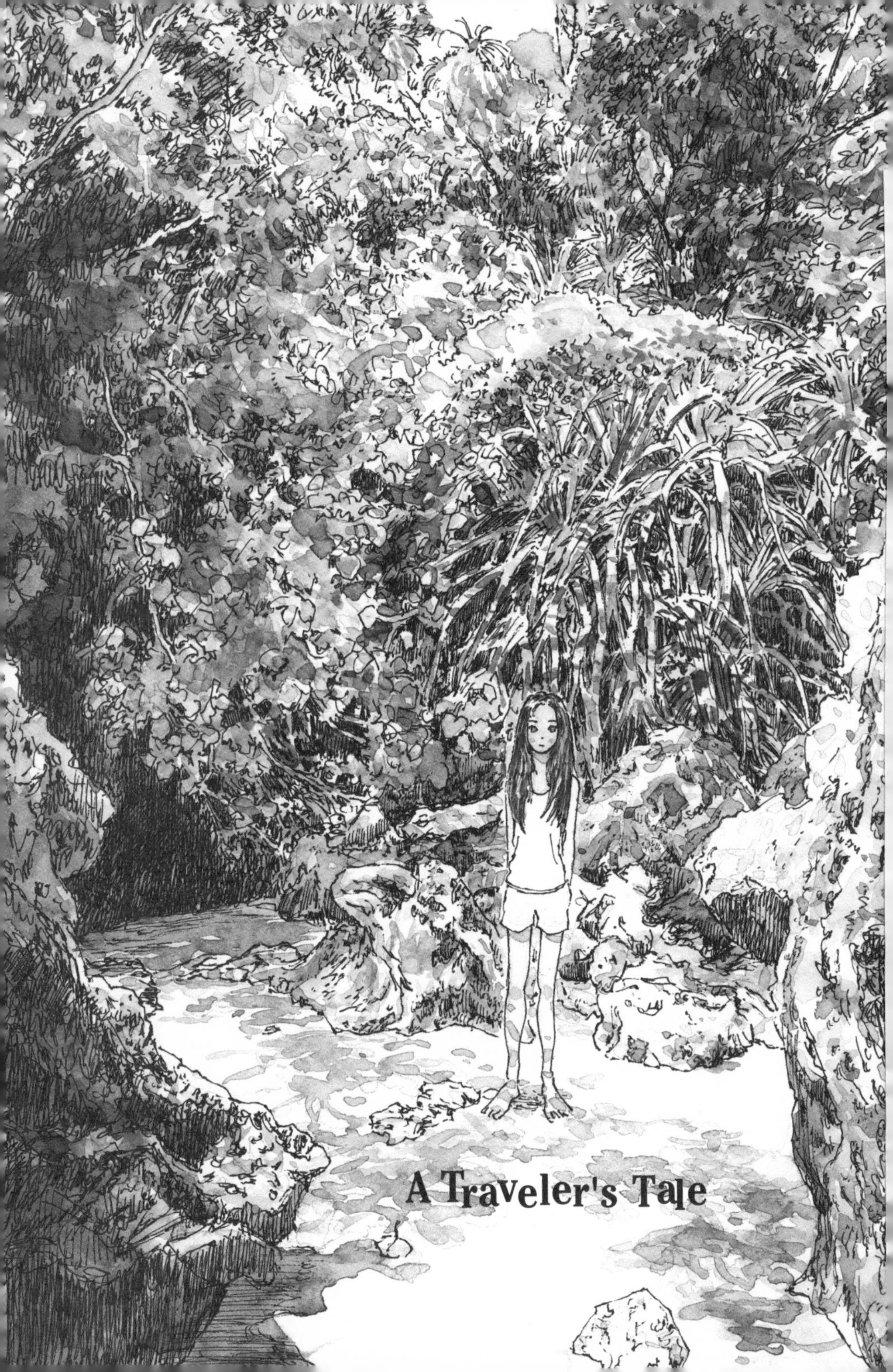
A Traveler's Tale

WHAT ARE YOU DOING HERE OF ALL PLACES?
WHAT ARE YOU DOING HERE?
I WAS HERE ONCE...
...AND I MADE A VERY IMPORTANT PROMISE.

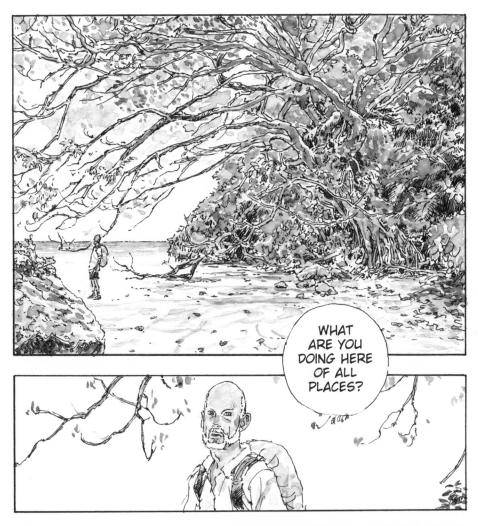

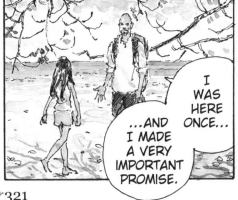

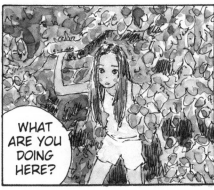

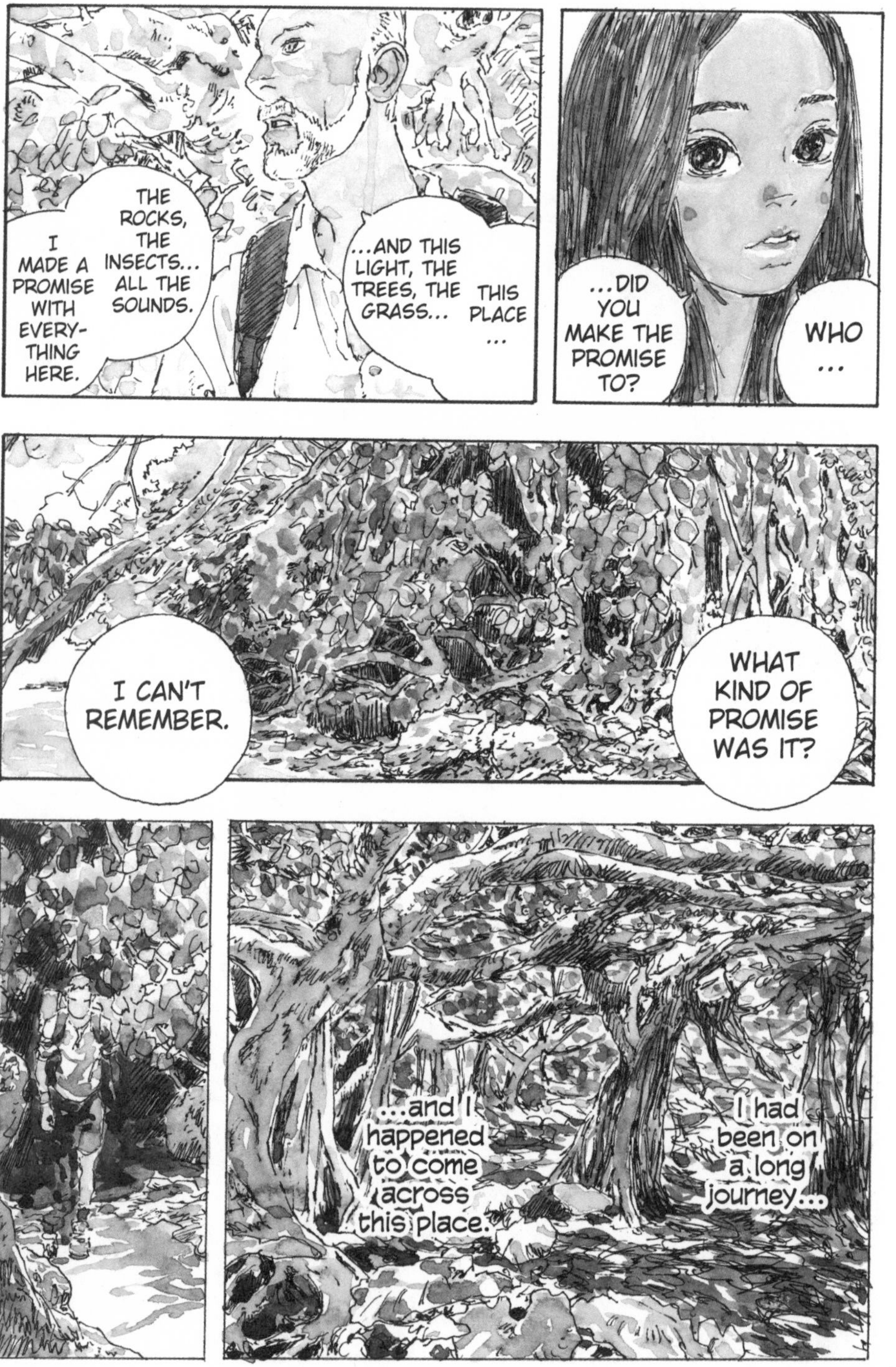
WHO ...
...DID YOU MAKE THE PROMISE TO?
I MADE A PROMISE WITH EVERY-THING HERE.
THE ROCKS, THE INSECTS... ALL THE SOUNDS.
...AND THIS LIGHT, THE TREES, THE GRASS...
THIS PLACE ...
WHAT KIND OF PROMISE WAS IT?
I CAN'T REMEMBER.
I had been on a long journey...
...and I happened to come across this place.

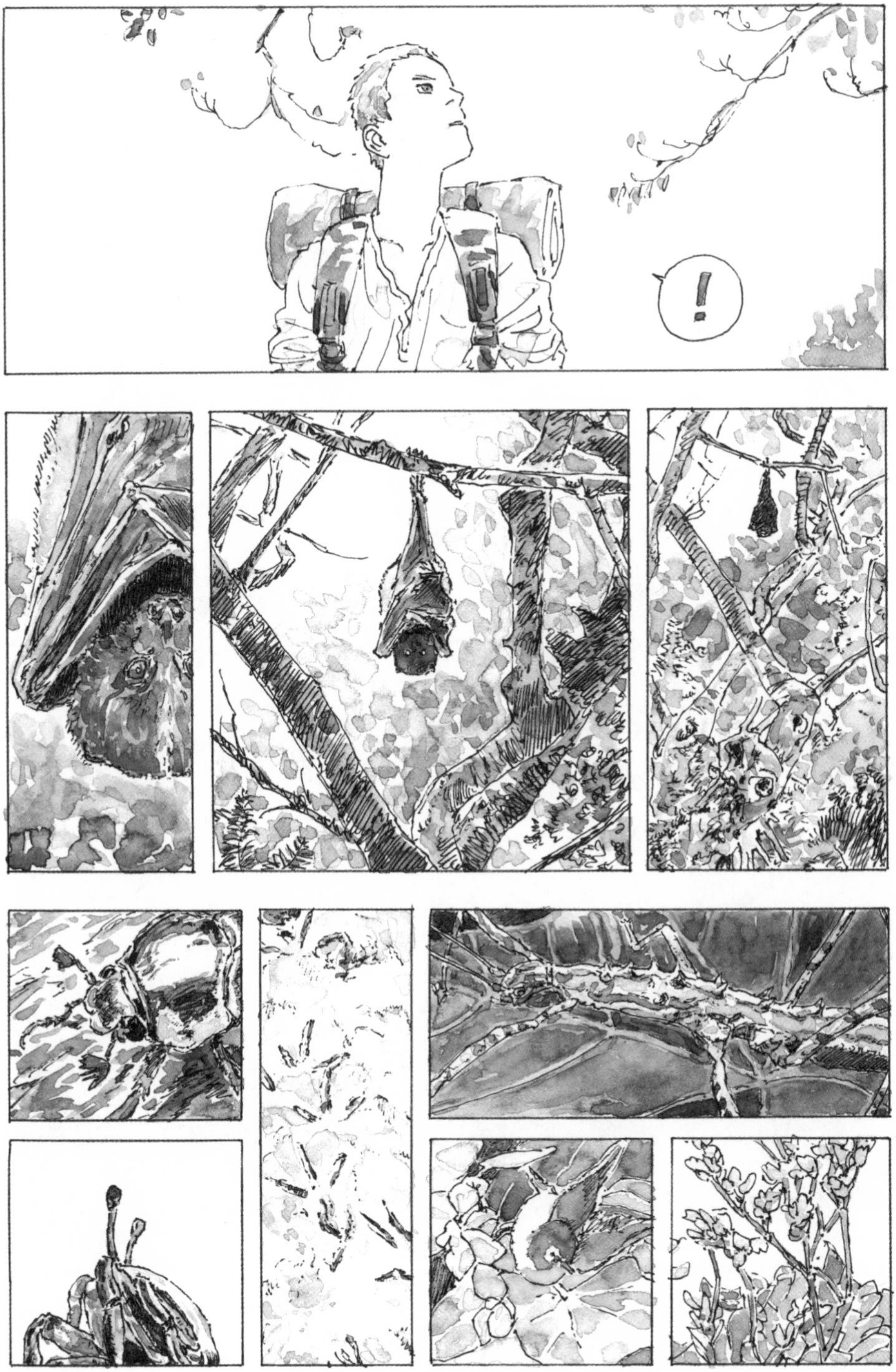
!

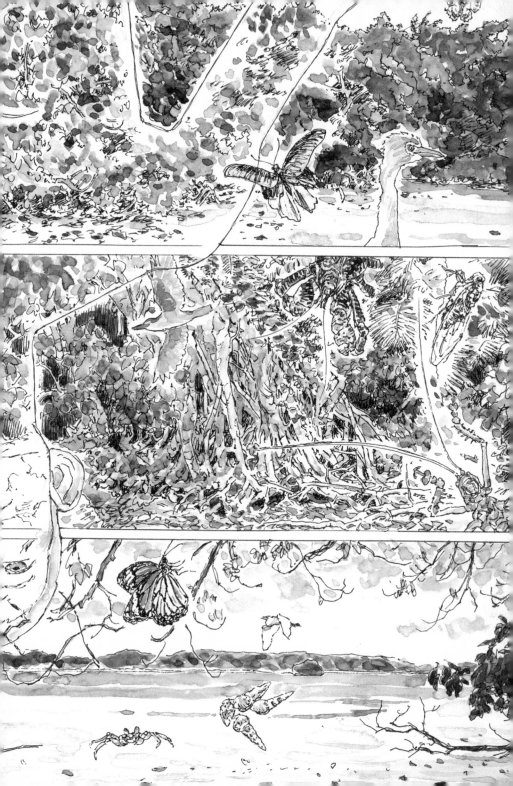

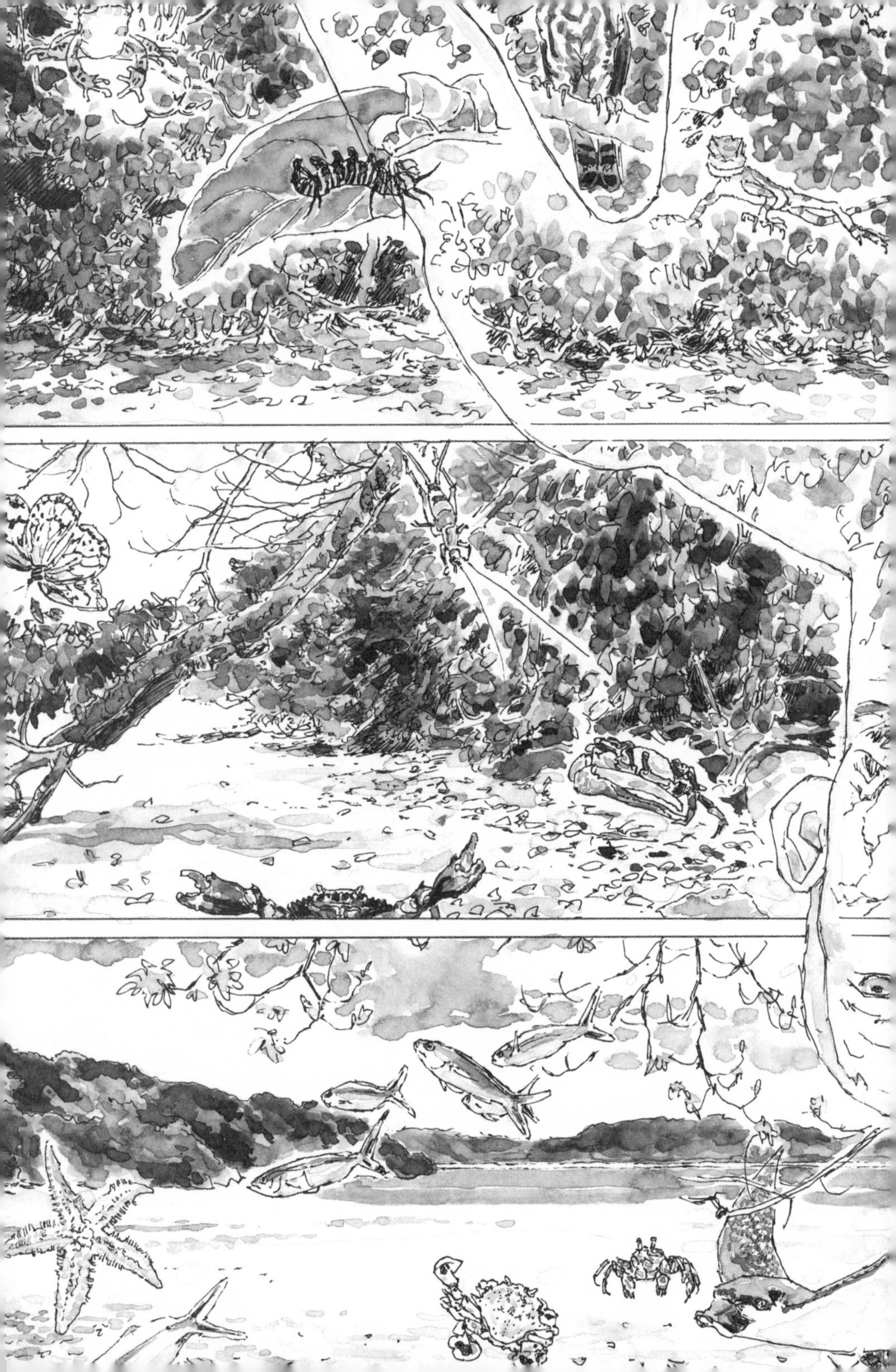

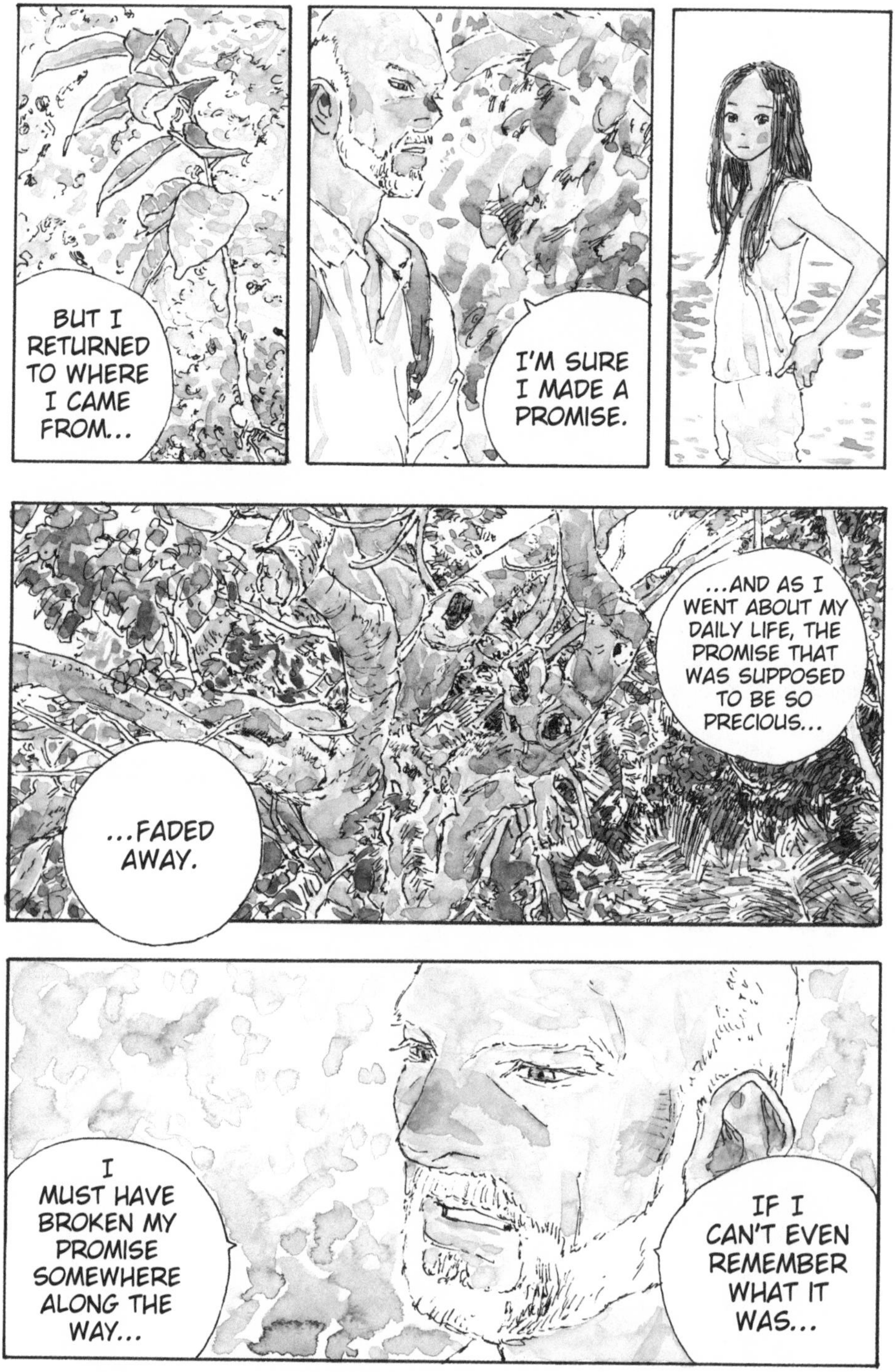
I'M SURE I MADE A PROMISE.
BUT I RETURNED TO WHERE I CAME FROM...
...AND AS I WENT ABOUT MY DAILY LIFE, THE PROMISE THAT WAS SUPPOSED TO BE SO PRECIOUS...
...FADED AWAY.
IF I CAN'T EVEN REMEMBER WHAT IT WAS...
I MUST HAVE BROKEN MY PROMISE SOMEWHERE ALONG THE WAY...

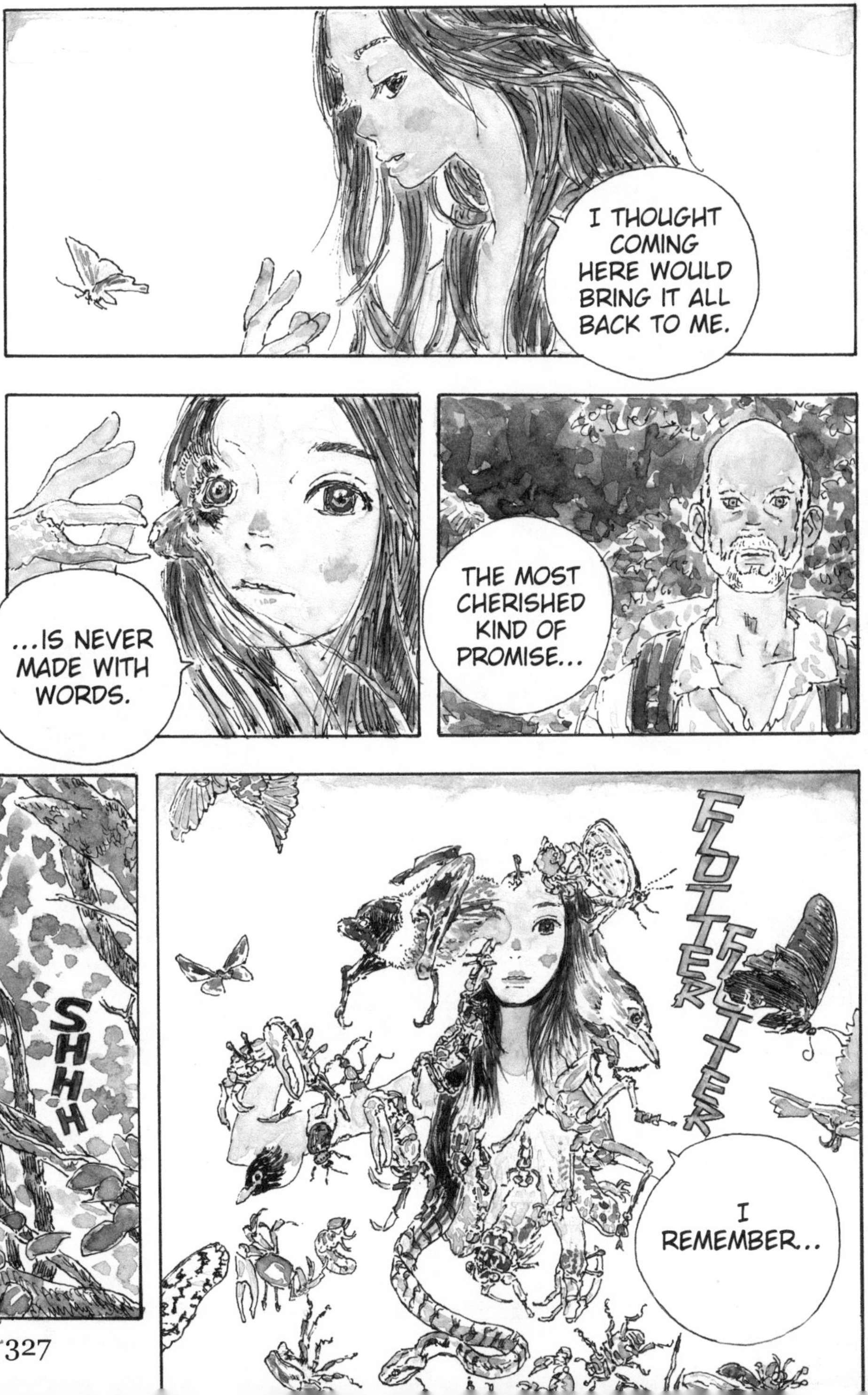
I THOUGHT COMING HERE WOULD BRING IT ALL BACK TO ME.
THE MOST CHERISHED KIND OF PROMISE...
...IS NEVER MADE WITH WORDS.
FLUTTER
FLUTTER
I REMEMBER...
SHHH

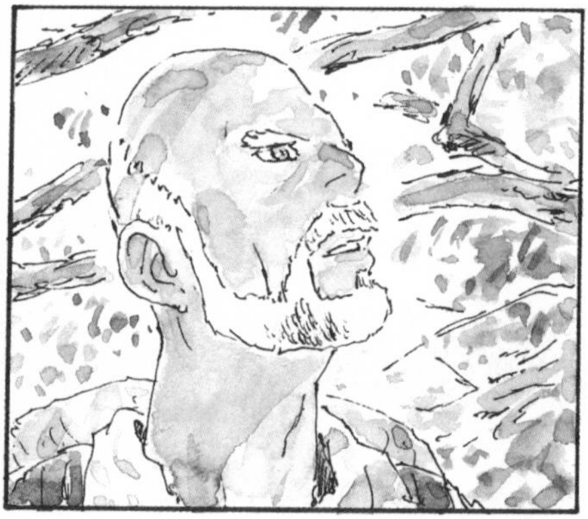
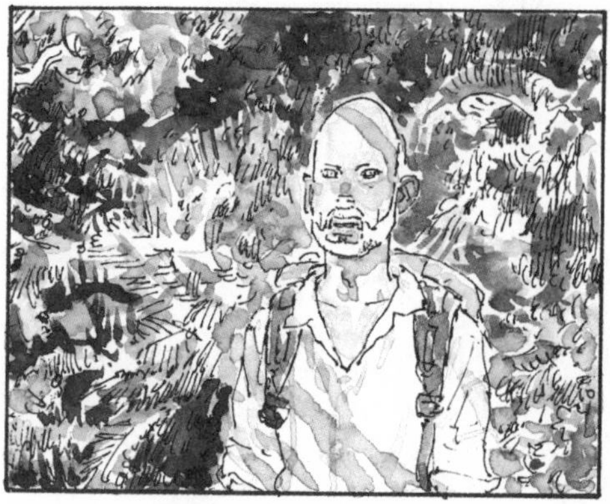
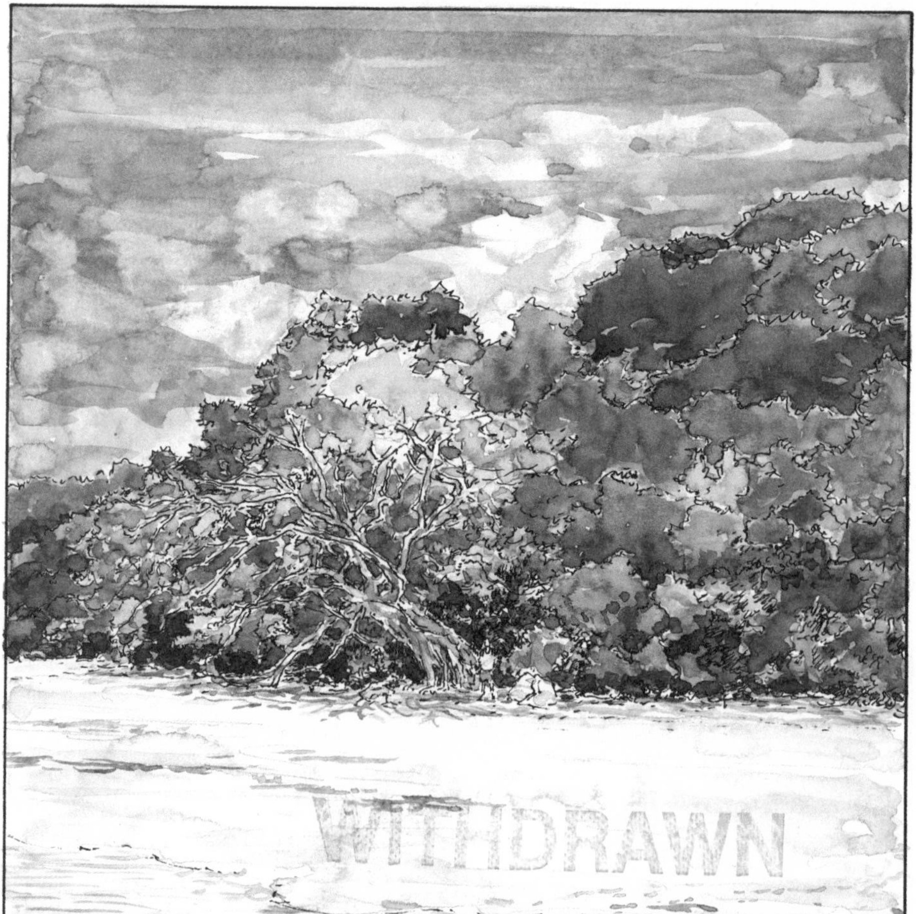

The End

CHILDREN OF THE SEA

Volume 5
VIZ Signature Edition

STORY AND ART BY DAISUKE IGARASHI

KAIJU NO KODOMO Vol. 5
by Daisuke IGARASHI

Original Japanese edition published by SHOGAKUKAN.
English translation rights in the United States of America and Canada arranged with SHOGAKUKAN.

Original Japanese cover design by chutte

Cooperation and assistance from Enoshima Aquarium

TRANSLATION = JN Productions
TOUCH-UP ART & LETTERING = Annaliese Christman
DESIGN = Fawn Lau
EDITOR = Pancha Diaz

Printed in Canada

Published by VIZ Media, LLC
P.O. Box 77010
San Francisco, CA 94107

www.viz.com

RATED T+ FOR OLDER TEEN
PARENTAL ADVISORY
CHILDREN OF THE SEA is rated T+ for Older Teen and is recommended for ages 16 and up. Contains disturbing imagery.
ratings.viz.com

IKKI
www.sigikki.com

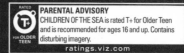

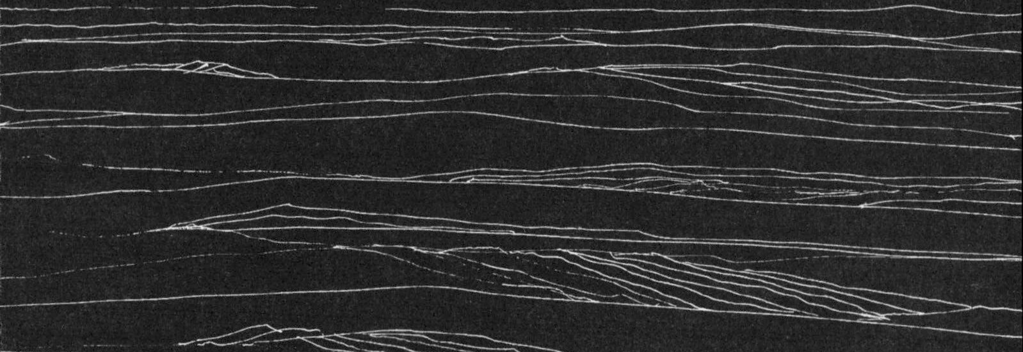

10 9 8 7 6 5 4 3 2 1
First printing, June 2013

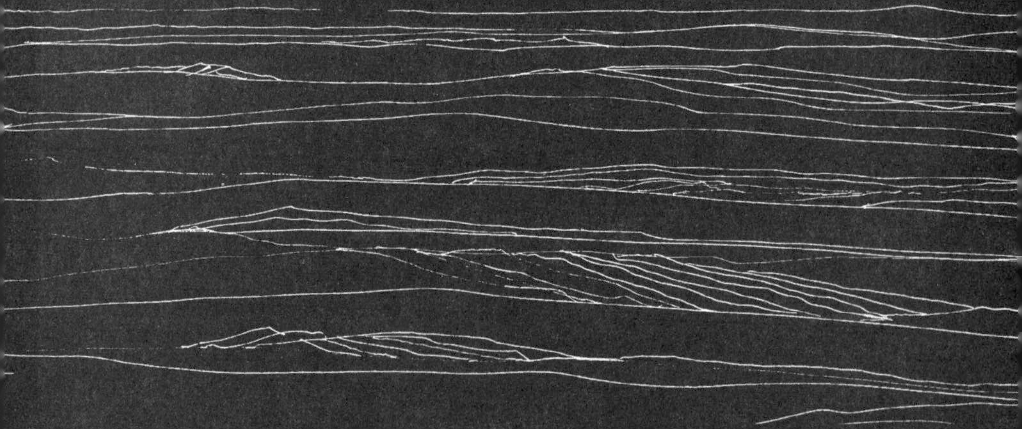

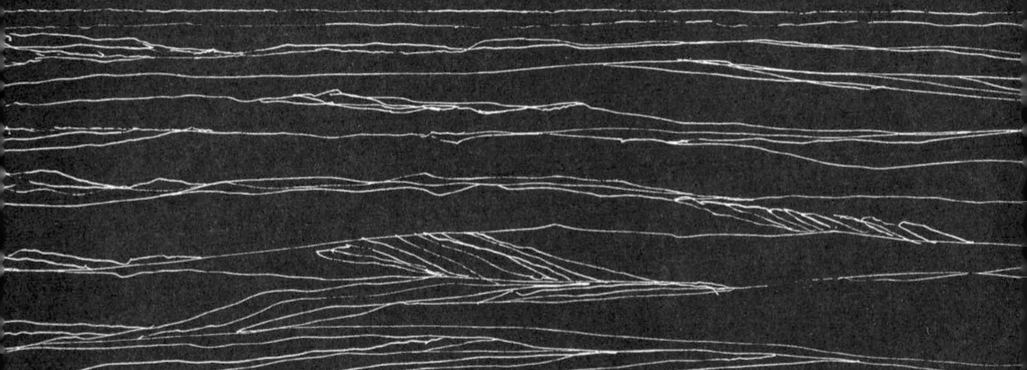

This is the **LAST PAGE** of this book.

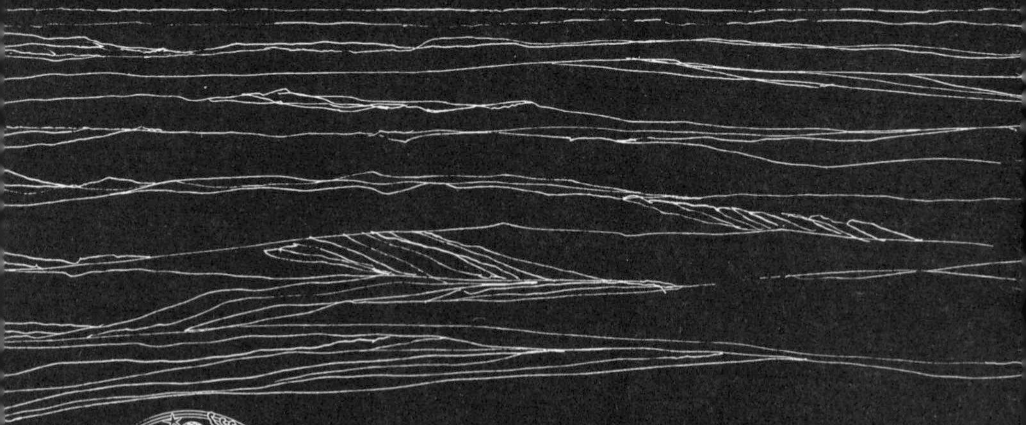

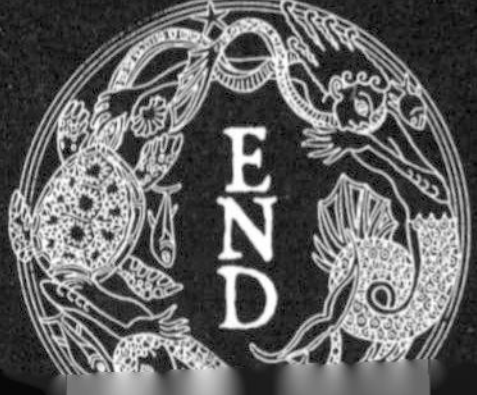
END

CHILDREN OF THE SEA
is printed from RIGHT TO LEFT in the original Japanese format in
[redacted]